Julian Soh
Anthony Puca
Marshall Copeland

ISBN: 978-0-7356-7823-1

Fourth Printing: December 2014

Printed and bound in the United States of America.

Microsoft Press books are available through booksellers and distributors worldwide. If you need support related to this book, email Microsoft Press Book Support at *mspinput@microsoft.com*. Please tell us what you think of this book at *http://www.microsoft.com/learning/booksurvey*.

Acquisitions and Developmental Editor: Kenyon Brown

Production Editor: Kara Ebrahim

Technical Reviewers: Darryl Kegg, Scott Wold, Stephen Jones, and Mark Ghazai

Copyeditor: Barbara McGuire

Indexer: BIM Publishing Services

Cover Design: Twist Creative • Seattle

Cover Composition: Ellie Volckhausen

Illustrator: Rebecca Demarest

Contents at a glance

PART 2: Office 365 Foundations: Identity Management

Chapter 3
Active Directory Federation Services 71

Chapter 4
Directory synchronization 137

PART 3: Office 365 Foundations: Monitoring and Automation

Chapter 5
Monitoring Office 365 with System Center. . 207

Chapter 6
Customizing Operations Manager
reports and dashboards for Office 365 283

Chapter 7
Automating Office 365 management
using Orchestrator. 325

Chapter 8
Office 365 and Service Manager
automation 351

Chapter 9
Windows PowerShell for Office 365. 395

Chapter 12
Mailbox migration and administering
Exchange Online 565

Chapter 13
SharePoint Online 631

Chapter 14
Lync Online 699

Chapter 15
Office 365 Professional Plus. 759

PART 5: Advanced topics: Incorporating Office 365 with Windows Azure

Chapter 16
Advanced concepts and scenarios for
Office 365 781

PART 6: Appendix

Appendix
Windows PowerShell scripts for
Office 365 813

Table of contents

Design conventions xix
Acknowledgments. xxi
Support & feedback xxiii
Errata xxiii
We want to hear from you xiv
Stay in touch xxv

PART 1: Introducing Office 365

Chapter 1:   **The business case for the cloud. 3**
Consumer vs. enterprise. 3
Office 365. 4
Licensing overview. 5
Office 365 terminology 8
Tenant. 8
Tenant name 8
Vanity domain name 9
Waves. 9
Hybrid. 9
Examples and screen shots. 9
Government Community Cloud 10
Business case for Office 365 10
Subscription model 10

What do you think of this book? We want to hear from you!

Microsoft is interested in hearing your feedback so we can improve our books and learning resources
for you. To participate in a brief survey, please visit:

http://aka.ms/tellpress

Economies of scale. 11
Scalability. 11
Redundancy. 11
Core competency 12
Trust Center 12
Certifications 13
Regulatory compliance 14
Summary. 15

Chapter 2:   **Planning and preparing to deploy Office 365. . . . . 17**

Approach to planning and evaluating Office 365. 17
Foundational planning and remediation tasks. 18
Service-specific planning and remediation tasks. 18
Office 365 planning, deployment, and troubleshooting tools 18
Office 365 Service Descriptions 19
Office 365 Deployment Guide 20
Microsoft Office 365 Deployment Readiness Toolkit 21
Network planning and analysis 26
Quality vs. quantity 27
Misconception about distance. 28
Speed test 28
Basic traffic analysis 35
Putting it all together 38
Alternative approach to email traffic analysis. 39
Network requirements for SharePoint Online. 43
Network requirements for Lync Online 44
Microsoft Remote Connectivity Analyzer. 46
Microsoft Online Services Diagnostics and Logging Support Toolkit 48
Windows PowerShell 52
Microsoft Online Services Module 54
Microsoft Windows PowerShell Integrated Scripting Environment (ISE) 3.0. 66
Summary. 68

PART 2: Office 365 Foundations: Identity Management

Chapter 3:   **Active Directory Federation Services 71**

Different types of user accounts 71
Cloud identity. 72
Federated identity 72
Integrating Active Directory with Office 365. 73
Adding your domain name to Office 365 74
Active Directory Federation Services. 82
Single sign-on experience. 83
Single sign-on requirements 84
Remediating the UPN suffix. 86
Installing IIS on the AD FS server. 92
Requesting and installing certificates. 92

Planning the AD FS architecture 99
Installing and configuring AD FS 2.0. 101
Testing the federation server 112
Converting the domain from standard authentication to identity federation . . . 113
Updating the federation URL endpoint 117
Removing Active Directory Federation Services 122
Converting a domain from identity federation to standard authentication 123
Completely uninstall AD FS 2.0 125
Summary 135

running SQL Server 151
Installing directory synchronization with Windows Internal Database 163
Configuring directory synchronization 168
Verifying directory synchronization. 176
Verifying directory synchronization using the admin center. 176
Verifying directory synchronization service status. 177
Using the Synchronization Service Manager. 178
Checking the Event Viewer. 181
Forcing an unscheduled directory synchronization 182
Understanding run profiles and management agents 182
Initiating an unscheduled directory synchronization using
Synchronization Service Manager. 183
Initiating an unscheduled directory synchronization using Windows
PowerShell. 191
Changing the directory synchronization schedule 194
Troubleshooting common directory synchronization errors 195
Directory synchronization is not running 195
Directory synchronization data problems 198
Troubleshooting directory synchronization using the MOSDAL toolkit. 198
Summary. 203

PART 3: Office 365 Foundations: Monitoring and Automation

Chapter 5:   **Monitoring Office 365 with System Center. 207**

Introduction to System Center components and licensing 209
System Center 2012 Configuration Manager 210
System Center 2012 Operations Manager. 212
System Center 2012 Data Protection Manager. 214
System Center 2012 Virtual Machine Manager 214

System Center 2012 Orchestrator 216
System Center 2012 Service Manager 217
System Center 2012 Endpoint Protection 218
System Center 2012 App Controller 219
Concepts and planning for monitoring Office 365 221
Evaluating what to monitor 222
Administering the monitoring solution 224
Monitoring targets 225
Deploying the SCOM infrastructure and importing the Office 365
Management Pack 225
Installing the System Center 2012 Operations Manager Service Pack 1
prerequisites 225
Downloading the System Center 2012 Operations Manager Service
Pack 1 media 236
Installing System Center 2012 Operations Manager 238
Importing the Office 365 Management Pack 253
Creating alert notifications 262
Creating alert recipients 263
Creating a subscription 270
Summary 281

Chapter 6:   **Customizing Operations Manager reports and dashboards for**
Office 365 . . . . **283**
Identifying Office 365 dependent servers 283
Customizing System Center 2012 Operations Manager state views 287
Customizing System Center 2012 Operations Manager alert views 289
Tuning the Office 365 management pack and reducing false alarms 291
Configuring the watcher nodes 300
System Center 2012 Operations Manager report customization 305
Dashboard creation for technical and business owners 311
Operator console dashboards 311
How to create a custom Office 365 dashboard 312
Office 365 service level agreement dashboards 317
Summary 323

Chapter 7:   **Automating Office 365 management using Orchestrator** **325**
System Center 2012 Orchestrator 325
Orchestrator overview and concepts 326
Introducing Orchestrator 326
Applying the runbook concept to Office 365 327
Using Orchestrator components 329
Installing Orchestrator 330
Prerequisites for installing Orchestrator for testing 331
Installing prerequisites for Orchestrator 332
Installing Microsoft SQL Server 334
Completing the installation for Orchestrator 335

Using Integration Packs with Office 365 automation 344

Creating a new runbook for Office 365 email accounts. 346

Summary. 350

Chapter 8:   Office 365 and Service Manager automation 351

System Center 2012 SP1 Service Manager 351

Service Manager components 352

Installing Service Manager 353

Installing the Self-Service Portal 358

Service and request offering in the Self-Service Portal. 392

Summary. 393

Chapter 9:   Windows PowerShell for Office 365 395

Windows PowerShell underlying services. 395

Preparing the Windows PowerShell environment. 396

Windows PowerShell pre-configured for the workstation or server. 396

Configuring Windows PowerShell and WinRM settings 401

Connecting Windows PowerShell to the Office 365 service. 403

Windows PowerShell as the future interface 405

Windows PowerShell Integrated Scripting Environment 406

Starting the ISE from Windows 8. 407

Starting the ISE from within Windows PowerShell. 407

Starting the ISE from Windows 7. 407

Navigating the ISE 409

Office 365 examples and exercises 414

Establishing a Windows PowerShell session with Exchange Online 414

Updating Windows PowerShell Help files 416

Granting mailbox access 417

Validating permissions 418

Changing time zones. 418

Viewing groups. 419

Creating distribution groups 419

Using the Admin Audit log. 421

Viewing retention policies 422

Creating retention policies 423

Summary. 425

PART 4: Integrating and using Office 365 Services

Chapter 10:   **Introducing Exchange Online** **429**

Multiple service descriptions 430
Exchange Online plans 431
Exchange Online core workloads and concepts 432
    Mailboxes and calendaring 433
    Exchange Online Archiving mailbox 434
    Email handling and transport 435
    Email filtering 438
    Secure email 438
Exchange Online capabilities 439
    Messaging limits 439
    Backup and recovery 439
    Exchange Online service availability and redundancy 441
Forefront Online Protection for Exchange 442
    Layered protection 443
    Anti-Spam 444
    Message quarantine 445
    FOPE policies 445
    Message handling 446
    Reporting 447
Exchange Online Archiving 448
    Archive size 449
    Backup and recovery 449
    EOA access 450
    Compliance 451
Exchange Hosted Encryption 451
Exchange Online implementation options 452
    Hybrid mailboxes 452
    Hybrid archiving model 454
    Hybrid mail protection and routing 455
New capabilities 456
    Data Leakage Prevention 456
    Rights Management Service 457
Summary 458

Chapter 11:   **Planning and deploying hybrid Exchange** **459**

Planning an Exchange hybrid deployment 460
    Understanding capabilities 460
    Requirements 461
    Using the Exchange Server Deployment Assistant 462
Installing Exchange hybrid deployment prerequisites 471
    Preparing the Exchange Management Console 471
    Certificates 482
    Configuring Exchange Web Services 508
Configuring an Exchange hybrid model 513

Establishing a hybrid relationship 514
Configuring a hybrid deployment. 517
Troubleshooting hybrid configuration 534
Autodiscover service 534
Virtual directory security settings. 537
Resetting the Autodiscover virtual directory. 539
Finalizing the Exchange hybrid deployment 542
Testing a mailbox creation 542
Testing a mailbox move. 5 4 9

Migration using remote Windows PowerShell 589
Migration with an Exchange hybrid environment 591
Microsoft Exchange PST Capture 592
Third-party migration tools 601
Migration best practices 601
Moving mailboxes back to on-premises Exchange. 603
Mailbox originally created on-premises. 603
Mailbox originally created in Exchange Online. 605
Decommissioning on-premises Exchange 607
Administering Exchange Online 608
Exchange Management Console. 609
Exchange Online remote Windows PowerShell 611
Exchange Online administration user interface 612
Compliance, Legal Hold, and eDiscovery concepts 621
Preserving content. 621
Automated deletions. 621
Enforced retention 621
Putting it all together 622
Personal archive 622
Messaging Records Management. 622
Holds. 623
Multi-mailbox search (eDiscovery) 627
Summary. 629

Chapter 13:   **SharePoint Online** **631**
Understanding SharePoint capabilities. 631
Introducing SharePoint Online 632
SharePoint Online concepts 633

SharePoint Online capabilities 633
SharePoint Online capacity limits 635
SharePoint hybrid model 637
Managing SharePoint Online 638
SharePoint Online 2013 638
SharePoint Online 2010 642
SharePoint Store 646
Permissions and adding apps to sites 655
Managing app licenses 657
SkyDrive Pro 659
Storage 660
External collaboration 660
Mobility 669
Office Web Apps 670
Achieving compliance with SharePoint eDiscovery Center 674
SharePoint Online Management Shell 694
SharePoint search in a hybrid environment 696
One-way outbound topology 697
One-way inbound topology 697
Two-way topology 698
Summary 698

Chapter 14:   **Lync Online** **699**
Lync terminology 700
Session Initiation Protocol and SIP addressing 700
Peer-to-peer voice vs. Enterprise Voice 700
Lync Online overview and licensing 701
Lync client 702
Lync meetings 704
Lync mobile 707
Lync Web App and Outlook Web App 708
Lync Online capabilities and concepts 712
Lync Online features 713
Lync Federation 713
Hybrid Lync Online 714
Dial-in audio conferencing 717
Lync Online planning and deployment 718
Test network bandwidth and latency 719
Determine ports and protocols 722
Allow outgoing connections 723
Create DNS entries 723
Configuring and managing Lync Online 728
Lync Online 2013 728
Lync Online 2010 736
Lync IM conversation history and policy 742
Configuring hybrid Lync 754

Migration considerations. 757
Summary. 757

Chapter 15:   **Office 365 Professional Plus. 759**

Introduction to the Microsoft Office editions 760
Office ProPlus Service Description. 762
Deploying Office 365 ProPlus. 762
Office Click-to-Run and activations 764
   Customizing Click-to-Run 769

Office 365 ProPlus common errors 777
   Microsoft Office subscription error. 777
   Office subscription removed 777
   No subscription found. 777
   Activation error. 778
Summary. 778

PART 5: Advanced topics: Incorporating Office 365 with Windows Azure

Chapter 16:   **Advanced concepts and scenarios for Office 365 . . . . 781**

Trusts. 783
   One-way forest trusts 785
   Two-way forest trusts 785
Introduction to Forefront Identity Manager 786
Office 365 and FIM architecture to support multi-forest scenarios. 788
Windows Azure 793
   Office 365 on-premises dependencies supported in Windows Azure 793
   Identity and SSO for Office 365 in Windows Azure. 794
   Scenario 1: All Office 365 identity management components deployed
   in Windows Azure 796
   Scenario 2: Office 365 on-premises identity management components
   duplicated in Windows Azure for disaster recovery and failover 797
   Virtual machine sizing. 798
Multi-factor authentication. 799
   Setting up Azure Multi-Factor Authentication 800
   First time user experience. 802
   Subsequent user experience 805
Summary. 809

PART 6: Appendix

Appendix A: **Windows PowerShell scripts for Office 365** **813**

Introduction 813

Determining the subscription name 813

Creating cloud identities from a .csv file 814

Generating a user list 815

Generating a subscription assignment report 815

Swapping licenses 818

Activating certain services in a suite SKU 819

Purging deleted users 820

Sending bulk email to users 820

Office 365 Windows PowerShell resources 822

Index **823**

Foreword

W HEN I think back at why I got into IT, it came down to a constant thirst for innovation and helping solve problems with technology. Innovation can take on two forms: refinement or outright change. Technology really exists to solve problems and can take any form.

Now we are seeing the pendulum swing to where many of the technology services are turning into commodities and things that used to take thousands of dollars of infrastructure to accomplish have been simplified into a few clicks. The automation we spent building in the last decade has turned into service and account hydration. The virtual machines, clustered services, and live migrations have been woven into the fabric of cloud services. It means the building and sizing of infrastructure is real-time and logic-based. As infrastructure people, we've watched this evolve and the elasticity of everything is really cool and getting better with more advances in security, rapid failover, and most other aspects each day.

Office 365 is a leader in the charge to take advantage of the infrastructure and automation improvements to provide highly available services. As the workloads in Office 365 (Exchange, SharePoint, Lync, Yammer, and Office) continue to develop, Office 365 removes the complexity of building out infrastructure and keeping software up to date. The rapid innovation of these services and the evolution of technology they build upon is a reflection of that spark that led many of us into technology careers.

Like any platform, it is extensible, configurable, and manageable. For the seasoned IT pro, many of the aspects around directory service management, user provisioning, PowerShell automation, email, and site administration are consistent with what you've probably been doing. As an IT pro, your stake and role is more valuable than ever. With a background in Exchange or SharePoint, you have a unique view into the inner workings of the services, without the painstaking work of provisioning and de-provisioning servers, patch management, and major upgrades.

Microsoft Office 365 Administration Inside Out is your guide to navigate the landscape to Office 365 from the IT pro lens. It goes much deeper and thoughtfully into the specifics of managing Office 365 workloads. The great thing with this book is that once you start a trial, you can hit the ground running and start getting hands-on. The other great side effect of cloud services is that you generally don't need to worry about test virtual machines or hosted hands-on labs. It's all there, so roll up your sleeves and get started.

—Jeremy Chapman
Director Office 365 Product Management

Introduction

WELCOME to *Office 365 Administration Inside Out*. This book was written specifically for enterprise-level customers who want to adopt Office 365. There are other books that cover the use of Office 365, but this book focuses on the actual integration of Office 365 with on-premises technologies. This integration is often necessary for organizations that already have, and might need to continue to have, some level of

of email functions in Office 365. These are all examples of enterprise-level decisions that organizations face, and this book addresses these types of real-world implementations and administration.

Who this book is for

This book is intended for Information Technology (IT) system architects who need to integrate Office 365 with existing on-premises technologies. It is also intended for subject matter experts in Exchange, SharePoint, and Lync who design migration and hybrid implementations of these specific Office 365 services. Although this book contains a lot of technical information, it can also serve IT leaders and decision makers such as Chief Information Officers (CIOs) by providing insight to the level of planning and effort required to integrate Office 365 with existing technologies. With that insight, IT leaders and CIOs can plan and budget their Office 365 projects accordingly. There are also security and compliance topics that security professionals will find useful because there are new and specific security considerations for adopting cloud services. This book is not intended for the typical end user or business user, nor is it intended to cover all the functionalities of Exchange, SharePoint, Lync, and Office.

Regardless of your role, we hope this book helps you methodically plan, integrate, and deploy Office 365 services in your organization. We also hope you will get a better understanding about deploying technologies that can make the Office 365 experience a great one for end users and administrators.

Assumptions about you

This book is designed for readers who have a fundamental understanding of Office 365 services, but possess technical expertise in the administration and configuration of the on-premises technologies equivalent to those services. Because Office 365 covers a breadth of technologies including SharePoint, Lync, Exchange, and Office, this book assumes that the audience for each of these technologies has the relevant expertise in configuring and administering these technologies prior to Office 365. In addition, this book includes information that can serve multiple audiences; because of this, it can serve as a great resource for an Office 365 implementation team of experts. During implementation, there is foundational work to complete in the areas of identity management, network assessments, security analysis, and migration planning. As such, this book assumes the readers in these areas have the operational expertise for managing AD, running network assessments, and making configuration changes to networking services such as Domain Name System (DNS), proxies, and firewalls. While not required, readers will benefit most from this book if they have a lab environment to implement the concepts covered in the book.

Conventions

This book uses special text and design conventions to make it easier for you to find the information you need.

Text conventions

Convention	Meaning
Bold	Bold type indicates keywords and reserved words that you must enter exactly as shown. Microsoft Visual Basic understands keywords entered in uppercase, lowercase, and mixed case type. Access stores SQL keywords in queries in all uppercase, but you can enter the keywords in any case.
Italic	Italicized words represent variables that you supply.
Angle brackets < >	Angle brackets enclose syntactic elements that you must supply. The words inside the angle brackets describe the element but do not show the actual syntax of the element. Do not enter the angle brackets.

Convention	Meaning
Brackets [ ]	Brackets enclose optional items. If more than one item is listed, the items are separated by a pipe character (|). Choose one or none of the elements. Do not enter the brackets or the pipe; they're not part of the element. Note that Visual Basic and SQL in many cases require that you enclose names in brackets. When brackets are required as part of the syntax of variables that you must supply in
Underscore _	You can use a blank space followed by an underscore to continue a line of Visual Basic code to the next line for readability. You cannot place an underscore in the middle of a string literal. You do not need an underscore for continued lines in SQL, but you cannot break a literal across lines.

Design conventions

INSIDE OUT   **This statement illustrates an example of an "Inside Out" heading**

These are the book's signature tips. In these tips, you get the straight scoop on what's going on with the software—inside information about why a feature works the way it does. You'll also find handy workarounds to deal with software problems.

Sidebar

Sidebars provide helpful hints, timesaving tricks, or alternative procedures related to the task being discussed.

TROUBLESHOOTING

This statement illustrates an example of a "Troubleshooting" problem statement

Look for these sidebars to find solutions to common problems you might encounter. Troubleshooting sidebars appear next to related information in the chapters. You can also use "Index to Troubleshooting Topics" at the back of the book to look up problems by topic.

Cross-references point you to locations in the book that offer additional information about the topic being discussed.

CAUTION

Cautions identify potential problems that you should look out for when you're completing a task or that you must address before you can complete a task.

Note
Notes offer additional information related to the task being discussed.

Acknowledgments

Writing a technical book is a challenging yet rewarding experience. Writing a technical book that covers a new technology offering that is rapidly changing and covers the core Microsoft enterprise software takes the experience to an entirely different level. After reading this book, we hope you can appreciate how innovative Office 365 really is. It is a well-planned service with technologies and options to address almost every business scenario.

made every attempt to continually update the information as we developed the book. However, due to the rapid update cadence of Office 365, the screen shots and information presented here might vary from your environment. Even so, the significant core concepts should remain consistent with the current Office 365 offering.

There are a number of people who have made this project possible. First, the authors would like to thank the great teams at O'Reilly Media and Microsoft Press for the opportunity to write this book. We also would like to thank Kenyon Brown, our senior editor, for his patience and valuable guidance throughout the project; Kara Ebrahim, our production editor, and her team for making the book look so aesthetically pleasing; and Barbara McGuire, our copy editor, for her excellent edits and valuable comments. We want to thank all our technical reviewers and subject matter experts, who behind the scenes validated all the material and provided very important feedback and corrections. They are Scott Wold, Darryl Kegg, Mark Ghazai, Stephen Jones, Jeremy Chapman, Yann Kristofic, Andreas Kjellman, and Darren Carlsen. We want to thank King County's CIO Bill Kehoe and many other IT leaders and technical experts in other organizations who have been willing to share their experience with us and give us the opportunity to work on their Office 365 projects. Without the vision and courage of these early adopters, it would not have been possible to provide all the real world experience we tried to capture in this book. We also thank the executive management at Microsoft for their support of this project, especially Jeff Tozzi, Dave Rogers, Javier Vasquez, Tori Locke, Dean Iacovelli, and Keith Olinger. Last but not least, we would like to thank the wonderful account teams at Microsoft we worked with, especially Steve Finney, Abel Cruz, Mark Wernet, Chris Wilch, Benjamin Callahan, Steve Kirchoff, Steven Fiore, Tara Larson, Bjorn Salvesen, Arshad Mea, Rick Joyer, Dan Crum, and Adam Loughran.

Julian Soh

This book has been one of the most challenging projects I have ever undertaken. There is so much material that we struggled to keep the scope of the book in check. This book truly has given me the opportunity to gain a deeper appreciation for the innovation, intricacies, and the possibilities that Office 365 offers.

This experience has helped me grow professionally, and I appreciate all the authors who have come before me because it is a huge personal investment in time and commitment for any author. Most importantly, I have been humbled by so many experts who have helped make this book possible. I sincerely would like to thank the efforts of my co-authors Marshall Copeland and Anthony Puca. Not only are they experts in their field, they have been great friends. I am humbled by their expertise and professionalism. I will always treasure this journey we have shared together, and I feel very blessed to have friends like you. I want to personally thank my Office 365 field team for making it such a great place to work and for your unselfish sharing of information. So thank you Bob Ballard, Carl Solazzo, Chuck Ladd, Dennis Guzy, Erika Cheley, Jed Zercher, Joel Martin, Michael Icore, Mike Hacker, Monica Hopelian, Scott Derby, Tim Gade, Stephen Jones, Brian Burns, and Scott Wold.

Finally, I would be remiss if I did not thank my family. I spent many days away from them. They also put up with my multi-tasking between writing chapters and trying to participate in family events. My wife Priscilla has been ever supportive and selfless in taking on all the extra work around the house. Thank you to my daughters Jasmine and Makayla for their understanding and for sacrificing some of our time together for this project. Jasmine, thank you for all the green tea you made me while I was busy typing away late into the night and for taking over the mowing of the yard.

To all these very important people in my life, I dedicate this book to you.

Marshall Copeland

Writing a book is a tremendous undertaking, and I would like to thank my beautiful wife Angela for her patience during the many evenings and weekends I spent hovered over a keyboard. She supports my hectic work with travel for public and customer speaking while keeping me grounded with incredible insight on what's important. For Cecil, Frances, and Barbara. We miss you.

Words are not enough to thank Julian Soh for offering me a seat on this voyage. It became very clear that to be a subject matter expert is quite different from trying to teach others by writing about a subject. Julian, merely saying "thank you" can't express my gratitude enough. Also, I want to thank Anthony Puca for his daily expertise with System Center and the insight he offered during our many conversations. A big thank you to Keith Olinger and Jeff Tozzi for their support during the writing of this book and for being two great people with amazing guidance to help me grow. You both pour so much effort into everyday work that our entire team is lifted, and we thank you.

Thank you to the many customers who continue to ask "what if" questions and allow me to provide insight to help each of you move forward. Thank you to Bill Gates and Steve Ballmer for building a fantastic company called Microsoft, the best place to work. A special thank you to Charles Fox for helping me see the right direction when I could not. Thank you to Mark Ghazai for all the Windows PowerShell guidance and Hyper-V understanding

When two friends, Julian Soh and Marshall Copeland, asked me to accompany them on this effort, I was honestly flattered. Special thanks go to Julian for coming up with the idea and driving it through; we could not have done this without you. Thank you, Marshall and Julian, for being my sounding board, for providing sanity checks and peer reviews, and for all the insightful conversations during those late night and weekend calls.

Working at Microsoft has given me access to some of the most talented, brightest, and passionate people in information technology. Thank you to all of you who contributed in some fashion. Thank you to Keith Olinger, Dave Rodgers, Bob Ballard, and their teams for their support. Thank you to Mark Ghazai and Marek Tyszkiewicz for all the Windows Power-Shell scripting. Thank you to Anna Timasheva for your System Center Operations Manager (SCOM) expertise. Thank you to Jeff Tozzi for growing an amazing group that supports state and local government in the U.S. Thank you to my account teams who remind me of the value these things provide to the customers and public: Mark Starr, Nathan Beckham, Todd Strong, Adam Loughran, Elisa Yaros, Bobby Bliven, Don Born, and Kris Gedman.

Support & feedback

The following sections provide information on errata, book support, feedback, and contact information.

Errata

We've made every effort to ensure the accuracy of this book and its companion content. Any errors that have been reported since this book was published are listed on our Micro-soft Press site:

http://aka.ms/Office365_Admin_IO_errata

If you find an error that is not already listed, you can report it to us through the same page.

If you need additional support, email Microsoft Press Book Support at *mspinput@microsoft. com*.

Please note that product support for Microsoft software is not offered through the addresses above.

We want to hear from you

At Microsoft Press, your satisfaction is our top priority, and your feedback our most valuable asset. Please tell us what you think of this book at:

http://www.microsoft.com/learning/booksurvey

The survey is short, and we read every one of your comments and ideas. Thanks in advance for your input!

Stay in touch

Let's keep the conversation going! We're on Twitter: *http://twitter.com/MicrosoftPress*

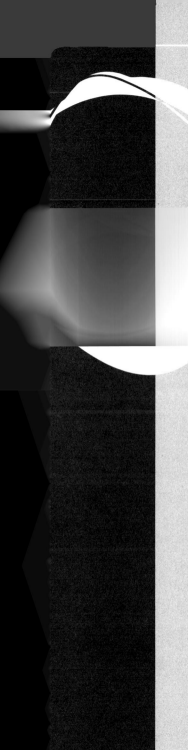

PART 1

Introducing Office 365

Planning and preparing to deploy Office 365 17

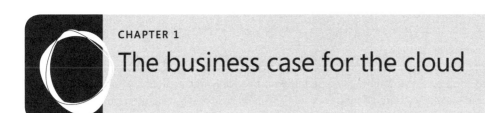

The business case for the cloud

Consumer vs. enterprise 3   Trust Center. 12

thereby maximizing economies of scale like never before.

The cloud has leveled the playing field between large and small organizations by making access to enterprise-class computing resources—technologies that otherwise are accessible only to organizations with big IT budgets—available to small companies. Competition to provide cloud services has further benefitted customers by driving down the cost of cloud computing. However, the most important aspect of cloud computing is that it makes IT more sustainable than ever before.

The cloud and the competition have also made technology companies more aggressive in providing better and more robust solutions. There are many cloud offerings in this decade, such as the introduction of Software as a Service (SaaS) and Infrastructure as a Service (IaaS). To a great extent, most of us in the IT world are speeding down a path toward "everything as a service."

Consumer vs. enterprise

The concepts of *consumer* and *enterprise* are important to keep in mind because the cloud has different meanings for different audiences. A consumer simply might want a convenient way to share files, while an enterprise might need to ensure security and audit trails in addition to the ability to share files. There are free services that offer features that are paid by advertisers, and then there are the very same features that might have to be purchased because they are not subsidized by advertising. After all, an enterprise might have a strong negative reaction if employees get distracted with non-work related advertising or, worse yet, advertising that might be deemed inappropriate to the mission of the organization.

With that in mind, one might come to appreciate the dual-pronged strategy that Microsoft has adopted. For example, some people wondered why Microsoft acquired Skype when there is already a Lync offering with similar capabilities, or why Microsoft provides SkyDrive in addition to SharePoint SkyDrive Pro. The reason is because enterprises typically have different needs from consumers. The fact is that enterprises require better controls from their IT services as well as other features that might not be relevant to the average consumer.

Office 365

This brings us to the introduction of Office 365. Of all the different types of cloud services, one that stands out very prominently and is clearly designed for the enterprise is the Microsoft cloud known as Office 365. Now in its third release, Office 365 is the overarching brand name of Microsoft's flagship business products offered through the cloud:

- **Office 365 ProPlus**   A full version of Office

- **Exchange Online**   For hosted messaging

- **SharePoint Online**   For hosted file sharing and collaboration

- **Lync Online**   For hosted communications

These business and productivity tools are rich in features by themselves, but when combined they become an integrated platform of capabilities that very few other solutions can match. If implemented on-premises and as these features continue to grow, evolve, and integrate with each other, the demand for the IT backend infrastructure to deliver and maintain the service becomes more and more complex. Organizations are constantly in need of evaluating IT costs and their return on investment (ROI), and the most important realization by organizations is that there needs to be a more sustainable way of delivering IT. Cloud computing has also become a reality because the infrastructure in most parts of the world have improved to the point where the Internet has the capacity and reliability to deliver business critical IT systems.

At the time of writing, Microsoft recently announced the launch of Project Online and Team Foundation Services (TFS) Online. If your organization requires these capabilities, they can be acquired separately and as add-ons to Office 365. Project Online and TFS Online leverage and integrate with the core Office 365 technologies. While this book will focus only on the core Office 365 technologies, it is important to note that the Microsoft technology roadmap includes the continued integration of other Microsoft technologies with Office 365.

Licensing overview

There are four core technologies in Office 365: Exchange, SharePoint, Lync, and Office ProPlus. As with many Microsoft licensing options, Office 365 provides multiple paths for adoption.

Just like the on-premises versions of the software, there is a standard edition as well as an enterprise edition for Exchange, SharePoint, and Lync. In the online world, these are known

- SharePoint Online

- Plan 1

- Plan 2

- Lync Online

- Plan 1

- Plan 2

- Office 365 ProPlus (no different plans)

Office 365 stand-alone purchases

The Plan 1 and Plan 2 categories represent the foundation of the flexible Office 365 licensing model. You can purchase any core technology and its associated plan as a stand-alone component. For example, if your organization is interested only in adopting a cloud-based email solution, you can acquire either Exchange Plan 1 or Exchange Plan 2, depending on the desired features. You do not need to acquire any of the other core technologies, such as Lync Online or SharePoint Online. We cover the different capabilities included in Plan 1 and Plan 2 for each of the core technologies in Office 365 in their respective chapters in this book.

Office 365 suites

Some organizations might be interested in multiple technologies. For these organizations, Microsoft provides bundled options known as Office 365 suites. There are different types of suites designed for different types of organizations:

- Enterprise suites

- Government suites

- Education suites

- Kiosk plans (created for enterprise customers that have employees without an office or desk)

- Office 365 Small Business Premium (best for organizations with 1 to 10 employees; see *http://office.microsoft.com/en-us/business/office-365-small-business-premium-office-online-FX103037625.aspx*)

- Office 365 Midsize Business (created for organizations with 11 to 250 employees; see *http://office.microsoft.com/en-us/business/office-365-midsize-business-productivity-software-FX103037683.aspx*)

- Office 365 Home Premium (see *http://office.microsoft.com/en-us/home-premium/*)

Chapter 1

Figure 1-1 shows the different K and E suites and the individual plans contained within the suites.

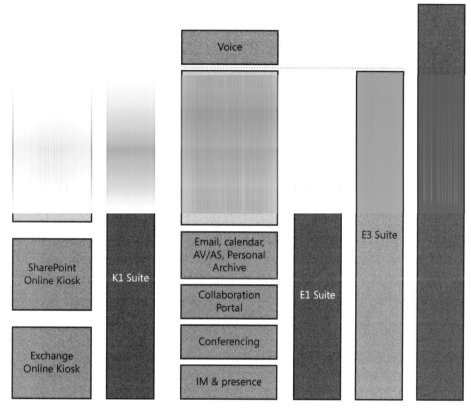

Figure 1-1 Office 365 K and E suites.

INSIDE OUT   Where is the E2 suite?

When the E suites were created, there were four E suites. E1 provides SharePoint Plan 1, Exchange Plan 1, and Lync Plan 1. However, it does not provide Office Professional Plus or Office Web Apps. The E2 suite provided Office Web Apps without Office Professional Plus. The E3 suite provides Office Professional Plus. Recently, Microsoft modified the plans by combining E1 and E2 into a single suite. The revamped E1 suite now has Office Web Apps. That is why there is no longer an E2 suite.

Office 365 suites combine some or all of the Office 365 core technologies and plans. Because this book focuses on the enterprise, we will use the Enterprise (E) and Government (G) suites as an example of how the suites combine the core technologies. The E and G suites are intended to be similar offerings except that the latter is designed for government organizations and provisioned through the Government Community Cloud (GCC), which we will introduce in the "Government Community Cloud" section later in this chapter.

Financially, it is more advantageous to acquire a suite than acquire the core technologies individually. Aside from the financial incentive, Office 365 core technologies are also implemented in such a way that they are already integrated with each other.

> **Note**
>
> You can find detailed information about the plans at *http://office.microsoft.com/en-us/pc/redir/XT104063440.aspx.*

Office 365 terminology

There are several new terms that are used in Office 365. You will frequently hear these terms when Office 365 is discussed, so it is important to understand what they mean. These terms are also used extensively throughout this book.

Tenant

An Office 365 subscription is often referred to as a *tenant*. The tenant refers to the licensing model, but might also refer to the deployed platform. For example, when you purchase an Office 365 E3 subscription, you will have an E3 tenant, which refers to your licensing model. It also might be referred to as an E-tenant, meaning that your Office 365 tenant is an enterprise subscription, which differentiates it from a government subscription, also known as a G-tenant.

Tenant name

The tenant name, sometimes referred to as the Office 365 domain name, is the onmicrosoft.com name of your tenant. When you sign up for an Office 365 subscription and create a tenant, you will be asked to select an organization name. This name, if available, will be pre-appended to the onmicrosoft.com domain name and becomes the name of your tenant. For example, if you pick Adatum as the name, and if it is available, your tenant name will be adatum.onmicrosoft.com. Your tenant name does not preclude you from adding your true domain name to your tenant.

Vanity domain name

Your true domain name is referred to as the *vanity domain name*. Continuing with the preceding example, if you have a tenant called adatum.onmicrosoft.com, your users can have an email address in the form of *<User>*@adatum.onmicrosoft.com. However, often this is not desirable. Your organization's email address in this case might be *<User>*@adatum.com. Therefore, you need to add adatum.com as a vanity domain name to your adatum.

which is to refer to Office 365 with the version number of the software component. For example, if we are referring to Exchange Online 2010, we will refer to it as Office 365 with Exchange Online 2010 or simply as Exchange Online 2010.

Hybrid

Hybrid is frequently used in the context of the different Office 365 services. The term refers to the implementation of on-premises Exchange, SharePoint, and Lync coexisting and working with the respective online deployments. For example, Exchange in a hybrid environment is the integration of on-premises Exchange with Exchange Online; in this scenario, an enterprise could have some mailboxes hosted on-premises and others hosted online. We will discuss hybrid scenarios that are specific to individual services in later chapters. *Hybrid* can also refer to on-premises technology coexisting with a different Office 365 service. For example, you might want to continue hosting Exchange on-premises but would like to introduce Lync capabilities through Office 365. The ability to integrate Lync Online with on-premises Exchange is another example of a hybrid configuration involving different technologies.

Examples and screen shots

The examples, instructions, and screen shots in this book are based on Office 365 with the 2010 versions of the software as well as 2013 versions when they were in preview and final release. However, the majority of the focus is on Office 365 with 2013 software. Due to the rapid evolution of Office 365, your screen might not match some of the screen shots in this book. We plan to regularly update this book to address significant changes in Office 365.

Government Community Cloud

Microsoft recently announced a special version of Office 365 called the Government Community Cloud (GCC). The GCC is specifically created for United States government entities. A subscription to the GCC is sometimes referred to as a G-tenant. All US federal, state, and local government entities are eligible to sign up for the GCC instead of a traditional enterprise Office 365 subscription, which is sometimes referred to as an E-tenant because of the E1, E3, and E4 plan names associated with the commercial offerings for enterprises. Like the E plans, the GCC has corresponding G1, G3, and G4 plans.

The GCC was introduced to address very specific government regulatory requirements, such as the need for special auditing or for additional background checks and security clearances of Office 365 personnel. These requirements are unique to government entities and are not required for enterprise customers. It does not mean that the GCC is more secure than the commercial Office 365 subscriptions. While the GCC is reserved for government entities, it is not a requirement for a government organization to register for a G-tenant. Government organizations can choose to use an E-tenant if they do not require the special requirements found in the GCC.

It is important to stress that certain regulatory requirements are achievable only in the GCC. One example of this is the ability to host Criminal Justice Information Services (CJIS) data in Office 365. There is a specific process to accomplish this, but it can be done only within the GCC. We will discuss CJIS in the "Regulatory compliance" section later in this chapter.

Business case for Office 365

Technologists and technology leaders likely are already familiar with Office 365 as a technology platform. However, some might believe that Office 365 only provides cost-savings opportunities. Cost savings, tangible and intangible, form the basis for a business case to consider Office 365 over traditional technology adoption. However, there are other aspects of Office 365 that make it a compelling solution to consider adopting. The following sections highlight some of the more significant features of an Office 365 business case.

Subscription model

The subscription model for licensing software is an industry trend and not just applicable to Office 365. However, what Office 365 does is to make it more cost effective to access new technologies. It also makes it flexible for organizations to license software only at a level that matches their organization's consumption. This is sometimes known as a *pay-what-you-use* model. Office 365 provides the ability for organizations to add and remove licenses, and enterprises are billed on an annual basis. Office 365 also makes it flexible and cost effective for enterprise customers in two important ways:

- Office 365 licensing serves as the user client access license (CAL) for on-premises and cloud-based services.

- Office 365 ProPlus is licensed per user instead of per device, and provides each user with the ability to install and activate up to five copies of Office ProPlus.

The basis of Office 365 subscriptions originates from the SaaS model. While it is a big departure from the mindset of owning software, the benefits include a substantial cost sav-

adopted by large corporate organizations as well as many government entities throughout the world. As such, it has reached a level whereby the economy of scale allows Microsoft to lower the cost of operations and pass the savings to customers. To lower the cost of operations, Microsoft has invested significantly in efficient data center designs and renewable energy sources. These investments benefit customers as well as the environment.

Scalability

The sizeable investment in data center operations that support Office 365 is on a scale that is beyond the economic feasibility of many organizations, particularly if the organization's core business is not IT. Adopting Office 365 provides access to world-class data centers; the most current software can be scaled rapidly in response to business needs. There is no need to excessively build on-premises capacity. An organization that acquires more capacity than needed will incur a higher cost of operations as well as unnecessary acquisition expenses. On the other hand, if you do not build enough capacity in your data centers, you run the risk of having an undersized infrastructure that could impact the business. Finding the right level of data center capacity is challenging, and most IT organizations will err on the side of caution by choosing to have more capacity than needed. Office 365 eliminates this problem for IT organizations.

Redundancy

Office 365 data centers are geo-redundant and are configured as active-active pairs. Therefore, Office 365 customers inherit true redundancy because the infrastructure is not only duplicated, it is also distributed in geographically disparate locations to minimize the risk of outages due to natural disasters. Investing in geo-redundancy disaster recovery options is a significant financial challenge for many organizations and a near impossibility for many small organizations prior to Office 365.

Core competency

Microsoft is the largest software company and is the developer of all the software offered in Office 365. As the manufacturer of all the software from the operating system to the applications, offering the latest Microsoft technologies through Office 365 is definitely a core competency. As such, Office 365 customers benefit from the best trained data center operations personnel and can expect higher levels of availability and the shortest resolution time for problems compared to full reliance on in-house supported data center operations.

INSIDE OUT   From the desk of a Chief Information Officer

"Moving from a traditional on-premise environment to the cloud has been a great journey that will continue into the foreseeable future. Cloud technology in my view is only going to continue to mature and be of greater benefit to government and all industries as we are able to take advantage of the economies of scale, scalability, and redundancy that cloud platforms like Office 365 provide that we cannot duplicate within our own data centers. The benefits that the cloud platforms provide outweigh the current constraints. However, there are lessons to be learned from early adopters on how best to make the transition from an on-premise environment to a cloud Office 365 environment that should be understood before making the leap. This book will assist you in understanding how best to make the transition to O365 so that you have a smooth transition and understand the investment of resources and budget."

William Kehoe, Chief Information Officer (CIO)
King County, Washington

Trust Center

Microsoft is very serious about security and privacy. Therefore, Microsoft created the Office 365 Trust Center to ensure transparent and efficient communication about the security and privacy of Microsoft cloud services.

> **Note**
> The Microsoft Office 365 Trust Center is located at *http://office.microsoft.com/en-us/business/office-365-trust-center-cloud-computing-security-FX103030390.aspx*. It is important to ensure that the Trust Center topics apply to your subscription. For more information, see *http://www.microsoft.com/online/legal/v2/?docid=36&langid=en-us*.

- Compliance

- Service Continuity

The information includes easy-to-understand topics and videos, so you do not need to be a subject matter expert to grasp the principles.

Certifications

Microsoft uses certifications and third-party verifications of various standards and regulatory requirements to differentiate Office 365 as an enterprise cloud service. This is one area where Microsoft leads other large, public cloud providers. In most cases, it is already a fact that the level of investment, geographic footprint, and specialization in this field far exceed the IT standards required by any current or potential Office 365 customer. Most organizations are not in the business of running data centers, which really exist only to support the real core business of the organization.

The key Office 365 certifications to take note of are the following:

- ISO 27001

- SOC 2 Type 1

- EU Safe Harbor

- Statement on Standards for Attestation Engagements No. 16, which is the successor to SAS 70 and ISAE 3402

- Federal Information Security Management Act (FISMA)

> **Note**
>
> For more details about Office 365 certifications, see *http://www.microsoft.com/online/legal/v2/?docid=27*.

Regulatory compliance

Office 365 meets the standards and requirements that are outlined in certain regulatory compliance standards such as the following:

- Health Insurance Portability and Accountability Act (HIPAA)

- Family Education Right and Privacy Act (FERPA)

- Gramm Leach Bliley Act (GLBA)

INSIDE OUT   Criminal Justice Information Services

The newest regulatory compliance pursued by Microsoft is the Criminal Information Services (CJIS) Security Addendum. This is available only for the Government Community Cloud and needs to be achieved at the state level for each state. CJIS is an interesting requirement because it is applicable only to law enforcement agencies that consume CJIS data. Therefore, Microsoft works with each state's CJIS representative to achieve the necessary requirements, such as adjudication and background checks of personnel, to jointly meet CJIS requirements with the state. After that is accomplished, all law enforcement organizations in the state can use Office 365 and still meet CJIS requirements. States that have worked with Microsoft to jointly sign the CJIS Addendum include Texas and, most recently, New York. Microsoft Office 365 is the only major cloud service that currently has this capability. To read the press release regarding Texas and CJIS, see *http://www.microsoft.com/en-us/news/Press/2013/Feb13/02-15TexasO365PR.aspx*.

The key difference between certifications and regulatory compliance is that the latter does not have a formal certification process. Instead, regulatory compliance standards rely on scheduled audits to ensure adherence.

An organization that is required to adhere to such standards will find that the standards tend to cover all aspects of their operations, including organization policies, processes, security, and technology portfolio. Because Office 365 adheres to these standards, an organization can adopt Office 365 services and be assured that the security, technology, and services in Office 365 meet those requirements.

It is important to note that it does not mean the organization becomes compliant with the standards just by adopting Office 365; instead, it means that the organization can maintain or achieve the regulatory compliance with Office 365 as part of their portfolio. It is necessary to make this distinction because portions of the standards might cover requirements that are not part of Office 365. For example, a particular requirement might dictate that records are kept for only 365 days, after which they must be destroyed. This is an organization process. Office 365 meets this requirement because it provides the tools and methods that can easily implement this requirement. However, it might be up to the organization

Summary

This chapter discussed the core principles upon which Office 365 is built: privacy, transparency, security, and compliance. The core principles and economic relevance of Office 365 have made the cloud a significant and permanent part of any organization's IT portfolio. The following chapters will dive into the technical details and lessons learned by organizations that have adopted Office 365 since its debut as the Business Productivity Online Services (BPOS).

Planning and preparing to deploy Office 365

Approach to planning and evaluating Office 365 17   Network planning and analysis 26

L required for enterprise customers who want to leverage existing on-premises infrastructure, such as Active Directory (AD) identity management.

In this chapter, we start with the planning for foundational technologies and requirements for Office 365 as a whole and gather information to develop a sound project plan.

Later, in the chapters where we discuss implementation of a specific service, we cover service-specific planning and preparation tasks.

In Chapter 3, "Active Directory Federations Services" and Chapter 4, "Directory Synchronization," we dive into integration with AD, using Directory Synchronization and federating with Office 365. The goal is to provide enterprise users with the best possible experience, which can be described as users not even realizing that the site they are accessing is in the cloud or that their mailbox is not on an email server located somewhere in the building. A successful Office 365 deployment is defined as the seamless integration of Office 365 with your enterprise, and that is what we want to accomplish. Success is also defined as an outcome that leads to a reduction in meaningless workload for IT professionals.

Approach to planning and evaluating Office 365

Planning for Office 365 might seem like a daunting task. It definitely is not a small or simple project. To make it more manageable, we grouped the planning and remediation tasks into two major categories:

- Foundational planning and remediation tasks

- Service-specific planning and remediation tasks

Foundational planning and remediation tasks

Foundational planning refers to the initial steps we need to take to ensure that Office 365 services will work properly. Remediation tasks refer to tasks we need to complete to avoid the degradation of the end-user experience or IT administrator experience with the services. Foundational planning and remediation tasks are common requirements that affect all services.

A good example of a foundational issue you must address is whether you have enough network bandwidth to support an Office 365 initiative. Another example is Identity Management because you need to know how users will be managed. How does Office 365 make use of information in AD? If your organization is not using AD, what are your user management options in Office 365? Is AD healthy and ready for Office 365? These are all questions that need to be answered during the planning and evaluation phase. As you can see, this is independent of the type of service you want to use in Office 365.

Service-specific planning and remediation tasks

Because Office 365 is a suite of tools—Exchange Online, SharePoint Online, Lync Online, and Office Professional Plus Subscription—there are tasks we need to perform from a planning perspective that are specific and unique to each service. Thus, as the name implies, service-specific planning and remediation tasks pertain to specific Office 365 services.

For example, if a user mailbox is migrated from the on-premises Exchange email server to Office 365 Exchange Online, will the user still be able to see the free and busy times of others whose mailboxes might still reside in the on-premises Exchange email server? If users have non-Windows mobile devices, will they be able to use the new Lync Online communication capabilities that come with the Office 365 suite the company is planning to purchase? These questions are all service related, and while they might span across multiple services and are just as important, they are not considered part of the foundational technologies.

Office 365 planning, deployment, and troubleshooting tools

Microsoft and third-party vendors make a number of tools available to enterprise customers. The following list shows the common tools you can use:

- Office 365 Service Descriptions

- Office 365 Deployment Guide

- Microsoft Office 365 Deployment Readiness Toolkit

- Lync Online Transport Reliability Probe (*http://trippsn2.online.lync.com/*)

- Microsoft Remote Connectivity Analyzer

- IP mapping service to determine data center locations (*http://iplocation.net*)

- Microsoft Online Services Diagnostics and Logging (MOSDAL) Support Toolkit

There is also an abundance of Office 365 content that is available online. One such resource

Depending on the size of your organization and licensing agreement with Microsoft, you might have a Microsoft Account Team assigned to you. If you know you have a Microsoft Account Team, you should contact your Microsoft Account Executive. Because of the complexity associated with enterprise customers, Microsoft conducts technical briefings and workshops that are designed to help customers better understand Office 365, its integration with existing technologies, and navigating licensing scenarios. Oftentimes, these pre-sales engagements do not cost you anything, and you will come out of them with a much better understanding of how to evaluate, plan for, and ultimately deploy Office 365 successfully.

Office 365 Service Descriptions

Microsoft Office 365 Service Descriptions are the most overlooked documents, which is unfortunate because these are very good documents that answer a lot of basic questions about each of the Office 365 services: SharePoint Online, Exchange Online, Lync Online, and Office Professional Plus Subscription. They have a surprising amount of detailed information that your organization will be interested in knowing. For example, in the Service Descriptions you can find answers to the following questions:

- How is the financially backed 99.9 percent Service Level Agreement (SLA) calculated?

- How much storage space will you get with SharePoint Online?

- What capabilities are in SharePoint Online versus the SharePoint on-premises server?

- Are there throttling limits in Exchange Online? If so, what are they?

- Do you get charged for shared and resource mailboxes?

- Can you federate Lync Online with other solutions?

- How do you manage Office Professional Plus Subscription licenses?

- What is the difference between Plan 1 and Plan 2?

- What is E-Suite versus Kiosk?

These questions represent just a small sampling of the valuable information found in the Service Descriptions. Another important point to make is that the Service Descriptions are considered the authoritative source of Office 365 capabilities, and they are updated on a regular basis.

> **Note**
>
> You can download the Office 365 Service Descriptions at *http://www.microsoft.com/ en-us/download/details.aspx?id=13602* in Microsoft Word and PDF formats.

INSIDE OUT   Keep the Service Descriptions close to you

You will be surprised by how many questions we are able to answer just by referring to the Service Descriptions. As consultants and architects, we carry them with us on our Surface and other electronic devices. They are our top reference materials.

Office 365 Deployment Guide

The Office 365 Deployment Guide is a very useful resource that organizes all the project planning information and tools available. It provides high-level guidance on tasks and the recommended order, phases, and best practices. Since being migrated to an online resource at *http://technet.microsoft.com/en-us/library/hh852466.aspx*, it has become more effective as a planning tool because it is easy to navigate within the document.

One valuable use of the Office 365 Deployment Guide is the guidance on the different types of deployment models. For example, if you are going to deploy a hybrid Exchange environment, there are prescriptive guidelines on how you should approach such a project. If you have to migrate from Lotus Notes to Exchange Online, there is targeted information pertaining to this type of project. Therefore, if you have a good idea about how your Office 365 project might look, you should start by reviewing the Deployment Guide for specifics pertaining to your type of requirements. Or, if you are uncertain about the requirements for your project, you could scan the Deployment Guide to get an overall sense of how to begin formulating those requirements.

Figure 2-1 shows an excerpt from the Office 365 Deployment Guide that explains how to approach a migration project. You can find this excerpt at *http://technet.microsoft.com/ en-us/library/hh852410.aspx*.

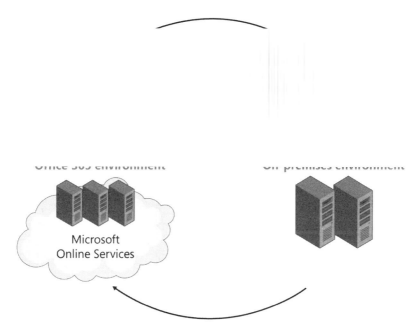

3. Migrate
- Migrate and synchronize Exchange mailbox content, calendars, and contacts
- Use third-party tools to migrate Lotus or GroupWise mailboxes
- Configure mobile device connectivity
- Perform service validation testing

Figure 2-1 Excerpt from the Office 365 Deployment Guide that outlines the main phases of a migration project.

Microsoft Office 365 Deployment Readiness Toolkit

As with most major projects, the first question is often, "Where do we even begin?" To help answer this question, in this section we show you how to download and begin using the Microsoft Office 365 Deployment Readiness Toolkit. The reason we like this toolkit is because it does a good job of gathering all the baseline information about your environment, and then it proceeds to tell you how ready your environment is for Office 365.

The information that the Deployment Readiness Toolkit gathers might include service-specific information. For that reason, we will revisit this tool and cover it in greater detail in the chapters covering each of the services.

You can download the Microsoft Office 365 Deployment Readiness Toolkit from the Microsoft Download Center at *http://www.microsoft.com/en-us/download/default.aspx* or from the Microsoft Office 365 Community website at *http://community.office365.com/en-us/forums/183/p/2285/8155.aspx*.

After you have downloaded the toolkit, follow these steps:

1. Identify a computer on which you will install the toolkit. The computer must to be joined to the domain.

2. Copy the downloaded toolkit to the domain-joined computer, unzip the package, and run the executable (.exe).

3. When the installation is complete, the toolkit will launch your browser and start analyzing your environment, as shown in Figure 2-2. Depending on the size of AD and the number of objects, the tool might take some time to gather the required information.

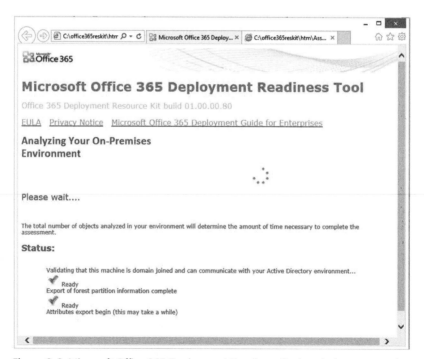

Figure 2-2 Microsoft Office 365 Deployment Readiness Tool analyzing your environment.

After the tool has finished gathering all the information, the page in the browser will be updated accordingly, as shown in Figure 2-3.

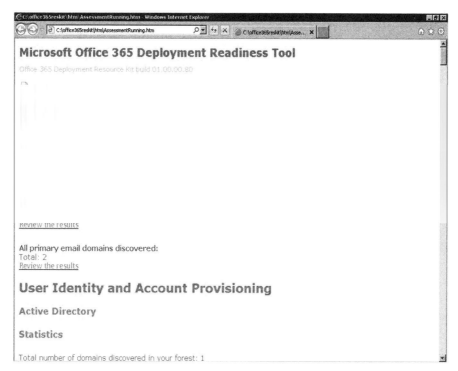

Figure 2-3 Results from the Office 365 Deployment Readiness Tool.

Review the results from the tool. You will notice the following information has been gathered:

- Information about email domains

- Number and names of AD forests and domains discovered

- Number of users, contacts, groups, and mailboxes

- Estimated number of AD objects to be synchronized

- AD forest schema and functional level

- Any detected clean-up tasks that need to be remediated in AD

- Any issues that might impact specific services, such as SharePoint Online, Lync Online, and Exchange Online

- Information on network IP addresses, trace route results, DNS records, and ports

Informational content is denoted by a blue icon that looks like a stylized "i." If there are notes, those will be denoted with an icon resembling a notepad. Areas that are ready and have no issues are denoted by a green check mark. Issues are denoted with a yellow triangle with an exclamation point inside. Figure 2-4 shows a sample report.

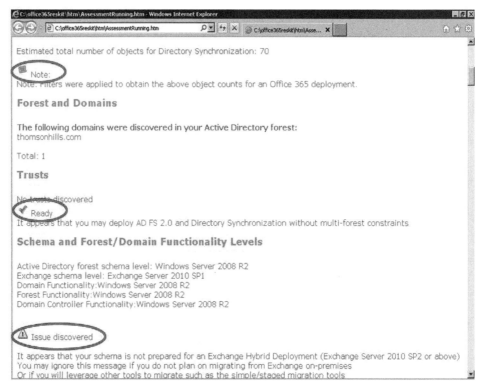

Figure 2-4 Information and issues discovered.

As shown in Figure 2-5, there are Quick Links at the top of the report that take you directly to specific sections of the report. For example, if you are interested only in information related to tasks you need to undertake to prepare your AD for Office 365, click the Active Directory Clean Up link. If you are interested in issues that need to be remediated in order to incorporate Exchange Online, click the Exchange Online link.

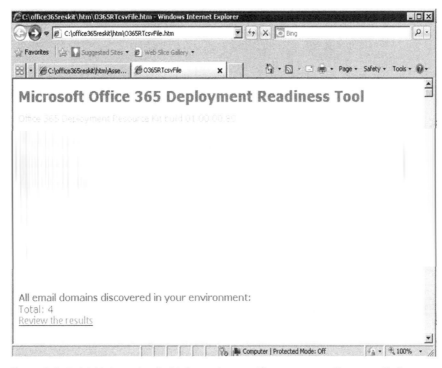

Figure 2-5 Quick Links to detailed information specific to areas needing remediation.

There is one particular Quick Link titled CSV File Maker. This link exports additional information to .csv files and saves them in your c:\office365reskit\do_not_modify directory, as shown in Figure 2-6. An example of the type of information that is exported to .csv files includes a list of user names and their corresponding user principal names (UPN). In fact, the report might refer you to a specific .csv file for additional information. In one report that we ran, we were told that a particular user name had a UPN that was too long, and we were referred to the employeeid.thomsonhills.com file. When we opened the file, all user identities were listed, and we were able to easily identify the user with the long UPN.

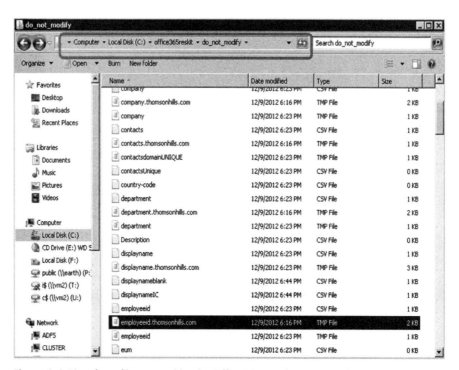

Figure 2-6 List of .csv files created by the Office 365 Deployment Readiness Tool.

The Office 365 Readiness Toolkit will generate a lot of information. You likely will spend a significant of time remediating issues and re-running the tool several times until all the issues have been remediated.

Network planning and analysis

The topic of network requirements is one of the most frequently asked questions whenever we talk to organizations about Office 365 mainly because of the emphasized dependency on the Internet for services to be rendered. IT departments often are very concerned about whether they need to have more bandwidth to deploy Office 365.

Before you sign a long-term contract for an increase in bandwidth, let us set some context for this topic:

- Quality is just as important as quantity. You might have enough bandwidth, but your network latency might be too high.

- You might not need as much bandwidth as you might imagine.

Quality vs. quantity

Two of the most miscommunicated concepts in networking are bandwidth and latency. The quality of your Internet connection is really a composite of both bandwidth and latency, which is a combination of the size of the pipe plus the time it takes to move data through that pipe.

For example, your Internet service provider (ISP) might provide you with a 1.5 megabits

and routers. You can increase your bandwidth by purchasing more or by combining multiple pipes. It is more difficult to reduce latency because you might not have control over the connection medium, but you might have control in reducing the number of intermediate devices or making those devices more efficient by upgrading the network cards in the devices. You also might be able to work with your ISP to reduce the number of hops or use a different ISP that might be closer to the Internet backbone or is part of the Internet backbone. We will discuss the importance of the Internet backbone in the "Misconception about distance" section later in this chapter.

To measure the quality of your network connection, you need to fully measure the throughput in terms of bits per second (bps), Mbps, and gigabits per second (Gbps).

TROUBLESHOOTING

A popular network topology is a star topology where the Internet connection might be located at the corporate headquarters or some central location. Branch offices might need to traverse point-to-point network connections such as fiber, T1/DS3, frame relay, microwave, or other types of leased lines to get to the corporate Internet gateways. We have seen many customers focus only on their Internet connection and overlook these point-to-point connections between branch offices. Office 365 is designed to be a secure solution so all transmissions are encrypted through a Secure Sockets Layer (SSL) or Transport Layer Security (TLS). This adds overhead. Furthermore, if you employ network acceleration technologies, these might no longer work in Office 365 because many network acceleration technologies need to have the ability to look inside the packets in order to apply compression algorithms. Encrypted packets prevent the ability to look inside packets, thus rendering network acceleration technologies ineffective. These are examples of impacts to the corporate network that you need to pay attention to, especially if you have multiple branch or remote offices.

Misconception about distance

One misconception about Office 365 is the notion that the nearest data center is still so far away. While it is easy to think of distance as a factor that inversely affects quality and latency, it really is less of an issue at the Office 365 level. This is because the Office 365 data centers are built in strategic locations throughout the world and are placed on Tier 1 networks, also known as the Internet backbone. Tier 1 networks are owned by large government and private organizations that have either scale or peering agreements in place with other Tier 1 network providers. Peer Tier 1 networks have direct point-to-point connections, which is often the case with fiber across countries, oceans, and continents. The Internet backbone is the fastest connection on the Internet, hence its name.

With Office 365 data centers sitting along the Internet backbone, the moment that network traffic reaches any point on the backbone, that traffic will take the fastest route to the nearest Office 365 data center. The slowest link will be from your on-premises gateway, to the ISP, and from the ISP to the backbone, if the ISP is not already part of the backbone.

For security reasons, Microsoft does not disclose the locations of all its data centers, although some are commonly known, such as the largest one in Chicago. Figure 2-7 illustrates how the data centers are located along the Internet backbone. However, note that it is not an accurate representation of the locations or number of data centers throughout the world. This figure is meant to serve only as a visual representation of the point-to-point, multiple, redundant connections that constitute the Internet backbone and how the Office 365 data centers are situated along these connections.

Aside from speed, the Internet backbone is also built with redundant connections managed by algorithms that optimize speed and availability. In other words, the Internet backbone is capable of self-repairing through re-routing and recovery. Thus, there is redundancy designed into the Internet backbone and, as a result, Office 365 data centers benefit from the redundancy as well.

Speed test

Now that we have discussed the importance of network speed (latency) and all the factors that affect speed, we need a plan to test the speed of your network connection from your organization to the nearest Office 365 data center.

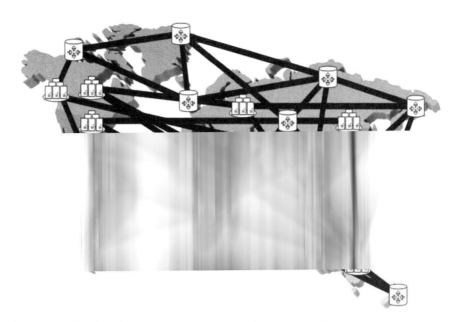

Figure 2-7 Office 365 data centers located along the Internet backbone.

The simplest approach for testing network speed is to use an online tool such as the tool available at *http://www.speedtest.net*. The problem with some online speed test tools is that they might not accurately represent your true speed, especially if these tools are provided by your ISP. For example, if your ISP developed and provided an online speed test tool, it might invariably yield a higher performance than what you are truly experiencing because the tool might be measuring your network location to another location owned and operated by the same ISP. This is akin to measuring an internal network, and of course we hope that any reputable ISP would at the very least have a snappy internal network!

The pairing of an IP address to a geographical location is known as geolocation. Therefore, the first step for a more valid test is to determine the geolocation between you and a point on the Internet backbone that is closest to an Office 365 data center. Next, you can use a tool that allows you to custom select a point closest to the geolocation of that data center and run the test. Here are the steps:

1. First, you need to determine the Office 365 data center that will respond to you. Open a command-prompt window and type **ping outlook.com**, as shown in Figure 2-8. Outlook.com will not respond, so you will get a Request timed out error message. However, simply take note of the IP address, which is 157.56.237.251 in this example.

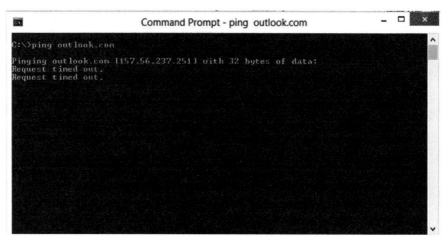

Figure 2-8 Pinging outlook.com

2. Open a browser and go to *http://www.iplocation.net.*

Your IP address should be detected, but what you need to enter is the IP address of outlook.com, which was served from a data center that responded to you. That address is the one you noted from Step 1, which is 157.56.237.251 in our example. Type your address from Step 1 and click Query, as shown in Figure 2-9.

Figure 2-9 Geolocation information for outlook.com.

3. Iplocation.net will consult up to three lookup sources to determine the location from which an IP address is being served. Take note of this location. In the example shown in Figure 2-9, the geolocation information for outlook.com is in Redmond, Washington.

4. Go to *http://www.speedtest.net*. Notice that speedtest.net automatically detected your IP address, and you have the option to begin the test. Without any configuration, speedtest.net will use your IP address and pair it with the geolocation of the closest speedtest.net server to conduct the test. However, we would like to select a server whose geolocation is the closest to the Office 365 data center that we were directed to. In this example, it is Redmond, WA. So instead of clicking Begin Test, click Settings, as shown in Figure 2-10.

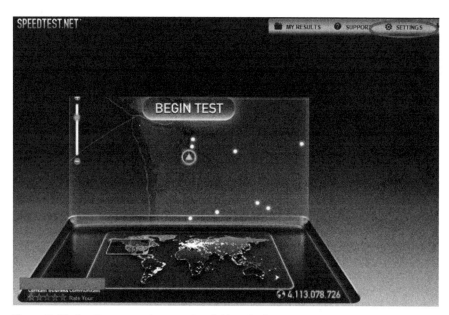

Figure 2-10 Configure speedtest.net by clicking Settings.

5. At the lower right of the Settings page, as shown in Figure 2-11, click the Preferred Server drop-down box and select a location of a speedtest.net server that is closest to the Office 365 data center location revealed by iplocation.net. In our example, we selected Seattle, WA., which is very close to Redmond, WA.

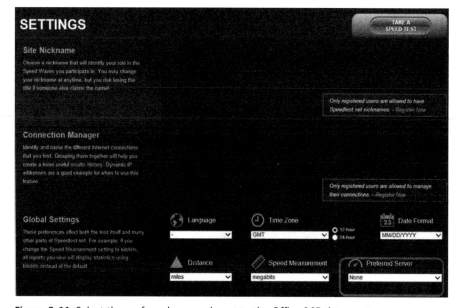

Figure 2-11 Select the preferred server closest to the Office 365 data center.

6. After you have selected your preferred server, click Save at the bottom of the screen, then click the Take A Speed Test button at the top of the screen, as shown in Figure 2-12.

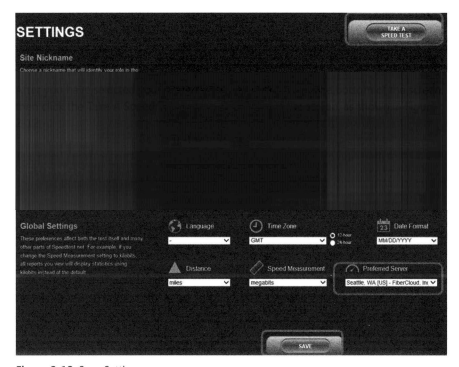

Figure 2-12 Save Settings.

7. You will return to a screen similar to the one you began with, except that you now have the option to click Begin Test with either the recommended server or your preferred server, as shown in Figure 2-13. Click Begin Test with your preferred server.

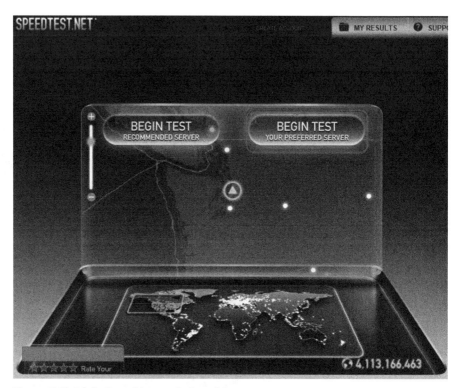

Figure 2-13 Begin Test with Your Preferred Server.

   8.   The results of your speed test will be available shortly and will be similar to Figure
            2-14.

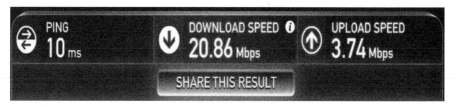

Figure 2-14 Results from speedtest.net.

In summary, this exercise helped you determine the performance of Office 365 with respect
to network speed through the following actions:

   ●   Determining the Office 365 data center that likely will serve your organization by
       pinging outlook.com.

   ●   Using iplocation.net to identify the geolocation of the Office 365 data center.

- Customizing the settings of speedtest.net so you can run a speed test between your location and a geolocation that is closest to the Office 365 data center.

In this example, our speed test results reveal that we have 20.86 Mbps available in download speed and 3.74 Mbps available in upload speed. The 10 ms ping result is the latency of the network. In the next section, where we calculate the network demands of Office 365 services, we can determine whether you have adequate network performance to support a good experience for your users when you migrate them to Office 365. If not, we might

more congested at that time. It might taper off significantly at lunch time and around quitting time at 5:00 P.M. If your organization is using commercial broadband, other ISP customers also might contribute to network congestion at different times of the day. Therefore, it is a good idea to conduct your speed test exercise during different times of the day, especially during known peak times, so that you can get an average of your network performance as well as the level of peak demand. If you have intelligent network gear in your organization, most of this information can be collected automatically as part of the network gear's capabilities, or you might use tools like a Fluke meter to collect network statistics. The extra effort and time you put in to diligently baseline your network utilization will help you be more accurate in predicting the experience with Office 365 and thus help you determine whether network remediation is required.

Basic traffic analysis

You should have some basic traffic information about your organization. For example, you should have some idea as to the types of traffic on your network and how much bandwidth each type of traffic is consuming. Most enterprise networks should have undergone at least one Quality of Service (QoS) analysis exercise that would yield the information you require. From the earlier exercise, you should also have an idea of your Internet speed.

Let us go through a basic traffic analysis so we can demonstrate how to create a baseline idea of the amount of bandwidth you would need for your environment. Figure 2-15 shows a network diagram that depicts the types of network traffic found in the different network segments.

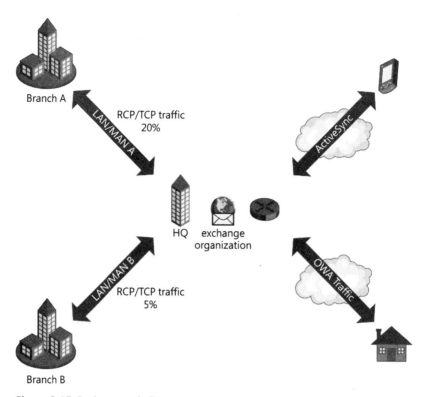

Figure 2-15 Basic network diagram.

Using purely hypothetical numbers for illustrative purposes, Figure 2-15 shows an organization with two branch offices connected to the Exchange server located at headquarters (called HQ in the figure) through a Local Area Network (LAN), Metropolitan Area Network (MAN), or some type of point-to-point network connection such as frame relay or fiber. After collecting traffic information from your network devices, you are able to determine that 20 percent of the traffic between Branch A is from Outlook communicating with the Exchange server. For Branch B, that volume is only 5 percent.

You might also have users who are accessing email through the web from outside your organization using Outlook Web App (OWA), and you determined that 25 percent of your Internet bandwidth is spent serving OWA access. You might also have a growing number of users with smartphones, and they are using ActiveSync to check their email. This might occur even though they are physically in one of the office buildings, which is why it is not surprising that 30 percent of your Internet bandwidth is spent on ActiveSync connections.

What Figure 2-15 tells us is that 55 percent of your Internet bandwidth is used to connect to the corporate Exchange server. The 25 percent email traffic from both branch offices is not a factor to your Internet connection because the offices are connected directly to HQ through other types of connections (LAN/MAN).

Now let us introduce Office 365 and evaluate just the email workload. With Office 365 Exchange Online, we will move mailboxes to Office 365. Figure 2-16 shows how your network diagram will change to reflect the new environment.

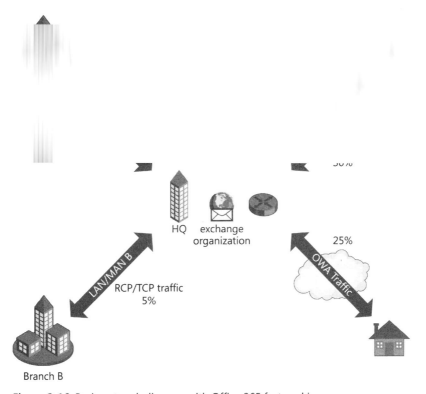

Figure 2-16 Basic network diagram with Office 365 factored in.

Assuming negligible changes in network traffic, with the introduction of Office 365 into the environment and shifting email workload to the cloud, the ActiveSync and OWA traffic is now no longer consuming your Internet bandwidth just to get to an on-premises Exchange server. Therefore, in this example we have offloaded 55 percent (30 percent + 25 percent) of the previously consumed bandwidth.

However, because Branch A and Branch B users now need to access their mailboxes in Office 365, their traffic is being passed through your Internet gateway, thereby consuming 25 percent (20 percent + 5 percent) of the Internet bandwidth, which in this case still results in a net savings of 35 percent (55 percent - 25 percent) of your Internet bandwidth consumption.

This is different for different organizations because it really depends on your network utilization, which basic traffic analysis and information gathering should yield. What is important in this exercise is to illustrate that bandwidth utilization will shift with the introduction of Office 365, and it might not necessarily mean you must always increase bandwidth because of Office 365. Due diligence in gathering and documenting the network traffic information can help you better determine how much traffic is in each segment and where they would apply after Office 365 is introduced.

INSIDE OUT   Bring your own device (BYOD)

We all have heard of the BYOD phenomenon. Every smartphone requires a data plan and, in the United States, carriers mandate data plans for subscribers who purchase smartphones. More and more people are demanding access to corporate email from their smart phones, and they are very comfortable reading and responding to emails from the devices. Most of the organizations we work with indicated a dramatic increase in ActiveSync traffic because of the proliferation of BYOD.

This sample exercise takes into consideration only a single service, which is Exchange Online. You will have to go through a similar exercise with the other services, SharePoint Online and Lync Online. Office Professional Plus Subscription is installed on desktops; therefore, it does not impact your Internet bandwidth. The only time Office Professional Plus Subscription impacts bandwidth is if you are streaming deployments from Office 365 directly to client computers. However, that typically is temporary traffic as a result of the deployment and not constant like email traffic. Your enterprise-class Internet connection might also have a provision for a certain amount of "burstable" bandwidth that would be very useful in such scenarios.

We will stick with the email scenario for a little longer before proceeding to the bandwidth requirements analysis for SharePoint Online and Lync Online.

Putting it all together

In finalizing our example, let us put together the information we were able to collect. In the preceding exercise, we determined that our network speed is 20.86 Mbps down and 3.74 Mbps up.

Let us also assume we are satisfied with the performance of email with our current on-premises Exchange server, and that is the only workload we are concerned with at this time. We want to ensure that users will not experience performance degradation with email when we move to Office 365 Exchange Online.

From Figure 2-15, we know that users are currently accessing the on-premises Exchange server with OWA and ActiveSync from outside our network. This is putting a load on our Internet gateway to the tune of 55 percent of our available bandwidth. Our on-premises Exchange is primarily serving up information to these devices, so to be more specific, 55 percent of our 3.74 Mbps (2.06 Mbps) is used to serve up OWA and ActiveSync requests. That leaves only 1.683 Mbps available for everything else.

By moving to Office 365 Exchange Online, we would free up 2.06 Mbps of OWA and

Mbps down, this increase does not look like it will be a significant impact.

In reality, there will also be an increase in the outgoing connection (up) because internal users are also sending emails, and they need to send them through to Office 365 Exchange Online. This is an example where if we do the due diligence to gather that information, we can more accurately determine whether this increase will offset the savings of 2.06 Mbps we saved from offloading OWA and ActiveSync traffic.

Alternative approach to email traffic analysis

Let us consider a scenario where you do not have the ability to collect granular traffic information about your network environment. It is still important for us to come up with a strategy to intelligently estimate the network requirements needed to support email through Office 365 Exchange Online. It is not a good strategy to "make a wild guess." Nor is it fiscally prudent to over-provision bandwidth so that network capacity will never be a factor, although the latter strategy can guarantee user experience will not be impacted.

For a scenario where you need to make an intelligent estimate of the network traffic requirements for email, you will have to at least know your users' behavior. We will introduce the concept of profiling your users and then applying behavior data to come up with an intelligent estimate.

You can download a very comprehensive Excel workbook to help you with estimating the amount of client email traffic.

> **Note**
>
> This workbook is located at *http://gallery.technet.microsoft.com/office/Exchange-Client-Network-8af1bf00* and as of this writing, it is still in beta. Even though it is still in beta, the workbook is very useful and can immediately help you estimate Exchange client traffic. This was developed by the Microsoft Exchange team, and you can find detailed instructions on how to use the workbook on the team's blog site at *http://blogs.technet.com/b/exchange/archive/2012/02/10/announcing-the-exchange-client-network-bandwidth-calculator-beta.aspx*.

When you open the workbook, you will notice there are several tabbed spreadsheets within the workbook. The first tab is where the instructions are located. The most important thing we want to point out is that the workbook is designed with Office 365 in mind. Therefore, as shown in Figure 2-17, make sure you select Office 365 as the service you will be using this workbook for. You can also change the other values according to the profile of your organization. Just read the instructions at the top of this spreadsheet.

By selecting Office 365 in the first tab, when you go to the second tab titled Client Mix, only the supported clients in Office 365 are highlighted. If you did not select Office 365, all the other clients, such as Outlook 2003, will be dimmed to indicate that those values should not be considered in an Office 365 scenario. You might still want to track this data by not selecting Office 365 in the first tab and using the Office 365 icon next to the supported clients in this tab to help with identifying which clients are supported in Office 365. This approach is particularly useful if you want to maintain a comprehensive representation of your organization, which might include legacy clients that need to be migrated. Figure 2-18 shows the client columns that have been dimmed because they are not supported in Office 365. Notice the Office 365 logo at the top of the columns with clients that are supported.

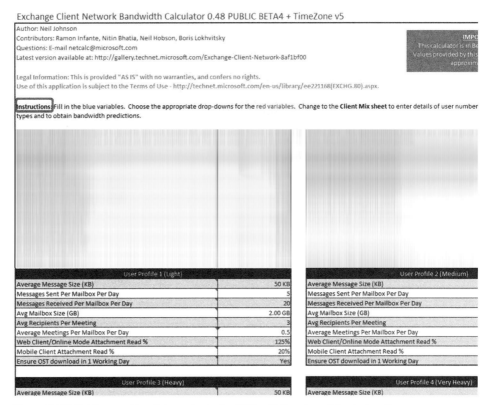

Exchange Client Network Bandwidth Calculator 0.48 PUBLIC BETA4 + TimeZone v5

Author: Neil Johnson
Contributors: Ramon Infante, Nitin Bhatia, Neil Hobson, Boris Lokhvitsky
Questions: E-mail netcalc@microsoft.com
Latest version available at: http://gallery.technet.microsoft.com/Exchange-Client-Network-8af1bf00

Legal Information: This is provided "AS IS" with no warranties, and confers no rights.
Use of this application is subject to the Terms of Use - http://technet.microsoft.com/en-us/library/ee221168(EXCHG.80).aspx.

Instructions: Fill in the blue variables. Choose the appropriate drop-downs for the red variables. Change to the **Client Mix sheet** to enter details of user number types and to obtain bandwidth predictions.

User Profile 1 (Light)	
Average Message Size (KB)	50 KB
Messages Sent Per Mailbox Per Day	5
Messages Received Per Mailbox Per Day	20
Avg Mailbox Size (GB)	2.00 GB
Avg Recipients Per Meeting	3
Average Meetings Per Mailbox Per Day	0.5
Web Client/Online Mode Attachment Read %	125%
Mobile Client Attachment Read %	20%
Ensure OST download in 1 Working Day	Yes

User Profile 2 (Medium)	
Average Message Size (KB)	
Messages Sent Per Mailbox Per Day	
Messages Received Per Mailbox Per Day	
Avg Mailbox Size (GB)	
Avg Recipients Per Meeting	
Average Meetings Per Mailbox Per Day	
Web Client/Online Mode Attachment Read %	
Mobile Client Attachment Read %	
Ensure OST download in 1 Working Day	

User Profile 3 (Heavy)	
Average Message Size (KB)	50 KB

User Profile 4 (Very Heavy)	
Average Message Size (KB)	

Figure 2-17 Set the workbook to evaluate for Office 365 and read the instructions.

Site Definition				2011	2010		2007		2003	
Site	Site User Profile	TimeZone	Concurrency	MAC (EWS)	OA-Cached		OA-Cached			
Site 1	Light	GMT	100%		50		234			
Site 2	Medium	GMT	100%	200			43			
Site 3	Light	GMT	100%				456			
Site 4	Light	GMT	100%							

Figure 2-18 Client columns are not highlighted because they are not supported in Office 365.

As you fill out the number of clients in each location and the types of users (light, medium, heavy, or very heavy), the network requirements for the site are displayed, as shown in Figure 2-19.

Network Predictions				
Total	Network Bandwidth (Exchange to Client)	Network Bandwidth (Client to Exchange)	Recommended Maximum Network Latency	TCP Connections (Aproximation)
304	1.03 Mbits/sec	0.07 Mbits/sec	320 ms	2069
265	1.40 Mbits/sec	0.31 Mbits/sec	320 ms	576
456	1.28 Mbits/sec	0.10 Mbits/sec	320 ms	3283

Figure 2-19 Network predictions.

You can always split a site into two rows if you have detailed enough profile information for a site whereby you know the number of light users and the number of heavy users. For example, you can rename "Site 1" to "London heavy users" and "Site 2" to "London light users" and provide the appropriate values for each row.

In this tab, there is also a graph, as shown in Figure 2-20, that depicts the traffic distribution throughout the day. This is patterned based on information you entered in the Input tab, such as the value of Working Day (hours).

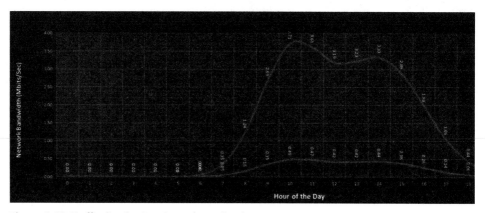

Figure 2-20 Traffic distribution throughout the day.

The Data Tables tab, as shown in Figure 2-21, is where the traffic demands are associated to the different types of users: light, medium, heavy, and very heavy. We recommend you not change these values unless you know for certain that your definitions for such users are different from Microsoft's general profile. The values in the Data Tables tab are used in other parts of the workbook, primarily the Client Mix tab, to calculate the charts and tables.

User Profile 1 (Light) [Sent: 5 Recv: 20 AvgMsg: 50 KB]				User Profile 2 (Medium) [Sent: 10 Recv: 40 AvgMsg: 50 KB]			
Client	kB/Day	kB/s (Peak)	kbps (Peak)	Client	kB/Day	kB/s (Peak)	kbps (Peak)
Outlook 2010 (OA-Cached)	2408.8	0.18	1.42	Outlook 2010 (OA-Cached)	3674.9	0.27	2.17
Outlook 2010 (MAPI-Cached)	2354.1	0.17	1.39	Outlook 2010 (MAPI-Cached)	3573.3	0.26	2.11
Outlook 2010 (MAPI-Online)	2037.4	0.15	1.20	Outlook 2010 (MAPI-Online)	3783.5	0.28	2.23
Outlook 2007 (OA-Cached)	2393.7	0.18	1.41	Outlook 2007 (OA-Cached)	3644.0	0.27	2.15
Outlook 2007 (MAPI-Cached)	2357.2	0.17	1.39	Outlook 2007 (MAPI-Cached)	3579.7	0.26	2.11
Outlook 2010 (OA-Cached)	6207.2	0.46	3.66	Outlook 2010 (OA-Cached)	8733.3	0.64	5.15
Outlook 2010 (MAPI-Cached)	6011.7	0.44	3.54	Outlook 2010 (MAPI-Cached)	8450.2	0.62	4.98
Outlook 2010 (MAPI-Online)	7273.3	0.54	4.29	Outlook 2010 (MAPI-Online)	10763.1	0.79	6.35
Outlook 2007 (OA-Cached)	6144.6	0.45	3.62	Outlook 2007 (OA-Cached)	8645.2	0.64	5.10
Outlook 2007 (MAPI-Cached)	6024.7	0.44	3.55	Outlook 2007 (MAPI-Cached)	8469.7	0.62	4.99
Outlook 2007 (MAPI-Online)	6539.9	0.48	3.86	Outlook 2007 (MAPI-Online)	9663.0	0.71	5.70
Outlook 2003 (OA-Cached)	4771.0	0.35	2.81	Outlook 2003 (OA-Cached)	6592.9	0.49	3.89
Outlook 2003 (MAPI-Cached)	4638.4	0.34	2.73	Outlook 2003 (MAPI-Cached)	6445.8	0.48	3.80
Outlook 2003 (MAPI-Online)	5081.0	0.37	3.00	Outlook 2003 (MAPI-Online)	7527.2	0.55	4.44
OWA 2007	7822.9	0.58	4.61	OWA 2007	11681.5	0.86	6.89
OWA 2010	7229.3	0.53	4.26	OWA 2010	10823.4	0.80	6.38
Windows Mobile 6.x	1119.0	0.08	0.66	Windows Mobile 6.x	1640.8	0.12	0.97
Windows Phone 7.x	1017.7	0.08	0.60	Windows Phone 7.x	1488.9	0.11	0.88
Outlook 2011 (EWS)	9167.6	0.68	5.41	Outlook 2011 (EWS)	13085.5	0.96	7.72

Figure 2-21 Data tables for light, medium, heavy, and very heavy users.

After you have determined the traffic requirements based on user profiling, you can use the calculated values and compare them to what is available in your environment to determine the likelihood of the need for a network upgrade.

Remember that while this is a very comprehensive workbook, its accuracy depends on how good a job you did with user profiling.

Network requirements for SharePoint Online

So far, we have covered only email traffic. SharePoint Online is another service that will consume network resources because it is your collaboration solution. Users will be using SharePoint to store, retrieve, share, and co-author documents. As such, the network requirements for SharePoint Online might be significant. The good news is that estimating SharePoint Online traffic is less complex than Exchange Online.

To estimate SharePoint Online traffic resource requirements, we first need to state the following baseline metrics provided by the Microsoft Online Services team:

- Each SharePoint Online page transfer consumes approximately 100 KB.

- On average, a typical user transfers approximately 36 pages an hour.

- About 10 percent of your organization's users will be using SharePoint Online simultaneously throughout the day.

Now that we know the metrics for typical SharePoint Online use, let us start profiling a sample organization to use as an example.

Example

A. Datum Corporation has 5,000 employees, and we need to estimate the network resources required for SharePoint Online.

Number of simultaneous users at any time = (0.1 x 5,000) = 500 users.

Network consumption per user = 36 pages/hour x 100,000 bytes x 8 bits/byte x 1hour/3,600seconds = 8,000 bps.

Organization's network requirements for SharePoint Online = 500 users x 8,000 bps/user = 4 Mbps.

Network requirements for Lync Online

The network requirements for Lync Online are also relatively easy to calculate. First, it is important to understand that, with the exception of multi-party virtual meetings where there is no multicast support, all other Lync communications will require only the Lync server to initiate the connection, after which the Lync clients communicate directly with each other. Therefore, internal Lync communications might not traverse your organization's Internet connection after the session has been initiated.

You can find the requirements for Lync Online in Appendix A of the Lync Online Service Description, and we have also listed them in Table 2-1.

TABLE 2-1 Lync Online bandwidth requirements

Feature	Bandwidth Requirements
Data	56 Kbps minimum / 56 Kbps high quality
Voice	50 Kbps minimum / 80 Kbps high quality
Video	50 Kbps minimum / 250 Kbps for CIF / 600 Kbps for

> **Note**
>
> The Lync Transport Reliability IP Probe is located at *http://trippsn2.online.lync.com/*.

This probe tests your network connection to determine a variety of characteristics including latency, jitter, packet loss, and the ability to sustain a consistent data stream, which is important for voice quality. Figure 2-22 shows the results of the Lync Online Transport Reliability IP Probe. The tabs along the left side provide a wide range of information to help you determine the quality of the Lync Online service based on your organization's network capabilities. As with all the testing tools we have introduced, you should run this tool during different times of the day to get a more accurate idea of your network performance during the course of the day.

Lync Online

Transport Reliability IP Probe

This reliability tool tests your Internet connection to a Microsoft Lync Online Service data center and measures the response times, bandwidth, allowed ports, route taken, and overall connection quality with respect to Real Time Media. The results can help you evaluate your network configuration for potential use with the Microsoft Lync Online Service. This tool does not engage any of the offerings from Microsoft Lync Online Service. Instead, it focuses on the quality of your connection to the Microsoft Lync Online Service data center.

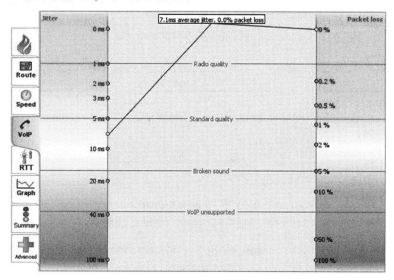

Figure 2-22 Lync Online Transport Reliability IP Probe.

TROUBLESHOOTING

For Lync Online, sustained reliability of the network connection is the most important component. Other services, such as SharePoint Online and Exchange Online, are more tolerant of variable network quality. Packet loss might be negligible because email will still eventually be delivered and the user will still get to a website. However, packet loss in Lync Online will result in poor voice quality in Lync calls. Poor voice quality is a very noticeable impact to customer experience. Therefore, if you are planning to deploy Lync Online, pay close attention to network latency and packet loss. It is a good practice to plan for QoS if possible.

Microsoft Remote Connectivity Analyzer

The Microsoft Remote Connectivity Analyzer, as shown in Figure 2-23, is an online tool that tests connectivity and connectivity requirements. It originated as a tool designed only for Exchange, which is why it still can be found at *http://testexchangeconnectivity.com*.

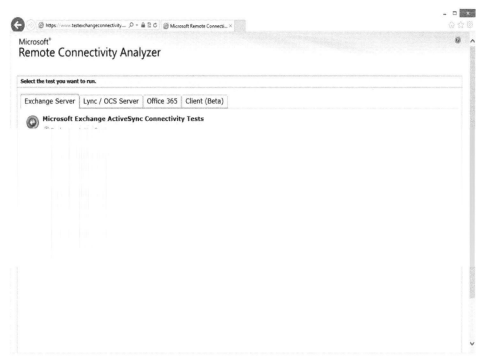

Figure 2-23 Microsoft Remote Connectivity Analyzer Tool.

Over time, however, the tool has evolved and more features have been added to it. Today, it can also be used to test the connectivity and connectivity requirements for Lync Online and Office 365. You might notice from Figure 2-23 that a new Client (beta) tab has been added to the analyzer. This is an example of new features continually being added to this analyzer.

The Microsoft Remote Connectivity Analyzer is an example of a service-specific tool, and as such we will dive deeper and demonstrate the use of this tool in later chapters that cover Exchange Online and Lync Online. For now, we just want to introduce this analyzer so you have a comprehensive list of tools in your toolkit and provide you with a quick overview of the types of connectivity tests this analyzer carries out.

There are many requirements for connectivity that the analyzer checks for. The tests that the analyzer conducts include the following:

- Checking to make sure that DNS lookup is successful. This is very useful for trouble-shooting split-DNS and reverse-DNS environments.

- Ensuring the necessary DNS records are present; for example, the SRV records.

- Making sure that Autodiscover is properly configured.

- Determining that valid certificates are issued.

- Checking that required ports are open.

- Testing ActiveSync.

- Testing a remote procedure call (RPC).

- Testing Simple Mail Transfer Protocol (SMTP) mail flow.

TROUBLESHOOTING

Many connectivity issues are because of closed ports, firewall Access Control Lists (ACLs), or misconfigured DNS, especially if you have a split-DNS model. Therefore, you should always check these first. Other issues we have encountered are self-signed certificates and certificates that are not issued by a trusted third-party certification authority (CA). Use the Remote Connectivity Analyzer to narrow down the communication errors, and then check the ports, DNS settings, firewall, and certificates associated with the service to try and troubleshoot the problem.

Microsoft Online Services Diagnostics and Logging Support Toolkit

The Microsoft Online Services Diagnostics and Logging (MOSDAL) Support Toolkit performs tests and collects data for Microsoft Online Services Support professionals and IT professionals to troubleshoot Office 365 configuration issues. The tests are broken down by categories, such as Exchange, Lync, and Applications. The types of information that MOSDAL collects include the following:

- System configuration information

- Network configuration information

- Registry entries pertinent to Office 365

- Network ports

- HTTPS requests

- Information about Office 365 applications; for example, Office Professional Plus Subscription

> **Note**
>
> MOSDAL comes in 32-bit and 64-bit versions and can be downloaded at *http://www.microsoft.com/en-us/download/details.aspx?id=626*, as shown in Figure 2-24.

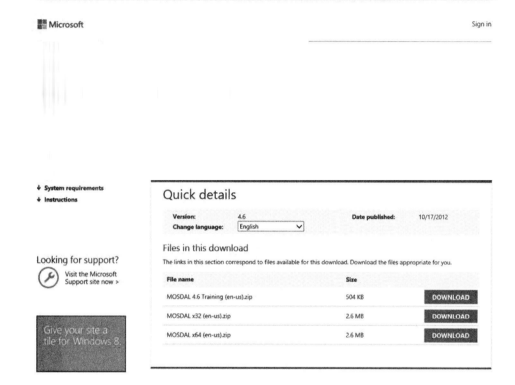

Figure 2-24 32-bit and 64-bit versions of MOSDAL are available.

After you have downloaded MOSDAL, you can unzip the package and install it on a Windows 7 workstation or a Windows Server 2008. MOSDAL can actually be installed on many versions of Windows.. A comprehensive list of systems that support MOSDAL is listed at the bottom of the MOSDAL download page.

After you have installed MOSDAL, you will need to launch it as an administrator or some of the tests will fail. After it is launched, you should see the screen with the test options grouped under the Office 365 and BPOS tabs. BPOS, otherwise known as the Business Productivity Online Standard Suite, is an older version. Microsoft has migrated every customer off BPOS, so the tests under that tab are mainly deprecated. You should focus on only the Office 365 tests, as shown in Figure 2-25.

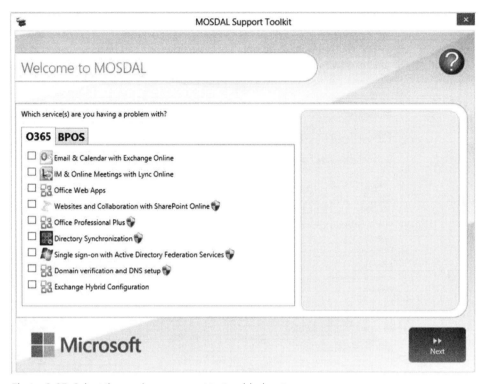

Figure 2-25 Select the services you want to troubleshoot.

As you hover over any item on the list, the pane to the right will be populated with information on what types of data will be gathered and if there are any requirements. For example, the tool might require your Office 365 credentials; if so, this information will be indicated accordingly.

After you select the services you would like to troubleshoot and click Next, MOSDAL will request your Office 365 logon credentials, as shown in Figure 2-26. Although you can skip this step and not provide your Office 365 logon credentials, you might limit the troubleshooting capabilities of MOSDAL. Therefore, for a comprehensive analysis, you should provide an Office 365 global administrator credential.

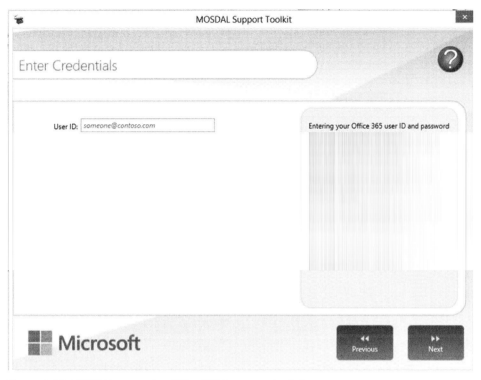

Figure 2-26 MOSDAL requesting Office 365 logon credentials.

Depending on the number of services you selected, MOSDAL might take some time to collect information to be used for troubleshooting. After it has gathered all the information, you will be provided with the option to open the file location where all the information is exported into organized folders and files. If you run MOSDAL multiple times, the data will be organized in folders with respective timestamps, as shown in Figure 2-27.

	Name	Date modified	Type	Size
☆ Favorites				
■ Desktop	📁 MOSDALREPORT	12/15/2012 2:59 PM	File folder	
📥 Downloads	📁 REPORTS_12_15_2012_2_03_48_PM	12/15/2012 2:08 PM	File folder	
📋 Recent places	📁 REPORTS_12_15_2012_2_20_08_PM	12/15/2012 2:21 PM	File folder	
☁ SkyDrive	📁 REPORTS_12_15_2012_2_28_59_PM	12/15/2012 2:31 PM	File folder	
📷 SharePoint Sites	📁 REPORTS_12_15_2012_2_36_06_PM	12/15/2012 2:38 PM	File folder	
☁ SkyDrive Pro	📁 MOSDALREPORT	12/15/2012 2:41 PM	Compressed (zipp...	28,701 KB
📚 Libraries				
📄 Documents				
🎵 Music				
🖼 Pictures				
🎬 Videos				

Figure 2-27 MOSDAL reports and data pertinent to troubleshooting Office 365 services.

MOSDAL collects a lot of information, and it is sometimes difficult to locate and interpret the data. From the MOSDAL download site, you should download and read the MOSDAL training manual, which will walk you through the types of data being gathered, where to locate the data, and how the data can be used for troubleshooting purposes. Figure 2-28 shows the "Introduction & Overview" section from the training manual.

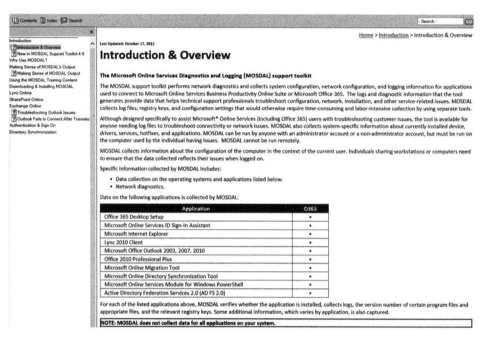

Figure 2-28 MOSDAL Training Guide.

Windows PowerShell

One last important task before we dive into Office 365 is the preparation of your Office 365 management environment. Office 365 is designed to be very oriented to Windows PowerShell. In fact, starting with Chapter 3, we will be working in Windows PowerShell. Not all administration tasks are available through the Office 365 Administration Portal's Graphical User Interface (GUI), but they are all available through Windows PowerShell. Therefore, Windows PowerShell is the superset administration tool and a definite requirement in your toolkit.

As we progress through the chapters, you will become more and more familiar with Windows PowerShell. It is the intent of this book to help you learn Windows PowerShell through immersion.

For now, if you are not familiar with what Windows PowerShell is, it is a non-GUI, command-line environment where you can either script a series of commands or issue the commands verbosely to make configuration changes. Windows PowerShell is built on the .NET Framework. Not only is it the management tool of choice for Office 365, it is also the direction for all Microsoft technologies. For example, in the latest release of Office 365, Exchange Server 2013 on premises and Exchange Online both will no longer have the Exchange Management Console (EMC). Exchange 2013 and Exchange Online will be man-

365.

INSIDE OUT   What is Windows PowerShell remoting?

You might sometimes hear that Office 365 administration is being carried out through Windows PowerShell remoting. What this means is simply that the Windows PowerShell cmdlets are being executed remotely from your workstation to affect changes to the Office 365 services located remotely in Microsoft data centers. You are not running the Windows PowerShell scripts directly from the servers themselves.

These are the two Windows PowerShell tools we have in our toolkit that you need to, at a minimum, also have in yours:

- Microsoft Online Services Module

- Windows PowerShell Integrated Scripting Environment (ISE) 3.0

The next two sections walk you through downloading, installing, and learning how to use these tools. After you have gone through the process, you will be ready to use these tools to complete the exercises in the book and to administer your Office 365 tenant.

Microsoft Online Services Module

The Microsoft Online Services Module is a downloadable component that should be installed on the workstation you will be using to manage Office 365. The following list shows the minimum requirements for your management workstation:

- Windows 7 or Windows Server 2008 R2

- Microsoft .NET Framework 3.5.1

- All current Office 365 updates

Follow these steps to install the Microsoft Online Services Module on your management workstation:

1. Verify that your workstation's operating system (OS) is either Windows 7, Windows Server 2008 R2, Windows 8, or later.

2. Click Start, and then click Control Panel.

3. On the View by menu at the top right, select Category, as shown in Figure 2-29. Then select Programs.

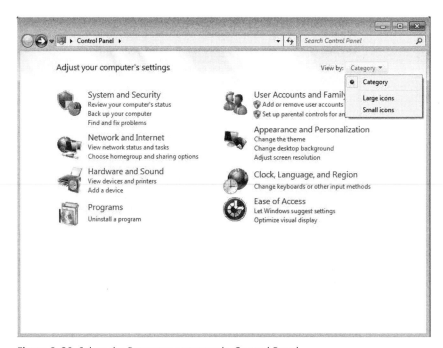

Figure 2-29 Select the Programs category in Control Panel.

4. In the Programs menu, select Turn Windows features on or off, as shown in Figure 2-30.

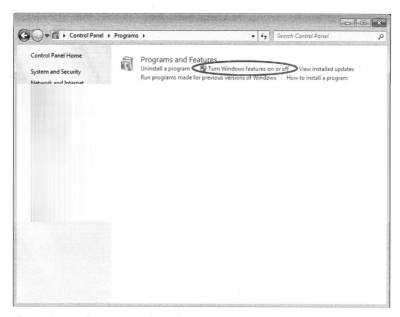

Figure 2-30 Select Turn Windows features on or off.

5. Select the Microsoft .NET Framework 3.5.1 check box, as shown in Figure 2-31. Then click OK.

Figure 2-31 Select the Microsoft .NET Framework 3.5.1 check box.

6. Download the Microsoft Online Services Sign-in Assistant.

> **Note**
>
> The 32-bit version of the Microsoft Online Services Sign-in Assistant can be
> downloaded at *http://go.microsoft.com/FWLink/p/?Linkid=236299*. To download
> the 64-bit version of the Microsoft Online Services Sign-in Assistant, see *http://
> go.microsoft.com/FWLink/p/?Linkid=236300*.

7. Install the Microsoft Online Services Sign-in Assistant by running the downloaded msoidcrl.msi file.

8. Read and accept the Microsoft Online Services Sign-in Assistant license agreement, as shown in Figure 2-32. Then click Install.

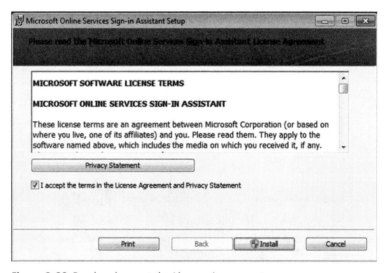

Figure 2-32 Read and accept the License Agreement.

9. Download the Microsoft Online Services Module.

Note

The 32-bit version of the Microsoft Online Services Module can be downloaded at *http://go.microsoft.com/FWLink/p/?Linkid=236345*. To download the 64-bit version of the Microsoft Online Services Module, see *http://go.microsoft.com/FWLink/p/?Linkid=236293*.

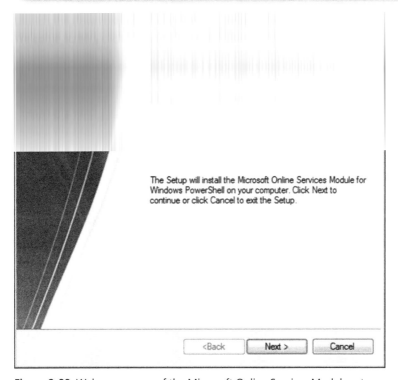

The Setup will install the Microsoft Online Services Module for Windows PowerShell on your computer. Click Next to continue or click Cancel to exit the Setup.

<Back   Next >   Cancel

Figure 2-33 Welcome screen of the Microsoft Online Services Module setup.

11. Read and agree to the software licensing terms, as shown in Figure 2-34. Then click Next.

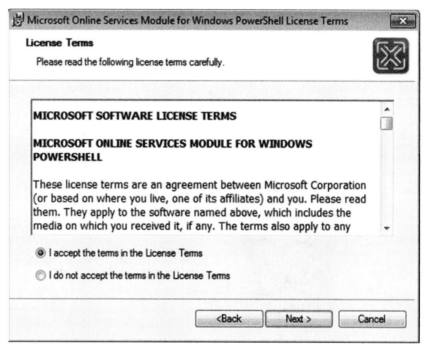

Figure 2-34 License terms for the Microsoft Online Services Module.

12. Select the default installation location or specify a different path, as shown in Figure 2-35. Check the box to create a shortcut (icon) on the desktop, if that is your preference. Then click Next.

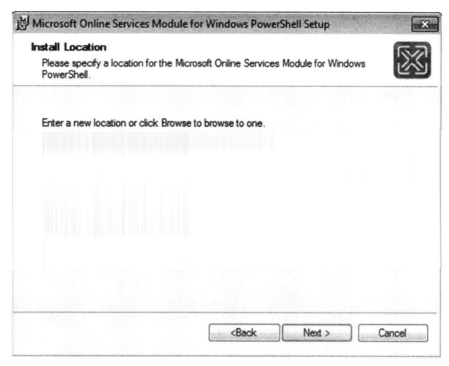

Figure 2-35 Installation location.

13. Click Install to begin the installation.

14. Click Finish when the installation is complete.

15. The Microsoft Online Services Module is an icon that looks like a blue parallelogram with a ">_" symbol, as show in Figure 2-36.

Figure 2-36 Icon for the Microsoft Online Services Module.

Testing the Microsoft Online Services Module

After you have successfully installed the Microsoft Online Services Module, it is time to test it. Before you proceed, make sure you have either purchased an Office 365 subscription or signed up for a trial subscription. Then follow these steps to execute your first Office 365 Windows PowerShell commands:

1. Launch the Microsoft Online Services Module by right-clicking the icon and running it as an administrator. You should see a command-prompt window similar to the one in Figure 2-37.

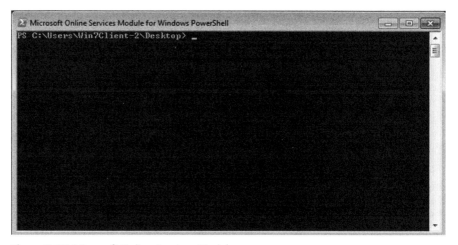

Figure 2-37 Microsoft Online Services Module.

2. Enter the following command, which will produce a login prompt for a user name and a password:

```
$cred = Get-Credential
```

The credentials you provide will be stored in the variable called *$cred*. When you see the login prompt, use your Office 365 global administrator account, as shown in Figure 2-38. Your Office 365 global administrator account will be something like *<yourname>@<yourcompany>.onmicrosoft.com*. Cmdlets are not case sensitive.

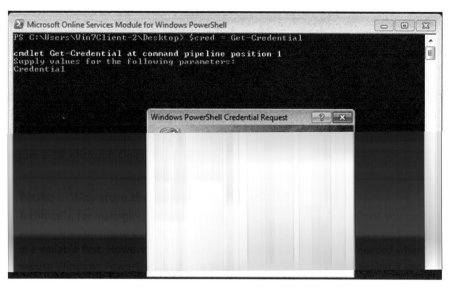

Figure 2-38 Microsoft Online Services prompt for logon credentials.

> **Note**   Why store the credentials in a variable?
>
> Technically, for managing identity and licenses with Windows PowerShell, you can just use the command *Connect-MsolService* without having to save the credential in a variable first. However, we are doing it here because this will be needed when we use Windows PowerShell for Exchange Online, so we are simply keeping it consistent throughout the book.

3.   Enter the following command, which is also shown in Figure 2-39:

```
Connect-MsolService -Credential $cred
```

This command will attempt to connect and authenticate to an Office 365 tenant using the login credentials that you stored in *$cred*.

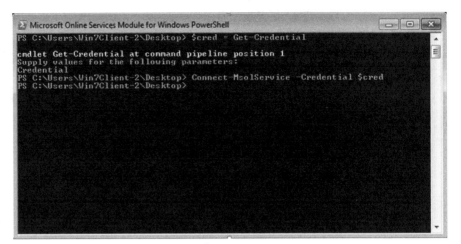

Figure 2-39 Connect-MsolService cmdlet.

4.   Lastly, enter the following command to see your subscription information:

`Get-MsolSubscription`

Figure 2-40 shows the results of the command. Notice that the cmdlet shows you the type of subscription (SkuPartNumber) and the total number of licenses you own (TotalLicenses).

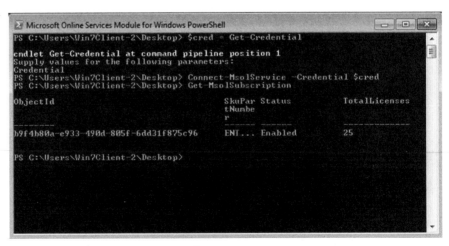

Figure 2-40 Get-MsolSubscription cmdlet.

As you can see, the Microsoft Online Services Module allows you to verbosely issue cmdlets to accomplish administrative tasks. However, we do not want to have to retype commands for every task. We want to be able to script the commands so we can automate administrative tasks.

To script the cmdlets, follow these steps:

1. Create the script in a script editor or with an application such as Notepad, and save the script as a file with a .ps1 extension. We used Notepad and the preceding example commands to recreate the entire script. We saved it as GetO365LicInfo.ps1, as shown in Figure 2-41.

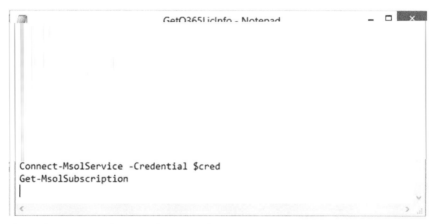

GetO365LicInfo - Notepad

```
Connect-MsolService -Credential $cred
Get-MsolSubscription
```

Figure 2-41 Notepad was used to write the script.

2. Run the script by referencing the full path to the script. Or, as shown in Figure 2-42, if the script was saved in the current directory you are in, type the following:

`.\GetO365LicInfo.ps1`

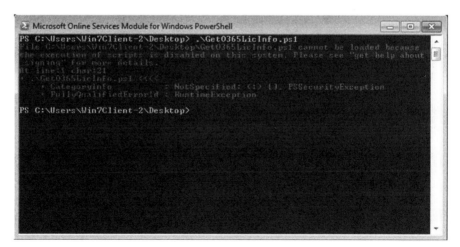

Figure 2-42 Executing the GetO365LicInfo.ps1 script.

> **Note** Execution of scripts is disabled
>
> You might receive an error message in red, as shown in the preceding Figure 2-42. The error message states the following: GetO365LicInfo.ps1 cannot be loaded because the execution of scripts is disabled on this system.
>
> The reason for this error is because of the security built into Windows PowerShell. The ability to run scripts is part of this security and is known as the execution policy. The execution policy determines whether scripts are allowed to be executed. By default, it is set to restricted. A restricted execution policy prevents scripts from running.

3. Confirm the security policy for your system by entering the following command, as shown in Figure 2-43:

```
Get-ExecutionPolicy
```

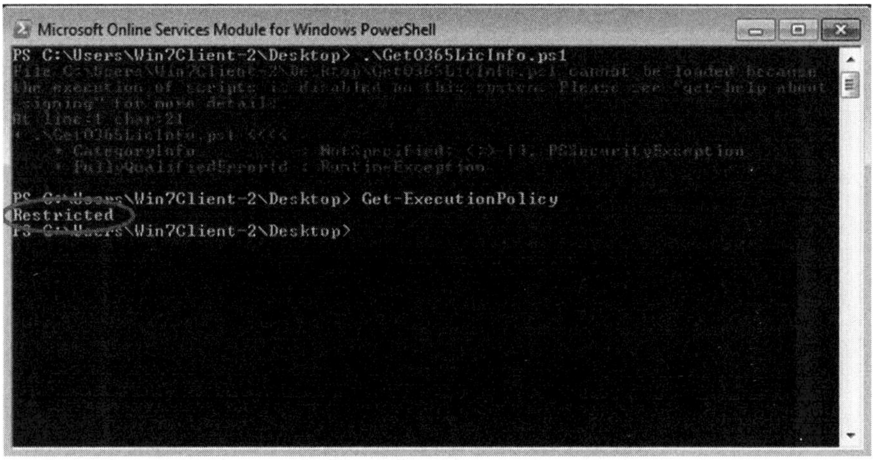

Figure 2-43 Execution policy revealed by the Get-ExecutionPolicy cmdlet.

4. Change the execution policy to unrestricted so you can run scripts. Do this by entering the following command:

```
Set-ExecutionPolicy –ExecutionPolicy Unrestricted
```

> **Note**   Permissions error
>
> You might get an error message stating you do not have the correct permissions to change the execution policy. This happens if you did not launch the Microsoft Online Services Module as an administrator. Close the Microsoft Online Services Module, then right-click the icon and select Run as administrator.

Figure 2-44 Confirm changing the execution policy to unrestricted.

6.   Run the GetO365LicInfo.ps1 script again. With the execution policy set to unrestricted, the script will now run, as shown in Figure 2-45.

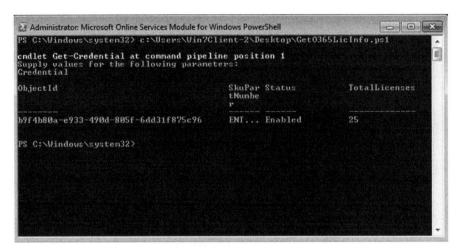

Figure 2-45 Executing the GetO365LicInfo.ps1 script.

Microsoft Windows PowerShell Integrated Scripting Environment (ISE) 3.0

There is a better way to write scripts than to use Notepad. In this section, we will introduce you to the Windows PowerShell Integrated Scripting Environment (ISE) 3.0. The ISE is an ideal scripting environment for several reasons. Here are some of them:

- It is designed for Windows PowerShell scripting, so it has all the necessary Help files.

- It has built-in Intellisense.

- It highlights cmdlets and variables in color for a more visible scripting experience.

- It provides both a scripting pane and a console pane that you can also use for viewing results or entering commands verbosely.

- It has debugging capabilities.

> **Note**
>
> The Windows PowerShell ISE 3.0 is included in Windows 8 but can be downloaded at *http://www.microsoft.com/en-us/download/details.aspx?id=29939* for Windows 7 SP1, Windows Server 2008, and Windows Server 2008 R2.

1. Download and install the Windows PowerShell ISE 3.0, if needed.

2. Launch the ISE.

3. Copy our GetO365LicInfo.ps1 script and paste it into the ISE, as shown in Figure 2-46.

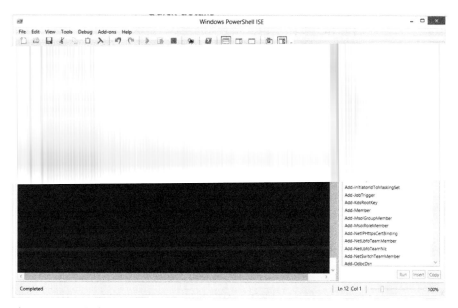

Figure 2-46 Windows PowerShell ISE 3.0 with the GetO365LicInfo.ps1 script.

Let us explore the ISE. Notice that the ISE includes the following areas:

- A script authoring pane

- A verbose console pane

- A command-list pane

To run the script, just click the Play button located on the toolbar across the top. If you need to verbosely enter cmdlets, you can do so in the console pane at the bottom. You can hide or show any of the panes by using the View menu.

Detailed use of the ISE is beyond the scope of this book. This brief introduction to the ISE should help you get started with using it to administer Office 365 and to follow along with the examples and exercises throughout this book. However, you will find the ISE to be a very useful and intuitive tool. As consultants, we use it extensively.

INSIDE OUT   Script Collection and other editors

It is a good idea to save all your scripts so you can re-use or modify them for other purposes. As you spend more time with Windows PowerShell and Office 365, you will find that a comprehensive script library will help you efficiently carry out tasks. To get you started and to aid you with Office 365 deployments, Microsoft has provided a collection of helper scripts. You can download these helper scripts at *http://www.microsoft.com/en-us/download/details.aspx?id=29568*. There are third-party Windows PowerShell editors you can try. As an example, other consultants we work with also use Quest Software's PowerGUI and Idera's PowerShell Plus.

Summary

In this chapter we covered how to plan and prepare for your Office 365 deployment. We reviewed the Office 365 Deployment Readiness Kit, how to analyze your network performance to determine your ability to adequately connect to your hosted Office services, and the significance Windows PowerShell plays in Office 365 deployment and administration. You probably spent a lot of time remediating issues and calculating network capacity. The good news is that we are now ready to go to the cloud!

In the next few chapters, we will dive right into what we consider the most important part of the Office 365 deployment, which is Identity Management. After all, the user is the most important part of the equation.

To the cloud...

PART 2

Office 365 Foundations: Identity Management

CHAPTER 3

Active Directory Federation Services 71

CHAPTER 4

Directory synchronization 137

Active Directory Federation Services

Different types of user accounts 71   Active Directory Federation Services 82

logon.

SSO through AD FS is not mandatory for Office 365, but enterprise customers usually implement it because of the need or desire to leverage existing identity management solutions such as AD. Remember, too, that we said the user is the most important part of the equation. SSO optimizes the users' experience because they don't need to provide credentials multiple times.

AD FS is commonly considered and discussed together with directory synchronization, which is covered in Chapter 4, "Directory Synchronization."

> **Note**
> Office 365 SSO is not available for Office 365 for professionals and small businesses or for Office 365 Small Business Premium Preview. For more information, see KB article 2662960 at *http://support.microsoft.com/kb.2662960*. SSO is available only for Office 365 Enterprise Suites.

Different types of user accounts

Before we dive into AD FS, we need to introduce the different types of user accounts and authentication methods available in Office 365.

As with any computer system, a user needs an account to access Office 365. This chapter covers the different ways in which user accounts can be created and maintained. We also describe the user experience when accessing Office 365 based on the different account types.

There are essentially two classes of user accounts:

- Cloud identity

- Federated identity

Cloud identity

Cloud identities are user accounts that are created directly in Office 365 through the admin center. The passwords associated with cloud identities are also stored in Office 365. Cloud identities can be managed through the admin center as well as through Windows Power-Shell. Windows PowerShell provides you with account management capabilities that might not be available through the admin center. For example, you can assign user passwords or remove password expiration dates by using Windows PowerShell, but these options are not available in the admin center. Windows PowerShell also opens the door for automation and bulk processing of accounts. We will dive deeper into Windows PowerShell in later chapters because Windows PowerShell is definitely the tool of choice for administering Office 365 at the enterprise level.

When a user tries to access an Office 365 service, she will be prompted for a logon name and a password, as shown in Figure 3-1. The user name and password will be validated by Office 365 before access to services is granted. For cloud identities, Office 365 is the authoritative authentication source known as standard authentication.

Federated identity

Federated identities refer to user accounts that are maintained outside of Office 365, such as in AD. Federated identities are the most commonly used accounts in an enterprise because most enterprises already have an identity management solution such as AD. Because Office 365 is built to be enterprise-ready, it will leverage your AD environment. We discuss other non-AD identity management solutions in later chapters, but for now we will assume AD as the authoritative identity source.

There are many benefits to leveraging your AD environment. For one, AD is most likely mature and you have already configured features such as Group Policy Objects (GPOs) that define password complexity requirements. Furthermore, from a day-to-day management standpoint, you and your administrators are probably using tools such as the Active Directory User and Computer (ADUC) management console. In this scenario, if you introduce cloud identities with Office 365, you would have to maintain a second set of user accounts in Office 365, thereby doubling your workload.

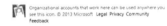

Figure 3-1 Office 365 logon window.

For example, let's say you create a new user account for a new employee in AD and that user requires access to Office 365. Without federated identities, you will have to manually create and maintain a corresponding user account in Office 365 for the new employee. Whenever an employee leaves your organization, you will have to ensure you delete, or disable, the user account in Office 365 in addition to deleting or disabling the employee's account in AD. Therefore, while cloud identities can be used in an enterprise and are easy to implement, they are definitely not the best approach from a long-term, administration standpoint.

Integrating Active Directory with Office 365

To fully leverage AD in Office 365, follow these general steps:

- Add your domain name to your Office 365 tenant.

- Set up and configure SSO through AD FS (optional; we cover this process later in this chapter starting with the "Active Directory Federation Services" section).

- Install and configure the Directory Sync tool (covered in Chapter 4).

> **Note**
>
> If you know you will be implementing SSO, we recommend you implement it prior to installing the Directory Sync tool. However, it is not uncommon for organizations to first implement directory synchronization before AD FS. In fact, in our experience, this has been quite a common approach.

The first step to integrating AD with Office 365 is to add your domain name to your Office 365 tenant. To do so, you first need to own a fully qualified domain name (FQDN). A fully qualified domain name is defined as a routable Internet domain name, such as .com, .net, or .org. A non-routable domain name, such as .lcl or .local, cannot be added.

Adding your domain name to Office 365

You can add your domain name to Office 365 through Windows PowerShell scripting. For now, we will use the graphical interface to accomplish this task:

1. Log on to your Office 365 admin center at *https://portal.microsoftonline.com* and click the domains link, as shown in Figure 3-2.

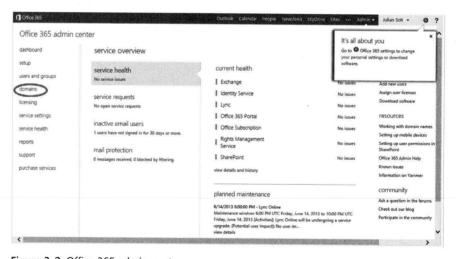

Figure 3-2 Office 365 admin center.

The domains page shows all the domains your Office 365 tenant is associated with and their respective status. As you can see, you can associate multiple domains to a tenant. However, once a domain has been associated to an Office 365 tenant, you will not be able to associate that same domain to another Office 365 tenant. By default, you should at least see the domain name that you used to first sign up for Office 365. It should be in the form of <Name>.onmicrosoft.com.

2. To associate a domain to this tenant, click the Add a domain link, as shown in Figure

Figure 3-3 Add a domain.

3. Click Specify a domain name and confirm ownership.

4. Enter your domain name in the text box and click next, as shown in Figure 3-4.

    Remember that you can add only an Internet routable domain, and the domain you specify must not have been previously associated with another Office 365 tenant. Do not worry if you do not remember whether a domain has been associated with another tenant. You will be notified if that is the case.

5. After you click next, Office 365 informs you if the domain has been previously associated. If not, you can proceed to the next task, which is to verify the domain.

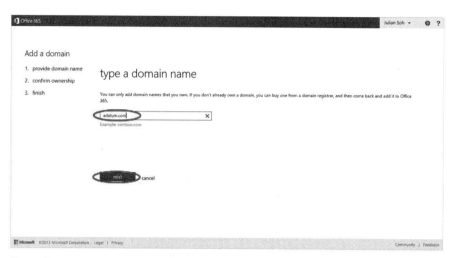

Figure 3-4 Enter your domain name.

You now need to confirm you own the domain and have the authority to add this domain name to Office 365. Office 365 asks you to create a TXT record in your Domain Name Service (DNS) server that is authoritative for the domain you just added. Office 365 also lists instructions on how to do this if your DNS is hosted by an Internet Service Provider (ISP) or registrar such as Go Daddy.

1. Select your ISP to view the specific instructions or select General Instructions if you are hosting your own DNS, which is often the case for an enterprise. In this example, we will select General Instructions. Figure 3-5 shows the list of available instructions.

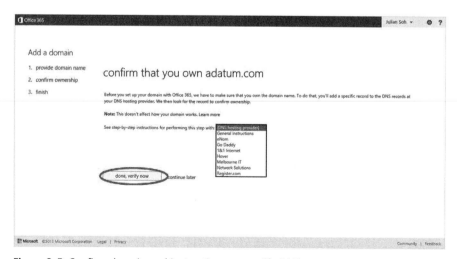

Figure 3-5 Confirm domain and instructions to modify DNS.

2. When you have selected the instruction that applies to you, the instruction will appear on the same page. In this example, when we selected General Instructions, we were given the option to create either a TXT record or an MX record in DNS that contains a unique number. During verification, Office 365 will resolve the domain through DNS and will attempt to locate these records. Personally, we have always used a TXT record instead of an MX record, but both options are available to you. Figure 3-6 shows information for General Instructions.

Figure 3-6 General Instructions to modify DNS.

3. Next, make the changes to your DNS. When you are done, click the done, verify now button. If you need more time or need to rely on someone else to make the DNS changes for you, just close the window. You can come back and verify the domain later.

Entering a DNS TXT record

In this section, we show you how to add the required TXT record to a Windows DNS server.

1. Log on to your DNS server. Using the Microsoft Management Console (MMC) for DNS, right-click the domain you are adding to Office 365 and select the Other New Records option, as shown in Figure 3-7.

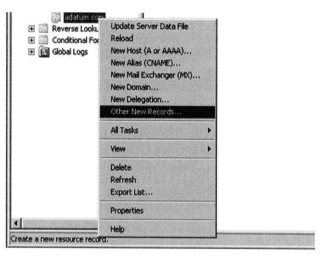

Figure 3-7 Microsoft Management Console for DNS server.

2. In the Resource Record Type dialog box, scroll down until you locate the Text (TXT) record type. Select it and click Create Record, as shown in Figure 3-8.

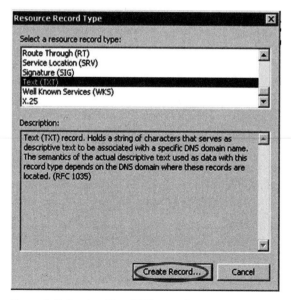

Figure 3-8 Create a Text (TXT) record type.

3. Lastly, as shown in Figure 3-9, leave the Record name field blank. In the Text field, enter the TXT record as instructed by Office 365 (see Figure 3-6, General Instructions to modify DNS). This usually takes the form of MS=ms1234567. When you are done, click OK.

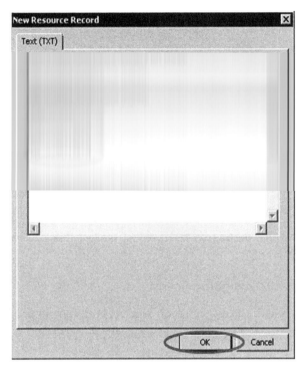

Figure 3-9 Creating the Text (TXT) record.

Verifying the domain

Now that we have created the TXT record, Office 365 will be able to verify that you have the authority to add the domain to your tenant. There is no need to wait for DNS convergence because Office 365 does not cache its DNS lookup of TXT records for domain verification purposes, so you can immediately start the verification process.

If you are still on the Office 365 page waiting for domain verification (see Figure 3-6) and if it has not yet timed out, you can click the done, verify now button. If you have to log on to the admin center again, follow these steps to confirm ownership:

1. From the admin center, click domains in the left pane, and then click the Setup in progress link in the Status column, as shown in Figure 3-10.

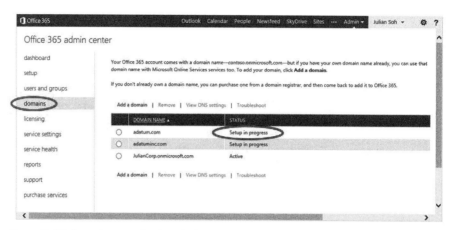

Figure 3-10 Domains page in the admin center.

2. Click Specify a domain name and confirm ownership.

3. Click the done, verify now button.

After your domain has been successfully verified, the next task is to specify how users will be added to Office 365.

Adding users and assigning licenses

We will explain how to add users through directory synchronization in Chapter 4. Therefore, we need to specify that users will be added at a later time. Follow these steps to specify that you will add users later:

1. If you are on the Add a domain page of Office 365, skip to the next step. Otherwise, from the admin center, click domains, and then click the Setup in progress link in the Status column, as shown in Figure 3-10.

2. On the Add a domain to Office 365 page, notice that the link in Step 2, which is Add users and assign licenses, is now active. Furthermore, the link in Step 1, which is Specify a domain name and confirm ownership, is no longer active and a check is shown for that step. This indicates you have completed the task. Click the Add users and assign licenses link.

3. Select the I don't want to add users right now option and click next.

You are now ready to finish the third task, which is to define the domain purpose and configure DNS.

Setting the domain purpose and configuring DNS

Setting the purpose of the domain means defining whether the domain will be used for Exchange Online, Lync Online, or SharePoint Online. Follow these steps to set the domain purpose:

1. If you are on the Add a domain to Office 365 page, skip to the next step. Otherwise, from the admin center click domains, and then click the Setup in progress link in the

domain purpose will look similar to the one shown in Figure 3-11. Select the services you want to associate with the domain and click next.

Figure 3-11 Set domain purpose.

4. Setting the domain purpose in the preceding step allows Office 365 to determine the necessary records you need to add to your DNS server, as shown in Figure 3-12. Office 365 does not manage DNS records but still provides services that require specific DNS entries for them to work. Add the records to your DNS server, then click done, go check. Office 365 will check that the DNS records are correctly created and will inform you if any errors are found. If there are no errors, you will receive a

message that the domain is ready to work with the Office 365 services you selected. The domain status will then be changed to Active instead of Setup in progress.

Figure 3-12 DNS settings for services that are associated to a verified domain.

> **Note**
>
> Choosing to specify SharePoint Online as a service associated to your domain name provides you the capability to host a public-facing website. However, a public-facing SharePoint Online website is currently not intended to be a full-featured web content management solution. If you do choose to use a public-facing site, and also want to use Exchange Online and Lync Online, you will need to first associate Exchange and Lync. Save the changes and configure your DNS for Exchange Online and Lync Online, then come back to specify SharePoint Online as a service to associate with the domain name.

Active Directory Federation Services

AD FS is a role in Windows Server. The most prominent and primary reason to use AD FS with Office 365 is that it allows an AD user to seamlessly access Office 365 without having to re-supply her credentials again. As mentioned earlier, this ability is often referred to as single sign-on (SSO). AD FS is an optional implementation and is not required for Office 365. However, if your organization decides to implement AD FS, the minimum AD FS version required by Office 365 is version 2.0; thus, it is often referred to as AD FS 2.0.

However, aside from SSO, there are other benefits of AD FS. Because AD FS facilitates the authentication of users through AD, you can take advantage of group policies. AD FS can also control location-based access to Office 365. For example, if you want to allow employees to be able to access Office 365 only from the corporate environment and not from

Single sign-on experience

Before we begin to install and configure AD FS 2.0, let us first take a look at the end-user experience when SSO with Office 365 is and is not in place.

Scenario 1: No single sign-on experience

In this scenario, a user is not authenticated through SSO. Each time the user attempts to access Office 365, he is prompted to supply a valid user name and password, whether he is attempting to access Office 365 from within the corporate network or from a public network logon.

Scenario 2: User is logged on at work

In this scenario, a user is at work and logs on to the corporate network. The enterprise AD authenticates the user so she has a valid claim token. When the user accesses Office 365 services, by opening Outlook to access email or by opening a browser to access the corporate intranet that is hosted in SharePoint Online, the Office 365 federation gateway will acknowledge the claim token and will not produce a logon prompt. This provides an SSO experience because the user does not need to present her logon credentials again.

Scenario 3: Remote worker on a virtual private network connection

A remote worker or teleworker is one who is not on the corporate network. Traditionally, these workers will use a technology such as a virtual private network (VPN) client to securely create an encrypted communication channel between their personal computers and the corporate network. This is known as a tunnel within the public network. Because it is encrypted, the communication is deemed secure.

In this scenario, a user presents his logon credentials during the VPN session initialization. The credentials are passed to the corporate network. After authenticated, the user possesses a claims token, as in Scenario 2. At this point, if the user opens his email or accesses the corporate intranet that is hosted in Office 365, the situation will be the same as it is for the worker in Scenario 2. That is, the user will not be prompted for his logon credentials again.

Scenario 4: Remote worker is not logged on to the corporate network

In this scenario, a remote worker has access to the Internet through a non-corporate network, such as her home office or the public Internet provided by a hotel. She can choose to log on through VPN, but for the sake of discussion let us assume this user does not do so because she does not need to access any corporate resources on the corporate network. Instead, she only wants to read email or access the corporate intranet that is hosted in Office 365. So she opens a browser and enters the uniform resource locator (URL) of the corporate intranet. Because she is not authenticated by AD, either locally or through VPN, she does not possess a valid token.

Office 365 presents the user with the Office 365 logon window, as shown in Figure 3-1. The user attempts to log on using her User Principal Name (UPN) user name. Office 365 recognizes that the user is trying to log on with a UPN suffix belonging to a domain that is federated and thus redirects the user to the AD FS server, as shown in Figure 3-13. The federation server presents a logon window to obtain the user's credentials. The user successfully enters her credentials and is issued a valid claim token. She then is redirected back to Office 365, where she is now granted access to Office 365 services.

In light of the different scenarios, it is a good idea to have a communication plan so you can communicate to your users what they will see when AD FS and SSO are in place.

Single sign-on requirements

The minimum requirements for setting up SSO with AD FS for Office 365 are divided into AD requirements and AD FS server requirements.

The server requirements to install the AD FS role are straightforward:

- AD FS must be installed on a server that is joined to a domain and running either Windows Server 2008 or Windows Server 2008 R2.

- AD FS 2.0 or above must be installed on a domain controller (DC).

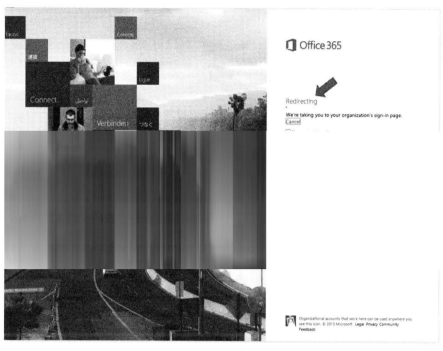

Figure 3-13 Office 365 logon portal redirecting you to sign in through the AD FS server.

- Internet Information Server (IIS) must be installed.

- Deployment of an AD FS 2.0 or above proxy server if you plan to allow users to connect from outside the company network. While an AD FS proxy is recommended, it is not required. Furthermore, the AD FS proxy and AD FS server cannot be set up on the same machine.

AD requirements to implement AD FS 2.0 for Office 365 can be more complex and impactful. The following are the AD requirements:

- AD with a minimum functional level of Windows Server 2003 in mixed or native mode.

- AD default UPN must be identical to the domain name you added in the preceding section.

For more information about AD FS requirements, see *http://technet.microsoft.com/en-us/library/dn151311.aspx.*

> ## Note
>
> User Principal Name (UPN) is the most common problem we see in AD. Most com-
> panies implemented AD many years ago when the Internet was still young and cloud
> computing was virtually unheard of. The Internet was considered the wild west with all
> its promises and dangers. Back then, a common security best practice was to give AD
> a non-routable UPN. The common UPN suffix used is typically .lcl or .local. The reason
> why Office 365 requires a valid UPN suffix is twofold. One, we will be creating a federa-
> tion between Office 365 and the local AD during the AD FS installation. This requires the
> domain to be added to Office 365 as we saw earlier in the chapter. Adding the domain
> to Office 365 requires the validation of a TXT or MX record through DNS, so the domain
> needs to be valid and routable. Second, when we install directory synchronization, the
> user name for an Office 365 account is in UPN format (example *<User Alias>*@adatum.
> com). The Directory Sync tool uses the UPN of the local AD to create the user account
> in Office 365. If the UPN of the local AD is not added and verified in Office 365, as will
> be the case with a non-routable UPN, then the user will be created with the default
> onmicrosoft.com UPN suffix that was created when the Office 365 tenant was created
> (example: *<User>*@adatum.onmicrosoft.com).

Follow these general steps to implement SSO using AD FS:

- Remediate your AD UPN suffix.

- Install IIS on the server that will host AD FS.

- Protect IIS with an Secure Sockets Layer (SSL) certificate.

- Install and configure AD FS 2.0.

Remediating the UPN suffix

The good news about remediating the UPN suffix in AD is that you do not need to replace
your old UPN suffix if it is not federated with Office 365. In fact, you are not able to replace
the original UPN that was used when you first created a forest.

A common reason why you need to add a UPN might be because the current one is not routable or you might not want to federate it for some reason. The solution is to add an alternate UPN suffix to your AD forest. To do so, you can use Windows PowerShell or the Active Directory Domains and Trusts MMC. The following steps show how to add a UPN with the Active Directory Domains and Trusts MMC:

1. Start the Active Directory Domains and Trusts MMC, as shown in Figure 3-14.

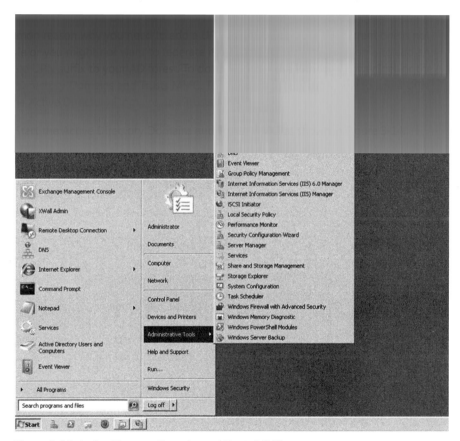

Figure 3-14 Active Directory Domains and Trusts MMC.

2. Right-click Active Directory Domain and Trusts and select Properties, as shown in Figure 3-15.

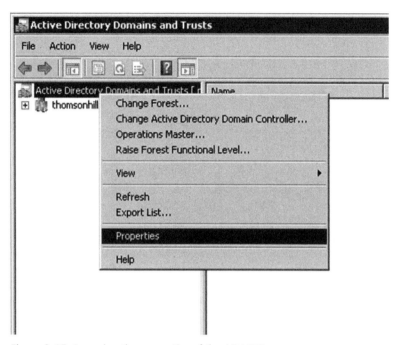

Figure 3-15 Accessing the properties of the AD UPN.

3. On the UPN Suffixes tab, enter the domain name you associated with Office 365 and click Add. Do not type @ before the UPN suffix because it will be added automatically. For example, to add adatum.com as an alternate UPN suffix, type adatum.com and not @adatum.com, as shown in Figure 3-16.

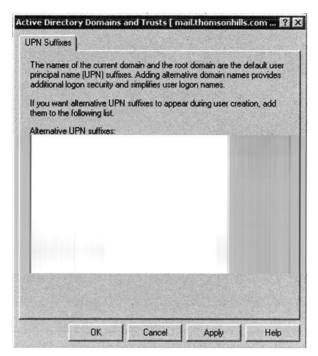

Figure 3-16 Adding an alternative UPN to the forest.

   4.   Click OK.

Now that you have added an alternative UPN to the forest, it will appear as an option in the user logon name settings in the Active Directory User and Computers (ADUC) MMC when you create a new user, as shown in Figure 3-17. All the UPN suffixes listed here will be associated with the user logon, but the one that is selected is known as the default UPN suffix. The default UPN suffix is the one that will be used by the Directory Sync tool to create the user in Office 365, so it is important to select the correct default UPN suffix when creating the user.

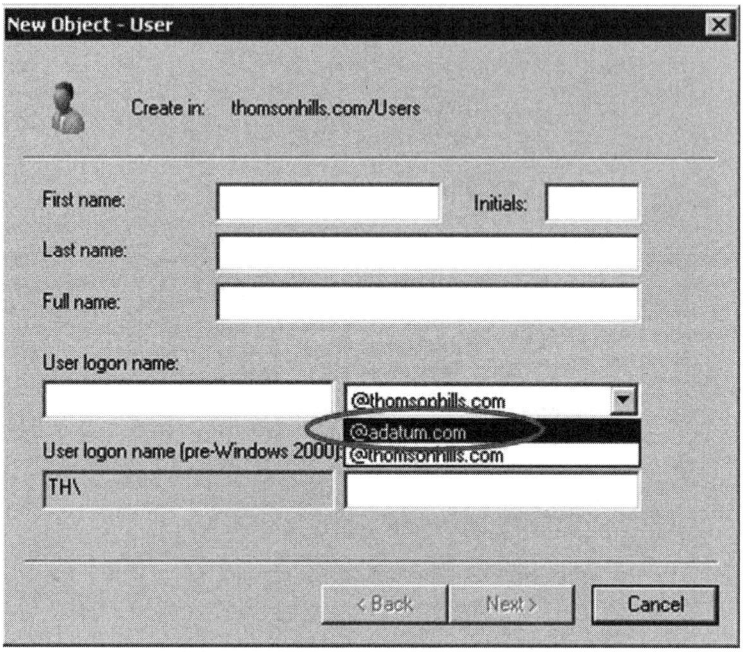

Figure 3-17 Setting the default UPN suffix when creating a user in ADUC.

It is not possible to change the default UPN suffix because it is associated with the AD forest when the forest was first created. Therefore, you will need a way to properly set the UPN suffix of all previous users to the correct default UPN suffix so that Directory Sync can correctly create the Office 365 account. You will also need to select the correct UPN suffix for new users at the time they are created. This can be done manually, as shown in Figure 3-16. This can also be automated using several methods such as Windows PowerShell or through Forefront Identity Manager (FIM). Automation is the preferred approach because it is easy to forget to set the correct default UPN suffix for new users.

Windows PowerShell is also the method you will use to bulk set users' default UPN, either organization-wide or by OU.

The following Windows PowerShell script updates the UPN suffix of all users in a particular OU:

```
#Script to update the UPN suffix
#Replace the fields indicated with <> with actual field names

import-module ActiveDirectory

Get-ADUser -SearchBase "ou=<OU Name>,dc=<domain name>,dc=<com or org or net>"
-SearchScope OneLevel -filter * |
ForEach-Object {
```

```
        $newUPN = $_.UserPrincipalName.Replace('<currentUPNsuffix>', '<newUPNsuf-
fix>')
        $_ | Set-ADUser -server <servername> -UserPrincipalName $newUPN
        }
```

The next sample script updates an entire domain, instead of just a single OU, to replace the default UPN suffix of thomsonhills.com to adatum.com. The -*whatif* parameter is used so that when the script is run, it shows the effects of the script without actually making any

```
        Set-ADUser -server mail -UserPrincipalName $newUPN -whatif
        }
```

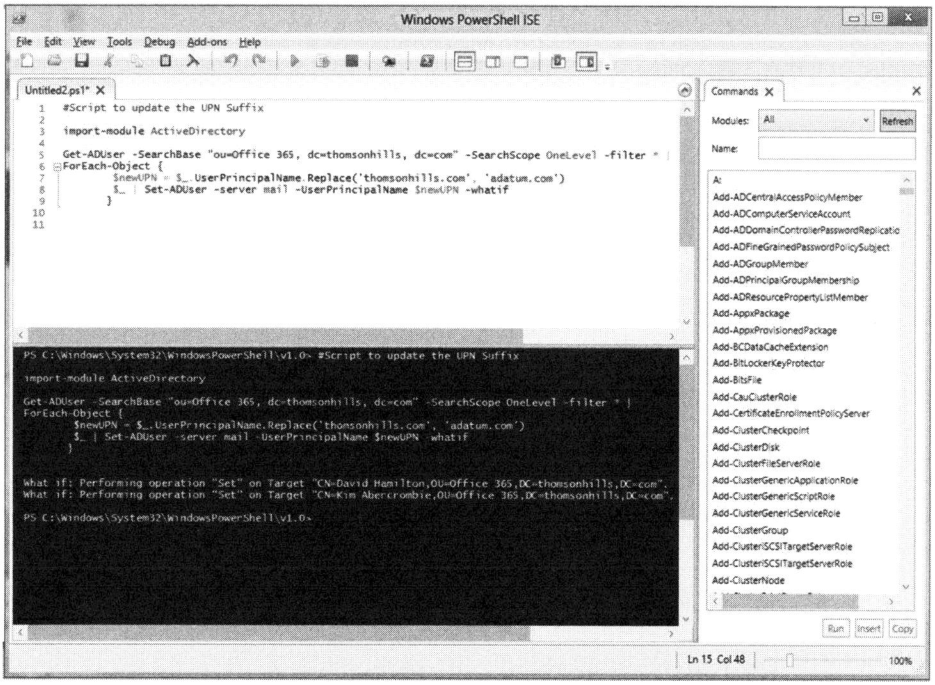

Figure 3-18 Windows PowerShell Integrated Scripting Environment (ISE) modifying the UPN suffix.

> **Note**
>
> A user can authenticate to AD through the UPN or by the legacy NetBIOS method (*Domain\Username*). Adding an alternate UPN suffix and changing the default UPN suffix for users will not affect the NetBIOS logon method. When you add multiple alternate UPN suffixes, a user can log on with any of the UPNs, but Directory Sync will use only the default UPN suffix from the Office 365 account creation process. That is why it is important to make sure the default UPN is set to the domain associated with Office 365 or it will not be able to create the user with that UPN. Instead, Directory Sync will create the account with the default initial Office 365 UPN suffix, which is in the form of @*<CompanyName>*.onmicrosoft.com.

Aside from the UPN suffix in AD, it is important to remember that Office 365 relies on AD attributes for information. For example, the Global Address List (GAL) information for users as well as distribution lists (DLs) rely on AD information. Therefore, you will need to ensure these attributes are populated in AD so the information will be available in Office 365.

Installing IIS on the AD FS server

AD FS requires the IIS role on the server. Install the IIS role by following these steps:

1. In Control Panel, select the Turn Windows features on or off option.

2. Select Roles in the Server Manager MMC.

3. In the Roles Summary pane, see if Web Server (IIS) is listed as an installed role. If you see it, then you are done and can skip the rest of the steps and go straight to the "Requesting and Installing Certificates" section.

4. If you do not see it, click the Add Roles link in the Roles Summary pane on the right.

5. Let the Add Roles Wizard guide you. When you are prompted to select roles to install, select the check box for Web Server (IIS).

6. Let the wizard guide you through the rest of the installation. Once complete, the IIS role will be installed.

You are now ready to protect the IIS Server with an SSL certificate for the default website.

Requesting and installing certificates

Now that we have IIS installed on the AD FS server, we need to address the issue of security certificates before we can install AD FS 2.0.

You need a security certificate to protect your AD FS server. AD FS relies on the IIS default website, which needs to be protected by an SSL certificate, to secure the communications between the client computer and the AD FS server.

Credentials are transmitted over this SSL connection, so it is important that the connection is encrypted. The SSL certificate also identifies the federation server, giving users confidence that they are authenticating to the organization and not a server impersonating as the organization.

Creating the certificate request

Follow these steps to create a certificate request:

1. Click Start, click Administrative Tools, and then click Internet Information Services (IIS) Manager.

2. In the IIS MMC, select the IIS server. In the middle pane, scroll down until you see Server Certificates, then double-click the icon, as shown in Figure 3-19.

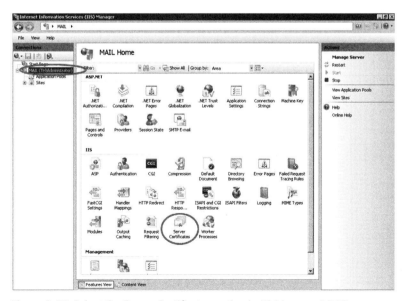

Figure 3-19 Select the Server Certificates option in IIS Manager MMC.

3.   In the Actions pane, select Create Certificate Request, as shown in Figure 3-20.

Figure 3-20 Create Certificate Request.

4.   Complete all fields in the Distinguished Name Properties page of the Request Certificate Wizard, as shown in Figure 3-21. Note that in the Common name text box, you should enter the fully qualified domain name (FQDN) of the federation service. For example, if you plan to refer to your federation service as *fs1.adatum.com*, then enter that FQDN in the text box. All fields are required. Click Next when you are done.

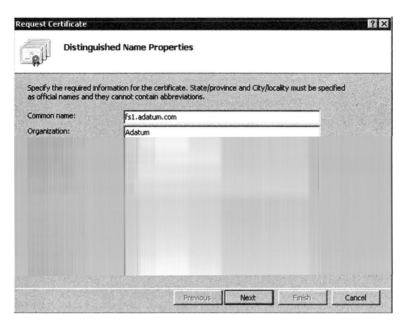

Figure 3-21 Information required for the certificate.

INSIDE OUT   The controversy about wildcard certificates

Consider using wildcard certificates because they provide you the flexibility and con-venience to change the host or service name without having to reissue the certificate. However, there is a long, ongoing debate about avoiding wildcard certificates as a security best practice. Whether you are a proponent of wildcard certificates or not will depend on your security posture and professional stance on this topic; however, this is beyond the scope of discussion for this book. We are simply pointing out that there are benefits to using wildcard certificates whenever there are name changes to servers and services involved, including the AD FS service.

Chapter 3

TROUBLESHOOTING

Be careful of name duplication

It is important to make sure the FQDN federation service is NOT the same as the server name in AD. In fact, it should not be the same as any other server in AD. For example, let us say you want to refer to your federation service as fs1.adatum.com, but when you set up this server and joined it to AD you also named it fs1. In this case, you will need to change the server name to something else or the AD FS installation wizard will not be able to set the SPN during installation. For more information, see "AD FS 2.0: Guidance for Selecting and Utilizing a Federation Service Name" at *http://social.technet. microsoft.com/wiki/contents/articles/4177.aspx.*

5. On the Cryptographic Service Provider Properties page, we recommend that you select the Microsoft RSA SChannel Cryptographic Provider with a bit length of 2,048, as shown in Figure 3-22. Although a 1,024 bit length is acceptable, it is more susceptible to cryptanalytic attacks. For more information about certificates for AD FS, see *http://technet.microsoft.com/en-us/library/adfs2-help-certificates(v=WS.10). aspx.*

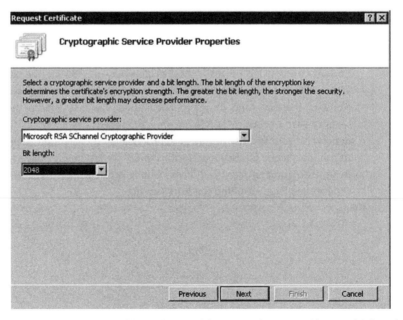

Figure 3-22 Cryptographic Service Provider Properties page with 2,048 bit length.

6. Lastly, specify a file name for the certificate request, which you will use with a third-party certificate provider or with your enterprise certificate authority.

7. Purchase an SSL certificate from a third-party certificate provider or use your enterprise PKI infrastructure if you have one. If you plan to purchase a certificate, skip the following "Using your enterprise certificate authority to issue a certificate" section and go to a domain registrar such as Go Daddy to purchase the certificate.

Command Prompt and select Run as administrator.

2. In the Command Prompt window, enter the following command:

```
certreq -submit -attrib "CertificateTemplate:WebServer" <path and file name of
Certificate Request file>
```

As shown in Figure 3-23, we issued the command and used Request.txt because that is the file name we used when we generated the certificate request earlier.

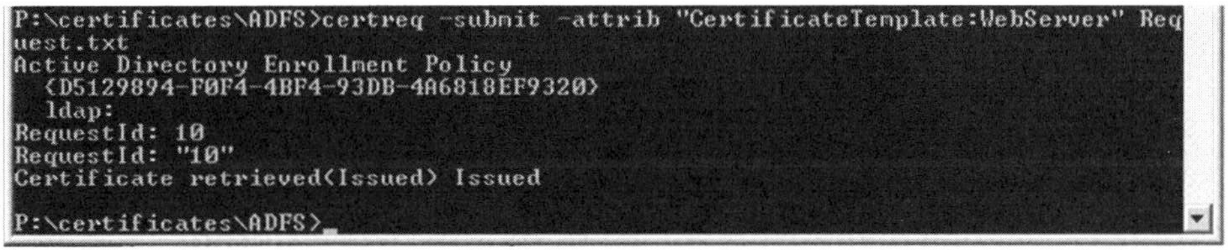

Figure 3-23 Using the *certreq* command on the CA server to issue a certificate.

Installing the certificate on IIS

Regardless of whether you purchased a certificate from a domain registrar or had your CA issue it, you should now have in your possession a certificate file, which usually has a .cer extension as part of the file name. Follow these steps to install the certificate on your IIS server:

1. On the AD FS server, start IIS Manager.

2. In the Connections pane, select the AD FS server, double-click Server Certificates in the middle pane, and click Complete Certificate Request in the Actions pane, as shown in Figure 3-24.

Figure 3-24 Complete Certificate Request in IIS Manager.

3. When prompted for the file name, browse to where you stored your .cer certificate file and select it. Give it a friendly name that will allow you to easily recognize it later, and complete the installation of the certificate.

Protecting the default website with the certificate

Now that we have installed the certificate, we need to use it for the default website. Follow these steps to apply the certificate to the default website:

1. From the AD FS server, start IIS Manager.

2. In the Connections pane, expand the ADFS server node, and then expand the Sites node. Right-click Default Web Site and select Edit Bindings, as shown in Figure 3-25.

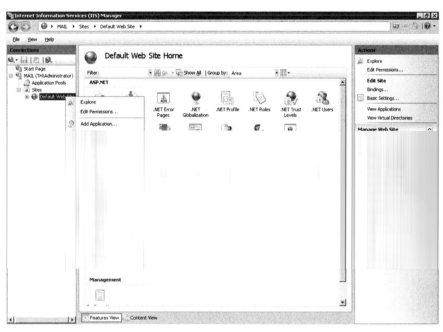

Figure 3-25 Edit the bindings of the Default Web Site.

3. Select the HTTPS protocol in the Site Bindings window, and then click Edit.

4. In the drop-down box for SSL certificate, select the certificate you installed in Step 3. You should be able to recognize it by the friendly name you gave the certificate when you installed it.

5. Click OK when you are done, and then click Close.

Now the IIS server is ready to host the AD FS service. Next, we will plan for our AD FS infrastructure and carry out the installation.

Planning the AD FS architecture

When planning for AD FS, there are several considerations from a design standpoint:

- The number of AD FS servers in the farm

- Whether or not to deploy an AD FS proxy

- Whether to use the Windows Internal Database (WID) that comes with AD FS or use a dedicated SQL server for the AD FS database

Chapter 3

AD FS server farm

The number of AD FS servers in the farm, which in turn determines the availability of the farm, is by far the most important design consideration because AD FS is the enabler for authentication through AD. There are other factors that might affect AD FS availability, such as network availability, that you also will need to take into consideration when designing your AD FS deployment. After you deploy AD FS for Office 365, if your AD FS servers are inaccessible, then access to Office 365 will not be possible. Therefore, it is important to build redundancy at the network and server layers.

At the very minimum, two AD FS servers in a single farm that is front ended with a load balancer will provide the needed redundancy. If one server is down for maintenance or for any other reason, authentication through the AD FS farm will still be possible and access to Office 365 will not be interrupted.

AD FS proxy

An AD FS proxy role is recommended if you plan to allow users to connect to Office 365 with SSO from outside the corporate network. Implementing an AD FS proxy is not required in this scenario, but it is a security best practice. Figure 3-26 shows a typical AD FS architecture.

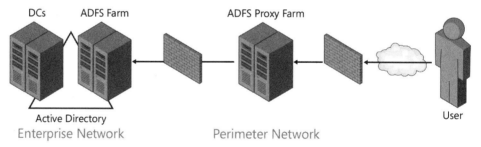

Figure 3-26 Typical AD FS and AD FS proxy implementation in an enterprise.

Implementing an AD FS proxy is beyond the scope of this book because it is more an of on-premises network and server infrastructure discussion rather than an Office 365 discussion. Therefore, we do not cover the process of implementing an AD FS proxy or how to implement redundancy through the deployment of server farms and failover clusters. However, in the following sections we show you how to install AD FS 2.0 on a server and how to establish the relationship with Office 365 to reap the benefits of SSO and extend enterprise controls into Office 365.

INSIDE OUT   Leveraging Windows Azure

Many decision makers in organizations realize the benefits of AD FS and regard it as a requirement rather than an optional component. At the same time, they are concerned that introducing AD FS adds a single point of weakness in the implementation of Office 365 because the 99.9 percent service level agreement (SLA) for Office 365 is meaning-

AD FS database

When deploying AD FS 2.0, you have the opportunity to use either the Windows Internal Database (WID) that comes with AD FS, which is the default, or a dedicated SQL server. The first AD FS server in the farm is known as the *primary federation server*, and subsequent AD FS servers are known as *secondary federation servers*.

The AD FS database, regardless of whether you choose to deploy WID or SQL, is used to store configuration information. The information in the database is replicated across the AD FS servers in the farm. The database on the primary federation server is a read-write data-base, while the ones on the secondary federation servers are read-only. In the event that the primary federation server becomes permanently unavailable, you will need to promote a secondary federation server to a primary federation server. There can be only one pri-mary federation server in the farm.

Deciding whether to use WID or a dedicated SQL server requires you to be aware of the limitations of using WID. Using WID limits your AD FS farm to five servers. For most orga-nizations, except the largest of enterprises, this is usually not a problem. There are other limitations when using WID that are not applicable to Office 365, such as being limited to only 100 trust relationships. This limitation might become an issue if you are planning to leverage your AD FS farm for other purposes besides Office 365.

Installing and configuring AD FS 2.0

Before starting the installation for AD FS 2.0, make sure you have completed all the preced-ing tasks. At this point, you already should have completed the following:

- Be familiar with the SSO experience your users will see and have a communication plan prepared.

- Understand the requirements for AD FS.

- Remediate your AD by ensuring you have the right UPN suffix added.

- Ensure existing users have the correct primary UPN suffix.

- Install IIS on the AD FS server.

- Create and install the security certificate for the default website in IIS on the AD FS server.

TROUBLESHOOTING

Download AD FS from Office 365
Do not directly add the AD FS role to the server through the Turn Windows features on or off link in Control Panel. Download and use AdfsSetup.exe instead.

When you have completed the preceding tasks, you are ready to install AD FS 2.0:

1. Create a service account for AD FS. In AD, create a service account that the AD FS service will use. Make sure this service account is part of the Administrators group of the local AD FS server. No special AD group memberships are required for this account; Domain Users is sufficient. We assume you know how to create AD service accounts and assign group membership in AD, so we do not provide details about how that is done.

2. Download the AD FS 2.0 software. The AD FS software package is a single executable file called AdfsSetup.exe. You can download it from the Microsoft Download Center at *http://www.microsoft.com/en-us/download/details.aspx?displaylang=en&id=10909*, as shown in Figure 3-27. Follow the instructions at the Download Center, which eventually will lead you to a list of the AdfsSetup.exe options. Select the package that applies to your server operating system.

Figure 3-27 Microsoft Download Center with the AD FS 2.0 software.

3. Run AdfsSetup.exe.

4. Click Next at the Welcome to AD FS 2.0 Setup Wizard page.

5. Read and accept the Microsoft Software License Terms and click Next, as shown in Figure 3-28.

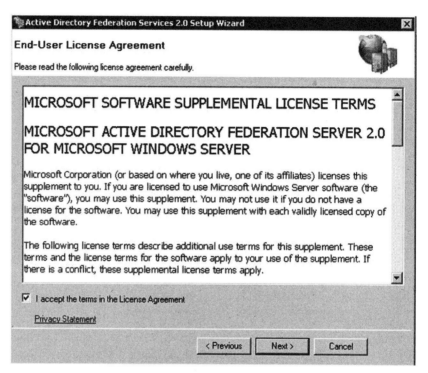

Figure 3-28 Accept the Microsoft Software License Terms for AD FS.

6. In the Active Directory Federation Services 2.0 Setup Wizard, select the Federation server option, as shown in Figure 3-29, and then click Next.

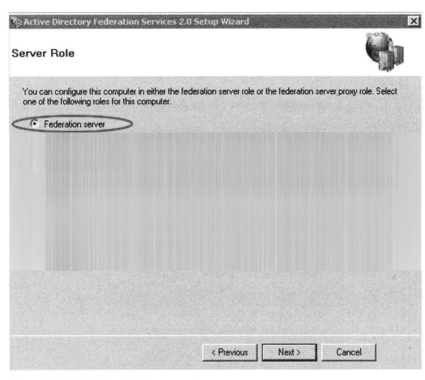

Figure 3-29 Install the AD FS server role.

7. As shown in Figure 3-30, the wizard will check for AD FS prerequisites and will install the required components if needed. Take note of the components the wizard will install, and then click Next.

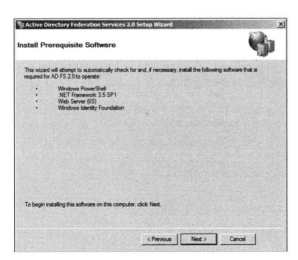

Figure 3-30 Installing AD FS prerequisites.

8. After the installation is complete, select Start the AD FS 2.0 Management snap-in when this wizard closes, as shown in Figure 3-31, and then click Finish.

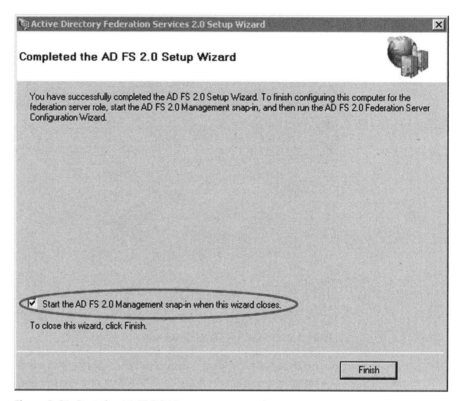

Figure 3-31 Start the AD FS 2.0 Management snap-in.

9. Because we selected the check box to start the AD FS Management snap-in in the preceding step, it will start at this time. Click the AD FS 2.0 Federation Server Configuration Wizard link in the middle pane, as shown in Figure 3-32.

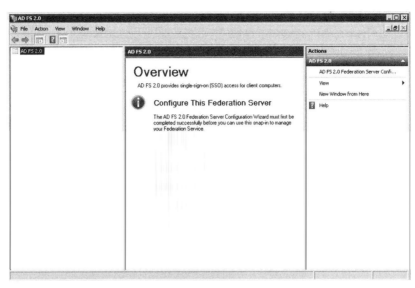

Figure 3-32 AD FS 2.0 Federation Server Configuration Wizard.

10. Because this is the first and primary federation server, select the Create a new Federation Service option, as shown in Figure 3-33, and then click Next.

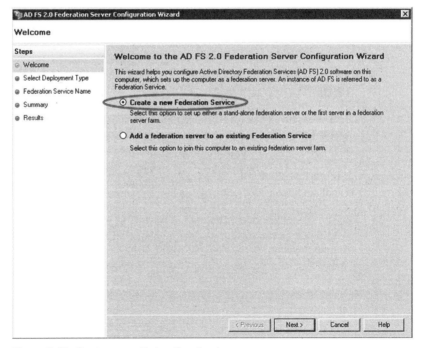

Figure 3-33 Create a new Federation Service.

11. In the Select Stand-Alone or Farm Deployment page, select New federation server farm, as shown in Figure 3-34, so you have the option to add more servers to the farm later.

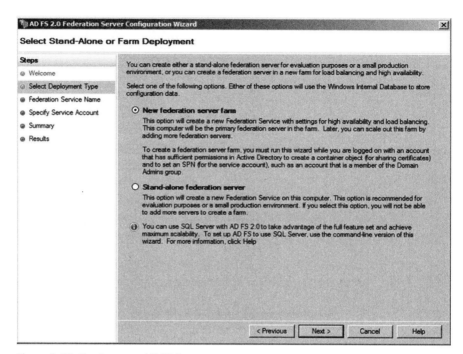

Figure 3-34 Create a new AD FS farm.

TROUBLESHOOTING

Problem with a stand-alone AD FS server

Remember our discussion earlier about AD FS potentially being a weak link for Office 365? For that reason, you should build an AD FS farm for a production environment. A stand-alone AD FS server will not allow you to add additional servers later.

12. The wizard will query the default website in IIS and should select the certificate you installed on the default website, as shown in Figure 3-35. Click Next.

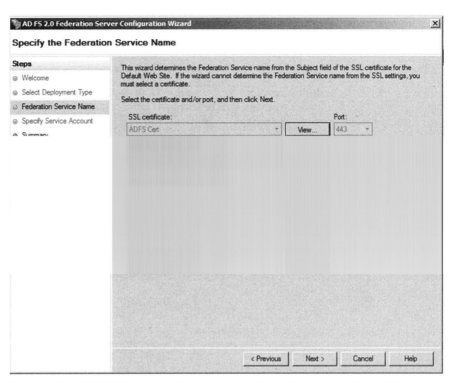

Figure 3-35 AD FS 2.0 Federation Server Configuration Wizard detects the certificate for the Default Web Site.

13. On the Specify a Service Account page, select the AD FS service account you created earlier, as shown in Figure 3-36. If you did not create the service account, you can use Active Directory Domain Services (AD DS) or Windows PowerShell to create the account. As a reminder, the service account must be a member of the Local Administrators group of the AD FS server. Click Next.

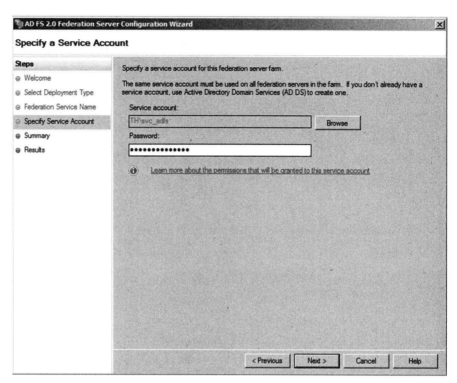

Figure 3-36 Select the AD FS service account.

14. On the Summary page, click Next to begin the AD FS configuration. When the configuration is complete, a Configuration Results page will appear that reports any issues, similar to the one shown in Figure 3-37.

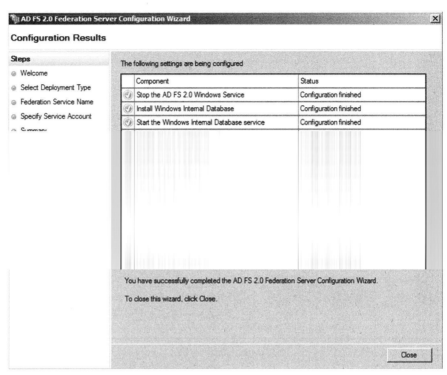

Figure 3-37 Configuration Results page showing AD FS 2.0 was successfully installed.

TROUBLESHOOTING

SPN was not set

You might be required to set the SPN for the service account manually. A common problem that occurs is when your host name is the same as the certificate issued to the default website. You can either change the server host name or revoke and reissue the certificate. The first option is usually simpler. Once you have done so, run the following command in a command line window as an administrator:

```
setspn -a host\<fully qualified servername> <domain>\<service account>
```

For example, if the fully qualified host name is fed.adatum.com and the service account is adatum\svc_adfs, the command will be the following:

```
setspn -a host\fed.adatum.com adatum\svc_adfs
```

15. Download and install the current AD FS 2.0 update rollup. For more information about the update rollup, see Knowledge Base (KB) article 2681584 at *http://support. microsoft.com/kb/2681584*.

Testing the federation server

Now that we have installed AD FS 2.0, we need to test that it is responding. Use a client computer located in the same forest as the AD FS server. From the client's browser, enter the URL of the AD FS server and append /FederationMetadata/2007-06/FederationMeta-data.xml to the end of the URL. For example, if your federation server's URL is https://fed. adatum.com, enter the URL in the client's browser, as shown in the following example:

```
https://fed.adatum.com/FederationMetadata/2007-06/FederationMetadata.xml
```

If the federation server is responding correctly, you will see an XML document similar to the one shown in Figure 3-38.

Figure 3-38 XML document and service description when accessing the AD FS server's URL.

Converting the domain from standard authentication to identity federation

Now that we have installed IIS, bound the AD FS service to the IIS server, applied the necessary certificates applied to the IIS server, tested AD FS, and can see the XML schema, it is safe to say that AD FS is now operational and can service authentication requests.

that best describes your environment.

AD FS server is installed on Windows Server 2008 R2

1. Download and install the Windows Azure Active Directory Module for Windows PowerShell cmdlets, formerly known as the Microsoft Online Services Module for Windows PowerShell cmdlets. The 32-bit version of the Windows Azure Active Directory Module for Windows PowerShell is located at *http://go.microsoft.com/FWLink/p/?Linkid=236298* and the 64-bit version is located at *http://go.microsoft.com/FWLink/p/?Linkid=236297*.

2. Start the Windows Azure Active Directory Module for Windows PowerShell cmdlets.

3. Enter the following command, which will produce a logon prompt for a user name and password:

   ```
   $cred = Get-Credential
   ```

4. The credentials you provide will be stored in the *$cred* variable. At the logon prompt, use your Office 365 Global Administrator account name.

> **Note**   Why save a credential in a variable?
> Technically, when managing identity with Windows PowerShell you can simply use the command *Connect-MsolService*. You do not need to save the credential in a variable first. However, we saved the credential in a variable in our example because we will need it when we use Windows PowerShell for Exchange Online, so we are just keeping it consistent throughout the book.

5. Enter the following command, which will attempt to connect and authenticate to an Office 365 tenant using the logon credentials you stored in *$cred*:

```
Connect-MsolService -Credential $cred
```

6. Lastly, enter the following command to convert the domain from standard authentication to identity federation in Office 365. Note that the *-SupportMultipleDomain* parameter is optional. Use it only if you will be federating other top-level domains (TLDs) with this Office 365 tenant.

```
Convert-MsolDomainToFederated -DomainName <domain name> -SupportMultipleDomain
```

If you do not receive any Windows PowerShell error messages, which are usually red in color, then your domain now supports identity federation. We will verify this in the "Verifying a successful conversion of a domain" section.

The AD FS server is installed on Windows Server 2008 SP2 or on a remote Windows 7 workstation

1. Download and install the Windows Azure Active Directory Module for Windows PowerShell cmdlets, formerly known as the Microsoft Online Services Module for Windows PowerShell cmdlets. The 32-bit version of the Windows Azure Active Directory Module for Windows PowerShell cmdlets is located at *http://go.microsoft.com/FWLink/p/?Linkid=236298* and the 64-bit version is located at *http://go.microsoft.com/FWLink/p/?Linkid=236297*.

2. Install the Windows Azure Active Directory Module on a remote server running Windows 2008 R2 or on a Windows 7 workstation.

3. On your AD FS server, right-click the shortcut to Windows PowerShell and run it as an administrator. Next, enter the following command:

```
Enable-PSRemoting -force
```

> **Note**
>
> The *Enable–PSRemoting* command creates a Windows Remote Management (WinRM) listener service on all IP addresses on the server using the HTTP protocol through port 5985. It also creates the required Windows Firewall rules to allow the Windows Remote Management application to go through port 5985. This allows a remote workstation or server to execute remote Windows PowerShell commands against this server.

4. To confirm that the Windows Remote Management service has been configured, execute the following command to see the configuration details:

```
winrm enumerate winrm/config/listener
```

5. Return to the remote server or workstation on which you installed the Windows Azure Active Directory Module and start the module.

6. Enter the following command, which will produce a logon prompt for a user name and a password:

    ```
    $cred = Get-Credential
    ```

    The credentials you provide will be stored in a variable called *$cred*. When you see

7. Enter the following command, which will attempt to connect and authenticate to an Office 365 tenant using the logon credentials that you stored in *$cred*:

    ```
    Connect-MsolService -Credential $cred
    ```

8. Enter the following command to set the context to that of the AD FS server:

    ```
    Set-MsolAdfscontext -Computer <FQDN of federation server>
    ```

9. Lastly, enter the following command to convert the domain from standard authentication to identity federation in Office 365:

    ```
    Convert-MsolDomainToFederated -DomainName <domain name> -SupportMultipleDomain
    ```

    Note that the *-SupportMultipleDomain* parameter is optional. Use it only if you will be federating other top-level domains (TLDs) with this Office 365 tenant.

    If you do not receive any Windows PowerShell error messages, which are usually red in color, then your domain is now a federated domain. We will verify this in the "Verifying a successful conversion of a domain" section.

Verifying a successful conversion of a domain

There are two main ways you can verify that federation has been successfully accomplished:

●   Using Windows PowerShell

●   Using the AD FS 2.0 Management snap-in

Windows PowerShell

You can verify your federation settings for the domain by issuing the following Windows PowerShell command after you have connected to Office 365 by using the *Connect-Msol-Service* command, as shown in Figure 3-39.

```
Get-MsolDomainFederationSettings –DomainName <your domain name FQDN>
```

For example:

```
Get-MsolDomainFederationSettings –DomainName thomsonhills.com
```

If you execute *Get-MsolDomainFederationSettings* without passing the *–DomainName* parameter, you will be verbosely prompted for a domain name.

Figure 3-39 Results after entering a command with the *Get-MsolDomainFederationSettings* cmdlet.

AD FS 2.0 Administration snap-in

You can also verify that a federation trust has been established between AD and Office 365 by looking at the trust relationships in the AD FS 2.0 Administration console. Follow the steps below:

1. Start the AD FS 2.0 Administration console.

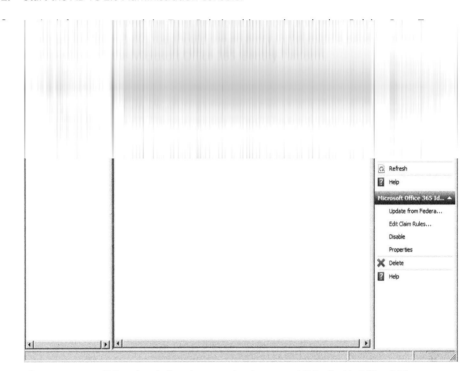

Figure 3-40 Verifying that federation trust has been established with Office 365.

Updating the federation URL endpoint

The federation URL endpoint is the FQDN of the federation server or service that Office 365 will redirect a user to once it detects the user is trying to log on with a UPN suffix that is associated to an identity federated domain.

If for any reason you need to change the federation URL endpoint, you can do so by following these steps:

1. Start the AD FS 2.0 Management console.

2. Right-click the AD FS 2.0 root node and select Edit Federation Service Properties from the drop-down box, as shown in Figure 3-41.

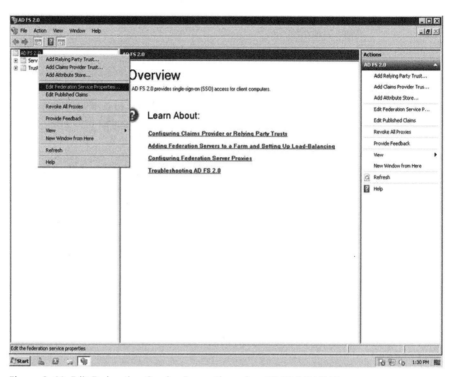

Figure 3-41 Edit Federation Service Properties using AD FS 2.0 MMC.

3. Edit the three properties of the federation service, as shown in Figure 3-42.

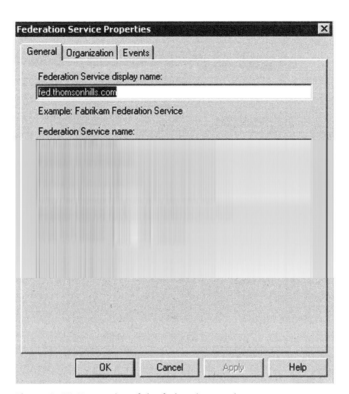

Figure 3-42 Properties of the federation service.

> **Note**   SSO lifetime
>
> AD FS 2.0 issues Security Assertion Markup Language (SAML) tokens that Office 365 consumes through the use of authentication cookies. Authentication cookies facilitate SSO in Office 365. The period of time that each authentication cookie can be used is represented by the SAML token's lifetime, which can be modified through the Web SSO lifetime setting, as shown in Figure 3-42. In the preceding example, once a user has been authenticated by AD FS the user will not be prompted for credentials for 480 minutes. If the user logs off and logs on again before 480 minutes, the SSO lifetime is reset.

4. Click OK to save the settings and restart the AD FS 2.0 service, as shown in Figure 3-43.

Figure 3-43 Restart the AD FS 2.0 service from the Services MMC.

5. If you have a wildcard certificate, you do not need to do anything with the certificate, assuming you did not change the domain name of your AD FS service. However, if you do not have a wildcard certificate and need to add a new certificate, you will first need to issue the following Windows PowerShell command from your AD FS server to turn off the AD FS automatic certificate rollover feature:

```
Set-ADFSProperties -AutoCertificateRollover $False
```

6. Skip this step if you do not need to update your certificate. Acquire or generate your new certificate.

7. Skip this step if you do not need to update your certificate. From the AD FS 2.0 Management console, expand the Service node under the root node, and then click Certificates. In the Actions pane, click Add Token-Signing certificate and add your new certificate. Click Add Token-Decrypting certificate, and then click Set Service Communications. See Figure 3-44.

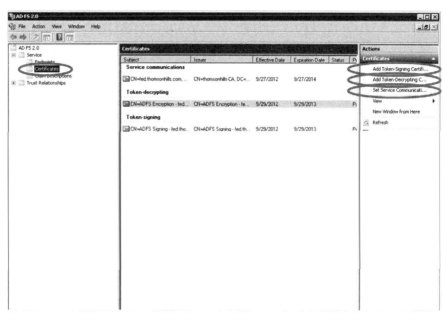

Figure 3-44 Add Token-Signing Certificate, Add Token-Decrypting Certificate, and Set Service Communications.

8. Lastly, enter the following Windows PowerShell command from the Windows Azure Active Directory Module:

```
Update-MSOLFederatedDomain -DomainName <YourFederatedDomain FQDN>
```

> **Note**
>
> By this time, you should be somewhat familiar with Windows PowerShell. Thus, for Step 8 we omitted the Windows PowerShell commands you would normally use to connect to Office 365 first, namely the *Get-Credential* and *Connect-MsolService* commands. Furthermore, if you are executing these commands from a remote server running Windows 2008 R2 or a Windows 7 workstation and not from your AD FS server, remember you need to also execute the *Set-MsolAdfsContext* command. Refer to previous sections if you need to refresh your memory.

9. Issue the following Windows PowerShell command from the Windows Azure Active Directory Module to determine if the federation URL endpoint is successfully updated:

```
Get-MsolDomainFederationSettings -DomainName <your domain FQDN>
```

Removing Active Directory Federation Services

In the event you need to remove AD FS and disable SSO for a domain in your tenant, there are a few important things you need to know:

- As with most actions, you will use the Windows Azure Active Directory Module and Windows PowerShell to convert the federated domain in Office 365 back to a standard domain.

- Previously federated user accounts, if they existed prior to federation, will not revert to using the original Office 365 passwords they had prior to federation.

- Temporary passwords will be generated for all federated users.

- The temporary passwords are stored in a file. You will specify the path and the name of the file as one of the parameters.

- Users will have to log on with their new temporary password and will be prompted to provide a new permanent password.

- If you choose to uninstall the AD FS role from your server, the virtual directories in the default website will not be removed. This must be done manually.

- If you choose to uninstall the AD FS role from your server, the AD FS database will not be removed. This can be done manually.

- Disabling SSO is also known as converting a domain from identity federation to standard authentication.

TROUBLESHOOTING

Accounts affected by reverting from identity federation to standard authentication
After you convert a domain in Office 365 from identity federation to standard authentication, all the user accounts associated with that domain will become unusable until you either convert the domain back to identity federation or until the users are also converted. Another word of caution is that the users will need to be assigned new passwords.

Converting a domain from identity federation to standard authentication

The first step you need to take to break federation is to convert the domain from federated to standard using Windows PowerShell. The second step, which is optional, is to uninstall AD FS 2.0 from the server.

The following scenarios show how to convert a domain from federated to standard. Ch...

you will use to supply your Office 365 credentials, and store the credentials in a variable named *$cred*:

```
$cred=Get-Credential
```

3. Enter the following command, which will attempt to connect and authenticate to an Office 365 tenant using the logon credentials you stored in *$cred*:

```
Connect-MsolService -Credential $cred
```

4. Enter the following command to remove the Rely Party Trust information from the Office 365 authentication system federation service and the on-premises AD FS 2.0 server:

```
Convert-MsolDomainToStandard -DomainName <domain name> -SkipUserCoonversion
[$true|$false] -PasswordFile:<path and filename>
```

5. If the *-SkipUserConversion* parameter is set to *$true*, a password file will not be generated and the user accounts that are associated with the domain will become unusable until either the domain is converted back to identity federation or each account is converted using the *Convert-MSOLFederatedUser* cmdlet, which we will discuss shortly. An actual command might look something like this:

```
Convert-MsolDomainToStandard -DomainName adatum.com -SkipUserConversion $false
-PasswordFile c:\TempPwd.txt
```

> **Note** Why not convert users?
>
> Why would you use *Convert-MsolDomainToStandard* with the *–SkipUserConver-sion $true* parameter so as not to convert users? One such scenario might be when you need to re-establish the Relying Party Trust. There have been a few occasions where we had to remove the Relying Party Trust because of an AD FS issue, and then turn around and use the *Convert-MsodDomainToFederated* to re-establish the Relying Party Trust. In such a scenario, we really do not want to convert the users.

6. Now that we have removed the Relying Party Trust, we need to reset the authentication setting for the domain. Enter the following command to accomplish this:

```
Set-MsolDomainAuthentication –Authentication Managed –DomainName <domain name>
```

7. If you need to manually convert user accounts to standard authentication because you used the *–SkipUserConversion $true* parameter, then enter this command:

```
Convert-MsolFederatedUser –UserPrincipalName <user@domain-name> -NewPassword
"<password>"
```

An actual command will look something like this:

```
Convert-MsolFederatedUser –UserPrincipalName julian@adatum.com –NewPassword
"Office365Rocks"
```

INSIDE OUT   Bulk conversion of user accounts

It might not be feasible for you to manually convert each user by repeatedly issuing the Windows PowerShell command, as shown in Step 6. To bulk convert users, you will have to write a script to iterate through a list of users and manually convert them. We use the following example script:

```
#Script to bulk convert users
#after Domain has been converted from
#Identity Federated to Standard Authentication

Cred$=Get-Credential
Connect-MsolService –Credential Cred$

Get-MsolUser –All | ForEach-Object {
    Convert-MsolFederatedUser –UserPrincipalName $_.UserPrincipalName –NewPass-
word "Temp-pwd"
}
```

Completely uninstall AD FS 2.0

The following process completely removes AD FS:

- Determine the location of the Certificate Sharing Container in Active Directory.

- Uninstall AD FS from the server(s) in the farm.

Determining the location of the Certificate Sharing Container in Active Directory

When we run the AD FS Configuration Wizard during installation to create a new AD FS server and farm, it creates a Certificate Sharing Container in Active Directory. When you uninstall, the Certificate Sharing Container is not automatically deleted, so we will need to do this manually.

The actual removal of the Certificate Sharing Container will be carried out later. For now, we just need to determine the container's location. We do this now because the Windows PowerShell commands to reveal the location of the container have to be run prior to uninstalling the last AD FS server in the farm.

To determine the location of the Certificate Sharing Container, follow these steps:

1. From an AD FS server, start Windows PowerShell.

2. Execute the following Windows PowerShell commands:

   ```
   Add-PsSnapin Microsoft.Adfs.Powershell
   Get-AdfsProperties
   ```

3. Take note of the *CertificateSharingContainer* property, as shown in Figure 3-45. We will use this information at a later step. In the example below, the pertinent information revealed by the Windows PowerShell script is CN=ADFS,CN=Microsoft,CN=Program Data,DC=thomsonhills,DC=com.

The GUID for the AD FS farm in this example is CN=2e9a65b9-3a14-43e1-b9ec-d965fb6272c5. Take note of the GUID of your farm.

Figure 3-45 Take note of the value for the CertificateSharingContainer.

Now that we know the location of the Certificate Sharing Container, we can start uninstalling AD FS 2.0 from the servers in the farm.

Uninstalling AD FS 2.0

As mentioned earlier in the chapter, if you need to remove the AD FS 2.0 role from your server, you will need to follow these steps:

1. Open Control Panel and in the Category view, click Programs.

2. Select the View Installed Updates link and search for the Active Directory Federation Services 2.0 component.

3. Select the Active Directory Federation Services 2.0 component and click Uninstall, as shown in Figure 3-46.

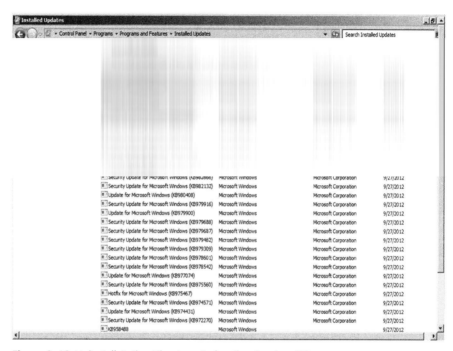

Figure 3-46 Uninstall Active Directory Federation Services 2.0.

Restoring IIS

Uninstalling AD FS 2.0 does not restore IIS to its original state. When you installed AD FS 2.0, the setup created virtual directories in IIS and an application pool for AD FS. These are not removed as part of the uninstall process, so you will have to do this manually. The virtual directories that were created in IIS are /adfs and /adfs/ls, and the application pool that was created is named ADFSAppPool, as shown in Figure 3-47.

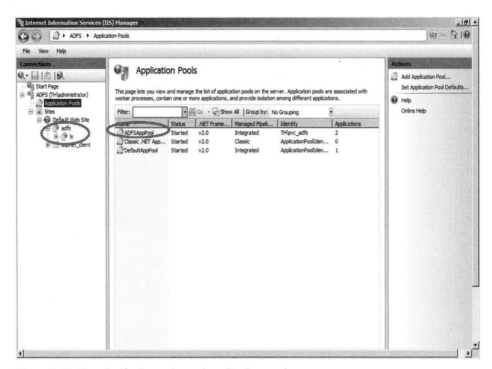

Figure 3-47 Virtual adfs directories and application pool.

To remove the application, application pools, and directories, follow these steps:

1. In IIS, navigate to the /adfs/ls directory.

2. Right-click the directory and select Remove, as shown in Figure 3-48.

Figure 3-48 Remove the application in /adfs/ls.

3. Repeat the same steps for the /adfs directory.

4. Select the Application Pools node and locate the ADFSAppPool application pool. Right click it and select Remove, as shown in Figure 3-49, or simply select Remove on the Actions pane.

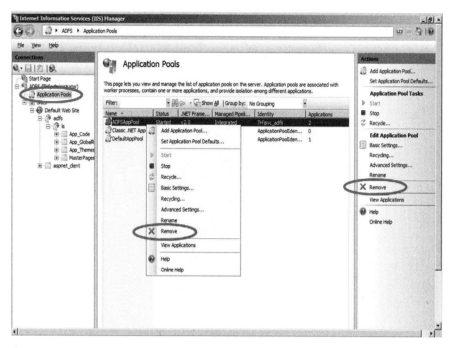

Figure 3-49 Remove the ADFSAppPool application pool.

5. Lastly, we need to remove the actual directories. Open Windows Explorer and navigate to %systemdrive%\inetpub.

6. Right-click the \adfs directory and select Delete, as shown in Figure 3-50.

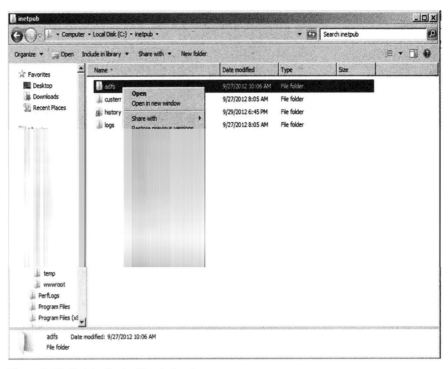

Figure 3-50 Delete the \adfs subdirectory.

Removing the Certificate Sharing Container

From an earlier step, you should have gathered the location information for the Certificate Sharing Container. We will now use that information to manually remove the container from AD by following these steps:

1. From a Windows 2008 or later Server that has the Active Directory Domain Services role installed, click Start. Click Run, and then type ADSIEdit.msc, as shown in Figure 3-51.

    If you need to install ADSIEdit on a server that is not running Windows 2008 or on a workstation, see "ADSI Edit (adsiedit.msc)" at *http://technet.microsoft.com/en-us/library/cc773354.aspx*.

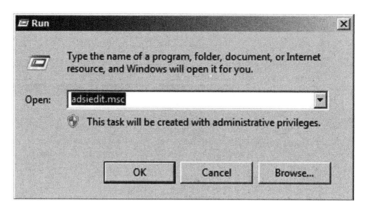

Figure 3-51 Run ADSIEdit.msc.

2. Right-click ADSI Edit and select Connect to, as shown in Figure 3-52.

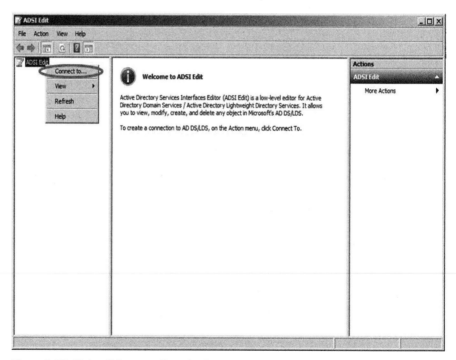

Figure 3-52 Right-click ADSI Edit and select Connect to.

3. Under Connection Point, click Select a well-known Naming Context, as shown in Figure 3-53. Then click OK.

Figure 3-53 Select the default naming context.

4. Refer to the location information of the Certificate Sharing Container you collected at the very beginning. In our example, we noted that the container is at CN=ADFS,CN=Microsoft,CN=Program Data,DC=thomsonhills,DC=com.

Applying this information to our example, and reading backward starting from DC=thomsonhills,DC=com, expand CN=Program Data, followed by CN=Microsoft, and finally CN=ADFS. Navigate in that order, as shown in Figure 3-54.

Chapter 3

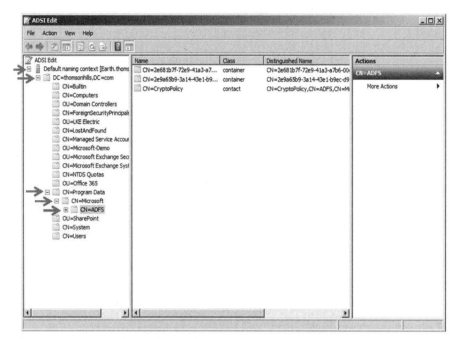

Figure 3-54 Locating the Certificate Sharing Container in ADSIEdit.msc.

5. Look for the GUID of the farm. You should already have that information from an earlier step. In our example, the GUID we are looking for is 2e9a65b9-3a14-43e1-b9ec-d965fb6272c5, as shown in Figure 3-55. Right-click the appropriate GUID and select Delete.

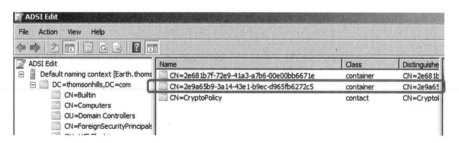

Figure 3-55 Locate, right-click, and delete the GUID that matches the AD FS farm.

You have now completely uninstalled AD FS and manually cleaned up all the objects and settings that were not removed by the uninstallation process.

Summary

In this chapter, we undertook and implemented SSO, a key component that is unique to enterprises and available only in the Office 365 Enterprise (A1/G1/E1, A3/G3/E3, or A4/G4/E4) suite offerings. There are many technologies that made this possible, the most important of which is a healthy Active Directory.

It is also important to stress that when you turn on SSO, you are in fact deferring authentication to your on-premises AD FS farm. Therefore, if the AD FS farm is unreachable for whatever reason, Office 365 services will be unavailable for users who are not yet authenticated. Invest in the time and architecture to build a robust AD FS farm and consider alternative and redundant options such as Windows Azure IaaS to supplement your AD FS farm.

Chapter 3

Directory synchronization process. 140   Forcing an unscheduled directory synchronization . . . 182

access. If they have not been authenticated by AD, they will be presented with the Office 365 portal logon screen, and they will need to supply a user name in UPN format.

If a federated UPN suffix is supplied, Office 365 automatically redirects the authentication request to your AD FS service. If it is not a federated UPN suffix or if the suffix is *.onmicrosoft.com, then Office 365 is responsible for the authentication. Collectively, this addresses the authentication process for Office 365. However, we still need to address how accounts are created in the Office 365 tenant. A corresponding Office 365 account needs to exist for each user needing access to Office 365.

The theme throughout this book is automation. As an enterprise, the last thing we want to do is manually maintain a second set of user accounts in Office 365. Office 365 user account automation comes in the form of directory synchronization.

During the directory synchronization process, a corresponding Office 365 account is created for each user account in AD, as shown in Figure 4-1.

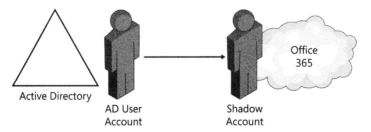

Figure 4-1 Directory synchronization with the Directory Sync tool.

Directory synchronization is accomplished through a free piece of software known as the Windows Azure Active Directory Sync tool, which is supplied by Microsoft specifically for use with Office 365 subscriptions. Under the covers, directory synchronization is really a customized distribution of Microsoft Forefront Identity Manager (FIM) 2010. FIM is used for more advanced directory synchronization scenarios that we will cover in Chapter 16, "Advanced Scenarios and Azure." You will hear the terms directory synchronization, DirSync, and Windows Azure Active Directory Sync used interchangeably. DirSync is used more frequently because of its brevity. We will generally reference it as directory synchronization throughout the book.

Directory synchronization is provided as a software tool, which means minimal configuration is required for directory synchronization to work. The important facts to know about directory synchronization are the following:

- Directory synchronization creates a copy of AD accounts in Office 365.

- A new directory synchronization option allows you to configure directory synchronization to synchronize AD passwords to Office 365. This is sometimes known as *same sign on*.

- Without implementing AD FS, directory synchronized accounts will require their own passwords in Office 365. This is accomplished by manually administering passwords in Office 365 or by using the new password sync option in directory synchronization.

- Accounts that are directory synchronized in Office 365 are not automatically granted access to Office 365 services. A separate action, manual or automated, must occur to assign Office 365 licenses to accounts. So, it is not uncommon to have more accounts in Office 365 than what you have licenses for because not all accounts require Office 365 access.

- Directory synchronization is a required prerequisite for SSO, Lync Online and Lync on-premises coexistence, and Exchange hybrid deployments.

- Directory synchronization is also responsible for the synchronization of other AD objects, such as distribution lists (DLs), photos, and security groups.

For the most part, directory synchronization is a one-way push of information from AD to Office 365. However, if you require a hybrid scenario for Exchange, a two-way synchronization needs to occur because directory synchronization needs to write some information back to AD to facilitate mail flow for a hybrid environment, where some mailboxes reside in Office 365 while others reside on-premises. We will take a deeper look at all the two-way synchronization occurrences in Chapter 11, "Incorporating Exchange Online in the Enterprise," which focuses on Exchange Online.

Directory synchronization synchronizes a number of AD attributes into Office 365, and you can configure it to include other attributes. At a minimum, directory synchronization requires the following attributes to contain values before the account can be synchronized:

- *CN*

- *Members* (if the object is a group)

INSIDE OUT   Leverage both identities

You might think you must choose to use either cloud identities or federated identities, but be aware there is no reason why you cannot use both. For example, in many enterprise organizations with AD, there might be a reluctance to create and maintain accounts for non-employees because of security and licensing concerns. These non-employee accounts might belong to vendors, business-to-business (B2B) partners, or contractors for whom you want access to Office 365 because you are doing business with them. This is a classic example of an extranet. There is a special class of cloud identity that allows for partner access to Office 365 at no cost. These are called Partner Access Licenses (PALs), and each Office 365 tenant comes with a number of PALs. PALs allow you to invite external users so they can access content stored in SharePoint Online. For more information about PALs, see the SharePoint Online Service Description. On the other hand, if you want to provide non-employees with other Office 365 services but do not want to create an account for them in AD, you can create a cloud identity for the non-employees and assign them access to Office 365. The important thing to note here is that cloud identities can coexist alongside federated identities in the same Office 365 tenant.

Directory synchronization process

As mentioned earlier, directory synchronization creates a user account in Office 365 by replicating the AD account in its UPN format and attempting to create an Office 365 account using that UPN. If it is not able to complete the process, then directory synchronization will create the account using the tenant's default domain name, which is usually *<Org.Name>.onmicrosoft.com*. For example, directory synchronization copies the object and properties for *marshall@adatum.com* and tries to create an account called *marshall@adatum.com* in an Office 365 tenant. However, if adatum.com is not a domain that is added to the Office 365 tenant, directory synchronization will not be able to create *marshall@adatum.com*. Instead, it will create the account as *marshall@adatum.onmicrosoft.com*. The onmicrosoft.com name is defined at the time you created your Office 365 tenant.

Figure 4-2 shows how an AD account is handled when it is synchronized with Office 365. It is important to note that directory synchronization synchronizes changes to existing accounts as well as the creation of new accounts. Directory synchronization also synchronizes accounts that were deleted in AD. (Figure 4-2 does not show the synchronization of deleted accounts).

When the directory synchronization process is completed, new accounts created in AD that do not exist in Office 365 will be created in the tenant. Existing AD accounts previously synchronized with Office 365 will be checked for changes since the last time directory synchronization ran, and any changes will be updated in Office 365. Finally, if an account in AD was deleted, the corresponding Office 365 account will also be removed.

It is also important to note that the very first time directory synchronization runs, a complete synchronization between AD and Office 365 is performed. Thereafter, each directory synchronization run is only an incremental pass that addresses the delta changes between AD and Office 365. By default, directory synchronization is scheduled to run every three hours, but this can be configured accordingly. You will see how this is accomplished later in the chapter.

Activating directory synchronization

Before installing the Windows Azure Active Directory Sync tool, you first need to activate directory synchronization in your Office 365 tenant. We can accomplish this by using Windows PowerShell or the Office 365 admin center.

However, before activating directory synchronization, if you are planning on implementing Exchange Online in a hybrid scenario, you need to update your AD schema with Exchange 2010 SP3. Although this is a service-specific task, and we will mention it again in Chapter 11, you should update the schema now if this scenario applies to you.

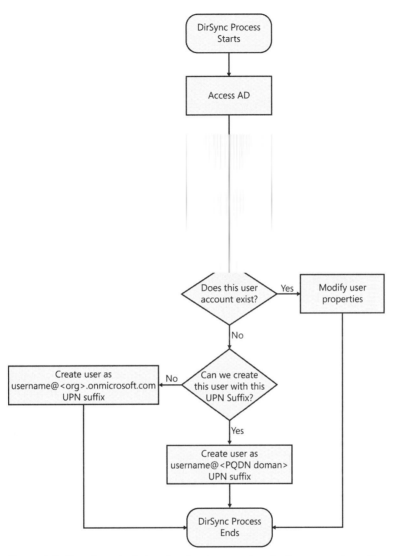

Figure 4-2 Flowchart depicting the directory synchronization account creation and update process.

Updating the AD schema

Updating the AD schema to include updates from Exchange 2010 SP3 makes it easier to deploy and manage Exchange Online in a hybrid scenario. It also allows you to manage email attributes in AD, and directory synchronization will replicate them to Office 365.

To update the AD schema, follow these steps:

1. Log on to your Exchange server with an account that has enterprise schema rights.

2. Click Start, click All Programs, click Accessories, and then click Command Prompt.

3. Enter the following command and make a note of the schema version:

```
dsquery * CN=ms-exch-schema-version-pt,CN=schema,CN=configuration,DC=<yourdomai
n>,DC=com -scope base -attr rangeupper
```

   Figure 4-3 shows an example of this command being executed and the corresponding results.

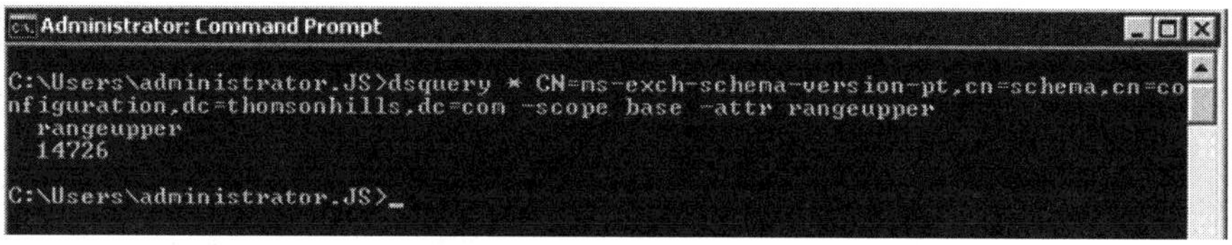

Figure 4-3 Determine the schema version number for Exchange.

4. Update your schema version if it is less than 14734. If it is 14734 or higher, your AD schema is already updated and you can skip the rest of the steps.

5. Download Exchange 2010 SP3 from the Microsoft Download Center at *http://www.microsoft.com/en-us/download/details.aspx?id=36768*. You can also read about the new features in Exchange 2010 SP3 from the Microsoft Exchange Team blog at *http://blogs.technet.com/b/exchange/archive/2013/02/12/released-exchange-server-2010-sp3.aspx*.

6. Extract the files into a directory.

7. Start a command prompt and navigate to the directory containing the extracted files.

8. As shown in Figure 4-4, run setup to prepare all domains in the forest for Exchange 2010 SP3 by using the */pad* parameter:

```
setup.com /pad
```

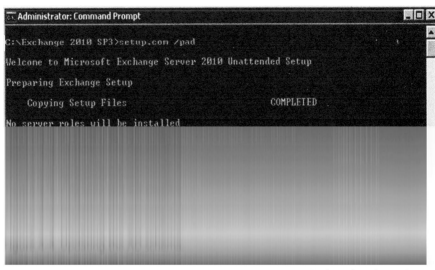

9. Extend the AD schema by issuing the following command, which is also shown in Figure 4-5:

```
setup.com /prepareschema
```

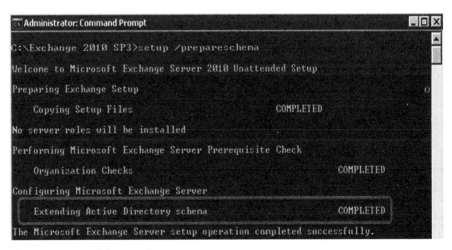

Figure 4-5 Extend the AD schema.

10. Rerun *dsquery*, as depicted in Step 3, to confirm that the AD schema is now version 14734, as shown in Figure 4-6.

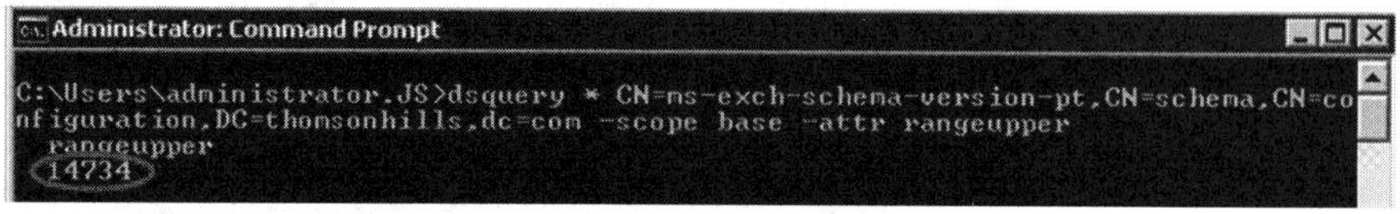

Figure 4-6 AD schema extended for Exchange 2010 SP2.

Now that the AD schema has been extended for Exchange 2010 SP3, you can proceed with activating directory synchronization for the Office 365 tenant.

Activating directory synchronization with Windows PowerShell

To activate directory synchronization, follow these steps:

1. Start the Online Services Windows PowerShell module.

2. Enter the following command, which will produce a logon prompt for a user name and a password:

```
$cred = Get-Credential
```

The credentials you provide will be stored in a variable called *$cred*. When you see the logon prompt, provide your Office 365 Global Administrator account. Remember that saving the credentials to a variable is optional because you can connect to Office 365 through Windows PowerShell just by using the *Connect-MsolService* command. Storing the credentials in a variable is needed for managing Exchange Online with Windows PowerShell and other scripting scenarios, so we are including this step to stay consistent with all the examples throughout the book.

3. Enter the following command, which will attempt to connect and authenticate to an Office 365 tenant using the logon credentials that you stored in *$cred*:

```
Connect-MsolService -Credential $cred
```

4. Finally, enter the following command to activate directory synchronization for the tenant:

```
Set-MsolDirSyncEnabled –EnableDirSync $true
```

5. To confirm directory synchronization is activated, enter the following command:

`(Get-MsolCompanyInformation).DirectorySynchronizationEnabled`

Figure 4-7 shows an example of the result. If the command returns a value of *True*, then directory synchronization is enabled. Otherwise, the value returned will be *False*.

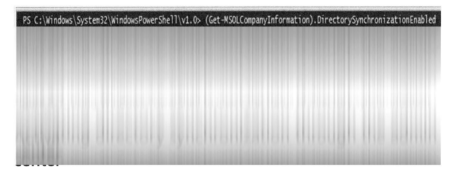

Alternatively, you can activate directory synchronization through the Office 365 admin center by following these steps:

1. Log on to the Office 365 admin center at *https://portal.microsoftonline.com*.

2. Click users and groups, as shown in Figure 4-8.

3. Click the Set up link for Active Directory synchronization, also shown in Figure 4-8.

Figure 4-8 Set up Active Directory synchronization for the Office 365 tenant.

4. Locate Step 3 on the Set up and manage Active Directory synchronization page and click activate, as shown in Figure 4-9.

Figure 4-9 Click activate to activate directory synchronization.

5. As shown in Figure 4-10, you will receive notification that after directory synchronization is activated, synchronized objects can be edited only on-premises. This simply means that AD becomes authoritative and you need to make changes to objects in AD and not in Office 365, which is our goal. Click activate.

Figure 4-10 Click activate to proceed with activating directory synchronization for the tenant.

> **Note**
> Although the message in Figure 4-10 states that Active Directory synchronized
> objects can be edited only on-premises, remember that you can still create cloud
> identities using any UPNs from domains that are verified and associated to your
> Office 365 tenant. Properties for cloud identities can be edited from the admin
> center or through Windows PowerShell. Furthermore, after directory synchroniza-
> tion is activated, it might take up to 24 hours before it is truly enabled. Therefore

AD objects you will be synchronizing. At the time of this writing, directory synchronization
is limited to 20,000 AD objects.

However, this does not mean you cannot synchronize more than 20,000 AD objects. This
limit was imposed so the Office 365 team will be aware of any large-scale synchronization.
Therefore, if you have more than 20,000 AD objects to synchronize, please contact your
Microsoft representative. Microsoft will work with your organization to help synchronize
more than 20,000 objects. Microsoft might also use this awareness to ensure that your
Office 365 tenant is provisioned in a way that it can optimally support more than 20,000
objects.

Directory synchronization was available in both 32-bit and 64-bit versions when it first
debuted for Business Productivity Online Services (BPOS). However, for Office 365, you
need to install the 64-bit version of the Windows Azure Active Directory Sync tool. In fact,
the 32-bit version is no longer available for you to download. If you have the 32-bit version
installed, it is recommended that you upgrade to the 64-bit version because the 32-bit version is no longer supported.

Chapter 4

> **Note**
>
> The 64-bit version of directory synchronization, now also known as Windows Azure Active Directory Sync, has the same core functionality as the 32-bit version but with added enhancements such as password sync. However, the database schemas for the two versions are different. Therefore, it is not possible for you to do an in-place upgrade from the 32-bit version to the 64-bit version. You will be required to re-install the 64-bit version of directory synchronization.

You can download the Windows Azure Active Directory Sync tool from the Microsoft Download Center at *http://go.microsoft.com/FWLink/?LinkID=278924* or from the Office 365 admin center.

Next, you need to know the system requirements for directory synchronization. The following are core system requirements for directory synchronization:

- 64-bit edition of Windows Server 2008 R2 SP1 Standard or Enterprise, or Windows Server 2008 Datacenter or Windows Server 2008 R2 Datacenter. 64-bit edition of Windows Server 2012 Standard or Datacenter.

- Joined to a domain.

- Not a domain controller.

- Either a Windows Internal Database (WID) or a computer running SQL Server.

- The server on which you intend to install directory synchronization will need the .NET Framework 3.5.1 and the Microsoft Online Services Sign-on Assistant.

These are the core requirements for directory synchronization. For more information, see *http://technet.microsoft.com/en-us/library/jj151831.aspx#BKMK_ComputerRequirements.*

INSIDE OUT   Use a virtual machine

Directory synchronization is not a resource-intensive process, so it is perfectly fine to use a virtual machine. Furthermore, consider the impact of the availability of directory synchronization. You might subconsciously think that directory synchronization needs to be high availability, and thus you might start thinking about strategies such as cluster-

new users. However, it is not necessary for you to overly invest in high availability strategies for directory synchronization. It is much more important to invest in high availability for AD FS than for directory synchronization, so you should invest your limited system resources accordingly. As an example, we had a customer with over 25,000 AD accounts, and the customer experienced some AD issues that were unrelated to Office 365. However, as part of the AD troubleshooting process, we had to shut down directory synchronization for a few days. Office 365 services were unaffected during that period of time.

Follow these steps to download and install directory synchronization:

1. Log on to Office 365 as a global administrator and from the admin center, click users and groups.

2. Click the Set up link for Active Directory synchronization, as previously shown in Figure 4-8. However, this time locate Step 4 of the process and click the download button, as shown in Figure 4-11. Notice that if directory synchronization is not yet fully activated, there will be a banner at the top of the screen stating that Active Directory synchronization is being activated and that the process might take up to 24 hours to complete.

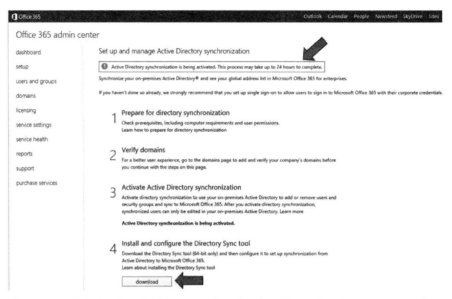

Figure 4-11 Click the download button to install and configure the Directory Sync tool.

3. Ensure you have the proper credentials before beginning the directory synchronization installation process:

   ❍ An AD account with Enterprise Administrator permissions

   ❍ An Office 365 account with the Global Administrator role

> **Important**
>
> Security alert! At this point, you or your organization's Chief Security Officer (CSO) might be concerned about requiring AD Enterprise Administrator privileges, which might constitute a roadblock. Therefore, it is worth spending some time looking into how the AD Enterprise Administrator account is used. We mentioned earlier that directory synchronization is intended to be a software tool with minimal configuration. The AD Enterprise Administrator account is part of that plan because the account is used only once during the directory synchronization setup process to simplify configuration. It is used to create a service account with the appropriate minimum set of privileges. After that, directory synchronization does not use the Enterprise Administrator account again, and neither does it retain the AD Enterprise Administrator's credential information anywhere in its configuration. The new service account created in AD by directory synchronization will take the form MSOL_*<some_numeric_value>*, such as MSOL_1234567.

Before starting the directory synchronization installation process, you need to decide whether directory synchronization will use a dedicated computer running a SQL Server instance to store configuration data or whether it will use WID, which comes with it. You should try to use WID if you have fewer than 50,000 objects in your AD because this makes your directory synchronization installation more like a network appliance and easier to maintain. There are also fewer components to troubleshoot and monitor; for example, it is easier to manage the communication between the directory synchronization server and the

SQL database in an enterprise setup because that is what we have been conditioned to do. However, the guidance is that if your AD has fewer than 50,000 objects to be syn-chronized, you can use directory synchronization with its built-in SQL 2008 Express. Use a dedicated computer running SQL Server only if you need to synchronize more than 50,000 objects. Continue to follow the installation instructions in this section, and we will show you how to configure directory synchronization for SQL 2008 Express or for a dedicated computer running SQL Server.

The next two sections outline the two options for installing directory synchronization:

- Install directory synchronization with a dedicated computer running SQL Server

- Install directory synchronization with WID

Select the option that applies to you and follow the steps outlined in that section.

Installing directory synchronization with a dedicated computer running SQL Server

Skip this section and refer to the next section if you choose to install directory synchroniza-tion with WID. Otherwise, follow these steps:

1. Navigate to the location where you downloaded the Directory Sync tool and launch it with the */fullsql* parameter:

    ```
    Dirsync /fullsql
    ```

Chapter 4

2. You will see a progress bar as files are being extracted. The Welcome page of the Directory Sync Setup Wizard will appear, as shown in Figure 4-12. Click Next.

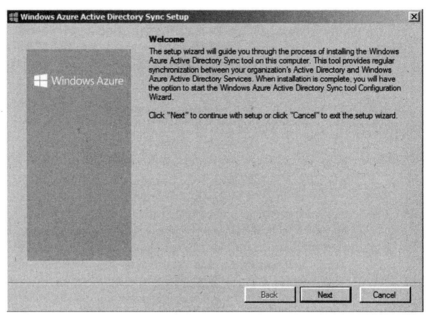

Figure 4-12   Welcome page of the Directory Sync Setup Wizard.

3. Read and accept the Microsoft Software License Terms for the Directory Sync tool. Select I accept and click Next, as shown in Figure 4-13.

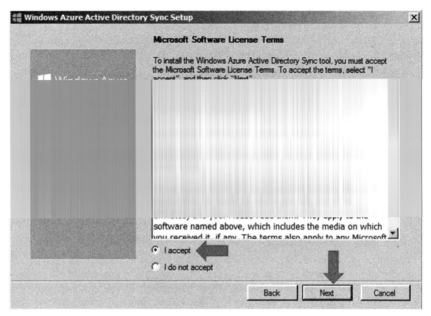

Figure 4-13 Microsoft Software License Terms for the Directory Sync tool.

Chapter 4

4. Specify the location to install directory synchronization or choose the default location, as shown in Figure 4-14. Click Next.

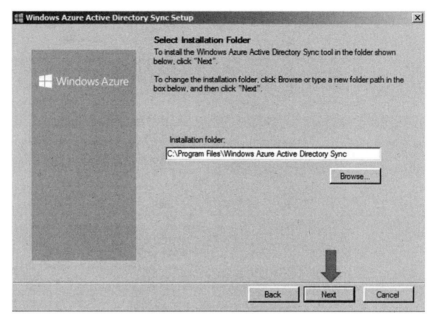

Figure 4-14 Specify the directory synchronization installation folder.

5. After the directory synchronization components have been installed, click Next, as shown in Figure 4-15.

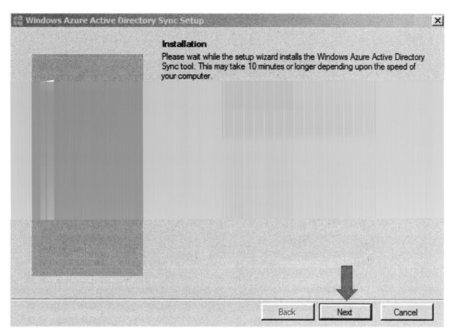

Figure 4-15 Click Next after the installation is complete.

6. As shown in Figure 4-16, after setup is complete, the Finished page appears with confirmation that you installed directory synchronization with the */FullSQL* option. It also directs you to instructions provided by Technical Support to complete the directory synchronization configuration. The Start Configuration Wizard now option is not available. Click Next.

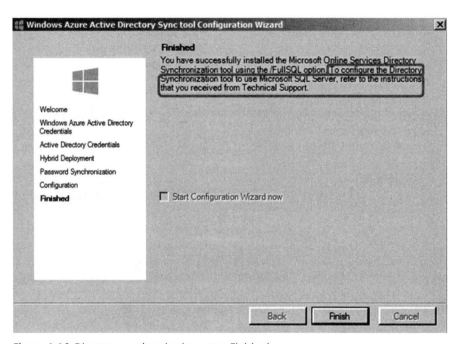

Figure 4-16 Directory synchronization setup Finished page.

7. Install the SQL Server Native Client on the directory synchronization server by running sqlncli.msi or by installing the client and administration tools. The sqlncli.msi is located in the \setup directory of your SQL Server installation package or DVD. Click Next at the Welcome page, as shown in Figure 4-17.

For more information about installing the SQL Server Native Client, see *http://tech-net.microsoft.com/en-us/library/ms131321(v=SQL.105).aspx.*

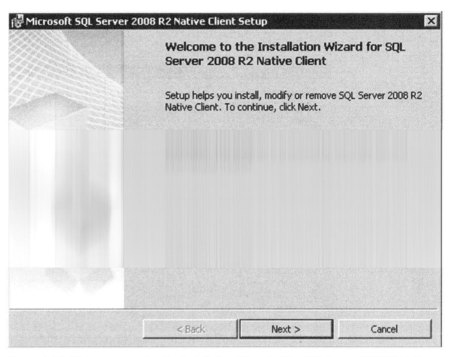

Figure 4-17 Welcome page for the Installation Wizard of the SQL Server 2008 R2 Native Client Installation Wizard.

8. Read and accept the Microsoft Software License Terms, then click Next.

9. As shown in Figure 4-18, accept the default, which is to install the Client Components but not the SQL Server Native Client SDK. Click Next.

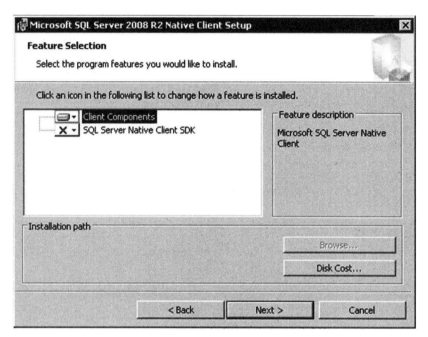

Figure 4-18 Install Client Components. The SDK is not required.

10. When the SQL Server Native Client Setup is completed, click OK to end the installation.

11. On the computer where directory synchronization is installed, navigate to the directory where directory synchronization is installed. In our example, we used the default directory during installation, which is C:\Program Files\Windows Azure Active Directory Sync.

12. Locate the file named DirsyncInstallshell.psc1, as shown in Figure 4-19, and double-click it.

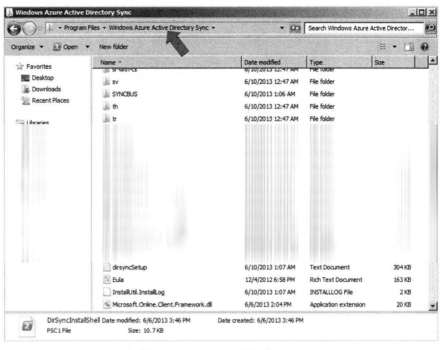

Figure 4-19 Locate and double-click DirSyncinstallshell.psc1.

13. As shown in Figure 4-20, at the Windows PowerShell prompt, enter the following
    command to configure directory synchronization for use with a dedicated computer
    running a SQL Server installation and instance:

```
Install-OnlineCoexistenceTool -UseSQLServer -SqlServer <SQLServerName>
-ServiceCredential(Get-Credential) -SqlServerInstance < >
```

Figure 4-20 shows our demo environment; in this example, our computer running
SQL Server is named sql.thomsonhills.com and the SQL instance is named CorpSQL.
Substitute these values for ones that apply to your environment.

Chapter 4

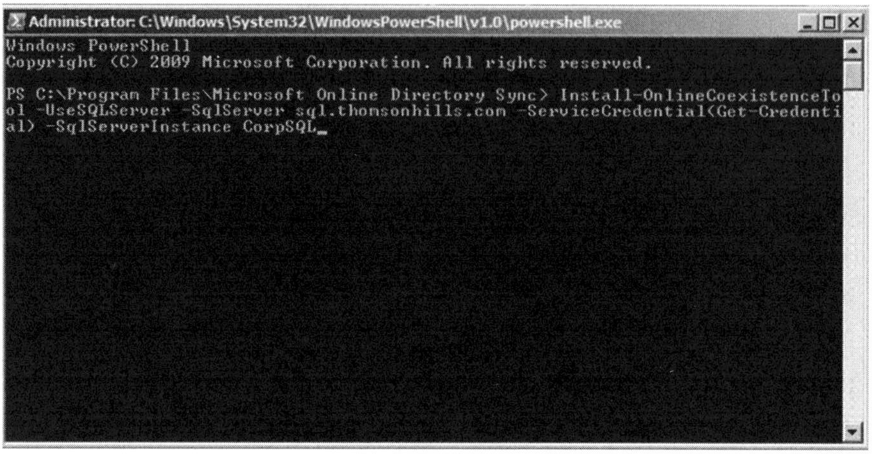

Figure 4-20 Enter the *Install-OnlineCoexistenceTool* command with SQL parameters.

INSIDE OUT
Other directory synchronization installation options if you change your mind

If at this time you change your mind and would like to install directory synchronization using other database options, it is still not too late. Use one of these options:

- To configure directory synchronization to use a dedicated computer running SQL Server, enter the following:

```
Install-OnlineCoexistenceTool -UseSQLServer -SqlServer <SQLServerName>
-ServiceCredential(Get-Credential) -SqlServerInstance <SqlInstanceName>
```

- To configure directory synchronization to use a different remote installation of SQL Server 2008 Express, enter the following:

```
Install-OnlineCoexistenceTool -UseSQLServer -SqlServer <SQLServerName>
-ServiceCredential(Get-Credential) -Verbose
```

- To configure directory synchronization to use an existing SQL Server 2008 Express installation that is already on the same machine, enter the following:

```
Install-OnlineCoexistenceTool -UseSQLServer -Verbose
```

14. When you see the logon window, as shown in Figure 4-21, provide your SQL Server logon credentials.

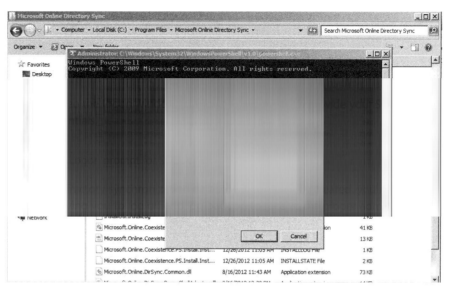

Figure 4-21 Logon prompt for SQL Server.

15. When the directory synchronization database is successfully created, you will see a screen notifying you to log off and log back on to receive the proper administrative access for directory synchronization. Go ahead and log off and log back on to the directory synchronization server, as shown in Figure 4-22.

TROUBLESHOOTING

Directory synchronization generates an error when connecting to the remote SQL database

If directory synchronization generates an error when connecting to the remote SQL database and you are sure your logon credentials are correct, the SQL Server Native Client might not have been properly installed. You might also find an entry in the event log with error number 1603. Check that the SQL Server Native Client has been installed (see Step 7). Make sure that the .NET Framework 3.5.1 has also been installed.

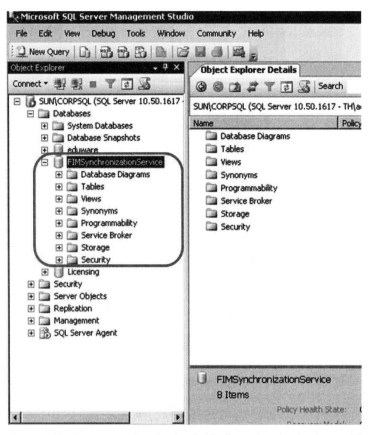

Figure 4-22 Directory synchronization finished creating the database, with a warning.

16. Confirm that the directory synchronization database was created. Log on to your SQL server and start the Microsoft SQL Server Management Studio, or if you have the SQL management tools installed on your workstation, start the Microsoft SQL Server Management Studio on your workstation and remotely connect to the SQL server.

17. The database was successfully created if you see the FIMSynchronizationService database, as shown in Figure 4-23.

Directory synchronization installation is now complete. At this point, you should have completed the following tasks:

- Installed directory synchronization on a dedicated computer running SQL Server

- Verified that the directory synchronization database was created successfully

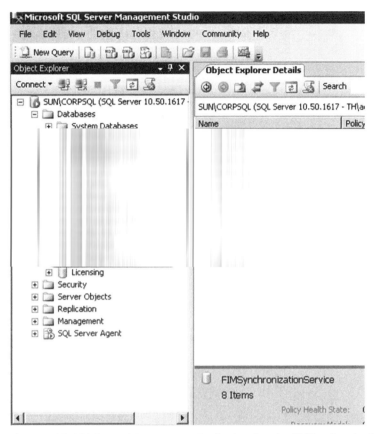

Figure 4-23 SQL Server Management Studio showing the FIMSynchronizationService database.

The next section outlines the steps required to install directory synchronization with WID. If you have installed directory synchronization on a dedicated computer running SQL server, you can skip the next section and go to the "Configuring directory synchronization" section.

Installing directory synchronization with Windows Internal Database

Skip this section and refer to the preceding section if you choose to install directory synchronization with a dedicated SQL database instead of WID. Otherwise, follow these steps:

1. Navigate to the location where you downloaded directory synchronization and start the dirsync installation package by double-clicking it, as shown in Figure 4-24.

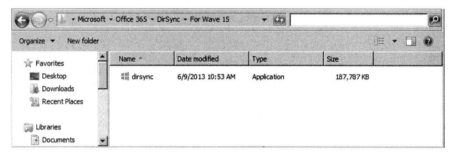

Figure 4-24 The downloaded dirsync package.

2. You will see a progress bar as files are being extracted. The Welcome page of the Directory Sync Setup Wizard will appear, as shown in Figure 4-25. Click Next.

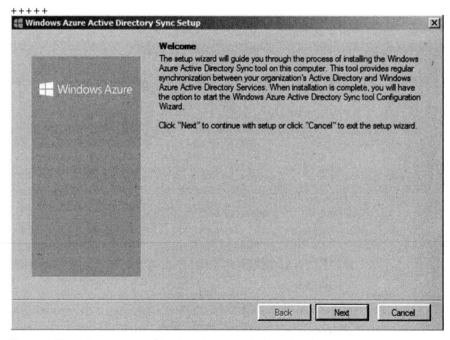

Figure 4-25 Welcome page of the Directory Sync Setup Wizard.

3. Read and accept the Microsoft Software License Terms for the Directory Sync tool. Select I accept and click Next, as shown in Figure 4-26.

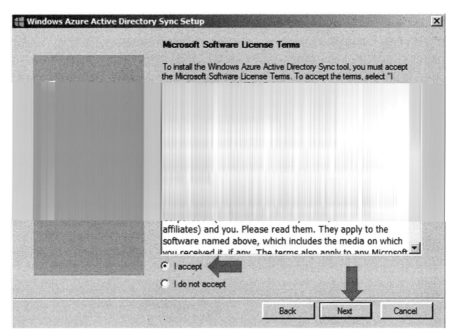

Figure 4-26 Microsoft Software License Terms for the Directory Sync tool.

4. Specify the location to install directory synchronization or choose the default location, as shown in Figure 4-27. Click Next.

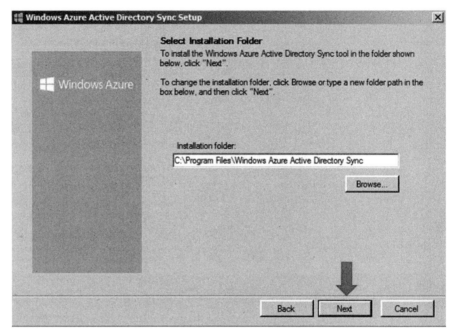

Figure 4-27 Specify the directory synchronization installation folder.

5. After the directory synchronization components have been installed, click Next, as shown in Figure 4-28.

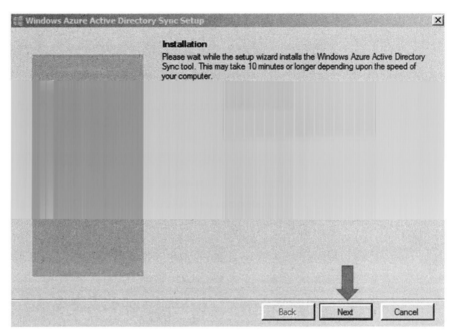

Figure 4-28 Click Next after installation is complete.

6. Select the Start Configuration Wizard now check box, as shown in Figure 4-29. If you choose to do so later, you can clear the check box and run the Configuration Wizard later by starting the executable at *<Drive>*:\program files\Windows Azure Active Directory Sync\ConfigWizard.exe.

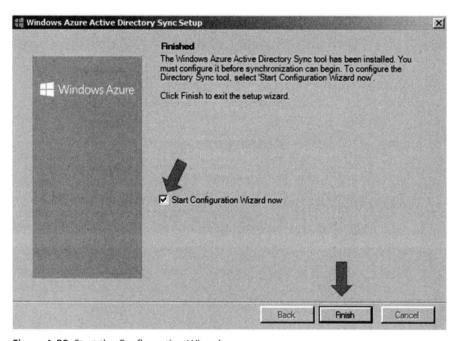

Figure 4-29 Start the Configuration Wizard.

Configuring directory synchronization

You are now ready to configure directory synchronization using the Windows Azure Active Directory Sync tool Configuration Wizard. If the Configuration Wizard is not already running, you can start it by following these steps:

1. On the directory synchronization server, open Windows Explorer and navigate to the directory synchronization directory. In our example, we used the default installation location for directory synchronization, which is c:\Program Files\Windows Azure Active Directory Sync.

2. Run the directory synchronization Configuration Wizard by locating and starting ConfigWizard.exe, as shown in Figure 4-30.

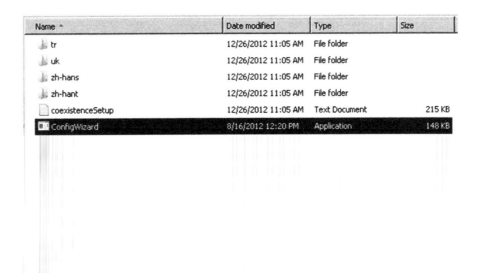

TROUBLESHOOTING

You receive a permissions error

If you receive a permission error, as shown in Figure 4-31, it is most likely because you did not log off and log back on again. The permissions do not take effect until the user logs off and logs back on.

Chapter 4

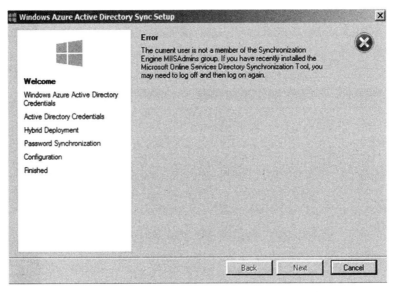

Figure 4-31 Windows Azure Active Directory Sync Setup Wizard permissions error.

Follow these steps to complete the directory synchronization configuration:

1. Click Next on the Welcome page of the Configuration Wizard, as shown in Figure 4-32.

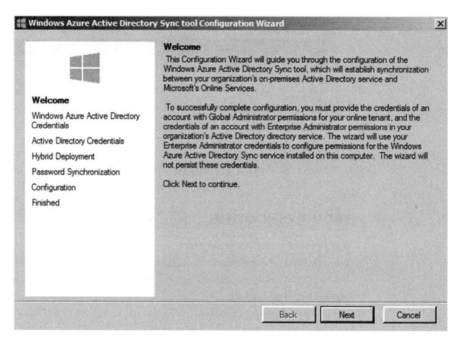

Figure 4-32 Welcome page of the Configuration Wizard.

2. Provide your Windows Azure Active Directory administrator credentials, as shown in
Figure 4-33. Notice that the user name is in UPN format. As such, the credentials you
provide should take the form *<Username>*@*<Organization>*.onmicrosoft.com.

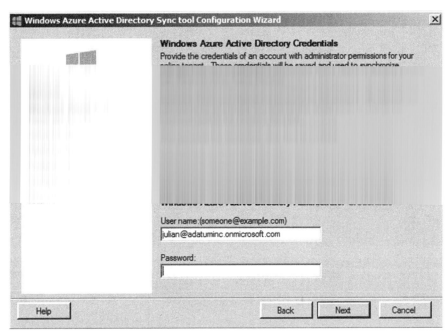

Figure 4-33 Directory administrator credentials required by the Configuration Wizard.

3. Next, as shown in Figure 4-34, you will be asked for an AD enterprise administrator credential. As mentioned earlier, the enterprise administrator credential provided will be used only once to create a service account and security group in AD. Notice that you can provide the AD credentials in UPN or down-level logon name (*Domain\ username*) format.

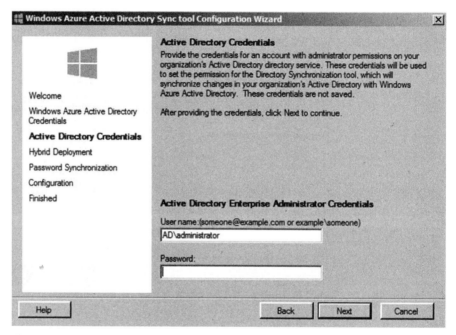

Figure 4-34 AD Enterprise Administrator credentials requested by the Configuration Wizard.

The next step in the configuration depends on whether you will be configuring a hybrid Exchange environment. Remember, in the case of a hybrid Exchange setup, directory synchronization will have to write information back to AD. Table 3-1 shows the list of attributes that are written back to AD by directory synchronization.

TABLE 3-1 Attributes that are written back to AD to enable Exchange coexistence

Attribute	Description
SafeSendersHash **BlockedSendersHash** **SafeRecipientHash**	Writes back to on-premises filtering and online safe and blocked sender data
msExchArchiveStatus	Identifies mailbox archive status in Exchange Online

Attribute	Description
ProxyAddresses	Identifies the corresponding address of a mailbox that has been migrated to Exchange Online
msExchUCVoiceMailSettings	Used by an on-premises Lync server to identify users that have voice mail capabilities (Exchange Unified Messaging, or Exchange UM) in Exchange Online

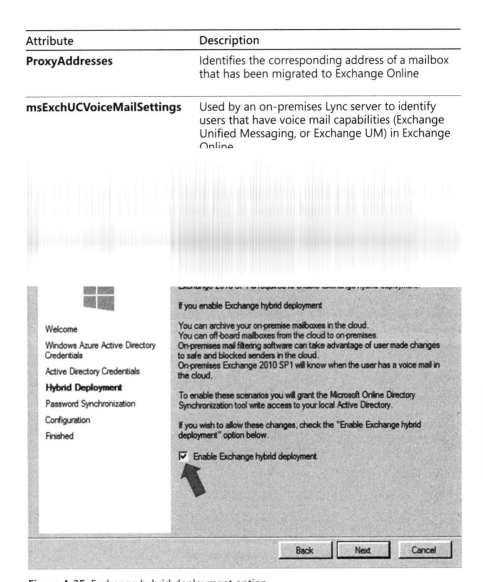

Figure 4-35 Exchange hybrid deployment option.

5. You now will be provided with the option to configure directory synchronization to synchronize AD passwords to Office 365, as shown in Figure 4-36. This is a new directory synchronization capability. If you want to implement SSO, do not select the Enable Password Sync check box. Otherwise, you have the option of implementing same sign on instead of having to manually set and maintain passwords in Office 365.

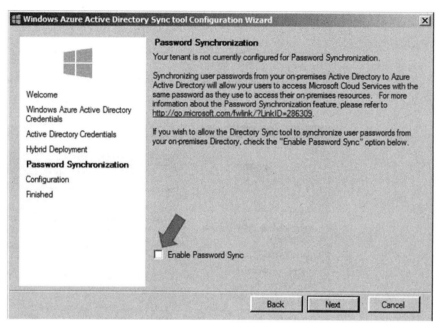

Figure 4-36 Password Synchronization.

6. At this point, the Configuration Wizard has sufficient information to configure directory synchronization. It might take several minutes to complete the configuration. When it is done, you can click Next.

7. In the final step of the Configuration Wizard, you will have the option to start synchronizing directories, as shown in Figure 4-37. Select the Synchronize directories now check box, and then click Finish. Directory synchronization will immediately start synchronizing your AD with Office 365.

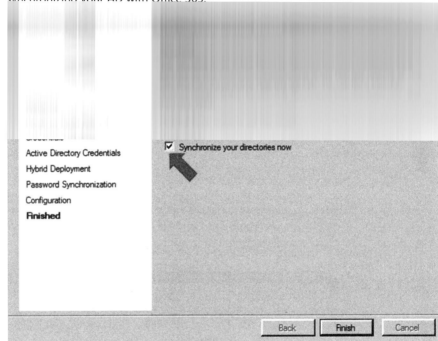

Figure 4-37 Synchronize directories immediately after configuration is complete.

Remember that by default, directory synchronization runs every three hours. The first synchronization will be a full synchronization of your AD with Office 365. Subsequent synchronizations will address only AD changes. The three-hour interval between synchronizations is based on the previous synchronization run and not on a set time. Alternatively, you can change this three-hour window or force an unscheduled synchronization run. You will see how this is done later in this chapter, in the "Forcing an unscheduled directory synchronization" section.

Chapter 4

Verifying directory synchronization

After directory synchronization is configured and set to run, you need to verify that it is indeed running. There are several ways to confirm the status of directory synchronization:

- Verify directory synchronization using the admin center.

- Verify directory synchronization service status using the Services MMC.

- Use the Synchronization Service Manager.

- Check the event log.

Verifying directory synchronization using the admin center

One way to verify directory synchronization status is through the Office 365 admin center:

1. Log on to the admin center.

2. Click users and groups to see objects from your AD populating this page. As shown in Figure 4-38, synchronized objects are identified with the Synced with Active Directory status, while cloud IDs are identified with the In cloud status. At the top of the page, under Active Directory synchronization, it also shows the last synchronization time. In our example, synchronization occurred less than an hour ago.

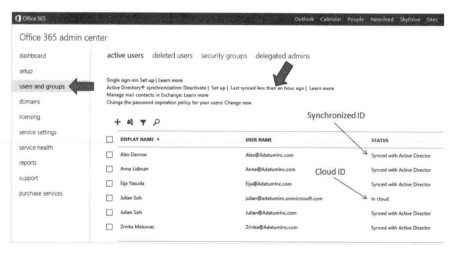

Figure 4-38 Differentiating between cloud identities and directory synchronized identities.

3. Click the name of an account that has been synchronized and select details, as shown in Figure 4-39. Notice that the fields cannot be edited, and you are informed that changes can be made only through AD.

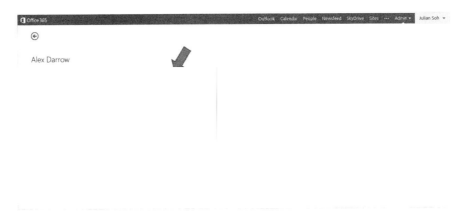

Figure 4-39 Fields are unavailable for user objects that are synchronized with Active Directory.

Verifying directory synchronization service status

Another way to determine the status of directory synchronization is to look at its service status. The directory synchronization service is listed as the Windows Azure Active Directory Sync Service:

1. On the directory synchronization server, click Start, click Administrative Tools, and then click Services.

2. In the Services MMC, locate Windows Azure Active Directory Sync Service and verify that the service is started, as shown in Figure 4-40.

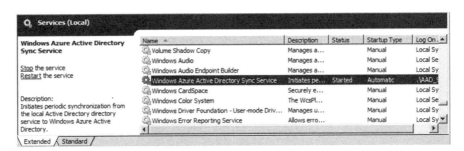

Figure 4-40 Windows Azure Active Directory Sync Service.

> **Note**
>
> The Windows Azure Active Directory Sync Service was created when you installed directory synchronization, and it uses a service account that was created as part of the installation, as shown in Figure 4-41. The service is configured to start automatically, and any errors resulting from the inability of the service to start will be logged in the event log.

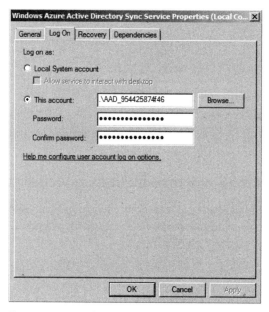

Figure 4-41 Windows Azure Active Directory Sync Service Properties.

Using the Synchronization Service Manager

You can also use the directory synchronization graphical client, Synchronization Service Manager, to see the status of directory synchronization as well as other information. To use the Synchronization Service Manager, follow these steps:

1. Navigate to *<Drive>*:\program files\Windows Azure Active Directory Sync\SYNCBUS\ Synchronization Service\UIShell and locate miisclient.exe, as shown in Figure 4-42.

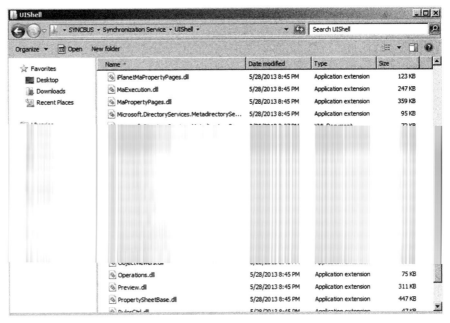

Figure 4-42 Synchronization Service Manager.

2. Start miisclient.exe.

TROUBLESHOOTING

Unable to connect to the Synchronization Service
Immediately after installing or running the directory synchronization Configuration Wizard, if you try to launch Synchronization Service Manager, you might encounter the error shown in Figure 4-43. This occurs even though you are using an administrator account with sufficient rights. This is because the account's security token is not yet updated. Simply log off and log back on, then re-run miisclient.exe and you should be able to access the directory synchronization client console. You should also check that the Windows Azure Active Directory Sync Service started correctly.

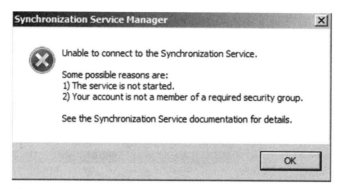

Figure 4-43 Error when trying to access the miisclient.exe graphical UI.

3. Explore the Synchronization Service Manager window. It shows key information about the directory synchronization service status, as shown in Figure 4-44. For example, under the Operations tab you can see the success or failure status of each directory synchronization run as well as the start and end time. The bottom left pane shows the export summary information in terms of number of accounts that are deleted, added, or updated. The bottom right pane displays the connection status and connection errors, if any.

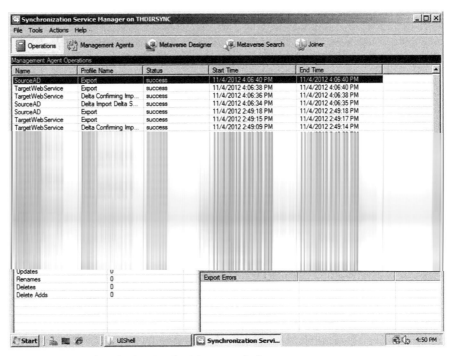

Figure 4-44 Synchronization Service Manager window.

Checking the Event Viewer

Directory synchronization writes entries to the event log every time it runs. Follow these steps to view the status of directory synchronization through entries in the event log:

1. On the directory synchronization server, click Start, click Administrative Tools, and then click Event Viewer.

2. In Event Viewer, expand the Windows Logs node.

3. Select the Application log and locate entries where the source is directory synchronization. If there are no errors, you should see a message that says "Export has completed," as shown in Figure 4-45.

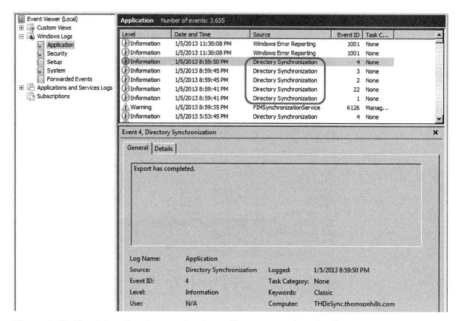

Figure 4-45 Event log showing entries from directory synchronization.

Forcing an unscheduled directory synchronization

As mentioned earlier, the default setting for directory synchronization is to run every three hours. You can initiate an unscheduled synchronization using the Synchronization Service Manager or Windows PowerShell. Using Windows PowerShell is the quickest and easiest way, while using the Synchronization Service Manager provides more verbose synchronization details.

Understanding run profiles and management agents

Run profiles are the pre-programmed operations defined for a management agent (MA). An MA is an identity source, such as Active Directory or Office 365. These pre-programmed operations usually involve data import and export. It is important to have an understanding of run profiles and operations because these can be used for troubleshooting purposes, as we will see later.

The available types of operations for MAs are the following:

- Delta Import

- Full Import

- Delta Synchronization

- Full Synchronization

- Delta Import/Delta Synchronization

- Full Import/Delta Synchronization

- Full Import/Full Synchronization

- Export

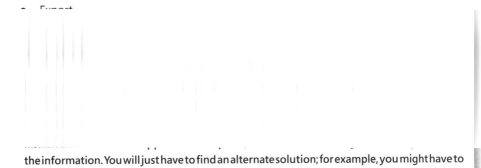

the information. You will just have to find an alternate solution; for example, you might have to rely on Full Imports.

After data is imported, it can be synchronized. Synchronization affects objects and attributes. Delta synchronization will affect only objects and attributes that have changed since the last synchronization. Full synchronization affects all objects and attributes. The import and synchronization steps are usually combined as a single process.

Initiating an unscheduled directory synchronization using Synchronization Service Manager

Using the Synchronization Service Manager to initiate directory synchronization is a two-phase effort, or four phases if we need to write information back to AD because of a hybrid Exchange setup:

- Synchronize (read) changes from AD

- Synchronize (write) changes to Office 365

- Synchronize (read) changes from Office 365 for fields associated with hybrid Exchange setups (only for hybrid scenarios)

- Synchronize (write) changes to AD for fields associated with hybrid Exchange setups (only for hybrid scenarios)

Chapter 4

With the preceding list in mind, if you need to force directory synchronization to run before the next scheduled time, follow these steps:

1. Using Windows Explorer, navigate to the directory synchronization installation at *<Drive>*:\program files\Windows Azure Active Directory Sync\SYNCBUS\ Synchronization Service\UIShell and locate miisclient.exe, as shown in Figure 4-42.

2. Launch the Synchronization Service Manager by double-clicking miisclient.exe.

3. Click the Management Agents tab, as shown in Figure 4-46.

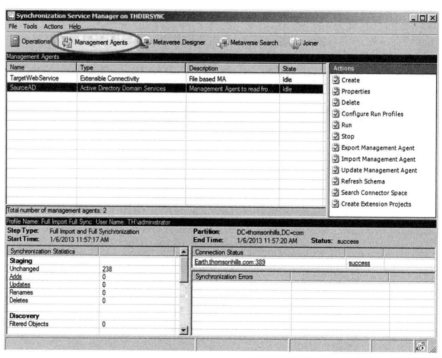

Figure 4-46 Synchronization Service Manager Management Agents tab.

4. Select SourceAD. We do this because we want Synchronization Service Manager to discover changes in AD.

5. From the Actions menu, select Run, as shown in Figure 4-47.

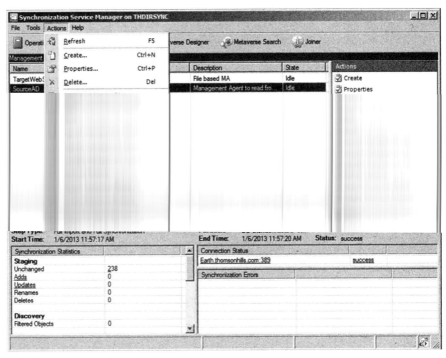

Figure 4-47 Synchronization Service Manager running a SourceAD update.

6. In the dialog box that appears, confirm that SourceAD is the selected Management Agent. Then select Delta Import Delta Sync for the run profile, as shown in Figure 4-48.

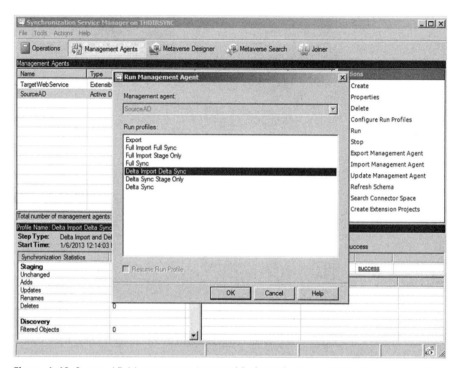

Figure 4-48 Source AD Management Agent with the Delta Import Delta Sync run profile.

7. Click OK.

8. Make sure the agent is running by looking at the status of SourceAD, as shown in Figure 4-49.

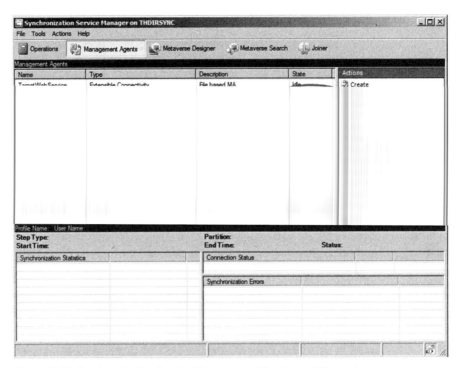

Figure 4-49 Synchronization Service Manager and the SourceAD agent running.

9. When synchronization is complete, the state of the SourceAD Management Agent reverts to Idle. When the state changes to Idle, look at the status of the synchronization to make sure it is successful, as shown in Figure 4-50. Other interesting information includes the Start Time and End Time, so you know how long it took to run the synchronization.

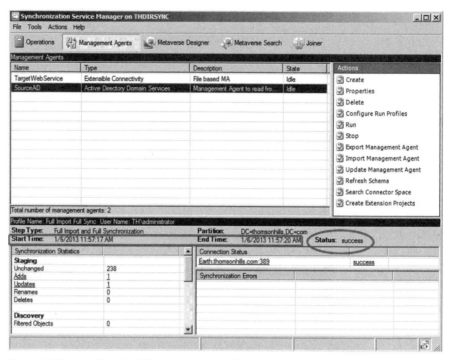

Figure 4-50 Start Time, End Time, and Status of the synchronization with AD.

10. Directory synchronization is now aware of the changes in AD. Look at the Synchronization Statistics pane located at the bottom left of the window, as shown in Figure 4-51. This pane shows changes and additions in AD detected by directory synchronization since the last time it ran. For example, as a demonstration, we modified a user account and added a new user account in AD. As expected, the Synchronization Statistics shows one Add and one Update.

Figure 4-51 Synchronization Statistics.

11. If you made changes, additions, or deletions in AD, the links in the Synchronization Statistics pane become active. As shown in Figure 4-51, only the Adds and Deletes links are active because we modified one account and added a new account. Click the links to see details on the additions, deletions, or updates. For example, Figure

4-52 shows the information for our modified account after we clicked the Update link.

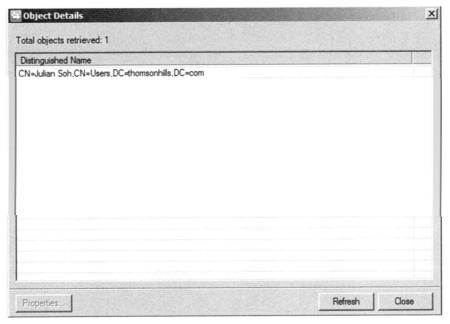

Figure 4-52 Details of a recently modified AD object.

12. Select the object, and then click Properties.

13. The metadata of the object is shown, and you can continue to drill down to additional details if a field has multiple values, such as the *proxyAddresses* field.

14. Close all open windows to return to the main Synchronization Service Manager window.

15. Now that directory synchronization is aware of the changes in AD, it is time to run a second process to update Office 365. From the Synchronization Service Manager window, select the Management Agents tab again, just as you did earlier (see Figure 4-46).

16. This time, instead of selecting the SourceAD Management Agent, select TargetWebService instead.

17. From the Actions menu, select Run, as shown in Figure 4-47.

18. Confirm the selected management agent is TargetWebService, then select Export as the run profile, as shown in Figure 4-53.

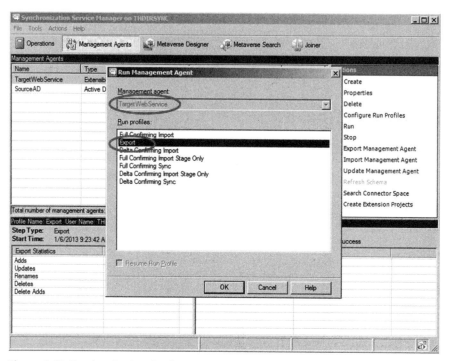

Figure 4-53 Synchronization Service Manager running the Export profile for TargetWebService.

19. Click OK.

20. This time, the state of TargetWebService changes from Idle to Running. When it is done, review the Synchronization Statistics, Start Time, End Time, Status, and Export Errors.

21. Remember, if this is a hybrid Exchange environment, we need to write changes back to AD. If this is not applicable, you can skip the rest of the steps in this section. However, if this applies to your organization, you need to initiate the write-back process by clicking the Management Agents tab again.

22. Select TargetWebService.

23. From the Actions menu, select Run.

24. In the Run Management Agent dialog box, select Delta Confirming Import, as shown in Figure 4-54.

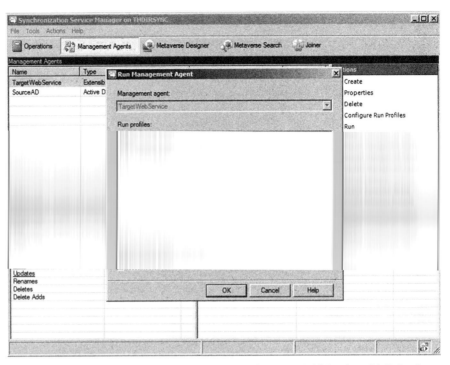

Figure 4-54 Synchronization Service Manager running TargetWebService with Delta Confirming Import.

25. Click OK and wait for the synchronization state to return to Idle.

26. When the state for TargetWebService is back to Idle and if no synchronization errors are reported, we can initiate the AD write-back process. Select the SourceAD Management Agent.

27. From the Actions menu, select Run.

28. In the Run Management Agent dialog box, select Export.

29. Click OK and wait for the synchronization state to return to Idle.

30. Verify that no errors were reported.

Initiating an unscheduled directory synchronization using Windows PowerShell

The other way to force directory synchronization to run is to use Windows PowerShell. Note that it is much simpler and quicker to use Windows PowerShell. Initiate an unscheduled directory synchronization through Windows PowerShell by following these steps:

1. From the directory synchronization server, navigate to *<Drive>*:\program files\ Windows Azure Active Directory Sync\.

2. Locate DirSyncConfigSell.psc1 and double-click the file. This will open Windows PowerShell with the correct directory synchronization modules loaded, as shown in Figure 4-55.

3. Enter the following command:

```
Start-OnlineCoexistenceSync
```

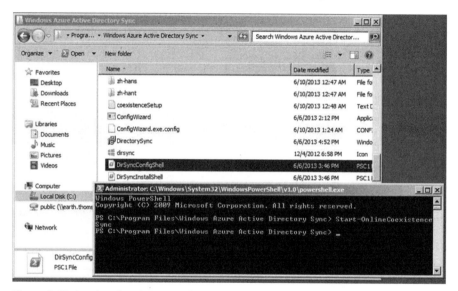

Figure 4-55 Starting the DirSyncConfigShell.psc1 file and entering the *Start-OnlineCoexis-tenceSync* command.

4. Using Windows Explorer, navigate to the directory synchronization installation at *<Drive>*:\program files\Windows Azure Active Directory Sync\SYNCBUS\ Synchronization Service\UIShell and locate miisclient.exe, as shown in Figure 4-42.

5. In the Synchronization Service Manager window, click the Operations tab near the top.

The Operations tab lists all the directory synchronization operations. Note that the *Start-OnlineCoexistenceSync* cmdlet created four synchronization operations, as shown in Figure 4-56.

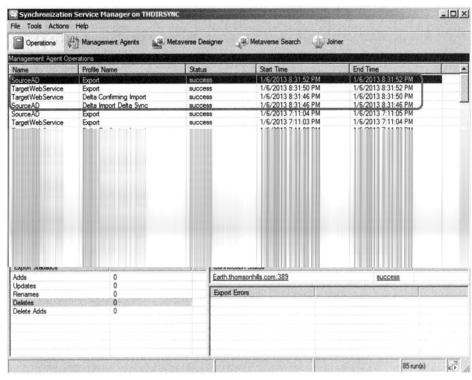

Figure 4-56 Synchronization Service Manager showing four recent synchronization operations.

The four synchronization operations are the following:

- SourceAD Delta Import Delta Sync

- TargetWebService Export Sync

- TargetWebService Delta Confirming Import Sync

- SourceAD Export Sync

These operations represent the bi-directional synchronization between AD and Office 365. Compare the execution of a single Windows PowerShell cmdlet to the lengthier, manual process you need to use with the Synchronization Service Manager.

INSIDE OUT Script to Force directory synchronization

We find it useful to have a shortcut on the desktop of the directory synchronization server so we can double-click the shortcut to force a directory synchronization. We use the following script:

```
Add-PSSnapin coexistence-configuration -ErrorAction SilentlyContinue

Start-OnlineCoexistenceSync
```

Changing the directory synchronization schedule

By default, directory synchronization runs every three hours. However, this interval is configurable. To change how often directory synchronization runs, you need to modify the directory synchronization scheduler file by following these steps:

1. From the directory synchronization server, navigate to *<Drive>*:\program files\ Windows Azure Active Directory Sync and locate the file Microsoft.Online.DirSync. Scheduler.exe.Config, as shown in Figure 4-57.

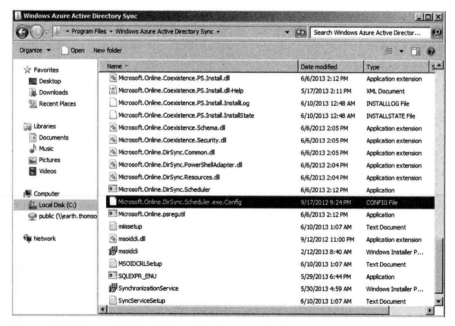

Figure 4-57 Microsoft.Online.DirSync.Scheduler.exe.Config.

2. The configuration file is simply a text file. Use an editor such as Notepad to open it.

3. Modify the *SyncTimeInterval* key value. The format is hours:minutes:seconds. Notice the default is 3:0:0, which indicates three hours, as shown in Figure 4-58.

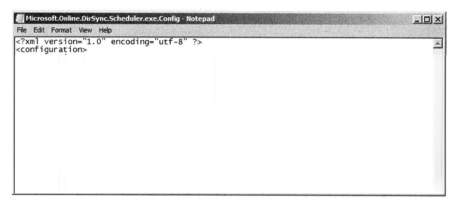

Figure 4-58 Modifying the SyncTimeInterval value with Notepad.

4. Save the file.

5. Restart the server or restart Windows Azure Active Directory Sync Service.

Troubleshooting common directory synchronization errors

Directory synchronization is a fairly robust procedure not normally prone to errors. The common problems are usually related to account access rights, network connectivity, and errors specific to the objects being synchronized.

In later chapters, we will dive deeper into monitoring strategies, which will include health and monitoring for directory synchronization using System Center. For now, let us look at some basic directory synchronization troubleshooting strategies.

Directory synchronization problems can be classified into one of these categories:

*   Issues that prevent the directory synchronization process from running as scheduled

*   Directory synchronization not able to synchronize certain objects or attributes

Directory synchronization is not running

If directory synchronization is not running, you probably will notice that Office 365 is not reflecting changes in AD or that directory synchronization did not run at the interval you scheduled through the Office 365 admin center. You also might receive an email notification from Office 365, as shown in Figure 4-59.

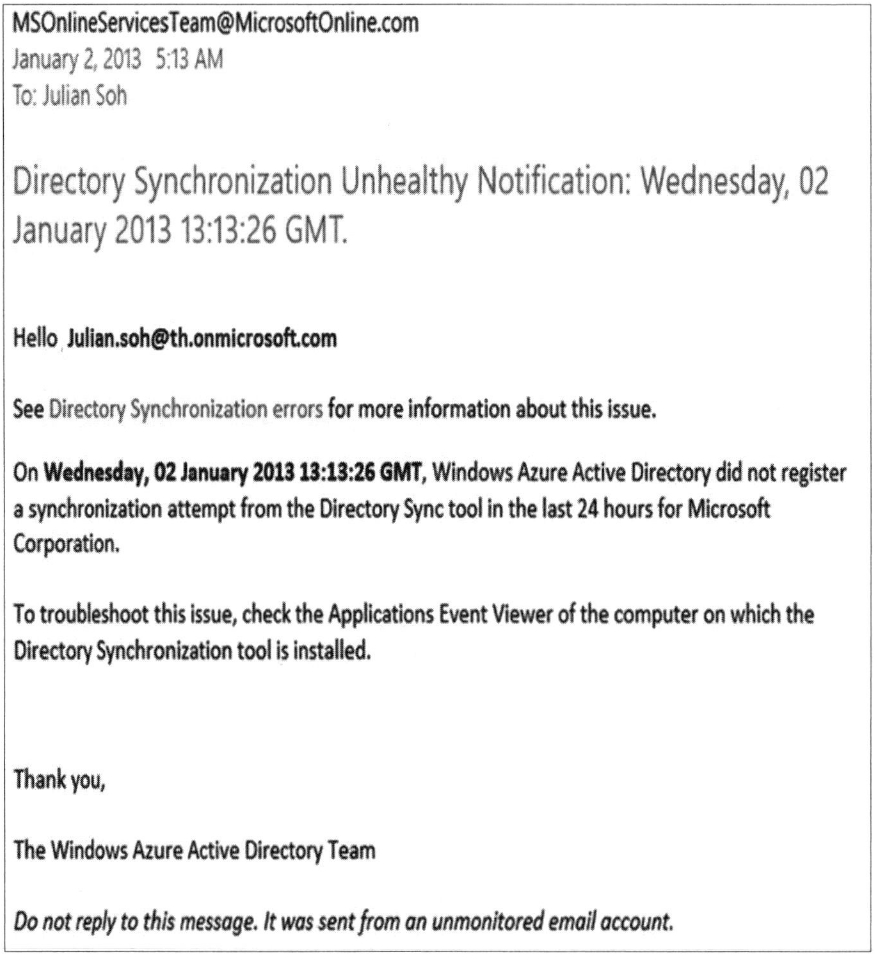

MSOnlineServicesTeam@MicrosoftOnline.com
January 2, 2013 5:13 AM
To: Julian Soh

Directory Synchronization Unhealthy Notification: Wednesday, 02 January 2013 13:13:26 GMT.

Hello Julian.soh@th.onmicrosoft.com

See Directory Synchronization errors for more information about this issue.

On **Wednesday, 02 January 2013 13:13:26 GMT**, Windows Azure Active Directory did not register a synchronization attempt from the Directory Sync tool in the last 24 hours for Microsoft Corporation.

To troubleshoot this issue, check the Applications Event Viewer of the computer on which the Directory Synchronization tool is installed.

Thank you,

The Windows Azure Active Directory Team

Do not reply to this message. It was sent from an unmonitored email account.

Figure 4-59 Email notification because of directory synchronization problems.

INSIDE OUT Provide a technical contact

It is not mandatory for you to provide a technical contact. However, notifications such as the one shown in Figure 4-59 will automatically be sent to the technical contact on file. Therefore, it is important for you to diligently designate a technical contact for your tenant.

When a notification is received that directory synchronization potentially might be unhealthy, review the event log and locate all directory synchronization messages. Directory synchronization events can be identified by sorting the Source column and looking for messages generated by directory synchronization.

The following sections provide solutions to troubleshoot directory synchronization if it is not running.

Check the directory synchronization AD service account

Validate that the directory synchronization service account credential in AD is still valid. By default, this is the MSOL_<*Numeric Identifier*> account, which can be identified in Active Directory Users and Computers.

Check the directory synchronization Office 365 account

When you first configured directory synchronization using the Configuration Wizard, you provided Office 365 Global Administrator account credentials. This account is used to log on to Office 365 for export and synchronization purposes. The Global Administrator account is a cloud ID and, by default, the password will expire every 90 days. Validate that this account has not expired.

If directory synchronization is not able to log on to Office 365 because its account credentials have expired, the event log will show errors similar to this:

```
Source: directory synchronization
Your Credentials could not be authenticated. Retype your credentials and try again.
GetAuthState() failed with -2147186688 state. HRsesult( 0x80048800)
```

Consider setting the directory synchronization Office 365 account credentials not to expire. Do this by issuing the following Windows PowerShell commands:

```
Import-Module MSOnline

$cred = Get-Credential

Connect-MSOLService –Credential $cred

Set-MSOLUser –UserPrincipalName <User Account> -PasswordNeverExpires $true
```

Chapter 4

Directory synchronization data problems

If directory synchronization is running but you notice anomalies, such as accounts not being replicated accurately, this can be attributed to data quality issues.

Unrecognized or invalid data in Active Directory

The data in the properties of objects synchronized into Office 365 are checked to make sure they are well-formed. There are specific criteria for these attributes; for example, email addresses cannot contain certain characters and cannot be more than 256 characters in length. Invalid data types can lead to objects or properties not being synchronized. To ensure that AD does not contain unsupported data, run the Microsoft Office 365 Deployment Readiness tool, as discussed in Chapter 2, "Planning and preparing to deploy Office 365."

You might also receive email notifications that state specific problems. The following errors might be reported:

- A synchronized object with the same proxy address already exists in Office 365.

- Unable to update this object because the user ID is not found.

- Unable to update this object in Windows Azure Active Directory because the following attributes associated with this object have values that might already be associated with another object in your local directory.

To troubleshoot data quality errors, you have two tools at your disposal:

- Microsoft Online Services Diagnostics and Logging (MOSDAL) Support Toolkit

- Microsoft Office 365 Deployment Readiness Toolkit

We covered the Microsoft Office 365 Deployment Readiness Toolkit in Chapter 2. You can re-run this tool again to identify which AD objects have data quality issues that might be affecting directory synchronization.

We also introduced MOSDAL in Chapter 2, but in the next section, we will use MOSDAL specifically to troubleshoot directory synchronization.

Troubleshooting directory synchronization using the MOSDAL toolkit

Use the MOSDAL toolkit specifically to troubleshoot directory synchronization:

1. Refer to Chapter 2 for download and installation instructions for MOSDAL if needed, and then start MOSDAL. For this exercise, MOSDAL must be installed and started from the directory synchronization server.

2. Click the O365 tab and select the directory synchronization check box, as shown in Figure 4-60. Click Next.

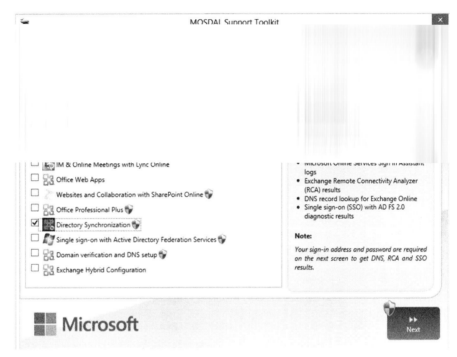

Figure 4-60 MOSDAL with the directory synchronization option.

3. Provide the Office 365 account credential that directory synchronization uses and make sure you do not select the I want to skip this step check box, as shown in Figure 4-61. Click Next. Although MOSDAL does not require you to supply Office 365 credentials, this is needed for a comprehensive directory synchronization test.

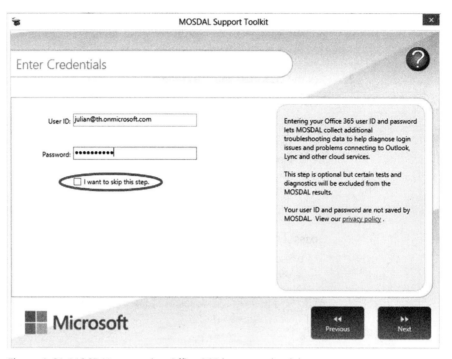

Figure 4-61 MOSDAL requesting Office 365 logon credentials.

4. Click Next to start the testing process. Ignore the instructions on this page because you do not need to restart any applications for this particular test.

5. When the test is complete, click Exit And Show Files.

6. Windows Explorer will open and show the MOSDAL directories. The reports are organized by the date and time stamp of the test. Open the folder with the date and time stamp that corresponds to your test.

7. Open the Admin_Applications folder.

8. Open the Directory_Synchronization_Tool folder.

9. Locate a text file titled MOSDALLog_Directory_Synchronization_Tool. Open this log file with any text editor. This is the log file that details the directory synchronization test steps. Take note of any errors encountered by the test. We included details on how to resolve two of the most common errors in the Troubleshooting sidebar. Close the MOSDALLog_Directory_Synchronization_Tool file.

TROUBLESHOOTING

Common MOSDAL errors

If you open the Directory_Synchronization_Tool folder and see only one file, the MOSDALLog_Directory_Synchronization_Tool file, that usually means the directory synchronization test encountered a problem. Open the MOSDALLog_Directory_Synchronization_Tool file with a text editor to determine the error. One common error is the account used to run MOSDAL does not have sufficient privileges. The MOSDAL

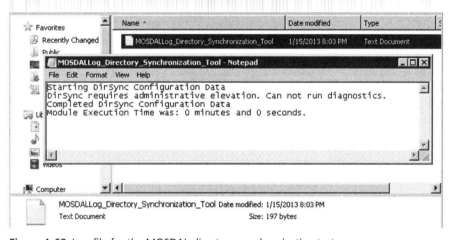

Figure 4-62 Log file for the MOSDAL directory synchronization test.

To resolve errors related to the need for administrative elevation, you need to add the account you are using to run MOSDAL to the local FIMSyncAdmins group:

1. From the directory synchronization server, click Control Panel, and then click User Accounts.

2. Select Give other users access to this computer.

3. Lastly, click Add to add a user or select an existing user, click Properties, and then select the Group Membership tab.

Chapter 4

4. Select Other and make the user part of the FIMSyncAdmins group, as shown in Figure 4-63.

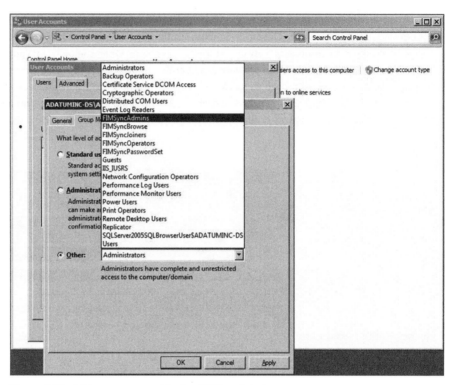

Figure 4-63 Add a user account to the FIMSyncAdmins group.

Another common problem with MOSDAL and the directory synchronization test arises if you do not run the test from the directory synchronization server. In this case, you will get an error stating that a directory synchronization key cannot be found in the registry, which will be listed in the MOSDALLog_Directory_Synchronization_Tool log file. The directory synchronization MOSDAL test requires the directory synchronization (FIM) tool. Therefore, it needs to be executed from the directory synchronization server.

1. In the same directory, locate and open DirSyncObjects.xml.

   DirSyncObjects.xml lists the objects that directory synchronization attempts to synchronize to Office 365 and lists any objects with duplicate UPNs and missing proxy addresses.

2. Resolve issues with duplicate UPNs and missing proxy addresses.

Summary

At this point, we have completed the foundational work for Office 365. In the last three chapters, we have covered the following tasks:

- Planning, preparing, and remediating your enterprise environment for Office 365, specifically regarding AD

start configuring and deploying the individual Office 365 services, which are Exchange Online, SharePoint Online, Lync Online, and Office 365 Professional Plus. You can proceed directly to any of the chapters that are specific to the services you want to use. The great thing about Office 365 is that there is no specific order to deploy the services. There is also no need for you to deploy all the services. You can pick and choose the services that are appropriate for your enterprise needs.

Alternatively, you can continue with Chapters 5, 6, and 7 to leverage System Center as an optional, but recommended, enterprise management suite of tools to build additional automation and monitoring for your Office 365 deployment. You could also choose to start deploying services first, and then return to the System Center chapters.

The point is that the deployment can proceed in any direction after the foundational services have been established. This is also a good testament to the flexibility of Office 365 workload adoption and deployment.

Chapter 4

PART 3

Office 365 Foundations: Monitoring and

CHAPTER 5

Monitoring Office 365 with System Center 207

CHAPTER 6

Customizing Operations Manager reports and dashboards for Office 365 283

CHAPTER 7

Automating Office 365 management using Orchestrator 325

CHAPTER 8

Office 365 and Service Manager automation 351

CHAPTER 9

Windows PowerShell for Office 365 395

Introduction to System Center components

Deploying the SCOM infrastructure and importing

Consider that if the on-premises Exchange Client Access Server (CAS) goes down, then Exchange Online users might not be able to view the free and busy times of those users whose mailboxes are still on-premises. If the on-premises AD FS infrastructure fails because of the AD FS servers, SQL server, or Internet Information Services (IIS) server, then users might not be able to log onto Office 365 altogether. A more comprehensive list of technologies that Office 365 is dependent on will be listed later in the "Evaluating what to monitor" section of this chapter, when it is time for us to determine what needs to be monitored.

Aside from monitoring, there is also the need to deploy software and make configuration changes to workstations so they work seamlessly with Office 365. For these reasons, it is important to have an enterprise-level monitoring and management solution, which is why we are introducing Microsoft System Center 2012 for consideration as part of an Office 365 deployment. The current version of System Center is 2012 with Service Pack 1, which was released in December, 2012.

System Center is a suite comprising eight components. Each of these eight components plays a crucial role in various aspects of Information Technology (IT) management. System Center was created to help companies with the management of physical and virtual machines, on-premises and off-premises cloud applications, people management tasks such as provisioning, request tracking, and the automation of processes to make organizations more productive and cost efficient.

The eight components within System Center cover all aspects of IT management, from applications and infrastructure to service delivery and automation, as shown in Figure 5-1.

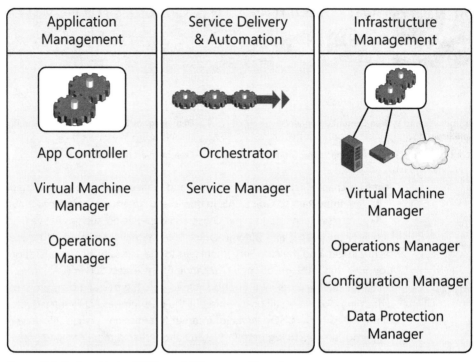

Figure 5-1 System Center 2012 capabilities across IT services.

System Center 2012 is an integrated management platform that helps you to easily and efficiently manage your datacenters, client devices, and hybrid cloud IT environments. System Center 2012 is the only platform to offer comprehensive management of applications, services, physical resources, hypervisors, software-defined networks, configuration and automation in a single offering.

System Center Configuration Manager is not generally recognized as a monitoring solution. However, underneath the covers, System Center Configuration Manager monitors a series of events, such as users who log on to workstations at the agent level or a configuration item being tracked by the agent in case of any deviations from the organization's standard configuration.

System Center Data Protection Manager is primarily responsible for data protection. To do so, it constantly monitors changes on the workloads it is protecting.

System Center Orchestrator is responsible for monitoring system events that will trigger and execute pre-defined procedures known as runbooks.

System Center Service Manager is an incident management component and thus monitors for changes to incidents and executes workflows accordingly.

System Center Virtual Machine Manager manages a variety of components on physical hosts and virtual machines. System Center Virtual Machine Manager can also determine if hosts are over-subscribed and migrate virtual machines in real time to different hosts to maximize performance and resources.

Finally, System Center App Controller monitors the state of private cloud services, applications deployed in Windows Azure PaaS, and virtual machines in Windows Azure, which an Infrastructure as a Service (IaaS) is offering. This is a significant element because Office 365

Introduction to System Center components and licensing

In this section we will briefly cover the eight System Center 2012 components, their capabilities, and their use cases as they relate to Office 365. Figure 5-2 shows all eight System Center components.

Figure 5-2 The eight System Center components.

Chapter 5

System Center 2012 Configuration Manager

System Center 2012 Configuration Manager is the oldest System Center product, dating back to 1994 with the release of Systems Management Server (SMS) 1.0. System Center 2012 Configuration Manager is the fifth full version in the evolution of the product and provides organizations with the controls needed to better manage desktop and data center environments. It provides extensive administration capabilities across operating systems, applications, and mobile devices, at the same time enforcing corporate compliance specifications. This is important for Office 365 because there are required desktop configurations as well as the deployment and management of the Office Professional Plus productivity suite subscription. At the server and data-center level, Configuration Manager can manage the on-premises and off-premises server components that are important to Office 365, such as domain controllers, AD FS, and on-premises Exchange servers. Configuration Manager is optimized for Windows and is extensible, making it the best choice to gain enhanced insight into, and control over, your Office 365-connected systems.

From a single console, Configuration Manager allows management of a wide range of mobile devices, including non-Windows based assets such as Android devices, iOS devices, and Linux and Mac OS computers. Configuration Manager provides a robust solution for the deployment of operating systems (OS) in a number of scenarios including, but not limited to, the following:

- **New PC** This is the ability to boot a new PC and deploy the full corporate OS image onto a new device with minimal user and administrator interaction. This means aside from booting the device from a USB, DVD, thumb drive, or Preboot Execution Environment (PXE), no other input is required to get the system ready.

- **Refresh PC** This scenario covers Configuration Manager's ability to backup all user data and preferences. Preferences, sometimes referred to as system states, are settings such as wallpapers and other customizations. Configuration Manager enables you to install the new OS image, join the system to the appropriate Active Directory domain and organizational unit, install applications that are not in the OS image but are specific to the user or department, and finally restore user data and state, all in a matter of minutes.

- **Replace PC** This is a combination of the Refresh PC and New PC scenarios because Configuration Manager will move the user data and state from an old PC to a new one.

- **Depot PC** This is Configuration Manager's ability to pre-stage systems *en masse* so they can be deployed quickly, with minimal administrator or user intervention required during setup.

INSIDE OUT Why does deploying an OS matter to Office 365?

Deploying an OS is an important activity because it relates to Office 365 if you are
planning to deploy the Office Professional Plus subscription. This is because the Office
Professional Plus subscription in Office 365 is the 2013 version of the Office suite, which
requires at least the 32-bit or 64-bit version of Windows 7. We have encountered a
number of Office 365 projects that combine the refresh of corporate computers as part

organization can choose to let users acquire Office through this portal. This is a significant
workload because the Office Professional Plus subscription now allows users to install and
activate Office on up to five devices. Without having a way for users to self-deploy Office,
the effort to deploy Office can exponentially increase. Figure 5-3 shows the capabilities of
System Center 2012 Configuration Manager.

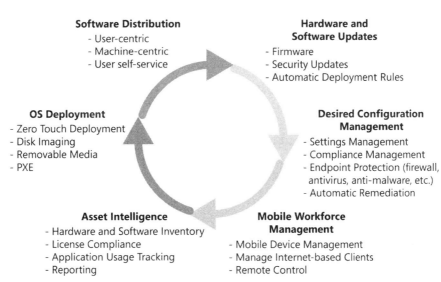

Software Distribution
- User-centric
- Machine-centric
- User self-service

**Hardware and
Software Updates**
- Firmware
- Security Updates
- Automatic Deployment Rules

OS Deployment
- Zero Touch Deployment
- Disk Imaging
- Removable Media
- PXE

**Desired Configuration
Management**
- Settings Management
- Compliance Management
- Endpoint Protection (firewall,
  antivirus, anti-malware, etc.)
- Automatic Remediation

Asset Intelligence
- Hardware and Software Inventory
- License Compliance
- Application Usage Tracking
- Reporting

**Mobile Workforce
Management**
- Mobile Device Management
- Manage Internet-based Clients
- Remote Control

Figure 5-3 System Center 2012 Configuration Manager's core capabilities.

Configuration Manager also provides organizations with the ability to centrally manage anti-virus, anti-malware, vulnerability prevention, and remediation through its patch

Chapter 5

management and Security Compliance Management technology, regardless of device type or connection medium. By leveraging the built-in Configuration Manager reporting that runs on top of SQL Reporting Services, your organization can run reports giving you insights to the states and statuses of devices in the environment. It also provides administrators with real-time alerting about threats such as detection of viruses, virus outbreaks, and spyware.

INSIDE OUT   Full featured mobile device management for Exchange Online

Office 365 Exchange Online provides limited mobile device management capabilities through Exchange ActiveSync Services (EAS). These capabilities, such as the enforcing of passwords on mobile devices before they can connect to Exchange Online, are identified as minimum requirements to enforce the security of the service. A solution such as Configuration Manager is required for a more comprehensive set of capabilities to manage mobile devices, which is a topic that comes up frequently in an Office 365 deployment planning project. Another alternative for hosting mobile device management is through Windows InTune, which supports Windows 8, Windows RT, iOS, and Android devices with full integration into System Center 2012 Configuration Manager. Windows InTune is out of scope for this book and will not be covered. For more information about Windows InTune, see *http://www.microsoft.com/en-us/windows/windowsintune*.

System Center 2012 Operations Manager

System Center 2012 Operations Manager is the fourth full version of the Operations Manager monitoring solution. Operations Manager is a monitoring framework, which means it can monitor almost anything in any given scenario. Operations Manager is capable of monitoring Windows, Linux, UNIX, Solaris, and non-OS based systems that are accessible through Simple Network Management Protocol (SNMP) or through any scripting language. Examples of these include the following:

- Windows Server and workstations

- Various Linux OS servers and workstations

- SNMP-capable routers, firewalls, and switches

- SNMP-capable generators, door-entry systems, and smart Heating Ventilation and Air Conditioning (HVAC) systems

- Any system you can run a script against in any language and determine the state of the entity you are monitoring

Operations Manager, scripting, and Office 365

Operations Manager's ability to use scripting to monitor systems is very applicable

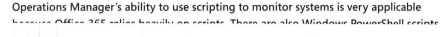

are most relevant to Office 365 because they are needed for Directory Synchronization and Single Sign-On. Monitoring these workloads is very important because if any of these fail, it could render Office 365 inaccessible.

MPs that are specific to Microsoft technologies are developed by the individual product teams responsible for the respective technology. Therefore, the actual development group that produces the technology is also the one that specifies the parameters that are impor-tant for the health of that technology. No other group is more authoritative or is in a better position to define an MP than the product group.

In 2010, Microsoft acquired AVIcode, Inc., which was recognized as a leader in the .NET Framework application performance monitoring. AVIcode was essentially an MP develop-ment company. For many years, the products of AVIcode were focused on the real-time monitoring of the .NET Framework application performance and diagnostics.

Operations Manager has agents based on the .NET Framework that run on Microsoft oper-ating systems as well as OpenPegasus agents that run on the Linux/UNIX/Solaris versions of operating systems. For monitoring of devices such as routers or Uninterruptable Power Supplies (UPS), SNMP polling is done in agentless mode. Agentless monitoring is also avail-able for Windows-based systems with a subset of the full monitoring potential available.

Therefore, if Office 365 is dependent on on-premises systems, and the systems are in turn dependent on non-Microsoft components such as UPS devices, Operations Manager can manage the entire technology stack so that a failure in one area can be quickly identified as the root cause of an outage. We will cover the planning, installation, basic operations, and

Chapter 5

best practices of Operations Manager later in the "Deploying the SCOM infrastructure and importing the Office 365 Management Pack" section of this chapter.

System Center 2012 Data Protection Manager

System Center 2012 Data Protection Manager, frequently referred to as DPM, is Microsoft's third full release of data protection technology. It originally debuted in 2005. DPM is different from traditional backup technologies because it provides near-continuous protection of the data, where typical "backup" technologies merely grab a snapshot copy at a specific point in time. Legacy backup software typically backs up data using one of the following three configurations:

- **Full Backup**   This configuration makes a full copy of everything targeted at the time the job is run.

- **Incremental Backup**   This configuration makes a copy of any file that has changed since the last full or incremental backup.

- **Differential**   This configuration makes a copy of the files that have changed since the last full backup.

DMP takes a different approach that gives it the ability to restore data to within 15 minutes. DPM does this by protecting files at the byte-level. The deltas are then copied to a secondary disk, which in turn is copied to another disk, tape, or cloud backup provider, as shown in Figure 5-4.

DPM provides the best protection and most Microsoft-supportable restore scenarios from disk, tape, and cloud, and in a scalable, amendable, and cost-effective way. It also provides the capability to protect virtual machines in your IT environment, as well as the applications running inside those VMs.

DPM leverages the Volume Shadow Service (VSS) API to intelligently access the data while at rest or in use. It also integrates into existing ticketing and workflow systems, scales to the largest enterprise sizes, and integrates tightly into the other System Center 2012 components. Most importantly, if there is a need to restore data in AD, SQL, or Exchange on-premises, DPM can do so, thereby protecting the integrity and preserving continued access to Office 365.

System Center 2012 Virtual Machine Manager

System Center 2012 Virtual Machine Manager is the third full release of Virtual Machine Manager, a product that Microsoft debuted in 2007. Virtual Machine Manager, frequently referred to as VMM, is the Microsoft System Center component for managing large numbers of virtual machine host servers based on Microsoft Hyper-V, VMware's ESX, or Citrix's

XenServer. Virtual Machine Manager allows administrators to manage both the virtual hosts and the virtual machines, or "guests" as they are frequently referred to.

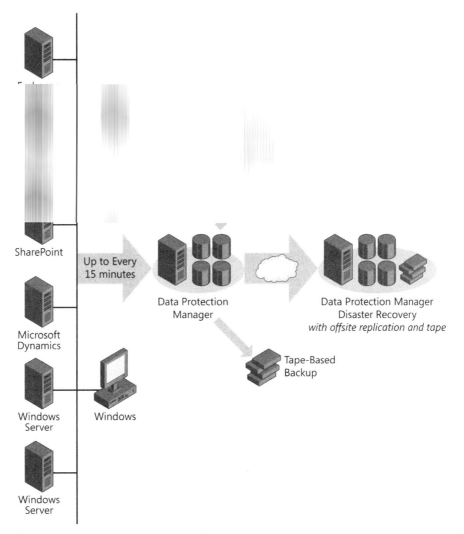

Figure 5-4 System Center Data Protection Manager disk-to-disk architecture.

Virtual machines are an entire operating system running within a partition on a hypervisor, which emulates the hardware an operating system is required to run on. This allows for multiple operating systems to run in parallel on the same physical hardware. This type of virtualization reduces the cost of hardware and provides operational flexibility. It also creates unique backup and restoration capabilities by isolating the operating system from the hardware.

Chapter 5

Virtualization is an important topic as it pertains to Office 365 because all the on-premises workloads that support Office 365 can be virtualized. This reduces the cost of managing on-premises technologies that support Office 365. Virtual Machine Manager's ability to provide numerous high-availability and disaster recovery options such as live migration, which is the ability to move a virtual machine from one virtual host to another with no downtime, allows zero downtime to Office 365 if there is ever a need to replace hardware.

System Center 2012 Orchestrator

System Center 2012 Orchestrator (SCO) is the second full release of the product formerly known as Opalis. Microsoft acquired Opalis, the industry leading IT workflow automation company, in 2009 and rebranded it as System Center Orchestrator. SCO is a workflow management solution for the data center. Orchestrator enables your organization to automate the creation, monitoring, and deployment of resources in your environment.

Orchestrator also provides a workflow management solution for the data center. This ability to automate activities, known as runbooks, can be used across Microsoft and third-party products. These runbooks are created in the Runbook Designer console and deployed through the deployment manager. They are run, or triggered, and monitored locally or remotely through the Orchestrator Console, System Center Service Manager, and System Center Operations Manager.

Orchestrator can tie disparate tasks and procedures together by using the graphical user-interface Runbook Designer to create reliable, flexible, and efficient end-to-end solutions in the IT environment. By using Orchestrator, your organization can do the following:

- Automate processes in your data center, regardless of hardware or platform

- Automate IT operations and standardize best practices to improve operational efficiency

- Connect different systems from different vendors with minimal knowledge of scripting and programming languages

Integration Packs, frequently referred to as IPs, extend the power and capability of Orchestrator by providing prebuilt activities that perform a wide variety of functions specific to the technologies the Integration Packs are for. This saves time by not having to manually create activities. Integration Packs can be downloaded from the Microsoft Download Center, CodePlex website, or third-party vendors developing IPs for different products such as the products at *http://www.kelverion.com*.

Remember from previous chapters that there are many steps involved in provisioning and de-provisioning Office 365 users. After a user object is synchronized into Office 365, it does not mean that the user immediately has access to Office 365 services. A separate action to provision Office 365 licenses to a user account needs to take place. This otherwise manual process can be replaced by automation. Therefore, SCO is an option to help with the automatic provisioning and de-provisioning of users in Office 365. SCO also can provide a self-service and provision method through a self-service portal called System Center 2012 Service Manager Service Offering.

System Center 2012 Service Manager

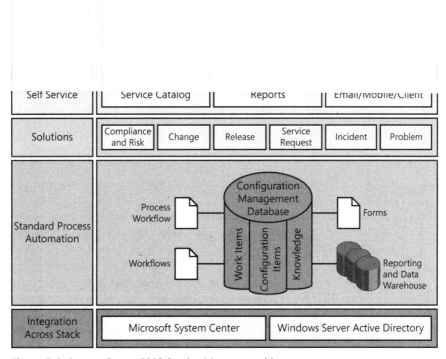

Figure 5-5 System Center 2012 Service Manager architecture.

Service Manager has six key solutions in its architecture, which are based on the ones found in the Microsoft Operations Framework (MOF) and the IT Infrastructure Library (ITIL):

- Compliance and Risk

- Change Management

- Release Management

- Service Request Fulfillment

- Incident Management

- Problem Management

Service Manager has an automated workflow engine for incident management, problem management, SLA management, and service request fulfillment. It also provides a user self-service portal through a Service Catalog and support access through mobile devices. Service Manager also comes with pre-built connectors for the following:

- **Active Directory**   For user data such as email, phone number, manager, office location, and group membership

- **System Center Configuration Manager**   For detailed hardware and software inventory of the devices the users have, applications they have installed, and versions

- **System Center Operations Manager**   For alerts that generate incidents within Service Manager and for sending status updates back to Operations Manager

- **Exchange**   For communication and notification purposes or automated creation of tickets through the email system

It is Service Manager's self-service portal that has the greatest relevance to Office 365. As mentioned before, there is software, such as the Office Professional Plus subscription, that a user can install directly from the Office 365 portal. Users can directly download the Office suite from the Office 365 portal, but that version uses Microsoft Update for patching. It's possible to customize Office Professional Plus to use a local network location to check for updates. To do so, customize the Office Professional Plus installation package with the Office Deployment Tool. After the Office installation package has been customized, you can publish it to the Service Manager's service offering catalog so users can access it from the self-service portal.

System Center 2012 Endpoint Protection

System Center 2012 Endpoint Protection is the second major release of Microsoft's anti-malware agent that is managed by System Center Configuration Manager. Endpoint Protection is frequently referred to as SCEP. Originally, Endpoint Protection was part of the Forefront suite of security products and named Forefront Endpoint Protection 2010, or FEP.

The reason we have included SCEP in this discussion is because Office 365 does not provide client protection. There might be confusion because of Forefront Online Protection for Exchange (FOPE), which provides anti-malware, anti-virus, and anti-spam protection. However, this protection is offered as a service-level protection, which means that FOPE is designed to prevent threats from entering the network and client through the email system. In reality, there are other ways in which malicious software can affect a system and, as such, these will not be within the scope of FOPE's protection.

Protecting the integrity of endpoints is an important topic because it ultimately protects your organization as well as Office 365 services.

Endpoint Protection allows you to consolidate desktop security and management into a single solution because it is built on System Center 2012 Configuration Manager. When

- Create and deploy Windows Firewall settings to groups of computers. This is important because there are specific firewall and browser settings required for Office 365.

- Use Configuration Manager software updates to automatically download the latest anti-malware definition files to keep client computers up-to-date.

- Control who manages the anti-malware policies and Windows Firewall settings by using the Endpoint Protection Manager Security role. This reduces the chance that Windows Firewall settings become misconfigured, thereby affecting access to Office 365.

- Use email notifications to alert you when computers report that malware is detected.

- View summary and detailed information from the Configuration Manager console and reports.

System Center 2012 App Controller

System Center 2012 App Controller is the newest System Center component in the suite. App Controller provides a common, self-service experience that can help your organization easily configure, deploy, and manage Windows Azure Applications (PaaS), Windows Azure Virtual Machines Services (IaaS), and service template deployments to on-premises private clouds through System Center 2012 Virtual Machine Manager. App Controller empowers administrators to perform the following tasks:

- Connect their data center or organization to public or private clouds

- Connect their data center or organization to a hosting provider in System Center 2012 SP1

Chapter 5

- Remove connections to public or private clouds

- Manage certificates on VMM library servers

- Delegate cloud administration to users

- Change account permissions

- Change public or private cloud properties

- View public or private cloud usage

- Manage cloud certificates

- Manage multiple Windows Azure subscription settings

- View the status of jobs

- View and deploy services from multiple VMM servers

App Controller is a web-based management solution that provides the extension of many of the on-premises virtualization capabilities to Windows Azure cloud services. We are introducing this concept here because we will be covering Windows Azure cloud services in Chapter 17, "Office Professional Plus Subscription." Windows Azure can be leveraged in an Office 365 deployment in lieu of implementing on-premises technologies. Therefore, it is important to cover the options to manage Windows Azure from System Center.

Figure 5-6 shows how App Controller can deploy, monitor, and manage systems in Windows Azure. These virtual machines can be provisioned within minutes and are an excellent choice to create redundancies for dependent, on-premises Office 365 technologies such as AD, AD FS, SQL, IIS, and Exchange.

Windows Azure securely provides your organization's on-premises corporate network the ability to deploy and manage Windows Azure virtual machines and published applications in Windows Azure IaaS and PaaS. In essence, this effectively extends your organization's data center and allows it to leverage the financially backed 99.95 percent uptime SLA of Windows Azure. This now aligns your on-premises Office 365 dependencies with the same level of SLA as Office 365 services.

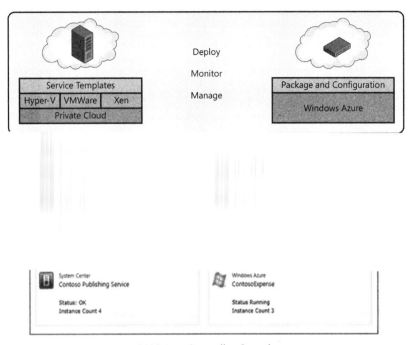

Figure 5-6 System Center 2012 App Controller Console.

Concepts and planning for monitoring Office 365

Microsoft's Office 365 puts Exchange, SharePoint, and Lync in the cloud. It also delivers Office Professional Plus through click-to-run technology and is responsible for activation. In this section, we will introduce some key concepts and explore how System Center 2012 Operations Manager can be used to monitor these critical business systems. Like any project, the usual elements, such as business case and communication plans, are recommended best practices. Because this book is not about project management, we will cover only concepts that are specific to System Center and Office 365.

To successfully deploy Operations Manager into a production environment, a few key steps must be accomplished. The IT group within the organization must ensure the following tasks are carried out:

- Procure System Center licensing.

- Become familiar with the technical requirements of Operations Manager.

Chapter 5

- Plan to provision physical and or virtual servers to deploy Operations Manager.

- Decide on the need for high availability in the System Center infrastructure.

- Identify the on-premises and off-premises technologies that need monitoring.

- Identify if there is overlap with existing technology and evaluate whether that technology can be replaced by Operations Manager.

- Validate that the network can handle the additional traffic of the monitoring solution.

- Determine whether network changes will need to be made.

- Determine whether there are special security requirements.

- Design a proof of concept for Operations Manager.

- Determine what the pilot deployment of Operations Manager will entail, and define milestones and success criteria.

- Implement a production deployment plan, which might entail an upgrade of the pilot system or a complete rebuild.

For the sake of brevity, we will use a single server implementation of Operations Manager to monitor our existing AD, Windows operating systems, and other technologies that Office 365 depends on.

Although running Operations Manager in Windows Azure Virtual Machines is an option, we will use the on-premises model for the exercises covered in this chapter.

Evaluating what to monitor

As part of the Office 365 project, the design scope of monitoring will have to be focused on Office 365 technologies. That is not to say you should limit the monitoring infrastructure to just the technologies that Office 365 is dependent on. Leveraging System Center to monitor other technologies is a good strategy to maximize your Return on Investment (ROI). However, if the core focus is on making sure Office 365 and its dependent workloads are properly monitored, it is important that your organization prioritizes which technologies to monitor. There is a key distinction between "need to monitor" versus "want to monitor." We make this distinction because we have seen many customers allow scope creep to take over when they realize there are over 300 Management Packs (MPs) available for download. The end result could be either a project that becomes too overwhelming or a monitoring infrastructure that produces so much data that the effective monitoring of Office 365 becomes lost in the mountain of data.

To understand what needs to be monitored for Office 365, we need to understand which technologies Office 365 depends on. Here is a list of those technologies:

- Server hardware

- Windows Server

- Virtualization hosts, if applicable

- IIS

- Microsoft Exchange Server for certain hybrid deployment scenarios

- Microsoft SharePoint Server for certain hybrid scenarios, such as Search

- Microsoft Lync Server

- SQL Server and or Windows Internal Database (WID)

- DirSync Server or Forefront Identity Manager (FIM) server

Now that we have identified many of the key technologies required by Office 365, we need to understand and document what the SLAs are for each part of this solution so we can accurately monitor and track them.

Chapter 5

INSIDE OUT   SLA reminder

It is important to remember that Office 365 is only as good as the SLA of a dependent on-premises technology. Even though the Office 365 SLA is 99.9 percent, if AD FS is implemented to facilitate Single Sign-On (SSO), and your organization can guarantee only 99.7 percent, then the Office 365 SLA is also reduced accordingly because if AD FS is not available, then access to Office 365 might also become unavailable to users who are not already authenticated. That is the reason we stress the importance of monitoring and why we dedicate several chapters in this Office 365 book to a monitoring solution such as Microsoft System Center 2012.

We will use the preceding list as the basis for the MPs we will download and import into System Center Operations Manager in the "Deploying the SCOM infrastructure and importing the Office 365 Management Pack" section of this chapter.

Administering the monitoring solution

Microsoft has incorporated Role Based Access Control, frequently referred to as RBAC, into Operations Manager. You should be familiar with this term after reading this book because RBAC also is used extensively in Office 365 administration.

Like in Office 365, RBAC in System Center allows the delegation of permissions within System Center Operations Manager so that users can be granted rights to various workspaces and objects to be administered through the Operations Manager console.

The design of RBAC can be based on your organization's current administrative practices. Whether it is a tiered or centralized structure, RBAC can be designed to accommodate any organizational administration style. However, instead of completely mirroring your current organization's administration model in RBAC, it might be prudent to appreciate that your organization's current model might be a result of the lack of RBAC-based administrative tools in the past. Therefore, with the introduction of Operations Manager, and the increased scope with respect to Office 365, your organization might want to take the opportunity to redesign the process, if applicable.

There are many RBAC roles available in Operations Manager. The following list shows some of the roles:

- Operations Manager administrators

- Authors

- Operators

- Report users

Monitoring targets

We identified the technologies that need to be monitored earlier in this chapter. We now need to identify the actual monitoring targets. Monitoring targets are the actual things we

In this section, we'll take you through the deployment of System Center 2012 Operations Manager. We will assume you have an existing server running Windows Server 2012 with SQL Server installed, and thatthe SQL Server and SQL Server Agent services are running and set to start automatically. The server should be a member server in the AD domain that is associated with your Office 365 tenant.

Installing the System Center 2012 Operations Manager Service Pack 1 prerequisites

The following list shows the prerequisites that must be met prior to installing Operations Manager. Most, but not all, of the roles and features are installed by means of the Server Manager Add Roles and Features Wizard:

- IIS with the following role services:

  - IIS 6 Metabase Compatibility

  - Windows Authentication

  - Request Monitor

  - HTTP activation under the .NET Framework 4.5

  - ASP.NET 3.5 – This is installed through Microsoft Updates on Windows Server 2012, not through the Add Roles and Features Wizard

  - Microsoft Report Viewer 2010 Redistributable Package

> **Note**
> You can download the Microsoft Report Viewer Redistributable Package at *http://www. microsoft.com/en-us/download/details.aspx?displaylang=en&id=6442*.

Follow these steps to install the prerequisites:

1. On the server running Windows Server 2012, where you will install System Center Operations Manager 2012, open Server Manager.

2. On the Manage menu, click the Add Roles and Features Wizard. The wizard will appear, as shown in Figure 5-7. Click Next to continue.

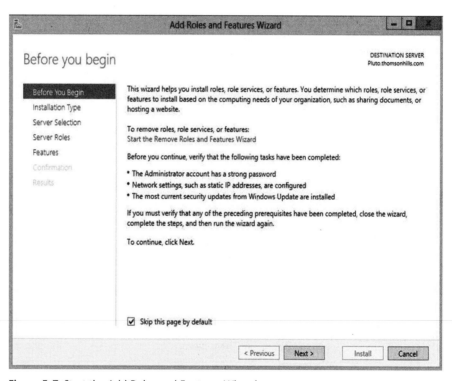

Figure 5-7 Start the Add Roles and Features Wizard.

3. Select Role-based or feature-based installation, as shown in Figure 5-8. Click Next.

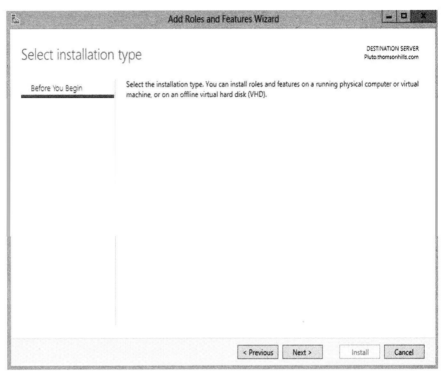

Figure 5-8 Select Role-Based or feature-based installation.

4. Select the server on which you will install System Center 2012 Operations Manager, as shown in Figure 5-9. You might have more than one server listed if Server Manager is being used for multi-server management. Click Next to continue.

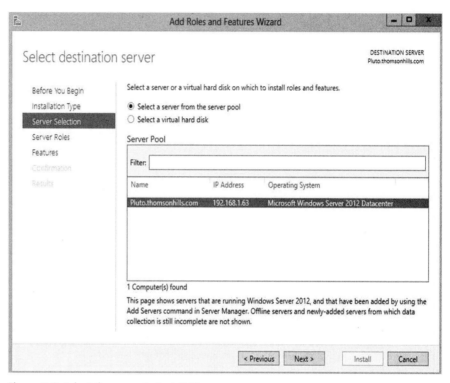

Figure 5-9 Select the server to install IIS.

5. Select the Web Server (IIS) role, as shown in Figure 5-10.

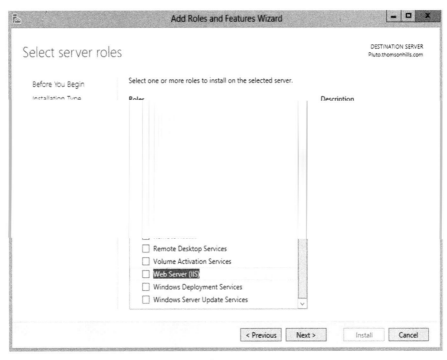

Figure 5-10 Select the Web Server (IIS) role.

6. Click Add Features, as shown in Figure 5-11.

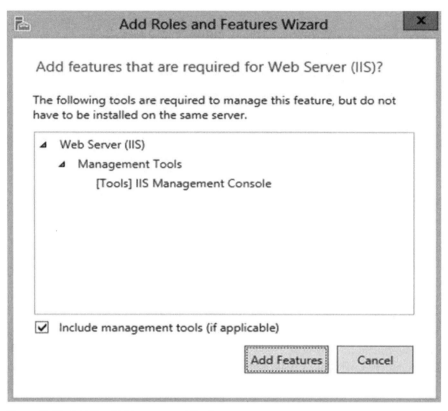

Figure 5-11 Add the IIS Management Tools.

7. On the Select features page, as shown in Figure 5-12, locate and expand the .NET Framework 4.5 node and select everything. Also select the check boxes for IIS 6 Metabase Compatibility, Windows Authentication, and Request Monitor. Click Next to continue.

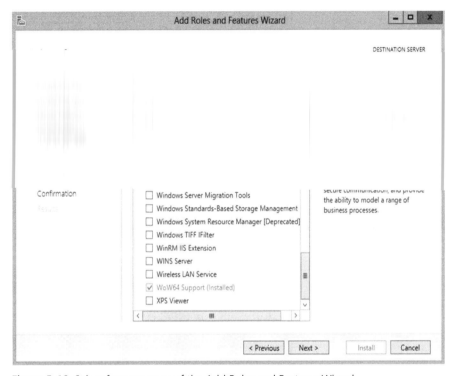

Figure 5-12 Select features page of the Add Roles and Features Wizard.

8. The Web Server Role (IIS) page will appear, as shown in Figure 5-13. This page is informational only. Click Next to continue.

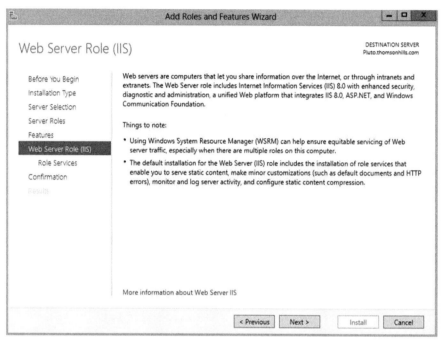

Figure 5-13 Web Server Role (IIS) page.

9. On the Select role services page, as shown in Figure 5-14, select the following check boxes, then click Next to continue:

- ❍ Default Document
- ❍ Directory Browsing
- ❍ HTTP Errors
- ❍ Static Content
- ❍ HTTP Logging
- ❍ Request Monitor
- ❍ Request Filtering
- ❍ Static Content Compression

❍ Web Server (IIS) Support

❍ IIS 6 Metabase Compatibility

❍ ASP.NET

❍ Windows Authentication

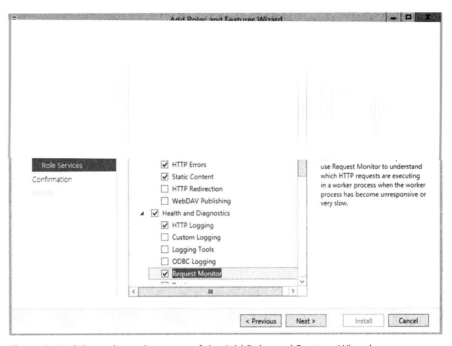

Figure 5-14 Select role services page of the Add Roles and Features Wizard.

10. On the Confirm installation selections page, as shown in Figure 5-15, click Install to start the installation of the selected roles and features.

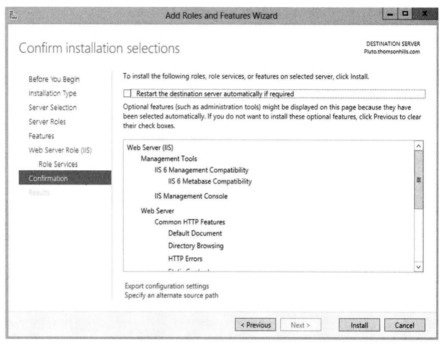

Figure 5-15 Confirm installation selections page of the Add Roles and Features Wizard.

11. When the installation completes, click Close, as shown in Figure 5-16.

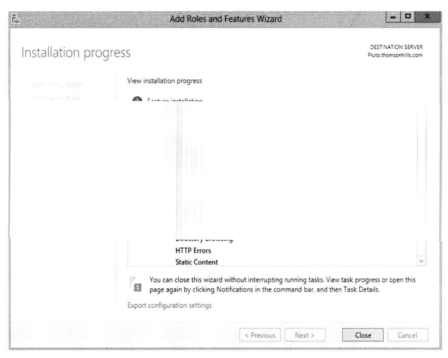

Figure 5-16 Installation progress page of the Add Roles and Features Wizard.

12. Start Control Panel and run Windows Update. This will download and install the .NET Framework 3.5.

This completes the installation of IIS and all the prerequisites for System Center 2012 Operations Manager.

Downloading the System Center 2012 Operations Manager Service Pack 1 media

Microsoft has published System Center 2012 Operations Manager Service Pack 1 as slip-streamed media to both the Microsoft Developer Network (MSDN) and to Volume Licensing customers. For the latter, Operations Manager with SP1 can be downloaded from the Volume Licensing website at *http://www.microsoft.com/licensing*. Figure 5-17 shows Operations Manager with SP1 from MSDN.

> **Note**
> The exercise in this book uses an MSDN copy, which is not licensed to be used for production deployments.

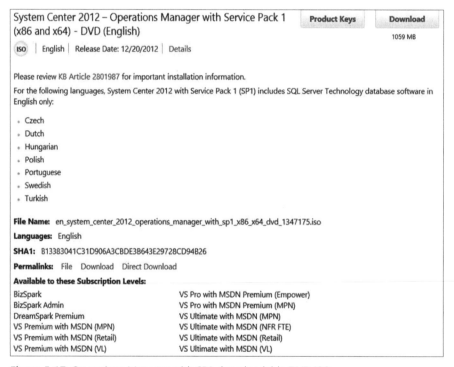

Figure 5-17 Operations Manager with SP1 downloadable DVD ISO.

After you have downloaded the Operations Manager DVD ISO , you can insert it in your Microsoft Hyper-V virtual machine, as shown in Figure 5-18.

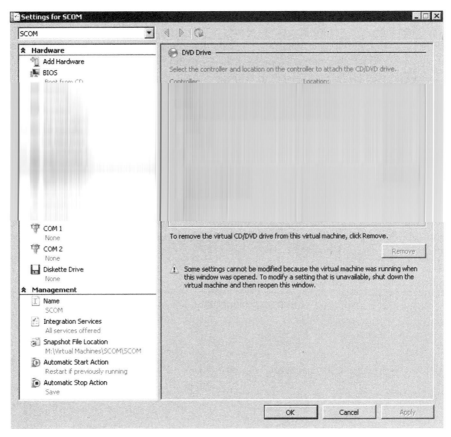

Figure 5-18 Inserting the System Center 2012 Operations Manager ISO into a Hyper-V VM.

Installing System Center 2012 Operations Manager

After you have successfully mounted the System Center 2012 Operations Manager Service Pack 1 DVD ISO to the virtual machine, you can begin installation by following these steps:

1. Start the virtual machine on which you will be installing Operations Manager and on which you have mounted the Operations Manager DVD ISO.

2. When the virtual server is started, log on to the virtual machine, then navigate to the virtual CD drive using the virtual server's Windows Explorer and start Setup.

3. Setup will start the System Center 2012 Operations Manager Service Pack 1 startup screen, as shown in Figure 5-19.

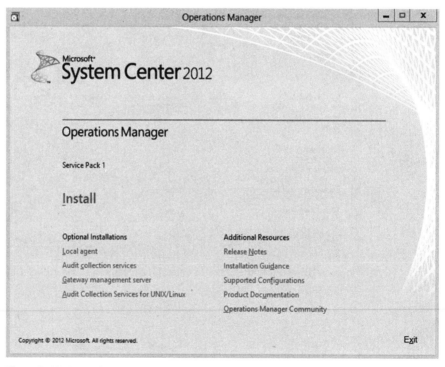

Figure 5-19 Operations Manager installation startup screen.

4. Click Install.

5. Select the features you want to install. To simplify the illustration, we will install all
    the features on the same server. In a real production environment, you might choose
    to install the features on different servers. Click Next after you have selected the
    features, as shown in Figure 5-20.

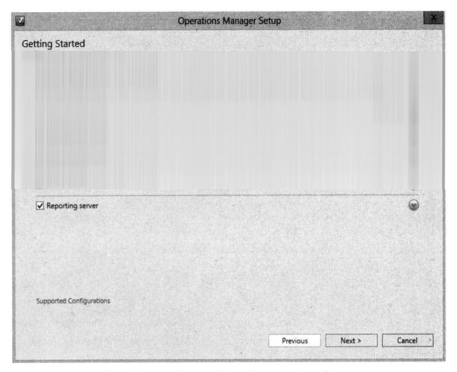

Figure 5-20 Operations Manager Setup – Select features to install.

6. Specify the path to install System Center 2012 Operations Manager or accept the default path, as shown in Figure 5-21. Click Next to continue.

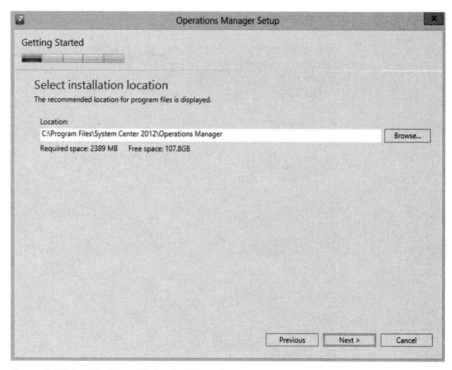

Figure 5-21 Installation path for the Operations Manager installation.

7. Wait for Operations Manager Setup to verify that all prerequisites have been installed, as shown in Figure 5-22. Click Next when Setup is done verifying.

Figure 5-22 Operations Manager Setup verifying prerequisites.

8. In the event the hardware is not compatible or if any prerequisites are missing, the relevant information will be displayed and Setup will indicate it cannot continue, as shown in Figure 5-23. If you encounter this page, read the information and follow the instructions to remediate the deficiencies, then click Verify Prerequisites Again. If no issues are found, proceed to Step 9.

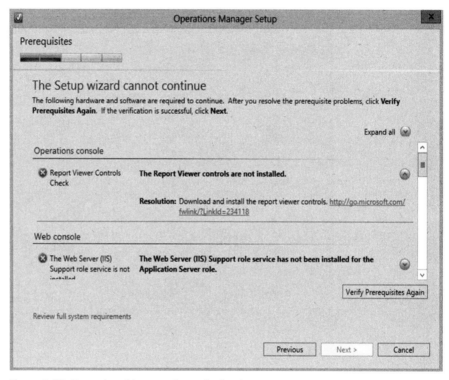

Figure 5-23 Operations Manager Setup finding issues.

9. If Operations Manager Setup does not find any issues that will prevent Operations Manager from installing, you will see the confirmation page, as shown in Figure 5-24. The page in Figure 5-24 has a low memory warning that does not prevent Operations Manager from being installed. However, it does recommend an increase in the amount of memory. Click Next to continue.

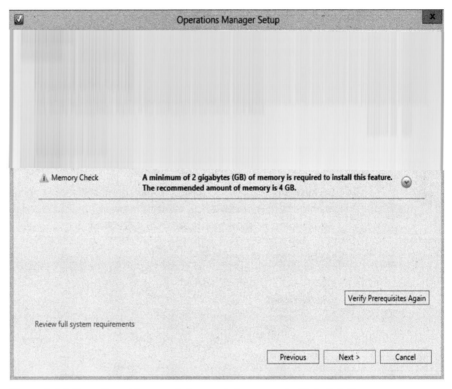

Figure 5-24 Operations Manager Setup ready to proceed with installation.

INSIDE OUT Hyper-V Dynamic Memory configuration

If the Windows Server 2012 Hyper-V Dynamic Memory setting is being used for hosting System Center 2012 Operations Manager, it's recommended to configure the startup RAM equal to the amount of maximum RAM for the virtual machine. This will force Hyper-V to allocate the maximum amount of RAM specified for the VM upon the VM's boot. This excess RAM will be released back to the host because it won't be needed immediately. This will suppress any prerequisite warnings related to the System Center 2012 component installation process and make the guest operating system's performance counters accurately reflect their state.

For more information on this dynamic memory recommendation, refer to the TechNet blog at *http://blogs.technet.com/b/mghazai/archive/2013/05/28/virtual-machine-ram-and-windows-server-2012-hyper-v-dynamic-memory.aspx.*

10. Because this is our first Operations Manager installation, select Create the first Management server in a new management group option and provide a management group name, as shown in Figure 5-25. Click Next to continue.

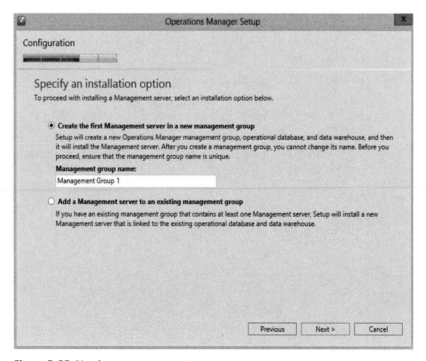

Figure 5-25 Naming a management group.

11. Read and accept the license agreement terms by checking the box, as shown in Figure 5-26. Click Next.

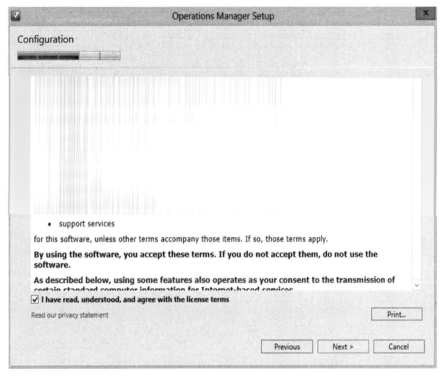

Figure 5-26 Licensing terms.

12. Review the Installation Summary and click Install, as shown in Figure 5-27.

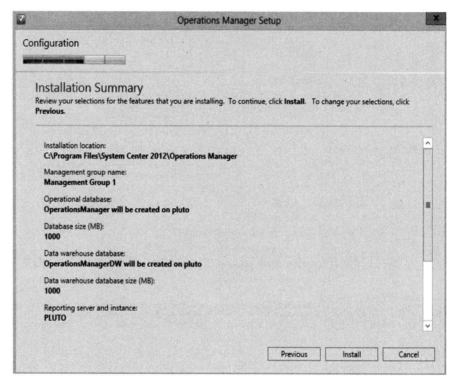

Figure 5-27 Installation Summary page.

13. Enable Microsoft Update, as shown in Figure 5-28, to keep System Center 2012 Operations Manager up-to-date. Click Next to continue.

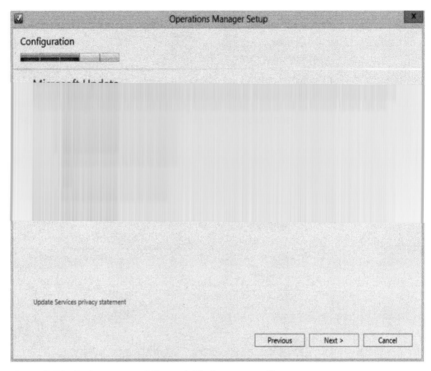

Figure 5-28 Option to turn Microsoft Update on or off.

14. Choose whether to participate in the Customer Experience Improvement Program, as shown in Figure 5-29. Click Next to continue.

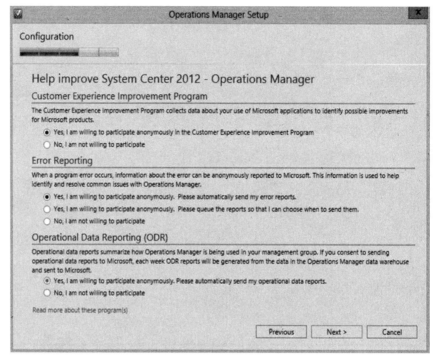

Figure 5-29 Customer Experience Improvement Program.

15. As shown in Figure 5-30, select the Domain Account option for the following three account names: Management server action account, Data Reader account, and Data Writer account (also known as the Data Warehouse Write account). Provide the domain and user name by using the down-level logon format *(Domain\User Name)*, and provide your account credentials. The System Center Configuration service and System Center Data Access service can use the Local System account, or you can create new AD service accounts. Click Next to continue.

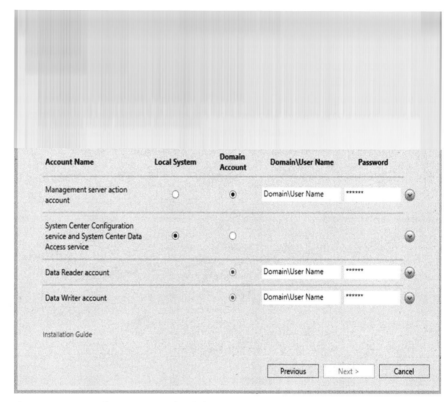

Figure 5-30 Provide account credentials.

16. Operations Manager uses SQL Server Reporting Service (SSRS) for reporting. You can use a separate SSRS instance or one that is installed on the local server. As mentioned prior to this exercise, we assume that you have access to a SQL Server instance. Specify the SQL Server instance, as shown in Figure 5-31. Click Next to continue.

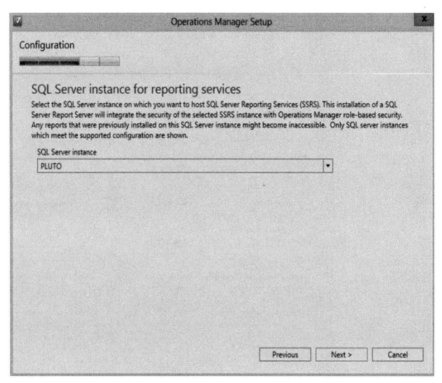

Figure 5-31 Select SQL Server instance.

17. Provide the SQL Server and database settings so that Setup can create the databases, as shown in Figure 5-32. You can specify the SQL Server port, database name, size, and database file and log locations. Click Next to continue.

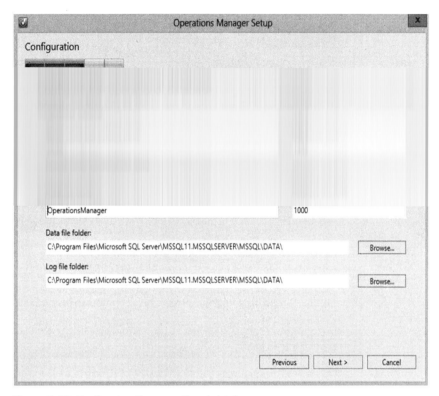

Figure 5-32 Configuring the operational database.

18. The same information is requested for the data warehouse database, as shown in Figure 5-33. Click Next to continue.

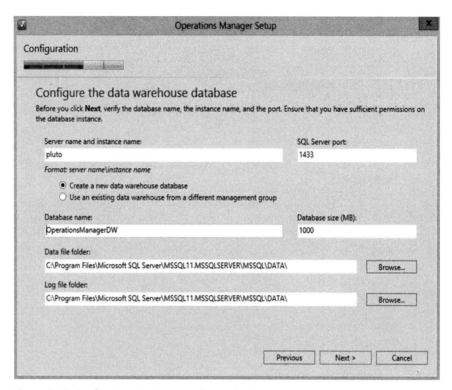

Figure 5-33 Configuring the data warehouse database.

19. At this point, Operations Manager is being installed and the installation progress is being displayed, as shown in Figure 5-34. Operations Manager will be installed after Setup finishes processing.

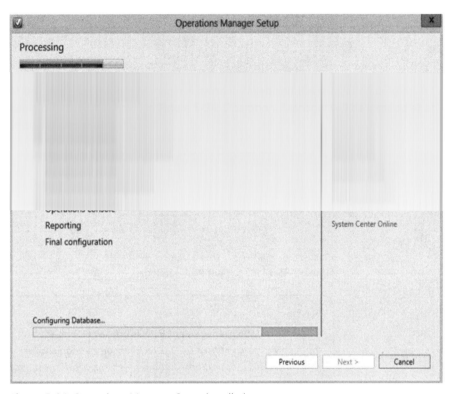

Figure 5-34 Operations Manager Setup installation progress.

Importing the Office 365 Management Pack

Management Packs are core to Operations Manager because they tell Operations Manager how to monitor a particular technology. Follow these steps to import an MP from the catalog into Operations Manager:

1. Download from the Management Pack catalog at *http://systemcenter.pinpoint. microsoft.com* and extract the files. Figure 5-35 shows the Management Pack catalog when you type **Active Directory** in the search box.

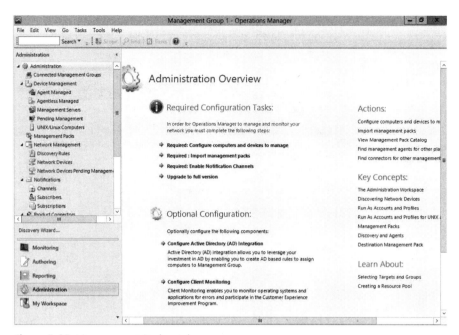

Figure 5-35 Management Pack catalog.

Note

A new Office 365 Management Pack is now available. You can download it from the TechNet Blogs at *http://blogs.technet.com/b/mghazai/archive/2013/06/17/system-center-2012-operations-manager-web-application-monitoring-example.aspx*.

2. We will use the Office 365 MP for this exercise. The URL we provided in the previous note will direct you to download a file named 3302.Office.xml. Rename this file Office.xml, as shown in Figure 5-36.

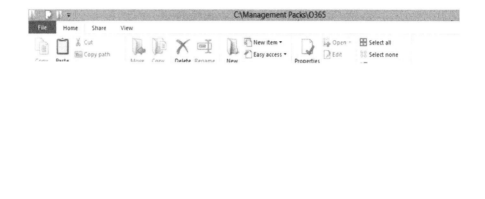

Figure 5-36 Office 365 Management Pack.

3. Start Operations Manager.

4. On the Operations console, click the Administration workspace.

5. In the Administration pane, expand the Administration node, expand the Device Management node, and then select Management Packs, as shown in Figure 5-37.

Figure 5-37 Administration Workspace.

6. Click Import Management Packs.

7. On the Select Management Packs page, click Add, as shown in Figure 5-38.

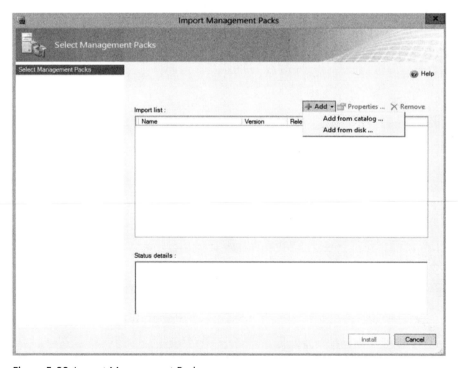

Figure 5-38 Import Management Pack.

Note

Figure 5-38 shows that the Add drop-down menu gives you the option to add from the catalog. So, even though we went to the catalog through a browser, we could have accessed the catalog directly from this page instead. If you chose to download an MP, similar to what we did with the Office 365 MP, you will select Add from disk.

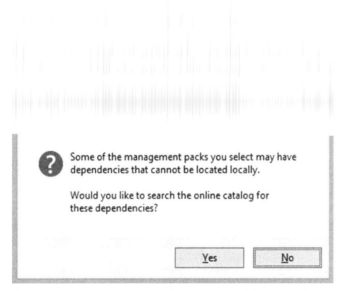

Figure 5-39 Dialog box asking whether to search for dependencies.

10. Select the file you named Office.xml in Step 2. Then click Open, as shown in Figure 5-40.

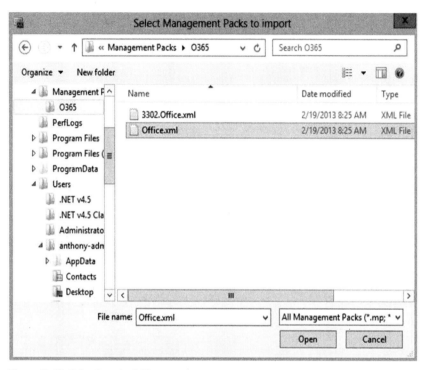

Figure 5-40 Selecting the MP.

11. The Office 365 MP will be validated. After it has been validated, it is ready for import, as shown in Figure 5-41.

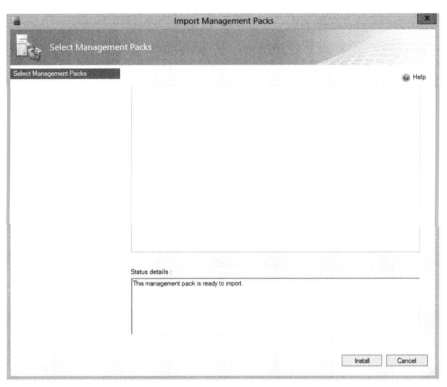

Figure 5-41 MP ready for import.

12. Click Install. Operations Manager will begin importing the MP, as shown in Figure 5-42.

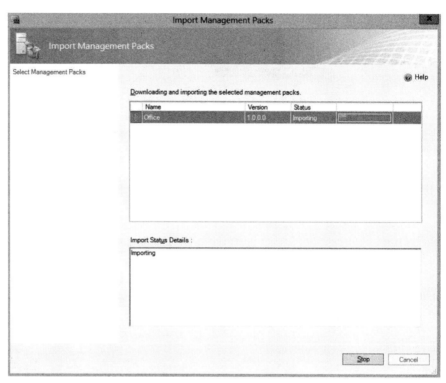

Figure 5-42 MP import progress.

13. After the Office 365 MP has been imported, you can verify there are no errors and the import was successful, as shown in Figure 5-43. Click Close.

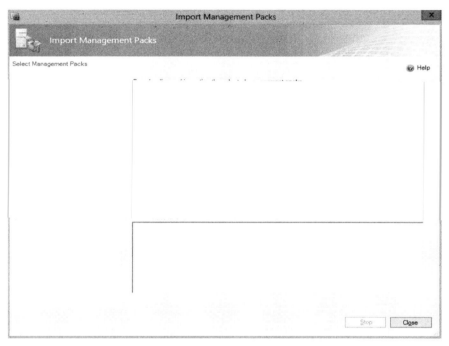

Figure 5-43 MP import completion.

14. View the MP in the Monitoring Overview pane of Operations Manager, as shown in Figure 5-44.

Figure 5-44 Viewing the Office 365 MP.

Creating alert notifications

In this section you will create System Center 2012 Operations Manager notifications. You will configure these notifications to be sent to the designated team responsible for the monitoring and management of Office 365 services. Notifications are usually in the form of emails, but can also be text messages. Alerts are classified by severity levels:

- Informational

- Warning

- Critical

In this exercise you will configure email notifications only for Critical alerts. To accomplish this, you need to create alert recipients and subscriptions.

Creating alert recipients

Follow these steps to create a recipient:

1. Start Operations Manager.

2. Right-click the Notification node in the Administration pane, as shown in Figure 5-45, and select New subscriber.

Figure 5-45 Creating a new subscriber.

3. In the Subscriber Name text box of the Notification Subscriber Wizard, provide the down-level logon name *(Domain\User name)* of the user you want to send notifications to, as shown in Figure 5-46. Click Next.

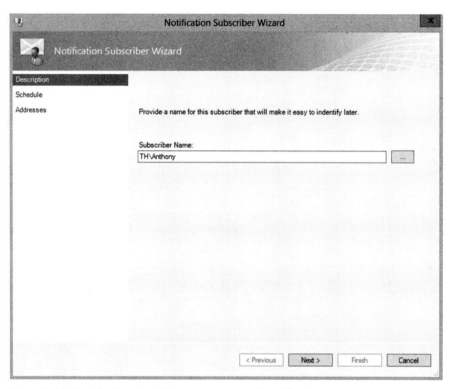

Figure 5-46 Provide down-level logon name to send notifications to.

4. On the next screen, as shown in Figure 5-47, determine when you want notifications
    to be sent. Select the option to send notifications as alerts come up or select the
    option to send notifications only during certain timeframes. After you have made
    your selection, click Next.

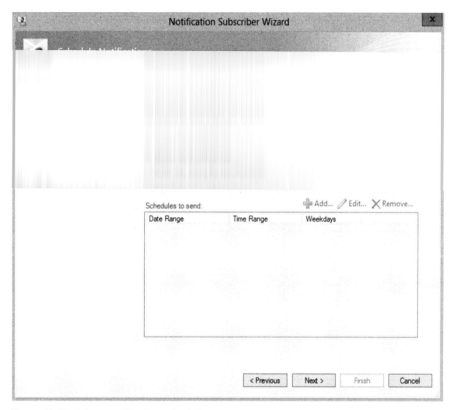

Figure 5-47 Select notification schedule.

5. In the third and last screen of the Notification Subscriber Wizard, as shown in Figure 5-48, you can associate specific addresses to specific notification times. As stated by the guidance on this screen, you can send notifications to an email address from 8:00 A.M. to 5:00 P.M. and send notifications to a cell phone outside those hours. Determine how you want notifications to be sent during different time frames. Click Add to create a new notification type.

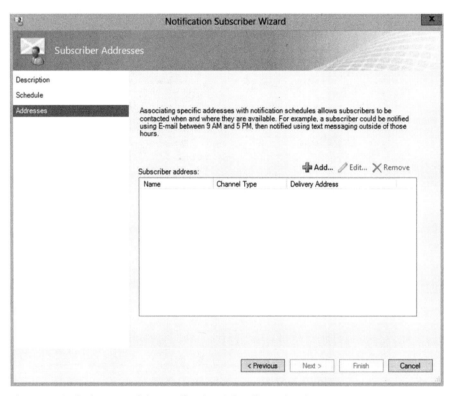

Figure 5-48 Final screen of the Notification Subscriber Wizard.

6. Provide a name for this notification in the Address name text box, as shown in Figure 5-49, and click Next.

7. Select the Channel Type. In this exercise, because we will be sending an email alert through this channel, select E-Mail (SMTP) in the Channel Type drop-down box. Leave the Command Channel text box blank, and type in the email address in the Delivery address for the selected channel text box, as shown in Figure 5-50. Click Next.

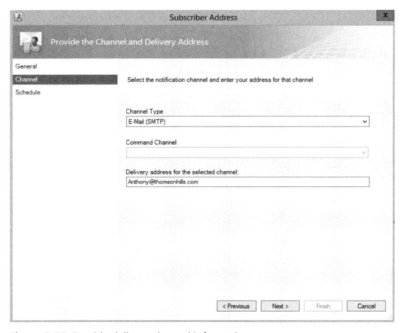

Figure 5-50 Provide delivery channel information.

8. Specify whether this channel will always receive notifications or whether to restrict notifications to a date and time range. Then click Finish, as shown in Figure 5-51.

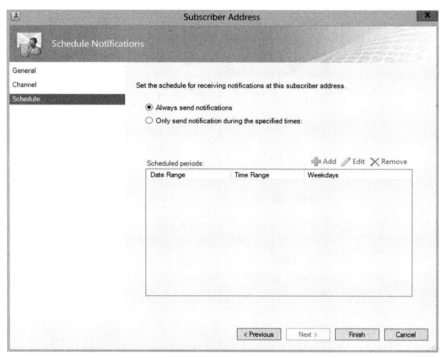

Figure 5-51 Define the schedule for the notification recipient.

9. Repeat Steps 5 through 8 if you need to create more recipients; otherwise, click Finish, as shown in Figure 5-52.

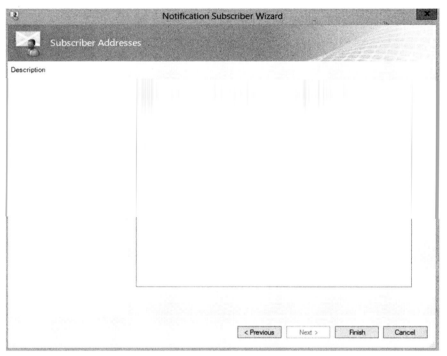

Figure 5-52 Subscriber Addresses page to add more channel subscribers.

10. You should see a screen notifying you that channels are saved, as shown in Figure 5-53. Click Close.

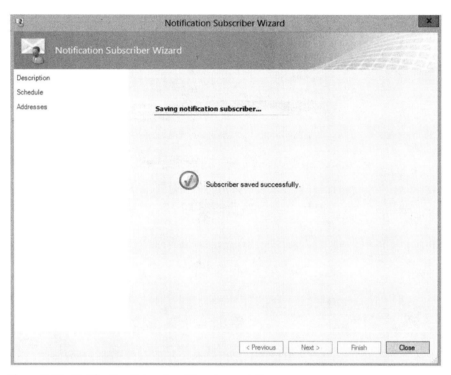

Figure 5-53 Notification Subscriber Wizard completion.

You have now successfully created an alert and the channels that the alerts will be sent to. You also saw that there can be different channels for the alerts, and each channel can have its own notification schedule and method.

Creating a subscription

Subscriptions are designed to facilitate users getting notifications without having the administrator maintain the notifications on a per-user basis. The subscription allows the administrator to specify the devices that send the notifications and the formats in which they are sent. In this section, we will create a subscription for alerts with an Error severity from any of the Office 365 or infrastructure servers.

1. Right-click the Notification node in the Administration pane, as shown in Figure 5-45, and select New Subscription.

2. Provide a name for the new subscription, as shown in Figure 5-54, then click Next.

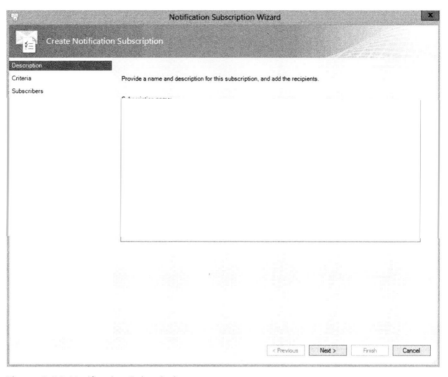

Figure 5-54 Notification Subscription name.

3. On the Subscription Criteria page, shown in Figure 5-55, define the certification criteria. For this exercise, check the following boxes:

    ❍ raised by any specific instance in a specific group

    ❍ of a specific severity

    ❍ with specific resolution state

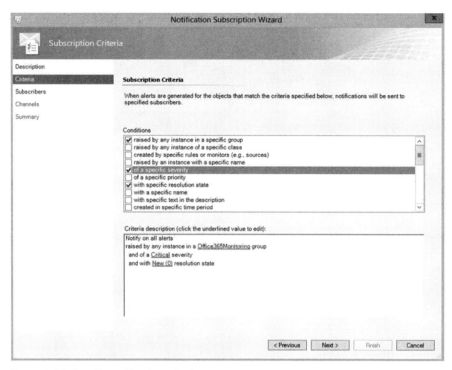

Figure 5-55 Specify notification criteria.

4. In the Criteria description section, click the first hyperlinked "specific," as shown in Figure 5-56. A Class Search window will appear.

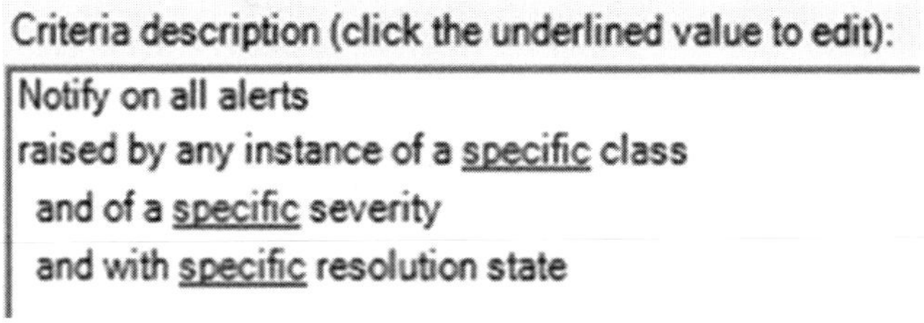

Criteria description (click the underlined value to edit):

Notify on all alerts
raised by any instance of a <u>specific</u> class
  and of a <u>specific</u> severity
  and with <u>specific</u> resolution state

Figure 5-56 Subscription criteria details.

5.   In the Class Search window, in the Management pack drop-down box, click the drop-down arrow and select the Office 365 MP. Then click Search, as shown in Figure 5-57, which will populate the Available classes box.

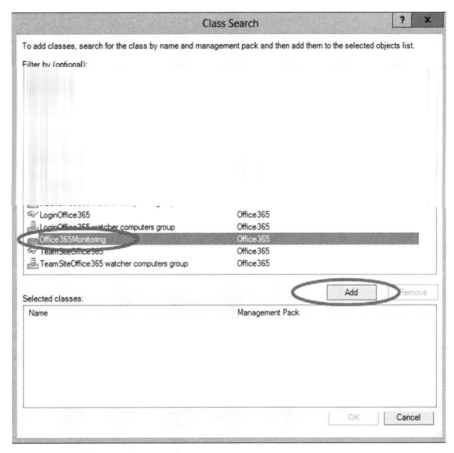

Figure 5-57 Office365 Class Search.

6.   Select Office365Monitoring in the Available classes box and click Add, as shown in Figure 5-57. Click OK to close the Class Search window.

7.   Click the second hyperlink titled "specific," as shown in Figure 5-56.

8. In the Alert Type window, select Critical, as shown in Figure 5-58, then click OK.

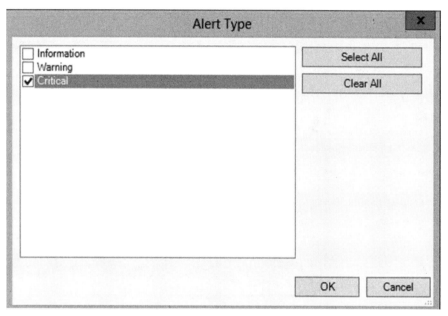

Figure 5-58 Alert Type.

9. Click the third hyperlink titled "specific," as shown in Figure 5-56.

10. In the Resolution State window, select New (0), as shown in Figure 5-59, then click
OK.

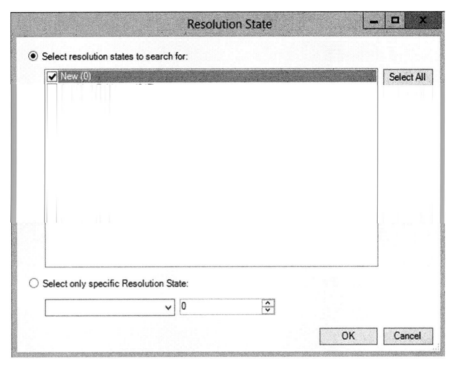

Figure 5-59 Select new resolution states.

11. The final Criteria description portion of the Notification Subscription Wizard should
now look like what is shown in Figure 5-60. What you have done is defined a
subscription that will raise an alert only on new and critical issues detected by the
Office 365 MP. Click Next.

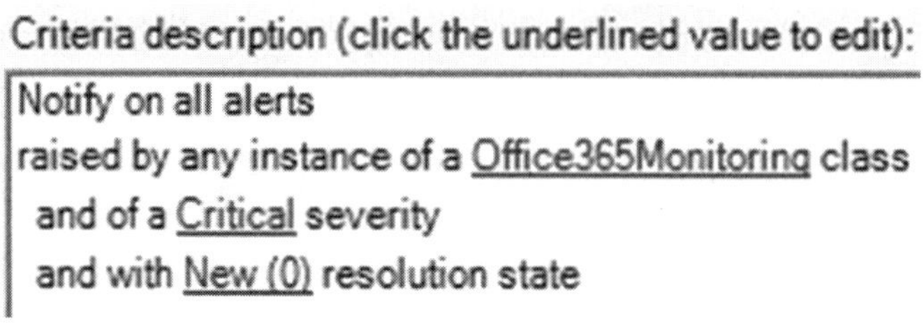

Criteria description (click the underlined value to edit):

Notify on all alerts
raised by any instance of a <u>Office365Monitoring</u> class
  and of a <u>Critical</u> severity
  and with <u>New (0)</u> resolution state

Figure 5-60 Criteria description.

12. On the Subscriber page, click Add.

13. In the Subscriber Search window, click Search. This will populate the Available subscribers box, as shown in Figure 5-61.

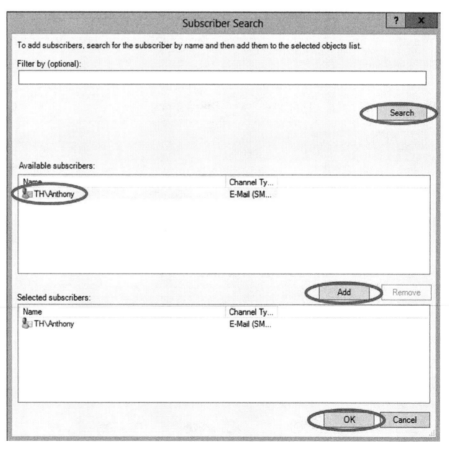

Figure 5-61 Select subscribers.

14. The selected user will appear in the Selected subscribers box, as shown in Figure 5-62. Click Next.

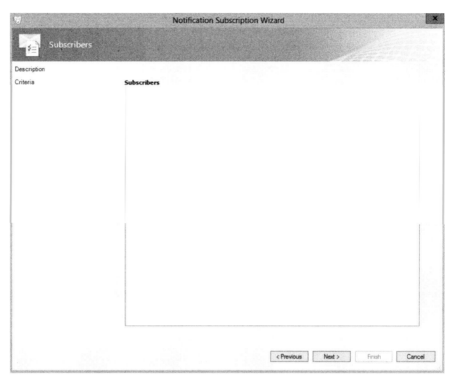

Figure 5-62 Selected subscribers.

15. On the Channels page, click Add.

16. In the Channel Search window, click Search. This will populate the Available channels box, as shown in Figure 5-63.

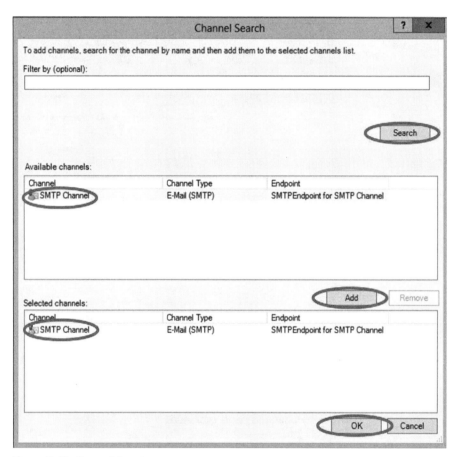

Figure 5-63 Channel Search.

17. Select the SMTP Channel from the Available channels list and click Add, as shown in Figure 5-63.

18. The SMTP Channel will now be listed in the Selected channels box, as shown in Figure 5-63. Click OK.

19. The SMTP Channel is now selected as a channel on the Channels page of the
Notification Subscription Wizard. In the Alert aging box, select the Send notification
without delay option, as shown in Figure 5-64, then click Next.

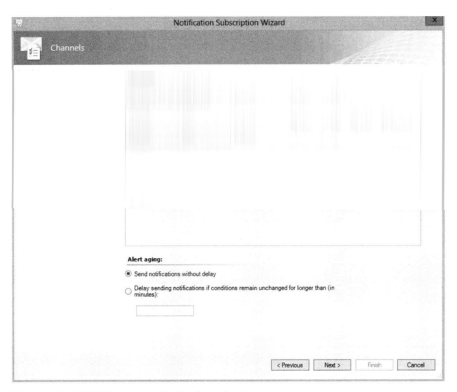

Figure 5-64 SMTP Channel added to the subscription.

20. On the Summary page, select Enable this notification subscription and click Finish, as shown in Figure 5-65.

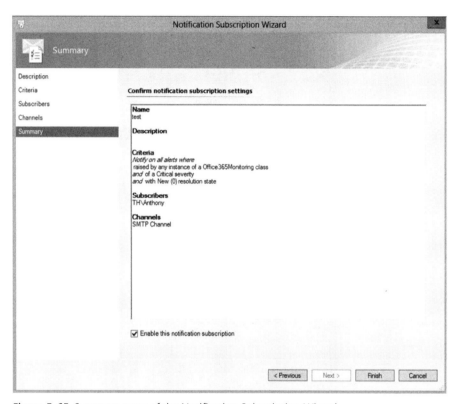

Figure 5-65 Summary page of the Notification Subscription Wizard.

Office 365 notifications are now set up. In this exercise, you enabled notification for a single user. However, you also can enable notification for an Active Directory distribution list or mail-enabled group. Using Active Directory groups allows you to add or remove members, which in turn will update the notifications list.

> **Note**
>
> For more information on System Center 2012 Operations Manager notifications, see the following resources:
>
> - "How to Enable an Email Notification Channel" at *http://technet.microsoft.com/ en-us/library/hh212914.aspx*.

This chapter demonstrated why System Center is relevant to Office 365, with a particular focus on Operations Manager to monitor the Office 365 workload. You learned the concept of Management Packs and that there is one designed for Office 365.

Although we focused on Operations Manager, remember that the other System Center 2012 suite components also play significant roles that help you manage Office 365. For example, Configuration Manager's software deployment capability can be used to deploy the Office Professional Plus subscription to desktops.

If you already have System Center in your organization, you can leverage your investment and extend your enterprise monitoring and management capabilities to include Office 365. If you do not have System Center, we hope you learned how each of the suite components will benefit Office 365. Furthermore, like AD FS, the solution can be leveraged for other non-Office 365 applications and systems in your organization.

This Office 365 book is not intended to extensively cover the capabilities of System Center; we are only scratching the surface in terms of its capabilities. There are other books and resources dedicated to the System Center 2012 suite. However, we hope you gained insight and knowledge on how to configure Operations Manager and how to use the Office 365 MP to monitor your Office 365 subscription.

Chapter 5

Customizing Operations Manager reports and dashboards for Office 365

Identifying Office 365 dependent servers 283   Tuning the Office 365 management pack and

System Center 2012 Operations Manager (SCOM) and walked through the process of downloading and importing the Office 365 management pack for SCOM.

In this chapter, we will continue to customize Operations Manager to monitor and create Office 365 reports and dashboards. We will cover utilization statistics, availability, and trending reports, as this is commonly requested information. These reports target business owners, technical support professionals, and users. Finally, we will demonstrate how to build various types of dashboards. Monitoring Office 365 is an important function because Office 365 will make up a significant portion of most organizations' IT services portfolio.

Identifying Office 365 dependent servers

Before we configure monitoring and customizing reports, you must first identity the servers that Office 365 is dependent on. At a minimum, these will be your domain controllers (DCs), AD FS, directory synchronization, and FIM servers. Follow these steps to create a server group in SCOM:

1. Start the SCOM Operator console. Select the Authoring workspace on the navigation pane, select Groups on the left pane, and then click Create a New Group from the Tasks pane, as shown in Figure 6-1.

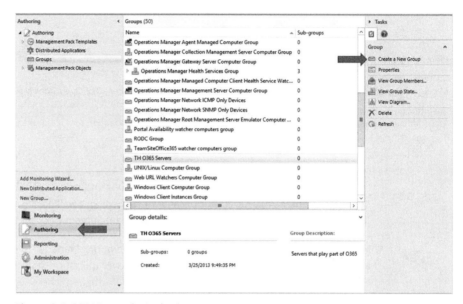

Figure 6-1 SCOM console Authoring pane.

2. On the General Properties page of the Create Group Wizard, provide a group name, provide a description, and select the Office365 management pack, as shown in Figure 6-2, and then click Next.

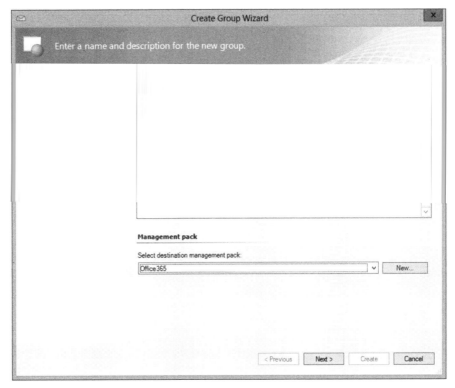

Figure 6-2 General Properties page of the Create Group Wizard.

3.   On the Choose Members from a List page, select Explicit Members, and then click
      Add/Remove Objects. On the Object Selection page, either search by object, search
      by service, or enter the name of the server you want to add to the group, as shown in
      Figure 6-3. Click Add.

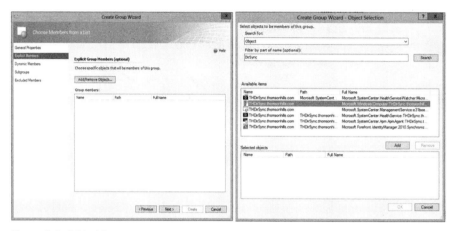

Figure 6-3 Add objects to a group.

4.   Repeat Step 3 and add all the Office 365 dependent servers. Click OK when you have
      added all the servers, and then click Next.

5.   On the Dynamic Members page, leave the defaults and click Next. You will not be
      using a formula to identify servers or services.

6.   On the Subgroups page, leave the defaults and click Next again because you will not
      be defining subgroups.

7.   On the Excluded Members page, click Create.

You have now created a group that contains the servers that Office 365 depends on. Later
in the chapter, as you create dashboards and reports, you will use this group as the targeted
scope. By doing so, the dashboards and reports will be based on the servers in this group.

Customizing System Center 2012 Operations Manager state views

In this exercise, you will modify a state view in the System Center 2012 Operations Managers console to include some key pieces of configuration data and health. A state view allows you to view the current health of servers and hardware that impact Office 365, such as AD FS and Microsoft Exchange Client Access Servers (CAS) servers. Follow these steps to con-

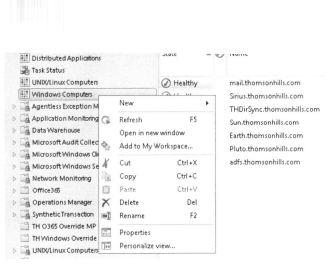

Figure 6-4 Personalizing System Center 2012 Operations Manager state views.

2. Select the fields you want to modify. For example, in Figure 6-5, we selected Logical Disk, Network Adapter, Physical Disk, and Processor. If any of these CAS hardware components fail, it might adversely impact Office 365. Click OK.

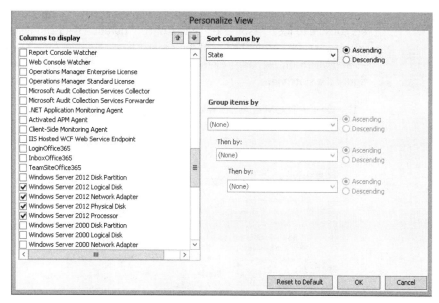

Figure 6-5 Column selection for display in the Windows Computer state view.

As shown in Figure 6-6, notice that the final result is a view that includes all the servers being managed and the health of the various hardware we selected, which in this case is the virtual hardware evidenced by the host column designating which server is running the virtual machines.

Figure 6-6 Customized Windows Computer state view.

Customizing System Center 2012 Operations Manager alert views

Next we'll demonstrate how to add the Repeat Count value to an alert view to help notify administrators of ongoing issues. Follow these steps to create an alert:

1. On the System Center Operations workspace, right-click the Active Alerts view and

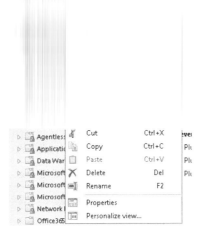

Figure 6-7 Personalizing System Center 2012 Operations Manager alert views.

2. Scroll down to the end of the list and select Repeat Count, as shown in Figure 6-8.

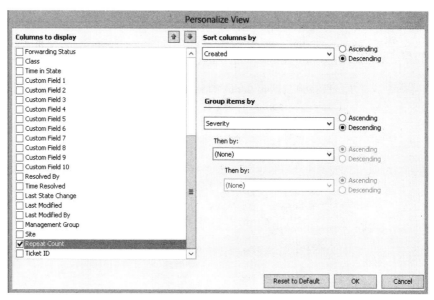

Figure 6-8 Column selection for the Active Alerts alert view.

3. The screen shot in Figure 6-9 shows the number of times the alert has been generated. This provides valuable insight for administrators.

Figure 6-9 Active Alerts view after it has been personalized.

Tuning the Office 365 management pack and reducing false alarms

The Office 365 management pack is only one of several that you will use to monitor Office 365 and its relevant infrastructure. This management pack is merely an example of what can be monitored with the SCOM Web Application Monitoring Wizard. The Office 365

- Accessing an Office 365 team site

Important

Logging on to and accessing an Office 365 mailbox might validate its database availability. However, within an Office 365 tenant mailboxes are spread across numerous databases, meaning other mailboxes might not be online and hence SCOM would generate a false positive. The Office 365 solution abstracts this from the user intentionally, which differs from how Exchange on-premises works. SCOM has no ability to monitor Microsoft Exchange databases in Office 365 currently.

Accessing the Office 365 team site is a valid monitoring test, but is also dependent upon a customer's network infrastructure, Internet Service Provider, and a variety of other variables including power, routing, and so on. Because monitoring any cloud solution from on-premises involves these risks, care should be taken when investigating whether an outage was flagged because of a cloud solution problem, an on-premises problem, or something between your data center and the cloud solution.

Chapter 6

To accurately monitor the Office 365 tenant availability, the service health dashboard in the Office 365 admin center should be used. This dashboard details the health and availability of all Office 365 services and their sub-services, such as email and calendar access under Exchange Online. The ideal monitoring solution for Office 365 is to query the service health dashboard today column on an interval and map the 9 possible states in the Office 365 service health status legend to SCOM monitor states. Monitoring the Office 365 service health dashboard is an evolving topic that we will continue to cover by providing regular updates at the following blog: *http://blogs.technet.com/b/mghazai/archive/2013/06/17/system-center-2012-operations-manager-web-application-monitoring-example.aspx.*

In summary, while monitoring Office 365 from your on-premises monitoring solution is a viable option, there are many factors that might cause your uptime to appear differently than what the cloud solutions uptime actually is. This could work both against or for you. This topic is discussed at the System Center Central website at *http://www.systemcentercentral.com.*

SCOM monitoring performs synthetic transactions, which are like user requests. These transactions run on a scheduled interval by using a SCOM watcher node. A watcher node is a SCOM agent-managed system designated to test synthetic transactions against remote systems. The result from each test is then validated to ensure that a response indicating a successful transaction was received. When such a response is received, the watcher node determines the service is healthy; otherwise, the watcher node will trigger an alert.

To enable monitoring of your Office 365 environment, perform the following steps:

1. Create an account that will be used by SCOM to access Office 365 to make sure services are available. Ensure that the account is replicated to Office 365 if directory synchronization is implemented. Make sure to assign the account an Office 365 license. Provide the account the correct level of access rights to SharePoint online. For this exercise, we have created an account called O365TesterAccount and provided it with an Office 365 license and access rights to the SharePoint Online team site.

> **Note**
>
> It's a best practice to set the test account, used by SCOM to access Office 365, to not expire so that the synthetic transaction will not fail and skew reports and Service Level Agreement (SLA) monitoring.

2. On the SCOM Operator console, click the Administration workspace.

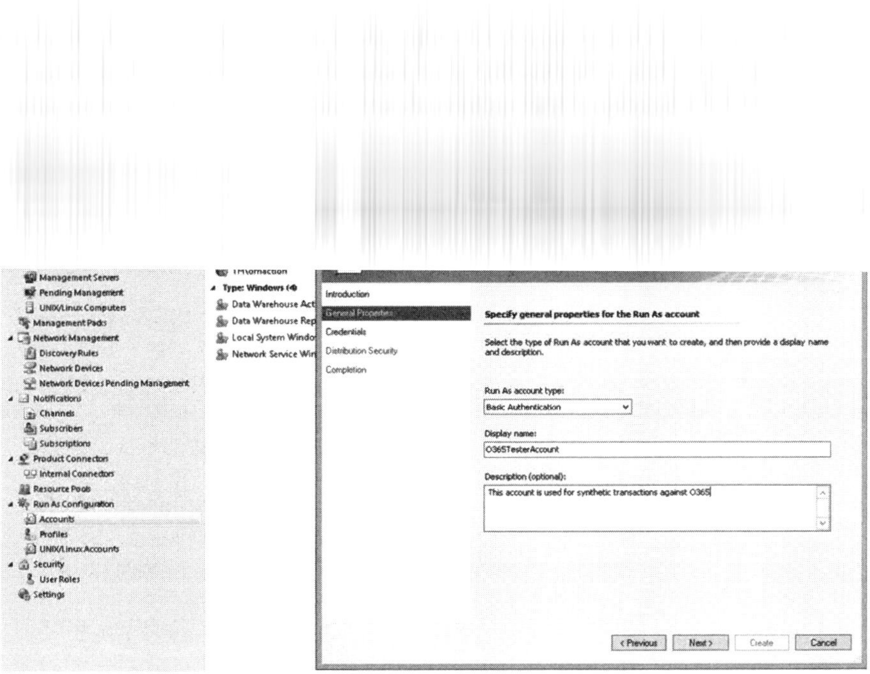

Figure 6-10 Office 365 MP Run As account type and Display name.

4. Enter the account name and password, as shown in Figure 6-11. Click Next.

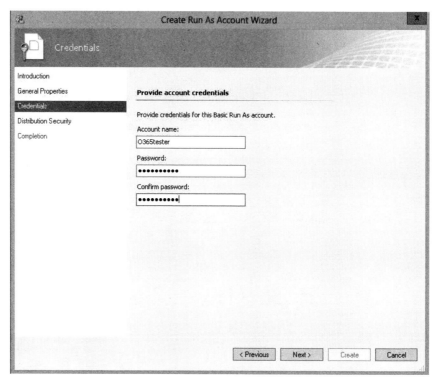

Figure 6-11 Office 365 MP Run As Account Credentials page.

5. Select the credential distribution method, as shown in Figure 6-12. In this exercise, we have chosen Less secure, which distributes the run-as account to all managed systems. This allows any system to act as an Office 365 watcher node.

6. Click Create.

Note

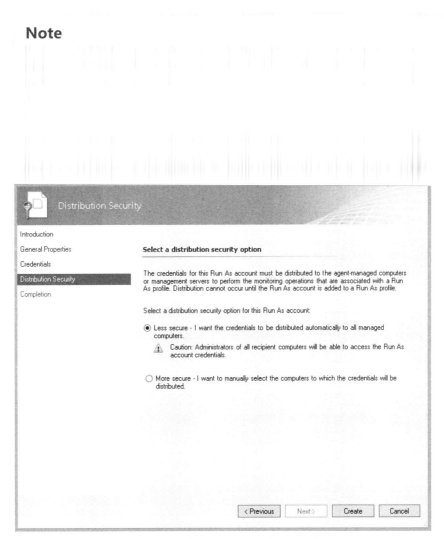

Figure 6-12 Office 365 MP Run As Account Distribution Security page.

7.   The Run As account will be created and, if successful, you will receive a confirmation, as shown in Figure 6-13. Click Close.

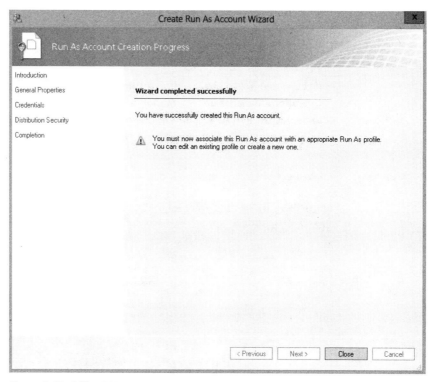

Figure 6-13 Office 365 MP Run As Account Creation Progress page.

You must now link the Office365Profile Run As profile with the Run As account you just created. The Office 365 Run As profile was created when the O365 Management Pack was imported into SCOM.

8.   On the SCOM console, click Administration on the navigation menu, expand the Run As Configuration node, and click Profiles.

9.   On the Profiles pane, locate and double-click Office365Profile. The Run As Profile Wizard will start.

10. Click Next on the Introduction page.

11. On the General Properties page, enter a description and change the display name if you choose to do so. Click Next.

12. On the Run As Accounts page, if you see a [Deleted account] listed, as shown in Figure 6-14, remove the [Deleted account] account.

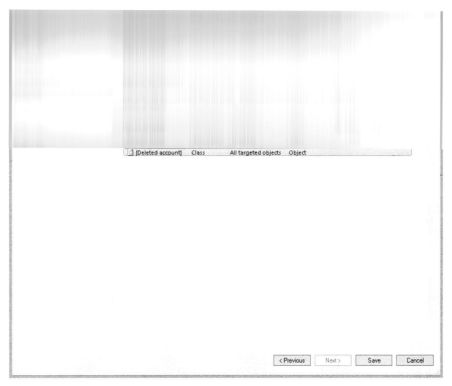

Figure 6-14 Office 365 MP Run As Accounts page of the Run As Profile Wizard.

13. Add the O365TesterAccount. Leave the default setting of All targeted objects, then click OK, as shown in Figure 6-15.

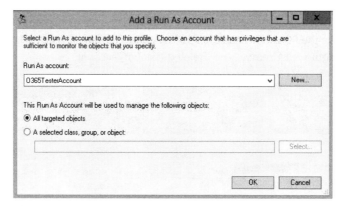

Figure 6-15 Office 365 MP Add a Run As Account selection.

14. Click Save, as shown in Figure 6-16, to finish the account configuration for the Office 365 MP.

Figure 6-16 Office 365 MP Run As Profile selected account.

INSIDE OUT   Check the Run As account by using it once manually

The Office 365 Run As account will need to be licensed within your Office 365 environment. It will also need to have a valid mailbox in Office 365 and access to the team site you will be testing against. Make sure to log on to the mailbox online at least once before testing to configure the time zone settings, otherwise the Inbox monitoring will fail until this is completed because it is expecting a mailbox web page, not the time zone selection page.

Configuring the watcher nodes

As mentioned earlier, a watcher node is an agent that runs monitors and rules that test an application or feature on a remote system. In this case, you will be using a watcher node to monitor and test Office 365.

INSIDE OUT **Why is it a best practice to use watcher nodes to monitor Office 365?**

Watcher nodes can validate that access to Office 365 is healthy, and it also can collect a slew of metrics in the process. For example, a watcher node can determine how long it took to connect to Office 365, resolve the resource, and traverse the network to it. It also can provide the total round trip response time from the resource. This can help provide insight to the end-user's experience with Office 365.

Follow these steps to configure the Office 365 MP to have a single watcher node for all three Office 365 monitoring scenarios for InboxOffice365, LoginOffice365, and TeamSiteOffice365:

1. On the SCOM console navigation pane, click Authoring and expand the Management Pack Templates node. Then click Web Application Transaction Monitoring, as shown in Figure 6-17.

    ### Note
    The three test synthetic transactions are already created through the Office 365 MP import process.

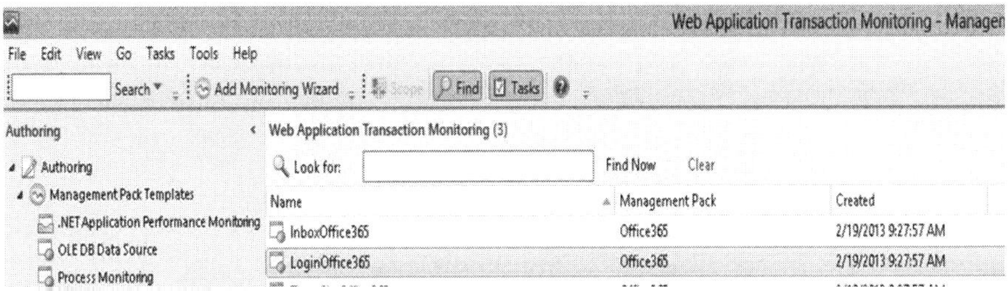

start the Web Application Editor, as shown in Figure 6-18.

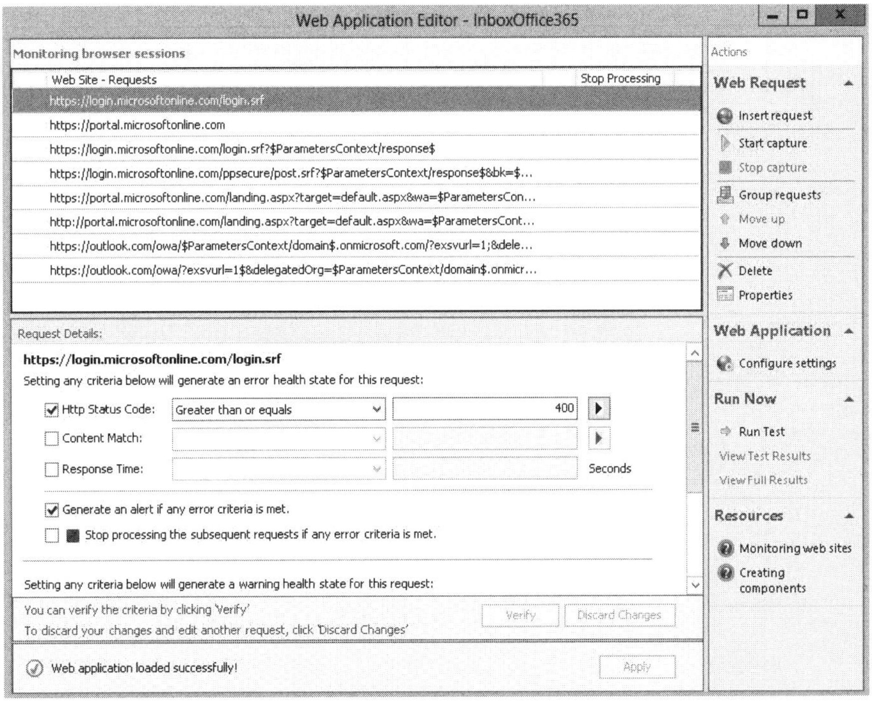

Figure 6-18 Office 365 MP LoginOffice365 transaction properties.

On the Actions pane, click Configure Settings and select the Watcher Node tab in the Web Application Properties dialog box, as shown in Figure 6-19.

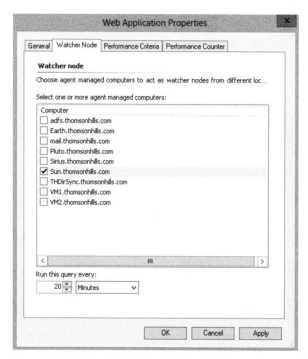

Figure 6-19 Office 365 MP LoginOffice365 Transaction Watcher Node settings.

3. Select the server or servers you want to be the watcher node(s), and set the monitoring interval by specifying a time for the Run the query every option. In this example, the watcher node will test the inbox availability every 20 minutes. Click OK.

> **Note**
>
> If the interval is less than 10 minutes, false alerts might occur.

4. Click Apply to commit the changes and note the confirmation that the web application loaded successfully, as shown in Figure 6-20.

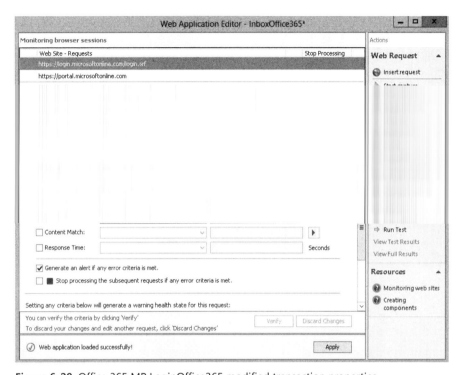

Figure 6-20 Office 365 MP LoginOffice365 modified transaction properties.

5. Repeat these steps to configure the watcher node and set the synthetic transaction frequency for the InboxOffice365 and TeamSiteOffice365 web application transactions.

Now that you have configured the watcher nodes, give the system some time to capture statistics. The captured statistics will be displayed in dashboards. Follow these steps to view the statistics:

1. On the SCOM Operator console, click the Monitoring workspace on the navigation pane.

2. Expand the Office365 MP and select the StateAlertPerformance dashboard. The Office365 MP populated the Alert, State, and Performance views into a single dashboard view, as shown in Figure 6-21. Notice that in the 24-hour graph, you are capturing the number of seconds each transaction takes as they run every 20 minutes.

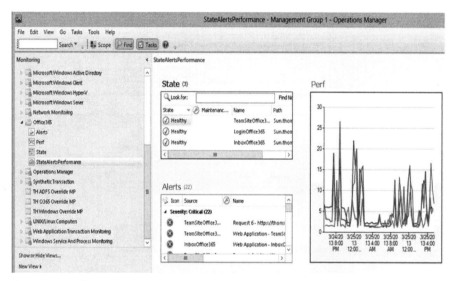

Figure 6-21 Office365 MP State, Alerts, and Performance dashboard.

> ## Note
>
> For additional guidance about how to monitor Office 365 with this MP, see the System Center Central Operations Manager blog at *http://www.systemcentercentral.com/scom-monitoring-office-365/#comment-2298*.

System Center 2012 Operations Manager report customization

Installing reporting is an option during the initial SCOM installation. When selected, the reporting installation creates a SCOM data warehouse called OperationsManagerDW. This data warehouse stores all the monitoring data System Center 2012 Operations Manager collects. By default, most of the data is stored for 400 days, which is approximately 13

Reporting is accessed through the Reporting pane on the SCOM console, as shown in Figure 6-22. Most MPs imported into SCOM will include reports. These reports are usually specific to the technology the MP is designed to monitor, although some are generic enough that they can be used for a variety of purposes and are easily customizable.

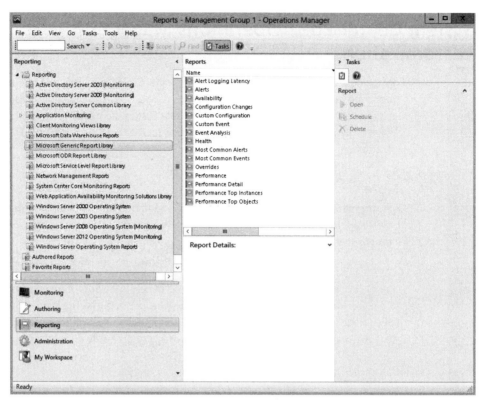

Figure 6-22 Operator console Reporting workspace and list of reports.

Reports are also accessible directly on the Report Tasks pane on the SCOM Monitoring workspace. The Report Tasks pane on the Operator console is context sensitive. Figure 6-23 shows the Microsoft Active Directory Reports available directly on the Monitoring workspace.

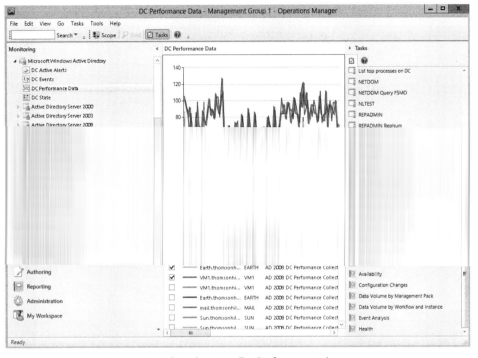

Figure 6-23 Active Directory MP domain controller Performance view.

As you select different items to monitor, notice that the list of available reports changes. Follow these steps to customize a report:

1. Select TeamSiteOffice365 and pick the Availability report to see the availability of TeamSiteOffice365, as shown in Figure 6-24.

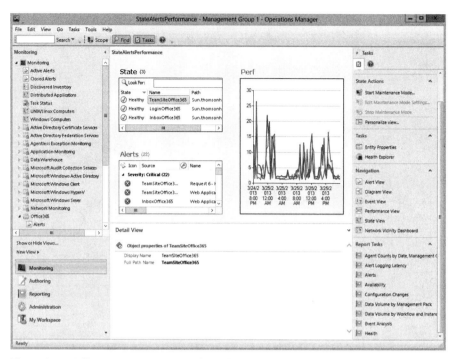

Figure 6-24 Office 365 MP reports available from the dashboard view.

2.   Once the Availability report has opened, select the start and end points you want to report against. Figure 6-25 illustrates configuring a report for the last 24 hours.

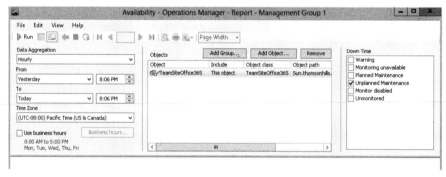

Figure 6-25 Office 365 MP Availability report smart header options.

3. Once you have configured the report, click Run in the upper-left corner. This will generate a SQL Reporting Services report, as shown in Figure 6-26. The report can also be exported to XML, CSV, PDF, MHTML, Excel, TIFF, or Word format. Because these reports are generated by SQL Reporting Services, they can also be scheduled and sent to an email account, UNC share, or SharePoint documents list. This is great for being able to go back, look at trends retroactively, and identify peak utilization times.

Figure 6-26 Office 365 TeamSiteOffice365 Availability report.

4. Click the Availability Tracker to see the outage details, as shown in Figure 6-27. This illustrates how we can see that the Office 365 site has been available only 94.65 percent of the time in the last 24 hours and when it was down.

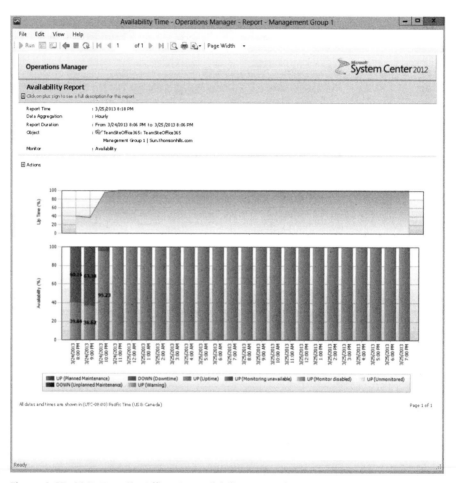

Figure 6-27 O365 TeamSiteOffice365 Availability report detail.

As you explore the reports, note that you navigate using the browser and hyperlinks. What we have shown is an easy way to report on the SLA of Office 365 and valuable insight into the overall SLA of Office 365 as well as the dependent on-premises technologies. This can also be used to validate your uptime and determine if Office 365 is meeting the advertised SLA. The reports also provide insight as to which dependencies might be affecting the SLA of Office 365.

Dashboard creation for technical and business owners

An alternative or supplement to reports is the concept of dashboards. Dashboards are graphical views of system and service status. The term was derived from vehicle dashboards where all the important pertinent information is displayed for the driver. If there are any problems with the vehicle, warning indicators will light up on the dashboard to help the driver take the necessary actions.

lished to Microsoft SharePoint Portal Server. They provide in-depth system state and alerts and are tailored for system administrators.

INSIDE OUT **Why do some System Center 2012 Operations Manager graphs not provide any counters to select?**

Whenever a dashboard is created and a graph is selected, if no counters show up below, this is an indication that the counter for this graph is currently not being collected.

Figure 6-28 shows an Office 365 dashboard. It shows the state of the team site, alerts, alert details, and performance. This is an example of an Office 365 dashboard that you will be building.

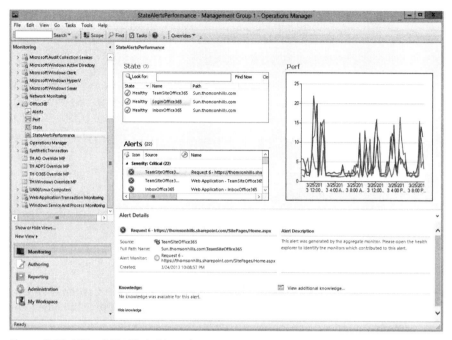

Figure 6-28 Office 365 MP dashboard.

How to create a custom Office 365 dashboard

In this section we will walk through the process to create a custom dashboard for your Office 365 subscription. Follow these steps to begin customizing your first dashboard:

1. On the SCOM Operator console, click the Monitoring workspace.

2. On the Monitoring workspace, right-click the Office365 MP and click New. Select Dashboard View, as shown in Figure 6-29.

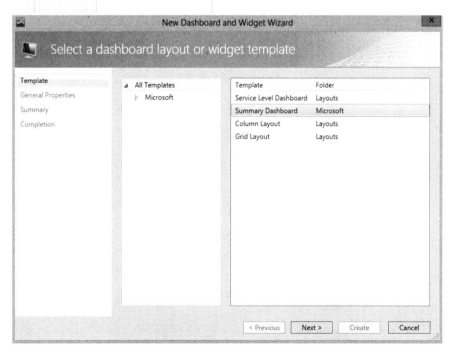

Figure 6-30 Choosing a dashboard template from the New Dashboard and Widget Wizard.

4. Provide a title for the dashboard and click Next, as shown in Figure 6-31.

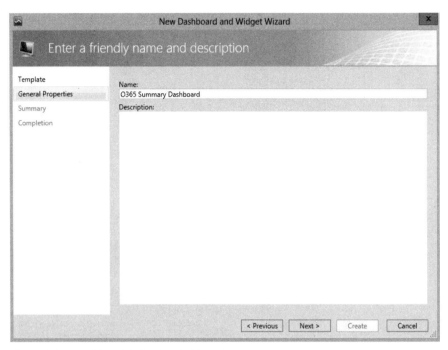

Figure 6-31 Provide a title for the dashboard.

5. Click Create.

6. Click Close. The dashboard will be rendered in the Operator console under your Office 365 MP, as shown in Figure 6-32. At this point most of the views are blank.

7. By clicking the gear icon at the upper-right corner of each display, as shown in Figure 6-32, you can click Configure and set the options for the dashboard.

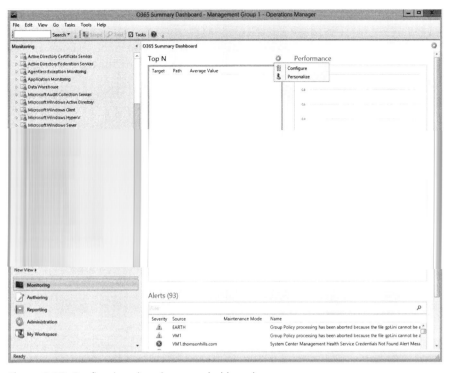

Figure 6-32 Configuring views in a new dashboard.

8. At the beginning of this chapter, you created a group of servers and named the group Office 365 Servers. Now you will use this group to scope each of these views. Click the respective gear on the upper-right corner of each dashboard pane, and select Configure from the drop-down menu.

9. On the General Properties page of the Update Configuration Wizard, modify the title and description if necessary, and then click Next.

10. On the Scope page, click Add to target this dashboard to a group of computers. This is where you will use the Office 365 Servers group. In the Add Groups or Objects dialog box, enter the name of the group in the text box, as shown in Figure 6-33. Select the group from the Available items list, and then click Add. Click OK.

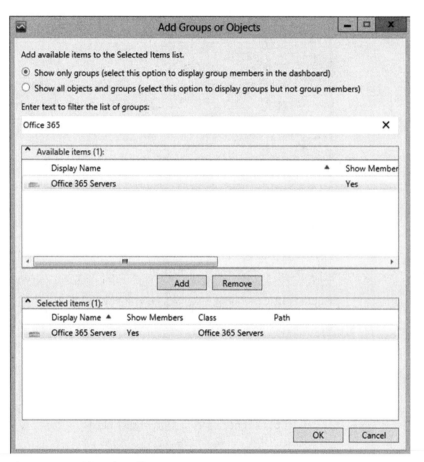

Figure 6-33 Adding the Office 365 Servers Group.

11. At this point, you can click Next to make modifications to the Criteria and Display properties of this dashboard, or you can click Finish to complete the configuration. For this exercise, click Finish.

12. The configured dashboard, based on monitoring information targeted at the servers in the Office 365 Servers group, is now displayed, as shown in Figure 6-34.

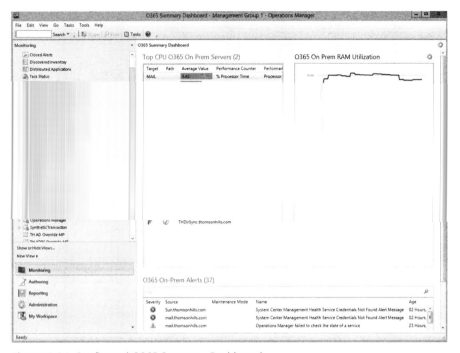

Figure 6-34 Configured O365 Summary Dashboard.

Office 365 service level agreement dashboards

Office 365 has a financially backed 99.9 percent service level agreement (SLA) for availability. You can create a dashboard to track this SLA so you can promptly request subscription credits in the event that your subscription to Office 365 fails to meet the SLA.

Remember, too, that the 99.9 percent SLA of Office 365 is meaningless if the on-premises technologies that it depends on fail. The bottom line is that monitoring Office 365 is an important activity, which at the very least is documented proof of satisfactory service delivery to your business.

SLA dashboards are easy to create in SCOM. Follow these steps to create SLA dashboards:

1. On the SCOM Operator console, select the Authoring workspace and expand Management Pack Objects.

2. Right-click Service Level Tracking and select Create from the menu.

3. On the General page of the Service Level Tracking Wizard, provide a name for this SLA dashboard. For this exercise, we will use O365 SLA as the name, as shown in Figure 6-35. Click Next.

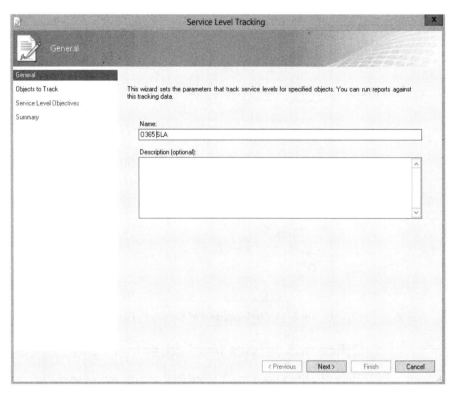

Figure 6-35 Creating service level tracking.

4. On the Objects to Track page, click Select.

5. On the Select a Target Class page, select All in the Search result filter drop-down box. Then enter Team in the Look for box. Finally, select TeamSiteOffice365 in the results list, as shown in Figure 6-36. Click OK.

Figure 6-36 Select TeamSiteOffice365 to monitor for SLA adherence.

> **Note**
> You can use this same process to monitor non-Office 365 websites, such as *www. bing.com*. This will monitor your Internet connection and trend the SLA of your ISP, which is an important Office 365 dependency.

6. Click Next.

7. On the Service Level Objectives page, click Add and select Monitor state SLO, as shown in Figure 6-37.

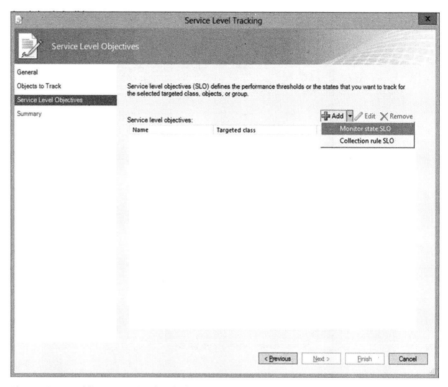

Figure 6-37 Adding a service level objective.

8. Provide a name, set the Monitor field to Availability, and set the Service level objective goal to 99.900, as shown in Figure 6-38.

9. As shown in Figure 6-38, select the following states to monitor: Unplanned maintenance, Unmonitored, and Monitoring unavailable. Click OK.

Figure 6-38 Service Level Objective threshold and state settings.

10. Click Next, and on the Summary page, click Finish.

The preceding steps walked you through the creation of an SLA that monitors the availability of the Office 365 team site, which essentially monitors the availability of SharePoint Online. You can repeat these steps to create an SLA definition for Exchange Online.

The final step is to create a dashboard based on the SLA definition for the Office 365 team site (SharePoint Online):

1. On the SCOM console, select the Monitoring workspace.

2. Right-click Office 365, select New, and then select Dashboard View.

3. On the New Dashboard and Widget Wizard page, select Service Level Dashboard as the template. Click Next.

4. Name the dashboard and provide a description if desired. Click Next.

5. On the Scope page, click Add.

6. In the Add SLA dialog box, select an SLA from the Available items list. The SLA you created during Steps 1 through 11 should be listed. Click Add, and then click OK.

7. Click Next.

8. On the Summary page, click Create. Figure 6-39 shows the SLA dashboard that will be created.

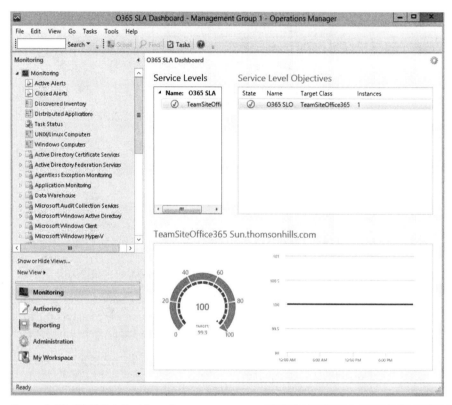

Figure 6-39 O365 SLA Dashboard.

Refer to TechNet or other books on SCOM if you want to learn more about monitoring and dashboard creation using SCOM. This book and chapter is focused only on customizing SCOM to monitor Office 365.

Summary

In this chapter we took a more in-depth look at monitoring and creating reports and dashboards for Office 365 using System Center 2012 Operations Manager. SCOM is a very powerful enterprise monitoring solution. If your organization already has SCOM, this chapter showed you how to leverage and extend SCOM to monitor Office 365 using the Office 365 MP. If your organization does not currently have a monitoring solution or is in the

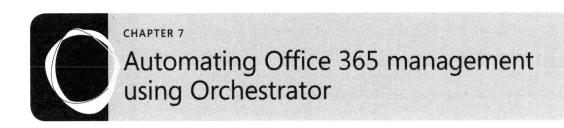

Automating Office 365 management using Orchestrator

System Center 2012 Orchestrator 325   Installing Orchestrator. 330

Orchestrator is a software solution that provides workflow automation for almost any business process, known in the industry as IT process automation (ITPA). Forward-thinking companies embrace automation to provide services and accomplish more with less. The support for Microsoft Office 365 automation with Orchestrator is not limited to your organization's data center, but also expands automation used to complete any cloud services.

When deciding to automate a business process, the rule-of-thumb to remember is return on investment (ROI). A business process, such as manually creating an Office 365 email account, might add 15 to 20 minutes a day. That process might be a good candidate for automation and provides a great ROI. A new Office 365 account creation time using Orchestrator is less than five minutes. In addition, a human resources (HR) task worker can start the process without IT staff involvement. In this chapter, we focus on automating the creation of Office 365 email accounts, but you can use Orchestrator to automate many other administrative tasks, such as password changes or providing user information such as a location or a name.

Orchestrator is designed for the enterprise because it uses the cloud model to deliver automation for services so business application owners have greater flexibility and freedom to grow their industries. Orchestrator includes the Runbook Designer component, which is used to create and publish Orchestrator runbooks. The Runbook Server is the component responsible for "running" the runbooks. The Management Server component is used to import Integration Packs (IPs). After an IP is imported, the Management Server makes the IP available to the Runbook Server.

Orchestrator can provide the following benefits:

- Greater opportunity to grow business

- Faster response to business needs

- Better use of IT staff

- Improved customer service

Orchestrator, formerly known as Opalis, has continually improved, with many of the work-flow automation technologies integrated into the System Center suite. In 2009, Opalis Software became a subsidiary of Microsoft Corporation. The ITPA in Opalis provided commanding capability to assist in IT operations. Opalis removed the associated overhead of manual IT responses to business problems. The acquisition of Opalis Software and the three-year integration into the System Center suite included the rebranding of Opalis to System Center 2012 Orchestrator. Orchestrator complements Microsoft's IT service delivery of building, managing, monitoring, and now automating data centers and cloud services.

In this chapter, you will learn how to install and use Orchestrator in System Center 2012 SP1 to automate Office 365 management tasks. We will narrow our process to building an automated runbook to create an Office 365 account for a new user. In Chapter 8, "Office 365 and Service Manager automation," we will show you how to use the Self-Service Portal in System Center 2012 Service Manager to make the Orchestrator runbook available to an HR department.

Orchestrator overview and concepts

Orchestrator is a server service that, at its core, is designed for automation by supporting the need for business process orchestration. Orchestrator is based on the IT Infrastructure Library (ITIL) and Microsoft Operations Framework (MOF). Both ITIL and MOF are frameworks for efficiency and best practices of IT operations.

Introducing Orchestrator

In Orchestrator, you can automate IT processes using the Runbook Designer interface to link activities (icons) by selecting them individually and dragging and dropping them onto the designer interface. An activity can be thought of as an icon that has software properties. These properties are unique to each activity and allow specific software functions such as querying Active Directory, reading a text file, or sending email. Each activity performs a specific task when it is activated, or runs. The activity is built in a runbook that is created in the Runbook Designer. A runbook can consist of a single activity or multiple activities. You can connect multiple activities together by linking them together. Figure 7-1 shows a representation of a runbook with four activities linked together.

Figure 7-1 Orchestrator runbook example that has four activities.

match of numbers and text. Once the Find Text criteria are met, the Write Web Page activity will run. This activity uses the text information from the preceding Find Text activity and appends data to a web page or creates a new web page based on an HTML template. The final activity, the Send Mail activity, sends an email notification to an email address with a message that the runbook has finished.

Applying the runbook concept to Office 365

In Figure 7-1, the Monitor Folder activity has properties that would search for a file with any name. The file could be a text file that contains information about a user account. It could contain the user's User Principle Name (UPN), first name, and last name. The second activity in the runbook could be configured to read the information and pass it in a variable to the next activity. You could then use this runbook to create a new account in Office 365 using a Windows PowerShell cmdlet. You will learn more about Office 365 Windows PowerShell cmdlets in Chapter 9, "Windows PowerShell for Office 365."

Now, instead of writing data to a web page as the third activity, we will run a Windows PowerShell cmdlet instead. Figure 7-2 shows the minor change in the runbook to support the Run Program activity. The change in our activity to a run program provides the capability to create the new user account in Active Directory and then run the *DirSync* command to synchronize the account in Office 365, followed by the Windows PowerShell cmdlet to assign Office 365 licenses to the user account.

Monitor   Find Text   Run Program   Send Email
Folder

Figure 7-2 Orchestrator runbook example using the Office 365 DirSync Windows PowerShell cmdlet as an option.

After the new Office 365 account is created, email will be sent to the Office 365 administrator to notify her that a new account was created successfully.

The runbook shown in Figure 7-2 is the basis for creating business automation in IT. This simple example of quickly automating a mundane task can be expanded to support almost any complex process.

Orchestrator includes standard activities, such as monitors, tasks, and other runbook controls. The standard activities are organized into IPs. The IPs supported by Microsoft are included with System Center. Orchestrator has been extended to include additional functionality for third-party products and technologies to support more complex IT automation in other IPs. Additional IPs to extend into third-party products are created by partners or created by in-house developers using the System Center 2012 Orchestrator Software Development Kit (SDK). Many third-party IPs are obtained separately.

INSIDE OUT   Licensing System Center Integration Packs

Virtual Server hosts are licensed using System Center 2012 Datacenter licenses and physical servers are licensed with System Center 2012 Standard. Both of these are licensed per physical processor (not core). Both licensing models provide all the System Center components in the suite, including Orchestrator, with all Integration Packs supported by Microsoft. For more information, see *http://download.microsoft.com/download/8/7/0/870B5D9B-ACF1-4192-BD0A-543AF551B7AE/System%20Center%20 2012%20Licensing%20FAQ.pdf.*

Orchestrator includes many Integration Packs. The following list is a sample of popular Integration Packs:

- Active Directory

- Exchange Admin

- Exchange Users

- VMware vSphere

- Windows Azure

- All Microsoft System Center components

Using Orchestrator components

As shown in Figure 7-3, Orchestrator has several useful components. The Runbook Designer is used to create, modify, and publish Orchestrator runbooks. The Runbook Designer publishes all runbooks to the runbook server, and the runbook server executes the runbooks. The management server imports the IPs. After an IP is imported, the management server makes the IP available to the runbook server. The runbook server is where individual activities in the runbook are executed.

The Orchestration database is a Microsoft SQL Server database that stores all the data, runbooks, and log files. The Orchestrator web service is a Microsoft Internet Information Services (IIS)-based website that provides a web interface into the Orchestration database. The Orchestration console uses the IIS web service to access data.

These are all the major components of Orchestrator. Other features necessary for a more complete architectural deployment include the Runbook Tester, which is part of the Runbook Designer interface. Additional runbook servers can be added for load distribution and high availability in a large enterprise.

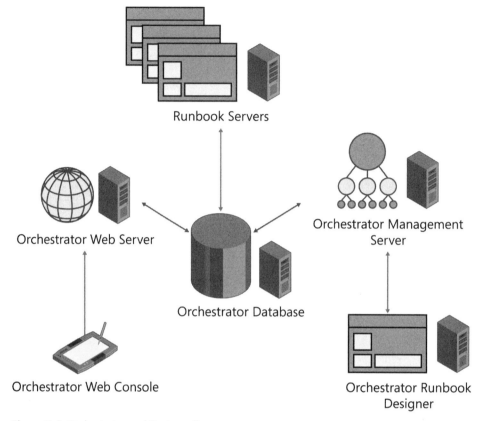

Figure 7-3 Orchestrator architecture diagram.

Installing Orchestrator

We now need to better understand Orchestrator automation, specifically so we can build Office 365 runbooks. You need to understand what the requirements are for a test server and how to set it up for testing. After you've finished the next few exercises, you will be able to move forward with a proof of concept (POC) or a small pilot deployment.

If you follow these steps and examples, you will begin to see how easy Orchestrator automation can be performed without writing a single line of code. That does not mean that if you are continuing to build your Windows PowerShell scripting library, that scripts cannot be used. You can use Windows PowerShell, C#, and other scripts in Orchestrator to help improve almost any business processes with IT automation.

Prerequisites for installing Orchestrator for testing

You need the following hardware to install Orchestrator in System Center 2012 SP1 on a single computer:

- 1 gigabyte (GB) of random access memory (RAM) (2 GB recommended)

- 200 megabyte (MB) of hard drive (500 MB recommended)

There are additional considerations for our test server:

- Orchestrator requires only the basic Microsoft SQL Server found in the database engine service. No additional SQL features are required.

- Orchestrator cannot be installed on an Active Directory domain controller server.

The following are other software and network configuration requirements to complete during the Windows Server installation for your single computer installation testing:

- Microsoft .NET Framework 3.5 SP1

- Microsoft .NET Framework 4.0 (included as a feature in Windows Server 2012)

- Optional: enabled IIS for Orchestrator web services

- Optional: Internet connection for Office 365 communication

INSIDE OUT   Microsoft TechNet guidance and downloads

For more information about installing individual Orchestrator components, see *http://technet.microsoft.com/en-us/library/hh420348.aspx*.

Installing prerequisites for Orchestrator

Identify or build a computer running Windows Server on which to install Orchestrator and follow these steps to install prerequisites:

1. Connect to the server (the name of our server in this example is SCO). Select Add roles and features from the Server Manager Dashboard, as shown in Figure 7-4.

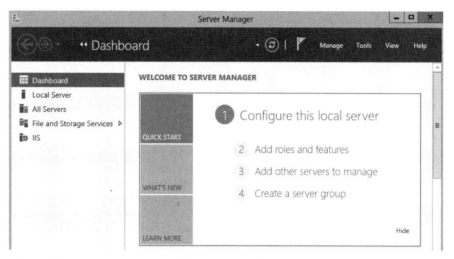

Figure 7-4 Windows Server 2012 Add roles and features.

2. Select the Add roles and features option, select the Server Name, then click Next.

3. Select the Enable the Web Server (IIS) component and allow any additional features required during this installation, as shown in Figure 7-5.

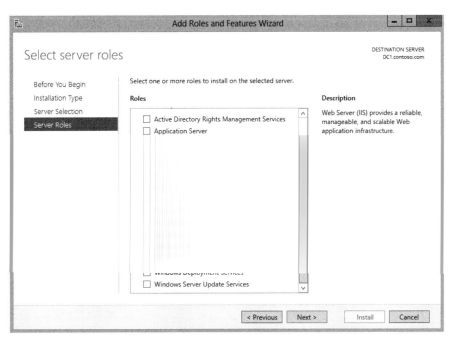

Figure 7-5 Windows Server 2012 Add Roles and Features Wizard.

4. Restart the computer to allow the Web Services role to finish installing.

5. Next, click Features and then select .NET Framework 3.5 Features (installed), as shown in Figure 7-6.

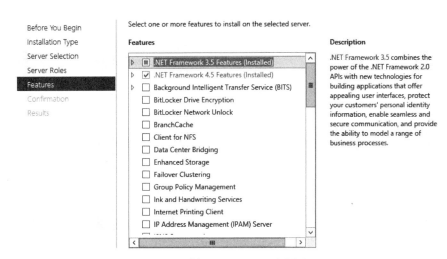

Figure 7-6 Windows Server 2012 Add .NET Framework 3.5 Features.

Installing Microsoft SQL Server

Now we will need to install SQL Server 2008 R2 or SQL Server 2012. Orchestrator requires only the SQL Database framework, so no additional SQL features are required. For the installation in our example, we will use SQL Server 2008 R2.

1. Connect to the Orchestrator server, insert the SQL Server installation DVD, and notice that the default option is Planning, as shown in Figure 7-7. Click the second option, Installation, to start the SQL Server Installation Wizard.

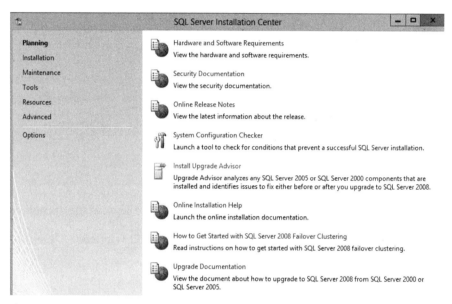

Figure 7-7 SQL Server Installation Center.

2. Choose the option to install a new SQL Server stand-alone installation, as shown in Figure 7-8.

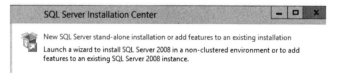

Figure 7-8 SQL Server new stand-alone installation.

3. Choose the SQL Server Data Server installation, accept all defaults, and finalize the installation. Allow Microsoft Windows Update Server to update the SQL Server database, and then restart the server.

Completing the installation for Orchestrator

Follow these steps to install Orchestrator in System Center 2012 SP1:

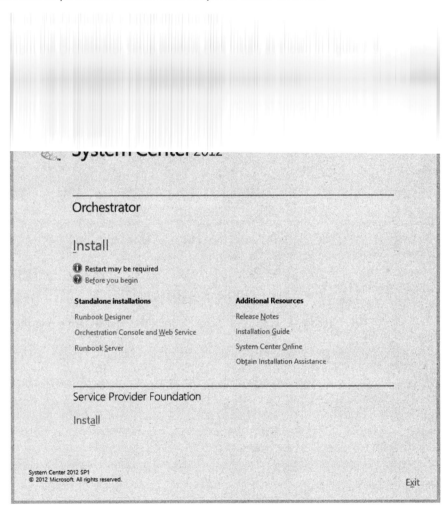

Figure 7-9 Orchestrator Setup.

3. On the Product registration page, enter the name and organization, as shown in Figure 7-10.

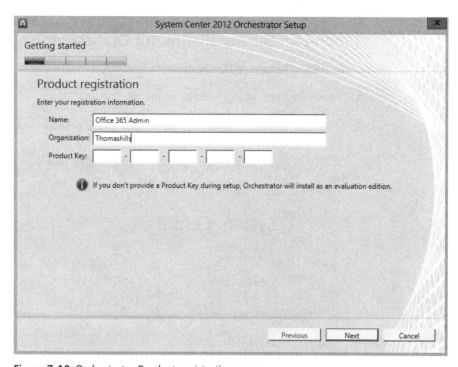

Figure 7-10 Orchestrator Product registration page.

4. Read and accept the Microsoft Software License Terms, and then click Next.

5. Notice all features for installation are enabled, as shown in Figure 7-11, so simply click Next.

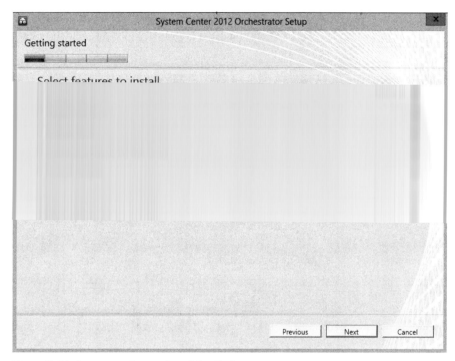

Figure 7-11 Feature options to install for Orchestrator.

6. The Orchestrator installation validates that all prerequisites are complete. After validation, the Configure the service account page appears. On this page, enter the user name (service account) and password, and select the domain from the drop-down box, as shown in Figure 7-12. Click Test to validate the account name and password. Clicking the Next button also runs the validation test for the account name and password.

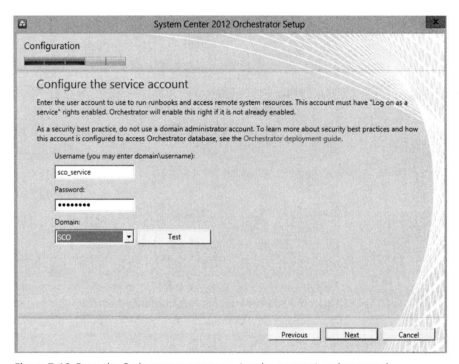

Figure 7-12 Enter the Orchestrator user name (service account) and password.

7. Specify the server name, specify the port number, and confirm that the default Windows Authentication method is selected, as shown in Figure 7-13. In our example, SQL Server is installed on the Orchestrator server, and there is no need to change the default port. Click Next.

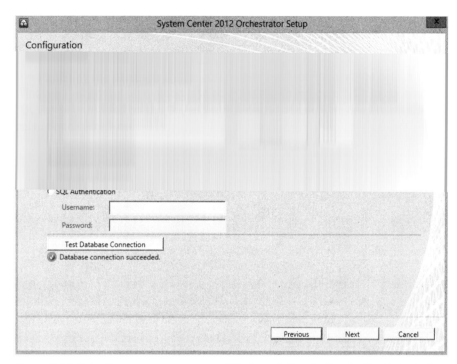

Figure 7-13 Enter the server name and use Windows Authentication for the Orchestrator database.

8. Create a new database for Orchestrator, as shown in Figure 7-14, then click Next.

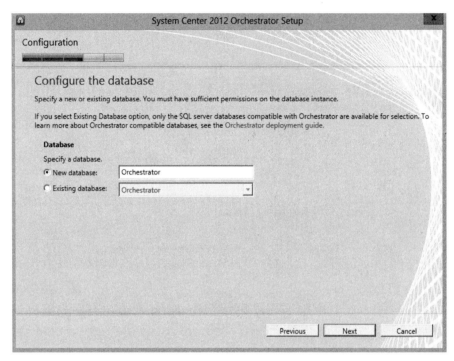

Figure 7-14 New installation with Orchestrator as the database name.

9. Take note of the name of the default user group for Orchestrator, and select the Grant remote access to the Runbook Designer check box, as shown in Figure 7-15. Click Next.

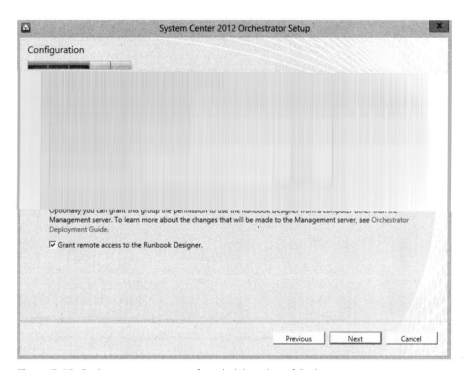

Figure 7-15 Options to grant access for administration of Orchestrator.

10. Take note of and accept the default ports for both the Web Service port and the Orchestration console port, as shown in Figure 7-16, and then click Next.

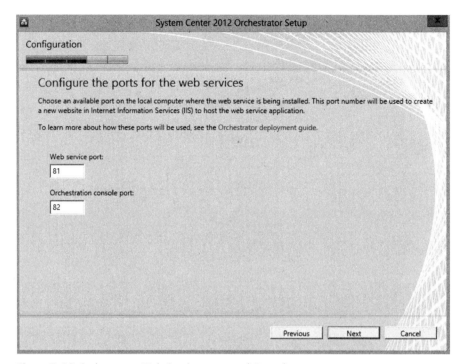

Figure 7-16 Orchestrator Web Services port and Console port.

11. Accept the default location to install on the C: drive, and then click Next.

12. Choose whether to provide feedback to Microsoft, and then click Next.

13. On the Summary page, review the installation information and click Next to start the installation. When Orchestrator is successfully installed, you will be notified that setup completed successfully, as shown in Figure 7-17.

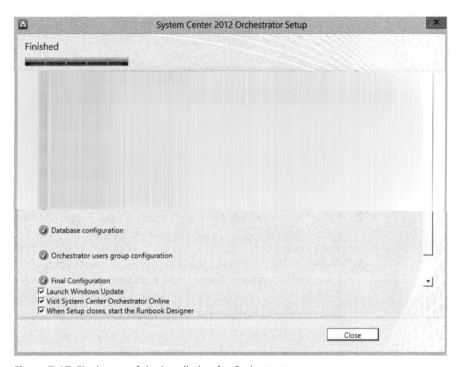

Figure 7-17 Final page of the installation for Orchestrator.

Now that you have Orchestrator installed, you need to complete a few more steps to enable some of the IPs before we can start building our Office 365 runbook.

Using Integration Packs with Office 365 automation

At this point, we are ready to download the necessary IPs. Several IPs are automatically imported during the download process. You can see the list of the default downloads at *http://www.microsoft.com/en-us/download/details.aspx?id=34611*. For our Office 365 automation, we need to import additional IPs:

- Active Directory Integration Pack

- Orchestrator Exchange Admin Integration Pack

- Service Manager Integration Pack

1. Go to the download site for System Center 2012 SP1 – Orchestrator Components Add-ons and Extensions at *http://www.microsoft.com/en-us/download/details. aspx?id=34611*.

2. Move the compressed file and un-compress the Integration Pack file on the Orchestrator server so it can be imported for use.

3. As part of our installation, the Deployment Manager component was installed. Now open the Orchestrator Deployment Manager console interface, as shown in Figure 7-18. With the console open, right-click the Integration Packs folder, and select the Register IP with the Orchestrator Management Server option.

Figure 7-18 Register IP with the Orchestrator Management Server.

4. On the Welcome screen, click Next.

5. Select Active Directory, Exchange Admin, and System Center 2012 Service Manager Integration Packs, as shown in Figure 7-19. Click Next.

Figure 7-19 Integration Packs selected for importing into Orchestrator.

6. Finish the integration of the Integration Pack files selected.

7. Validate that all the files were imported.

8. Right-click the Integration Packs folder, as shown in Figure 7-20, and select the Deploy IP to Runbook Server or Runbook Designer option.

Figure 7-20 Deploy the IP to Runbook Server or Runbook Designer.

9. The Browse for Computer dialog box appears, as shown in Figure 7-21. Click OK to deploy Integration Packs from an available Orchestrator Runbook Designer server(s).

Figure 7-21 Select the Orchestrator server that will use the Integration Packs.

10. Select Orchestrator Server and click OK.

11. Click Next, then choose to schedule or deploy now the Integration Packs. This page supports the requirement of maintenance windows for production. Click Next, and then click Close.

At this stage, all the Integration Packs we need are imported and should be available in the System Center Orchestrator Runbook Designer. Next, we will build the runbook for automating the creation of an Office 365 email account for a new user.

Creating a new runbook for Office 365 email accounts

Now that we have implemented the foundation for automation with the installation of System Center Orchestrator, it's time to create your first runbook. The next few steps support two specific goals. The first is to provide an introduction to the basics of Orchestrator and the second is to enable the automation framework to be used with Microsoft System Center Service Manager. We show you how to enable the automation framework in Chapter 8.

Follow these next steps to create the Orchestrator runbook for a new Office 365 account. However, you will not configure any of the activities. The configuration of each activity depends on a few parameters in System Center 2012 SP1 Service Manager, which we will discuss in Chapter 8.

1. Open the Runbook Designer, as shown in Figure 7-22.

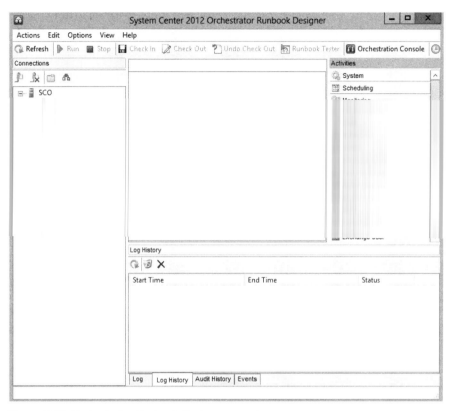

Figure 7-22 Orchestrator Runbook Designer console.

2. Expand the SCO folder, as shown in Figure 7-23, and right-click Runbooks. Select New, and then select Folder to create a new folder. In our example, we labeled the folder O365Admin. Right-click the new folder, select New, and then select Runbook.

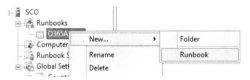

Figure 7-23 Creating a folder and runbook name for our Orchestrator project.

3. From the Orchestrator Runbook Designer menu, select Check Out Runbook, and then select and rename the runbook. For this exercise, we renamed the runbook NewOffice365Account.

4.   On the right side of the Runbook Designer, expand the Runbook Control Integration Pack folder, as shown in Figure 7-24. Select the Initialize Data activity, and then drag and drop the activity to the far left of the screen. Double-click the activity and select the Add button.

Figure 7-24 Selection of the first Orchestrator activity from the runbook IP on the Activities menu.

5.   Double-click Parameter 1 in the details pane, change the name to ActivityGUID, and click OK. ActivityGUID is used to identify the Service Manager ID. Click Finish to close the Details Information window.

6.   On the right side of the Runbook Designer, expand the Active Directory folder, select the Create User activity, and drag and drop the activity next to the Initialize Data activity.

7.   Click the Initialize Data activity. Now move your mouse to the right of the activity until the mouse turns into a crosshair. With the mouse pointer as a crosshair, click and drag to connect the Initialize Data activity with the Create User activity, as shown in Figure 7-25. This is how you link one activity to the next.

Figure 7-25 Placement and linking of the first two Orchestrator activities.

8. On the right side of the Runbook Designer, expand the Active Directory IP folder and select the Enable User activity. Drag and drop it next to the Create User activity. Link the Get Object activity to the Get Relationship activity.

9. Expand the System IP folder to choose another activity. Select the Run .Net Script activity and drag and drop it next to the Enable User activity. Link the Enable User Activity to the Run .Net Script activity. Right-click the Run .Net Script activity and change the name to DirSync PowerShell.

activities.

12. In Runbook, expand the System IP folder. Select the Run .Net Script activity. Drag and drop the activity next to the Update SR Progress activity. Right-click the Run .Net Script activity and change the name to Assign Licenses. Link these two activities.

13. In Runbook, expand the SC 2012 Service Manager IP folder and select the Update Activity activity. Link the Assign Licenses activity to the Update Activity activity.

You have now created, but not configured, the activities using Orchestrator. We will config-ure the individual activities in Chapter 8 after we install and configure System Center 2012 SP1 Service Manager. Your finished runbook should resemble the one shown in Figure 7-26. Save your runbook so you can return to finalize the configuration.

Figure 7-26 Completed placement of our runbook activities.

In this chapter you have completed the first part of a two-part process. You installed Orchestrator in System Center 2012 SP1 and built the foundation of a runbook. In Chapter 8, we will install System Center 2012 SP1 Service Manager, which will enable us to provide work flow and create a self-service portal.

Summary

By following the steps in this chapter, you have installed Orchestrator in System Center 2012 SP1, integrated essential Orchestrator IPs, and built your first runbook. Many companies with data centers build automation processes to lower costs. This automation example supports Microsoft Office 365. Orchestrator supports automation in all local data centers and off-premises cloud solutions such as Office 365, Windows Azure, and other hosted services.

Office 365 and Service Manager automation

System Center 2012 SP1 Service Manager 351   Service catalog overview. 365

I Automating Office 365 management with Orchestrator," you were introduced to System Center 2012 Orchestrator, and you started building a foundation to support automation of Office 365 manual tasks. You installed Orchestrator, imported Integration Packs (IPs), and built a runbook. You did not configure the runbook activities to work with Service Manager because the system was not installed.

In this chapter, you will install System Center 2012 Service Manager and connect Orchestrator runbooks to Service Manager. You will install the Service Manager Self-Service Portal and "publish" the Office 365 service offering into the portal for the Human Resources (HR) department. You then will finalize the runbook that you created in Chapter 7 to securely support automation of an Office 365 account to individuals in the HR department. After that, we will show you how to connect the Orchestrator runbook to Service Manager to create a service offering that users can access in the Self-Service Portal.

The project in this chapter is the model for a number of Service Manager request offerings that you can continue to build for both Office 365 and internal requests. The following steps are involved in this end-to-end process:

1. Install Service Manager.

2. Enable a connector between Service Manager and Orchestrator.

3. Configure Service Manager automation:

   a. *Complete Orchestrator integration and finalize the runbook.*

   b. *Create a runbook automation activity template.*

   c. *Create a service request template.*

    d.   Create a request offering.

    e.   Create a service offering and publish.

Service Manager components

System Center 2012 Service Manager is an integrated platform for automating and supporting the IT Infrastructure Library (ITIL) and Microsoft Operations Framework (MOF) processes. Service Manager supports change management, incident management, problem management, release management, service delivery, and more. Through its configuration management database (CMDB) and process integration, Service Manager connects information from other System Center components, such as Orchestrator, Configuration Manager, and Operations Manager. In Figure 8-1, you can see the different services in a typical architecture using two servers.

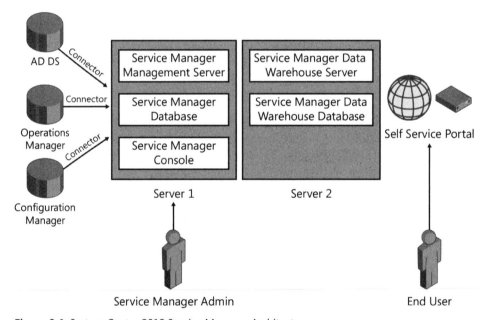

Figure 8-1 System Center 2012 Service Manager Architecture.

In Figure 8-1, Server 1 is the Service Manager management server. The management server is the primary server to manage incidents, changes, users, and tasks. The Service Manager database contains configuration items, work items, change requests, and the System Center Service Manager configuration. The Service Manager console is the user interface for both Service Manager administrators and help desk administrators. The console supports installation on local workstations as a stand-alone component.

Server 2 hosts the data warehouse management server and the data warehouse database, which provides long-term business data for key performance indicators (KPIs) and reporting. The Self-Service Portal is a web-based interface into Service Manager for creating an incident or requesting services from the published service offerings.

Installing Service Manager

You need to prepare two more virtual servers to install System Center 2012 Service Man-

ments for SQL Server. Many of the requirements are used in standard server offerings with some specifics highlighted here:

- The .NET Framework 3.5 or 4.5 (as required by the components)

- SQL Server Native Client

- Microsoft Report Viewer 2012 Runtime redistributable package

> **Note**
>
> For the complete list of hardware requirements for Service Manager, see *http://technet. microsoft.com/en-us/library/hh524328.aspx*. For the complete list of software requirements for Service Manager, see *http://technet.microsoft.com/en-us/library/hh519608. aspx*.

You begin the System Center 2012 Service Manager installation starting with Server 1, as shown in Figure 8-1. You need to create two domain service accounts, work flow service and service manager service, then grant those accounts local administrative access to both Server 1 and Server 2.

> **Note**
>
> To install SQL Server 2012, use the Installation Wizard instructions at *http://msdn.micro-soft.com/en-us/library/ms143219.aspx*.

After you have installed the operating system and SQL Server, follow these steps:

1. Insert the System Center 2012 Service Manager media to run as an administrator for the installation, as shown in Figure 8-2.

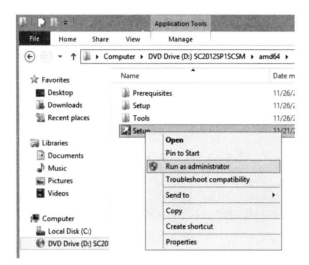

Figure 8-2 Service Manager Run As administrator.

2. Start the installation for Service Manager to start the Service Manager Setup Wizard and enter the appropriate information on the Product registration page. As shown in Figure 8-3, you can choose not to install a product key and instead install a 180-day evaluation version. Click Next.

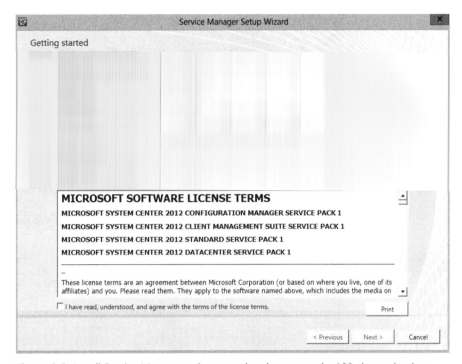

Figure 8-3 Install Service Manager using a product key or use the 180-day evaluation edition.

3. On the Installation Location page, accept the default location on the C: drive, and then click Next.

4. The prerequisites are checked by the Service Manager Setup Wizard on the following page. If the prerequisites are not met, the installation cannot continue. If you encounter a red circle with a white X indicating a requirement is not met, install the missing component by clicking the blue hyperlink text, as shown in Figure 8-4. After the installation of missing prerequisites is complete, click the Check prerequisites again button, and then click Next.

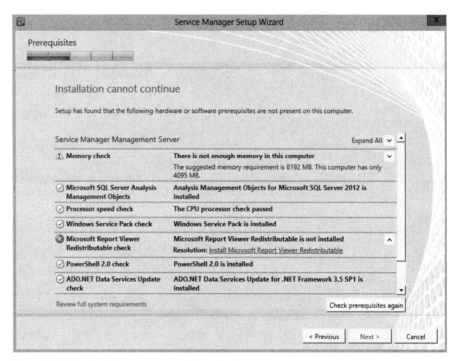

Figure 8-4 Service Manager prerequisites check.

5. The Service Manager Setup Wizard displays a page to configure the Service Manager database. A pop-up window indicates the SQL_Latin1_General collation is in use and not recommended for multilingual environments. Click OK to close the notification window, and then click Next to continue with the installation.

6. Configure the Service Manager management group name on the next page of the wizard. As shown Figure 8-5, a TH domain global group is selected to be the administrators of Service Manager. Rather than use the default administrators group, you might want to take a moment to create a group and add select members using the Browse button. Click Next after supplying the information.

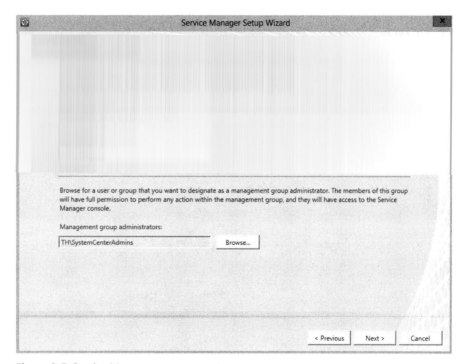

Service Manager Setup Wizard

Browse for a user or group that you want to designate as a management group administrator. The members of this group will have full permission to perform any action within the management group, and they will have access to the Service Manager console.

Management group administrators:

TH\SystemCenterAdmins   Browse...

< Previous   Next >   Cancel

Figure 8-5 Service Manager management group name.

7.   In the Service Manager Setup Wizard, enter the account for Service Manager services and the workflow account you created before Step 1, and then click Next. Continue through each page of the wizard, accepting the defaults, until you arrive at the summary page. Click the Install button to start the installation and wait for the Setup Wizard to finalize the installation, as shown in Figure 8-6.

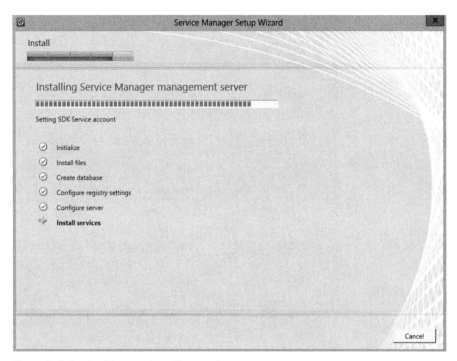

Figure 8-6   Service Manager installing services.

8.   After the installation is complete, the final wizard page prompts you to back up the encryption backup keys. Store the keys in a location other than the server and make sure they are backed up, should they need to be used in a recovery procedure.

9.   Proceed to Server 2 and start at Step 1. Choose the Install the Service Manager Data warehouse management server option. For our automation testing, the data warehouse server is not required.

Installing the Self-Service Portal

Currently, the portal server installation supports only the following versions of SharePoint:

- Microsoft SharePoint Foundation 2010

- Microsoft SharePoint Server 2010

- Microsoft SharePoint 2010 for Internet Sites Enterprise

SharePoint 2010 is not supported on Windows Server 2012, and therefore Windows Server 2008 R2 is required for the portal server operating system. You might be tempted to use SharePoint Foundation 2013 Server, which is supported on Windows Server 2012, but at the time of this writing SharePoint 2013 is not supported by System Center 2012 Service Man-

see http://technet.microsoft.com/en-us/library/hh519608.aspx.

Choose another virtual server as the Self-Service Portal. Install Windows Server 2008 R2 and SQL Server 2008 R2. The Self-Service Portal has specific web content requirements, so you must enable the following:

- Internet Information Services with IIS 6 metabase compatibility

- SQL Server 2012 Analysis Managed Objects (regardless of SQL version)

- A (self-signed) Secure Sockets Layer (SSL) certificate that can be used on the host

- Microsoft SharePoint Foundation 2010 (portal specific)

> **Note**
> To download Microsoft SharePoint Foundation 2010, see *http://www.microsoft.com/en-us/download/details.aspx?id=5970.*

To install SharePoint Foundation 2010 and the Self-Service Portal, follow these steps:

1. Log on to the server using an administrator account and install SharePoint Server 2010 by running the Products Configuration Wizard. Follow the prompts and accept the default settings, then restart the computer.

2. Insert the System Center 2012 SP1 Service Manager media and run as an administrator for the installation.

3. Start the installation for the Service Manager web portal under the Install (Optional) items Setup Wizard, enter the appropriate information on the Product registration page, and click Next.

4. The wizard displays the option to install the necessary parts for the Self-Service Portal. Select both options, Web Content Server and SharePoint Web Parts, because you have installed SharePoint Server Foundation 2010 on this server. Click Next.

5. The Service Manager Setup Wizard completes a system check and the results are displayed, as shown in Figure 8-7. You might receive a warning if the server does not have the recommended amount of memory. This warning is not critical for your testing, so click Next.

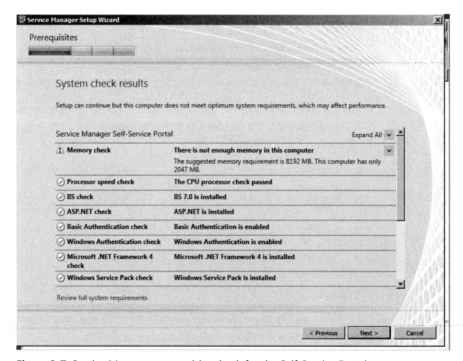

Figure 8-7 Service Manager prerequisite check for the Self-Service Portal.

6. Accept the default location for the virtual websites in the C:\inetpub\wwwroot folder. Click Next, and then select the option to use Port 443. Click the drop-down arrow to select the SSL certificate, as shown in Figure 8-8. Click Next to continue to select the database server. Enter the local server name, select the default server instance, accept the default database name, and then click Next.

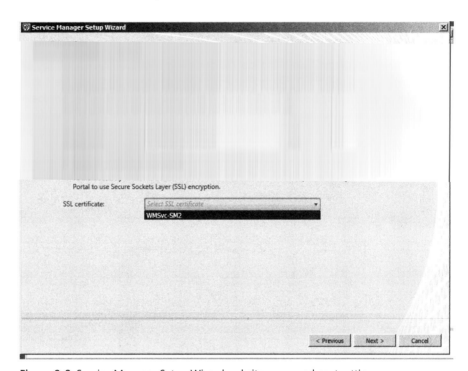

Figure 8-8 Service Manager Setup Wizard website name and port setting.

7. The next page in the Service Manager Setup Wizard requests the account for the Self-Service Portal. Instead of using the default option of Local System account, enter the Service Manager service account you created when the Service Manager service and database were installed. Click Next. Use the same account for the SharePoint Application Pool, and then click Next again.

8. The next page in the wizard is for configuring the SharePoint website, as shown in Figure 8-9. Notice the default port for SharePoint, select the Enable SSL encryption check box, and click the drop-down arrow to select the certificate chosen earlier. Accept the defaults for the SharePoint content site, and then click Next.

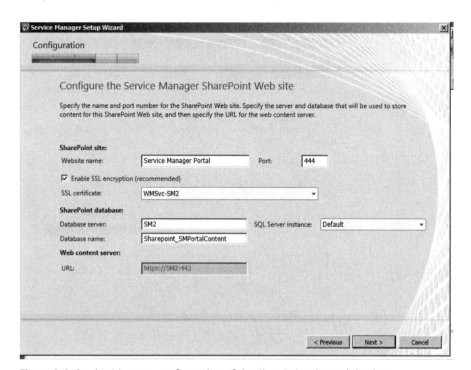

Figure 8-9 Service Manager configuration of the SharePoint site and database.

9. This wizard displays a page to use Microsoft Updates to secure the server. Select the Use Microsoft Update option, and then click Next. The next page in the wizard is the Installation summary page of all the selections. Click the Install button to begin the installation, as shown in Figure 8-10.

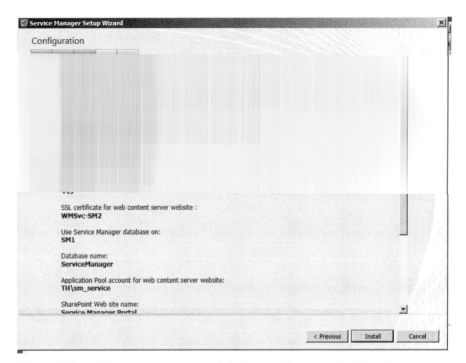

Figure 8-10 Installation summary page of the Service Manager Setup Wizard.

10. After the installation is complete, click the option to connect to the installed Self-Service Portal. If a self-signed SSL certificate has been used instead of a publicly trusted certificate, Internet Explorer will show you a warning that indicates a problem with the security of this site, as shown in Figure 8-11. Click Continue to this website.

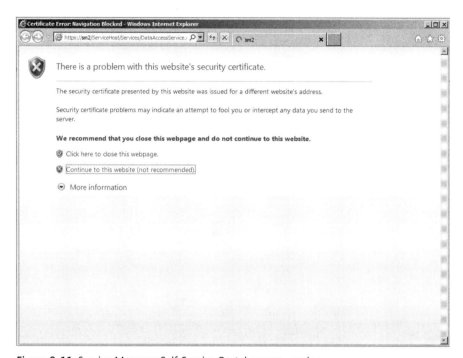

Figure 8-11 Service Manager Self-Service Portal access warning.

11. The portal shows a frame with blank information to the right of the pages. If Microsoft Silverlight is not installed on the computer accessing the site, you cannot see the default service request options until you download and install Silverlight, as shown in Figure 8-12.

> **Note**
> The Self-Service Portal requires Silverlight to show the objects that are created in
> the Service Manager console and published to the portal. To download Silverlight,
> see *http://www.microsoft.com/getsilverlight/get-started/install/default.aspx*.

Service catalog overview

Later in this chapter, we will show you how to use automation tasks to create a new Office
365 email account using a combination of the Service Manager Self-Service Portal as the
front end and System Center Orchestrator as the back end. As we continue to build this
automation service, you should understand a few Service Manager concepts.

The service catalog organizes requests using containers. These catalog containers are displayed in the Self-Service Portal. We use them as a method to organize the content that is
presented to the user. The service offering is the actual form used by the end user to create
an incident or a request for a specific service. The service offering is used to organize the
forms. For each category there is at least one and often more than one service offering.
Service Manager uses catalog item groups to maintain specific user groups, such as HR
Administrators, and gives the groups access to service offerings.

The portal is built as another site in SharePoint 2010 that contains pre-packaged web parts and takes advantage of Silverlight to display content. For our purposes in these exercises, it might be helpful to think of the Self-Service Portal as an interface to enable automation for Office 365 administrators. This portal provides access to the Configuration Management Database (CMDB) inside Service Manager. This is a website for end users to generate requests or review status of requests that have not been completed. The Self-Service Portal is used for many types of requests, some that are related to Office 365 and some that are not. Figure 8-13 shows an example of a fully populated Self-Service Portal. This example is used to demonstrate an organization that has completed many service offerings.

Figure 8-13 Service Manager Self-Service Portal catalog view with services.

Service request automation

Next, you will create a new Office 365 account using service request processes. You start the processes by entering data in the Self-Service Portal form. The connector of System Center 2012 Service Manager enables direct access to the runbooks of System Center Orchestrator and extends the automation beyond the reach of any typical service management solutions. Figure 8-14 shows the workflow to create automation between the Self-Service Portal, Service Manager, and Orchestrator. The Orchestrator connector syncs the runbook data to the Configuration Manager Database (CMD) inside Service Manager. The Orchestrator runbook activities and their properties are mapped to the properties in the Service Manager request templates. The request templates are added to the service offerings so end users can make a service request from the portal.

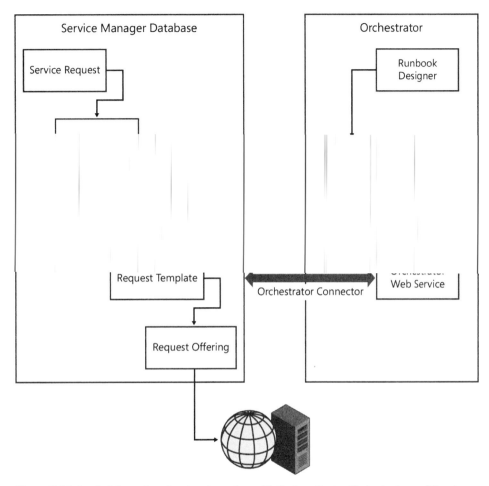

Figure 8-14 Logical flow of runbook automation with System Center Orchestrator and Service Manager.

Enabling the System Center Orchestrator connector

Now that you have a visual understanding of how automation between System Center Orchestrator and Service Manager flows, you need to enable the connector by following these steps:

1. Log on to the Service Manager server and open the Service Manager console. Navigate to the Administration workspace, as shown in Figure 8-15, right-click Connectors, expand Create connector, and select Orchestrator connector.

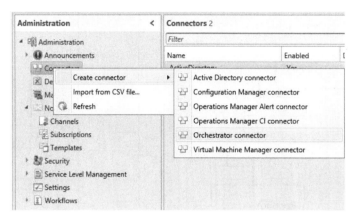

Figure 8-15 Use the Service Manager console to enable the Orchestrator connector.

2. The Orchestrator Connector Wizard appears. The wizard will help you step through the connector process. Use the information in Table 8-1 to complete the wizard. As you enter the information from the Wizard Item column, click Next to move through the wizard to the next item to complete.

TABLE 8-1 Completing the Orchestrator Connector Wizard items

Wizard Item	Item Configuration	Item Notes
Connector Name	Orchestrator Connector	Enable Connector
Web service URL	http://*Server*:81/Orchestra-tors2012/Orchestrator.svc	Change *Server* to Your Server Name
Credentials	*Domain*\SM_Service	Service Account
Sync Folder	Default is the root \ or \ O365Admin	Limit to Folder
Web Console URL	http://*Server*:82/	Change *Server* to Your Server Name

3. After filling in the appropriate information, the Summary page appears. Click the Create button to finalize the connection and close the wizard.

4. As you continue to build and test the Orchestrator runbooks, you will need to synchronize the information from Orchestrator and expose the runbooks and their activities to Service Manager for automation. Select the Synchronize Now option, as shown in Figure 8-16. To ensure that the CMBD of System Center 2012 Service Manager is updated with the latest information from the connector, System Center 2012 Orchestrator connector synchronizes with Service Manager on a daily basis. If any changes are made in the runbooks, you can also initiate the synchronization process manually by clicking Synchronize Now in the console or by using the

Update-SCSMConnector Windows PowerShell cmdlet in the System.Center.Service.
Manager Windows PowerShell module.

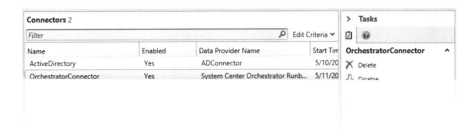

Configuring Service Manager automation

The automation foundation is now completed. The next few exercises show you how to create the automation components for the new Office 365 email account. In the Self-Service
Portal where user information is entered, the runbook is started and Active Directory
on-premises is synchronized with Office 365. Now that both System Center Service Manager and System Center Orchestrator are installed, you need to complete the integration
between the two systems. The runbook automation process for this example requires five
main steps:

1. Complete Orchestrator integration and finalize the runbook.

2. Create a runbook automation activity template.

3. Create a service request template.

4. Create a request offering.

5. Create a service offering and publish it.

INSIDE OUT   Unscheduled DirSync synchronization with Service Manager

In our example, you are expected to have AD FS enabled for AD to synchronize with
Office 365 in a two-phase process. The automation example can be modified based on
any of the scenarios discussed in Chapter 4, including the Exchange hybrid scenario.

Completing Orchestrator integration and finalizing a runbook

In Chapter 7, we created a runbook and did not configure the activities because Service Manager was not available. At this point, you can start the runbook automation with the first step in the process. Using System Center Orchestrator allows us to use the Orchestrator Data Bus. The Data Bus is a mechanism in Orchestrator that passes information from one activity in a Runbook to another activity.

This first step completes the integration between Service Manager and Orchestrator. To configure and complete the runbook activities, follow these steps:

1. Log on to the System Center 2012 Orchestrator server and open the Orchestrator Runbook Designer console. Expand Global Settings, click Variables, and right-click and create a new folder titled O365Settings. You should add 3 variables: Right-click the folder, select New Variable and type the name *ADFSserver*; right-click the folder a second time, select New Variable and type the name *AdminName*; finally, right-click the folder a third time and type the name *AdminPassword*, as shown in Figure 8-17. (Note the optional setting for the password to encrypt). Enter your information for each variable.

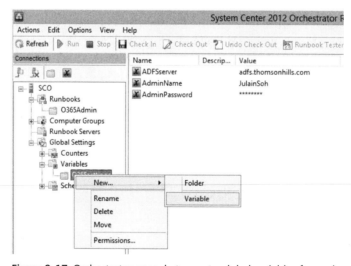

Figure 8-17 Orchestrator console to create global variables for runbook utilization.

2. On the Options menu, click SC 2012 Service Manager, as shown in Figure 8-18, to complete the integration.

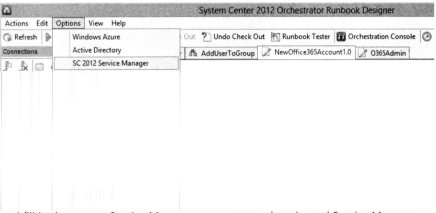

and fill in the correct Service Manager server name, domain, and Service Manager service account, as shown in Figure 8-19. Click the Test Connection button to validate that the server name and credentials are correct, then click OK to close the editing window. Click Finish to close the Connection dialog box for the Service Manager connector. The next step completes the Active Directory integration pack from Orchestrator.

Figure 8-19 Detailed view of Integration Pack configuration from Orchestrator.

4. Return to the Connection dialog box and click Add. Enter the name for the connector and fill in the correct Active Directory server name, domain, and Service Manager service account. Validate that the account password is correct, then click OK to close the editing window. Click Finish to close the Connection dialog box.

5. In the Orchestrator console, open the O365Admin runbook folder and use the Check Out option to edit the runbook we created in Chapter 7. Right-click the folder name and rename the runbook title New Office 365 Account 1.0.

> **Note**   **Best practice to name runbooks**
> Name your runbooks with effective subject titles and include version numbers such as 1.0, 1.1, 1.2 and so on to easily search for related runbooks and easily identify runbooks to the corresponding Service Manager workflow.

6. This step enables data entered in the Self-Service Portal to be consumed and processed by the Active Directory Integration Pack and the Service Manager Integration Pack in Orchestrator. Double-click the Initialize Data activity to edit the properties. This specific Orchestrator activity provides a starting activity for information received from Service Manager and specifically from the Self-Service Portal. As the Initialize Data Properties are displayed, as shown in Figure 8-20, click the Add button. Notice the default text is Parameter 1. Rename the text titled Parameter 1 to *ActivityGUID*. You need to add four more variable data string options for a total of five. As you add parameters, rename the default text:

    a. Click the Add button a second time and rename the default text parameter *FirstName*.

    b. Click the Add button a third time and rename the default text parameter *LastName*.

    c. Click the Add button a fourth time and rename the default text parameter *Password*.

    d. Click the Add button a fifth time and rename the default text parameter *UserAlias*. These five parameters are all that are required for this Office 365 runbook example.

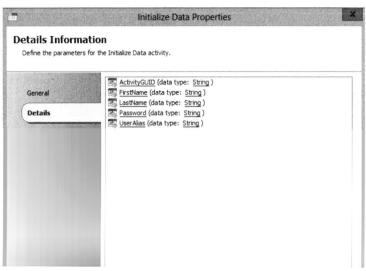

Figure 8-20 Runbook activity Initialize Data Properties page.

7. Validate that the Initialize Data icon is linked to the Create User icon, then double-click the Create User icon. On the Properties page, click the ellipsis button to the right of the Common Name box and select a domain controller. As shown in Figure 8-21, right-click next to the Common Name properties to open the menu, click Subscribe, then click Published Data.

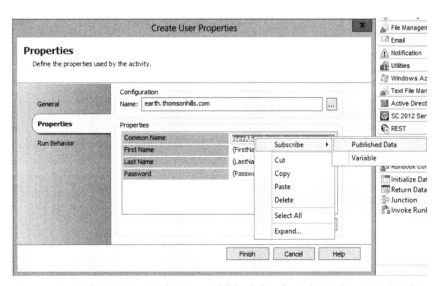

Figure 8-21 Orchestrator console using published data from the Orchestrator data bus.

8. Click the Optional Properties button to add the published data to include user alias, first name, last name, and password. Subscribe to published data using the values in Table 8-2 to finalize all the properties. Click Finish after the data is entered.

TABLE 8-2 Values to complete the Orchestrator properties and subscription to the data bus

Common Name	Published Data
Common Name	*UserAlias*
First Name	*FirstName*
Last Name	*LastName*
Password	*P@ssw0rd1234* (any strong password)

9. Now you need to configure the Enable User icon properties. Double-click the Enable User icon and connect to a domain controller. In the Distinguished Name box, right-click Subscribe and select Distinguished Name from the Create User icon. This data is passed automatically because of the integration with Active Directory through the System Center Orchestrator Active Directory Integration Pack.

10. On the Run .Net Script activity, right-click and rename the activity Run DirSync. With this Run DirSync activity, you need to run the DirSync Windows PowerShell script.

11. Double-click the Run DirSync icon and use the ellipses to the right of Type to select PowerShell, as shown in Figure 8-22.

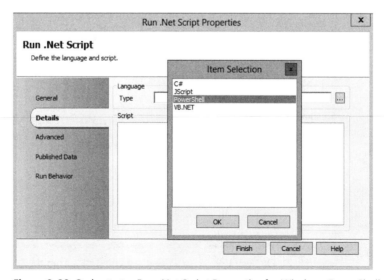

Figure 8-22 Orchestrator Run .Net Script Properties for Windows PowerShell.

12. Use a Windows PowerShell script to synchronize the newly created account in Active
Directory with Office 365. Enter the script (copy and paste) into the Script area of the
activity. Change the three variables (right-click Subscribe) created earlier for ADFS-
Server, Admin-Name, and Admin-Password for Office 365 access. Use the following
script in the Run .Net Script activity:

```
$ErrorActionPreference = "Stop"

try
```

```
Shell.psc1" -command "Start-OnlineCoexistenceSync"
        }
      $Result
}
catch
{
  Throw $_.Exception
}
```

13. Select the Get Relationship activity to update a manual step in Service Manager that indicates that the Windows PowerShell command completed successfully and the service request is in progress. Double-click the activity to configure the details. Figure 8-23 shows the parameters. Use the ellipses to expand the options and select the parameters. Right-click Object Guid and subscribe to the ActivityGUID from the Initialize Data activity.

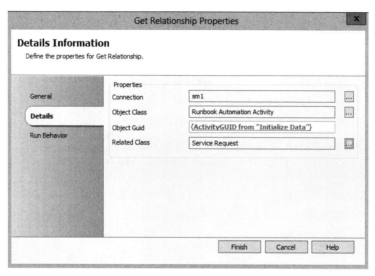

Figure 8-23 Orchestrator Get Relationship activity properties.

14. In the Details Information dialog box, double-click the Update Object activity to configure the properties. As shown in Figure 8-24, in the Connections drop-down box, select the name of the Service Manager server. In the Class drop-down box, select Service Request, which is the related object GUID from the Get Relationship activity. (In the preceding step, you passed the GUID from Initialize Data). We selected an option to update the text based on the last time the sync was finished. Click Finish to close the dialog box.

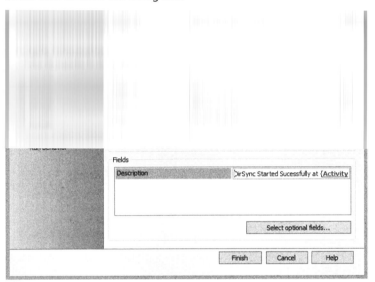

Figure 8-24 Orchestrator Update SR Progress Manual Task Properties.

15. For the second Run .Net Script activity, we will use the Windows PowerShell script in the .Net Script activity properties windows, as shown in Figure 8-22, to assign a license to a new user. Enter the following Windows PowerShell script. Change the three variables (right-click Subscribe) created earlier for ADFS-Server, Admin-Name, and Admin-Password for Office 365 access. Make sure to remove the quotes on each side:

```
$ErrorActionPreference = "Stop"

try

{

    $DomainPassword = ConvertTo-SecureString "ADMIN-Password" -AsPlainText
-Force

    $DomainCred = New-Object -TypeName System.Management.Automation.PSCredential
-ArgumentList  "Admin-Name",$DomainPassword

      $Result = Invoke-Command -ComputerName "ADFS-Server" -Credential $Domain-
Cred -ScriptBlock {

                    C:\Windows\System32\WindowsPowerShell\v1.0\powershell.exe
-command "& Connect-MsolService" "& Get-MsolUser -UnlicensedUsersOnly | Set-
MsolUser -UsageLocation us" "& Get-MsolUser -UnlicensedUsersOnly | Set-MsolU-
serLicense -AddLicenses uclabs:ENTERPRISEPACK"

        }

      $Result

}

catch

{

  Throw $_.Exception

}
```

16. The next action you need to complete is to update the Service Request in Service Manager to indicate that the runbook has completed and the service request is closed. In the Orchestrator activity, select Connection for your Service Manager server activity and then:

  a. Click the ellipses and select the manual activity.

  b. Select the Object Guid published data to ActivityGUID from Initialize Data.

  c. Click the Select optional fields button, then select status. Finally, in the status box click the ellipses and set the status to Completed.

This final activity in the runbook updates the request in Service Manager to close this instance of the request.

Creating a runbook automation activity template

The second step in the automation process is creating a runbook automation template. The workflow in Service Manager includes creating workflow through templates that provide internal integration through required steps and publishes the request into the Self-Service Portal. Follow these steps to create the activity template:

1   Log on to the Service Manager console. Click the Administration workspace, select

might sometimes expose a few minor changes you completed that the Runbook Designer did not update in the Orchestrator database. This is because of a known SQL cache issue. You might not notice this until you create the automation activity template. If you encounter this problem, correct it by opening the SQL Server Management Studio console and connecting to the computer running SQL Server that is hosting the System Center Orchestrator database. Select the Orchestrator database, click New Query, type the following query, and then run it:

```
TRUNCATE TABLE [Microsoft.SystemCenter.Orchestrator.Internal].Authoriza-
tionCache
EXEC [Microsoft.SystemCenter.Orchestrator.Maintenance].[EnqueueRecurrent-
Task] @taskName = 'ClearAuthorizationCache'
```

2. In the Service Manager console, click the Library workspace, expand the library, click Runbooks, and then select the runbook created earlier, New Office 365 Account 1.0. If the status is Invalid, simply delete the runbook from the Tasks pane and synchronize the Orchestrator connector again. Select the runbook with a single click of the mouse. From the Action pane, as shown in Figure 8-25, click Create Runbook Automation Activity Template.

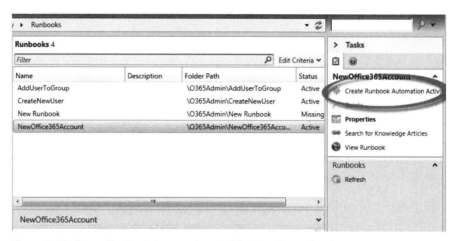

Figure 8-25 Create Runbook Automation Activity Template Wizard in Service Manager.

3. In the Create Template dialog box, provide a name, description, and class. Create a new management pack (MP) to save the information to. Use the data in Table 8-3 to create the new runbook first, using the New button on the side of the management pack prompt. Click OK to continue.

TABLE 8-3 Configuration details to complete the Service Manager management pack creation

Item	Configuration
Name	New Office 365 Account MP
Description	Office 365 automation service offering Management Pack

4. Use the data in Table 8-4 to create a new automation activity template. Enter the name and description, and then click OK to start the next step of the wizard. Figure 8-26 shows the results of this step.

TABLE 8-4 Configuration details to complete the Automation Activity Template

Item	Configuration
Name	New Office 365 Account Automation Activity Template
Description	Activity Template used in New Office 365 Account Creation
Class	Runbook Automation Activity (default)
MP	Name created from Table 8-3

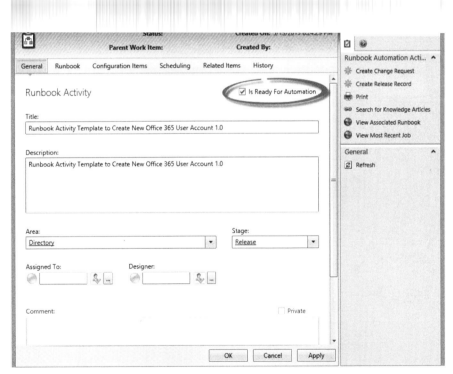

Figure 8-26 Service Manager Runbook Activity Template properties, ready for automation.

5. Click the Runbook tab to continue the configuration of the runbook activity template. The name of each parameter is mapped back to the parameters created in the Runbook Initialize Data activity. It is especially important to notice the Mapped to property Text# under each name. This is highlighted in Figure 8-27 because these text properties are used later in the Request Publishing Wizard.

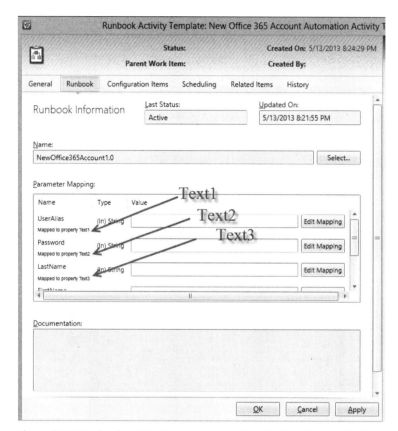

Figure 8-27 Runbook Activity Template properties highlighting text field mapping.

6. Next, use the scroll bar on the right side of the Parameter Mapping panes to scroll down to the parameter we created titled *ActivityGUID*. As shown in Figure 8-28, click the Edit Mapping button, select the Runbook Automation Activity option, expand Object, click Id, and change the Text5 mapping. Notice that the Mapping property is updated to the ID. Click Close.

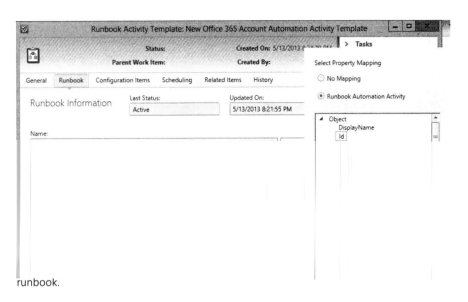

runbook.

7. Click OK to save the changes from the activity template to the management pack and close this form. The template can now be found in the Service Manager Library with the other templates if additional editing is required.

Creating a service request template

The third step in the automation process is creating a service request template. The request template is used to build the service request for the runbook processes and act as the workflow container for progress steps used in the request. To create a service request template, follow these steps:

1. In Service Manager, click the Library workspace, expand the Library node, and right-click Templates. Select the Create Template option, as shown in Figure 8-29.

Figure 8-29 Service Manager Create Template.

2. Use the Browse button to set the class to Service Request. If the MP changes, use the down arrow to select the New Office 365 Account Automation MP previously created. Enter the data using the values in Table 8-5. After entering the data, click OK to open the Service Request Template form.

TABLE 8-5 Items to complete the Create Template dialog box

Item	Configuration
Name	New Office 365 User Service Request Template
Description	New Office 365 User Service Request Template
Class	Service Request
MP	New Office 365 Account Automation Activity Template (MP)

3. Enter the data in the Service Request Template form, based on information from Table 8-6. Leave the Title box blank because it is updated from Orchestrator or the service offering.

TABLE 8-6 Items to complete the Service Request Template form

Item	Configuration
Title	BLANK
Description	Activity Stage for New Office 365 User Account
Urgency	Medium
Priority	Medium
Source	Portal
Area	Directory (for the Service Catalog)

4. Click the Activities tab at the top of the form to open the Activities pane in Service Manager. You need to add a new activity for this form. Select the green plus sign at the top right labeled Activities to select a template. The Service Manager template will invoke the runbook in the Orchestrator activity you created previously, as shown in Figure 8-30. Scroll down or search for the Runbook Activity Template and allow the form to open.

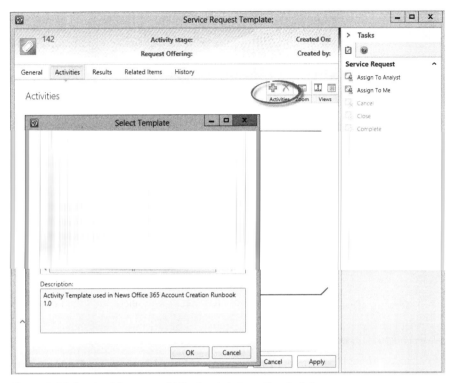

Figure 8-30 Service Manager add Runbook Automation Activity.

5. After the Runbook Activity Template form opens, you can validate the step. Click the Runbook tab and notice in the Parameter Mappings pane that the ActivityGUID, as shown in Figure 8-31, is incremented from the service request template. This is how Service Manager increments the workflow as each process is completed. Click OK to return to the Service Request Template form.

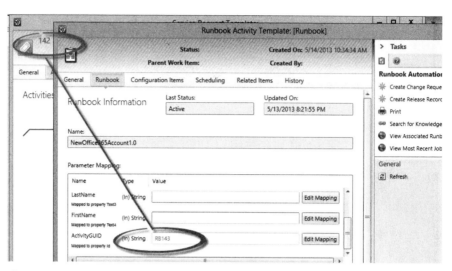

Figure 8-31 Runbook activity details highlighting the workflow numbering.

6. In the Service Request Template form, select the green plus sign at the top right labeled Activities. Select Default Manual Activity, as shown in Figure 8-32. Click OK to return to the view of the Manual Activity form.

    a. In the Title box, enter **Manual Activity for Runbook Invoke**.

    b. In the Description box, type **This Manual Activity waits for the final update from the Orchestrator Activity. When this Manual Activity form closes it also closes the service requests.**

    c. Click OK to close the Manual Activity form.

A manual activity created in the Service Manager form keeps the service request open until the Orchestrator runbook final activity is completed. This Service Manager manual activity updates the Service Manager form manual activity and closes it, which in turn closes the Service Manager service request.

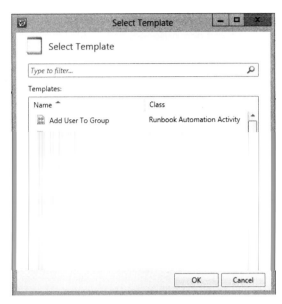

Figure 8-32 Service Manager Default Manual Activity selection.

7. Click the OK button to close the Service Request Template form.

Creating a request offering

The request offering is the fourth step in the automation processes and allows you to lever-age both the runbook automation template and the request template. To create a request offering, follow these steps:

1. Open the Service Manager console, click the Library workspace, expand Service Catalog, right-click Request Offering, and click Create Request Offering, as shown in Figure 8-33.

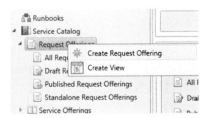

Figure 8-33 Service Manager Console view to start the Create Request Offering Wizard.

2. Click Next on the Before You Begin page of the Create Request Offering Wizard.

3. On the General page of the wizard, enter the title that matches the offering listing and provides a searchable name. The title is displayed in the catalog on the Self-Service Portal. Enter a description to help the user understand the title, as shown in Figure 8-34. In the Management pack drop-down box, select the New Office 365 User Service Request Template created in the previous process. Click Next.

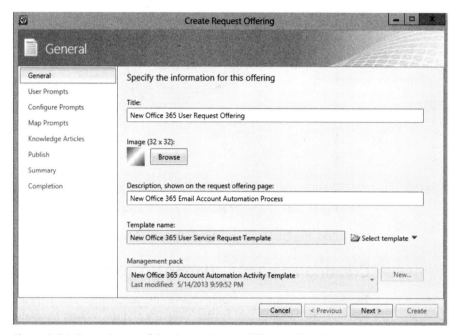

Figure 8-34 General page of the Create Request Offering Wizard.

4. The next page of the wizard is the User Prompts page. This page will appear in the Self-Service Portal when end users select the request. Enter instructions to aid end users and guide them through the steps. Click the green plus sign four times to enter the first name, last name, alias, and password, as shown in Figure 8-35. In the Enter prompts or information box, set Response Type to Required and Prompt Type to Text. Click Next.

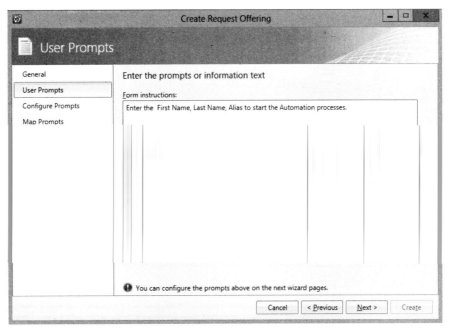

Figure 8-35 User Prompts page of the Create Request Offering Wizard.

5. On the Configure Prompts page, we don't need to make any changes. There should be a small green check that all prompts are configured. Click Next to continue.

6. On the Map Prompts page, you need to carefully match the text in the previous templates with the prompts that are displayed on the portal. Select the Runbook Activity Template. If you recorded the Text1, Text2, Text3, and Text4 fields earlier, enter them now. You can, however, hover your mouse cursor over any of the properties on the left to display the correct mapping. Figure 8-36 shows that Text1 corresponds to UserAlias. Map all prompts, and then click Next.

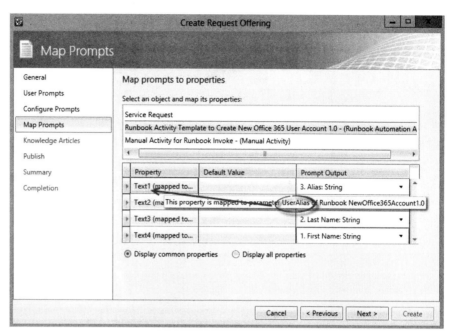

Figure 8-36 Map Prompts page of the Create Request Offering Wizard.

7. On the Knowledge Articles page, click Next. You have not created any knowledge
    articles to support this request offering.

8. On the Publish page, change the Offering status to Published. Click Next.

9. On the Summary page, click Create to finalize the selections. On the Completion
    page, click Close if the request completed successfully.

Creating and publishing a service offering

The fifth and final step in the automation process, which includes runbook automation with
Service Manager integration, is to create a Self-Service Portal service offering and publish
the entire automation process to the portal. To create the offering and publish it, follow
these steps:

1. Open the Service Manager console and click the Library workspace. Expand Service
    Catalog and use a single mouse click to select Service Offerings. As shown in Figure
    8-37, right-click Service Offerings and select Create Service Offering to start the
    wizard.

2. On the General page, enter the title and select the Access and Security category using the drop-down arrow. Enter the overview and description to clearly identify this service to the end user. Figure 8-37 shows each of the prompts. Click Next.

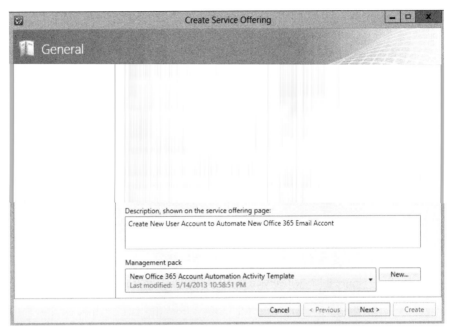

Figure 8-37 Create Service Offering Wizard.

3. The remainder of the pages in this wizard have options that support the Self-Service Portal request. Use the information in Table 8-7 to complete the wizard.

TABLE 8-7 Items to complete the publishing of the Service Offering Wizard

Wizard Page Title	Configuration
Detailed Information	None (No SLA, Links, or costs information)
Related Services	None
Knowledge Articles	None
Request Offering	Add, New Office 365 User Request Offering
Publish	Change offering Status to Published
Summary	Click Create

4. After the Create Service Offering Wizard has completed successfully, click Close to close the wizard.

Service and request offering in the Self-Service Portal

You have completed all the steps necessary to enable runbook automation from Orchestrator using the workflow in Service Manager. Figure 8-38 shows the publication in the portal.

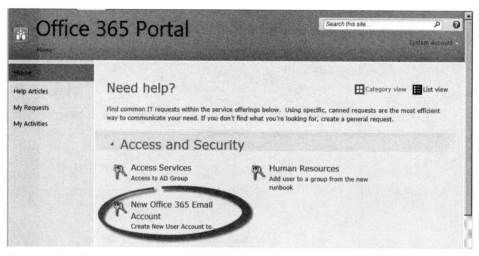

Figure 8-38 Self-Service Portal view of the service request in the Access and Security category.

When end users select the request from the catalog, they will be required to complete the necessary prompts, as shown in Figure 8-39. In our example, you can see data entered for first name, last name, alias, and password. Obviously, we have provided only the mechanics to publish the automation processes. You should allow time for troubleshooting as well as time to review each step to better understand how you can incorporate them into your company's enterprise processes.

Figure 8-39 Self-Service Portal with details used in the Service Request.

Summary

In this chapter, we introduced you to many of the Service Manager components and showed you how you can use System Center 2012 to automate Office 365 manual tasks. You learned how to easily install System Center 2012 Service Manager SP1. With Service Manager installed, you returned to finalize the System Center 2012 Orchestrator integration by configuring the System Center Orchestrator connector and building a runbook.

We walked you through each of the five steps to create a Service Manager automation project, including a runbook, service templates, and a service offering. This chapter focused on automating a single Office 365 manual task as a model to show you how to build additional automation for other Office 365 administration tasks.

Windows PowerShell for Office 365

Windows PowerShell underlying services 395   Windows PowerShell Integrated ....

are a few examples of common characteristics that differentiate an enterprise from the consumer:

- Size and complexity

- Compliance and regulatory requirements

- Management strategy, centralized or de-centralized

Windows PowerShell was introduced to specifically address automation and management issues because provisioning and managing users for more than a few identities can quickly become demanding for large or complex organizations. Windows PowerShell provides administrators with a more efficient and reliable way to deliver services in a predictable and repeatable fashion, thereby delivering services in a much shorter time. For example, if a bulk configuration change needs to happen for a large portion of the organization, manually effecting those changes would take significant time and effort and would be prone to misconfiguration.

This chapter is designed to help enterprises automate mundane administrative tasks for Office 365 as well as on-premises technologies that Office 365 relies upon, such as AD and AD FS. What are some of the things we can do with Windows PowerShell for Office 365? For many organizations, this begins with deployment, migration, administration and monitoring of Office 365 services. In this chapter, we will explore the main tasks of Office 365 services that can be managed with Windows PowerShell.

The easiest way to learn Windows PowerShell is through hands-on practice, which is how we present the material in this chapter. The exercises and examples in this chapter introduce Windows PowerShell commands that are specific to Office 365.

As an introduction to Windows PowerShell terminology, be aware that the most basic object in Windows PowerShell is a cmdlet (pronounced command-let). To use most of the commands, you will need administrative rights in Office 365 and a workstation configured to run Windows PowerShell commands.

Preparing the Windows PowerShell environment

In this section of the chapter, we will cover what is needed to use Windows PowerShell from a workstation to facilitate performing Office 365 tasks.

Windows PowerShell pre-configured for the workstation or server

We need to validate or prepare a version of the Windows operating system to support Windows remoting to use features discussed in this chapter. The ability to remotely administer services is not new to Microsoft. It was first introduced in the .NET Framework in 2002.

To run Windows PowerShell cmdlets on remote systems, you need to prepare your workstation or server by completing the following tasks:

- Configure your environment to run using administrator privileges.

- Get the most current Help files.

- Import the Office 365 Windows PowerShell module.

Windows PowerShell cmdlets are commonly issued from an administrator's workstation. Windows PowerShell commands are issued to Office 365 through a technology called Windows Remote Management (WinRM).

WinRM includes a scripting application programming interface (API) used to obtain data from remote computers that follow the Windows Server Management (WS-Management) protocol, which is why you will sometimes hear Windows PowerShell in Office 365 referred to as remote Windows PowerShell. In the simplest definition, WinRM has a listener service that runs on both the administrator's workstation and the remote server the commands are sent to. Without WinRM installed and correctly configured, the scripts will not run.

INSIDE OUT   WinRM versions

In Windows 7 or Windows Server 2008 R2, WinRM is 2.0 and is installed by default. Working in the field, we've discovered some customers' security practices might have removed this feature.

Windows 8 and Windows Server 2012 come with WinRM 3.0 and is installed by default.

Determining the WinRM version

Follow these steps to identify the version of WinRM installed on your administration workstation:

1. If you are using Windows 8 or Windows Server 2010, skip to Step 3. If you are using Windows 7 or Windows Server 2008 R2, click Start and type **cmd** in the search box. This should cause Windows to locate the Command Prompt program under Programs, as shown in Figure 9-1.

2. Right-click Command Prompt and select Run as administrator. If the Windows User Account Control (UAC) prompts whether to continue, select Yes and skip to Step 4.

Figure 9-1 Windows 7 Command Prompt running under administrator privileges.

3. If you are using Windows 8 or Windows Server 2012, open the Start screen and type **cmd**. Windows will find the Command Prompt, as shown in Figure 9-2. Right-click Command Prompt and select the Run as Administrator icon located at the bottom of the screen, also shown in Figure 9-2.

Figure 9-2 Windows 8 Command Prompt running with administrator privileges.

4. Type the following command and press Enter:

```
WinRM ID
```

The WinRM version, together with other information, will be displayed, as shown in Figure 9-3.

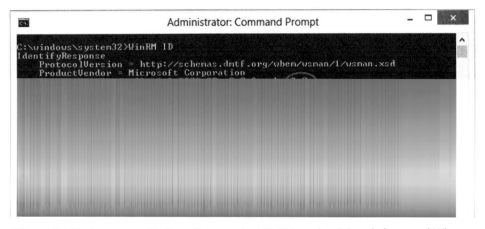

Office 365 Windows PowerShell cmdlets require WinRM version 2.0 and above and Windows PowerShell version 2.0 and above.

In this chapter, we will use Windows 8 as the administrator workstation so we can leverage Windows PowerShell 3.0 and its vastly improved Integrated Scripting Environment (ISE).

INSIDE OUT   Upgrade WinRM or Windows PowerShell for older operating systems

If you need to take additional time to update your version of WinRM, see *http://go.microsoft.com/FWLink/?LinkId=186253*. If you need to upgrade to Windows Power-Shell 2.0, see *http://help.outlook.com/en-us/140/cc952756.aspx*.

Verifying that WinRM is running

Follow these steps to verify that WinRM is running:

1. From the Start screen in the Windows 8 Enterprise workstation, type **Windows PowerShell**. Right-click Windows PowerShell in the Results window, as shown in Figure 9-4, and select Run as administrator. Click Yes if prompted by UAC.

Figure 9-4 Windows 8 Enterprise workstation Run as administrator.

2. Type the following command and press Enter:

   `winrm enumerate winrm/config/listener`

3. If you receive the error shown in Figure 9-5, it means WinRM is not running.

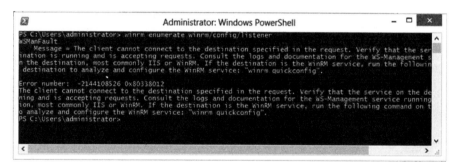

Figure 9-5 WinRM informing the user that it is not running.

4. If you need to start the WinRM service, type the following command and press Enter:

   `winrm quickconfig`

5. When prompted whether to start the WinRM server, type **Y** for yes. Repeat this step by typing **Y** to make the changes and **Y** to create a WinRM listener, as shown in Figure 9-6.

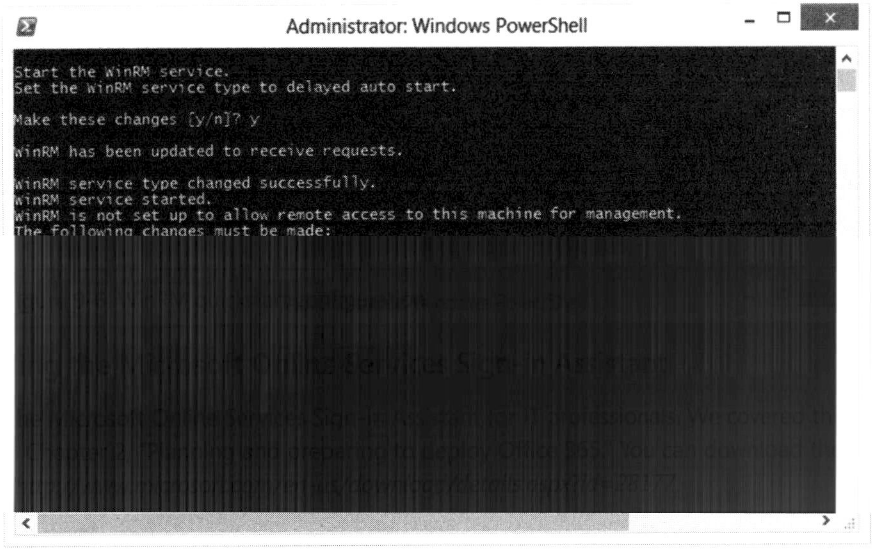

```
Start the WinRM service.
Set the WinRM service type to delayed auto start.

Make these changes [y/n]? y

WinRM has been updated to receive requests.

WinRM service type changed successfully.
WinRM service started.
WinRM is not set up to allow remote access to this machine for management.
The following changes must be made:
```

Figure 9-6 WinRM quickstart configuration.

Installing the Microsoft Online Services Sign-in Assistant

Install the Microsoft Online Services Sign-in Assistant for IT professionals. We covered this topic in Chapter 2, "Planning and preparing to deploy Office 365." You can download the files at *http://www.microsoft.com/en-us/download/details.aspx?id=28177*.

Installing the Windows Azure Active Directory Module for Windows PowerShell

Download and install the Windows Azure AD module for Windows PowerShell. We covered this topic in Chapter 2. You can download the module at *http://go.microsoft.com/FWLink/p/?Linkid=236297*.

Configuring Windows PowerShell and WinRM settings

With the correct versions of WinRM and Windows PowerShell installed and running, follow these steps to configure their settings:

1. At the Windows PowerShell command prompt, type the following command and press Enter:

   ```
   Get-ExecutionPolicy
   ```

   If the returned value displayed is not *RemoteSigned*, as shown in Figure 9-7, you will need to set the policy to allow *RemoteSigned* by entering the following command:

   ```
   Set-ExecutionPolicy RemoteSigned
   ```

Chapter 9

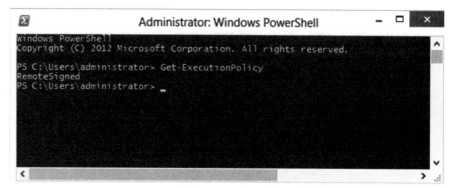

Figure 9-7 Windows PowerShell command prompt and the execution of the *Get-ExecutionPolicy* command.

2. If you had to make a change to the policy, verify that it is now correctly set to *RemoteSigned* by running *Get-ExecutionPolicy* again.

3. In Windows PowerShell, type the following command and press Enter. You should see returned values similar to what is shown in Figure 9-8:

```
winrm get winrm/config/client/auth
```

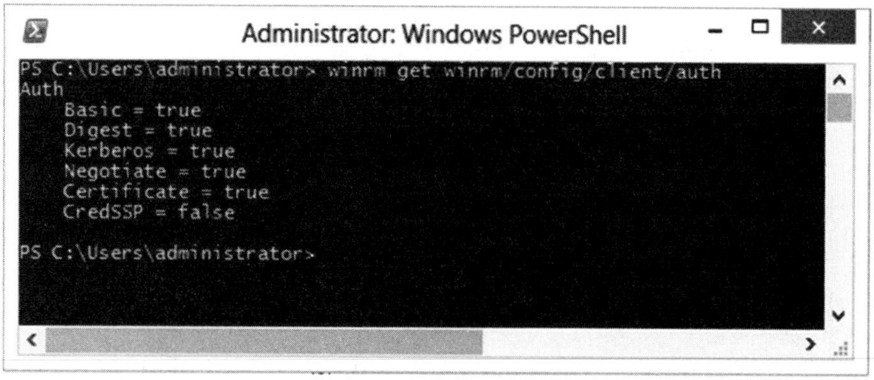

Figure 9-8 Validate that the WinRM listener service has authorization set to Basic.

4. In the results, as shown in Figure 9-8, look for the value of *Basic = true*. If the value is set to *Basic = false*, change the value to *true* by entering the following command:

```
winrm set winrm/config/client/auth @{Basic="true"}
```

Note that the string between the { } is case sensitive, so type it exactly as shown.

INSIDE OUT   Customizing the Windows PowerShell user interface

You can customize the font size and color in Windows PowerShell. This ability might help you visualize the text better or reduce eye fatigue. To change the font color, start Windows PowerShell as an administrator. Right-click the icon at the upper left of the window and select Properties. Click the Font tab and change the color or size of the text.

The Windows PowerShell on your local administrator workstation is called the *client-side session*. The client-side session has only the basic Windows PowerShell commands available. When we connect to the cloud-based services, we are connecting to the *server-side session* in the server environment. Once connected, we can leverage the Windows PowerShell commands used in the Office 365 server-side session with a few easy steps.

Follow these steps to establish connection with Exchange Online in Office 365:

1. Start Windows PowerShell.

2. Type the following command and press Enter:

    ```
    $LiveCred = Get-Credential
    ```

3. You will see a logon prompt, as shown in Figure 9-9. Provide your Office 365 administrator credentials.

Chapter 9

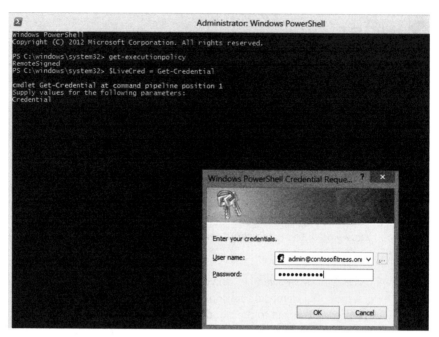

Figure 9-9 Credentials prompt after entering Windows PowerShell commands.

4. The credentials you provided in Step 3 are now stored in the *$LiveCred* variable. Open a Windows PowerShell session, also known as *PSSession*, to Exchange Online by entering the following command:

```
$Session = New-PSSession -ConfigurationName Microsoft.Exchange -ConnectionUri
https://ps.outlook.com/powershell/ -Credential $LiveCred -Authentication Basic
-AllowRedirection
```

Your *PSSession* should look similar to Figure 9-10.

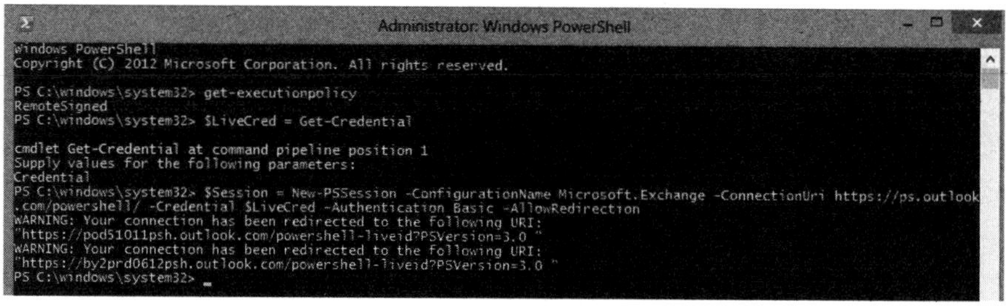

Figure 9-10 Windows PowerShell Command Prompt window after online sessions are connected.

5. Enter the following command to start using the session. After executing the command, your window should look similar to the one shown in Figure 9-11:

```
Import-PSSession $Session
```

```
PS C:\windows\system32>
PS C:\windows\system32> $Session = New-PSSession -ConfigurationName Microsoft.Exchange-ConnectionUri https://ps.outlook.
com/powershell/ -Credential $cred -Authentication Basic -AllowRedirection
WARNING: Your connection has been redirected to the following URI:
"https://pod51011psh.outlook.com/powershell-liveid?PSVersion=3.0 "
WARNING: Your connection has been redirected to the following URI:
"https://by2prd0612psh.outlook.com/powershell-liveid?PSVersion=3.0 "
PS C:\windows\system32> Import-PSSession $Session
```

6. At this point, you are connected and ready to manage your tenant. Normally, you will issue commands to manage your tenant, which we will explore in exercises later in this chapter. For now, we will end the session by entering the following command. This is what you will normally do when you are done with your administration tasks:

```
Remove-PSSession $Session
```

> **Important**
>
> It is important that you close a *PSSession* after you are done. The reason for closing a *PSSession* is because of the five-connection limit in place as a security measure. If you do not close a *PSSession*, you will need to wait for the session to time out. If there are five sessions of *PSSession* open, you will not be able to establish additional sessions.

Windows PowerShell as the future interface

With Office 365, you have the choice to use the admin center or Windows PowerShell. While many of the administrative tasks can be performed through the admin center, some tasks are difficult to do without Windows PowerShell and some tasks can be performed only with Windows PowerShell.

Office 365, like all Microsoft applications, has a primary Graphical User Interface (GUI), and the traditional Microsoft Management Console (MMC) continues to be available. However, Windows PowerShell is also here to stay and continues to grow in significance when it comes to service administration. In fact, Microsoft GUIs run Windows PowerShell behind

Chapter 9

the scenes, and in most cases the GUIs today also expose the Windows PowerShell scripts they are running in the back end. The next time you use a Microsoft wizard, such as the Setup Wizard, look at the progress screen. Often, the Windows PowerShell scripts are being exposed so you know what the GUI is doing. This is one way that Microsoft is helping customers with the transition to Windows PowerShell.

Windows PowerShell Integrated Scripting Environment

So far, you have been using the Windows PowerShell Command Prompt window. While efficient, the Command Prompt window is not very user friendly. To help improve the Windows PowerShell scripting experience, Microsoft provides a powerful Integrated Scripting Environment (ISE). In Chapter 2, we showed you how to download and install Windows PowerShell ISE 3.0 for Windows 7. ISE 3.0 comes with Windows 8 and Windows Server 2012.

The ISE is a graphical scripting console that comes with Intellisense, comprehensive Help files, multi-tabbed windows, and a pleasant authoring environment. It supports the same Windows PowerShell cmdlets for Office 365 and recognizes all the Windows PowerShell keyboard shortcuts. You can also set breakpoints by right-clicking a line of code for debugging. Figure 9-12 shows the ISE.

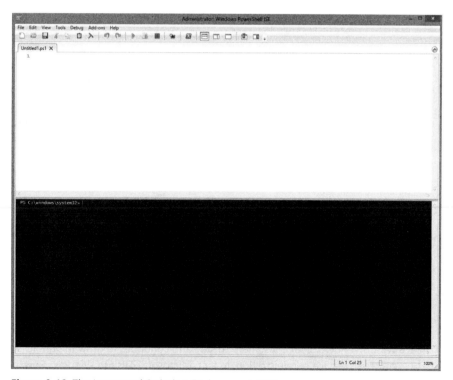

Figure 9-12 The Integrated Scripting Environment (ISE).

Starting the Windows PowerShell ISE is easy after you know exactly where to find the application. The following sections show you the different ways to locate and start the ISE.

Starting the ISE from Windows 8

If your administrator workstation is Windows 8, follow these steps to start the ISE:

1. From the Start screen in the Windows 8 Enterprise workstation, type **Windows**

Figure 9-13 Windows PowerShell ISE in Windows 8.

2. Right-click the Windows PowerShell ISE icon and select Run as administrator at the bottom of the screen. Click Yes if prompted to continue by UAC.

3. Consider pinning the ISE to the Windows Start menu so you do not have to search for it all the time.

Starting the ISE from within Windows PowerShell

If you already have the Windows PowerShell Command Prompt window open, you can start the ISE simply by entering the following command:

```
Start-Process PowerShell_ISE -Verb RunAs
```

Starting the ISE from Windows 7

If you are running Windows 7, follow these steps to start the ISE:

1. Click Start and type **Windows PowerShell ISE** in the search box.

2. Right-click Windows PowerShell ISE and select Run as administrator.

Chapter 9

The Windows PowerShell ISE console should appear and look similar to Figure 9-14. If it does not look similar, it might be because of the view. Click the View menu and configure the visibility and placement of windows in the ISE.

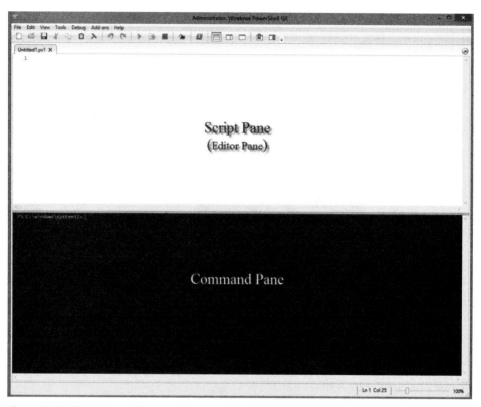

Figure 9-14 ISE window with two of the main areas displayed and identified.

The following are some of the new features included with ISE version 3.0:

- Intellisense, which provides dynamic, actionable menus for matching cmdlets, parameters, values, files, and folders as you type

- Editor and Help windows enhancements

- Restart Manager and Auto-Save, which support scripts to be automatically saved in the event of a restart

- Add-on tools, which provide additional controls for Windows Presentation Foundation (WPF) when using the object model

INSIDE OUT

Installing Windows PowerShell ISE on older operating systems

If you're running Windows 7, it comes with Windows PowerShell ISE version 2.0. You can upgrade it to ISE 3.0. For more information, see Windows Management Framework 3.0 in the Microsoft Download Center at *http://go.microsoft.com/FWLink/p/?LinkID=229019.*

If Windows Server 2008 R2 is the Operating System (OS) you are using to follow the

Navigating the ISE

Figure 9-15 shows the Windows PowerShell ISE console configured to display the Script Pane and Command Pane. Use the View menu to configure the placement and visibility of panes.

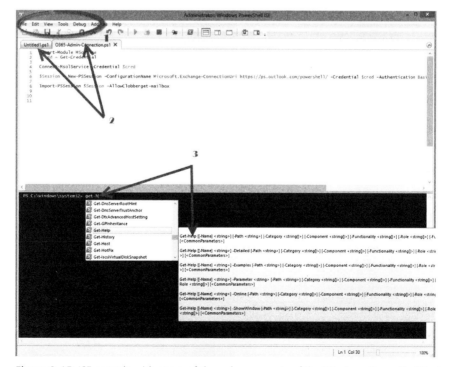

Figure 9-15 ISE console with some of the enhancements of the Windows PowerShell features.

When exploring the ISE, you will notice some familiar menus. We will be referring to the annotated screen shot shown in Figure 9-15 as we look at some of the new features in the ISE.

Along the top is the menu. In the screen shot, it is circled and labeled 1. Like any traditional menu, the menu allows you to access tools, debug scripts, open and save scripts, and configure the view of the ISE.

The next feature, which is labeled 2, shows the tabs of the ISE. The tabs enable you to have multiple scripts open at once.

An additional area to point out is the Command Pane. The Command Pane allows you to interactively issue commands similar to issuing commands in the traditional Windows PowerShell Command Prompt window. It also features IntelliSense, which is labeled 3 in Figure 9-15. As an example, notice that when we typed the first few characters of a cmdlet, in this case **Get-H**, IntelliSense produced a fly-out menu after the letter H and listed the cmdlets that begin with Get-H. This feature should be familiar to developers accustomed to the Microsoft Visual Studio Integrated Development Environment (IDE).

Next, notice that as we hold the mouse cursor over a cmdlet in the Intellisense menu, the parameters and methods associated with the cmdlet are exposed in a secondary menu.

These features are not limited to just the Command Pane. They are also available in the Scripting Pane, as shown in Figure 9-16.

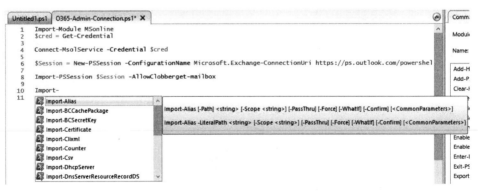

Figure 9-16 Intellisense in the Scripting Pane.

Another feature that is useful is the Command Add-on library. You can enable the Command Add-on pane by clicking the icon located on the toolbar, as shown in Figure 9-17.

Administrator: Windows PowerShell ISE
Show Command Add-on

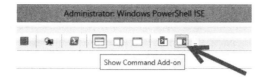

Figure 9-17 Menu options on the ISE toolbar.

Enable the Command Add-on feature to provide a method of searching for commands

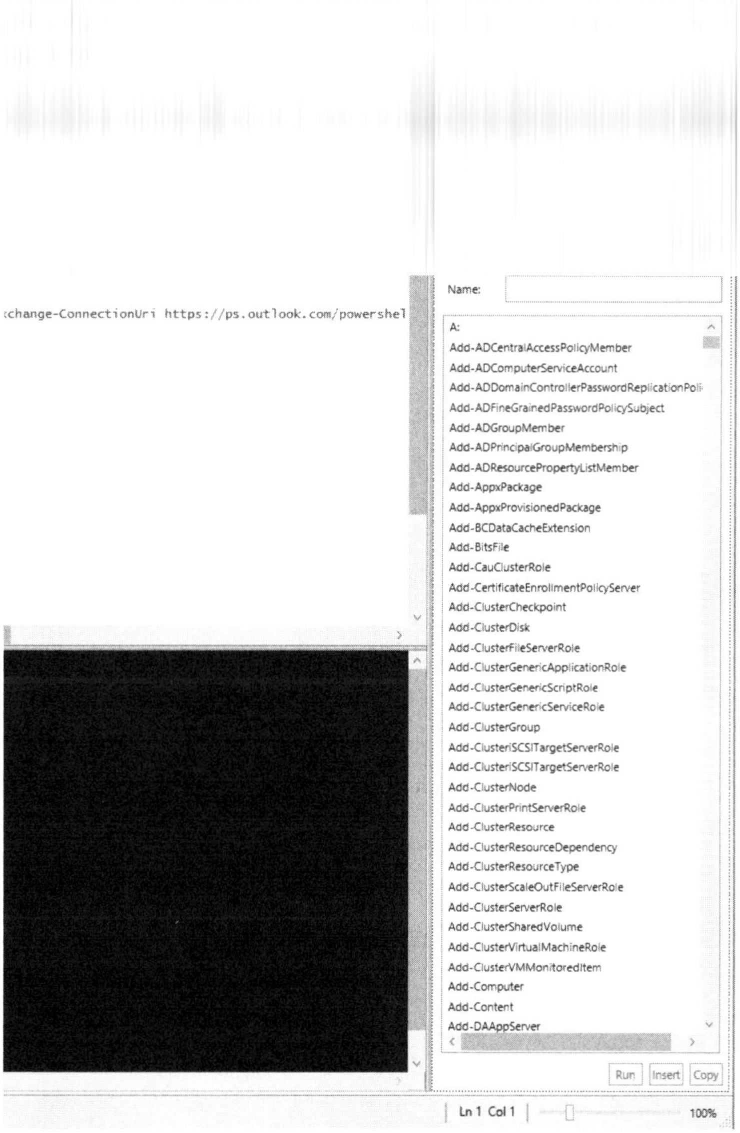

Name:
change-ConnectionUri https://ps.outlook.com/powershel
A:
Add-ADCentralAccessPolicyMember
Add-ADComputerServiceAccount
Add-ADDomainControllerPasswordReplicationPoli
Add-ADFineGrainedPasswordPolicySubject
Add-ADGroupMember
Add-ADPrincipalGroupMembership
Add-ADResourcePropertyListMember
Add-AppxPackage
Add-AppxProvisionedPackage
Add-BCDataCacheExtension
Add-BitsFile
Add-CauClusterRole
Add-CertificateEnrollmentPolicyServer
Add-ClusterCheckpoint
Add-ClusterDisk
Add-ClusterFileServerRole
Add-ClusterGenericApplicationRole
Add-ClusterGenericScriptRole
Add-ClusterGenericServiceRole
Add-ClusterGroup
Add-ClusteriSCSITargetServerRole
Add-ClusteriSCSITargetServerRole
Add-ClusterNode
Add-ClusterPrintServerRole
Add-ClusterResource
Add-ClusterResourceDependency
Add-ClusterResourceType
Add-ClusterScaleOutFileServerRole
Add-ClusterServerRole
Add-ClusterSharedVolume
Add-ClusterVirtualMachineRole
Add-ClusterVMMonitoredItem
Add-Computer
Add-Content
Add-DAAppServer
Run
Insert
Copy
Ln 1 Col 1
100%

Figure 9-18 ISE window after enabling the Command Add-on.

The Command Add-on enables you to quickly search for commands. Follow these steps to see for yourself:

1. Place your cursor in the Name box. Type **set-ps** and notice that as you type the list narrows to provide you with possible results.

2. You can also narrow your searches by modules instead of cmdlet name. Click the down arrow in the Modules drop-down box, as shown in Figure 9-19. Note the list of modules available.

Figure 9-19 Display the modules loaded in the ISE.

3. In the Modules drop-down box, select Microsoft.PowerShell.Core.

4. Scroll down to the *New-PSSession* cmdlet and hold your cursor over the command. Your ISE should look similar to the screen shot shown in Figure 9-20.

utlook.com/powershel

this cmdlet, as shown in Figure 9-21.

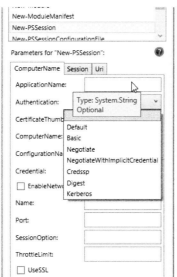

Figure 9-21 *New-PSSession* cmdlet parameters.

As you can see, the complexity of Windows PowerShell becomes a little less daunting if you leverage the ISE as an authoring tool. Aside from Intellisense and the Command Add-on, the ISE is also a more pleasant and productive way to write your scripts. We will use the ISE more when we begin our exercises in the next section.

Office 365 examples and exercises

For the remainder of this chapter, we will focus on using the ISE and combining it with some of the common Windows PowerShell cmdlets to manage Office 365.

As an introduction to Office 365 cmdlets, we will present several exercises that cover common Office 365 administration tasks. For these exercises, we will be using a different tenant, ContosoFitness.onMicrosoft.com, because this is our test tenant. After we understand the changes created with our Windows PowerShell cmdlets, they can be implemented in our production tenant.

INSIDE OUT   Testing

It is a best practice to have a test tenant with a few users so you can test your Windows PowerShell scripts. Alternatively, you can use your production tenant with test users. In both scenarios, the test users most likely will have to be assigned Office 365 licenses, at least during script testing. Microsoft does not provide free test tenants or free test user licenses.

Establishing a Windows PowerShell session with Exchange Online

This first exercise is a review of the cmdlets that enable you to establish a Windows Power-Shell session (*PSSession*) connection with Exchange Online in Office 365. Each of the following exercises builds on this exercise. Follow these steps to establish a *PSSession*.

1. Start the ISE.

2. Type the following commands in the Script Pane and press Enter, or you can download the additional files from the Office 365 admin center. On the Script Pane, open O365-Admin-Connections.ps1 and click the Run option on the ISE ribbon.

   ```
   Import-Module MSonline

   $cred = Get-Credential

   Connect-MsolService -Credential $cred
   ```

```
$Session = New-PSSession -ConfigurationName Microsoft.Exchange-ConnectionUri
https://ps.outlook.com/powershell/ -Credential $cred -Authentication Basic
-AllowRedirection

Import-PSSession $Session -AllowClobber
```

3. Enter the credentials to allow our client-side session to communicate with our service-side session, as shown in Figure 9-22.

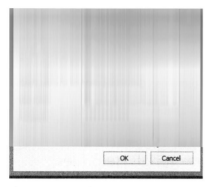

Figure 9-22 Authentication challenge response window.

4. Validate your connection by entering the following command in the ISE and pressing Enter:

```
Get-Mailbox
```

Figure 9-23 shows the result of the *Get-mailbox* command. Notice that the Office 365 server-side session redirects our requests. The ISE Command Prompt window you are using should look very similar.

```
WARNING: Your connection has been redirected to the following URI: "https://pod51011psh.outlook.com/powershell-li
veid?PSVersion=3.0."
WARNING: Your connection has been redirected to the following URI: "https://bv2prd0612psh.outlook.com/powershell-
liveid?PSVersion=3.0."

ModuleType Name                           ExportedCommands
---------- ----                           ----------------
Script     tmp_geltuvbi.jba               {Add-AvailabilityAddressSpace, Add-DistributionGroupMember, Ad...


PS C:\windows\system32> Get-Mailbox

Name                     Alias                ServerName       ProhibitSendQuota
----                     -----                ----------       -----------------
Anthony                  Anthony              bl2prd0611mb423  24.75 GB (26,575,110,144 bytes)
DiscoverySearchMailbox...  DiscoverySearchMa...  bluprd0611mb424  50 GB (53,687,091,200 bytes)
Julian                   Julian               ch1prd0610mb355  24.75 GB (26,575,110,144 bytes)
admin                    admin                bluprd0611mb424  24.75 GB (26,575,110,144 bytes)


PS C:\windows\system32>
```

Figure 9-23 The *Get-Mailbox* command and the output.

5. Use Windows PowerShell to learn the Exchange Online commands that are most helpful. This example shows you how to quickly search for cmdlets based on keywords. As shown in Figure 9-24, at the command prompt enter the following command and press Enter:

```
Get-Command -Noun Mailbox
```

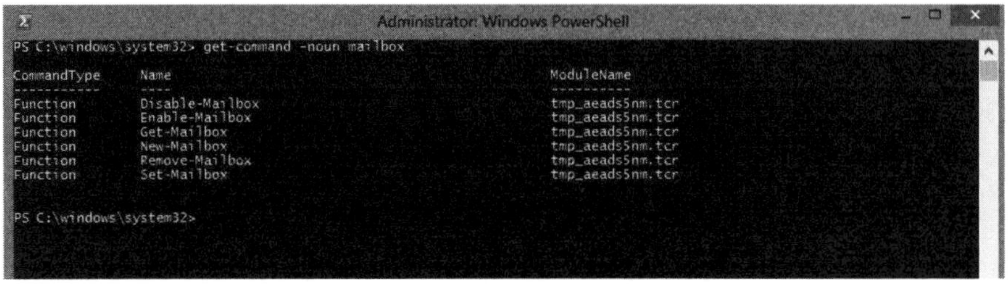

Figure 9-24 Results of the *Get-Command –Noun Mailbox* example.

In the next section, we will introduce other Windows PowerShell cmdlets.

Updating Windows PowerShell Help files

You need to occasionally update the Help files in Windows PowerShell to ensure you have the latest versions. Follow these steps to update the Windows PowerShell Help files:

1. Start the ISE and establish a *PSSession* if you do not already have one.

2. Enter the following command. Your window should look similar to the one shown in Figure 9-25:

    ```
    Update-Help
    ```

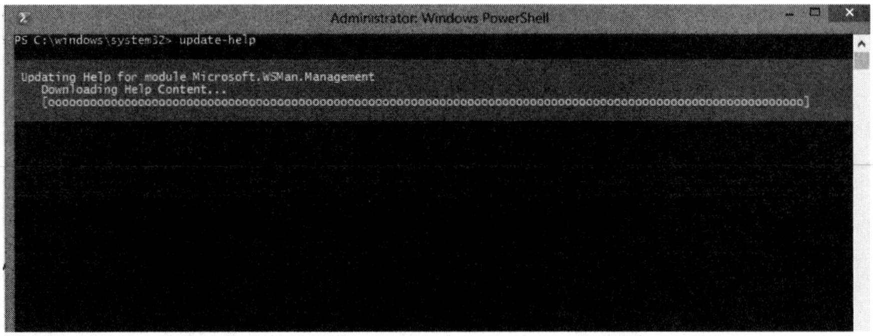

Figure 9-25 Updating Help from online sources is a new feature in Windows PowerShell 3.0.

Granting mailbox access

In this exercise, you will grant one user permissions to another user's mailbox. If you are continuing from the preceding exercise, you do not need to enable communications. Otherwise, follow the steps in the preceding exercise to establish a session with Exchange Online in Office 365.

To grant permissions, follow these steps:

1. Start the ISE and establish a *PSSession* if you do not already have one.

2. Enter the following cmdlet to view mailboxes and identify the users you want to provide permissions to:

   ```
   Get-Mailbox
   ```

3. For this exercise, we will grant user Julian full access to user Anthony's mailbox. We accomplish this by entering the following command. The result of this command is shown in Figure 9-26:

   ```
   Add-MailboxPermission -Identity julian@Contosofitness.onmicrosoft.com -User
   Anthony@ContosoFitness.onMicrosoft.com -AccessRights FullAccess -Inheri-
   tanceType All
   ```

> **Important**
>
> **Be careful when resetting the administrator password because it could affect your access to the tenant.**

Figure 9-26 Adding mailbox permissions to an Office 365 online account.

The *Add-MailboxPermission* cmdlet has several attributes, including the ability to select users and change their access rights. The information returned in the display indicates there were no syntax errors and the command completed successfully.

Validating permissions

Validating a user's permissions is another common administrative task. In this exercise, you will validate a user's access permissions to other mailboxes.

1. Establish a new *PSSession* if you do not already have one.

2. View the permissions of a mailbox by entering the following command. In the Office 365 development environment you are using, use an account name in place of Julian@ContosoFitness.onMicrosoft.com. The result should be similar to what is shown in Figure 9-27:

   ```
   Get-MailboxPermission -Identity Julian@ContosoFitness.onMicrosoft.com | Select
   User, AccessRights, Deny
   ```

Figure 9-27 View of the Office 365 mailbox rights from our development environment.

Changing time zones

It might be necessary to change the time zone for Office 365 mailboxes. If the time zone is incorrectly set for a user, it will affect the Exchange calendar. To change the time zone for a user, follow these steps:

1. Establish a *PSSession* if you do not have one.

2. To validate a user's time zone, enter the following command. Replace the user Anthony@ContosoFitness.onmicrosoft.com for one that applies to your environment:

   ```
   Get-MailboxRegionalConfiguration -Identity Anthony@ContosoFitness.onMicrosoft.
   com
   ```

3. To change the user's time zone, enter the following command. In this example, we will change the time zone for user Anthony@ContosoFitness.onmicrosoft.com:

```
Set-MailboxRegionalConfiguration -Identity Anthony@ContosoFitness.onMicrosoft.
com -TimeZone "Pacific Standard Time"
```

Viewing groups

Getting a list of groups in Office 365 is another common administrative task. Follow these

Figure 9-28 Show distribution groups using the *Get-Group* cmdlet.

Creating distribution groups

Creating a new Exchange distribution group requires additional information. In this exercise, you will see how the ISE can help you with the Windows PowerShell syntax by leveraging Intellisense. Follow these steps to create a new distribution group:

1. If the Command Add-on pane is not visible, enable it.

2. In the Name field, begin typing the command *New-DistributionGroup*, as shown in Figure 9-29. Notice that before you finish typing the command, the ISE will display the correct command.

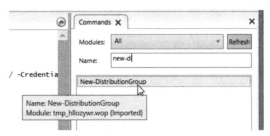

Figure 9-29 Finding a cmdlet in the ISE.

3.   Click the *New–DistributionGroup* cmdlet. A detailed section at the bottom of the Commands pane will appear, as shown in Figure 9-30.

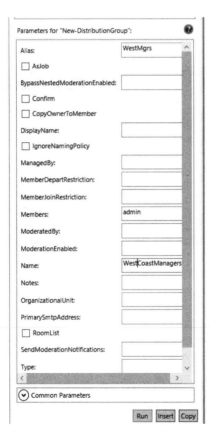

Figure 9-30 Parameter view of the ISE to help identify additional options used in the *New-DistributionGroup* cmdlet.

4.   Enter the parameters in the current Module view, click the Insert button, and then click the Run button at the bottom of the window. The ISE will build the Windows

PowerShell command for you. The output from the Command Pane should be similar
to the window shown in Figure 9-31.

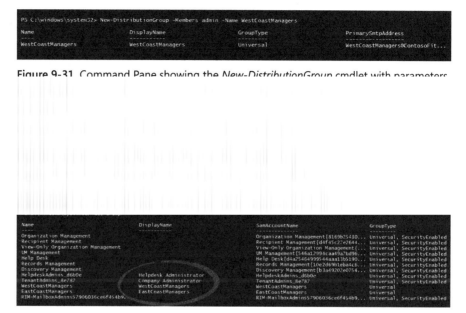

Figure 9-31 Command Pane showing the *New-DistributionGroup* cmdlet with parameters

Figure 9-32 Results of the *Get-Group* Windows PowerShell cmdlet after adding two new
distribution groups.

Using the Admin Audit log

The *Search-AdminAuditLog* cmdlet allows you to search the contents of the administrator
log. In this exercise, we will use *Search-AdminAuditLog* to search for newly created objects.

In the previous exercise, you created new distribution groups. You can use *Search-Admin-
Auditlog* to find information about these new groups by following these steps:

1.   Start the ISE and establish a *PSSession* if you do not already have one.

2.   In the Command Prompt window, type the following command and press Enter:

```
Search-AdminAuditLog -Cmdlets New-DistributionGroup
```

You should see the new distribution groups that were recently created. Your output
should look similar to what is shown in Figure 9-33.

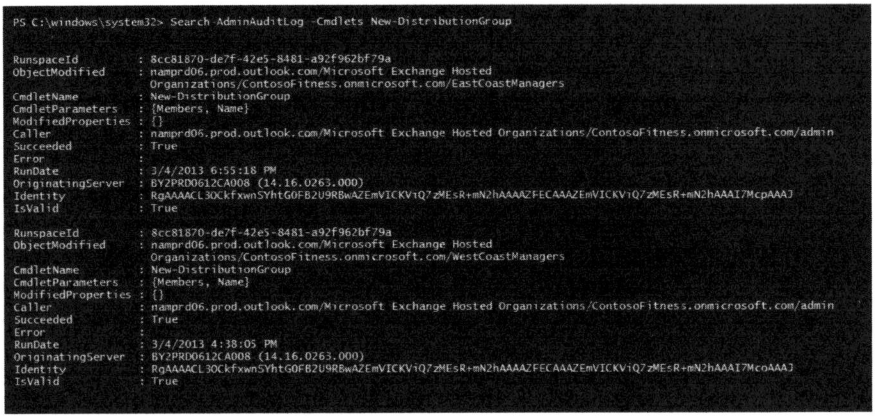

Figure 9-33 Results of the Windows PowerShell *Search-AdminAuditLog* command.

3. Search results might provide more data and the window might scroll beyond the current view. There is an option to redirect the output of any command to a text file. To redirect, or pipe, the output of command, modify the command by adding a > followed by the path and filename of the text file in which you want to store the output. For example, to redirect the output of the command in Step 2, enter the following command:

```
Search-AdminAuditLog -Cmdlets New-DistributionGroup > D:\Temp\AdminLog.TXT
```

Viewing retention policies

Most enterprises have compliance and regulatory requirements that require information to be deleted in a timely fashion. Exchange Online Messaging Records Management (MRM) is part of a larger compliance capability feature that helps ensure the timely removal of data. Compliance, MRM, Data Leakage Prevention, and In-Place Hold are discussed in greater detail in Chapter 11, "Incorporating Exchange Online in the Enterprise."

In this exercise, you will use Windows PowerShell to view retention policies by following these steps:

1. Start the ISE and establish a *PSSession* if you do not already have one.

2. At the command prompt, type the following command and press Enter:

```
Get-RetentionPolicy
```

3. The output from *Get-RetentionPolicy* should look similar to what is shown in Figure 9-34.

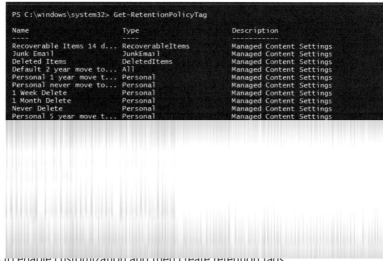

steps to enable customization and then create retention tags.

1. Start the ISE and establish a *PSSession* if you do not already have one.

2. At the command prompt, type the following command and press Enter:

    ```
    Enable-OrganizationCustomization
    ```

    You should see a progress bar similar to the progress bar shown in Figure 9-35 as the customization is being enabled.

Enable Configuration Customizations for Organization.
    Creating built-in Exchange Roles.

Figure 9-35 Progress bar showing customization being enabled.

3. Now create the retention tag using the *New-RetentionPolicyTag* cmdlet. In this exercise, we will create a 30-day retention tag to permanently delete items in the Deleted Items folder that are 30 days old. We will name this retention tag *FitnessTeams-DeletedItems*. As you will see in the command, the parameters for these properties are *–Type*, *-AgeLimitForRetention*, and *–RetentionAction*. Enter the following command into the ISE console and press Enter:

    ```
    New-RetentionPolicyTag "FitnessTeams-DeletedItems" -Type DeletedItems
    -RetentionEnabled $true -AgeLimitForRetention 30 -RetentionAction
    PermanentlyDelete
    ```

The result from the *New-RetentionPolicyTag* command should look similar to what is shown in Figure 9-36.

```
PS C:\windows\system32> New-RetentionPolicyTag "FitnessTeams-DeletedItems" -Type DeletedItems -RetentionEnabled $true -AgeLimitForRetention 30

Name                       Type            Description
----                       ----            -----------
FitnessTeams-DeletedItems DeletedItems     Managed Content Settings
```

Figure 9-36 Command Pane results after creating a new retention tag.

INSIDE OUT   Learn more Office 365 Windows PowerShell cmdlets

As we have stressed throughout the book, Windows PowerShell helps with automation and is the recommended way to manage Microsoft technologies and platforms. There are a number of tasks that do not have a user interface alternative because of the limited amount of screen real estate in a browser or MMC. The exercises covered in this chapter are only a starting point for Office 365 administration with Windows PowerShell commands. You should familiarize yourself with the many Office 365 remote Windows PowerShell commands, which can be found at *http://onlinehelp.microsoft.com/en-us/ office365-enterprises/hh125002.aspx*.

For information specific to Exchange 2013 Windows PowerShell commands, see *http:// help.outlook.com/en-us/140/dd575549.aspx*.

We recommend that you spend more time learning to use more of the Windows Power-Shell commands. One quick way to learn the details of Windows PowerShell is by exploring the Windows PowerShell Module view in the ISE console. Learn more commands using Internet Explorer by highlighting a Windows PowerShell command, right-clicking the command, and searching with Bing, as shown in Figure 9-37. Normally the results, especially those from TechNet, will provide the Windows PowerShell command details, syntax, and examples that can be copied and pasted into the ISE console.

Figure 9-37 Quick option to search with Bing to find details and example code for specific Office 365 and Exchange Online commands on TechNet.com.

Summary

As an Office 365 administrator, you can decide when to use Windows PowerShell and when to use the Office 365 admin center. The information in this chapter started you on your journey to learning Windows PowerShell. You should also now have a workstation that is capable of running Windows PowerShell and managing Office 365. Windows PowerShell is the foundation to implement automation in Office 365 as well as the on-premises tech-

dows PowerShell.

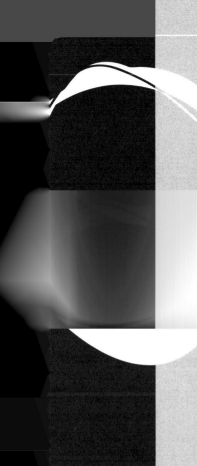

PART 4

Integrating and using Office 365 Services

Introducing Exchange Online 429

CHAPTER 11
Planning and deploying hybrid Exchange. . 459

CHAPTER 12
Mailbox migration and administering
Exchange Online 565

CHAPTER 13
SharePoint Online 631

CHAPTER 14
Lync Online. 699

CHAPTER 15
Office 365 Professional Plus. 759

Multiple service descriptions   430   Exchange Online Archiving   448

form that debuted in 1996. The primary role of Exchange Online is to facilitate email communications and provide calendaring and scheduling capabilities.

There are many hosted email services available in the marketplace today; some are even free of charge. However, unlike most hosted email services, Exchange is built for the enterprise and thus includes the required enterprise controls. The following are a few examples of the enterprise controls available with Exchange and Exchange Online:

- Mail journaling

- Messaging Records Management (MRM)

- Custom routing and handling

- Secure messaging

- Legal Hold, which has been renamed In-Place Hold

- Multi-mailbox electronic discovery (eDiscovery)

- Voice mail integration with Exchange Unified Messaging (UM)

Exchange Online is based on the equivalent on-premises Exchange technology. At the time of this writing, Exchange Online is based on the Exchange Server 2010 technology. Exchange 2013 was recently released to manufacturing (RTM); thus, Exchange Online will be upgraded accordingly. In fact, Microsoft announced that all new Office 365 customers after February 27, 2013 will be provisioned with Exchange 2013. Existing Office 365 customers still on the Exchange 2010 platform will be upgraded.

In this chapter, we introduce Exchange Online, Forefront Online Protection for Exchange (FOPE), Exchange Online Archiving (EOA), and the different deployment models. Chapter 11, "Incorporating Exchange Online in the Enterprise" covers planning, deployment, and administration of Exchange Online in detail.

Multiple service descriptions

Because Exchange Online has so many workloads, unlike the other Office 365 services, it is described in detail by multiple Service Descriptions. Each Service Description covers a specific significant workload. The Exchange service is described in these three Service Descriptions:

- Microsoft Exchange Online for Enterprises Service Description

- Microsoft Exchange Online Archiving Service Description

- Forefront Online Protection for Exchange (FOPE) Service Description

INSIDE OUT   When in doubt

Service Descriptions are the authoritative documents describing the capabilities and limitations of an Office 365 service. When in doubt or when you need to confirm the capabilities of a particular service, first read the Service Description. As consultants, we carry an updated copy of the Service Description whenever we are on site with customers. As of this writing, the Service Descriptions can be downloaded at *http://www.microsoft.com/en-us/download/details.aspx?id=13602*. However, with the release of the latest version of Office 365, the Service Descriptions have been moved to TechNet. As such, the Service Descriptions for the new Office 365 are located at *http://technet.microsoft.com/en-us/library/jj819284.aspx*.

This chapter will highlight only key information from the Service Descriptions. Furthermore, the capabilities of Office 365 continue to change as technology improves and as Microsoft responds to market and customer demands. As such, the overview of key capabilities in the following sections is subject to change. The Service Descriptions will also be updated accordingly to reflect such changes.

Exchange Online plans

Exchange Online is offered as part of a suite or as a stand-alone subscription. Regardless of how Exchange Online is acquired, it comes in three flavors:

- Exchange Online for Kiosk Workers

- Exchange Online Plan 1

is available.

Table 10-1 summarizes the major differences between Exchange Online plans.

TABLE 10-1 Comparison of Exchange Online plans

Exchange Online Plan 1	Exchange Online Plan 2	Exchange Online for Kiosk Workers
50 gigabyte (GB) total mailbox size shared between primary mailbox and online archiving	50 GB primary mailbox, unlimited online archiving	2 GB total mailbox size with no online archiving
Forefront Online Protection for Exchange, which will be upgraded to Exchange Online Protection	Forefront Online Protection for Exchange, which will be upgraded to Exchange Online Protection	Forefront Online Protection for Exchange, which will be upgraded to Exchange Online Protection
ActiveSync support	ActiveSync support	ActiveSync support
	Instant messaging capabilities in Outlook Web App (OWA); requires Lync integration	Instant messaging capabilities in Outlook Web App (OWA); requires Lync integration
	Exchange Unified Messaging (UM) capabilities	
	In-Place Hold and Legal Hold	

Chapter 10

INSIDE OUT Mix and match

Like all the other Office 365 workloads, you can mix and match Exchange Online plans, unless you acquired Exchange Online as part of a suite. Only one type of Exchange plan can be assigned to a user, and you can switch a user's plan without losing Exchange data. However, if you remove the Exchange Online plan license from a user for an extended period of time, the mailbox data for the user will be deleted. When a mailbox is deleted, you have to contact Microsoft Online Support within 30 days if you need the mailbox and its contents restored. After 30 days have passed, the mailbox and its contents cannot be recovered. When you change the Exchange Online plan for a user, the changes take effect immediately. This is important to know because in the event the change is a downgrade, the user might lose the ability to send or receive email. For example, if a user who has more than 2 GB of data in the mailbox is downgraded from Exchange Online Plan 1 to Exchange Online Plan for Kiosk Workers, the new 2 GB limit will take effect immediately and the overage caused by existing data in the mailbox will result in the user's inability to send or receive new messages. However, existing content in the mailbox will not be affected even though the limit is surpassed.

Exchange Online core workloads and concepts

To better understand Exchange Online, let us first list and define the different core email workloads:

- Mailboxes and calendaring

- Email archiving with EOA

- Email handling and transport with FOPE

- Email filtering, also with FOPE

- Secure email

INSIDE OUT FOPE to be replaced by EOP

With the latest release of Office 365, FOPE is being replaced by Exchange Online Protection (EOP). The service and SLA provided by EOP is the same as FOPE but the interface is different and more integrated with the Office 365 admin center. We will look at FOPE in this chapter and EOP in Chapter 12.

The reason why we feel it is important to identify these core workloads is because they each have unique configuration options, address specific security issues, and have elements used to define the different models of Exchange hybrid deployments that we will address in greater detail later in this chapter as well as in Chapter 11.

Mailboxes and calendaring

The primary mailbox is where the Inbox folder, which is the default email storage location

From a search perspective, the content stored in the primary mailbox enjoys the benefit of the new, always up-to-date mode, which means search performance and results are significantly improved over previous versions of Exchange.

Calendaring is the other significant capability that people rely on. Not only do Exchange Online calendars help you organize your day, they enable you to schedule meetings by allowing you to check on the availability of other people and resources.

INSIDE OUT   Email client vs. email server

Exchange Online is where content is stored and synchronized. It should not be confused with an email client. Examples of email clients are Microsoft Outlook, Apple iMessage and iCalendar applications, and even a browser. Outlook and Exchange are built to provide all the capabilities and maximize your email experience. However, it is important to note that Exchange Online supports more than just the Outlook email client. Through industry standard protocols such as ActiveSync, Post Office Protocol (POP), Internet Message Access Protocol (IMAP), and (Hypertext Transfer Protocol Secure) HTTPS, Exchange Online provides access to email and calendaring capabilities for many different devices, including non-Microsoft-based devices and clients.

Exchange Online Archiving mailbox

EOA is a new enterprise cloud-based archiving solution. It is designed to hold large amounts of data, to the point that if needed, there is an option for you to provision an unlimited amount of EOA storage for your organization.

EOA should be viewed as a solution to replace Personal Storage Table (PST) files. The .pst files have been around for a long time and have been a popular choice for archiving old emails. Over time, because .pst files have size limits, users have resorted to creating multiple .pst files to overcome these size limits. Multiple .pst files are then mounted in Outlook to access the contents. This approach allows users to have all their emails and the ability to drag and drop emails between the multiple .pst file locations and the primary mailbox.

However, .pst files have been seen as a major organization problem for the following reasons:

- The .pst files are local file-based storage and, despite the ability to password protect .pst files, they are a high risk for data loss.

- The .pst files cannot be easily searched from a central location if there is a need for electronic discovery.

- Legal holds cannot be placed on contents stored in .pst files.

- Records retention and management policies cannot be easily applied to contents stored in .pst files.

For users, there are inherent shortcomings as well. In today's world where it is likely that each person owns and uses more than one computing device, the localized nature of .pst files makes it difficult to synchronize the contents across multiple devices. The rise of mobility further limits the user because access to .pst contents is not possible through mobile solutions such as OWA.

EOA resolves both the requirement for organization compliance as well as the access challenges faced by users. EOA is also a consideration for organizations that have deployed third-party archiving solutions.

As an added benefit, EOA is available for Exchange Online and Exchange on-premises. We will examine these two configurations in Chapter 11. We provide a more detailed look at the features of EOA in the "Exchange Online Archiving" section later in this chapter.

Email handling and transport

Email transport is the end-to-end path of email transmission. Email transport is the responsibility of the Hub Transport server role in Exchange Online as well as FOPE. Email transport can be categorized into three communication types:

- Communication between clients and Exchange Online

- A web browser

- Outlook rich email client application

- Mobile communication devices such as smartphones

- iPads, tablets, and other mobile computing devices

- Blackberries, a proprietary form of communication device

Regardless of which device is used to connect to Exchange Online, Exchange Online is designed to ensure that the connections are all secured at the transport layer, as shown in Figure 10-1.

Outlook uses Remote Procedure Call (RPC) over an encrypted HTTPS channel to access email messages. HTTPS is the transport layer security that encrypts the communication channel.

If a browser is used, the OWA client is served by Exchange Online through HTTPS as well.

Exchange ActiveSync (EAS) is an Extensible Markup Language (XML)-based communication standard that is communicated through HTTP or HTTPS. The Exchange Online implementation of EAS is based on HTTPS, so the communication channel is also encrypted in this scenario.

If the mobile device does not have a client that can consume EAS, at the very least it would have a browser that can access OWA or OWA Light over HTTPS. Therefore, the communication channel is encrypted.

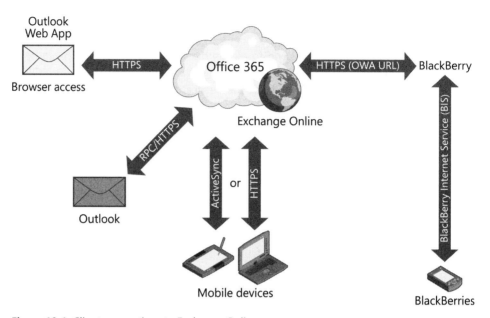

Figure 10-1 Client connections to Exchange Online

For Blackberry devices, Microsoft and Blackberry, formerly Research In Motion (RIM), have partnered to offer the Blackberry Internet Service (BIS) as a free service for Office 365 customers. Communication between Blackberry devices and Office 365 through BIS is encrypted.

Communication between Exchange Online and destination email servers

The only time that email might not be encrypted during transmission is the communication portion between Office 365 and the destination email system hosting the mailbox of the recipient, as shown in Figure 10-2. This is the Simple Mail Transmission Protocol (SMTP) portion and is not new in the world of email, which is the reason why email is generally not considered a secure method of transmitting information.

Figure 10-2 Unsecure SMTP traffic

While this is true for traditional email traffic, FOPE attempts to make email transmission more secure through the implementation of opportunistic Transport Layer Security (TLS).

As shown in Figure 10-3, Exchange Online, through the integrated Forefront Protection for Exchange, will first attempt to make a TLS connection with the destination email system. As depicted in Step 2 of Figure 10-3, the destination email system will either accept or reject the TLS connection request. Finally, in Step 3, if the destination email system accepted the TLS connection request, Exchange Online will transmit the email securely through the TLS

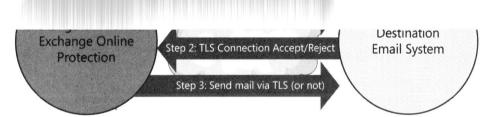

Figure 10-3 Opportunistic Transport Layer Security (TLS)

You can affect the email transport method. This is known as handling. Applied to the opportunistic TLS scenario, let us assume that you would like to change this setting for emails based on certain properties, such as destination or content. You can change the setting from opportunistic TLS to enforced TLS. By doing so, you have created a special handling circumstance.

Communication between Exchange Online customers

Communication channels between Office 365 data centers are all encrypted. Therefore, if a user in an organization that uses Exchange Online sends an email to another user in a different organization that also uses Exchange Online, the email will be delivered through an end-to-end encrypted connection, even if the Exchange Online service for both organizations reside in different data centers.

This also applies to customers who subscribe to Office 365 from different geographic locations. For example, a user in Singapore working for a Singapore-based company that uses Exchange Online sends an email to a user located in Washington working for a U.S.-based company that also uses Exchange Online. In this scenario, even though the users are working for two different companies that are geographically disparate, that email will be delivered through a secure transmission because they are both Exchange Online customers.

Email filtering

Forefront Protection 2010 for Exchange Server (FPE) implemented in Office 365 data centers is also responsible for protecting the Exchange Online servers. It takes care of the email filtering and email handling workloads. FPE can also be implemented as a stand-alone hosted service to protect an on-premises Exchange server. We will discuss this in greater detail later in this chapter.

When Forefront is acquired as a stand-alone service rather than as part of Exchange Online, it is known as Forefront Online Protection for Exchange (FOPE). At the time of this writing, FOPE is scheduled to be updated, and the next release will be renamed Exchange Online Protection (EOP).

Email filtering ensures email safety by dealing with possible threats and nuisance within emails, such as spam mail based on content, spam mail from known or suspicious sources, and messages that contain potentially dangerous attachments. Email-borne threats still rank the highest in terms of security risk, and the popularity of mobile devices as a result of the bring your own device (BYOD) phenomenon serves to exacerbate the problem.

EOP/FOPE forms a layer of separation between Exchange Online and the Internet, and it accepts and routes email on behalf of your organization. As such, EOP/FOPE is able to provide email filtering services through the traditional approach of scanning the headers and contents of inbound and outbound email.

EOP/FOPE is built upon thousands of servers spread across global data centers using a Microsoft proprietary algorithm to route traffic. In the event that a data center goes offline, the algorithm will reroute traffic accordingly. Therefore, your organization's email presence will benefit from the highest level of redundancy.

We provide a more detailed look at FOPE capabilities in the "Forefront Online Protection for Exchange" section later in this chapter.

Secure email

Secure email service is a solution built by a Microsoft partner, Voltage Security, and hosted in Office 365. This service is known as Exchange Hosted Encryption (EHE). Sensitive information such as trade secrets, product information, customer data, private health information protected by the Health Information Portability and Accountability Act (HIPAA), and credit card information are some examples of sensitive data that needs to be protected. We cover EHE in detail in the "Exchange Hosted Encryption" section later in this chapter.

Exchange Online capabilities

Exchange Online is primarily responsible for mailbox access and securely preserving contents. It is also responsible for initiating the delivery of email messages to internal and external recipients. Based on the Exchange Online plan your organization subscribes to, it is also responsible for storing voice mail content through its UM role.

As of this writing, the messaging limits are as follows:

- Maximum message size of 25 MB, including attachments.

- 10,000 recipients per day limit (where a distribution group is considered one recipient). Therefore, if you use two distribution groups with 10,000 recipients in each distribution group, Exchange Online sees that as two recipients when in reality the email is sent to 20,000 recipients.

- A single email can be addressed to a maximum of 500 recipients. A distribution group is again considered one recipient.

- Exchange Online throttles the rate of email delivery to 30 messages per minute for each mailbox. Anything beyond 30 messages will be queued for delivery in subsequent minutes. For example, if you send out 100 messages in rapid succession, the messages will be delivered over the course of slightly over three minutes: 30 messages will be sent immediately, 30 more will be sent the second minute, 30 the third minute, and the last 10 messages will be sent the fourth minute.

Exchange Online is not a mass-mailing service. If you need to send emails that are beyond the specified limits, there are third-party services to help you responsibly send out bulk emails and manage email campaigns.

Backup and recovery

Backups in Office 365 services are generally used to supplement disaster recovery measures. Services in Office 365 are provisioned in an active-active synchronized configuration between two data centers, which forms the first line of defense against data loss and service outage. Microsoft relies on backups as a supplemental strategy to recover from data corruption. As such, backups of Exchange Online data are not designed to respond to service requests for single-item recovery purposes. However, Exchange Online does have a single-item recovery feature, which we will cover shortly.

When a user deletes an item, it is stored in the user's Deleted Items folder until it is removed by the user or by a retention policy. Items deleted from the Deleted Items folder are stored in a Recoverable Items folder and can be recovered by the user for a period of 14 days before they are permanently purged from the system. Figure 10-4 shows the Recover Deleted Items option in the Outlook menu ribbon when the Deleted Items folder is selected.

Figure 10-4 Outlook Folder menu with the Recover Deleted Items option

INSIDE OUT   Recovering items

Recoverable items are stored on the server, and you need to be connected to the Exchange Online service to see items that can be recovered. If you are not connected to Exchange Online and attempt to see the recoverable items, you will receive a notification informing you that you need to connect to the server.

As mentioned, items in the Recoverable Items folder can be restored by the user within 14 days. A user can permanently delete items from the Recoverable Items folder by selecting items and clicking the Delete button, as shown in Figure 10-5.

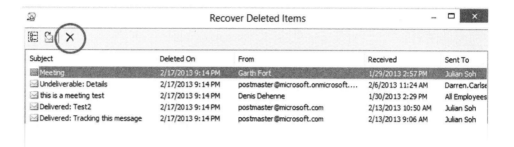

Recoverable Items folder by the user or by a retention policy, and is separate and beyond the 14-day period that an item resides in the Recoverable Items folder.

When you delete a user account in Active Directory (AD), remove the Exchange Online license from a user account, or delete the mailbox, the mailbox and its contents will be deleted. In the first scenario, the user account and the mailbox will be deleted during the next scheduled directory synchronization. In the second scenario, where the Exchange Online license has been removed, it will take some time before the actual mailbox and its contents are removed. Only the final scenario is more immediate. When you delete the mailbox directly through Windows PowerShell or through the administration portal, the action takes effect immediately.

If the mailbox and its contents are deleted by any of these three actions, you can submit a request within 30 days to Microsoft Online Services to restore the mailbox and its contents.

Exchange Online service availability and redundancy

Microsoft guarantees a 99.9 percent service availability that is calculated on a monthly basis and on a per-customer basis. The 99.9 percent also includes maintenance windows, which means there are no expected outages to Exchange Online due to planned maintenance.

Microsoft is able to accomplish this because of the geo-redundant infrastructure of Exchange Online. If the Service Level Agreement (SLA) is not met, Microsoft will be financially obligated to give you a reduction in your Exchange Online subscription costs for that month. The financial liability and public perception are very significant factors that motivate Microsoft to minimize slippages in meeting the SLA.

Chapter 10

INSIDE OUT   SLAs: More than meets the eye

When we meet with customers who are evaluating Office 365, they often tell us that 99.9 percent is really low for an industry standard. Some customers also say they have a greater than a 99.9 percent uptime requirement. During such conversations, we share two important things. The first is that the 99.9 percent is an SLA metric, not an engineering design. The SLA states that Microsoft is obligated to meet at least a 99.9 percent uptime. More often than not, the service surpasses 99.9 percent availability. The second thing we bring up is that there is a distinct difference between stating an SLA and meeting an SLA. Most organizations do not have the benefit of a geo-redundant footprint and the type of infrastructure to maximize the chances of meeting the SLA. In many cases, not meeting an internal SLA does not result in significant penalties aside from unhappy users. This is definitely not like the financial penalties that bind Microsoft. Furthermore, most SLAs exclude planned maintenance times; therefore, it might not be an equivalent comparison. It is not that the organizations' IT professionals are unable to maintain an Exchange environment, it is just that there is no comparison to Exchange Online because of the level of investment coupled with the technical expertise derived directly from Microsoft, the manufacturer of the Exchange technology. As you can see, Exchange Online is easily the best hosted Exchange service available in the market because of these unique characteristics of Office 365.

While service availability is very important, an often under-discussed topic is the speed of service restoration if a natural disaster destroys a data center. This is where the value of geo-redundancy comes into play. In the event that a disaster destroys a data center, Exchange Online is able to restore email services within one hour. This metric is known as the Recovery Time Objective (RTO). For Exchange Online, the RTO is only one hour because of the geo-redundant nature of the data centers.

Another closely related metric to RTO is the Recovery Point Objective (RPO). The RPO measures the amount of data at risk in the event of a disaster. For example, if an organization without geo-redundancy does backups every evening and the backup ends at 5:00 A.M. in the morning, if disaster strikes at noon, then the RPO for the organization is seven hours. In contrast, the geo-redundant and active-active configuration of Exchange Online makes it possible for a near instantaneous RPO.

Forefront Online Protection for Exchange

FOPE has the following key features:

- 99.999 percent financially backed uptime guarantee

- 100 percent protection against all known viruses

- Capture of at least 98 percent of all spam

- False positive commitment of 1 in every 250,000 messages

- Email delivery of less than one minute

Figure 10-6 shows the main page of the FOPE administrator console. It provides statistics as well as announcements related to the FOPE service. In this section, we show the key capa-

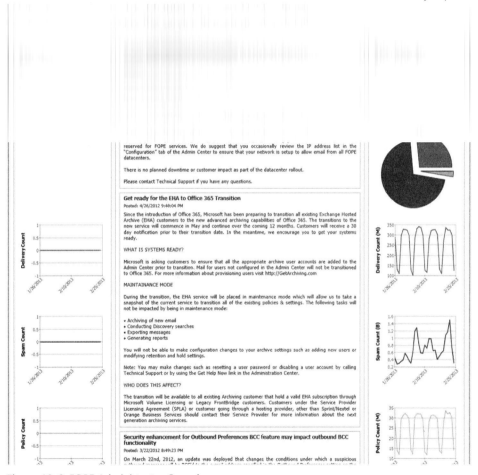

Figure 10-6 FOPE Administrator Console

Layered protection

The effectiveness of FOPE is attributed to its use of layered filtering. This is accomplished through the use of three scan engines with virus and malware strains provided by three different partners that specialize in anti-virus and anti-malware solutions. FOPE checks with these partners for signature updates every 15 minutes and incorporates new variants into FOPE filters accordingly.

INSIDE OUT   Three times the protection

Most organizations incorporate anti-virus and anti-spam filters, but most use only a single reputable solution provider. There are two important things to note with regards to FOPE multi-layer filtering. First, you get three times the protection. All email protection service providers react in a responsive manner and need to take time to develop and update their signature files in response to new variants. Having three providers gives FOPE the most effective and quickest turnaround time to respond to new variants. Secondly, it is the security partners who are providing the filters. That is their core competency, and Microsoft simply leverages and implements that into FOPE.

Anti-Spam

Spam mail affects users' productivity and consumes unnecessary network resources. Left unchecked, spam can easily make email systems unusable. FOPE uses all the industry spam detection methods, including the following:

- Internet Protocol (IP) and IP subnet reputation
- Connection analysis for suspicious or non-RFC compliant attempts
- Content analysis
- NDR backscatter prevention
- Customer reporting
- Industry spam lookup blacklists
- Directory-based blocking

These are just some of the more common and well-known methods. FOPE utilizes other methods to fight spam as well, but we will not examine every method and detail because these are covered in the FOPE Service Description and at TechNet. The important thing to note is that your organization does not have to maintain spam protection nor compromise on spam protection by using FOPE. Your organization will benefit from not having to manage and tweak every spam control method. This takes away the busy work so your email and network administrators can focus on more important tasks.

Message quarantine

To handle false-positives, FOPE has a quarantine feature. The FOPE quarantine area is accessed through the browser. You can also choose to grant users the ability to view their own quarantine area to review and release messages, or you can choose to keep that as a centralized administrative function. By default, messages in the quarantined area are kept for 14 days if no action is taken.

INSIDE OUT   Hub Transport or FOPE policies

With the overlap in routing capabilities, the question that often comes up is whether to use Hub Transport or FOPE to manage inbound and outbound emails. In the past, Hub Transport was the only available mechanism within Exchange to implement policies against inbound and outbound emails. With the introduction of FOPE, it is recommended that policies should be designed in FOPE because it is better suited to enforce policies. Therefore, it is recommended that existing Hub Transport rules be migrated to FOPE where applicable.

Figure 10-7 shows a comparison of the Hub Transport window to the FOPE policy window. Notice the overlap in capabilities between a transport rule and a FOPE policy. Also shown in Figure 10-7, FOPE policies can be developed based on the following email characteristics:

- Message content in the subject and body

- Recipients

- Attachment existence and type

- Domain details

- Message header information

- IP addresses

- Message size

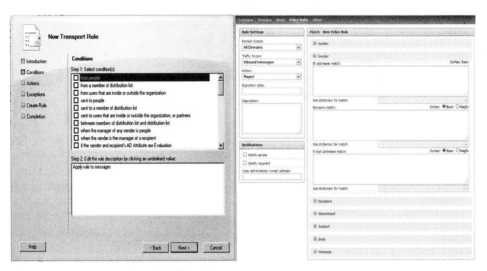

Figure 10-7 Transport rule and FOPE policy

Message handling

When a message satisfies a FOPE policy, whether it is spam or organization policy, you can control how the message is handled. Following are the message-handling capabilities of FOPE:

- Reject

- Allow

- Quarantine

- Redirect

- Deliver with Bcc

- Force TLS

In addition, you can also notify the sender or the recipients of the FOPE action as well as send a copy to an administrator with the information. Finally, you also have the ability to test FOPE rules before enforcing them. This is a feature that is not available in a Hub Transport rule. You can enable or disable a Hub Transport rule, but you cannot test a Hub

Transport rule before putting it into effect. Figure 10-8 shows the FOPE actions you can apply against specific policy rules.

Figure 10-8 FOPE actions with respect to policies

Reporting

FOPE provides reporting and analytics capabilities. You have the ability to create reports based on the following:

- Inbound and outbound delivery

- Spam and virus information

- Policy filtering

- Suspicious emails

Figure 10-9 is a screen shot of the FOPE report creation page. Note that you also have the ability to schedule reports for delivery through email.

Figure 10-9 FOPE report creation

Aside from reports, FOPE also provides you with the capability to trace email messages. This feature is handy when you need to find out what happened to an inbound or outbound message. Figure 10-10 shows the FOPE message tracing page.

Figure 10-10 FOPE Message Trace.

Exchange Online Archiving

As mentioned earlier, EOA is the hosted archiving workload. The detailed capabilities of EOA are covered in an EOA-specific Service Description, the Microsoft Exchange Online Archiving Service Description. This section highlights the major capabilities of EOA.

Built-in archiving is a new Exchange 2010 capability and is built as part of Exchange Online. It can also be deployed as an independent workload, which we will see in greater detail later in this chapter. Hosted archiving is known as EOA.

Archive size

One of the biggest benefits of EOA is the ability to provision a large amount of storage space for archiving purposes. Archiving, built into Exchange Online Plan 1, allows you to

unlimited storage, in reality only 100 GB per mailbox is initially provisioned. The reason for this is because EOA requires a valid size value, and zero, which is traditionally used to indicate unlimited size, is not a valid value and the field cannot be blank. Therefore, Microsoft Online Services chose 100 GB as an arbitrary high number. The service is still intended to be unlimited, so if any of your users reach the 100 GB limit, you will simply need to submit a service request to increase the limit. There will be no charge for any additional storage beyond the 100 GB limit. Secondly, it is important to note that size limit is separate from time limits. There is no time-limit dimension in EOA. Time limits are based on the Message Records Management (MRM) capabilities of Exchange Online. MRM leverages retention tags and retention policies to automatically delete messages. Without a defined MRM, EOA will retain all messages in the primary mailbox and in EOA unless a user manually deletes them.

Backup and recovery

EOA shares the same SLA as Exchange Online when it comes to service continuity and disaster recovery. Like Exchange Online, EOA backups are for disaster recovery purposes and not designed to respond to service requests for single-item recovery. All EOA recovery capabilities are based on the same Exchange Online recovery capabilities covered in the Exchange Online section earlier in this chapter. EOA provides 99.9 percent guaranteed service availability; the same one hour RTO and almost instantaneous RPO also apply.

Chapter 10

EOA access

The EOA mailbox is accessed as part of the user's email interface in Outlook 2007, 2010, and 2013. EOA can also be accessed through a browser through the OWA.

However, EOA cannot be accessed through Outlook 2003, Outlook 2011 for Mac, Office 2008 Entourage Web Services Edition, or OWA Light. From a protocol level, EOA cannot be accessed through the Post Office Protocol (POP) or Internet Message Access Protocol (IMAP). Finally, EOA mailboxes can be accessed only by the owner and cannot be delegated.

You can customize how EOA appears in the users' email interface by specifying the mailbox name. Figure 10-11 shows the ability to custom name the EOA mailbox, and Figure 10-12 shows the same EOA mailbox in the Outlook 2013 email interface.

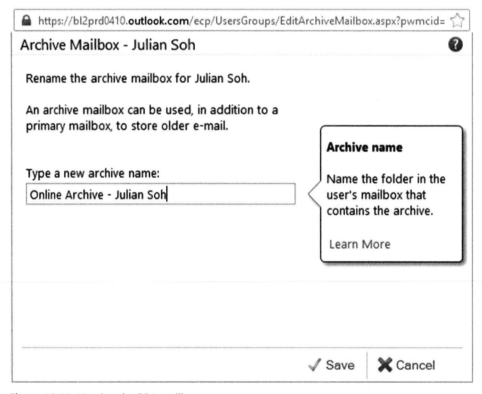

Figure 10-11 Naming the EOA mailbox

Figure 10-12 Outlook 2013 with EOA mailbox

Compliance

As mentioned earlier, prior to EOA, email content was preserved by .pst files or third-party storage solutions that take content out of the native Exchange mailbox environment. EOA provides enhanced compliance capabilities by leveraging MRM and Legal Hold capabilities.

The multi-mailbox search capability of Exchange Online can search EOA with the same kind of granularity and comprehensiveness that applies to primary mailboxes. In the next release of Exchange Online and EOA, Legal Hold is renamed In-Place Hold and provides greater granularity in holding content. We cover compliance and discovery in detail in Chapter 11.

Exchange Hosted Encryption

Emails containing sensitive content need special handling so that they are not transmitted through insecure SMTP. Traditionally, there are two ways to protect such content:

- Using a certificate-based solution, such as a private key infrastructure (PKI)

- Using a non-certificate-based solution

EHE is a solution that does not require the use of certificates. However, it does require FOPE email-handling capabilities to identify email content so that the EHE solution can be invoked. Therefore, FOPE is a prerequisite for EHE.

Chapter 10

EHE uses a technology known as Identity-Based Encryption (IBE). IBE uses recipients' email addresses as the public keys. When a message is redirected to EHE by FOPE, it stores the message and encrypts it with a private key, which will be made available to the recipient. At the same time, EHE notifies the recipient of the email and initiates a two-step, email-based verification process. Once a recipient's identity has been verified, the recipient can access the email through a clientless, browser-based reader, known as the Voltage Zero Download Messenger, over an HTTPS connection.

Exchange Online implementation options

Exchange Online is the most flexible service in Office 365. There are many ways in which you can implement Exchange Online. In fact, whenever the hybrid nature of Office 365 is mentioned, Exchange Online is the foremost that comes to mind.

To describe the flexible nature of Exchange Online, let us recall the core Exchange work-loads we just defined:

- Primary mailboxes

- Email filtering and handling with FOPE

- Email archiving with EOA

As the name implies, a hybrid implementation of Exchange is a combination of online and on-premises Exchange workloads. In a hybrid environment, the above workloads can be handled by on-premises infrastructure or Exchange Online in any combination. In this section, we review the different hybrid Exchange models. In Chapter 11, we cover the configuration and deployment details for these models.

Hybrid mailboxes

The hybrid mailbox model is the most commonly recognized configuration and is also the most complex of all the hybrid models. In this model, Exchange Online is deployed in such a way that the organization has some mailboxes on premises, while other mailboxes reside in Exchange Online. However, despite the disparate placement of mailboxes, the organization continues to retain its singular look and feel, and users are completely unaffected. This means that the organization and its users continue to have a single global address list (GAL) and the ability to share calendars and view free and busy times, regardless of where the mailboxes reside. The entire organization will also share the same SMTP namespace.

There are many reasons for an organization to set up a hybrid mailbox configuration, and it is quite a common occurrence. For example, if an organization already has an on-premises Exchange implementation and wants to migrate to Exchange Online over time, a hybrid model will have to be established. This is an example of a phased migration and is popular among large organizations where a cutover migration is not possible.

For some organizations, there might be business requirements, regulatory controls, or just political drivers that might make a hybrid mailbox configuration a more permanent setup. This is a more permanent hybrid model than the first scenario. Both the temporary and permanent hybrid mailbox configurations are fully supported deployment models.

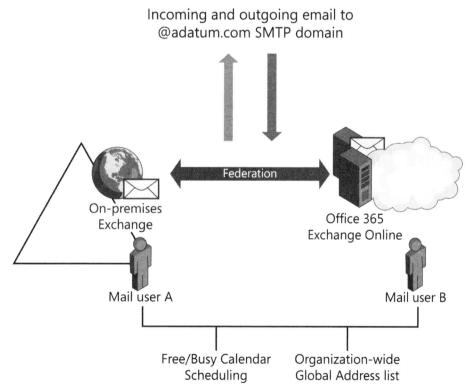

Figure 10-13 High-level graphic representation of a hybrid mailbox configuration

Hybrid archiving model

Another, less discussed hybrid model is the deployment of only the EOA workload to an on-premises Exchange implementation. In this scenario, an organization might, for whatever reason, choose not to move mailboxes to Exchange Online. However, they might consider just deploying the archiving workload by leveraging EOA.

If our example organization, Adatum, decides to implement archiving in the cloud without moving mailboxes, their configuration will look something like Figure 10-14.

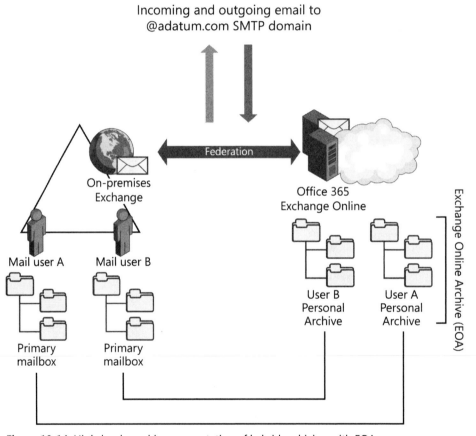

Figure 10-14 High-level graphic representation of hybrid archiving with EOA

Even though EOA is just one of the workloads in Exchange Online, your organization will immediately benefit from adopting this small workload, without having to move mailboxes.

For starters, if your organization is struggling with .pst files, EOA is a logical approach for solving the compliance and security issues associated with .pst files. Your users will also benefit from having a personal archive in EOA because they can now access the contents of their personal archive from multiple computers, including through OWA.

Alternatively, if your organization currently has an in-house, third-party central archival system for email, there is an opportunity for your organization to save hardware and licensing cost by implementing EOA. On-premises archival solutions require you to maintain and upgrade hardware, which at the very least are the hard drives that house the archive data. As with any enterprise storage solution, it is not just a matter of capacity, but also the need

The third hybrid model is another model that does not involve mailbox migration. Remember we mentioned earlier in the chapter that if your organization has its own on-premises Exchange implementation, or for that matter any type of email solution, you can acquire a Forefront-hosted email filtering service known as FOPE as a stand-alone solution.

This model affects only mail-flow capabilities by routing inbound or outbound email through FOPE. Figure 10-15 shows this type of configuration.

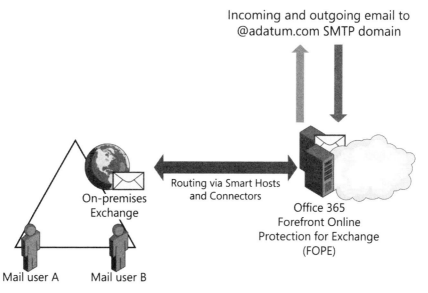

Figure 10-15 Hybrid mail protection leveraging FOPE

This model allows your organization to outsource only the email filtering service while continuing to maintain on-premises email servers. We have covered FOPE features earlier in this chapter, so this model allows your organization to enjoy all those features without mailbox migration.

New capabilities

The latest version of Office 365, released on February 27, 2013, uses the 2013 version of Exchange. Therefore, Exchange Online will have new capabilities as a result of the release. We discuss these new capabilities in this section.

Data Leakage Prevention

Data Leakage Prevention (DLP) is the ability of a system to automatically detect sensitive information. DLP is a new feature in Exchange Online and allows you to incorporate ISO-based templates. These templates allow Exchange Online to detect the following U.S.-specific data types in email:

- Federal Trade Commission (FTC) consumer rules

- Financial data

- Gramm-Leach-Biley Act (GLBA)

- Health Insurance Portability and Accountability Act (HIPAA)

- Patriot Act

- Personally identifiable information (PII) data

- State data breach notification laws

- Social Security information

Aside from U.S.-specific data types, there are also templates available for Australia and UK data laws. You can also import or customize a template. Figure 10-16 is a screen shot of the available DLP templates.

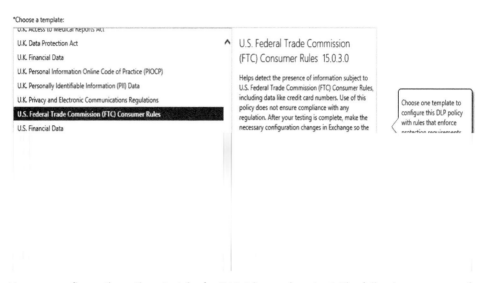

You can configure the actions to take for DLP-triggered content. The following are some of these actions:

- Block messages

- Force TLS transmission

- Allow sender to proceed with sending the message, but log the activity

Furthermore, you can configure different actions on DLP-triggered content depending on whether the recipients are internal or external.

Rights Management Service

Rights Management Service (RMS) is a Microsoft technology that can be applied to file systems, SharePoint, and Exchange. Traditionally, RMS is a Windows Server feature, and on-premises RMS can be deployed to protect on-premises and Office 365 content. In the latest release of Office 365, a hosted RMS offering is available for use with Exchange Online and SharePoint Online. Hosted RMS cannot be used to protect content stored on-premises.

RMS for Exchange Online allows the sender to specify how content should be handled to prevent the unauthorized re-transmission of email.

Summary

The key takeaway in this chapter is that hosted email in Office 365 is extensive and extremely configurable, as indicated by the different Service Descriptions dedicated to each workload. There are also different hybrid models that you can deploy. With that, you are now ready to plan and deploy Exchange Online.

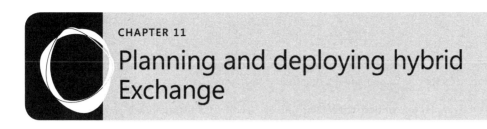

Planning and deploying hybrid Exchange

Planning an Exchange hybrid deployment 460   Configuring an Exchange hybrid model. 513

To recap, Exchange can be deployed as a fully on-premises solution, completely in Office 365, or as a hybrid. Because this is an Office 365 book, we will not be discussing fully on-premises Exchange implementations except in the context of a migration. Implementing a hybrid Exchange environment is an involved process and in some cases is a required pre-requisite for some mailbox migration scenarios. Mailbox migration is covered in Chapter 12, "Mailbox migration and administering Exchange Online."

This chapter is a more hands-on chapter where we will walk you through these tasks:

- Planning for the hybrid deployment of Exchange

- Prerequisites for the hybrid deployment of Exchange

- Configuring the hybrid deployment of Exchange:

    ○ Exchange hybrid environment

    ○ Exchange Online Archiving (EOA)

    ○ Mail flow

The first task will introduce all the different planning tools as well as factors that might influence your Exchange Online implementation model. We will also walk you through pre-paring the management environment and prerequisites for Exchange in a hybrid model.

In Chapter 12, we will cover mailbox migration options and how to manage Exchange Online as part of your enterprise. Because Exchange Online is based on Exchange on-premises technology, administration of the service is very similar between on-premises and online. This book is not intended to be an exhaustive Exchange administration book as there are other books focused solely on this topic. What we will cover are the administration tasks specific to managing a hybrid environment.

At the time of this writing, Office 365 with Exchange 2013 technology was recently released. Therefore, many existing Office 365 customers have not been upgraded to Exchange 2013. As such, where applicable, we will discuss both versions.

On that note, let us proceed to the planning phase.

Planning an Exchange hybrid deployment

Before you begin the planning process, take time to understand the core capabilities and requirements for an Exchange hybrid environment.

Understanding capabilities

To recap, the following list shows the capabilities of an Exchange hybrid deployment model:

- Single global address list (GAL).

- Ability to see free and busy schedules regardless of where the mailboxes reside.

- Ability to move mailboxes from Exchange on-premises to Exchange Online and vice versa.

- Availability of Outlook Web App (OWA) for both on-premises and online users.

- Client-side capabilities such as mail tips that are applicable to both on-premises Exchange and Exchange Online. For example, if a Data Leakage Prevention (DLP) rule is created to disallow emailing of sensitive information to external recipients, it will consider recipients who are on-premises and those who are online as part of the same organization.

INSIDE OUT   Temporary or permanent?

You can establish an Exchange hybrid environment as a temporary model to facilitate a phased migration with the end goal of being 100 percent in the cloud, or you can establish a permanent model with some mailboxes or workloads handled by Exchange on-premises and others by Exchange Online. Both models are fully supported strategies.

Requirements

An Exchange hybrid environment has the following requirements:

- You must always have an on-premises Exchange server to facilitate the hybrid model.

- You must install an Exchange 2010 SP3 Client Access Server (CAS) role in your Exchange 2003 or 2010 environment, or if you already have Exchange 2010, you

Office 365, only Exchange 2010 SP2 was required. SP3 facilitates hybrid models involving the latest version of Office 365, which features Exchange 2013 technologies.

- Directory synchronization should already be installed and configured for Active Directory write-back. This was covered in Chapter 4, "Directory synchronization". Refer to Figure 4-35 in Chapter 4.

- Access to a Domain Name System (DNS) for your domain to create the necessary DNS Autodiscover and service (SRV) records. If you want to route email through Office 365 instead of your on-premises Exchange Hub Transport server, you will need to modify your organization's MX records. We will create and modify DNS records shortly, so make sure you have the ability to make DNS changes for your organization.

- If you are planning a phased migration, identify which mailboxes will move to Exchange Online and which ones will remain on-premises.

> **Note**
>
> As you plan the placement of mailboxes, take special note of which mailboxes have delegate permissions. Delegate permissions, such as delegate access, folder permissions, and "send on behalf of" are not available unless the delegates coexist with the mailbox. Therefore, if a manager has an assistant with delegated rights to the manager's mailbox, you should plan on having both the manager's mailbox and the assistant's mailbox reside on-premises or in Office 365. Do not separate these two individuals' mailboxes.

Chapter 11

INSIDE OUT Exchange Pre-Deployment Analyzer

If you do not have Exchange 2010 in your environment and need to deploy Exchange 2010, download and install the Exchange 2010 Pre-Deployment Analyzer (ExPDA) at *http://www.microsoft.com/en-us/download/details.aspx?id=11636*. ExPDA performs a comprehensive topology scan of your environment to determine its readiness for an Exchange 2010 deployment.

Using the Exchange Server Deployment Assistant

Microsoft has provided an online Exchange Server Deployment Assistant to help you plan for an Exchange hybrid deployment. The great thing about this tool is that it generates all the checklist items required for your particular hybrid configuration model.

In this exercise, you will use the Deployment Assistant to generate a schematic and a check-list for our deployment model. Follow these steps to use the Deployment Assistant and to review the checklist it generates:

1. Go to *http://technet.microsoft.com/en-us/exdeploy2010/default(EXCHG.150). aspx#Index* and start the Deployment Assistant.

2. Select the Hybrid (includes Exchange Online Archiving) option, as shown in Figure 11-1.

Figure 11-1 Exchange Server Deployment Assistant.

3. The next two questions are specific to your organization, and they are questions as to what version of on-premises Exchange your organization currently has and whether you would like to configure an EOA-only model. For this exercise, we responded that we have an Exchange 2010 on-premises environment and do not want to deploy EOA only, as shown in Figure 11-2.

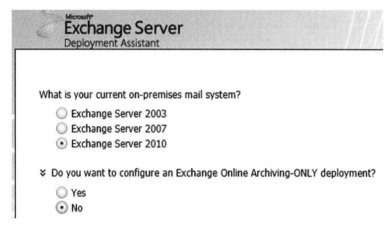

Figure 11-2 Telling the Deployment Assistant about your environment and intention.

4. Take note of the navigation options at the bottom right of the Deployment Assistant. On later pages of the assistant, a check box might also be provided, as shown in Figure 11-3. At this time, click the right arrow to go to the next page.

Figure 11-3 Navigation arrows and check box in the Deployment Assistant tool.

5. The next three questions are specific to your desired deployment model. Answer them accordingly. For this exercise, we have chosen to use on-premises credentials, also known as single sign-on (SSO), and to route email to and from external recipients through Exchange Online. We will not be using an Edge Transport server to route emails between Exchange Online and our on-premises Exchange environment. Figure 11-4 shows how we answered the three questions. Click the right arrow to go to the next page.

INSIDE OUT   Why did we answer this way?

The reason we chose to answer the five questions the way we did and selected this scenario for this exercise is because it is the most popular hybrid mailbox scenario, in our experience. Most customers we encounter would like to phase the deployment, which means some mailboxes remain on premises and others are in Exchange Online. Secondly, they do not want to cause degradation in experience for the users whose mailboxes are moved to Exchange Online; therefore, SSO is a non-negotiable requirement. Finally, most customers also want to offload the Hub Transport server role so they gain better fault tolerance for Internet email transport and at the same time take advantage of offloading the email protection workload because Forefront Online Protection for Exchange (FOPE)/ Exchange Online Protection (EOP) is integrated with Exchange Online.

6. Based on the answers provided thus far, the Deployment Assistant generated a schematic for our setup, as shown in Figure 11-5. Take the time to review the information and the schematic. Click the right arrow when you are ready.

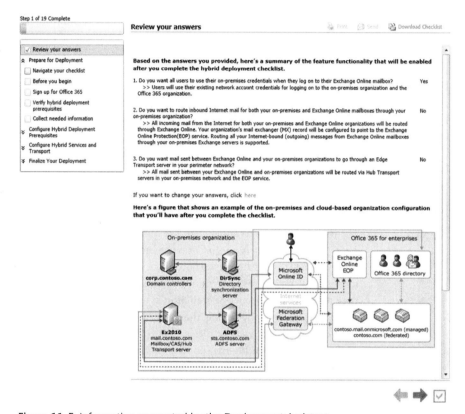

Figure 11-5 Information generated by the Deployment Assistant.

7. Read through the information as you navigate ahead in the Deployment Assistant. You should have fulfilled most of the prerequisites if you completed the tasks outlined in Chapter 2, "Planning and preparing to deploy Office 365", Chapter 3, "Active Directory Federation Services", and Chapter 4. Keep navigating ahead until you get to the Collect Needed Information page. Gather all the required information and complete the table that is found on that page. The table is reproduced as Table 11-1. Click the right arrow when you are done.

TABLE 11-1 Table of information needed for hybrid deployment

Description	Example value in checklist	Value in your organization
Active Directory forest root	corp.contoso.com	
Internal Exchange 2010 SP3 server host name (contains Mailbox, Hub Transport, and	EX2010	
Internal Active Directory Federation Services (AD FS) server host name (only for organizations choosing to deploy single sign-on)	ADFS	
External AD FS server fully qualified domain name (FQDN) (only for organizations choosing to deploy single sign-on)	sts.contoso.com	
Internal Active Directory synchronization server host name	DirSync	
On-premises Autodiscover FQDN	autodiscover.contoso.com	
Service tenant FQDN		

> **Note**
> You can choose only the subdomain portion of this FQDN. The domain portion must be onmicrosoft.com.

8. The next step is to configure SSO, which was covered in Chapter 3. Click the right arrow when you are done.

9. On the Configure Active Directory synchronization page, configure Active Directory synchronization, which was covered in Chapter 4. Click the right arrow.

10. On the Verify service configuration page, verify the service configuration for AD FS and DirSync. Verification and troubleshooting these services were covered in Chapters 3 and 4. Click the right arrow.

11. The next step is to configure DNS records. Use the table of examples on the Configure DNS records page to help you configure your DNS records. The table is recreated as Table 11-2. Gather the information, but do not make the changes at this time as we are only reviewing the checklist items. We will make the DNS changes later. Click the right arrow to go to the next page.

TABLE 11-2 Required DNS changes

Hybrid requirement	DNS record	DNS record type	Target/value
Required for all hybrid deployments	Autodiscover.contoso.com	CNAME or A	If using CNAME DNS: mail.contoso.com If using A DNS: External IP address of an Exchange 2010 SP3 Client Access server or firewall
Recommended as a best practice for all hybrid deployments	SPF	TXT	v=spf1 include:outlook.com include:spf.messaging.microsoft.com~all

12. The next checklist item in the Deployment Assistant is the configuration of Windows PowerShell and the Exchange Management Console (EMC). This will allow your organization to easily manage Exchange Online. If your organization has been using Exchange on-premises, the familiar EMC can also be used to manage both Exchange on-premises and Exchange Online. Furthermore, this will help facilitate mailbox moves between on-premises and online. We will walk you through the installation of EMC on a workstation and connect it to Exchange Online later in this chapter. For now, click the right arrow on the Configure management interfaces page to go to the next page.

13. The next item on the checklist is to obtain certificates. Certificates are used to secure communications between the on-premises Exchange environment and Exchange

Online. The checklist recommends that you select a common name (CN) for your certificate that is the same as the suffix of your organization's SMTP address. This certificate cannot be a self-signed certificate. It must be issued by a trusted third-party certificate authority. We will acquire the certificate and bind the services to the certificate later in this chapter. Click the right arrow on the Configure Exchange certificates page to proceed to the next page.

14. The last item on the checklist, prior to the actual deployment, is the configuration of

TABLE 11-3 Quick checklist

Task description	Completed [Y/N]
Ensure you have an Office 365 tenant provisioned with Exchange Online as part of the subscription.	
Ensure you have Office 365 administration capabilities (at least for Exchange Online).	
Review and understand Exchange hybrid model capabilities.	
Identify placement of mailboxes. Take special note of users' mailboxes that need to move or stay together.	
Install the Exchange 2010 SP3 CAS role if your environment is running Exchange 2003 or Exchange 2007. Install SP3 if you already have an existing Exchange 2010 CAS.	
Install the Exchange Management Console (EMC) from the Exchange 2010 SP3 package to a workstation if you will be using a workstation to manage Exchange and/or Exchange Online.	
Connect your organization's Exchange Online tenant to the EMC.	

Task description	Completed [Y/N]
Create autodiscover.*<Your-Org>*.com A or CNAME DNS record.	
Configure directory synchronization with write-back capabilities.	
Configure AD FS for SSO.	
Create a certificate signing request (CSR) and apply it to your Exchange server. Certificate type = Unified Communication.	
Configure Autodiscover on your Exchange server.	
Configure Exchange Web Services (EWS) on your Exchange server.	
Configure an offline address book (OAB) on your Exchange server.	
Run the Exchange Server Deployment Assistant at *http://technet. microsoft.com/en-us/exdeploy2010/default(EXCHG.150).aspx#Index* to confirm all required tasks.	
Test remote mailbox creation.	
Test remote mailbox move.	
Change MX record (optional depending on hybrid model).	
Enable centralized mail transport (optional and for rare compliance cases).	
Use Exchange Remote Connectivity Analyzer (ExRCA) to test mail flow settings.	

Now that we have an idea of the tasks involved, let us go through the exercise of implementing an Exchange hybrid environment. These tasks should look familiar to you because they were identified by the Exchange Server Deployment Assistant.

Installing Exchange hybrid deployment prerequisites

The first thing you need to do is to prepare your management environment. You will need this management environment to carry out administrative and configuration tasks. You will also be making configuration changes to your Exchange on-premises server to prepare for integration with Exchange Online.

can also be used to manage your organization's Exchange Online subscription.

EMC on a server

When you install Exchange 2010 on a server, the EMC will be installed as part of the installation process. While you can use the server's EMC to manage Exchange and also to carry out the Exchange hybrid implementation tasks, it is generally not a best practice to do so. Install and configure the EMC on a workstation for administration purposes.

EMC on a workstation

You might choose to install EMC on a workstation for remote management of Exchange rather than using a server-based EMC. The following list shows the prerequisites to install the EMC:

- Domain-joined computer

- At least one Exchange 2010 server installed in the forest

- Windows Vista x64 with SP2, Windows 7 x64, Windows 8 x64, Windows Server 2008 RTM x64 with SP2, or Windows Server 2008 R2

Follow these steps to install the EMC prerequisites. We will be using a Windows 8 workstation for this exercise:

1. Click Control Panel, and then click Programs.

2. Under Programs and Features, click Turn Windows features on or off.

Chapter 11

3. Expand the Internet Information Services node, expand the Web Management Tools node, and then expand the IIS 6 Management Compatibility node. Select the IIS 6 Management Console and IIS Metabase and IIS 6 configuration compatibility check boxes, and then click OK, as shown in Figure 11-6.

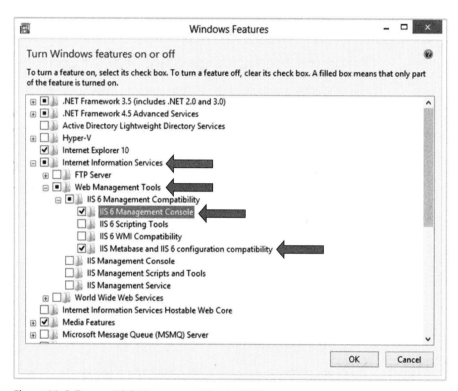

Figure 11-6 Turn on IIS 6 Management Compatibility.

4. After features have been added successfully, restart your computer.

5. Download Exchange 2010 Service Pack 3 and execute the self-extracting package.

> **Note**
> You can download Exchange 2010 SP3 at *http://www.microsoft.com/en-us/download/details.aspx?id=36768*.

6. Start the Exchange Server 2010 Setup Wizard and select Step 4: Install Microsoft Exchange, as shown in Figure 11-7.

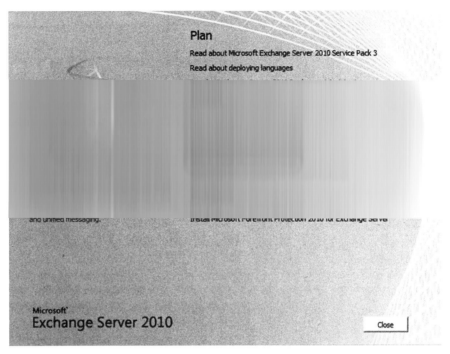

Plan

Read about Microsoft Exchange Server 2010 Service Pack 3

Read about deploying languages

and unified messaging.   Install Microsoft Forefront Protection 2010 for Exchange Server

Microsoft®
Exchange Server 2010   Close

Figure 11-7 Exchange 2010 SP3 installation screen.

7. On the installation Introduction page, click Next.

8. On the Microsoft Software License Terms page, read the license terms, select I accept the terms in the license agreement, and click Next.

9. On the Error Reporting page, choose whether you would like to report errors to Microsoft as feedback. Choose Yes or No, and then click Next.

Chapter 11

10. On the Installation Type page, as shown in Figure 11-8, select Custom Exchange Server Installation, select the Automatically install Windows Server roles and features required for Exchange check box, and then click Next.

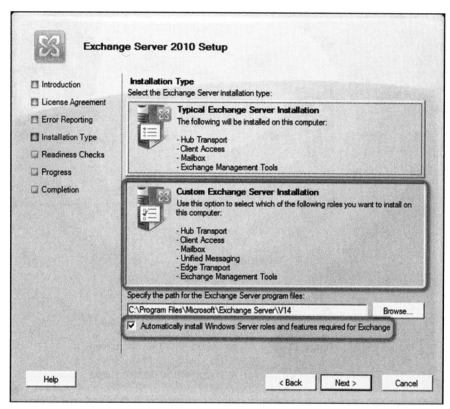

Figure 11-8 Exchange Installation Type page.

11. On the Server Role selection page, select Management Tools, as shown in Figure 11-9. Click Next.

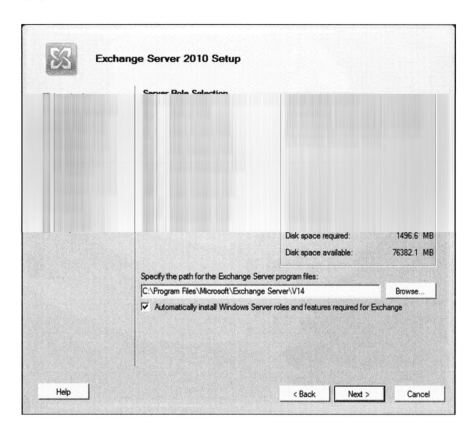

Figure 11-9 Server Role Selection page.

12. Setup will conduct a readiness check. After it has verified that the computer is ready to install the management tools, you can click Install. Figure 11-10 shows two Readiness Checks pages side-by-side. The one on the left shows that the readiness checks encountered issues and therefore cannot proceed, while the one on the right shows that the computer passed all checks and is ready to proceed with the installation of the management tools.

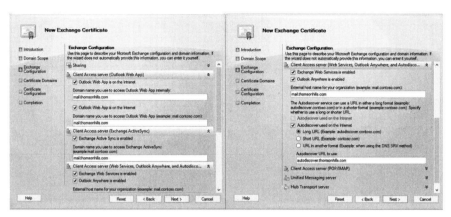

Figure 11-10 Readiness Checks page.

13. Setup will show the installation progress, as shown in Figure 11-11.

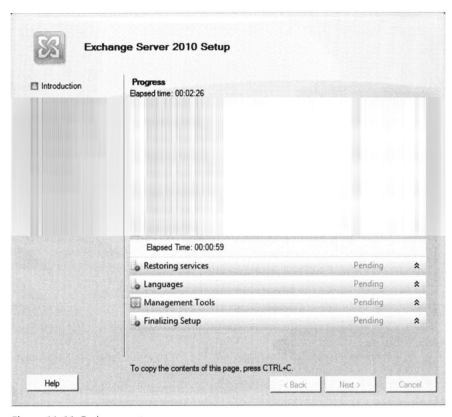

Figure 11-11 Exchange setup progress.

14. When setup is done, click Finish. Two new icons are now available in your Start
screen, as shown in Figure 11-12. One is the Exchange Management Shell and the
other is the Exchange Management Console.

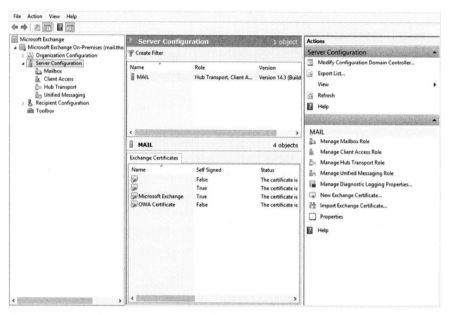

Figure 11-12 Windows 8 Start screen with the Exchange Management Shell and EMC.

Now that you have installed the EMC, it is time to add Exchange Online to the EMC. Click
the EMC icon from your Start screen to start the EMC.

Adding Exchange Online to the EMC

Adding your organization's Exchange Online to EMC so you can manage it is an easy exercise. Assuming that you already have an Office 365 subscription with Exchange Online as part of your tenant, follow these steps to add it to your EMC:

1. Start the EMC. Along the left, you will see the Exchange implementations you have access to, as shown in Figure 11-13.

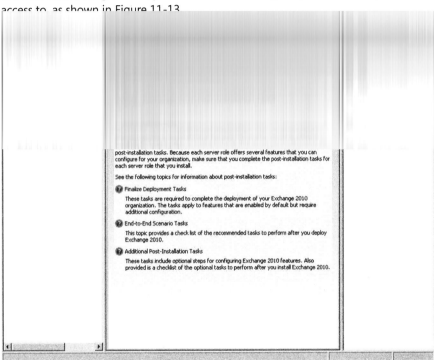

Figure 11-13 EMC showing available Exchange implementations.

2. On the Actions pane, click Add Exchange Forest.

3. In the Add Exchange Forest dialog box, provide a friendly name so you can identify this Exchange implementation.

4. In the Specify the FQDN or URL of the server running the Remote PowerShell instance drop-down box, click the drop-down arrow and select the only option available, which is Exchange Online, as shown in Figure 11-14.

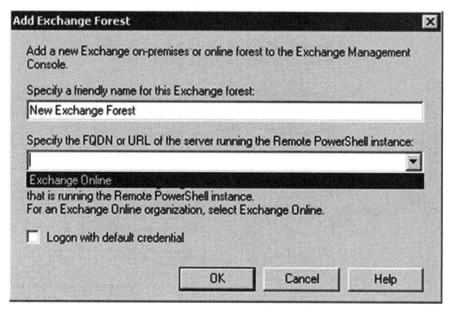

Figure 11-14 Adding a new Exchange forest.

5. If you have already installed AD FS and DirSync to enable SSO, you can select the Logon with default credential check box. Click OK.

6. Skip this step if you have SSO and you selected the Logon with default credential check box in Step 5. Otherwise, you will see the logon prompt shown in Figure 11-15. Enter your Office 365 credentials, and then click OK.

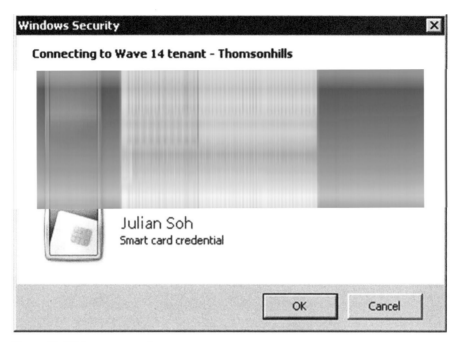

Figure 11-15 Logon prompt.

7. After your logon credentials have been validated, the EMC will show the Office 365 Exchange Online tenant in the navigation pane. Figure 11-16 shows a screen shot of the EMC after we added two separate tenants to the EMC.

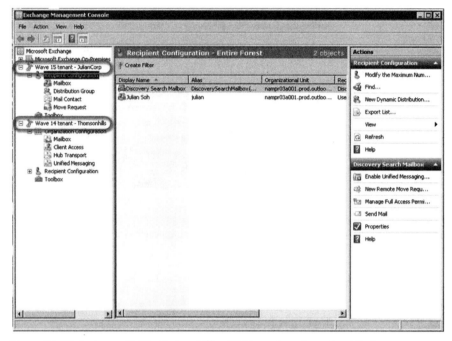

Figure 11-16 Exchange EMC with two Office 365 tenants and one local Exchange environment.

Certificates

Communication between your organization's on-premises Exchange environment and Exchange Online is protected with a digital certificate. This certificate cannot be a self-signed certificate. There are three tasks you need to carry out:

- Generate a new Exchange certificate signing request (CSR)

- Purchase the certificate from a trusted third-party certificate authority (CA)

- Import the newly purchased certificate and assign services

Generating a new Exchange certificate request

Generating a new Exchange certificate request is the first task you need to complete using the newly installed EMC. Follow these steps to create the certificate request:

1. Start the EMC, expand the Microsoft Exchange On-Premises node, click the Server
    Configuration node, and select New Exchange Certificate from the Actions pane, as
    shown in Figure 11-17. This will start the New Exchange Certificate Wizard.

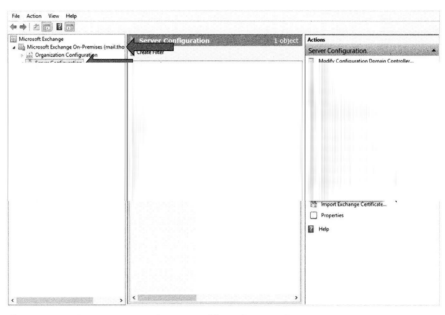

Figure 11-17 Create a new Exchange certificate from EMC.

2. On the first page of the New Exchange Certificate Wizard, provide a friendly name so you can easily identify the certificate. In this exercise, we chose to name our certificate Exchange Unified Communications Certificate, as shown in Figure 11-18. Click Next.

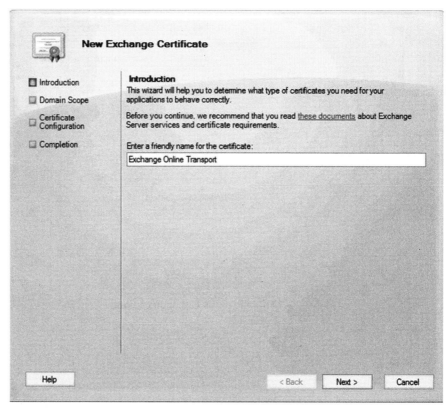

Figure 11-18 Friendly name for a new Exchange certificate.

3. On the Domain Scope page, determine if you would like to use wildcard certificates. Wildcard certificates provide you the flexibility to add subdomains without updating the certificate each time you add a subdomain. For this exercise, we will not be using wildcard certificates because we will not be adding subdomains. Leave the Enable wildcard certificate check box cleared and click Next, as shown in Figure 11-19.

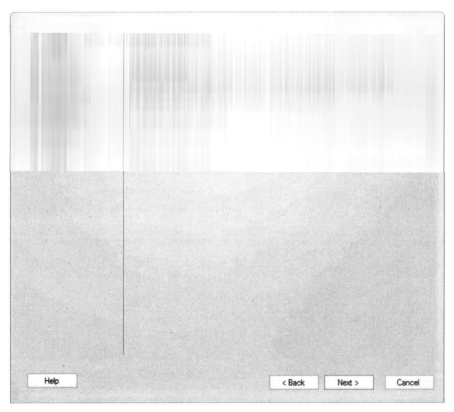

Figure 11-19 Wildcard certificate.

4. On the Certificate Configuration page, expand the Client Access server (Outlook Web App) group by clicking the down arrows next to the group. Select both boxes for Outlook Web App on the intranet and internet, as shown in Figure 11-20. Provide the FQDN of the OWA URL on the intranet and the internet. These are usually the same URL unless you are using different URLs with a split-DNS.

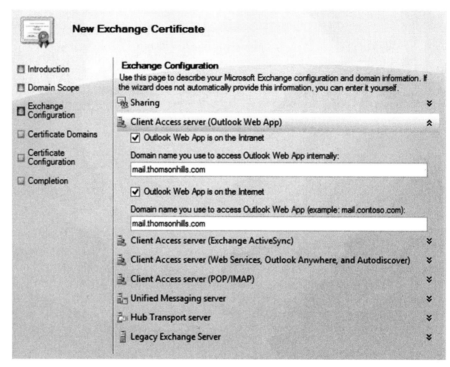

Figure 11-20 Exchange Configuration: Client Access server (OWA).

5. Next, expand the Client Access server (Exchange ActiveSync) configuration group and
    select the Exchange Active Sync is enabled check box, as shown in Figure 11-21. Enter
    the domain name for ActiveSync.

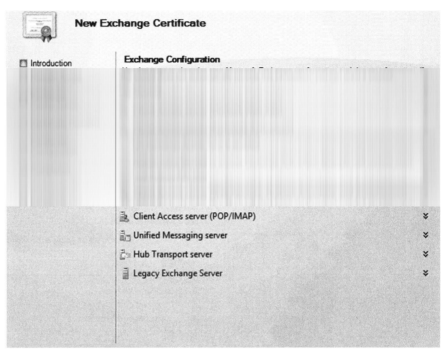

Figure 11-21 Exchange Configuration: Client Access server (Exchange ActiveSync).

6. Expand the Client Access server (Web Services, Outlook Anywhere, and Autodiscover) configuration group and select the Exchange Web Services is enabled check box and the Outlook Anywhere is enabled check box, as shown in Figure 11-22. Provide the external FQDN for your organization and also select the Autodiscover used on the Internet check box. Finally, select the Long URL option and enter the Autodiscover URL to use.

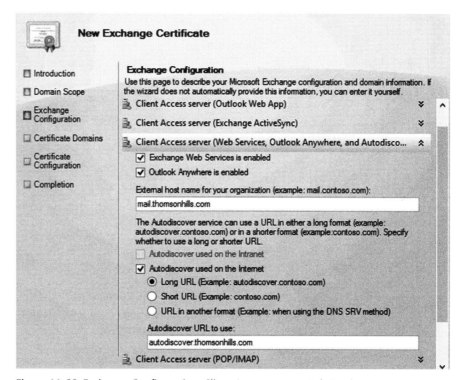

Figure 11-22 Exchange Configuration: Client Access server (Web Services)

INSIDE OUT   Common DNS issue

The FQDNs we selected, such as mail.<*Organization_Name*>.com and autodiscover.<*Organization_Name*>.com, are commonly used for these services. You can choose different host names as long as you remember to add these records to your organization's DNS service. Furthermore, if you use split-DNS, ensure that you have the right records in the right DNS service.

7. Finally, expand the Hub Transport server configuration group and select the Use mutual TLS to help secure Internet mail check box. Enter the FQDN of the on-premises Exchange server that hosts the Hub Transport role, as shown in Figure 11-23.

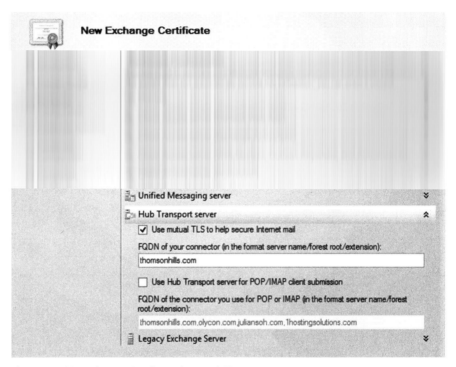

Figure 11-23 Exchange Configuration: Hub Transport server.

8. Click Next.

9. On the Certificate Domains page, review the domains that will be added to the certificate. Make sure all the FQDNs you specified are added to the certificate, especially the Autodiscover service and top-level domain name for your organization. The external FQDN needs to be set as the default CN. The default CN is in boldface. If the external FQDN is not in boldface, select it and click Set as common name. Figure 11-24 depicts the configuration for our exercise.

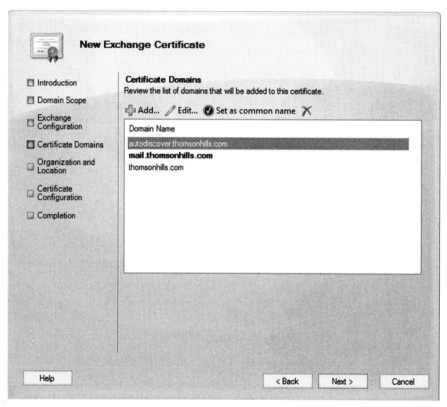

Figure 11-24 Certificate Domains.

10. Next, we need to add owa.*<Your_Organization>*.<com> as a domain. Click Add and enter the record, as shown in Figure 11-25. Click OK when you are done. Then click Next.

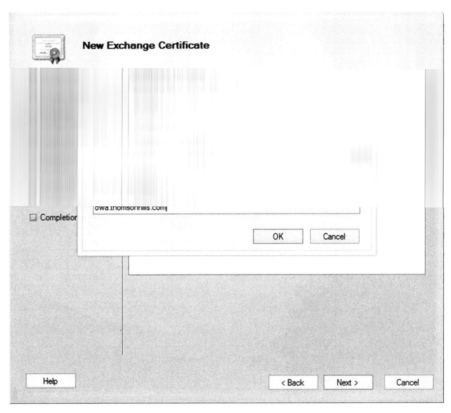

Figure 11-25 Adding an OWA domain.

11. On the Organization and Location page, enter your organization's information, then click Browse to select a location to save your certificate request file to, as shown in Figure 11-26. Click Next.

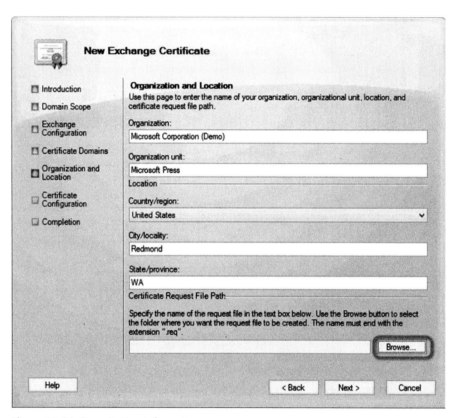

Figure 11-26 Organization information.

12. Review the certificate configuration information. If everything is in order, click New, as shown in Figure 11-27.

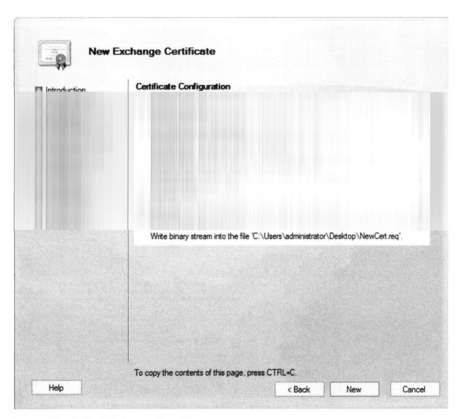

New Exchange Certificate

☑ Introduction

Certificate Configuration

Write binary stream into the file 'C:\Users\administrator\Desktop\NewCert.req'.

To copy the contents of this page, press CTRL+C.

Help   < Back   New   Cancel

Figure 11-27 Certificate Configuration summary.

13. After the wizard has created the file, take note of the type of certificate you need to purchase. It is always a Unified Communications certificate, as shown in Figure 11-28. Click Finish.

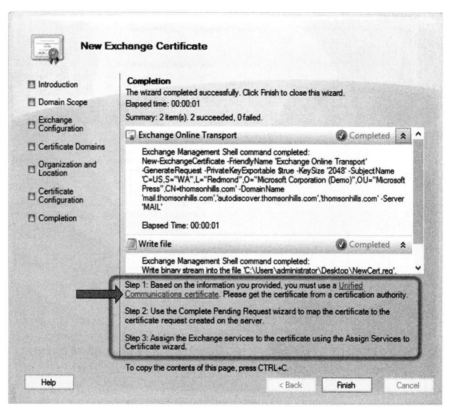

Figure 11-28 Unified Communications certificate required.

Acquiring a certificate

As noted in the previous exercise, you will need to acquire a Unified Communications certificate from a trusted third-party CA. DigiCert (*http://www.digicert.com*) is an example of a trusted third-party CA. We will use DigiCert as a CA for this part of the exercise, although you are free to use any trusted third-party CA.

This portion of the exercise might vary depending on which CA you use:

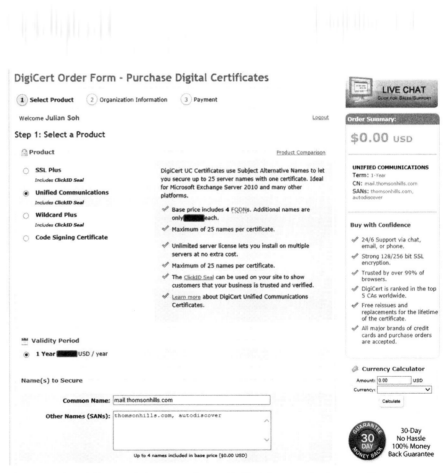

Figure 11-29 DigiCert website to purchase a Unified Communications certificate.

Chapter 11

2. Regardless of which CA you use, make sure you use the common name you specified when you generated the certificate request. This is usually mail.<*Your_Organization*>.<com>.

3. Include subject alternative names (SANs), especially Autodiscover, as shown in Figure 11-29.

4. The certificate will need to be bound to the certificate signing request (CSR) code that was generated when you created the request file in the previous exercise. Open the CSR in an editor such as Notepad and copy the text, as shown in Figure 11-30.

Figure 11-30 Certificate signing request.

5. Provide the CA with the CSR upon request. In most cases, this is part of the acquisition process. Figure 11-31 shows DigiCert's process allowing us to submit the CSR.

Figure 11-31 Submitting the CSR to the CA.

6. The CA will conduct a verification process. This process varies from CA to CA, but might involve sending emails to email addresses based on Whois lookup information of the domain. The goal of the CA is to verify that you have the authority to act on behalf of the domain from which you are trying to get a certificate issued. When the verification process is complete, you will receive a certificate file from the CA. After you receive that file, you are ready to complete the certificate installation.

Chapter 11

Importing a purchased certificate

After your certificate order has been processed by the CA, you will receive a certificate file through email, as shown in Figure 11-32.

Figure 11-32 Certificate file issued by a CA.

Follow these steps to complete the import of your certificate:

1. Start the EMC, expand the Exchange On-Premises node, and navigate to the Server Configuration node.

2. Select the certificate you created in the preceding exercise. In the preceding exercise, we named that certificate Exchange Unified Communications Certificate, as shown in Figure 11-33. Take note that the certificate is not self-signed, as indicated by False in the Self Signed column, and it is also pending, as indicated by the Status column.

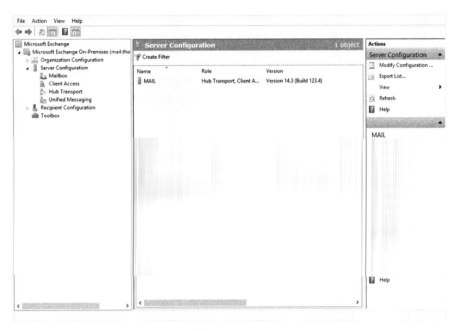

Figure 11-33 Complete pending certificate request.

3. On the Actions pane near the bottom right are the applicable actions for the certificate you selected. One of the actions should be Complete Pending Request, as shown in Figure 11-33. Click Complete Pending Request, which will invoke a wizard to help walk you through the steps.

4. In the Complete Pending Request Wizard, click Browse and locate the .cer certificate file you received from the third-party CA, as shown in Figure 11-34.

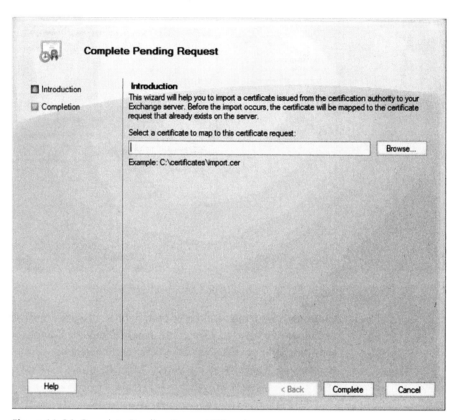

Figure 11-34 Complete Pending Request Wizard.

5. Click Complete.

6. Verify that the certificate request has completed successfully, as shown in Figure 11-35, then click Finish.

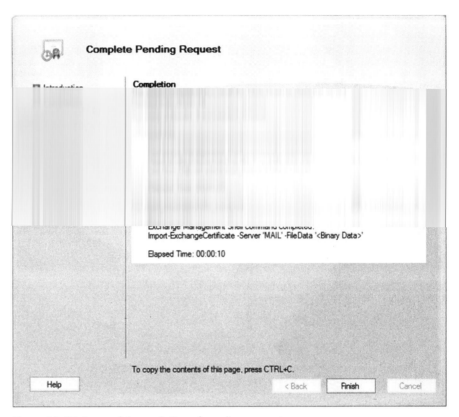

Complete Pending Request

Completion

Exchange Management Shell command completed:
Import-ExchangeCertificate -Server 'MAIL' -FileData '<Binary Data>'

Elapsed Time: 00:00:10

To copy the contents of this page, press CTRL+C.

Help   < Back   Finish   Cancel

Figure 11-35 Successful completion of pending request.

Chapter 11

INSIDE OUT   Windows PowerShell commands

We are a fan of Windows PowerShell, and it does make life easier. Microsoft is making it easier to adopt Windows PowerShell with the release of the Integrated Scripting Environment (ISE) that we have been using as an example throughout the book. Another way Microsoft is making it easier is to expose the Windows PowerShell commands that are used even if you use a GUI. For example, if you look at Figure 11-35 again, notice that the Windows PowerShell command that was used to import the certificate is *Import-ExchangeCertificate*.

7. We now need to assign services to the certificate. In the EMC, click the Unified Communications certificate you just imported.

8. On the Actions pane, click Assign Services to Certificate, as shown in Figure 11-36.

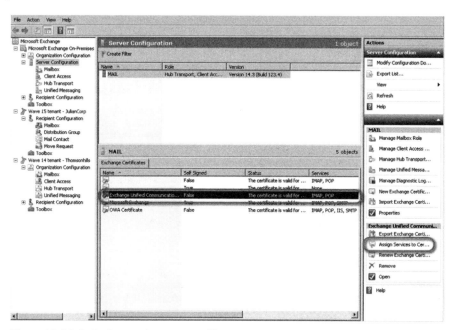

Figure 11-36 Assigning services to a certificate.

9. Select your organization's on-premises mail server and click Next, as shown in Figure 11-37.

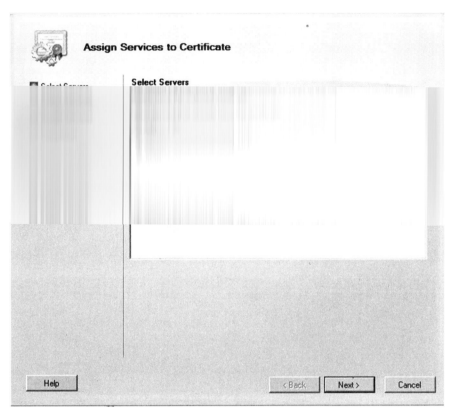

Figure 11-37 Assign Services to Certificate: Select Servers.

10. On the Select Services page, select the services you would like the certificate to protect. At a minimum, you need to select SMTP and IIS, as shown in Figure 11-38.

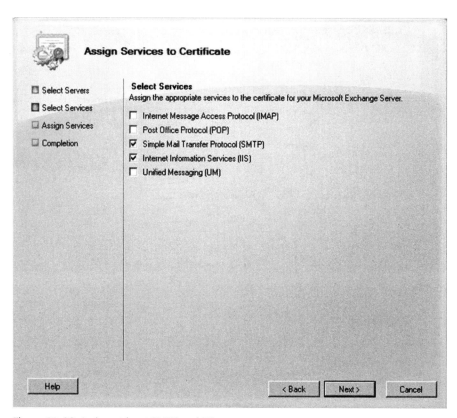

Figure 11-38 Assign at least SMTP and IIS.

11. On the Assign Services to Certificate page, confirm that the services you selected are listed to be assigned to the certificate. In this exercise, we selected SMTP and IIS, so they are listed on this page, as shown in Figure 11-39. Click Assign to confirm the assignment of these services to the certificate.

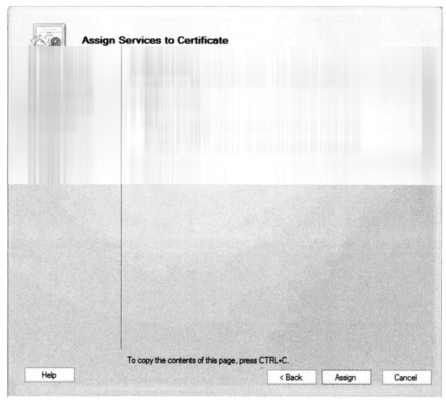

Figure 11-39 Assign Services.

12. On the Completion page of the Assign Services to Certificate Wizard, make sure the services are successfully assigned, as shown in Figure 11-40, and then click Finish.

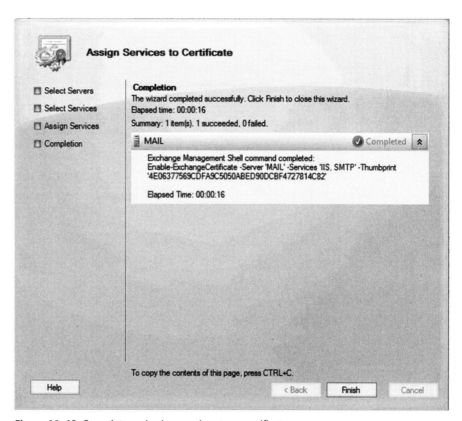

Figure 11-40 Complete assigning services to a certificate.

Verifying certificates and services

The final step is to verify the tasks you have completed thus far by confirming that the correct services are assigned to the proper certificates. You will use Windows PowerShell for this exercise. Follow these steps to confirm the assignment of services to the certificate:

1. Launch the Exchange Management Shell.

2. As shown in Figure 11-41, run the following Windows PowerShell command:

```
Get-ExchangeCertificate | Format-List *
```

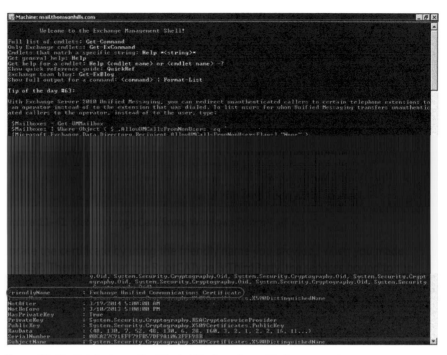

Figure 11-41 *Get-ExchangeCertificate* Windows PowerShell command.

3.   Locate the certificate by using the friendly name you provided when you made the CSR. Then verify that the RootCAType is ThirdParty, the services bound to the certificate are correct, and the status of the certificate is valid. For this exercise, we used the name Exchange Unified Communications Certificate. In Figure 11-36, notice that we located the certificate through the friendly name and verified that the RootCAType, services bound, and status of the certificate are all correct.

Configuring Exchange Web Services

For a hybrid deployment, external access to the on-premises CAS servers needs to be configured. Follow these steps to configure external access to the CAS:

1. Start the EMC, expand the Server Configuration node, select Client Access, and click Configure External Client Access Domain on the Actions pane, as shown in Figure 11-42.

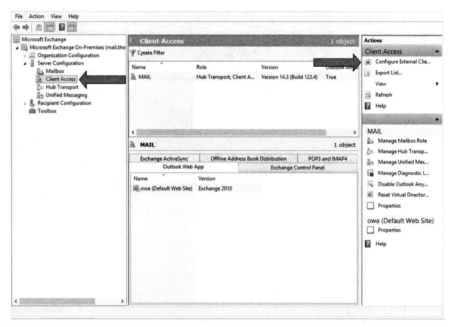

Figure 11-42 Using EMC to configure external access to CAS.

2. On the Server selection page, enter the external FQDN of the CAS, click Add, and then select the CAS server to associate the FQDN to, as shown in Figure 11-43. Click OK.

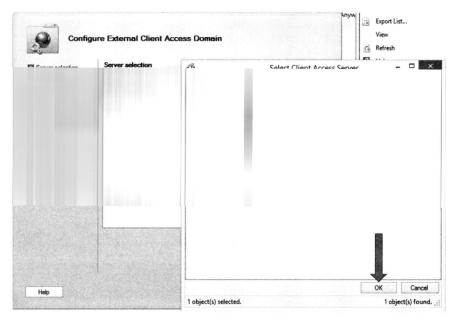

Figure 11-43 Selecting the CAS and associating it to the external FQDN.

3. Click Configure.

4. The wizard will configure the CAS. When done, the wizard will report the status of each configuration step, as shown in Figure 11-44. Confirm there are no errors, and then click Finish.

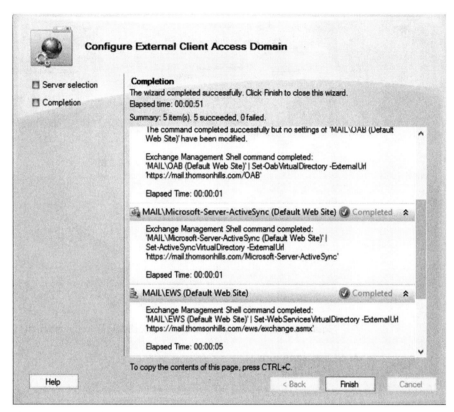

Figure 11-44 Configure External Client Access Domain Wizard: server configuration status.

INSIDE OUT   Common warning from the wizard

When you run the Configure External Client Access Domain Wizard, it configures the required services. However, if you have configured a previous service such as OWA, the wizard will warn you that the settings have not been modified, as shown in Figure 11-45.

Figure 11-45 Warning that settings are not modified.

Verifying CAS, EWS, OAB, and ActiveSync configuration

The preceding exercise configured your CAS so EWS and the required services are available externally. Follow these steps to confirm everything has been configured successfully:

1. Start the Exchange Management Shell.

2. Verify that the external URL for EWS has been set by entering the following Windows PowerShell command. The results should be similar to what is shown in Figure 11-46:

```
Get-WebServicesVirtualDirectory "EWS (Default Web Site)" | Format-Table Name,
ExternalURL
```

Figure 11-46 Windows PowerShell command to verify the external URL of EWS.

3. Next, verify that the external URL is set on the offline address book (OAB) virtual directory by entering the following Windows PowerShell command. The results should be similar to what is shown in Figure 11-47:

```
Get-OabVirtualDirectory "OAB (Default Web Site)" | Format-Table Name,
ExternalURL
```

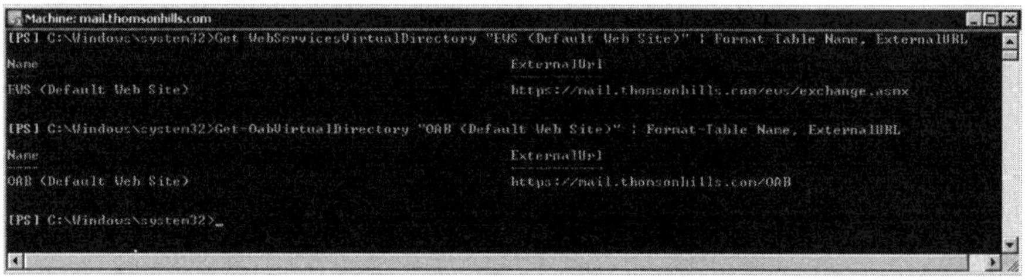

Figure 11-47 Windows PowerShell command to verify that the external URL is set for OAB.

4. Finally, verify that the external URL has been set for ActiveSync by entering the following Windows PowerShell command. The results should be similar to what is shown in Figure 11-48:

```
Get-ActiveSyncVirtualDirectory "Microsoft-Server-ActiveSync (Default Web Site)"
| Format-Table Name, ExternalURL
```

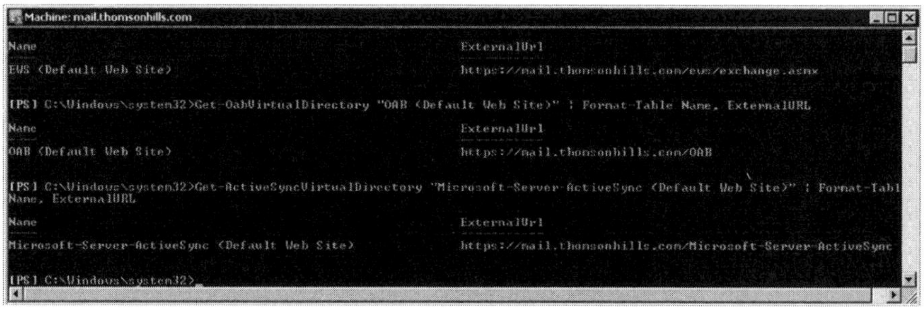

Figure 11-48 Windows PowerShell command to verify that the external URL is set for ActiveSync.

At this point, you have implemented all the prerequisites for your organization's Exchange hybrid deployment. You are now ready to proceed with establishing the hybrid configuration.

Configuring an Exchange hybrid model

One of the greatest advantages about Office 365 is that Microsoft fully embraces hybrid scenarios. Publicly, the company has announced that all their technology will be designed "for the cloud first." This is very evident in the new releases of Exchange and Exchange Online. Prior to this initiative, configuring an Exchange hybrid environment was a tedious and manual process. The release of Exchange SP2 made the deployment of an Exchange

- Configuring a hybrid deployment

Establishing a hybrid relationship

You will use the New Hybrid Configuration Wizard to establish a hybrid relationship with Office 365. This wizard creates the necessary objects in AD, specifically the *HybridConfiguration* object, to store all the configuration information. Follow these steps to create a new hybrid relationship:

1. Start the EMC, expand the Microsoft Exchange On-Premises node, and select Organization Configuration. Click New Hybrid Configuration on the Actions pane, as shown in Figure 11-49.

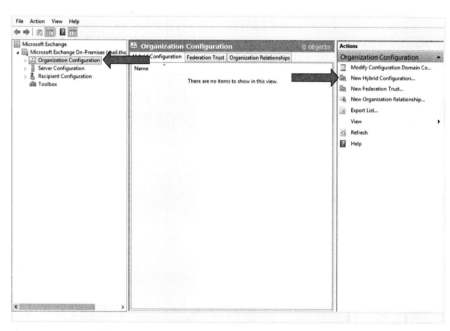

Figure 11-49 Use the EMC (SP3) to create a new hybrid configuration.

2. On the New Hybrid Configuration page, click New, as shown in Figure 11-50.

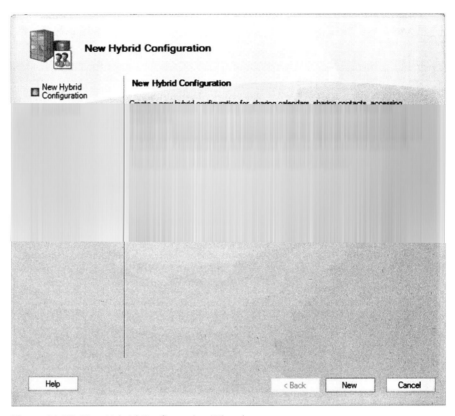

Figure 11-50 New Hybrid Configuration Wizard.

Chapter 11

3. The wizard establishes a trust with the Microsoft Federation Gateway, which can be translated as establishing a trust with Office 365. It also creates a self-signed certificate and saves the entire configuration as *New-HybridConfiguration*. The wizard's steps and progress are shown in Figure 11-51.

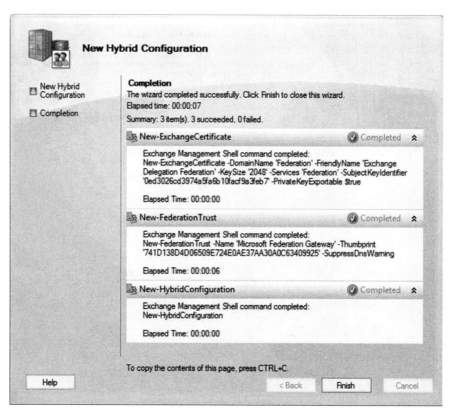

Figure 11-51 New Hybrid Configuration Wizard tasks and progress.

4. Verify that no errors were encountered and each of the three tasks was completed successfully. Click Finish.

Now that a new hybrid relationship with Office 365 has been established, it is time to configure the hybrid deployment.

Configuring a hybrid deployment

Follow these steps to configure the hybrid deployment:

> **Note**
>
> Keep in mind you can always change the hybrid configuration. Therefore, the settings
> you implement as you go through this exercise can be changed at a later date if needed.

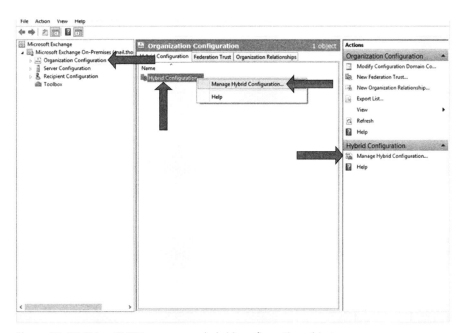

Figure 11-52 Using EMC to manage a hybrid configuration object.

2. Select the Hybrid Configuration object and either right-click and select Manage Hybrid Configuration or click Manage Hybrid Configuration on the Actions pane, as shown in Figure 11-52.

INSIDE OUT   Add the Exchange Online tenant first

When we walked you through the prerequisites, one of the exercises was to add your Exchange Online tenant to the EMC. If you have not done so, you will receive a message when you try to manage the hybrid configuration object, as shown in Figure 11-53. If you get this message, add your Exchange Online tenant to EMC before proceeding.

Microsoft Exchange

You must add your Exchange Online tenant as an additional forest before you can run the Manage Hybrid Configurtion wizard.

OK

Figure 11-53 Dialog box advising to add your Exchange Online tenant first.

3. On the Introduction page of the Manage Hybrid Configuration Wizard, as shown in
Figure 11-54, read the information, especially the Before using this wizard section.
If you have been following the steps in this chapter and in Chapters 2, 3, and 4, the
items listed would already have been addressed. Click Next.

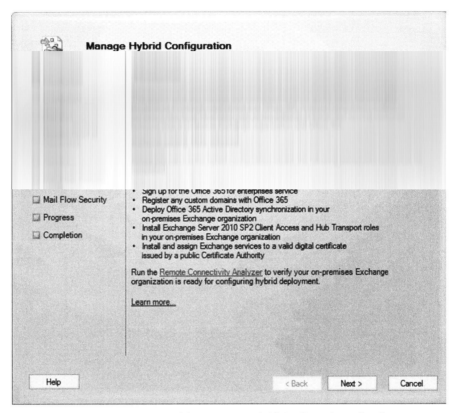

Figure 11-54 Introduction page of the Manage Hybrid Configuration Wizard.

4. On the Credentials page, supply your AD credentials in the top section and your Office 365 credentials in the bottom section. Select both Remember my credentials check boxes, as shown in Figure 11-55. Click Next.

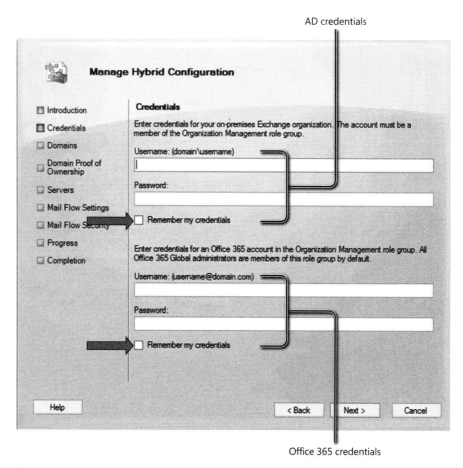

Figure 11-55 Credentials page of the Manage Hybrid Configuration Wizard.

5. On the Domains page, click Add, as shown in Figure 11-56.

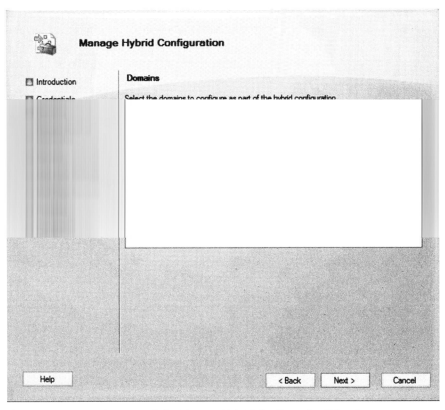

Figure 11-56 Domains page of the Manage Hybrid Configuration Wizard.

6. When you click Add, as shown in Step 5, the wizard will examine your Exchange configuration. A dialog box will appear containing a list of domains that your Exchange environment is authoritative for, as shown in Figure 11-57. It might take some time for the wizard to query your Exchange environment. Select the domains you want to add to the hybrid configuration. If you are selecting multiple domains, use the Shift and Ctrl keys to make multiple selections. Click OK.

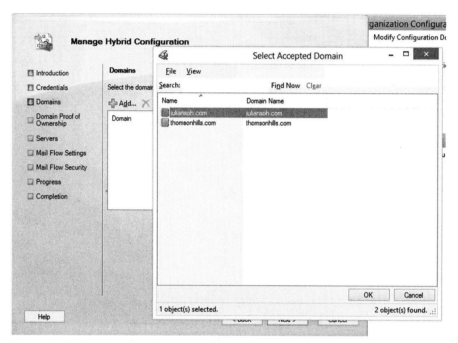

Figure 11-57 Select Accepted Domain dialog box of the Manage Hybrid Configuration Wizard.

7. The domains you selected should now be listed in the Domains list, as shown in Figure 11-58. Click Next.

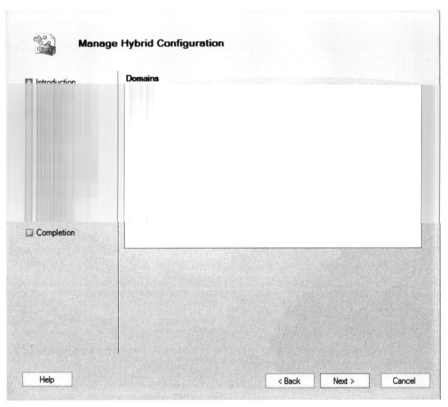

Figure 11-58 Domains selected on the Domains page of the Manage Hybrid Configuration Wizard.

8. On the Domain Proof of Ownership page, you will be provided with text strings for each of the domains you selected in Step 7, as shown in Figure 11-59. You need to create TXT records in your DNS server using these values. As you can see in Figure 11-59, these values are long and complex. Therefore, use CTRL+C to copy the information. We will paste it into an editor in the next step.

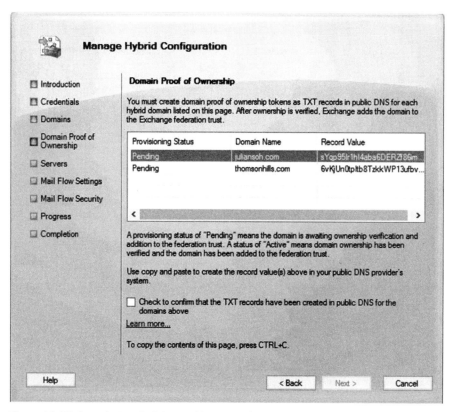

Figure 11-59 Domain Proof of Ownership page of the Manage Hybrid Configuration Wizard.

9. Launch an editor such as Notepad and paste the copied information from Step 8, as shown in Figure 11-60.

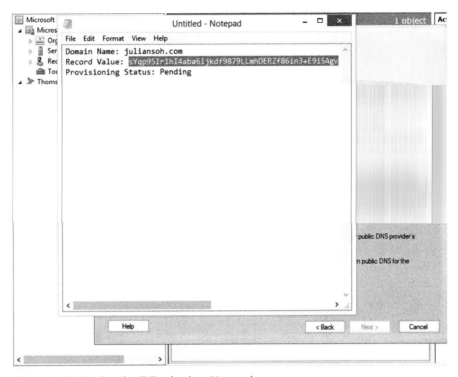

Figure 11-60 Pasting the TXT value into Notepad.

10. Do not close the EMC or the wizard. You now need to configure your public DNS. For this exercise, we will use Microsoft DNS Manager. Start DNS Manager on a DNS server.

11. Right-click the forward lookup domain that we need to create the TXT record for, select New Other Records, select Text (TXT), and click Create Record, as shown in Figure 11-61.

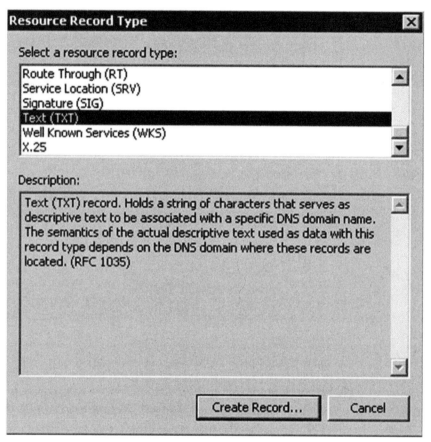

Figure 11-61 Creating a text (TXT) record type in Microsoft DNS Manager.

12. Copy the text value from Notepad that is associated to the domain and paste it into the Text box, as shown in Figure 11-62. Leave the Record name box blank. Click OK.

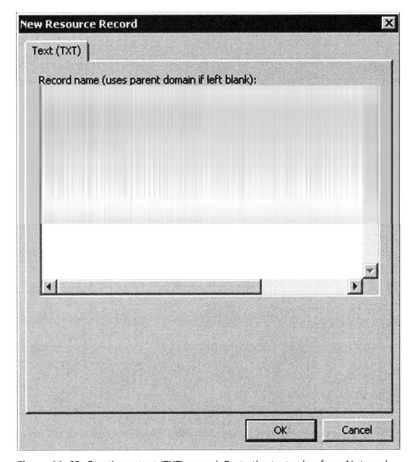

Figure 11-62 Creating a text (TXT) record. Paste the text value from Notepad.

13. Click Done.

14. Repeat steps 10 through 13 for the other domains if you are configuring for multiple domains.

> **Note**
> You might need to give DNS some time to propagate your DNS changes before proceeding with the rest of these steps.

Chapter 11

15. Return to the EMC and the Manage Hybrid Configuration Wizard, which was where we left off from Step 8. Select the Check to confirm the TXT records have been created in public DNS for the domain above check box, as shown in Figure 11-63.

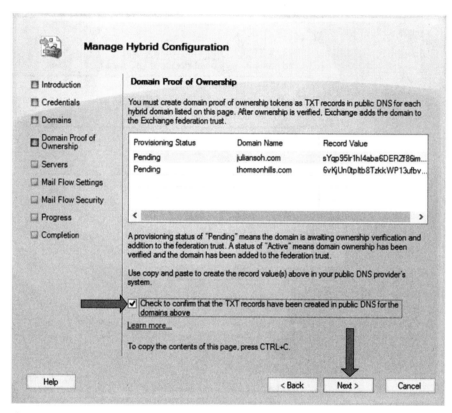

Figure 11-63 Check the box in the Manage Hybrid Configuration Wizard.

16. Click Next.

17. On the Servers page, select your organization's on-premises CAS server that will be participating in the hybrid configuration by clicking Add and selecting the CAS servers in the Select Client Access Server dialog box, as shown in Figure 11-64. Click OK.

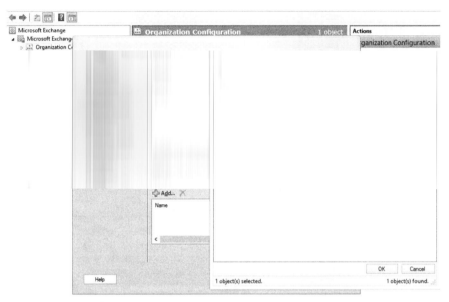

Figure 11-64 Selecting CAS in the Manage Hybrid Configuration Wizard.

18. Repeat Step 17 for the Hub Transport server. Click Next when both the CAS and Hub Transport servers have been selected.

19. On the Mail Flow Settings page, click Add and enter the public IP address for the Hub Transport server participating in the hybrid configuration, as shown in Figure 11-65. Click OK.

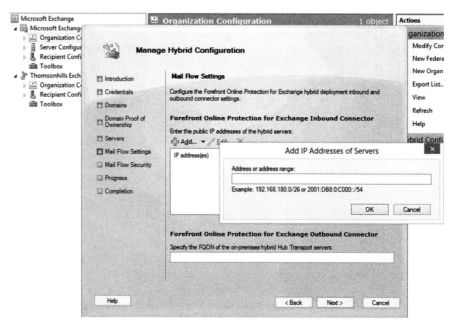

Figure 11-65 Mail Flow Settings page of the Manage Hybrid Configuration Wizard.

20. Repeat Step 19 if your organization has multiple Hub Transport servers participating in the hybrid configuration.

21. As shown in Figure 11-65, in the Forefront Online Protection for Exchange Outbound Connector box, also on the same page, enter the FQDN of the on-premises hybrid Hub Transport servers. Click Next.

22. On the Mail Flow Security page, select the certificate issued by the trusted third-party CA, as shown in Figure 11-66. Click View Certificate to verify that the correct certificate is selected.

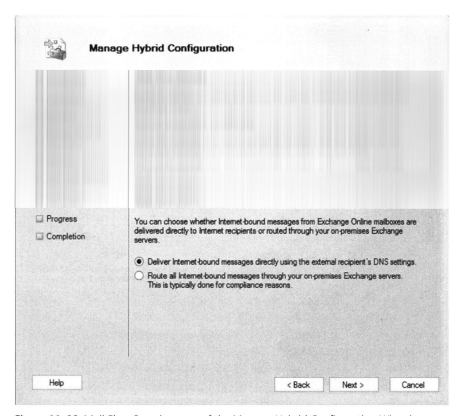

Manage Hybrid Configuration

☐ Progress

☐ Completion

You can choose whether Internet-bound messages from Exchange Online mailboxes are delivered directly to Internet recipients or routed through your on-premises Exchange servers.

◉ Deliver Internet-bound messages directly using the external recipient's DNS settings.

○ Route all Internet-bound messages through your on-premises Exchange servers. This is typically done for compliance reasons.

Help   < Back   Next >   Cancel

Figure 11-66 Mail Flow Security page of the Manage Hybrid Configuration Wizard.

23. For the Mail Flow Path settings located at the bottom half of the page, select whether to route internet-bound messages directly or to route them through your on-premises Exchange servers. For more information about these options, see the "Centralized Mail Transport" section later in this chapter. Click Next.

Chapter 11

24. The next page is the Progress page, which confirms the configuration details the
Manage Hybrid Configuration Wizard has collected so far, as shown in Figure 11-67.
Verify all the settings are correct, and then click Manage.

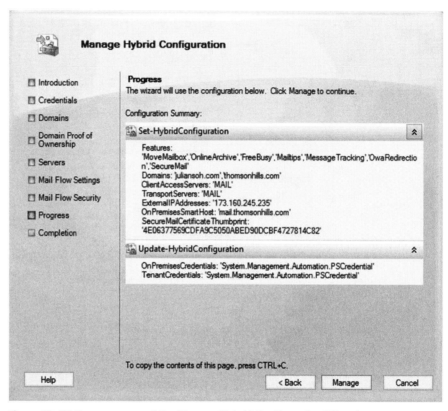

Figure 11-67   Progress page of the Manage Hybrid Configuration Wizard.

25. The wizard will update your hybrid configuration settings. When it is done, the status of the update tasks will be shown on the Completion page, as shown in Figure 11-68.

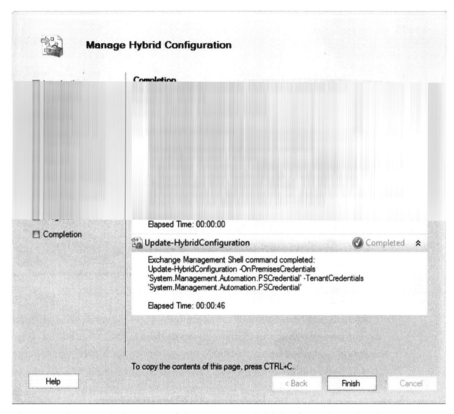

Manage Hybrid Configuration

Completion

☐ Completion

Elapsed Time: 00:00:00

Update-HybridConfiguration   ✅ Completed ≫

Exchange Management Shell command completed:
Update-HybridConfiguration -OnPremisesCredentials
'System.Management.Automation.PSCredential' -TenantCredentials
'System.Management.Automation.PSCredential'

Elapsed Time: 00:00:46

To copy the contents of this page, press CTRL+C.

| Help | | < Back | Finish | Cancel |

Figure 11-68 Completion page of the Manage Hybrid Configuration Wizard.

> ## Note
> If your hybrid configuration fails, take note of the error and see the "Troubleshoot-ing hybrid configuration" section of this chapter to see if your issue might be addressed there. We have included common issues that would cause the hybrid setup to fail, along with the troubleshooting and remediation approach.

Chapter 11

26. To verify that the hybrid configuration works, start an Exchange Management Shell session and enter the following Windows PowerShell command:

```
Get-HybridConfiguration
```

The returned result of a successful configuration is shown in Figure 11-69. Exit the Windows PowerShell window, and click Finish.

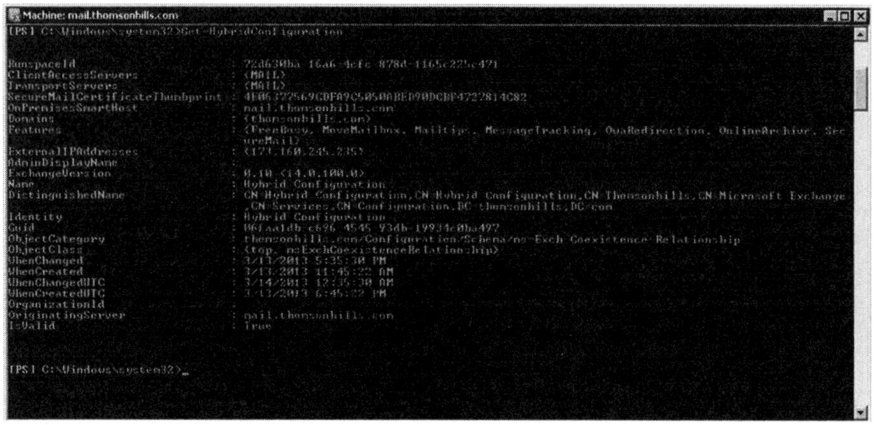

Figure 11-69 *Get-HybridConfiguration* command.

At this point, you have established a federation between your on-premises Exchange environment with Exchange Online through the Microsoft Federation Gateway for Office 365. If you do not need to troubleshoot any configuration issues, you can proceed to finalize and test your hybrid configuration.

Troubleshooting hybrid configuration

There are several common issues that can cause your hybrid configuration efforts to fail. We will discuss the common ones in this section.

Autodiscover service

A common problem involves the misconfiguration of the Autodiscover service and associated DNS records. To test the Autodiscover service, you should be familiar with the Microsoft Exchange Remote Connectivity Analyzer (ExRCA), which we introduced in Chapter 2. Although this tool began as an online analyzer to troubleshoot Exchange on-premises, it has evolved into a tool to test Office 365 as well as both Lync Online and Lync on-premises. You can access the analyzer at *https://www.testexchangeconnectivity.com/*.

Figure 11-70 shows the main page of ExRCA.

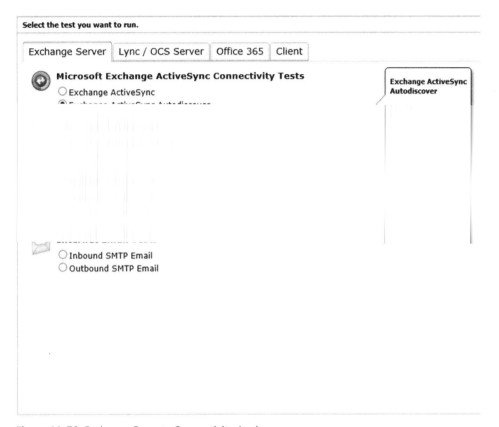

Figure 11-70 Exchange Remote Connectivity Analyzer.

Select the Exchange ActiveSync Autodiscover option to ensure that the Autodiscover service is properly configured and your certificates are valid. You will need to provide a valid
email address and logon credentials to a mailbox for this test to occur. The logon credentials simply need to be to a standard mailbox; it does not need to be an administrator
account. The process is identical to someone using her email address to add a new account
to a mobile device and relying on Autodiscover and ActiveSync to automatically configure
email settings. When the test is complete, you should see test results similar to the page
shown in Figure 11-71.

Chapter 11

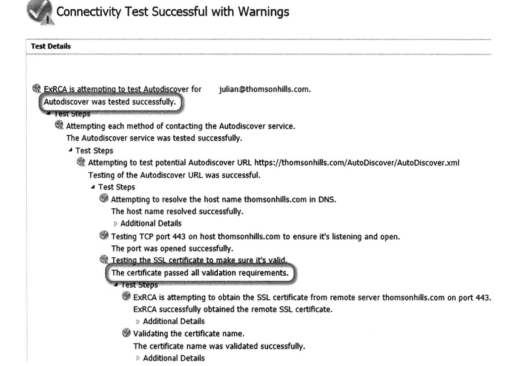

Figure 11-71 Test results for Autodiscover and certificate validation.

The two most important things to get out of the test are the following:

- Autodiscover is tested to be successful.

- The certificate validation passed.

If any of these tests fail, you will need to troubleshoot and resolve the issues accordingly. They might not be the only problems in your configuration, but they would definitely be issues that are preventing you from completing your hybrid Exchange deployment.

Check your DNS for the proper DNS records. Autodiscover might not be working because of improperly configured DNS. More commonly, we have seen issues related with split-DNS environments. In such a situation, the results from ExRCA will need to be verified because ExRCA is able to resolve Autodiscover as it is using your external DNS. However, your CAS server might have an internal IP address with Network Address Translation (NAT). As such, the internal DNS might not have the correct records. Use nslookup from your CAS server to ensure that Autodiscover is resolving to the correct address.

INSIDE OUT Certificates

We see a lot of issues related to certificates when working with customers. Some of the common certificate problems include self-signed certificates, certificates with incorrect names, certificates without the proper subject alternative names (SANs), and incorrect certificate types. Remember that you need to have a trusted third-party CA assigned Unified Communications certificate with the proper Autodiscover records included in

Virtual directory security settings

The virtual directory settings might sometimes cause the hybrid setup to fail. You might encounter this when the Hybrid Configuration Wizard tries to update the hybrid configuration. You might get an error message similar to the one shown in Figure 11-72.

```
Error:
Updating hybrid configuration failed with error 'Subtask Configure execution failed: Creating
Organization Relationships.

Execution of the Get-FederationInformation cmdlet had thrown an exception. This may indicate invalid
parameters in your Hybrid Configuration settings.

Federation information could not be received from the external organization.
   at Microsoft.Exchange.Management.Hybrid.RemotePowershellSession.RunCommand(String cmdlet,
Dictionary`2 parameters, Boolean ignoreNotFoundErrors)
'.

Additional troubleshooting information is available in the Update-HybridConfiguration log file located at
C:\Program Files\Microsoft\Exchange Server\V14\Logging\Update-
HybridConfiguration\HybridConfiguration_12_8_2011_18_2_52_634589641723224440.log.

Exchange Management Shell command attempted:
Update-HybridConfiguration -OnPremisesCredentials 'System.Management.Automation.PSCredential' -
TenantCredentials 'System.Management.Automation.PSCredential'

Elapsed Time: 00:02:56
```

Figure 11-72 Error updating hybrid configuration.

If you get this error, follow these steps to see if the virtual directory settings might be the issue:

1. Start the Exchange Management Shell and enter the following command:

   ```
   Get-FederationInformation <domain> -Verbose
   ```

2. You should see the details of the error, as shown in Figure 11-73. These errors, as pointed out in Figure 11-73, might be 401 and 403 errors, indicating problems with accessing the virtual directory to get the federation information.

Figure 11-73 401 and 403 errors from *Get-FederationInformation*.

3. If *Get-FederationInformation* is unable to retrieve information about the hybrid configuration, *Update-HybridConfiguration* would also encounter issues. *Update-HybridConfiguration* is the last Windows PowerShell command that the Hybrid Configuration Wizard attempts to execute. To resolve the 401 and 403 errors, you need to make sure that the Autodiscover virtual directory has the proper security settings. Enter the following command:

   ```
   Set-AutodiscoverVirtualDirectory -Identity 'autodiscover (Default Web Site)' -
   WSSecurityAuthentication $true
   ```

4. Enter the *Get-FederationInformation* command again. The 401 and 403 errors should be resolved. A successful resolution should produce results similar to the window shown in Figure 11-74.

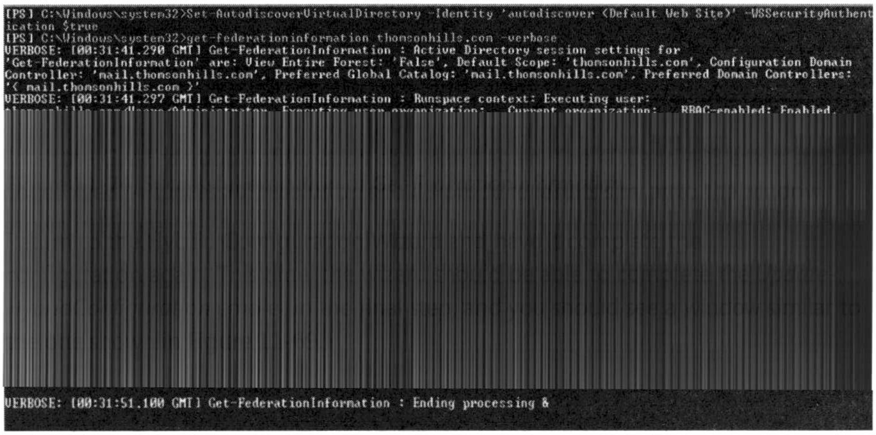

Figure 11-74 Successful execution of *Get-FederationInformation*.

5. Return to the Hybrid Configuration Wizard and have it complete the configuration again. This time, the wizard should be able to complete the *Update-HybridConfiguration* cmdlet in the final step, and you should see a window similar to the one shown in Figure 11-69.

Resetting the Autodiscover virtual directory

In some cases, there might be problems with your Autodiscover virtual directory due to incorrect parameters or corruption. Resetting the Autodiscover virtual directory involves a process that will delete the current virtual directory and recreate it with default settings.

Follow these steps if you determined that you need to reset the Autodiscover virtual directory:

1. Start the EMC and connect to your CAS server.

2. Expand the Microsoft Exchange On-Premises node, followed by the Server Configuration node, and then select Client Access. Click Reset Virtual Directory on the Actions pane, as shown in Figure 11-75.

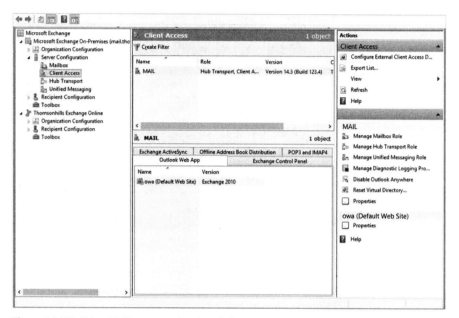

Figure 11-75 Using EMC to reset the virtual directory.

3. Click Browse, select Autodiscover, and then click OK, as shown in Figure 11-76. Click Next.

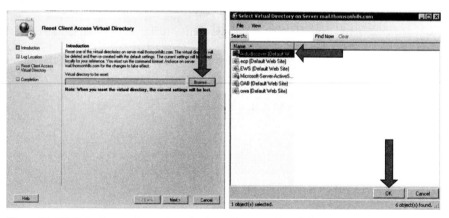

Figure 11-76 Selecting and resetting the Autodiscover virtual directory.

4. On the Log Location page, accept the default location or specify a location to save the log file. The log file will save the settings of the current virtual directory because by resetting the virtual directory, the current settings will be overwritten with default settings. Click Next.

5. The final page of the wizard is shown in Figure 11-77. The wizard lists the four tasks the wizard will complete: getting the Autodiscover virtual directory, reading and saving the current configuration to the log file, deleting the current Autodiscover

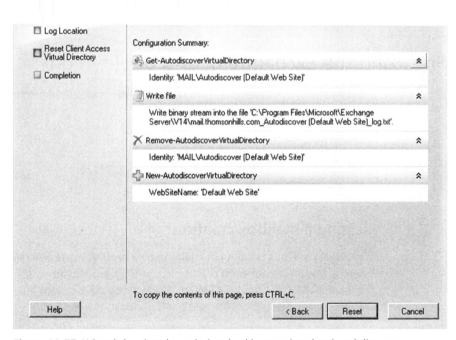

Figure 11-77 Wizard showing the tasks involved in resetting the virtual directory.

> **Note**
>
> Notice the Windows PowerShell cmdlets exposed by the Reset Client Virtual Direc-
> tory Wizard: *Get-AutodiscoverVirtualDirectory*, *Remote-AutodiscoverVirtualDirec-
> tory*, and *New-AutodiscoverVirtualDirectory*. This is an example of Microsoft MMCs
> and GUIs showing the Windows PowerShell commands so you can write scripts to
> automate administrative tasks.

6. After the Autodiscover virtual directory is successfully reset, you need to reset IIS by
entering the following command:

```
iisreset /noforce
```

7. You will also need to set the virtual directory security settings. Open the Exchange
Management Shell and enter the following command:

```
Set-AutodiscoverVirtualDirectory –Identity 'autodiscover (Default Web Site)' –
WSSecurityAuthentication $true
```

Finalizing the Exchange hybrid deployment

At this point, you are ready to start using your Exchange hybrid environment. The final
tasks involve the testing of mailbox operations:

- Testing mailbox creation

- Testing mailbox move

- Changing an MX record to affect mail flow

Testing a mailbox creation

Before we start bulk creations of mailboxes, we need to create a single test mailbox. In this
exercise, you will create a test mailbox to confirm the ability to do so in our new hybrid
configuration. You will use the EMC to create a new mailbox with the New Remote Mailbox
Wizard. Follow these steps to create a test mailbox:

1. Start the EMC, expand the Microsoft Exchange On-Premises node, and then expand the Recipient Configuration node. Select New Remote Mailbox on the Actions pane, as shown in Figure 11-78.

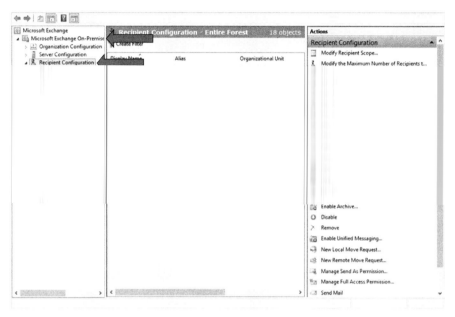

Figure 11-78 Using the EMC to create a new remote mailbox.

2. On the Introduction page of the New Remote Mailbox Wizard, select User Mailbox as the mailbox type to create, as shown in Figure 11-79. Take note, too, of all the other types of mailboxes you can create. Click Next.

INSIDE OUT   Licensing reminder

Remember that user mailboxes consume an Exchange Online license, but shared and resource mailboxes do not need an Exchange Online license.

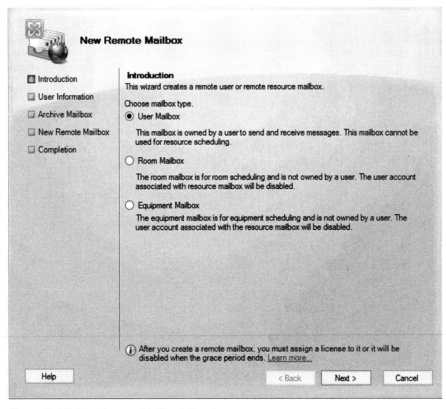

Figure 11-79 New Remote Mailbox Wizard.

3. Provide at least the first name, last name, user logon name, and password, as shown in Figure 11-80, and then click Next.

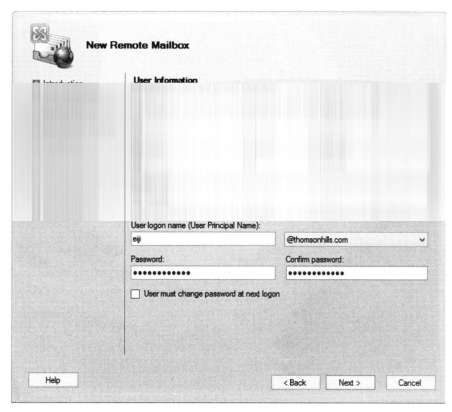

New Remote Mailbox

User Information

User logon name (User Principal Name):

| eiji | @thomsonhills.com |

Password: Confirm password:

| •••••••••••• | •••••••••••• |

☐ User must change password at next logon

| Help | | < Back | Next > | Cancel |

Figure 11-80 User information for the New Remote Mailbox Wizard.

4. On the Archive Mailbox page, if you would like to provide a personal archive for this mailbox, select the Add an archive mailbox check box, as shown in Figure 11-81. Click Next.

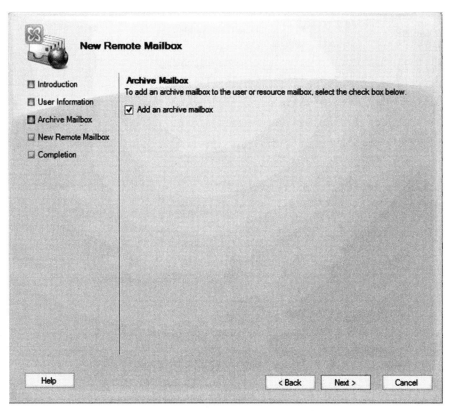

Figure 11-81 Archive Mailbox page of the New Remote Mailbox Wizard.

5. Review the information that the New Remote Mailbox Wizard will use to create the new remote mailbox, as shown in Figure 11-82. If everything is in order, click New.

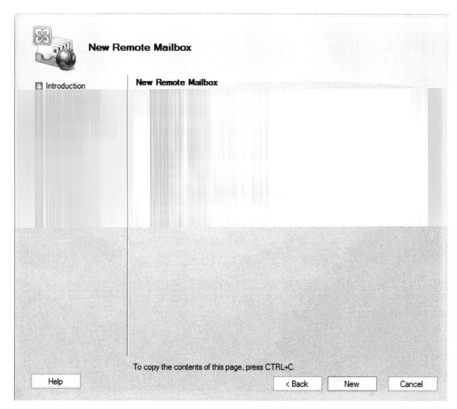

Figure 11-82 Configuration summary.

6. The New Remote Mailbox Wizard will attempt to create the mailbox in your Office 365 Exchange Online tenant. When the task is completed successfully, you will see a completion page similar to the one shown in Figure 11-83. Click Finish.

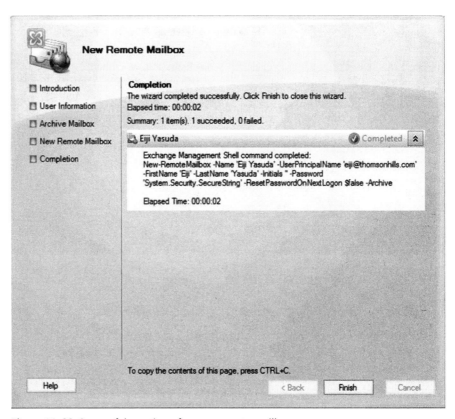

Figure 11-83 Successful creation of a new remote mailbox.

7. Even though the new remote mailbox was successfully created, as reported by the New Remote Mailbox Wizard, if you go to your Office 365 admin center at this point, you will not see the mailbox. The mailbox will appear after the next synchronization. Unless you changed the frequency for which DirSync runs, it is three hours by default. You can force directory synchronization to occur immediately by going to the DirSync server, navigating to C:\program files\Microsoft Online Directory Sync, and starting DirSyncConfigShell.psc1. Next, enter the following command:

Testing a mailbox move

In this test, you are ensuring the proper configuration of your hybrid configuration by test-ing the migration of an existing on-premises mailbox to your Office 365 Exchange Online tenant. This test is a prerequisite for bulk mailbox migration, which is covered in Chapter 12. Follow these steps to move one or more mailboxes:

1. Because DirSync and AD FS are prerequisites for an Exchange hybrid environment, the user whose mailbox you want to move should already be synchronized with Office 365. Log on to your Office 365 admin center and assign the user account with an Exchange Online license. Alternatively, you can use Windows PowerShell to assign the license.

2. Start the EMC.

3. Expand the Microsoft Exchange On-Premises node and expand the Recipient
    Configuration node. Click Mailbox and select the mailbox you want to move to Office
    365. Select the New Remote Move Request option on the Actions pane, as shown
    in Figure 11-84. You can use the Shift and Ctrl keys to select multiple mailboxes to
    move.

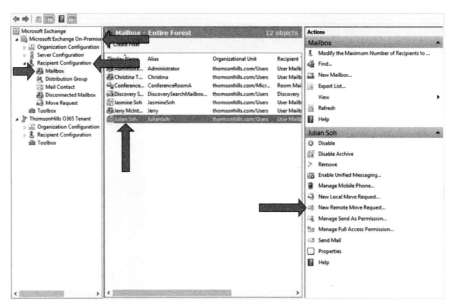

Figure 11-84 Using the EMC to create a New Remote Move Request.

4. On the Introduction page of the New Remote Move Request Wizard, choose to move only the archive mailbox or both the mailbox and the archive mailbox. In this exercise, we will move both the mailbox and the archive mailbox for this user, as shown in Figure 11-85. Click Next.

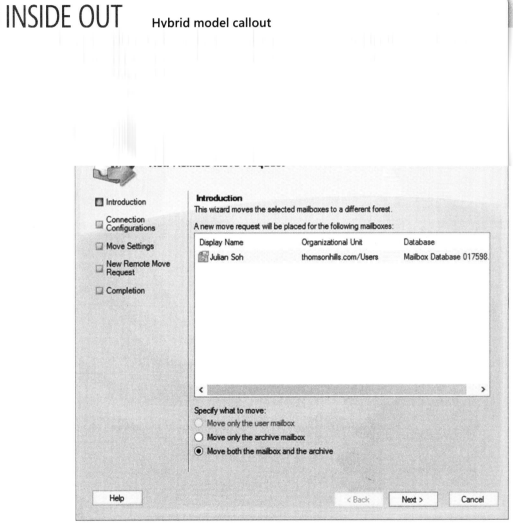

Figure 11-85 Specify the mailboxes to move through the New Remote Move Request Wizard.

5.   On the Connection Configurations page, your Office 365 tenant should already be
     selected in the Target forest box. If not, use the drop-down box to select your Office
     365 tenant as the target forest. The FQDN of the Microsoft Exchange Replication
     service is the FQDN of your CAS server. Finally, enter the credentials of a user with
     access rights to move mailboxes for your on-premises Exchange environment. Your
     input should look similar to the page shown in Figure 11-86. Click Next when done.

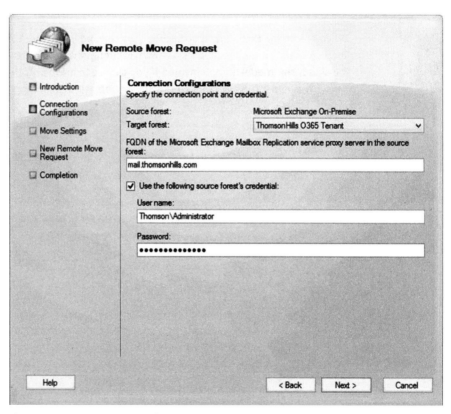

Figure 11-86 Connection Configurations page of the Remote Mailbox Move Wizard.

6. On the Move Settings page, click Browse to browse for the target delivery domain, and then select your email delivery domain. This should be the *<Domain>*.mail. onmicrosoft.com address. In this scenario, your on-premises Exchange will receive emails, so it will use this address for SMTP routing. In the Target Delivery Domain box, as shown in Figure 11-87, select the target delivery domain, click OK, and then click Next.

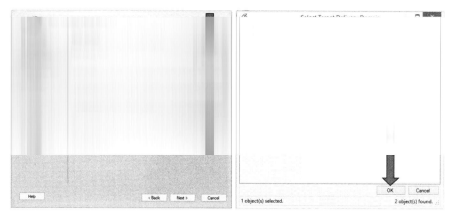

Figure 11-87 Select the target delivery domain.

7. Review the configuration details on the Summary page. Click New.

8.   The New Remote Move Request Wizard will initiate the mailbox move, and you should see the initiation of the move completed, as shown in Figure 11-88. Note that this is only the initiation of the move. The actual move takes time and is happening in the background. We will see how we can monitor the move in the next step. Click Finish.

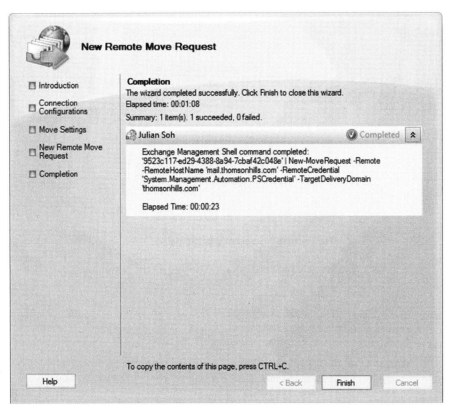

Figure 11-88   New Remote Move Request Wizard completed successfully.

9. You can track the progress of the mailbox move in the EMC. Expand the Office 365 node, and then expand Recipient Configuration. Click Move Request. The mailboxes for which you have initiated a move request, along with their statuses, will be listed on the main pane, as shown in Figure 11-89. The status of the move request for a mailbox is listed as Moving when it is in progress and Completed when it is done. If there are errors, the status might be Failed or Completed with Errors.

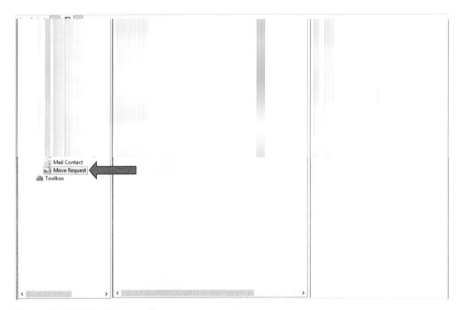

Figure 11-89 Checking mailbox move requests.

10. After a move request is completed, as indicated in the EMC, you need to clear the In-Transit flag. This is done by selecting the Clear Move Request action on the Action pane, as shown in Figure 11-89.

11. Click Yes to confirm clearing of the move request.

Let us examine the settings of a mailbox that has been moved. Figure 11-90 is a screen shot of one such mailbox. Start the EMC, open the mailbox that has been moved, and click the E-Mail Addresses tab. Scroll down the list and you should see the routing email address.

Figure 11-90 Routing email address of an Office 365 mailbox.

Notice that the routing email address takes the form of *<Domain>*.mail.onmicrosoft.com. This is how your on-premises Exchange will know to route the email to Office 365. This setting was placed there when you selected the target delivery domain in Step 6.

The email routing settings for mailboxes you created and mailboxes you moved should have the same *<Domain>*.mail.onmicrosoft.com routing email address. Inbound mail flow is shown in Figure 11-91.

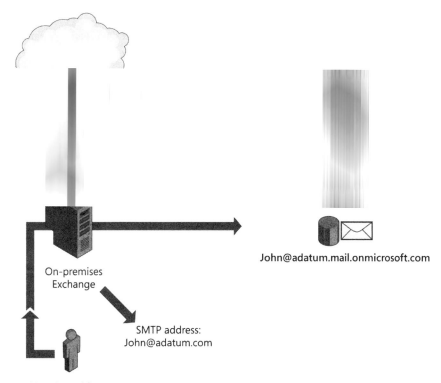

John@adatum.mail.onmicrosoft.com

On-premises
Exchange

SMTP address:
John@adatum.com

Routing address:
John@adatum.mail.onmicrosoft.com

Figure 11-91 Inbound mail flow.

In this configuration, we have outbound emails from the Office 365 mailbox go directly to the destination even though inbound emails go through the on-premises Exchange server. However, if needed, we can configure outbound emails to also go through the on-premises Exchange server.

Before proceeding, you should test mail flow to make sure inbound and outbound mail is working. You can use the Exchange Remote Connectivity Analyzer or just exchange test emails from an external mail service such as Hotmail. Make sure to test both on-premises mailboxes as well as online mailboxes. Send emails between on-premises mailboxes and online mailboxes as well.

Changing an MX record

At this point, you have the option to switch the MX record that is pointing to your on-premises Exchange environment to Exchange Online. This introduces an alternative hybrid scenario where email from the Internet will first go through FOPE, or EOP if you are on the latest release of Office 365. FOPE or EOP will scan the email for spam, viruses, and other threats before routing the mail to online and on-premises mailboxes. This is known as changing your organization's Internet mail ingress point.

The benefit of this scenario is the ability for you to take advantage of FOPE or EOP filtering and protection. By doing so, you can decommission your on-premises email filtering and protection solution.

To change your Internet mail ingress point from on-premises Exchange to Exchange Online, you will need to change the MX record. Locate the MX record for your organization and change it, using the example in Table 11-4 as a guide.

TABLE 11-4 DNS MX record

DNS record type	MX riority	Target
MX record	0	<Domain>.mail.eo.outlook.com

After you have made this change to your MX record, you can use the Exchange Remote Connectivity Analyzer (ExRCA) to test mail flow. ExRCA has an Internet email test that allows you to test inbound and outbound Internet email. Use the inbound test to ensure Internet-originated email messages make it to your online and on-premises mailboxes through FOPE or EOP.

Centralized mail transport

There are two configuration options available when routing emails through Office 365 Exchange Online:

- Route mail for both on-premises and online recipients through Exchange Online with centralized mail transport disabled (default setting).

- Route mail for both on-premises and online recipients through Exchange Online with centralized mail transport enabled.

Centralized mail transport disabled

Disabled centralized mail transport is the default setting. Disabling centralized mail transport basically means that FOPE or EOP process all inbound messages and are responsible for routing messages to on-premises mailboxes or online mailboxes.

Take, for example, an email addressed to two individuals, John and Eiji, at Adatum. Figure 11-92 depicts how mail is handled with centralized mail transport disabled:

1. An email arrives at Office 365 FOPE or EOP because Adatum's MX record has been changed. John's mailbox is in Exchange Online and Eiji's mailbox is on-premises.

2. When the email arrives at FOPE or EOP, it determines the location of John's and Eiji's mailboxes and makes a copy of the email.

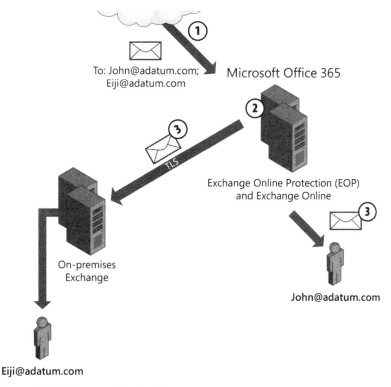

Figure 11-92 No centralized mail transport.

For outbound messages, emails sent from Exchange Online mailboxes to external recipients will be routed through FOPE or EOP. Emails sent from Exchange on-premises mailboxes for external recipients will be routed directly to the recipients.

Centralized mail transport enabled

With centralized mail transport enabled, inbound emails will still be received by FOPE or EOP first because of the change in MX records. Figure 11-93 depicts mail handling when centralized mail transport is enabled:

1. An email is sent to two recipients, John and Eiji. The email is first received by FOPE or EOP because the MX record has been changed accordingly.

2. FOPE or EOP scans the email for spam, virus, and other threats.

3. The email is sent by FOPE or EOP to Exchange on-premises.

4. Exchange on-premises receives the email and determines that Eiji's mailbox is on-premises and John's mailbox is in Exchange Online.

5. Exchange on-premises makes a copy of the email and sends one copy to Eiji's mailbox on-premises and routes the other copy, addressed for John, back to FOPE or EOP.

6. FOPE or EOP receives the message from Exchange on-premises and recognizes that it is destined for John, whose mailbox resides in Exchange Online.

7. FOPE or EOP delivers the email to John through Exchange Online.

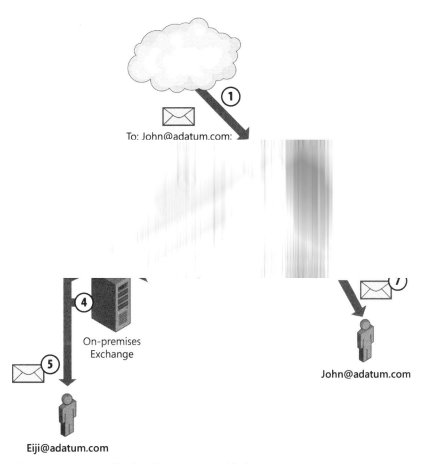

To: John@adatum.com:

On-premises
Exchange

Eiji@adatum.com

John@adatum.com

Figure 11-93 Centralized mail transport enabled.

For outbound messages, email sent from Exchange Online mailboxes to external recipients will be routed through your on-premises Exchange Hub Transport server if centralized mail transport is enabled. Emails sent from Exchange on-premises mailboxes for external recipients will also be routed directly to the recipients through DNS and the on-premises Exchange Hub Transport server.

INSIDE OUT Enable centralized mail transport: yes or no?

The reason most organizations enable centralized mail transport is because of special compliance requirements such as on-premises Data Leakage Prevention (DLP). However, with DLP now available in the latest release of Office 365, the reasons for enabling centralized mail transport are further reduced. Furthermore, this adds additional hops and latency to email delivery, not to mention your on-premises Exchange environment might be at risk of becoming a single point of failure. Therefore, unless you have specific compliance requirements that can be met only by having to route Internet-bound emails through your on-premises Exchange environment, the recommendation is that you should not enable centralized mail transport.

Enabling and disabling centralized mail transport

Before you change your MX record, decide whether to enable centralized mail transport. Remember, too, that centralized mail transport is not enabled by default. If you need to turn centralized mail transport on or off, you can do so with the EMC or through Windows PowerShell.

Enabling and disabling centralized mail transport with EMC

Follow these steps and refer to Figure 11-94 to enable or disable centralized mail transport with the EMC:

1. Start the EMC, expand the Microsoft Exchange On-Premises node, and click Organization Configuration.

2. On the main EMC pane, select the Hybrid Configuration tab.

3. On the Actions pane, click Manage Hybrid Configuration.

4. Because you are not changing anything else except for centralized mail transport, click Next on each page of the Manage Hybrid Configuration Wizard until you get to the Mail Flow Security page, as shown in Figure 11-94.

5. Under Mail Flow Path, choose to route email directly using DNS settings or route all Internet-bound email through your on-premises Exchange environment.

6. Click Next.

7. Click Manage.

8. Click Finish to exit the wizard after the successful modification of your hybrid configuration.

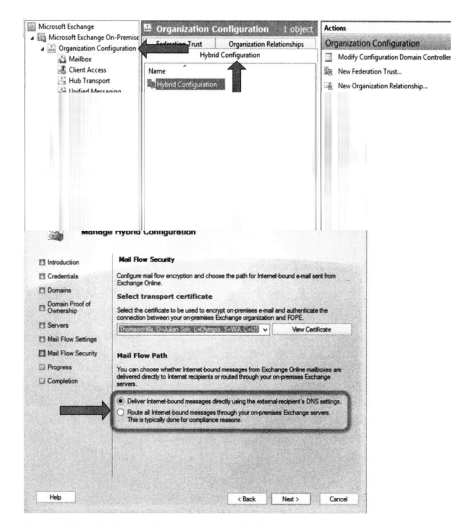

Figure 11-94 Modify hybrid configuration with EMC.

Enabling and disabling centralized mail transport with Windows PowerShell

The *Get-HybridMailFlow* cmdlet is used to show the hybrid mail flow configuration, and the *Set-HybridMailFlow* cmdlet is used to modify the configuration.

Chapter 11

To see the current hybrid mail flow settings for your environment, enter the following command without any parameters:

```
Get-HybridMailFlow
```

Get-HybridMailFlow will return a list of configuration information. Included in the list is *CentralizedTransportEnabled*, as shown in Figure 11-95.

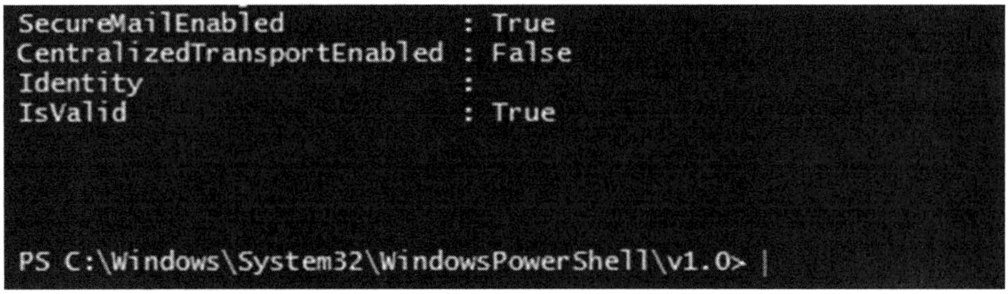

```
SecureMailEnabled           : True
CentralizedTransportEnabled : False
Identity                    :
IsValid                     : True



PS C:\Windows\System32\WindowsPowerShell\v1.0> |
```

Figure 11-95 Information returned by the *Get-HybridMailFlow* cmdlet.

Figure 11-95 confirms the default settings for secure mail and centralized mail transport. Secure mail is the TLS connection between your on-premises Exchange and Exchange Online, which is enabled by default, while centralized mail transport is not enabled. If you need to enable centralized mail transport, enter the following command:

```
Set-HybridMailFlow -CentralizedTransportEnabled $True
```

To disable centralized mail transport, enter the following command:

```
Set-HybridMailFlow -CentralizedTransportEnabled $False
```

Use the *Get-HyrbirdMailFlow* cmdlet before and after each time you make changes to your configuration.

Summary

Exchange Online is the most complex service in Office 365 to implement. This is because of the many implementation models and the different components that can be implemented independently. As we saw in Chapter 10, the other services are covered under a single Service Description, whereas Exchange Online workloads are covered by four Service Descriptions: Exchange Online, Exchange Online Archive (EOA), Exchange Online Protection (EOP), and Exchange Hosted Encryption (EHE).

Now that we have implemented Exchange Online, in the next chapter we will show you how to migrate mailboxes and subsequently manage the different Exchange workloads.

Mailbox migration and administering Exchange Online

Mailbox migration options. 565   Administering Exchange Online. 608

Now that you have incorporated Exchange Online in your environment, it is time to discuss mailbox migration options and administering the different messaging workloads. As we mentioned before, this book is about Office 365, so we will focus only on Exchange Online and hybrid administration topics in this chapter.

Mailbox migration options

There are three primary types of migration options:

- Cutover migration

- Staged migration

- Hybrid deployment migration

A cutover migration is a process where all on-premises mailboxes and contents are migrated as a single batch and is applicable to Exchange 2003, 2007, 2010, and 2013 with fewer than 1,000 mailboxes. You must disable directory synchronization if you would like to do a cutover migration.

A staged migration is a process where a subset of mailboxes and content is migrated in several batches over time and is applicable only to Exchange 2003 and 2007. A staged migration is typically the approach if you have more than 1,000 mailboxes. A special consideration for staged migration is that you need to identify mailboxes that must be in the same migration batch. The mailboxes of individuals participating in delegate permissions must be kept together. Therefore, they need to belong to the same batch when you plan a staged migration.

If your organization has Exchange 2010 or 2013 with more than 1,000 mailboxes, you will need to implement an Exchange hybrid deployment, which is what you implemented in Chapter 11.

Figure 12-1 shows a flowchart depicting migration options available to your organization based on your on-premises configuration.

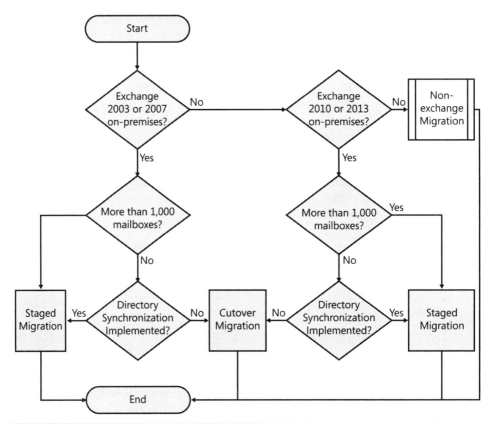

Figure 12-1 Migration options.

Cutover migration

A cutover migration is ideal for organizations with 1,000 mailboxes or less. The other important requirement for a cutover migration is that directory synchronization has not been established. The reason for this is because the cutover migration will create users in Office 365 as part of the process. Therefore, if directory synchronization is already synchronizing Active Directory (AD) objects to Office 365, you need to use a staged migration or migrate using a hybrid deployment.

A cutover migration is initiated through the Exchange admin center (EAC) for the latest release of Office 365. For organizations that are currently on Office 365 but have not been upgraded to the latest release, this is done through the Exchange Control Panel (ECP). You can also use Windows PowerShell to provision new Exchange Online mailboxes, and then migrate mailbox data from your on-premises Exchange to Exchange Online.

Before we look at how a cutover migration is set up, it is useful for you to know what happens when you execute a cutover migration. When a cutover migration is initiated, the fol-

cess is called initial synchronization.

- On-premises mailbox contents are synchronized with their corresponding online mailboxes every 24 hours. This part of the process is called incremental synchronization.

- When you are ready to complete the migration, change the MX record to start routing emails to the online mailboxes and end the migration. Exchange will conduct a final synchronization and notify the administrator through email that the migration is complete. The email notification will contain two reports:

  ○ **MigrationErrors.csv**   This report contains a list of mailboxes that failed to migrate and information about the error.

  ○ **MigrationStatistics.csv**   This report contains a list of mailboxes and the corresponding number of items migrated. The report also includes a unique password assigned to each mailbox that the user will need to change after initial log on. Remember that this is because the cutover migration creates new accounts as part of the migration process.

You have the option to use Autodiscover or manually configure connection settings prior to initiating the cutover migration. Configuring Autodiscover was covered in Chapter 11.

Chapter 12

Cutover migration with the ECP

Follow these steps to execute a cutover migration using the ECP:

1. Log on to Outlook Web App (OWA).

2. On the Options menu located at the upper-right corner of the OWA window, select See All Options, as shown in Figure 12-2.

Figure 12-2 Options menu in OWA.

3. Select the Manage Myself option, and then select My Organization, as shown in Figure 12-3. This will take you to the ECP.

Figure 12-3 Access the ECP through the Manage My Organization menu item.

4. When the ECP appears, select the E-Mail Migration tab on the Users & Groups page, as shown in Figure 12-4.

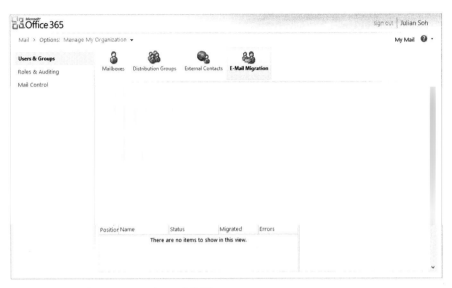

Figure 12-4 Exchange Control Panel (ECP).

5. The main pane shows migration processes and their corresponding statuses and errors. If there are any existing migration processes, you will see them listed here and you can edit, start, resume, pause, or delete the processes by using the controls on this page. To create a new cutover migration, click New.

6. Select whether to use Autodiscover, manually configure connection settings, or use IMAP for mailbox content migration, and then click Next.

7. Provide an administrator's email address, log on with a credential and password, and enter the number of mailboxes to migrate simultaneously. The default is to migrate three mailboxes simultaneously, and the maximum is 50. Click Next.

8. ECP will test the connection to your on-premises Exchange server with the Autodiscover or manual connection settings. When the connection is successful, you will be prompted to provide a name for the batch migration.

9. Provide email addresses that the migration report should be sent to by typing in the addresses or by using the Browse button to select from the global address list.

> **Note**
>
> For more information about migrating all mailboxes to Office 365 through a cutover migration, see *http://help.outlook.com/en-us/140/ms.exch.ecp.emailmigrationwizardex-changelearnmore.aspx.*

Cutover migration with EAC

If your organization is using the latest release of Office 365, the ECP will not be an available graphical user interface (GUI) option. Instead, you will use the EAC. To initiate a cutover migration using the EAC, follow these steps:

1. Access the Office 365 admin center at *https://portal.onmicrosoft.com.*

2. After authentication, select Exchange from the Admin menu, as shown in Figure 12-5.

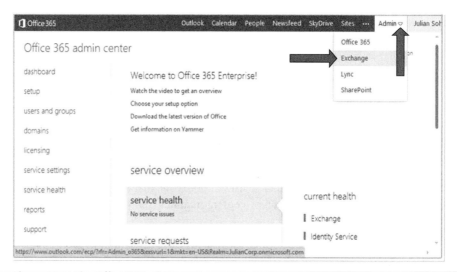

Figure 12-5 The Office 365 admin center.

3. In the EAC, select recipients on the pane on the left, and then click the migration tab, as shown in Figure 12-6.

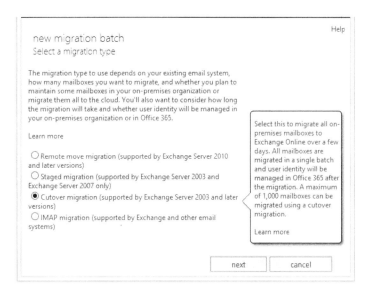

4. Select Migrate to Exchange Online. You will be provided with migration options, as shown in Figure 12-7. Select the Cutover migration option, and then click next.

Figure 12-7 Migration options in the EAC.

5. Provide the email address of any one of the mailboxes that will be migrated, and then provide an on-premises administrator credential, as shown in Figure 12-8. Click Next.

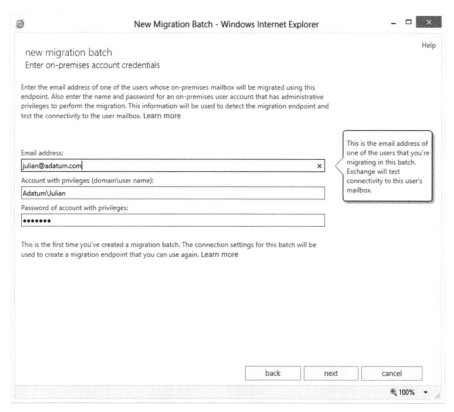

Figure 12-8 Credentials and email information for a new cutover migration batch.

6. Enter a name for the cutover migration, as shown in Figure 12-9, and then click Next.

Figure 12-9 Name the cutover migration.

7. Choose to either manually or automatically start the migration and provide email addresses that a report should be sent to after the migration is complete, as shown in Figure 12-10, and then click new.

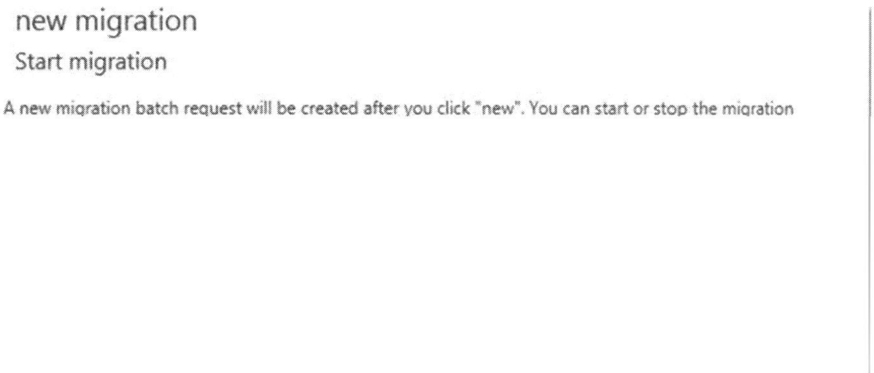

new migration
Start migration

A new migration batch request will be created after you click "new". You can start or stop the migration

Figure 12-10 Start migration and email address of administrators.

Staged migration

A staged migration is initiated through the EAC, the ECP, or through Windows PowerShell. It is similar to a cutover migration except that you have the ability to identify a subset of mailboxes to migrate through a .csv file. Staged migration is the appropriate migration method if directory synchronization is already implemented.

Before we examine how to set up a staged migration, it is useful for you to know what happens during a staged migration. When you initiate a staged migration, the following processes occur:

- The migration service checks that directory synchronization is configured, prompts for the .csv file, and checks that each entry in the .csv file is a mail-enabled user (MEU) in Office 365.

- The service then converts the MEUs into mailboxes and populates the *TargetAddress* property of the on-premises mailbox with the email address of the cloud mailbox.

- After the *TargetAddress* property has been updated for all mailboxes, you will receive an email with a list of mailboxes that have been successfully created and converted. Mailbox contents are not migrated yet, but the users can start using the mailbox without any MX record changes. This is because if emails arrive at the on-premises mailbox, they will be redirected to Exchange Online because of the *TargetAddress* property.

- The migration service then starts to migrate the contents, contacts, and calendar items from the on-premises mailboxes to their corresponding online mailboxes. When content migration is done, another report is emailed to administrators.

- At this point, you can create and start additional migration batches.

- When you are done with migration, change the MX records so that email will be directly delivered to the online mailboxes. You can then complete the migration. The migration service will carry out any necessary cleanup and checks to make sure every MEU that has a corresponding on-premises mailbox has been migrated. A final status report will then be sent to the administrator.

Creating a .csv file

The first order of business to carry out a staged migration is to create a .csv file containing the attributes of mailboxes you want to migrate. The first row of the .csv file is the header row and should contain only the following attribute names:

- *EmailAddress*   This is the SMTP address of the mailbox and is the only required attribute.

- *Password*   The password that will be set for the cloud-based mailbox after it is migrated. This is an optional attribute and is not required if single sign-on (SSO) is enabled. If you set the password in the .csv file and SSO is enabled, it will be ignored. Simply leave this box blank if it does not apply to your configuration.

- *ForceChangePassword*   This Boolean attribute specifies whether the user must change the password when first logging on to the cloud mailbox. The value is either *True* or *False*. This is also an optional attribute and is not required if SSO is enabled. If you set this attribute in the .csv file and SSO is enabled, it will be ignored. Simply leave this box blank if it does not apply to your configuration.

Figure 12-11 shows an example of a .csv file for a staged migration. This .csv file will cause the staged migration process to migrate five mailboxes, set the password for the new cloud mailboxes to NewPa$$word, and require only Anna and Scott to change their password upon initial logon to their respective cloud mailboxes.

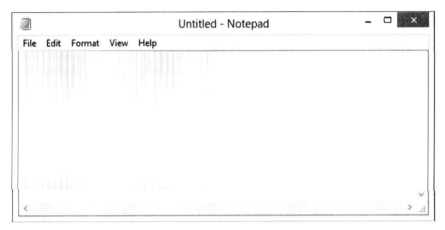

Figure 12-11 Contents of a .csv file for staged migration.

A .csv file is required regardless whether the staged migration is initiated through the ECP, the EAC, or Windows PowerShell. Furthermore, the .csv file can contain only these attributes.

INSIDE OUT   Support for non-ASCII characters

If you need to support non-ASCII or special characters in your .csv file, then save it with UTF-8 encoding.

Staged migration with ECP

Follow these steps to initiate a staged migration using the ECP:

1. Log on to OWA.

2. From the Options menu located at the upper-right corner of the OWA window, select See All Options, as shown in Figure 12-2.

3. Select the Manage Myself option, and then select My Organization, as shown in Figure 12-3.

4. When the ECP appears, select the E-Mail Migration tab on the Users & Groups page, as shown in Figure 12-4.

5. Click New to create a new migration batch and decide whether to use Autodiscover to detect settings or to manually specify the settings by selecting the option that applies to your scenario:

   ○ **Exchange 2007 and later versions**   Automatically detect connections settings with Autodiscover

   ○ **Exchange 2003 and later versions**   Manually specify connection settings

   ○ **IMAP**

6. Provide an administrator's email address, log-on credential, password, and the number of mailboxes to migrate simultaneously. The default is to migrate three mailboxes simultaneously, and the maximum is 50.

7. When prompted for the .csv file, click the Browse button to navigate to the location and file, and then provide a name for this staged migration batch, as shown in Figure 12-12. Note that by default, a report will be sent to the administrator's email address identified in Step 7. You can provide additional email addresses if you want to have the report directed to other administrators in addition to the administrator identified in Step 7. The batch name cannot contain spaces or special characters. Click Next.

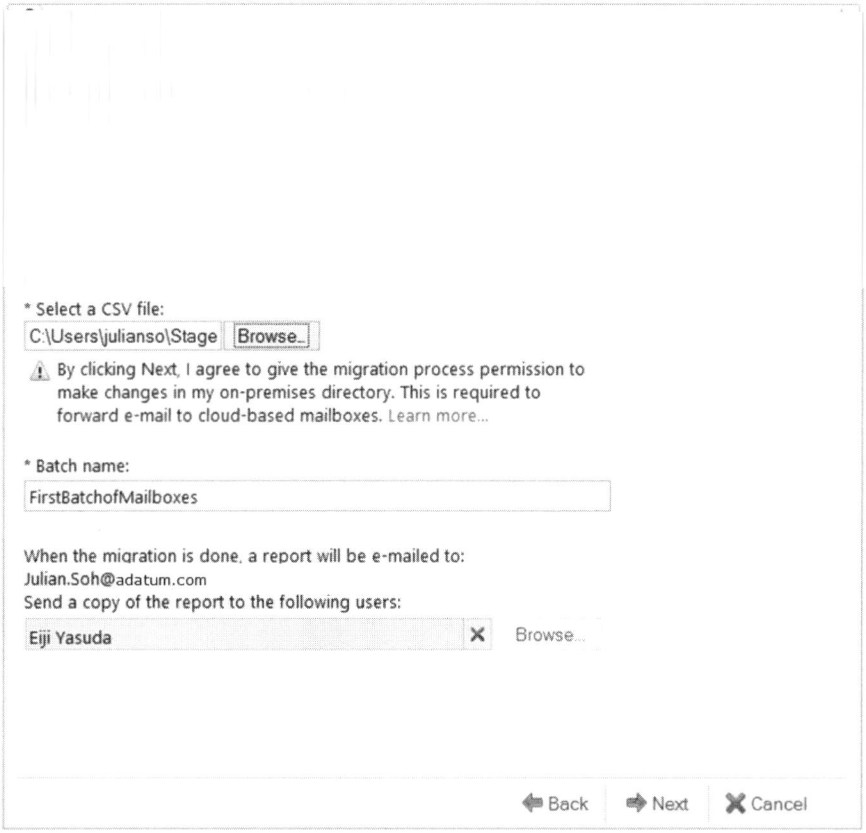

Figure 12-12 Upload a .csv file, a batch name, and a report.

8. The migration wizard will verify the .csv file and contents to make sure there are no errors before creating the migration batch. If there are validation errors, you will see a warning such as the one shown in Figure 12-13. Click the Show error details link to get detailed information about the errors. The errors could be invalid email addresses or formatting errors in the .csv file. In this particular case, we had an email address in the .csv file that was not properly formatted.

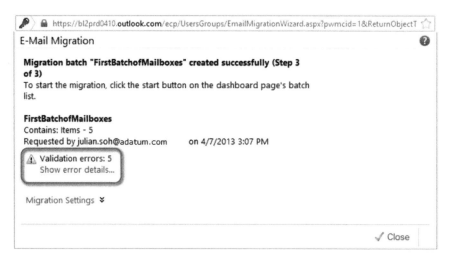

Figure 12-13 Validation errors with a .csv file.

9. Click Close.

10. On the E-Mail Migration page in the ECP, the staged batch migration you just created should be listed, as shown in Figure 12-14. Select it and click Start to begin the batch migration.

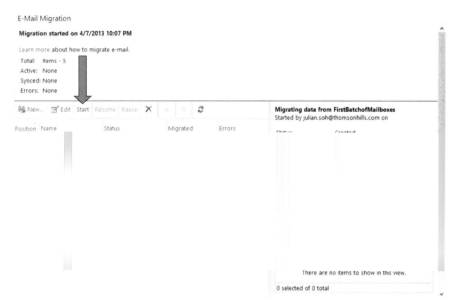

Figure 12-14 Starting a migration batch.

11. After you have started the migration, you can monitor the process by selecting the batch migration and looking at the statistics located in the right pane, as shown in Figure 12-14. The status of the migration, number of mailboxes migrated, and errors are also listed along with the migration batch.

Staged migration with EAC

Starting a staged migration from the EAC is similar to a cutover migration from the EAC. Follow these steps to initiate a staged migration from the EAC:

1. Access the Office 365 admin center at *https://portal.onmicrosoft.com*.

2. After authentication, click the Admin menu on the upper-right corner of the page and select Exchange, as shown in Figure 12-5.

3. In the EAC, select recipients on the pane on the left and then select the migration tab, as shown in Figure 12-6.

4.   Select Migrate to Exchange Online. You will be provided with migration options, one of which is a staged migration. Select it, as shown in Figure 12-15, and then click next.

Figure 12-15 Select Staged migration from the list of migration options.

5. Click the Browse button, navigate to the location of the .csv file, and select it. The wizard will read the .csv file, determine the number of mailboxes to be migrated, and display that information, as shown in Figure 12-16. Click next.

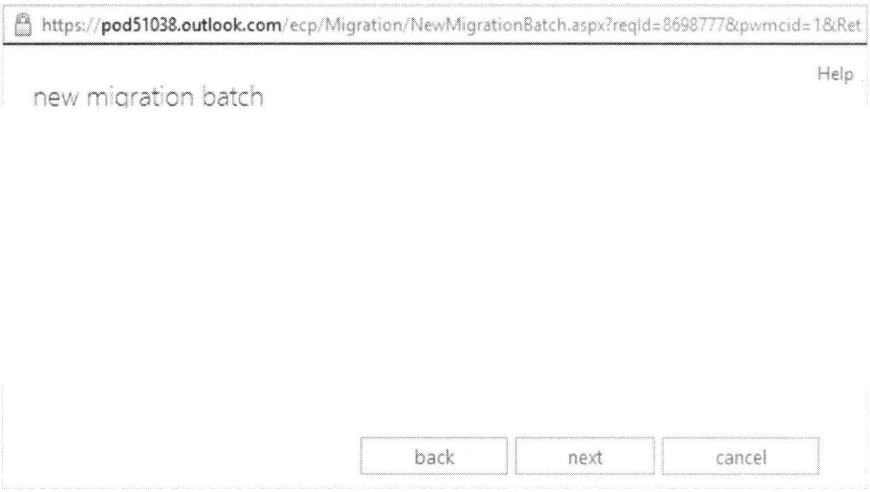

https://**pod51038.outlook.com**/ecp/Migration/NewMigrationBatch.aspx?reqId=8698777&pwmcid=1&Ret

Help

new migration batch

back   next   cancel

Figure 12-16 Selecting the .csv file in the EAC migration wizard.

6. Provide account credentials of an account that has access to the on-premises mailboxes that need to be migrated. The account is in the down-level format (*domain\user name*), as shown in Figure 12-17. Do not use the user principal name (UPN) as the account name. Click next.

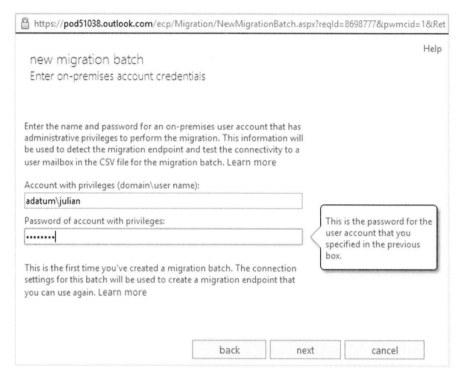

Figure 12-17 Provide credentials of an account with permissions to on-premises mailboxes.

7. The migration wizard will try to automatically detect settings. If it is not able to do so, you will need to manually provide your on-premises server settings, as shown in Figure 12-18. Enter the information, if requested, and click next.

https://**pod51038.outlook.com**/ecp/Migration/NewMigrationBatch.aspx?reqId=8698777&pwmcid=1&Ret

Help

new migration batch

migrating. For example, mail.contoso.com.

back   next   cancel

Figure 12-18 Connection settings in the event that automatic detection fails.

8. Give the migration batch a name, as shown in Figure 12-19, and then click next.

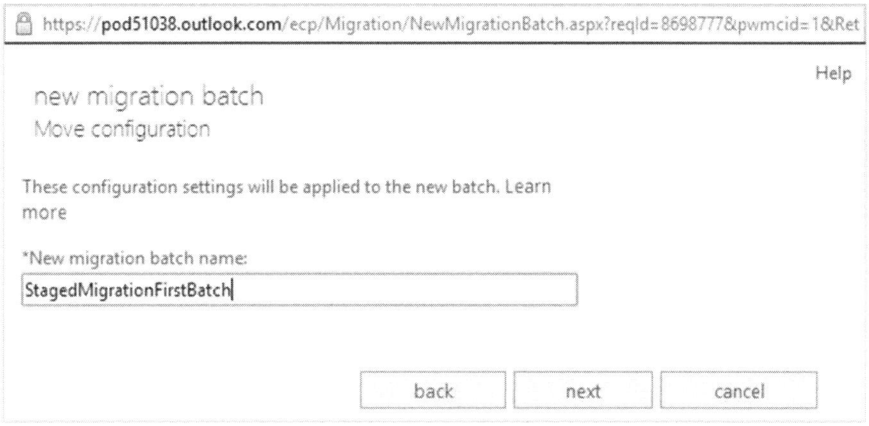

https://**pod51038.outlook.com**/ecp/Migration/NewMigrationBatch.aspx?reqId=8698777&pwmcid=1&Ret

Help

new migration batch
Move configuration

These configuration settings will be applied to the new batch. Learn more

*New migration batch name:

StagedMigrationFirstBatch

back   next   cancel

Figure 12-19 Provide a name for this phased migration batch.

Chapter 12

9. Click browse to select administrators who should receive a report when the migration is completed, as shown in Figure 12-20. Click new to create the migration batch.

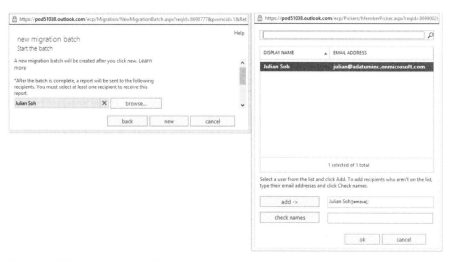

Figure 12-20 Select report recipients.

10. After the migration batch is created, you can view its status and start it from the EAC, as shown in Figure 12-21.

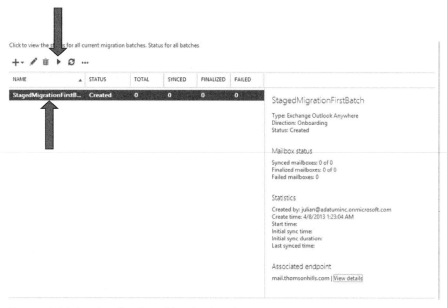

Figure 12-21 Starting the phased batch migration.

IMAP migration

An IMAP migration is commonly used in migrations from non-Exchange email systems to Exchange Online. As the name implies, the on-premises email system will need to have the IMAP protocol enabled to use an IMAP migration method. Prior to initiating an IMAP migration, there are two manual tasks you must perform:

●   Create the Exchange Online mailboxes for users whose mailbox contents you want to

Creating a .csv file

Create a .csv file to target the on-premises users' mailboxes whose content you want to migrate to Exchange Online. The first row of the .csv file is the header row and should contain only the following attribute names:

●   *EmailAddress*   This is the user ID for the user's cloud-based mailbox in UPN format. Note that this is not the SMTP address; this is the user ID in Office 365.

●   *UserName*   This is the user logon name for the on-premises mailbox on the IMAP server.

●   *Password*   This is the password for the user's account on the on-premises IMAP mailbox server.

The .csv file for an IMAP migration batch must not be larger than 10 MB and cannot contain more than 50,000 rows. Furthermore, all three attributes are required. Contacts, calendar items, and tasks cannot be migrated with the IMAP method.

IMAP migration with the ECP

Follow these steps if your organization has not been upgraded to the latest release of Office 365 and would like to use the ECP to initiate an IMAP migration. This section assumes you have created mailboxes in Exchange Online for the on-premises users for whom you want to migrate content.

1.   Log on to OWA.

2. From the Options menu located at the upper-right corner of the OWA window, select See All Options, as shown in Figure 12-2.

3. Select the Manage Myself option at the upper left, and select My Organization, as shown in Figure 12-03. This will take you to the ECP.

4. In the ECP, as shown in Figure 12-04, select E-Mail Migration under Users & Groups.

5. To create a new IMAP migration, click New, then select IMAP.

6. As shown in Figure 12-22, provide the fully qualified domain name (FQDN) of the on-premises email server in the IMAP server box. Select the authentication type, encryption level, and the IMAP port if it is not the standard port 993 for IMAP. Finally, specify the number of mailboxes to simultaneously migrate. Click Next.

Figure 12-22 IMAP server settings.

7. The migration wizard will test the connection settings by attempting to connect to the on-premises mail server with the IMAP protocol. If successful, it will prompt you for the .csv file.

8. Click the Browse button to navigate to the location and .csv file. Provide a name for the IMAP migration in the Batch name box. Batch names cannot have spaces or special characters.

12. Exchange Online will check the .csv file to ensure that no errors are detected. If there are no errors, you will be notified that the .csv file successfully passed the checks.

13. Review the information about the migration batch, and then click Close.

14. The IMAP migration batch should now appear in the list in the ECP E-Mail Migration window. Select it, and then click Start to initiate the migration.

15. After the migration is completed, change your MX records so that new mail will be delivered to the cloud mailboxes.

IMAP migration with the EAC

If your organization is using the latest release of Office 365 and would like to use the EAC, follow these steps to initiate an IMAP migration:

1. Access the Office 365 admin center at *https://portal.onmicrosoft.com*.

2. After authentication, click the Admin menu on the upper-right corner of the page and select Exchange, as shown in Figure 12-05.

3. In the EAC, under recipients, select the migration tab from the main pane, as shown in Figure 12-6.

4. Select Migrate to Exchange Online. You will be provided with migration options, one of which is IMAP migration. Select it, and then click next.

Chapter 12

5. Click the Browse button and navigate to the location and the .csv file. Click Open, and then click next.

6. Exchange Online will check the .csv file to ensure that no errors are detected. If there are no errors, you will see the number of mailboxes detected in the .csv file. Click next to continue.

7. As shown in Figure 12-23, provide the FQDN of the on-premises email server in the IMAP server box. Select the authentication type, encryption level, and the IMAP port if it is not the standard port 993 for IMAP. Finally, specify the number of mailboxes to simultaneously migrate. Click next to continue.

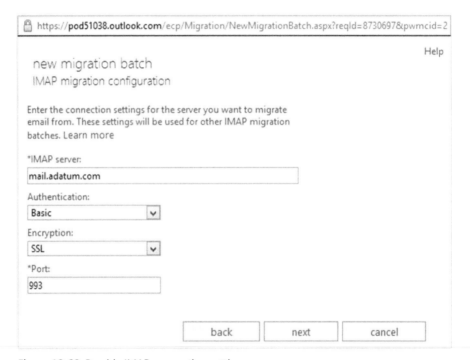

Figure 12-23 Provide IMAP connection settings.

8. If the IMAP settings in Step 7 are correct and Exchange Online can connect to the on-premises server through IMAP, the wizard will use the information to create a migration endpoint. On the Confirm the migration endpoint page, click next.

9. After the migration endpoint has been successfully created, the information about the endpoint will be displayed on the IMAP migration configuration page. Click next.

10. On the Move configuration page, provide a name for the migration batch, and then click next.

11. On the Start the batch page, click browse to select additional administrators to whom you would like to send a copy of the migration report once the migration is complete.

12. Select whether to automatically start the batch or to manually start it later. Click new to create the batch.

13. After migration is complete, modify your MX record to point to Office 365 Exchange

Online 2010

A cutover migration to Exchange Online 2010 can be done through remote Windows Pow-erShell by following these steps:

1. Connect to Exchange Online by creating a *PSSession* using the following commands:

```
Import-Module MSonline

$cred = Get-Credential

Connect-MsolService -Credential $cred

$Session = New-PSSession -ConfigurationName Microsoft.Exchange-ConnectionUri
https://ps.outlook.com/powershell/ -Credential $cred -Authentication Basic
-AllowRedirection

Import-PSSession $Session -AllowClobber
```

2. Create a connection string containing the migration settings:

```
$MigrationSettings = Test-MigrationServerAvailability -Exchange -Credentials
(Get-Credential) -ExchangeServer <on-premises Exchange fqdn> -RPCProxyServer
<external Outlook Anywhere fqdn>
```

3. When prompted, enter the on-premises credentials of a user who has full access privileges to the on-premises mailboxes.

4. Create the migration batch by entering the following command:

```
New-MigrationBatch -Exchange -Name <Batch Name> -ExchangeConnectionSettings
$MigrationSettings.ConnectionSettings -MaxConcurrentMigrations <number of
concurrent migrations> -TimeZone <TimeZone in double quotes, example "Pacific
Standard Time">
```

Chapter 12

5. Start the migration by entering the following command:

```
Start-MigrationBatch
```

6. During the migration, you can monitor the progress by entering the following command:

```
Get-MigrationBatch | fl Status
```

INSIDE OUT Cutover migration best practices

Plan to do a cutover migration over a weekend and change the MX record as soon as the cutover migration is successfully completed. Remember that cutover migrations are for organizations with 1,000 or fewer mailboxes, and even though there is a final synchronization, it is common for mailboxes to be missing items between synchronizations if a cutover migration is left in synchronized mode for an extended period of time. Therefore, plan to complete a cutover migration in a single pass and switch the MX records as soon as possible. It also helps if prior to the migration you set the Time to Live (TTL) for your MX records to be fairly short, thereby reducing the time required for Domain Name System (DNS) convergence. The *Complete-Migration* cmdlet is deprecated as of April, 2012. For more information, *see http://community.office365.com/en-us/blogs/ office_365_technical_blog/archive/2012/04/04/why-administrators-don-t-see-the-complete-migration-button-in-the-e-mail-migration-tool.aspx.*

Using remote Windows PowerShell with the latest release of Office 365 with Exchange Online 2013

Follow these steps to initiate a migration to Exchange Online 2013 using remote Windows PowerShell:

1. Open a new *PSSession* by entering the following commands:

```
Import-Module MSonline

$cred = Get-Credential

Connect-MsolService -Credential $cred

$Session = New-PSSession -ConfigurationName Microsoft.Exchange-ConnectionUri
https://ps.outlook.com/powershell/ -Credential $cred -Authentication Basic
-AllowRedirection

Import-PSSession $Session -AllowClobber
```

2. Enter the following command to create a new migration endpoint:

```
$SourceEndPoint = New-MigrationEndpoint -ExchangeOutlookAnywhere -Name
SourceEndPoint -Credentials (Get-Credential) -ExchangeServer <on-premises
Exchange FQDN> -RpcProxyServer <on-premises Outlook Anywhere FQDN>
-EmailAddress <SMTP address of an on-premises mailbox to be migrated>
```

3. To create a cutover migration batch, go to Step 4. To create an IMAP migration batch, go to Step 5. To create a *staged migration* batch, enter the following command:

5. To create an IMAP migration batch, enter the following command:

```
$IMAPBatch = New-MigrationBatch -Name
```

6. Start the migration batch automatically by adding the *–AutoStart* parameter to the commands in Step 3 or 4. Otherwise, you can manually start the migration batch by entering the following command:

```
Start-MigrationBatch -Identity $StagedBatch.Identity
```

or

```
Start-MigrationBatch -Identity $CutoverBatch.Identity
```

Migration with an Exchange hybrid environment

Migration after establishing an Exchange hybrid environment is one of the most popular approaches because, unlike the other methods we have covered so far, after you establish an Exchange hybrid environment, you can move mailboxes to the cloud and back to on-premises. Part of setting up an Exchange hybrid environment is to implement an Exchange 2010 Service Pack 3 (SP3) Client Access Server (CAS). This introduces the Mailbox Replication Service (MRS) that comes with the 2010 SP3 CAS. MRS is the service responsible for carrying out mailbox moves.

In Chapter 11, we discussed in depth how an Exchange hybrid model is implemented. As such, we will not be covering the steps again here.

Microsoft Exchange PST Capture

With Exchange Online, your users have large mailboxes with access to a personal archive. As mentioned before, this makes personal folders (.pst) files obsolete. If your organization has .pst files, in addition to migrating mailboxes you might have to search for .pst files on computers in your organization so you can incorporate the contents into personal archives. This can be accomplished with Microsoft PST Capture.

PST Capture works with Exchange on-premises and Exchange Online. Therefore, you have two import options:

- Discover .pst files and import contents to an on-premises Exchange server first, then migrate mailboxes to Exchange Online. In this scenario, the on-premises Exchange server must be Exchange 2010 or Exchange 2013.

- Discover .pst files and import contents directly to Exchange Online.

PST Capture comprises the following components:

- **PST Capture Central Service**   The Central Service maintains the list of .pst files found in your organization and manages the migration of the data into Exchange Online.

- **PST Capture Agent**   This is the component that needs to be installed on computers in your organization and is responsible for locating .pst files associated to the computer it is installed on. The agent is also responsible for transmitting the .pst file to the Central Service during import operations.

- **PST Capture Console**   The PST Console is the administrator interface to configure .pst discovery, configure the import process, and also import .pst files from network storage devices that do not have capture agents installed.

> **Note**
>
> For more information about Microsoft PST Capture, see *http://technet.microsoft.com/ en-us/library/hh781036(EXCH.141).aspx.* Pay special attention to the permissions required for PST Capture. The PST Capture Console and Agent also require the .NET Framework 4.5.

Installing and using PST Capture

Implementing a PST Capture strategy involves installing the PST Capture Console first. Follow these steps to install the PST Capture Console:

1. Download Microsoft PST Capture and PST Capture Agent from the Microsoft Download Center at *http://www.microsoft.com/en-us/download/details.aspx?id=36789*

distribution solution such as System Center Configuration Manager. You can start Windows installer with the following parameters to initiate an unattended installation:

```
Msiexec /I PSTCaptureAgent.msi /q CENTRALSERVICEHOST=<IP Address or FQDN of
Capture Console> SERVICEPORT=6674
```

4. After all the agents have been distributed to the computers on your network, start the PST Capture Console. As shown in Figure 12-24, there are two major actions: New PST Search and New Import List.

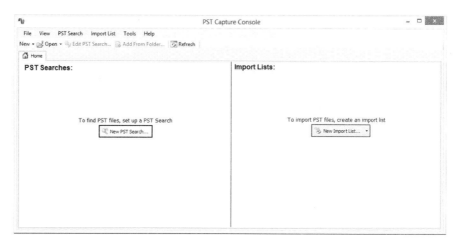

Figure 12-24 PST Capture Console.

5. Before searching for .pst files, you need to specify your online connection settings. From the Tools menu, select Settings.

6. On the Settings page, under Online Connection, provide the credentials of an Office 365 administrator account.

7. If you are migrating .pst content directly to Office 365 Exchange Online, select the The above is an Office 365 Server check box and provide the server name. To determine your Exchange Online server name, use the ECP by going to OWA, selecting Options, selecting See All Options, and clicking the Settings for Post Office Protocol (POP), IMAP, and SMTP access link, as shown in Figure 12-25.

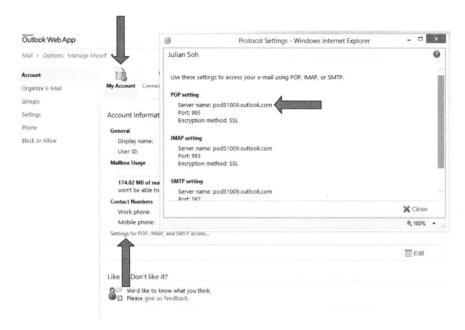

Figure 12-25 ECP showing your Exchange Online information.

8. After you have entered the information in the Online Connection Settings page, click Check. If the PST Capture Console can connect to Exchange Online with the credentials, you will see the "Successfully connected to Exchange Online" message, as shown in Figure 12-26. Click OK to save the settings and close the window.

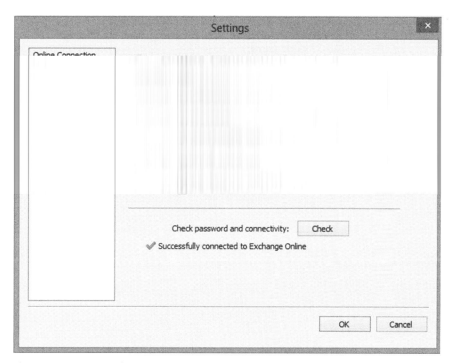

Figure 12-26 Successfully connected to Exchange Online.

9. Click New PST Search to invoke the New PST Search Wizard, as shown in Figure 12-27. Note that there are four steps. At the first step, select the Computers node, and then click Next.

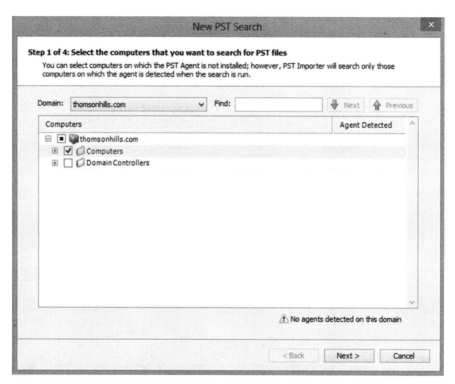

Figure 12-27   New PST Search Step 1 of 4.

10. In Step 2 of the New PST Search Wizard, specify the computers' storage locations to include and exclude when searching for .pst files, as shown in Figure 12-28, and then click Next.

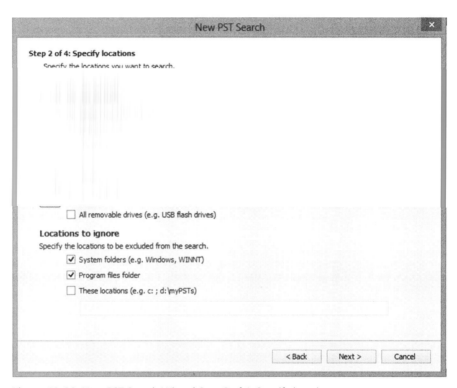

Figure 12-28 New PST Search Wizard Step 2 of 4: Specify locations.

11. In Step 3 of the New PST Search Wizard, you can choose to schedule this search at an off-peak time by specifying the date and time, or you can accept the default of No schedule so you can manually start this search. Click Next.

Chapter 12

12. In the last step of the New PST Search Wizard, give the search a name, as shown in Figure 12-29, and then click Finish.

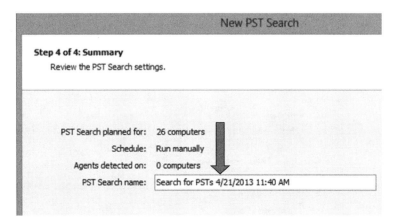

Figure 12-29 New PST Search Wizard Step 4 of 4: Provide a PST search name.

13. A new PST Search is created, and the details are displayed in a separate tab in the PST Search Console, as shown in Figure 12-30. Note the following key information: Number of computers included in the search scope, the status of each task, and whether the search is scheduled or not. Also, make sure the agent is detected for the computers that are in this PST Search. There is a Search All Now button you can use to invoke this search. Click this button to manually start the search now.

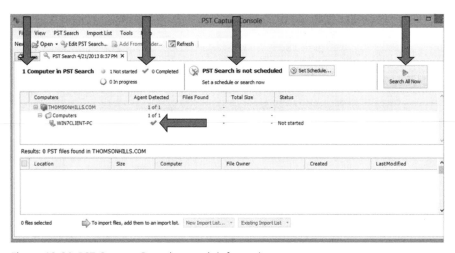

Figure 12-30 PST Capture Console: search information.

14. When the search is complete, the status beside each computer selected will be Completed and the number of PST files found, if any, will be listed in the Files Found column together with the total size of all the PST files found on the computer. Figure 12-31 shows the results of a computed PST search.

Figure 12-31 PST search results.

15. Select the .pst files you want to import by selecting the check boxes. Then click the New Import List button at the bottom of the page.

16. You will see a drop-down list with two options: Cloud Import List and OnPrem Import List. As mentioned before, you can use PST Capture to import content from .pst files to an on-premises Exchange server or directly into Exchange Online. For this exercise, select Cloud Import List.

Chapter 12

17. Set the .pst files to a destination mailbox by clicking the Set mailbox link, as shown in Figure 12-32. A list of mailboxes will be listed in a separate window. Select the destination mailbox from the list, and then click OK.

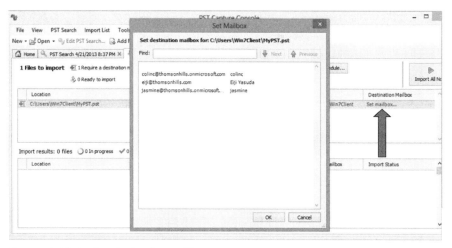

Figure 12-32 Setting destination mailbox.

> **Note**
>
> If you recently set the online connection settings (Step 8), the Set Mailbox window might be empty. This is because the PST Console has not retrieved a list of all the mailboxes on Exchange Online. Wait for a while, and then try again. Depending on the number of mailboxes in Office 365, it might take some time.

18. Click the Import All Now button to start importing .pst contents to the respective destination mailboxes.

Although we did not cover all the settings for the PST Capture Console, you can explore the different options available, such as setting the staging area, import tolerance, and whether to import non-mail items such as calendars. Click Tools from the PST Capture Console menu and select Settings. Next, review the available settings options and configure them to meet your organization's needs.

Third-party migration tools

If for some reason the existing tools and options provided by Microsoft do not meet your migration needs, there are always third-party tools you can turn to. Examples of third-party Exchange migration tools are Quest Software, Binary Tree, BitTitan, Cemaphore, and Metalogix. Exchange is a mature platform and has been around for some time. Therefore, third-party tools are readily available and are just as mature.

In most scenarios, you will want to route incoming email to Exchange Online. Therefore, before starting any of the migration tasks, regardless of whether it is a cutover, staged, or IMAP migration, change the Time To Live (TTL) of your MX records so as to improve the DNS convergence time when you do switch your MX records. The recommendation is that you change the TTL to 3,600 seconds, which is one hour.

Migration performance

There are many factors that affect migration performance, such as the size and number of items in the mailboxes, network bandwidth, network latency, and the on-premises mail servers. Migration performance can also be affected by the time of day and the number of users on the network. That is why you should carry out migrations after the work day is done or over weekends. As an example, after initial tests with a small staged migration batch, Microsoft Consulting Services generally aims to ramp up to a migration rate of 1,000 mailboxes a week, mostly conducted after business hours when network utilization is at the lowest level.

As we mentioned in Chapter 2, "Planning and preparing to deploy Office 365", bandwidth is not necessarily the only factor. Latency and sustained throughput are factors that are just as important when it comes to migration performance. For an idea on how much throughput is required for the different types of migration options we covered in this chapter, refer to the Migration Performance white paper referenced in the following Inside Out sidebar. In the Migration Performance white paper, an important metric to note is that past experience has shown that a 5 GB to 10 GB per hour rate of data migration can be reliably achieved, but depends on the Internet connection.

Chapter 12

INSIDE OUT "Migration Performance" white paper

Microsoft has provided an excellent TechNet article about migration performance based on experience and observations from actual customer migrations to Office 365. The "Migration Performance" white paper is located at *http://technet.microsoft.com/en-us/library/jj204570*.

If you are going to use Microsoft PST Capture, you can import the .pst files to your on-premises mailbox first and then do a migration, or you can import the .pst files directly to cloud mailboxes. PST imports are bandwidth-intensive operations, so you need to take that into consideration when scheduling and designing your PST import strategy.

Migration service throttling

In the migration exercises that you looked at earlier in this chapter, recall that you have the ability to specify the number of mailboxes that are migrated simultaneously, which by default is three. Specifying the number of mailboxes that should be simultaneously migrated is referred to as migration-service throttling.

Refer again to the "Migration Performance" white paper or test a single mailbox migration to determine the migration throughput. This will help you determine the optimum number of simultaneous migrations your network can support.

User throttling

User throttling mostly affects third-party migration tools. User throttling limits the number of mailboxes a user can access simultaneously and is designed to minimize risks and preserve resources. Therefore, if a migration tool uses a single service account with access to all mailboxes, Office 365 might throttle the service account if it starts to access too many mailboxes simultaneously during the migration process, thereby impacting migration performance. When you evaluate migration tools, make sure that performance will not be impacted by user throttling. Good migration tools generally use Exchange Web Services to impersonate user accounts so Exchange Online is not seeing a single user simultaneously accessing multiple mailboxes, but rather the users accessing their respective mailboxes. Thus, user throttling will not be triggered.

Moving mailboxes back to on-premises Exchange

Moving mailboxes back to on-premises can be facilitated only through an Exchange hybrid environment. Otherwise, you will need to rely on third-party tools. Unlike having the cutover and staged migration options from the EAC and ECP, when moving mailboxes to Office 365, there are no built-in options to carry out the reverse.

then migrated to the cloud, all you have to do is submit a new remote move request from the Exchange Online organization to the Exchange on-premises organization through the Exchange Management Console (EMC). Follow these steps to see how this is accomplished:

1. Start the EMC. Expand the Microsoft Exchange On-Premises node and navigate to the Recipient Configuration node. As shown in Figure 12-33, right-click the Recipient Configuration node, right-click a mailbox in the middle pane, and select New Remote Move Request from the drop-down menu.

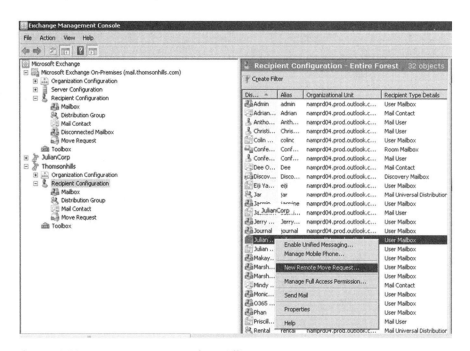

Figure 12-33 Remote Move Request from Office 365.

2. Follow the steps in the Remote Move Request Wizard, as in Chapter 11. When you get to the Move Settings page, select your on-premises domain in the Target Delivery Domain box. In the Remote Target Database box, if you are migrating to an Exchange 2010 server, use the format *<Server>\<Database Name>*, as shown in Figure 12-34. If you are migrating to an Exchange 2003 or 2007 server, use the format *<Server>\<Storage Group>\<Database Name>*; for example, MAIL\First Storage Group\Mailbox Database.

Figure 12-34 Move Settings page.

3. Complete the rest of steps in the New Remote Move Request Wizard, and then click New to initiate the move request.

Mailbox originally created in Exchange Online

If the Exchange Online mailbox you want to move back to on-premises Exchange was originally created in Office 365, you will need to first set the *ExchangeGUID* property on the associated on-premises mailbox. You need to do this because the *ExchangeGUID* property is not synchronized back to the associated on-premises mailbox if the mailbox was initially created in Office 365. For a remote move request to succeed, the value stored in the *ExchangeGUID* property must be the same for the mailbox in Office 365 and the associated on-premises remote mailbox.

Follow these steps to check and set the *ExchangeGUID* property for the on-premises remote mailbox:

1. Start the EMC on your on-premises Exchange hybrid server or management computer.

2. Check if the *ExchangeGUID* property on the on-premises remote mailbox is set by entering the following command. Figure 12-35 shows an example of the output as a result of issuing the command:

```
Get-RemoteMailbox <alias of cloud mailbox to migrate back on-premises> | For-
mat-List ExchangeGUID
```

Figure 12-35 Checking the value of *ExchangeGUID*.

3. If the return value for *ExchangeGUID* is **not** all zeros, as shown in Figure 12-35, then *ExchangeGUID* is set. You can immediately initiate a remote mailbox move back to on-premises Exchange by following the steps outlined in the "Mailbox originally created on-premises" section.

4. If the return value for *ExchangeGUID* is all zeros, then *ExchangeGUID* is not set. On a separate computer, start the Windows Azure Active Directory Module for Windows PowerShell and connect to Exchange Online. Do not use the Exchange Management Shell. As a reminder, you can use the following syntax to connect to Exchange Online through remote Windows PowerShell:

```
Import-Module MSonline

$cred = Get-Credential

Connect-MsolService -Credential $cred

$Session = New-PSSession -ConfigurationName Microsoft.Exchange-ConnectionUri
https://ps.outlook.com/powershell/ -Credential $cred -Authentication Basic
-AllowRedirection

Import-PSSession $Session -AllowClobber
```

5. Enter the following command to retrieve *ExchangeGUID* for the Exchange Online mailbox, and write down the returned value:

```
Get-Mailbox <alias of the cloud mailbox to migrate back to on-premises> \ For-
mat-List ExchangeGUID
```

6. Go back to the Exchange Management Shell window, and enter the following command to set the value of the *ExchangeGUID* property on the on-premises remote mailbox:

```
Set-RemoteMailbox <alias of cloud mailbox to move> -ExchangeGUID <GUID>
```

7. Start an unscheduled directory synchronization process using the *Start-OnlineCoexistenceSync* command. Refer to Chapter 4, "Directory synchronization", if you need a refresher on how to do this.

decommissioning all on-premises Exchange after all mailboxes and email workloads have been migrated. However, it is important to note that if your organization wants to manage Exchange Online with the EMC, a minimum of one Exchange on-premises CAS must still exist in the forest.

If directory synchronization is implemented, Active Directory is then the source of authority, and Microsoft recommends not removing the last Exchange 2010 on-premises server. By removing the last on-premises Exchange server, you will be unable to make changes to the mailbox objects in Exchange Online because the source of authority is defined as on-premises.

The bottom line is that you should keep one Exchange 2010 CAS on-premises, for now. A more detailed discussion about this topic is covered by the Microsoft Exchange team on their team blog referenced in the following Inside Out sidebar.

INSIDE OUT Microsoft recommendation on decommissioning Exchange on-premises

You can read about the Exchange team's recommendation to maintain on-premises Exchange 2010 CAS and the reasons on the Exchange Team Blog located at *http://blogs.technet.com/b/exchange/archive/2012/12/05/decommissioning-your-exchange-2010-servers-in-a-hybrid-deployment.aspx*.

Chapter 12

Administering Exchange Online

Because Exchange on-premises, Exchange Online, and the Exchange hybrid environment are based on a common set of technologies, the management tools and experience are similar across the different deployment models. The administration tools for Exchange are the following:

- 2010 SP3 Exchange Management Console (EMC)

- Windows PowerShell

- Office 365 admin center and the browser-based EAC, including managing Exchange Online Protection (EOP) in the latest release of Office 365 with Exchange Online 2013

- Forefront Online Protection for Exchange (FOPE) Administrator Console for Office 365 with Exchange Online 2010

This book does not cover all the intricacies of administering Exchange and messaging; there are dedicated Exchange books for that. What we will do is provide a summary of the different administration tools and focus on the specifics of administering Exchange Online and the Exchange hybrid environment and introduce you to the new capabilities in Exchange Online 2013.

Exchange Management Console

The EMC serves as a familiar interface for Exchange administrators. To manage Exchange Online through the EMC, you need to maintain an on-premises Exchange Client Access Server (CAS). To use EMC as the administration tool, simply add Exchange Online as a new organization into EMC, as shown in Chapter 11. However, note that there are differences between what you can administer in Exchange on-premises versus Exchange Online, and this is reflected in the EMC.

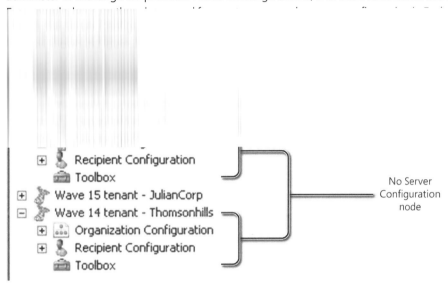

Figure 12-36 Difference between Exchange on-premises and Exchange Online in the EMC.

Implementation of an Exchange hybrid environment through Exchange 2010 SP3 CAS also provides the capabilities to create and manage the hybrid components as workloads, such as remote mailbox moves and managing the hybrid configuration, as shown in Figure 12-37 and through the tasks covered in Chapters 11 and 12, "Mailbox migration and administering Exchange Online".

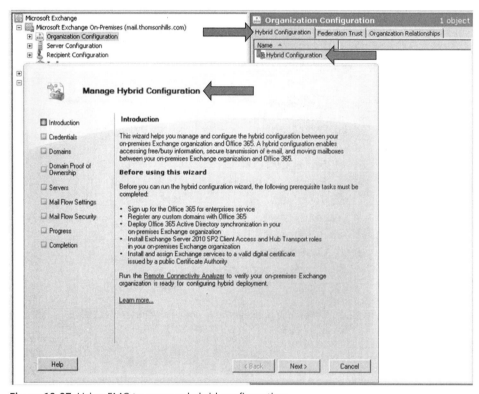

Figure 12-37 Using EMC to manage hybrid configuration.

Exchange Online remote Windows PowerShell

A majority of Office 365 Windows PowerShell cmdlets are for Exchange Online, and Windows PowerShell is the recommended approach to managing Exchange. To manage Exchange Online through remote Windows PowerShell, you first need to establish a new session. We use the following base script as a template in the Windows PowerShell ISE:

```
#Base script for managing Exchange Online




#

# <Exchange Online Management cmdlets> #

#

Remove-PSSession $Session
```

Between the *Import-PSSession* and *Remove-PSSession* commands, you can insert the vast array of remote Windows PowerShell cmdlets for Exchange Online.

> **Note**
>
> A reference to all the available Windows PowerShell cmdlets for Exchange Online is located at *http://help.outlook.com/en-us/exchangelabshelp/dd575549.aspx*.

INSIDE OUT   Clear your *PSSession*

It is important to always clear your session with the *Remove-PSSession* cmdlet because there is a maximum of three sessions per logon. Therefore, if you do not clear a session, you run the risk of running out of sessions and will need to wait for a session to timeout before you can open a new session.

Exchange Online administration user interface

Another management tool is a browser-based user interface (UI), which takes the form of the Exchange Control Panel (ECP) or the Exchange admin center (EAC), depending on which release of Office 365 your organization is using. One of the key new capabilities in Exchange is Role Based Access Control (RBAC). RBAC provides the ability to delegate administrative tasks, some of which may be handled by non-technical personnel. For example, the responsibility for conducting electronic discovery (eDiscovery) should belong to compliance or legal personnel. Therefore, there is a need for an easy interface to manage such functions without having to distribute special administrative software or grant excessive administrative privileges.

Exchange Control Panel

The ECP is hosted and accessed through the OWA. Accessing the ECP through OWA was covered earlier in this chapter. Figure 12-38 shows the ECP UI.

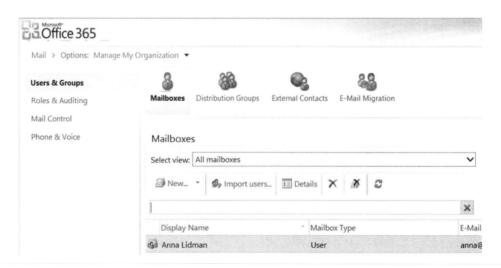

Figure 12-38 The ECP user interface.

Along the left side of the ECP is the navigation pane that groups the administrative functions. Figure 12-38 shows the administrative capability to manage mailboxes, distribution groups, and external contacts. Additionally, you can access the E-Mail Migration wizard on the Users & Groups page.

RBAC and compliance management capabilities are located on the Roles & Auditing page. A number of RBAC roles are available out of the box, as shown in Figure 12-39. However, you can modify the scope of each role's capabilities and create new RBAC roles.

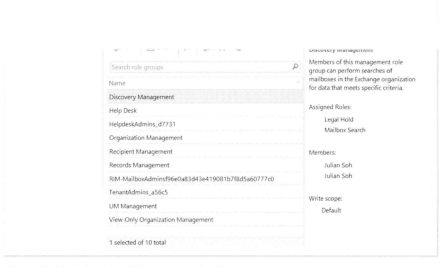

Figure 12-39 Roles & Auditing page in the EMC.

As mentioned earlier, we will leave the detailed administration of Exchange to other resources. However, before we leave this topic it is important to note that you can perform the majority of daily administrative functions through the ECP. As you explore the UI, notice that it is designed to be user friendly so that even non-technical administrators, such as the compliance and legal professionals we identified earlier, can perform administrative tasks.

At this point, we will leave the ECP and move on to discuss Forefront Online Protection for Exchange (FOPE).

Forefront Online Protection for Exchange administration

FOPE is responsible for email protection in Exchange Online 2010 and is a separate interface that is launched through the ECP. From the ECP, select Mail Control and click Configure IP safelisting, perimeter message tracking, and e-mail policies, as shown in Figure 12-40.

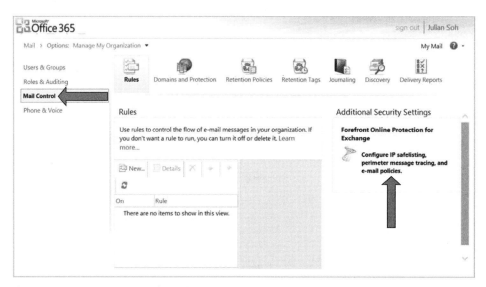

Figure 12-40 Accessing FOPE from the ECP.

This will start the FOPE administration interface, as shown in Figure 12-41. The FOPE administration interface provides statistics on mail hygiene and enables you to create reports, track messages, and create mail-handling policies.

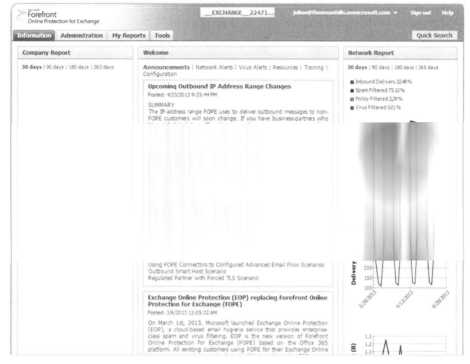

Figure 12-41 FOPE administration interface.

Your core activity in FOPE is the creation of mail policies. Follow these steps to see how mail policies are created and maintained in FOPE:

1. From the FOPE administration console, click the Administration tab, and then select Policy Rules.

2. Click New Policy Rule located under Tasks.

3. Set the domain scope, set the traffic scope, and select the policy's action, as shown in Figure 12-42.

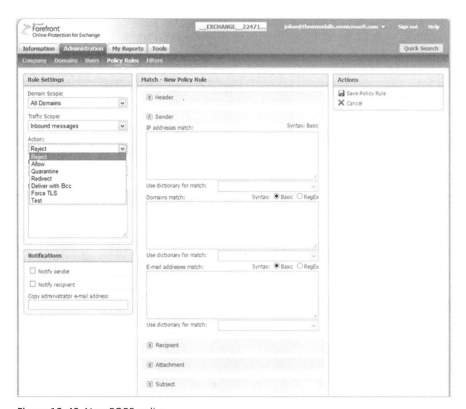

Figure 12-42 New FOPE policy.

4. Provide settings for the Expiration date field, if applicable, and determine if you want to send notifications whenever this rule is triggered.

5. In the Match pane, define the data patterns that would lead to the triggering of this policy. As you can see, you have the option to match by header, sender, and recipient IP addresses, domains, or e-mail address, attachment, subject, body, and message properties.

6. Click Save Policy Rule on the Actions pane to save this policy.

As with the ECP, there are other administrative functions for FOPE that we will let you explore on your own. This section serves only as an introduction to FOPE administration. We will now move on to look at the Exchange admin center (EAC).

Exchange admin center

The EAC is the successor to the ECP in the latest release of Office 365 and, like the ECP, it is a browser-based interface that organizes administrative functions into groups, as shown in Figure 12-43.

Figure 12-43 The EAC.

The main difference between the ECP and the EAC is the introduction of several new capabilities in Exchange Online 2013 and the respective administration functions that are exposed in the EAC. One of the new capabilities is Data Leakage Prevention (DLP) that is located on the Compliance Management page, as shown in Figure 12-44.

> **Note**
>
> DLP is a premium feature that requires an Exchange Online Plan 2 subscription. Exchange 2013 implemented on-premises requires an Exchange Enterprise client access license (CAL). In a hybrid Exchange implementation, Exchange Online Plan 2 users are covered for all premium features implemented on-premises, including DLP, and will not require a separate Exchange 2013 Enterprise CAL.

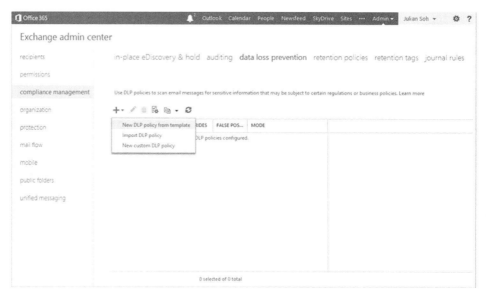

Figure 12-44 Data loss prevention in the EAC.

Prior to the latest release of Office 365, you had to rely on on-premises DLP solutions and have Exchange Online route all email through that solution. With the latest release of Office 365, Exchange Online 2013 provides DLP capability. You can create content triggers that rely on ISO-based templates to recognize data patterns. ISO stands for the International Organization for Standardization and is the internationally recognized entity that develops and publishes international standards. Following are a few examples of the included DLP templates:

- U.S. Health Information Portability Act (HIPAA)

- U.S. Personally Identifiable Information (PII)

- U.S. Social Security Act

- U.S. Financial Information

There are international DLP templates included as well. To see the full list of DLP templates, click the + icon, as shown in Figure 12-44, and then select New DLP policy from template from the drop-down menu. For example, if we create a DLP policy based on the HIPAA template and name the policy HIPAA Rules, this rule will show up in the DLP list of policies. At the same time, the corresponding rules that dictate how to handle emails that trigger this policy will be created in the mail flow section, as shown in Figure 12-45. Notice that you have the granular ability to define actions such as whether to allow overrides, different handling for internal versus external recipients, and how attachments should be handled.

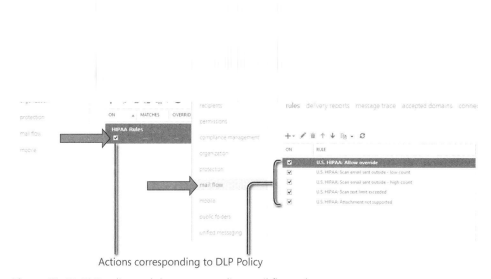

Actions corresponding to DLP Policy

Figure 12-45 DLP policy and the corresponding mail flow rules.

The new DLP feature is an important addition to Exchange Online because it further enhances the service by providing another built-in mechanism to prevent the accidental disclosure of sensitive information through email.

Exchange Online Protection

Exchange Online Protection (EOP), the successor to FOPE, does not have a separate user interface. EOP administration is now fully integrated into the EAC through the protection page, as shown in Figure 12-46.

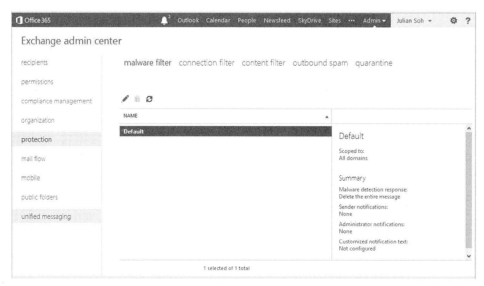

Figure 12-46 EOP management incorporated into the EAC.

As with the other administration tools, we will not go into the details of administration and instead will continue in the following sections to look at other new capabilities of Exchange Online.

Compliance, Legal Hold, and eDiscovery concepts

Compliance, eDiscovery, Legal Hold, and records management are very important topics for many organizations in the public and private sectors because of the legal and financial implications for not properly preserving or disposing of communication content in a timely fashion. Emails usually make up a significant, if not majority, of the content managed by an organization. Almost all legal cases allow or require the introduction of email content and

- Enforced retention

Preserving content

Preserving content is the capability to allow for the indefinite storage of content in a centralized location. A centralized storage location can serve as an authoritative data source that will ease management and eDiscovery efforts. Furthermore, if the centralized storage location is big enough, users will feel less compelled to delete content just to free up space, thereby reducing the risk of accidental deletions.

This capability is provided by the introduction of the personal archive, which we will discuss in detail shortly.

Automated deletions

To properly control the deletion of emails and to counter-balance the ability to indefinitely store them, Exchange introduces a concept called messaging records management (MRM). MRM consists of retention tags and policies, which help to automatically archive or delete email based on the age of the email timestamp. We will look at MRM in detail soon.

Enforced retention

Enforced retention is the capability to preserve email content to make it discoverable and yet permit the normal mailbox functions, including deletions and modifications. Enforced retention is accomplished by Exchange Online 2010 Legal Hold. In Exchange Online 2013, this is known as In-Place Hold. We will look at holds in detail shortly.

Putting it all together

As you can see, the three capabilities are designed to work together to form a comprehensive corporate compliance strategy. There is a centralized email storage location that makes search easier and an automated email archiving and deletion mechanism to help manage content without user intervention, thereby reducing human error or oversight. Finally, there is a mechanism to enforce preservation of content that overrides any other action to modify or destroy that content. Let us now look in detail at the actual technologies that provide these three capabilities.

Personal archive

We think of the personal archive as the foundational technology that supports compliance. The personal archive is sometimes referred to as the online archive or Exchange Online Archiving (EOA) if it is implemented as a stand-alone Exchange Online workload.

Before the introduction of the personal archive, users had limited mailbox sizes because of the need to manage the performance of Exchange. That is why Personal Storage Tables (PSTs) became popular. Users either delete emails to free up space in their mailbox or move them to .pst files. Both of these actions are major causes of concern when it comes to compliance.

Exchange Online Plan 1 provides a 25 GB storage that is shared between the primary mailbox and the archive mailbox. Exchange Online Plan 2 provides unlimited archive space that is separate from a 25 GB primary mailbox.

> **Note**
>
> Remember that Exchange Online Archiving provides each user with an unlimited amount of archive mailbox space that is initially provisioned as 100 GB, and it is accessible through Outlook and Outlook Web App.

Therefore, the first step to compliance remediation is to assign users a personal archive. You can choose to do this for every user or only for certain users. Provisioning a personal archive can be done through the EAC, ECP, EMC, or Windows PowerShell.

Messaging Records Management

After you have provided users with a generous personal archive, you might still need to implement MRM to automatically archive or dispose of email content. MRM is accomplished through retention tags and retention policies.

Retention tags

Retention tags are discrete actions that can be applied to email messages and folders. Retention tags are designed to be very granular. Here are a few examples of retention tags:

- Move items that are 180 days old from the Inbox to the Personal Archive.

- Permanently delete items in the Personal Archive that are older than 1,825 days (five

sequential actions on items, such as moving items from the primary mailbox to the archive mailbox if they are two years old, and then deleting them after five years. Using the three retention tag examples, you can combine all of them into a single organization retention policy and apply the retention policy to all mailboxes. If you do that, your organization's email compliance statement will look something like this:

Adatum Inc. Email Retention Policy

All emails that are 180 days old are automatically moved from your primary mailbox to your personal archive, where they will reside for 4.5 years, at which time they will be permanently deleted. Emails that are determined by the system to be junk mail are stored in the junk mail folder for 5 days, after which they will be deleted. However, if you believe that an email was accidentally identified as junk and you did not get to it within 5 days, you can recover it from your recycle bin within 14 days after it was automatically deleted.

Holds

Retention policies are sometimes misunderstood because of their name. It is easy to forget that retention tags and policies are responsible only for moving or deleting content to ensure the content does not exceed its retention schedule. Retention tags and policies do not actually preserve content. This means if a user decides to delete an email on the first day it arrives, the retention policy you just put in place does not prevent the user from doing so.

To enforce the preservation of email content, Exchange uses the concept of a Legal Hold (Exchange Online 2010) or an In-Place Hold (Exchange Online 2013). Another interesting concept about enforced preservation is that the user is not prevented from carrying out actions that modify or delete email content. This is by design because mailbox operations should continue to function normally. This is a very significant Microsoft strategy because it balances your organization's compliance requirements and at the same time does not affect the productivity of your users. When email content is on hold, it is discoverable.

A Legal Hold in Exchange Online 2010 is applied at the mailbox level and implemented through the EMC, ECP, or Windows PowerShell. While the concept of immutability can be accomplished through Legal Hold, the ability to apply it only at the mailbox level might not be granular enough because too much content might be placed on hold. Nonetheless, what is important is that content is immutably preserved and, with a large personal archive, the space consumption as a result of content preservation under Legal Hold is not an issue.

In Exchange Online 2013, Legal Hold is renamed In-Place Hold, and it now addresses the ability for you to be more granular in selecting the content to preserve by introducing two types of In-Place Holds:

- Time-based hold, including indefinite hold

- Criteria-based hold

Time-based hold

Time-based holds, sometimes referred to as rolling holds, work like an MRM retention tag in that the hold is applied based on the timestamp of an email. As long as the timestamp of the email falls within the limits of the time-based hold, the email content will be preserved and is discoverable through a multi-mailbox eDiscovery search. After the timestamp of the email falls outside the time-based holds, the content of the email will no longer be preserved and will be subject to the modification or deletion actions of the user or MRM.

Criteria-based hold

Criteria-based hold relies on keywords and Boolean logic to preserve content. Aside from a keyword criteria match, you can also specify source and recipients, date ranges, and message types (email, calendar items, and so on).

INSIDE OUT   Keyword Query Language

A new capability that is not very well advertised is the Keyword Query Language (KQL). KQL is a syntax that allows you to conduct proximity searches. The following is an example of KQL syntax:

```
"acquisition" NEAR(n=3) "debt"
```

cific individuals, or to distribution groups. If an email is subject to multiple holds, as long as any of the hold remains applicable to the email, then its contents will be preserved and is discoverable.

You can create time-based holds and criteria-based holds on the compliance management page of the EAC, as shown in Figure 12-47.

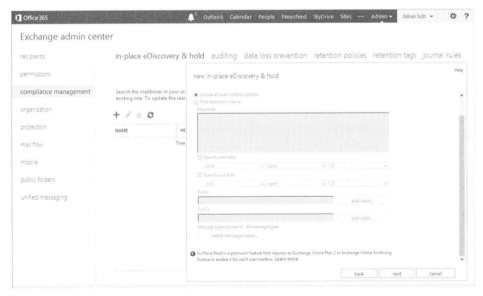

Figure 12-47 Creating In-Place Holds through the EAC.

When prompted for the holding period, you can choose to hold indefinitely or to hold for a certain number of days, as shown in Figure 12-48.

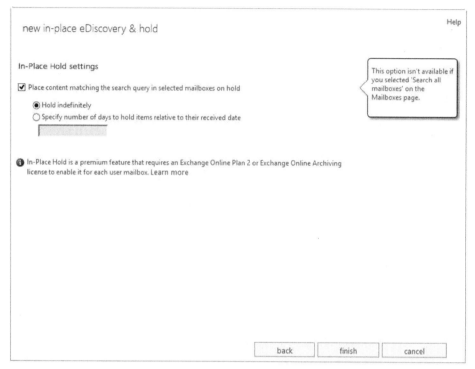

Figure 12-48 Define hold settings.

As an example of a corporate-enforced, In-Place Hold policy, an organization could choose to create an organization-wide, time-based hold by following these steps:

1. In the EAC, select compliance management, and then select in-place eDiscovery & hold.

2. Click the + icon to create a new in-place hold.

3. Provide a name for the hold, and then click next.

4. Select Specify mailboxes to search, and then click the + icon.

5. In the Global Address List (GAL) dialog box, select a distribution group, such as Everyone. Click add, and then click ok to close the GAL. Alternatively, you can simply select the Search all mailboxes option in Step 4. Click next.

6. On the Search query page, select Include all user mailbox content. This enforces the preservation of all email, regardless of content. Click next.

7. On the In-Place Hold settings page, select Place content matching the search query in selected mailboxes on hold. Select the Specify number of days to hold items relative to their received date option. Type 180 in the text box, and then click finish.

You have now implemented an organization-wide, time-based hold. In the event that you

mailbox. Each tenant is provisioned with a single Discovery mailbox, but you can create additional Discovery mailboxes. Furthermore, each Discovery mailbox is limited to 50 GB.

INSIDE OUT   Concurrent searches

It is not stated explicitly in the Service Description, but you are limited to two concurrent multi-mailbox searches. If you have the need for multiple concurrent searches, you can submit a request to Microsoft Online Support with a business case for the need to temporarily increase this limit.

An alternate option is to create all the required eDiscovery searches, and then write a Windows PowerShell script that checks the status of each search request and attempts to start it if the status of the search is Failed because two other searches are already running. We created a script and had it run every few minutes. The Windows PowerShell script to check the status of the search and attempt to start it is the following:

```
if((Get-MailboxSearch "<search job name>") status -eq "Failed"
   Start-MailboxSearch -identity "<search job name>" -Force }
```

Results of multi-mailbox searches are located on the same page as In-Place Holds. As you can see in Figure 12-49, by clicking on an existing time-based or criteria-based hold, the information including estimates of the search results are shown in the informational pane to the right.

Figure 12-49 Estimate of search results.

By clicking the magnifying glass icon, as shown in Figure 12-50, you can re-run the estimate for search results, preview the search results, or copy the search results.

Figure 12-50 Search results options.

Summary

We covered a lot of information in this chapter. We started by looking at the different mailbox migration options, including a strategy to migrate .pst content with PST Capture. We also covered the administration of Exchange and its different workloads, such as Forefront Online Protection for Exchange (FOPE), Exchange Online Protection (EOP), and Data Loss Prevention (DLP). Finally, we covered the compliance capabilities of Exchange Online in the form of In-Place Holds, multi-mailbox search, and Messaging Records Management (MRM).

What we covered in the last three chapters is very specific to Exchange in the cloud. We focused on Exchange hybrid models and mailbox migrations. We hope these chapters have provided you with a strong foundation to understand Exchange Online and how it integrates with your on-premises messaging solution.

Chapter 12

Because it is not possible for this book to be exhaustive on all aspects of Exchange administration, bear in mind that Exchange Online 2010 is equivalent to Exchange on-premises 2010, and Exchange Online 2013 is equivalent to Exchange on-premises 2013. Therefore, if you need to dive deeper into the topic of administering Exchange, there are many good books already in the market that focus solely on Exchange administration and all its workloads, and these should meet your needs.

In the next chapter, we will look at SharePoint Online, which is another service provided under Office 365.

Understanding SharePoint capabilities 631   Office Web Apps 670

2007 on-premises versus WSS 3.0 online, primarily because WSS was never designed for large, multi-tenant hosted environments. Since then, Microsoft introduced a "Cloud First" initiative and made it the company's top priority.

Microsoft SharePoint 2010 server technologies were retrofitted to better scale and support large, multi-tenant scenarios. Thus, with the introduction of Office 365, SharePoint 2010 server technologies were implemented in Office 365, not SharePoint Foundation. This resulted in a huge improvement of hosted SharePoint capabilities. Key capabilities previously missing in BPOS, such as InfoPath electronic forms, Business Connectivity Services (BCS), and FAST Search technology, are now available in SharePoint Online.

With the February 27, 2013 release of Office 365, SharePoint 2013 is the featured collaboration platform in the cloud. This is a significant milestone because the 2013 release of Microsoft's productivity tools was designed completely based on the Cloud First initiative and natively supports public and private multi-tenant cloud deployments. As you will see in this chapter, more features are now available in SharePoint Online 2013, and the gap between on-premises SharePoint and SharePoint Online continues to close. Even though we will include SharePoint Online 2010 in our discussion, we primarily will be focused on SharePoint Online 2013 and the new capabilities.

Understanding SharePoint capabilities

SharePoint Online is less complex to implement than Exchange Online. However, as a platform it pulls together a wide array of technologies designed to help people collaborate better. In fact, SharePoint can be thought of as a collection of capabilities, including the following:

- Intranet, extranet, and Internet portals

- A content management system (CMS) to better manage files, including the ability to facilitate synchronization and access of files across multiple devices

- A social platform consisting of blogs, wikis, newsfeeds, hash tags, and statuses

- An enterprise search tool

- A web-based document viewing, authoring, and co-authoring solution

- A business intelligence (BI) solution with capabilities to display dashboards and key performance indicators (KPIs) or to interact with pivot tables and charts using only a web browser

- An electronic forms and workflow solution that also allows for the incorporation of data from disparate data sources

There are many custom line-of-business (LOB) solutions based on SharePoint, such as Records Management, Case Management, Media Management Systems, and Personnel Management Systems. The list and possibilities for SharePoint are vast, which is why Share-Point has been, and remains, one of Microsoft's fastest growing products.

Introducing SharePoint Online

Like Exchange Server technologies, SharePoint on-premises is available in two flavors: Standard and Enterprise. SharePoint Online, like Exchange Online, also has two offerings: Plan 1 and Plan 2. SharePoint Online Plan 1 is akin to SharePoint Standard on-premises, and SharePoint Online Plan 2 is akin to SharePoint Enterprise on-premises.

> **Note**
> For a concise breakdown of SharePoint Online capabilities as well as the Standard versus Enterprise features, see *http://technet.microsoft.com/en-us/library/jj819267.aspx*.

Another important point to know about SharePoint Online and the tenant's domain name is how the latter is used in the SharePoint URL. For example, if you select Adatum as the domain name, your Office 365 domain will be Adatum.onmicrosoft.com. You can add ada-tum.com to your tenant, but SharePoint Online URLs for intranet or extranet use will still be *https://Adatum.sharepoint.com/sites/<site collection or site name>*. SharePoint Online does support a limited, public, anonymous site that can be used for an Internet presence. In this case, a vanity URL such as *www.Adatum.com* could be used for this site collection only.

SharePoint Online concepts

SharePoint administrators will be familiar with the SharePoint architecture, which comprises web applications in Internet Information Server (IIS) upon which site collections are created. Within site collections, there are sites followed by libraries, folders, and then the content at the cellular level of this information architecture. Figure 13-1 depicts this hierarchical structure.

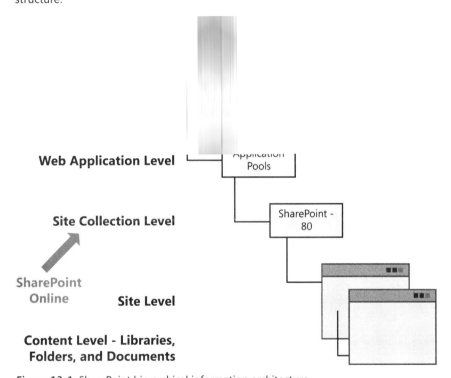

Figure 13-1 SharePoint hierarchical information architecture.

For SharePoint Online, the highest level of access in the SharePoint information architecture is the site collection level.

SharePoint Online capabilities

Like other services in Office 365, SharePoint Online is governed by an authoritative Service Description.

> **Note**
>
> You can download the Service Description for SharePoint Online 2010 by selecting Share-Point Online at *http://www.microsoft.com/en-us/download/details.aspx?id=13602*. You can view the Service Description for SharePoint Online 2013 at *http://technet.microsoft.com/en-us/library/jj819267.aspx*.

The SharePoint Online Service Description does a great job at listing all SharePoint features, grouped by functional categories, and specifying their availability. A snapshot of this information from the SharePoint Online Service Description is shown in Figure 13-2. For example, all the developer features are grouped together. The App Catalog feature is available in Office 365 Enterprise E3, Education A3, and Government G3 suites, but not available in Office 365 Small Business. The Business Connectivity Services (BCS) Profile Pages feature is not available across the board, which means that this feature is not available in SharePoint Online.

Developer features	Office 365 Small Business	Office 365 Small Business Premium	Office 365 Midsize Business	Office 365 Enterprise E1 Office 365 Education A2 Office 365 Government G1	Office 365 Enterprise E3 Office 365 Education A3 Office 365 Government G3	Office 365 Enterprise E4 Office 365 Education A4 Office 365 Government G4	Office 365 Enterprise K1 Office 365 Government K1	SharePoint Online Enterprise External Users
Access Services	Yes	Yes	Yes	Yes	Yes	Yes	Yes	Yes
App Catalog (SharePoint)	No	No	Yes	Yes	Yes	Yes	Yes	Yes
App Deployment: Autohosted Apps	Yes	Yes	Yes	Yes	Yes	Yes	Yes	Yes
App Deployment: Cloud-Hosted Apps	Yes	Yes	Yes	Yes	Yes	Yes	Yes	Yes
App Deployment: SharePoint-Hosted Apps	Yes	Yes	Yes	Yes	Yes	Yes	Yes	Yes
BCS: Business Data Webparts	No	No	No	No	Yes	Yes	No	Yes
BCS: External List	No	No	No	No	Yes	Yes	No	Yes
BCS: OData connector	No	No	No	No	Yes	Yes	No	Yes
BCS: Profile Pages	No	No	No	No	No	No	No	No

Figure 13-2 Excerpt of the features matrix from the SharePoint Online Service Description.

Many organizations continue to maintain SharePoint on-premises as well as adopting SharePoint Online, which is a viable strategy because this makes SharePoint a more scalable solution. This is often times referred to as hybrid SharePoint. However, on-premises

SharePoint and SharePoint Online are technically separate, even though there is limited hybrid functionality when implementing SharePoint Server 2013 on-premises with SharePoint Online 2013. Hybrid scenarios for SharePoint on-premises and SharePoint Online are discussed in the "SharePoint search in a hybrid environment" section later in this chapter.

INSIDE OUT   Application servers and point solutions

SharePoint Online capacity limits

In response to market and customer demands, Microsoft continuously reviews the capacity limits of all Office 365 workloads, including SharePoint Online. Therefore, it is important to refer to the SharePoint Online Service Description for updates on a quarterly basis.

Storage limits

Another important topic in the SharePoint Online Service Description is the amount of shared storage space available to your organization. Office 365 uses the following formula to determine the base SharePoint storage space, also known as pooled storage space, for each tenant:

(10 GB + 500 MB/user + purchased storage) $\leq$ 25 TB per tenant

Based on this formula, if your organization has 1,000 users and you purchase Office 365 E3, your SharePoint Online storage space will be the following:

10 GB + (500 MB x 1,000) = 10 GB + 500 GB = 510 GB

In addition to pooled storage, each of the 1,000 users gets 25 GB of space in SkyDrive Pro that is separate from the calculated pooled space. If you determine that the 560 MB of pooled SharePoint Online storage is insufficient, you can purchase additional space to add to the pooled storage, up to 25 TB for the tenant.

SharePoint Online 2013 introduces the ability to host an external website with content management capabilities. The default storage limit for the external website is 5 GB, but you can allocate up to 100 GB of storage space. The storage allocation for the external website draws from the pooled storage allocated for the tenant.

Site collection limits

Depending on the Office 365 plan, you will have one or more site collections. Refer again to Figure 13-1, and remember that the site collection is the highest level in the SharePoint information architecture. With the Office 365 Small Business plan, you get one site collection, and with the E3/A3/G3 Enterprise plans, you get 3,000 site collections. These limits are an example of the continuous change to SharePoint Online limits because in SharePoint Online 2010 the number of site collections was 300, so there is a tenfold increase to this limit between SharePoint Online 2010 and SharePoint Online 2013. Each site collection has a limit of 100 GB or 2,000 sites, whichever comes first.

INSIDE OUT   Managing sites and site collections

Even with the best planning and robust governance, there will be times when you might need to move a site from one site collection to another because of organizational changes or when you are approaching the 2,000 site limit or 100 GB limit. Moving sites between site collections potentially can be a challenging task, but thanks to a mature SharePoint ecosystem, there are now many affordable solutions in the marketplace that can make this an easy task. One such example is ShareGate at *http://www.share-gate. com*. You can use this tool to move sites and site collections between SharePoint Online tenants and between SharePoint on-premises and SharePoint Online. Reorganizing information is just one of the many capabilities of such tools. It is recommended that you have these tools in your toolkit for your organization's SharePoint administrators. When shopping for these tools, make sure they are capable of supporting SharePoint on-premises and SharePoint Online.

Number of users

SharePoint Online is designed to support large user communities. The default limit is 500,000 users, but if your organization has more than 500,000 users, contact your Microsoft representative or Office 365 Support to make arrangements to increase the user count limit. Another new concept introduced in SharePoint Online 2013 is the recognition of external users. External users are not part of your organization and include business partners, customers, or other external entities. The recognition of external users enables your organization to collaborate with external entities, which is facilitated through Partner Access Licenses (PALs). This is not the same as anonymous access. PALs allow you to identify and track access to SharePoint content. All SharePoint Online plans include 10,000

PALs. You have the ability to purchase more if required, with the exception of the E3/A3/ G3 Enterprise Plans, for which you can request additional PALs beyond 10,000 at no extra charge.

File upload size limit

The maximum size for files you can upload to SharePoint Online is 2 GB and is not configurable.

SharePoint hybrid model

Unlike Exchange Online, SharePoint Online has a limited set of hybrid configurations. If your organization currently has on-premises SharePoint farms, they are and will remain separate from SharePoint Online. The new hybrid model allows certain SharePoint capabilities to span across both the on-premises SharePoint farm and SharePoint Online. The capabilities that can span across both environments are the following:

- Search

- Business Connectivity Services

- Duet Enterprise Online for Microsoft SharePoint and SAP

Like all the other Office 365 hybrid services, the prerequisites for setting up a SharePoint hybrid environment include directory synchronization and Active Directory Federation Services (AD FS), which were covered in Chapter 2, "Planning and preparing to deploy Office 365," Chapter 3, "Active Directory Federation Services," and Chapter 4, "Directory synchronization."

> **Note**
>
> For more information about SharePoint hybrid environments, see *http://technet.micro-soft.com/en-us/library/jj838715.aspx.*

Of the three SharePoint capabilities that are supported in a hybrid configuration, search is the most common implementation. We will take a closer look at hybrid search in the "SharePoint search in a hybrid environment" section later in this chapter.

Managing SharePoint Online

As mentioned earlier, the highest level to which you have administrative access is the site collection level. You do not have access to SharePoint central administration as you do with SharePoint on-premises. Instead, you manage SharePoint Online through the Office 365 admin center at *https://portal.microsoftonline.com* or through the SharePoint Online Management Shell.

SharePoint Online 2013

Follow these steps to familiarize yourself with the SharePoint Online 2013 admin center in Office 365 by creating a new site collection:

1. Access the SharePoint admin center through the Office 365 admin center by clicking the Admin menu item at the upper right and selecting SharePoint from the drop-down menu, as shown in Figure 13-3.

Figure 13-3 Accessing the Office 365 admin center.

2. After you have selected SharePoint from the Admin drop-down menu, you will see
the SharePoint admin center, as shown in Figure 13-4.

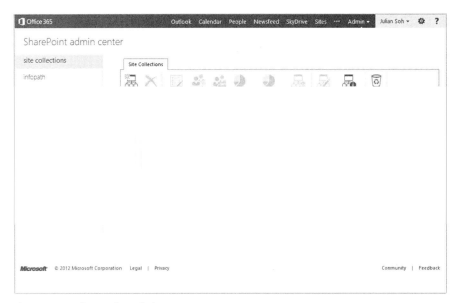

Figure 13-4 SharePoint admin center.

If you are familiar with SharePoint Online 2010, you will notice that there are new capabilities available in SharePoint Online 2013, such as Records Management, the SharePoint
Store (apps), and External Sharing located on the Additional Settings page. To extensively
cover all the features of SharePoint Online 2013 is beyond the scope of this book, but we
will take a close look at some of them in the "SharePoint Store," "SkyDrive Pro," and "Achieving compliance with SharePoint eDiscovery Center" sections later in this chapter.

To create a new site collection, select site collections from the left navigation pane. Click New and select Private Site Collection, as shown in Figure 13-5. If you choose to create a public website, remember you can create only one, after which the option will be unavailable.

INSIDE OUT Public websites in SharePoint Online

You have only ONE public website per tenant. After you have created a public website, this option will be unavailable whenever you click New. In SharePoint Online 2010, the public website is not as full featured as the public website in SharePoint Online 2013.

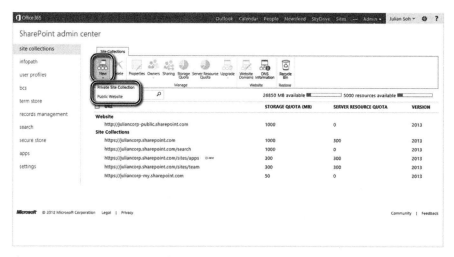

Figure 13-5 Create a new site collection in the SharePoint Online 2013 admin center.

3. You will see a dialog box prompting you for details regarding the new site collection you want to create, as shown in Figure 13-6. If you have experience with previous versions of SharePoint, this dialog box should be familiar. Provide the necessary information for the site collection, and then click OK to create it.

Figure 13-6 Creating a new site collection.

After you click OK, SharePoint Online will begin provisioning the site collection. You will see it appear in the Site Collections page with a spinning icon next to the site collection indicating that it is being provisioned. After provisioning is complete, an icon labeled new will appear next to it.

SharePoint Online 2010

Follow these steps to familiarize yourself with the SharePoint Online 2010 administration center:

1. For Office 365 with SharePoint Online 2010, you can access the SharePoint Online administration center by clicking Manage under the SharePoint section, as shown in Figure 13-7.

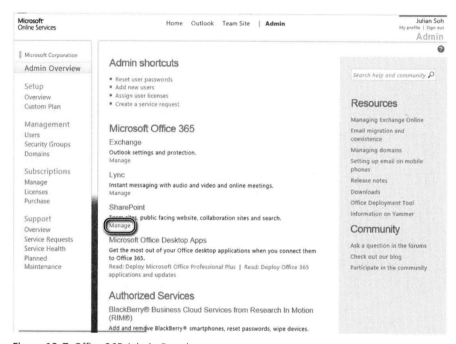

Figure 13-7 Office 365 Admin Portal.

2. As you can see, the SharePoint Online 2010 Admin Portal clearly exposes the capabilities available to you. Figure 13-8 shows the administration center with SharePoint Online 2010 capabilities clearly listed.

Figure 13-8 SharePoint Online 2010 administration center.

There are six capabilities you can manage from the administration center in lieu of Central Administration:

- Manage site collections

- Configure InfoPath Forms Services

- Manage User Profiles

- Manage Business Connectivity Services

- Manage Term Store

- Manage Secure Store Service Application

Going into the details of each of the preceding SharePoint capabilities is beyond the scope of this book, so we leave that to other resources that are dedicated to SharePoint.

The most common task in SharePoint Online is the creation of site collections. The relative simplicity of creating site collections and sites showcases the benefit of SharePoint Online. Follow these steps to create a new site collection:

1. Select Site Collections, click New, and then select Private Site Collection, as shown in Figure 13-9.

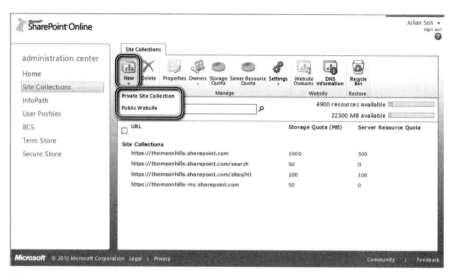

Figure 13-9 Creating a new site collection.

2. After you choose to create a new site collection, the New Site Collection dialog box appears, as shown in Figure 13-10. This dialog box is similar to one you will see if you create a site collection through SharePoint on-premises Central Admin. Give your site collection a title, name the URL, and provide the type of site collection and resources to allocate to the site collection. After you have provided all the necessary settings for this new site collection, click OK to create it.

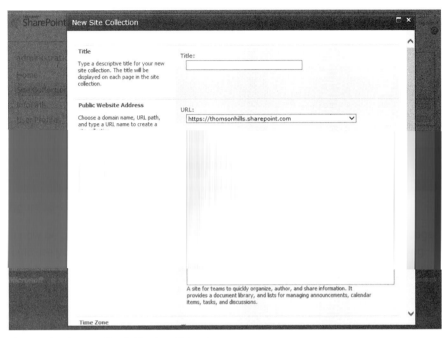

Figure 13-10 New Site Collection dialog box.

You will now be placed back at the SharePoint administration center's Site Collection page. You should see your site on the list, but there will be a spinning icon next to it indicating that it is in the process of being created. After it's created, you will see an icon labeled new next to the site collection. You can also manage existing site collections by selecting them from the site collections list.

SharePoint Store

The SharePoint Store is a new and exciting model that enables SharePoint Online to be extended through the use of apps, but it is available only in the latest release of Office 365 with SharePoint Online 2013. An app for SharePoint is a small, specialized, stand-alone application that is responsible for specific tasks that help you meet business needs. The SharePoint Store model allows you to accomplish several tasks:

- Purchase specialized apps to extend SharePoint Online

- Purchase specialized apps to extend Office

- Manage the licenses of purchased apps

- Manage app requests

- Appoint app managers

You can access the SharePoint Store on the apps page in the SharePoint Online admin center, as shown in Figure 13-11.

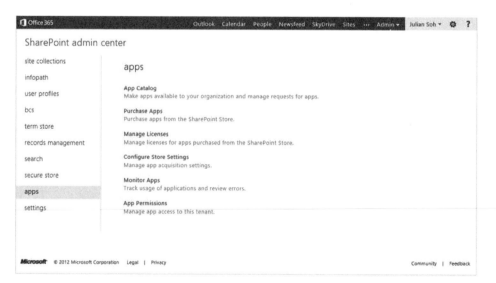

Figure 13-11 SharePoint Store.

Before acquiring apps for your organization, you need to first create an app catalog site, to which you will publish purchased apps for your organization's consumption. Follow these steps to make apps available to your SharePoint Online users:

1. On the SharePoint Online 2013 admin center, select apps, as shown in Figure 13-11.

2. Click App Catalog to create an app catalog site.

Figure 13-12 Creating a new app catalog site.

4. Provide a title for your app catalog site and URL. Designate an administrator and specify the quota for the site, as shown in Figure 13-13. Click OK. For this exercise, we have provided the following title for our app catalog site: Company Owned and Approved Apps.

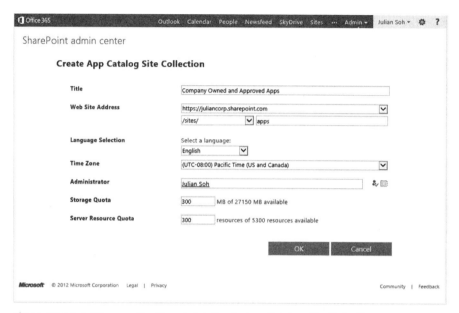

Figure 13-13 Settings on the SharePoint Create App Catalog Site Collection page.

5. After the app catalog site has been created, you can start it by means of its URL. As shown in Figure 13-14, the out-of-the-box master page for the app catalog site shows you three tasks you can undertake: Distribute apps for SharePoint, Distribute apps for Office, and Manage requests for apps.

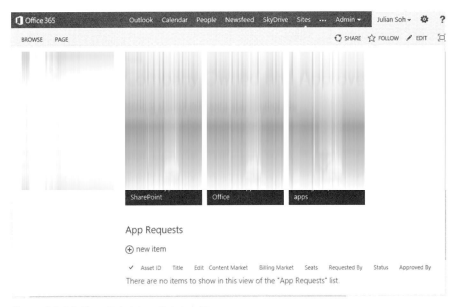

Figure 13-14 SharePoint App Catalog Site.

6. Next, we will show you how to purchase an app and make it available through our SharePoint app catalog. Click the Admin menu and select SharePoint to get to the SharePoint admin center.

7. On the SharePoint admin center, click apps to get to the SharePoint Store.

8. Select Purchase Apps.

9. The SharePoint Store will show you the featured apps and also will allow you to navigate by category, as shown in Figure 13-15. Select an app that interests you and click its tile.

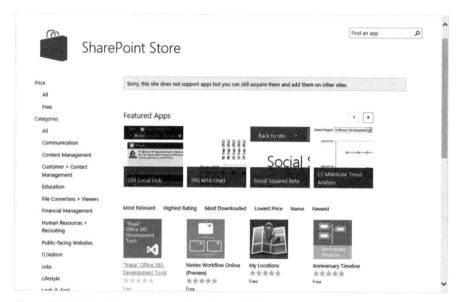

Figure 13-15 SharePoint Store showing the available apps.

10. For this exercise, we will choose a free app called Locations Mapper. Click the Locations Mapper tile to see information about the app, including details and reviews, as shown in Figure 13-16. Click the ADD IT button to add the app to your collection.

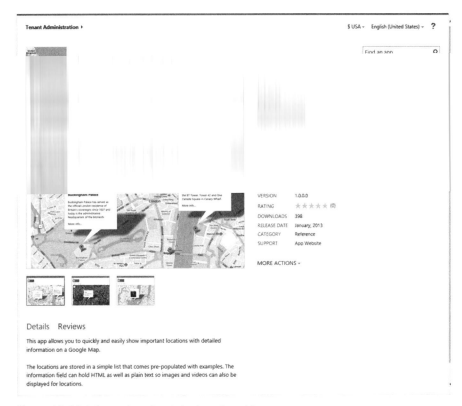

Figure 13-16 Information about the Locations Mapper app.

11. Confirm that you want to add the app by clicking the green Continue button.

12. After you acquire the app, click the Return to site link. This will take you back to the SharePoint admin center.

13. Click apps, and then select App Catalog.

14. Select Site Contents from the left navigation pane, and then click add an app, as shown in Figure 13-17.

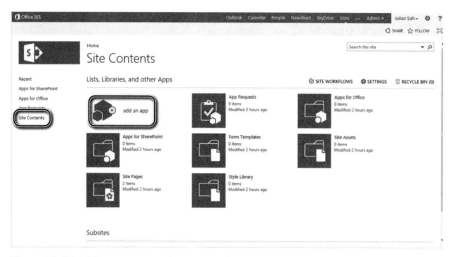

Figure 13-17 Adding an app to the App Catalog.

15. The app you purchased earlier should appear in the list of apps. In our exercise, we selected the Locations Mapper app, and as shown in Figure 13-18, that app appears on the list of apps that we can add to the App Catalog. Click the Locations Mapper app to add it to the App Catalog site.

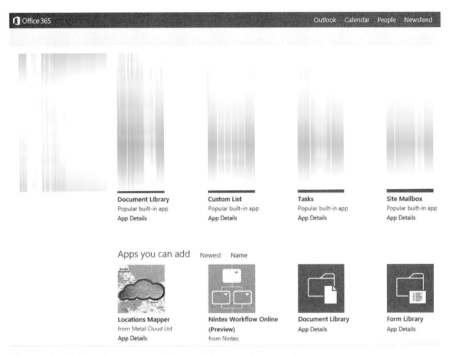

Figure 13-18 List of apps available to add to the App Catalog site.

16. You might be prompted to allow the app to access certain information. The terms, conditions, and privacy statements from the manufacturer of the app are disclosed to you, as shown in Figure 13-19. If you are satisfied with the terms, conditions, and privacy statement of the manufacturer of this app, click the Trust it button.

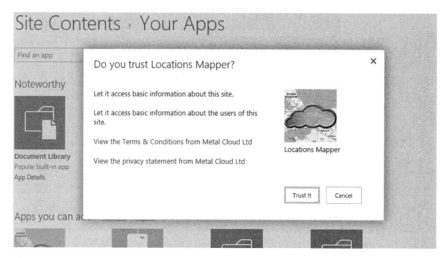

Figure 13-19 Trusting an app.

17. The app might take some time to install. You can see the progress by looking at the app's details, as shown in Figure 13-20. After it is done, a green icon labeled new! will be affixed next to the app's tiles.

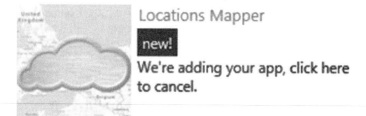

Figure 13-20 Status of an app.

Now that you have seen how to acquire an app from the SharePoint store, let us take a look at how site administrators can access the app.

Permissions and adding apps to sites

To add an app to a site requires the user to be part of the Site Owners group. Now that you have acquired the Locations Mapper app, follow these steps to see how site owners can use the app:

1. Create a site collection if you do not already have one. To assign access rights to a user, log on as the site collection administrator and click the icon of the gear at the

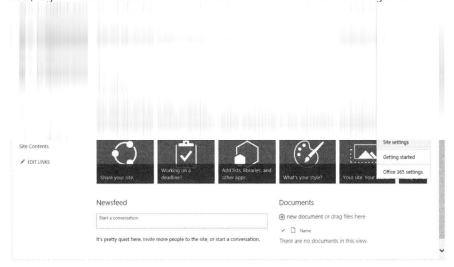

Figure 13-21 SharePoint Online Site settings.

2. Select Site permissions under Users and Permissions, and then click the Team Owners group.

3. Click New and select Add users to this group, as shown in Figure 13-22. Enter the name of a user you want to add to the Team Owners group so the user can use the Locations Mapper web part you acquired for your organization.

Figure 13-22 Adding users to groups.

4. Have the site administrator, who is now part of the Site Owners group, log on to the site. If it is a new site, there will be an Add lists, libraries, and other apps tile on the site. The site administrator can click this tile or, alternatively, click the gear icon and select Add an app.

5. The Locations Mapper app should be available to the site administrator, as shown in Figure 13-23.

Figure 13-23 Adding an app to a site.

Managing app licenses

The SharePoint Store allows your organization to manage app licenses. Follow these steps to see the app license management capabilities of the SharePoint Store:

1. Log on as an administrator and access the SharePoint Store.

2. Select Site Contents from the left navigation pane.

3. Click the ellipsis of an app and select Licenses, as shown in Figure 13-24. In this exercise, we will use the Locations Mapper app.

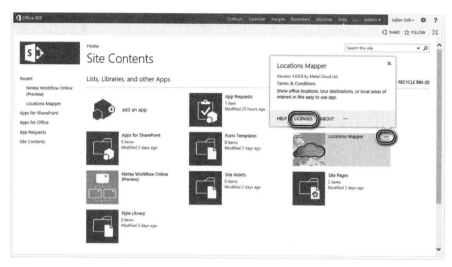

Figure 13-24 Accessing the license information of an app.

4. The license details for the app will be displayed, as shown in Figure 13-25. This includes people who have been assigned the license as well as people who can manage the licenses for this app. Click the ACTIONS link and select View in the SharePoint Store.

Figure 13-25 App License Management page.

5. Click MORE ACTIONS, as shown in Figure 13-26, to see all the options: Recover
    License, Manage License, Request License, and Report a Violation. With the exception
    of the Report a Violation option, go ahead and explore each of the other options on
    your own.

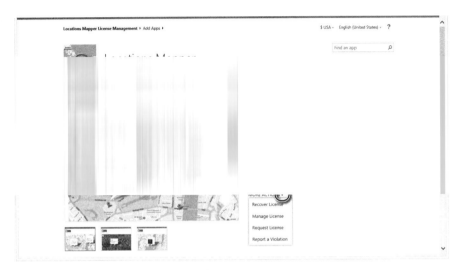

Figure 13-26 License management options.

As you can see, there are many new apps already in the SharePoint Store, and this is a great
model to extend SharePoint Online. Prior to SharePoint Online 2013, it was not possible to
extend SharePoint Online with third-party apps. Therefore, this is a significant new feature
of SharePoint Online.

SkyDrive Pro

The foremost designed use for SharePoint Online is to serve as a portal to improve the
collaboration and thus the productivity of employees. In fact, the main highlight of Share-
Point 2013 is the social aspect, which is designed with a focus on how people work and
communicate. In business terms, SharePoint Online is the perfect solution for intranets and
the replacement of file servers as document repositories, and this is all facilitated through
SkyDrive Pro.

SkyDrive Pro is an unfortunate naming convention that causes confusion with the consumer version of SkyDrive. It is important to state from the beginning that SkyDrive Pro is
not the same as SkyDrive.com. SkyDrive Pro is in fact the new and improved successor of
SharePoint MySites. Its core functionality is to provide an enterprise-class personal storage
location for users, thereby replacing the need for network home drives. This functionality

is similar to the consumer version of SkyDrive except that SkyDrive Pro provides corporate controls such as audit capabilities for content stored in SkyDrive Pro.

Storage

As a storage medium, SkyDrive Pro is SQL-based SharePoint storage that also provides all the organization controls that current SharePoint users are familiar with, such as version control, check-in, check-out, Legal Hold, and eDiscovery. These controls are not available in SkyDrive.com, and that is a key difference. SkyDrive Pro is offered as part of SharePoint Online and thus also inherits the security concepts highlighted in the Microsoft Office 365 Trust Center. As mentioned earlier, each user in SharePoint Online gets 25 GB of personal storage space through SkyDrive Pro, which is separate from the pooled SharePoint Online storage.

> **Note**
>
> At the time of this writing, SkyDrive Pro was updated and as a result, the storage limit was increased to 25 GB. Previously, the storage limit was 7 GB.

External collaboration

After files are stored in SkyDrive Pro, a number of new capabilities become available to your organization. One of the new capabilities is the ability to collaborate with external entities through the use of Partner Access Licenses (PALs) that are included in SharePoint Online. PALs are a unique concept because they balance the need to easily share files with external entities, provide a security mechanism, and yet free IT from having to manage access rights for external entities.

Follow these steps to explore the external collaboration capabilities of SharePoint Online:

1. Enable external sharing for your organization's Office 365 tenant by going to the SharePoint admin center and selecting settings. Select the type of external sharing to allow, as shown in Figure 13-27.

Figure 13-27 Turning on external sharing at the tenant level.

2. Log on to your Office 365 portal, and then click SkyDrive from the menu, as shown in Figure 13-28.

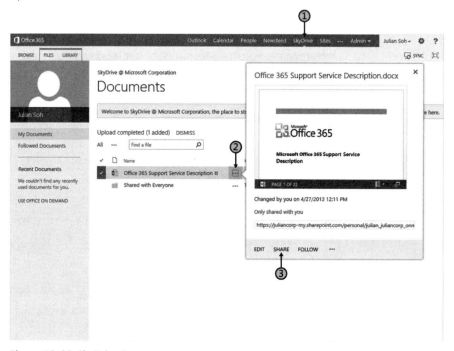

Figure 13-28 SkyDrive Pro.

3. Locate a file that is already stored in SkyDrive Pro and click the ellipsis to bring up the preview window, as shown in Figure 13-28. Notice that the preview window displays the document content with the options to Edit, Share, and Follow, plus other options you can access by clicking the ellipsis.

4. Click Share to bring up the Sharing dialog box, as shown in Figure 13-29. Enter the email addresses of users you want to invite to collaborate on this document. These users can be external users. In the drop-down menu, select the Can view option to restrict users to only view the document, or select the Can edit option to allow users to both view and edit the document.

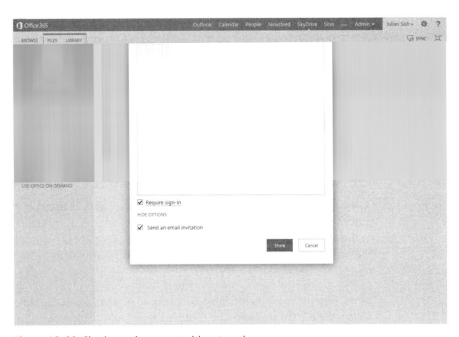

Figure 13-29 Sharing a document with external users.

5. If you would like to require users to sign in, select the Require sign-in check box. This is where SharePoint Online provides an option to provide a level of assurance that only the recipients on the original invitation are authorized. If you select the Require sign-in box, the email addresses of the people you invite must be associated with a Microsoft account, previously known as Windows Live ID. Authentication with the Microsoft account is required before access to the file is granted. Therefore, if the person you invite forwards the invitation to someone else, the third party would not have the correct Microsoft account to be authenticated before access is granted.

6. Click Save to create and send the invitation.

After the invitation is sent to an external entity and the entity accesses the shared file, a PAL is consumed. After an email address is associated with a PAL, other shared files with the same entity will not consume additional PALs. After all sharing has ceased for the email address, the PAL will be released and can then be used by another external user.

Managing external sharing

As an administrator, you have the ability to allow or deny external sharing. In Step 1 of the preceding exercise, you saw how you can turn sharing on or off for the entire organization at the tenant level. This needs to be done before you can turn external sharing on or off at the site collection level. The site collection is the lowest level at which you can control the ability for external sharing.

When external sharing is enabled, users can share sites, libraries, folders, and documents. Follow these steps to determine content sharing information and how to modify and remove sharing access:

1. For this exercise, we will use a document in SkyDrive Pro. Select a document in SkyDrive Pro and click the ellipsis.

2. In the document preview window, notice the sharing information, as shown in Figure 13-30. Click Open to anyone with a guest link.

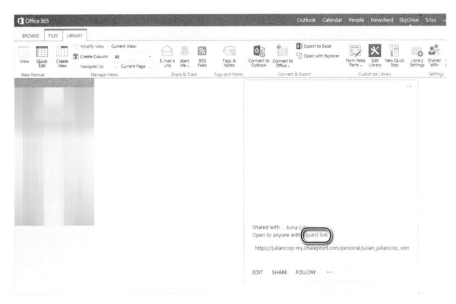

Figure 13-30 External sharing information.

3. In the window showing the guest link, as shown in Figure 13-31, you can click the delete icon to remove the ability for external users to access the document with the link.

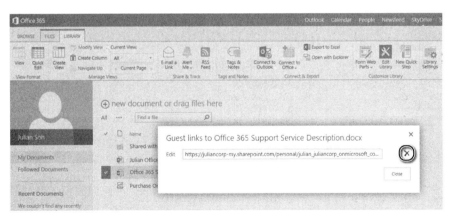

Figure 13-31 External sharing link.

4. Choose to disable the link or to keep it.

5.   To remove an external user, click the ellipsis at the end of the document's file name, click the ellipsis in the preview window, and then select Shared With from the drop-down menu, as shown in Figure 13-32.

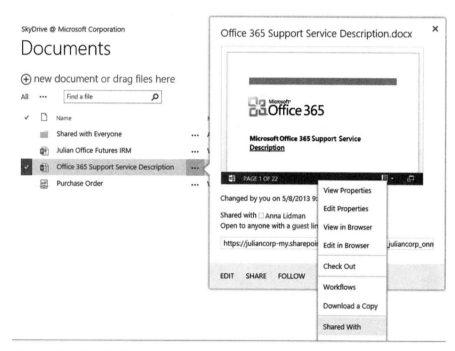

Figure 13-32 See all external sharing.

6. Click the ADVANCED option, as shown in Figure 13-33.

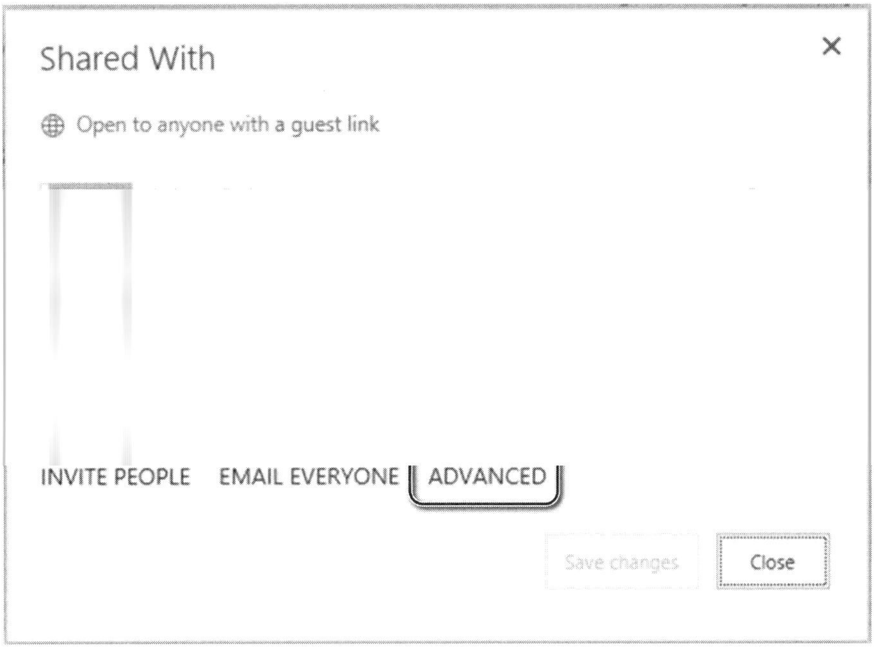

Figure 13-33 List of people the document is shared with.

7.   Click the PERMISSIONS tab and use the options along the top to add, remove, or modify users and their permissions, as shown in Figure 13-34.

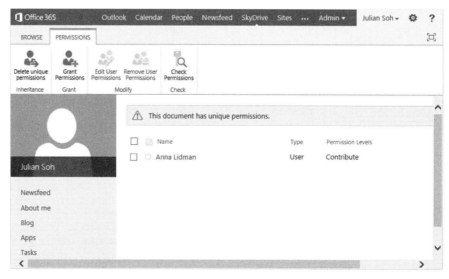

Figure 13-34 Permissions list.

Microsoft introduced the ribbon menu in SharePoint 2010, and this is carried forward into the current version of SharePoint Online. On most pages, the two major tabs are FILES and LIBRARY. As an alternative to the preceding exercise, you can also access and modify the sharing information from these tabs, as shown in Figure 13-35. The sharing option on the Files tab will be available only after one or more files have been selected, and the sharing settings will affect only the selected files. The sharing option and settings on the Library tab will affect the entire library.

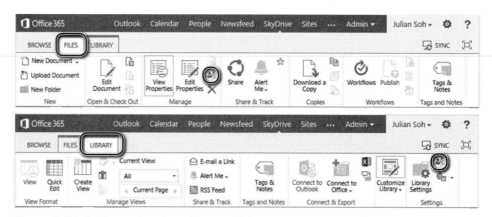

Figure 13-35 Sharing options from the menu ribbon.

INSIDE OUT   Best practices for external sharing

The ability to share content with external users creates the risk of over-sharing. Micro-soft has an article about managing external sharing and best practices at *http://office.microsoft.com/en-us/office365-sharepoint-online-small-business-help/manage-sharing-with-external-users-HA102849862.aspx.*

Because SharePoint Online is a web-based repository, users can access their documents through SkyDrive Pro from anywhere there is an Internet connection, as illustrated in Figure 13-36.

Figure 13-36 Anywhere access to documents stored in SharePoint Online.

SharePoint Online also supports mobility through the incorporation of SkyDrive Pro Win-dows Sync, previously SharePoint Workspace. SkyDrive Pro Windows Sync provides the abil-ity to synchronize files and folders in SkyDrive with local computing devices. Thus, users can access documents through Windows Explorer, and the documents and folders will synchro-nize with SkyDrive Pro whenever there is network connectivity. To create a synchronization relationship, click Sync from SkyDrive Pro, as shown in Figure 13-37. This will create a sync location on the hard drive and add a favorite in Windows Explorer.

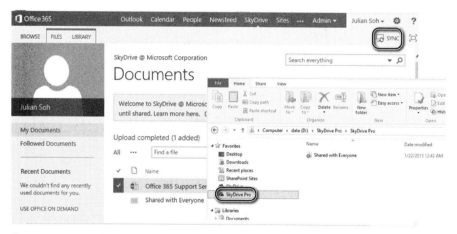

Figure 13-37 Synchronizing SkyDrive Pro with Windows Explorer.

Office Web Apps

SharePoint Online supports mobility by embracing the BYOD phenomenon through Office Web Apps. Unlike Office Professional Plus, which we will discuss in Chapter 15, "Office 365 Professional Plus", Office Web Apps is a SharePoint Online capability. Office Web Apps is the web-based version of Office. Follow these steps to see Office Web Apps in action:

1. From SkyDrive Pro, identify a file you want to edit. Click the ellipsis next to the file name to expose the preview window, as shown in Figure 13-38.

2. In the preview window, click the ellipsis to reveal a drop-down menu, and then select Edit in Browser, also as shown in Figure 13-38.

Figure 13-38 Edit in a browser using Office Web Apps.

Office Web Apps will be presented in the browser, as shown in Figure 13-39, with the familiar Word ribbon because we opened a Word document in this example. Because we shared this document with another entity in the earlier example, and if that entity is also editing the document, both entities can co-author the document at the same time. At the lower right of the browser window, if there are multiple co-authors, the number of co-authors will be shown. When expanded, the identities of the co-authors will be displayed.

INSIDE OUT   Co-authoring in Word and Excel

For Word documents, co-authors can use either the rich Word application or the Word Web App. Therefore, there is no need for all co-authors to be on one or the other to co-author. For Excel, co-authoring is possible only through the Excel Web App.

Figure 13-39 Co-authoring through the browser with Office Web Apps.

3. Save the document by clicking the disk icon at the upper left, and then close Office Web Apps by clicking the X at the upper-right corner.

4. On the SkyDrive Pro page, click new document, as shown in Figure 13-40. You will be prompted to select the type of Office document you would like to create.

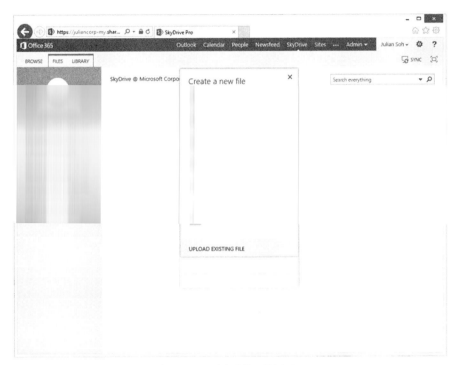

Figure 13-40 Creating a new document with Office Web Apps.

5. When prompted, provide a file name, and then click OK. The Office Web App needed to create your document will be launched in the browser.

As you can see, SharePoint Online facilitates mobility by allowing your users to edit and create documents through a browser. Therefore, as long as there is an Internet connection and a browser, your users can be productive. Instead of emailing attachments, your users can invite others, including external entities, to collaborate and co-author.

INSIDE OUT Configuring the iPad for Office 365

Office Web Apps, which are a function of SharePoint, make it possible for devices such as the iPad to edit Office documents through the browser. At the time of writing, there is no native Office product for the iPad. Mike Hacker and Julian Soh co-authored a blog detailing how an iPad will work with Office 365. See *http://blog.mikehacker. net/2012/01/19/configuring-and-using-an-ipad-with-office-365/*.

Achieving compliance with SharePoint eDiscovery Center

Another prominent new feature in SharePoint Online 2013 is a new site collection type called the eDiscovery Center. The eDiscovery Center provides the following compliance capabilities:

- Electronic discovery of documents in SharePoint Online, Exchange Online, and Lync Online through federated search

- Case management

- Legal Hold

- Removal of duplication and exporting of results

INSIDE OUT Access rights for eDiscovery

For eDiscovery purposes, the Compliance Officer's Office 365 account needs to have at least read-only access to the content in SharePoint Online. She must also be a member of the Discovery Manager group in Exchange Online if you want to allow her to include Exchange content as part of eDiscovery efforts.

Follow these steps to explore the eDiscovery Center:

1. Create an eDiscovery Center site collection by going to the SharePoint Online 2013 admin center.

2. Select site collections, click New, and then select Private Site Collection.

3. Provide a title for the site and a web site address, click the Enterprise tab under Template Selection, and then select eDiscovery Center, as shown in Figure 13-41.

Figure 13-41 Creating a new eDiscovery Center site collection.

4. Specify an administrator and the storage quota, and then click OK to create the site.

5. After the eDiscovery Center site collection is created, go to the site by using its URL. Your new eDiscovery Center should look similar to the one shown in Figure 13-42.

Figure 13-42 SharePoint Online eDiscovery Center.

6. Click the Create new case link and provide a name for the case in the Title box. Provide a URL name for the case as well. Notice that the URL is a site in the eDiscovery site collection. Therefore, using SharePoint terminology, a case is a site in the eDiscovery site collection. You can set the user permissions to inherit from the parent site or assign unique permissions to create a separation of duties between different case managers, as shown in Figure 13-43.

Figure 13-43 Creating a new case.

7. Click Create after you have completed the necessary information for the case site.

Chapter 13

After the case site is created, you will be directed to the site. Before we look at the case site, let us take a look at the hierarchical information structure for eDiscovery and introduce two new terms:

- eDiscovery sets

- Queries

As shown in Figure 13-44, an eDiscovery set is a collection of information sources, specifically SharePoint Online, Exchange Online, and/or Lync Online. Queries enable you to create subsets of information through filtered searches of eDiscovery sets.

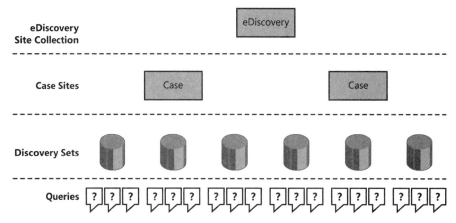

Figure 13-44 Information hierarchy of the eDiscovery site collection.

To demonstrate eDiscovery, consider the following scenario:

Adatum Inc. and Tailspin Toys are entering into an agreement. The organizations exchange emails. Some of those emails have attachments. There have also been meetings regarding the proposed partnership. Documents regarding the transactions between both organizations exist in SharePoint Online. A regulatory body has requested to see all communication between the two organizations related to contracts valued at $10,000. You are the Chief Compliance Officer (CCO) of Tailspin Toys and already have an eDiscovery Center established in SharePoint Online.

Now assume you are the CCO of Tailspin Toys. Follow these steps to discover content to comply with the regulatory body's request:

1. Because you need to search for emails, you first need to configure your eDiscovery Center site collection to enable federated search capabilities across SharePoint Online and Exchange Online. You need to do this only once for each eDiscovery Center site collection. From the eDiscovery Center site collection, click the gear icon located at the upper-right corner, and then select Site settings.

2. Under Site Collection Administration, click Search Result Sources.

3. On the Manage Result Sources page, click New Result Source, as shown in Figure 13-45.

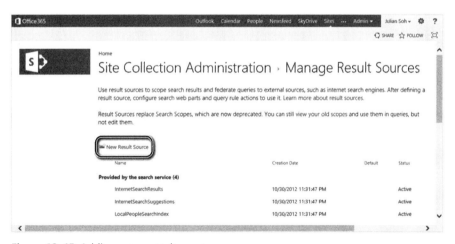

Figure 13-45 Adding a new result source.

4. Provide a name for the new data source. For this exercise, we will just use Exchange eDiscovery because this best describes it. Select Exchange and select the Use AutoDiscover check box, as shown in Figure 13-46, and then click Save.

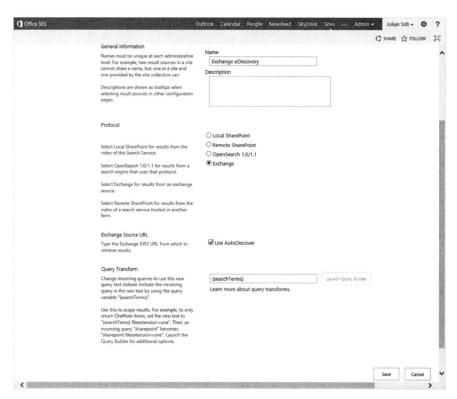

Figure 13-46 Adding an Exchange data source.

5. Click the logo or the Home link next to the logo to return to the eDiscovery Center's main page.

6. Click the Create new case link to create a new case. For this exercise, we will use Adatum as the case name.

7. After the case site has been created, click new item under eDiscovery Sets, as shown
in Figure 13-47.

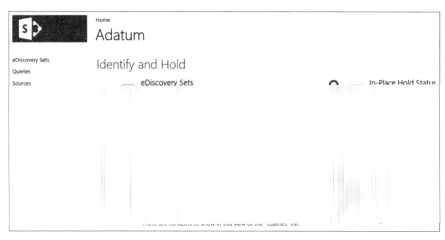

Figure 13-47 Creating a new eDiscovery Set.

8. On the New: eDiscovery Set page, provide a name in the eDiscovery Set Name box, and then click Add & Manage Sources, as shown in Figure 13-48. For this exercise, we will name our eDiscovery set All Adatum Communications.

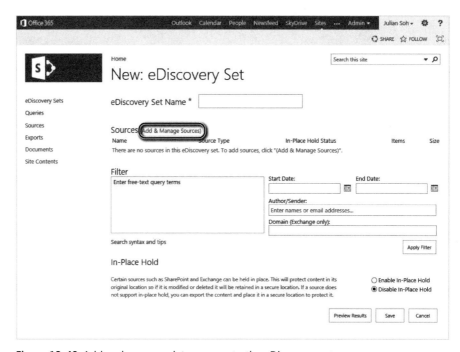

Figure 13-48 Add and manage data sources to the eDiscovery set.

9. Enter the email addresses or use the global directory icon to search for mailboxes to include in the eDiscovery set. Enter SharePoint URLs to include in the eDiscovery set, as shown in Figure 13-49. Click the check icons next to the fields to validate the email addresses, and then click OK to save the data sources.

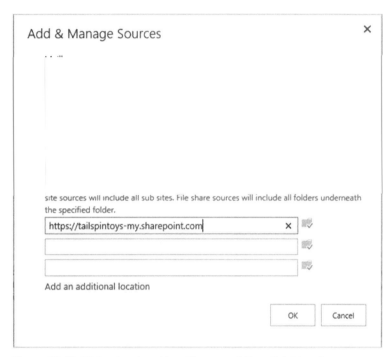

Figure 13-49 Dialog box to add mailboxes and SharePoint locations.

> **Note**
>
> As you can see in Figure 13-49, you can add additional mailboxes beyond the three that are seen on the page. However, it is not practical to add large number of mailboxes in the event you need to search all mailboxes. In these scenarios, you should add distribution groups to the eDiscovery set.

10. The number of discovered items in the mailboxes and SharePoint locations are shown on the New: eDiscovery Set page. By default, found items are not placed on hold. However, you have the option to implement In-Place Hold, as shown in Figure 13-50.

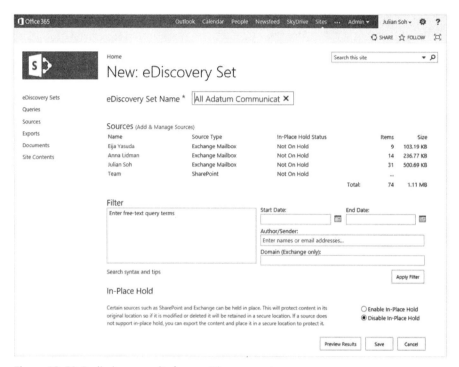

Figure 13-50 Preliminary results for an eDiscovery set.

You can further narrow down the number of items in the eDiscovery set by specifying additional filters in the Filter box. You can use Boolean logic and enclose phrases in quotes. You can also use Keyword Query Language (KQL) if you need to create more complex search criteria. For example, type the following to search for items where the terms *acquisition* and *debt* are no more than three words apart:

```
"acquisition" NEAR(n=3) "debt"
```

> **Note**
>
> For more information about KQL syntax, see the MSDN article at *http://msdn. microsoft.com/en-us/library/ee558911.aspx.*

11. Without putting in any filters, click Preview Results. You will see a results window listing all items found in the mailboxes and SharePoint site, as shown in Figure 13-51.

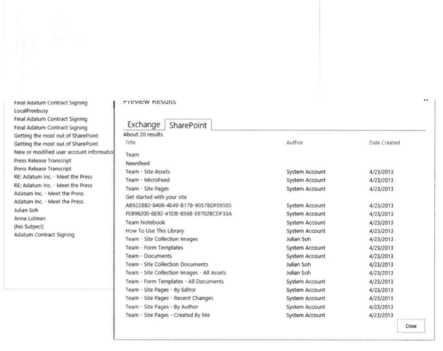

Figure 13-51 Preview results of the eDiscovery set.

12. Click the Close button to close the Preview Results window.

13. Create a Word document named Purchase Order, and create the document's content as a hypothetical invoice with an amount of 10,000. Upload the document to the SharePoint Team site, which is included in the eDiscovery set. You might have to give SharePoint Online some time to crawl the document. After the crawl has completed, proceed with this exercise.

14. Type the following terms in the Filter box and click Preview Results:

```
"contracts" OR 10000
```

15. You should notice that the result set for the eDiscovery set is much smaller, as shown in Figure 13-52. Click the SharePoint tab to view the results, and compare it to what it was before in Figure 13-51. Notice, too, that the results for SharePoint should include the document titled PurchaseOrder, even though we were not looking for the terms *Purchase* or *Order*. In this exercise, it shows that the eDiscovery set was able to find the value *10000* in the document.

Figure 13-52 Filtered results as shown on the Preview Results page.

16. Click the Close button to close the Preview Results page.

17. Click the Save button to save the results of this eDiscovery set.

In this exercise, you created an eDiscovery set to search three mailboxes in Exchange Online and one SharePoint Site. You also created a filter to search for the terms *contract* or *10000*, and you then saved the eDiscovery set. Therefore, you were able to fulfill the request from the regulatory body for communications between your organization and Adatum related to contracts or transactions that are worth $10,000. In the next exercise, we will look at the use of queries and how to export eDiscovery results.

Let us continue our case study with the following scenario:

Your organization's attorney wants to review only contract-related correspondence between Tailspin Toys and Adatum before the documents go to the regulatory body. She does not care about invoices, purchase orders, or any financial transaction documents unless they contain the term contract. The attorney wants you to place items that meet her request on legal hold and to send her a copy of the results on a DVD.

earlier.

3. On the Adatum case site, select eDiscovery Sets on the left navigation pane.

4. On the eDiscovery Sets page, select the eDiscovery set you created in the preceding exercise. If you have been following along with the preceding exercise, this will be the All Adatum Communications eDiscovery set.

5. On the All Adatum Communications eDiscovery set page, select Queries from the left navigation pane, and then click new item on the Queries page, as shown in Figure 13-53.

Figure 13-53 Creating a new query from the eDiscovery set.

6. Take note of the number of Exchange and SharePoint items at this time. Provide a name for this query. For our exercise, we will name it Contracts Only.

7. In the Query box, type the term **contract** and select Email as the only message type we want to find, as shown in Figure 13-54. Click the Exchange tab, and then select Apply under the Message Type heading.

Figure 13-54 Apply filters to a query.

8. After the filters are applied, the number of items will be reduced because of the more restrictive filters. Notice that all the meeting items in Exchange were eliminated because you specified only email communications, as shown in Figure 13-55.

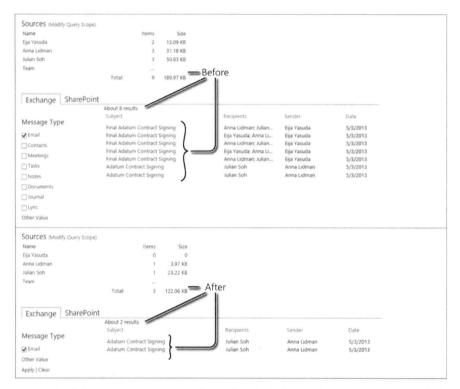

Figure 13-55 Before and after screen shots of results before and after filters were applied to a query.

9. Click the Save button to save this query. At the upper right corner, a small pop-up box will appear with the message "Query saved."

10. Click the Export button. On the Export page, set your export options, as shown in Figure 13-56. Notice that you have the option to include removing duplicate Exchange content. You can also choose to include SharePoint versions of content that might not have directly met your search criterion, but are versions of one that does. Lastly, you also have the ability to include encrypted or unknown content that SharePoint was able to determine is a possible match. For this exercise, select Remove duplicate Exchange content, and then click OK.

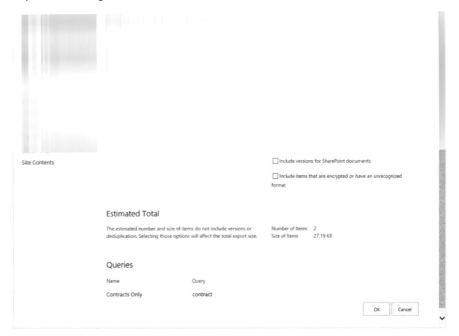

Figure 13-56 Settings for exporting items.

11. As shown in Figure 13-57, on the Export: Download page, you will see a Download Results button and a Download Report button. Click Download Results. This will launch an application. If you are prompted by a security warning that the publisher is unverified, click Run. This will launch the eDiscovery Download Manager application.

> **Note**
>
> A download report will create a report of only mailbox and SharePoint items that are found, not the actual content. The download results will create the report as well as return the actual content.

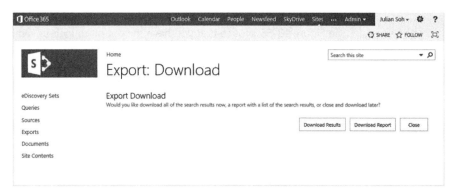

Figure 13-57 Download results and reports.

12. On the eDiscovery Download Manager page, click Browse to navigate to a location on your local computer to export the results, as shown in Figure 13-58. You will copy the contents of this location to the DVD for the attorney when the export is done. After you have selected a location, click OK.

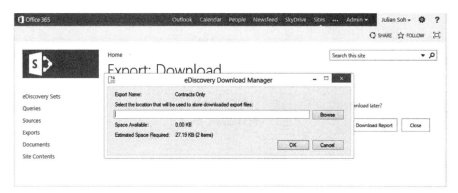

Figure 13-58 eDiscovery Download Manager application.

13. After the results have been exported, click Close to close the eDiscovery Download Manager application.

14. Open Windows Explorer and navigate to the export location, as shown in Figure 13-59. Notice that the eDiscovery Download Manager exported Exchange contents into the Exchange folder and SharePoint contents into the SharePoint folder. There is also a report summary that you can open in Excel. The eDiscovery Download Manager also created a Reports subfolder, which contain detailed reports about the export as well as any errors. These reports are also in Excel format. If you had selected Download Report in Step 11, this is the only folder that would have been created. Notice that the Exchange content has been exported to a .pst file in the Exchange subfolder.

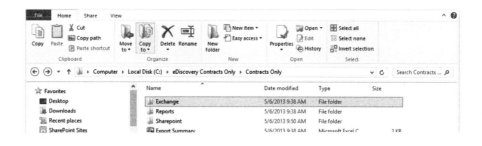

As you can see, the eDiscovery Center and federated search capability in SharePoint Online 2013 makes it easier for organizations to meet compliance and regulatory requirements.

INSIDE OUT   Exchange or SharePoint?

Exchange Online has eDiscovery capabilities because it needs to be able to provide that functionality for organizations that do not have SharePoint or SharePoint Online. However, if you do have SharePoint Online, the eDiscovery capabilities cover both SharePoint and Exchange content, so it is a superset level of eDiscovery capabilities that will better serve your needs. However, you will still need to use Exchange Messaging Records Management (MRM) to manage the content life cycle in Exchange.

SharePoint Online Management Shell

The SharePoint Online Management Shell is a Windows PowerShell module that allows you to manage SharePoint Online users, site collections, and sites. Before you can use the SharePoint Online Management Shell, you must first follow these steps to set it up:

1. On your management computer, download and install Windows Management Framework 3.0.

> **Note**
>
> **You can download Windows Management Framework 3.0 from the Microsoft Download Center at *http://www.microsoft.com/en-us/download/details. aspx?id=34595*.**

2. Download and install the SharePoint Online Management Shell.

> **Note**
>
> **You can download the SharePoint Online Management Shell at *http://www.microsoft.com/en-us/download/details.aspx?id=30359*. 32-bit and 64-bit versions of the shell are available.**

3. Start the SharePoint Online Management Shell from the Start menu, and type the following command to connect to your SharePoint Online tenant:

```
Connect-SPOService –URL https://<your-domain>-admin.sharepoint.com –Credential
<Admin UPN>
```

For example, if your tenant name is adatum.onmicrosoft.com and the UPN of an administrator is admin@adatum.onmicrosoft.com, then you would enter the following command:

```
Connect-SPOService –URL https://adatum-admin.sharepoint.com –Credential admin@
adatum.onmicrosoft.com
```

4. Enter the administrator password when prompted, and then type the following command to retrieve a list of all sites in your tenant. Figure 13-60 shows an example of the output:

```
Get-SPOSite
```

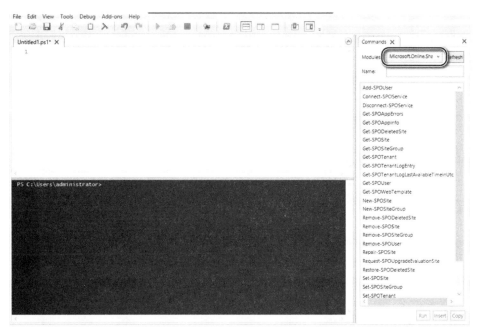

PowerShell cmdlets for SharePoint Online will be available on your computer. Start the Windows PowerShell ISE, select the Microsoft.Online.SharePoint.PowerShell module from the command browser, as shown in Figure 13-61, and you will be able to see the available Windows PowerShell cmdlets for SharePoint Online.

Figure 13-61 Windows PowerShell ISE with the Microsoft.Online.SharePoint.PowerShell module.

Chapter 13

As a reminder, if you want to know the use and parameters of a cmdlet, simply type the following:

```
Get-Help <cmdlet> -<Full|Examples|..>
```

For example, if we want to know how to repair a SharePoint Online site, we see that there is a *Repair-SPOSite* cmdlet. To find out how to use this cmdlet, type the following:

```
Get-Help Repair-SPOSite -Full
```

The *Get-Help* options are shown in Figure 13-62. Notice that Intellisense in Windows PowerShell ISE makes it easy for you to quickly become familiar with Windows PowerShell as a management tool for SharePoint Online.

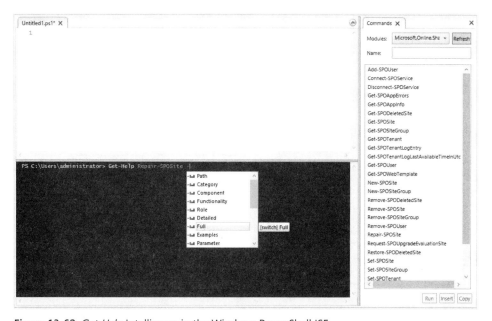

Figure 13-62 *Get-Help* Intellisense in the Windows PowerShell ISE.

SharePoint search in a hybrid environment

Of the three hybrid scenarios we mentioned earlier in the chapter, the most common one is the implementation of SharePoint search services. There are three architecture models for search in a SharePoint hybrid environment:

- One-way outbound topology

- One-way inbound topology

- Two-way topology

All three scenarios require the search service to be responsible for crawling and indexing the local domain's content so as not to impact network and computer resources. Therefore, a SharePoint on-premises search service is responsible for content stored in the on-premises farm, and the SharePoint Online search service is responsible for content stored in SharePoint Online. The results are then made available to each search service by means of federated search for each of the three topologies.

One-way outbound topology

- The SharePoint Online search service will be able to serve results based on content stored in SharePoint Online, but not content stored in the SharePoint on-premises farm.

This topology is useful when implementing an extranet solution whereby SharePoint Online serves as the extranet. External partners with access to SharePoint Online will not see results and content from SharePoint on-premises as you direct them to use only the SharePoint Online search service, while internal employees can see results from both environments.

One-way inbound topology

With the same prerequisites as the one-way outbound topology, the one-way inbound topology is the opposite in the following ways:

- The SharePoint on-premises search service can provide search results based on content stored on-premises.

- The SharePoint Online search service can provide search results based on content stored in SharePoint Online as well as content stored in SharePoint on-premises.

In this topology, the connection between SharePoint Online and SharePoint on-premises will need to go through a reverse proxy device.

Two-way topology

In a two-way topology, the SharePoint on-premises search service and the SharePoint Online search service will serve results based on content stored in both environments. Regardless of which search service a user accesses, the search results from both services will be based on content stored in both environments, as shown in Figure 13-63.

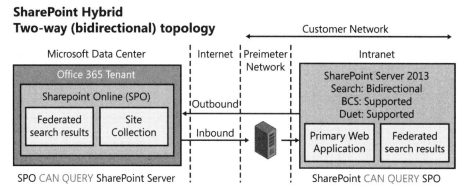

Figure 13-63 Topology of a hybrid two-way search.

INSIDE OUT   Configuring SharePoint for search

A detailed configuration of SharePoint on-premises and SharePoint Online hybrid search is outlined at *http://technet.microsoft.com/en-us/library/dn197168.aspx*.

Summary

There are so many capabilities in SharePoint Online that it is not possible to cover every single one in detail. This chapter was designed to provide you with the major highlights of SharePoint Online and the administrative capabilities of the new features in the latest release of Office 365 with SharePoint Online 2013. The key takeaway in SharePoint Online is that it is designed to be a great collaboration tool for both internal and external users, and it also supports mobility through the availability of Office Web Apps. The introduction of the SharePoint Store enables SharePoint Online 2013 to be more customizable and extensible than previous versions of SharePoint Online. Your organization also has the ability to manage and recover app licenses as well as the ability to delegate that functionality to other site administrators or the Help desk. In the next chapter, we will discuss Lync Online, a useful communication service for organizations.

Lync terminology 700   Configuring and managing Lync Online. 728

- Instant Messaging (IM)

- Virtual Meeting

- Point-to-Point Voice-over-Internet Protocol (VoIP) audio and video

- Replacement or integration with traditional telephony infrastructure, also known as Enterprise Voice (available only with Lync on-premises)

Lync is a viable Private Branch eXchange (PBX) and traditional voice integration or replacement option when implemented as an on-premises solution. A Lync project that integrates or replaces PBXs and traditional voice is known as an Enterprise Voice project. It is important to note that Lync Online provides all the capabilities except for Enterprise Voice. An Enterprise Voice project requires Lync on-premises servers and requires Lync Voice Client Access Licenses (CALs), sometimes referred to as Voice+ CALs. Even though Lync Online does not provide hosted Enterprise Voice capabilities, the solution can be licensed through Office 365, as we will see later in the chapter.

The latest Office 365 offers Lync Online based on Lync 2013 technology, which supports the Lync 2013 client and is also backward compatible with the Lync 2010 client. There are improvements in the Lync 2013 client over the 2010 client, such as the support of multi-party video and audio/video support in a new browser-based web meeting client. Aside from these improvements and some changes in the look and feel of the Lync client, the basic functionality remains very similar and will not pose a huge learning curve for users who are familiar with the Lync 2010 client. We will base our discussions and examples on the Lync 2013 client, but we also will cover the administration of Office 365 with Lync Online 2010.

Lync terminology

Before we take a closer look at Lync, let us introduce a few terms that are specific to Lync and the world of Unified Communications.

Session Initiation Protocol and SIP addressing

Session Initiation Protocol (SIP) is an industry standard protocol governed by the Internet Engineering Task Force (IETF) and is used for controlling multimedia communication sessions that often include voice and video over Internet Protocol (IP) networks. The SIP signaling layer is the "control" layer to all Lync communications. Call set-up, feature activation, call termination, and so on are all controlled through SIP signaling. Lync and Lync Online use Transport Layer Security (TLS) for security; therefore, all Lync SIP communications are encrypted with TLS, which is the successor to the Secure Sockets Layer (SSL) protocol.

The scope of a Lync deployment is defined by its SIP domain, sometimes referred to as the SIP namespace, and used interchangeably. A SIP namespace looks similar to an Simple Mail Transfer Protocol (SMTP) address, such as adatum.com. The Lync address of users in the SIP domain is known as their SIP Uniform Resource Identifier (SIP URI). Think of the SIP URI as the "Lync phone number" of a user, just like the SMTP address is the email address of a user. The SIP URI of a user is written in the following format:

```
sip:julian@adatum.com
```

INSIDE OUT   Lync SIP and Exchange SMTP

For full integration of Lync and Exchange, the SIP address and the SMTP address of a user should be the same.

The SIP domain is an important concept because it factors into hybrid scenarios and federation, which we will cover in the "Hybrid Lync Online" section later in the chapter. In addition, the SIP domain is used to create the appropriate Domain Name System (DNS) records, which we will also cover later in the chapter.

Peer-to-peer voice vs. Enterprise Voice

Sometimes known as Voice over IP (VoIP), peer-to-peer voice is a unicast session involving only endpoints that are connected through an IP network. We want to differentiate this from Enterprise Voice where the endpoints include devices connected to both an IP network and the public switched telephone network (PSTN).

Lync Online overview and licensing

Lync Online is the hosted version of Lync and is offered through Office 365. Like the Exchange Online and SharePoint Online services, Lync Online also comes in two flavors: Plan 1 and Plan 2. Plan 1 is akin to Lync Standard on-premises, and Plan 2 is akin to Lync Enterprise on-premises.

> **Note**
>
> For a matrix comparing Lync capabilities and plans, see *http://office.microsoft.com/en-us/lync/meeting-software-compare-lync-plans-FX103842081.aspx.*

As mentioned earlier, Lync Online does not provide a hosted Enterprise Voice workload. However, the E4, A4, or G4 Office 365 plans include Enterprise Voice CALs (Voice+) as part of Office 365 from a licensing standpoint. An organization under E4, A4, or G4 will still need to separately license and implement Lync servers on-premises, but the users' Voice+ CALs are covered under Office 365.

Perhaps the greatest benefit of Lync Online to organizations is the relative ease in introducing a very visible and tangible service to employees. As part of Office 365, Lync Online immediately integrates with all the other Office 365 services. For example, presence information is visible in both SharePoint Online and Exchange Online. Lync capabilities can also be integrated in other technologies such as System Center Service Manager, which will enable Help desk personnel to better assist users if presence information is available.

Just like the other services, the in-depth coverage of the capabilities of Lync is beyond the scope of this book. We will cover its main capabilities and focus on the deployment and management of Lync Online.

Lync client

Lync is most recognized by its rich client, which comprises your presence and the presence of other users. Presence is represented by a colored bar next to the silhouette or photo of a user, as shown in Figure 14-1.

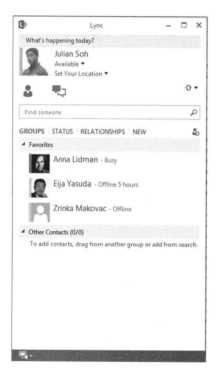

Figure 14-1 Lync 2013 client.

By default, presence in Lync Online is derived from the Exchange Online calendar or the current call state. However, users have the ability to override their statuses by simply click-ing the down arrow next to the current presence status and selecting a different one, also shown in Figure 14-1.

In the search box, you can type in a name to locate people. To communicate with someone, right-click the individual's name and select a communication method, as shown in Figure 14-2.

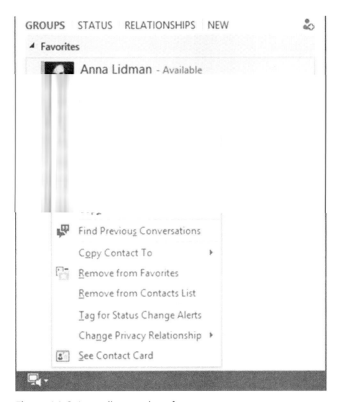

Figure 14-2 Lync client options for contacts.

As shown in the drop-down menu in Figure 14-2, the options include sending an IM, initiating a Lync call, starting a video call, sending an email message, and scheduling a meeting. Instant Messaging might be a new and perhaps more efficient communication method for your organization. When you send another person an IM, a window will pop up on the lower-right corner of his desktop, and he will have an opportunity to accept the IM session. IMs are carried out within an IM window, as shown in Figure 14-3.

Figure 14-3 Instant Messaging.

The controls for Lync IM conversations are located along the bottom of the IM window. As shown in Figure 14-3, the controls from left to right enable a user to do the following:

- Show or hide the IM chat window

- Initiate a voice call or switch an audio device

- Initiate a video call or preview a video before sharing

- Share a screen, whiteboard, poll, PowerPoint presentation, and more

- Show a list of participants in the conversation

The Lync client is very intuitive, and we have not seen it pose a steep learning curve for users who are new to Lync.

Lync meetings

A Lync meeting is a virtual meeting that usually involves multiple parties. Lync Online provides this feature as part of Lync Online Plan 2 or in the A3/E3/G3 Suite, but external attendees do not require a Lync license to attend a meeting organized by someone in your organization. Each Lync Online user is assigned their own conference bridge. Users do not share resources within your Office 365 tenant, and each user can have up to 250 attendees within a single conference bridge. When the Lync client is installed, a Lync meeting option becomes available in the Outlook client so you can easily schedule a Lync meeting, as shown in Figure 14-4.

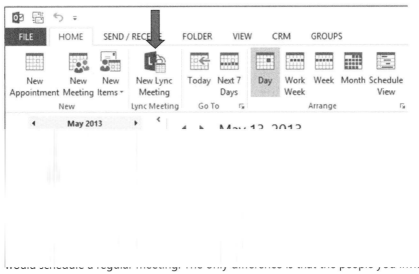

a meeting request with the option to Join Lync Meeting, as shown in Figure 14-5.

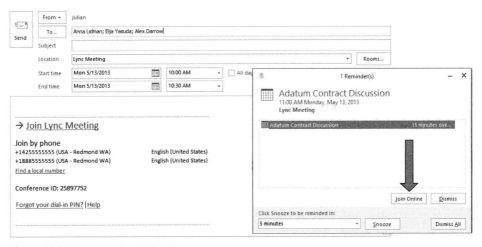

Figure 14-5 Lync meeting invitation.

When you are in a Lync meeting, you can view the attendees and presenters, and you can promote an attendee to a presenter and vice versa. A presenter can also record the meeting and control a participant's audio capabilities, as shown in Figure 14-6.

INSIDE OUT   Lync privacy

A presenter has control over a participant's audio capabilities in that a presenter can mute and unmute an attendee. However, for privacy purposes, a presenter cannot control a participant's video.

Figure 14-6 Presenter view of a Lync meeting.

As you can see, a Lync meeting brings together all the rich media capabilities to make the meeting as immersive as possible. There is audio, video, sharing of content, IM, and recording. Not only are Lync meetings efficient, they help reduce your organization's operating cost and carbon footprint. Lync is also a great training tool where meetings or presentations can be recorded and viewed later by attendees who are unable to attend.

External conference attendees

If you schedule a conference, you can send Lync meeting invitations to anyone with an email address; they do not have to be part of your organization. Lync Online conference attendees do not need to have an Office 365 account, nor do they need to have the Lync client installed. If an attendee attempts to join a Lync Online meeting and does not have the Lync client installed, she will be redirected to a web page to install the browser-based Lync Web App. We will take a closer look at the Lync Web App in the "Lync Web App and Outlook Web App" section later in this chapter. As mentioned earlier, you do not need to license external attendees for them to participate in a Lync meeting organized by someone in your organization.

Lync mobile

Lync Online is designed to promote mobility by providing Lync clients for mobile platforms such as the Windows Phone, Windows RT, iPad, iPhone, and Android phones. Figure 14-7 shows the Lync app for the iPad at the Apple App Store, which can be found at *https://*

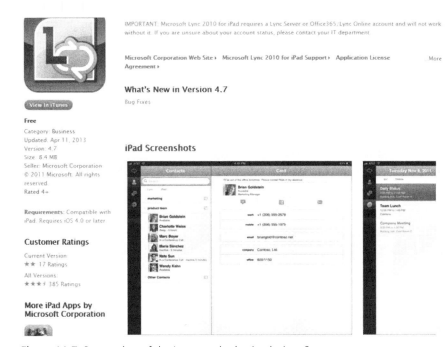

Figure 14-7 Screen shot of the Lync app in the Apple App Store.

Lync Web App and Outlook Web App

To further promote mobility, a mobile or external user without a Lync client can also attend Lync online meetings through a browser using the Lync Web App. The 2010 Lync Web App in Office 365 with Lync 2010 does not provide audio or video, just the screen sharing and IM portion of the meeting. The 2013 version of the Lync Web App in the latest version of Office 365 with Lync 2013 provides full audio and video capabilities through a plug-in, as shown in Figure 14-8.

Figure 14-8 Lync Web App plug-in to enable audio and video.

Participants to Lync meetings through the Lync Web App can be promoted to present-ers and have the ability to share video and content. The same controls are located along the bottom of the window, as shown in Figure 14-9. Compare the layout of the Lync Web App in Figure 14-9 to that of the Lync rich client in Figure 14-6, and note the similarities between them.

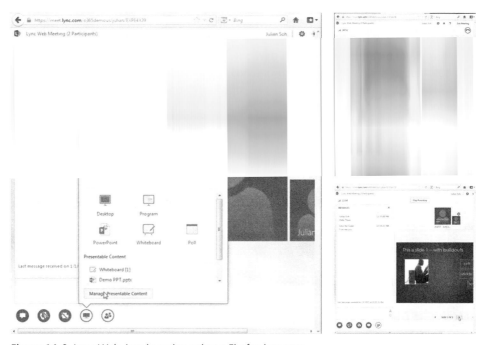

Figure 14-9 Lync Web App in action using a Firefox browser.

As shown in Figure 14-9, Lync Web App 2013 provides the same rich functionality found in the Lync rich client. Another method to access Lync Instant Messaging and presence is the Outlook Web App (OWA), as shown in Figure 14-10. Note the green bar indicating presence and the drop-down menu showing the Lync presence options.

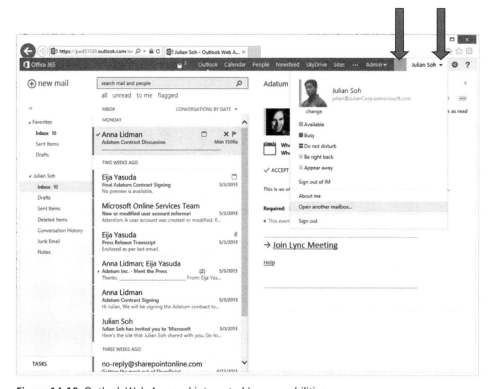

Figure 14-10 Outlook Web App and integrated Lync capabilities.

To initiate a chat, hover your cursor over a recipient in OWA and select the Send Instant Message icon, as shown in Figure 14-11. The IM window is a pop-up window in a new browser instance, also shown in Figure 14-11.

Figure 14-11 Initiating an IM from OWA.

Finally, if a user does not have Outlook but wants to schedule a Lync meeting, there is no equivalent option built into OWA 2010. Instead, to schedule a Lync meeting through the browser in OWA 2010, use the Lync Web Scheduler at *https://sched.lync.com*. The Lync Web Scheduler can be used for Lync Online 2010 and Lync Online 2013. However, for OWA 2013, which is the latest version provided in Office 365, your users have the option to directly schedule a Lync meeting in OWA without going through *https://sched.lync.com*. As shown in Figure 14-12, the screen shot on the right is the Lync Web Scheduler for Office 365 with Lync 2010. The screen shot on the left shows OWA 2013 and the Online meeting option, which allows you to schedule a Lync meeting. This provides a more streamlined approach to scheduling a Lync meeting through the browser and within OWA, thereby doing away with the need to schedule from a different web page.

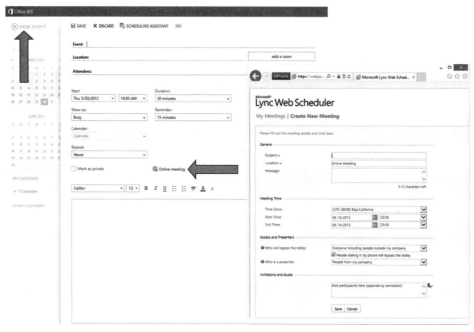

Figure 14-12 Lync Web Scheduler for Lync Online 2010 (right) and OWA 2013 (left).

INSIDE OUT   Lync Web App

Remember that the Lync Web App for Lync Online 2010 does not support audio or video, while Lync Web App 2013 does support audio and video through a browser plug-in.

Lync Online capabilities and concepts

Like the other services in Office 365, Lync Online capabilities are governed by an authoritative Service Description.

Note

You can download the Lync Online 2010 Service Description at *http://download.microsoft.com/download/0/9/6/096C9441-8089-4655-ABB3-DC0ABA01A98D/Microsoft%20 Lync%20Online%20for%20Enterprises%20Service%20Description.docx*. You can find the Lync Online 2013 Service Description at *http://technet.microsoft.com/en-us/library/ jj822172.aspx*.

Lync Online features

The most important aspect of the Lync Online Service Description is the matrix of capabilities available in the different Lync Online plans. In some cases, a particular Lync feature might be available only with an on-premises implementation of Lync. Figure 14-13 is a snapshot of the capability matrix showing what is available in Lync Online. For example, the Multiparty IM and Presence capability is not available in the Office 365 K1 plan, and the Persistent Chat feature is not provided by Lync Online and is available only for Lync

PC-to-PC IM and Presence	Yes	Yes	Yes	Yes	Yes	Yes	No	Yes	Yes
Multiparty IM and Presence	Yes	Yes	Yes	Yes	Yes	Yes	No	Yes	Yes
Contact Card Configuration	Yes	Yes	Yes	Yes	Yes	Yes	No	Yes	Yes
Picture Configuration	Yes	Yes	Yes	Yes	Yes	Yes	No	Yes	Yes
Contact List Configuration	Yes	Yes	Yes	Yes	Yes	Yes	No	Yes	Yes
Unified Contact Store	Yes	Yes	Yes	Yes	Yes	Yes	No	Yes	Yes
Address Book Search	Yes	Yes	Yes	Yes	Yes	Yes	No	Yes	Yes
Distribution List Expansion	Yes	Yes	Yes	Yes	Yes	Yes	No	Yes	Yes
Persistent Chat	Yes	No	No	No	No	No	No	No	No

Figure 14-13 Features and capabilities of Lync as outlined in the Service Description.

Lync Federation

Lync Federation is the external connection with other Lync implementations or other communication platforms. For example, if Adatum Inc. uses Lync Online and wants to federate with its business partner, Tailspin Toys, and if the latter has implemented Lync on-premises, then Lync Federation can be established between the two organizations.

When Lync Federation is established between organizations, users in the organizations can see each other's presence, communicate using IM, and make Lync-to-Lync audio and video calls. Lync Federation is specific to Lync and should not be confused with Active Directory Federation Services (AD FS) Identity Federation or Exchange Online Federation, both of which we covered in previous chapters.

Lync Federation can also refer to connectivity to other non-Lync platforms, such as Skype and Windows Live Messenger, although Live Messenger users are now in the process of being migrated to Skype. We will configure Lync Federation in the "Configuring hybrid Lync" section later in this chapter.

Hybrid Lync Online

The term *hybrid Lync* needs to be clearly understood because it is often misunderstood. Contrary to the initial assumption of the term *hybrid*, Lync workloads cannot be divided between Lync Online and Lync on-premises like you can with Exchange in a hybrid environment. Hybrid Lync is also used to describe the relationship between Lync Online and the Exchange or SharePoint technologies. These hybrid architectures are defined as the following:

- Lync Online and Exchange on-premises

- Lync Online and SharePoint on-premises

- Lync on-premises and Exchange Online

- Lync on-premises and SharePoint Online

Table 14-1 lists the capabilities associated with each of the four hybrid architectures, including the full list of capabilities for Lync on-premises with other on-premises implementations of Exchange and SharePoint.

TABLE 14-1 Capabilities based on hybrid architecture

	Exchange on-premises	Exchange Online	SharePoint on-premises	SharePoint online
Lync 2013 on-premises	Presence and IM in Outlook and Outlook Web App	Presence and IM in Outlook and Outlook Web App	Presence in SharePoint	Presence in SharePoint
	Schedule and join	Schedule and join	Skills search	
	Publish status based on Outlook calendar free and busy information	Publish status based on Outlook calendar free and busy infor-mation		
	Contact list	Contact list		
	Contact photo in Lync 2013 Client and Lync Web App	Contact photo in Lync 2013 Client and Lync Web App		
	Meeting delegation (when users are both on-premises or both online)	Meeting delegation (when users are both on-premises or both online)		
	Missed conversations history and call logs stored in Exchange mailbox	Missed conversations history and call logs stored in Exchange Online mailbox		
	Archiving content in Exchange	Archiving content in Exchange Online		
	Search archived content	Search archived content		
	Voice Mail	Voice Mail		

	Exchange on-premises	Exchange Online	SharePoint on-premises	SharePoint online
Lync online 2013	Presence and IM in Outlook Schedule and join Lync online meetings through Outlook Presence and IM in mobile clients Missed conversations history and call logs stored in Exchange mailbox Join Lync online meeting through mobile clients Contact photo in Lync 2013 client Publish status based on Outlook calendar free and busy information Meeting delegation (when users are both on-premises or both online)	Presence and IM in Outlook Schedule and join Lync online meetings through Outlook Presence and IM in mobile clients Missed conversations history and call logs stored in Exchange Online mailbox Join Lync online meeting through mobile clients Contact photo in Lync 2013 client Publish status based on Outlook calendar free and busy information Meeting delegation (when users are both on-premises or both online) Contact List Archiving content in Exchange Online Search archived content Voice mail	Presence in SharePoint	Presence in SharePoint

Prior to Lync 2013, the only way for Lync Online and Lync on-premises to co-exist was through the use of different SIP namespaces and leveraging Lync Federation. With Lync 2013 and the latest Office 365 with Lync Online 2013, it is possible to have both Lync implementations sharing the same SIP namespace in what is sometimes known as a split-domain scenario. However, even in a split-domain scenario Lync workloads cannot be divided. Therefore, users in the domain will need to be homed to either the Lync on-premises implementation or Lync Online, but not both.

INSIDE OUT   Reminder about hybrid Lync facts

It is important to remember that you can implement hybrid Lync (shared SIP domain) only when there is a Lync 2013 on-premises edge server and Lync Online 2013. Users homed to a 2010 Lync on-premises server can also take advantage of a hybrid Lync implementation as long as there is a Lync 2013 on-premises edge server. Earlier versions of Lync on-premises without a Lync 2013 edge server and Lync Online 2010 require

Dial-in audio conferencing

We mentioned earlier that Lync Online currently does not provide Enterprise Voice capabilities, which basically means you cannot connect a traditional telephone line. One exception to this is the ability to provide dial-in phone audio conferencing capabilities. Dial-in audio conferencing allows meeting attendees to dial into the meeting through a phone number to participate in the audio portion of a Lync online meeting. Office 365 Lync Online provides this capability through three certified dial-in conference providers:

- British Telecom (BT)

- Intercall

- Premiere Global (PGi)

If your organization wants to provide dial-in capabilities with Lync Online, you will purchase the service directly from one of the three providers.

INSIDE OUT Why choose a certified dial-in conference provider?

Your organization might already have a dial-in conference provider or might have that capability in-house. A common question that is often raised is why an organization would not just stay with an existing system even if it is not one of the three certified providers? It is fine to have a separate dial-in audio conferencing, but remember that in this scenario the dial-in audio conferencing portion remains separate from the audio portion of the Lync Online meeting. Therefore, the presenter will have to also be connected to the dial-in audio conference bridge to provide audio to attendees who have chosen to dial in. Furthermore, if recording is needed, the audio from the dial-in conference bridge will not be included in the recording. The three certified dial-in audio conferencing providers are connected to Office 365. Therefore, the dial-in audio is not separate from the Lync Online audio.

We will cover the configuration of dial-in audio conferencing through the Office 365 admin center in the "Configuring and managing Lync Online" section later in this chapter.

Lync Online planning and deployment

All the topics we have covered should be considered as part of your organization's Lync Online deployment planning. As a recap, we have discussed the following topics thus far:

- Understanding SIP addressing

- Understanding Lync Online capabilities and associated licensing plans

- Reviewing the Lync Online Service Description

- Understanding Lync Federation

- Understanding the different architectures for hybrid Lync

With your understanding of these topics, you should be able to determine the best Office 365 plan for your organization and have a good idea which architecture will most likely be applicable to meet your organization's needs. The most important item on the list so far is determining the SIP URI for your users. Where possible, align the SIP URI with SMTP because Outlook will use the default SMTP domain to retrieve Lync conference information. If the SIP URI is not the same as SMTP, the integration will fail.

The next task to accomplish in your Lync Online deployment planning is to test whether your organization's network has the correct ports open and sufficient bandwidth, which we will discuss in the following section.

Test network bandwidth and latency

An in-depth analysis of your organization's network, such as a network assessment, is highly recommended. Furthermore, if you currently have network-based voice, audio, and video solutions already deployed in your organization, the performance and quality of existing solutions can serve as a good baseline of your network's bandwidth and latency.

Microsoft provides a web-based analysis tool you can use to determine your network's abil-

puter resides on. Therefore, if you have several network subnets or different geographic locations, you should at a minimum run the probe from all the locations and during different times of the day.

When you launch the Transport Reliability Probe, you might be prompted to install Java if it has not been installed on your machine. On the main window, you have the option to click the Start Test button. When you click the Start Test button, you will be asked to provide a Session ID. The Session ID is just a name for the test. We generally use the name of the subnet or location to identify the test results, as shown in Figure 14-14. After you have provided a name for the Session ID, click OK and the test will begin.

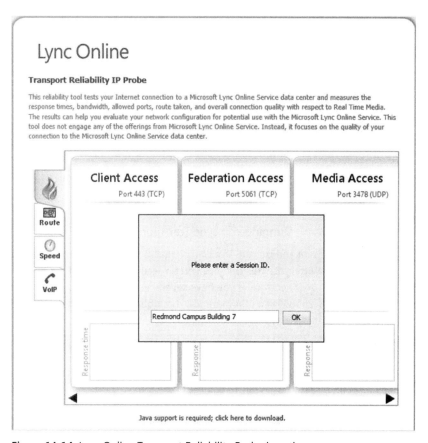

Figure 14-14 Lync Online Transport Reliability Probe in action.

The Transport Reliability Probe is a Software as a Service (SaaS) test of your network and provides in-depth insight into network issues that might affect the quality of Lync calls. As mentioned in Chapter 2, "Planning and preparing to deploy Office 365 ", bandwidth is only one factor. Another important factor that can affect the quality of Lync is network latency. Use the tabs along the side of the Transport Reliability Probe to look at each of the test results. Pay particular attention to the following information because it significantly affects all VoIP solutions, including Lync:

- Number of hops

- Response time for each hop (latency)

- Bandwidth

- Sustained throughput

- Packet loss

Figure 14-15 shows the report from a sample network analysis. Notice that this network has sufficient bandwidth but faces latency issues with one of the hops. Therefore, a potential problem is exposed and should be remediated prior to deploying Lync Online.

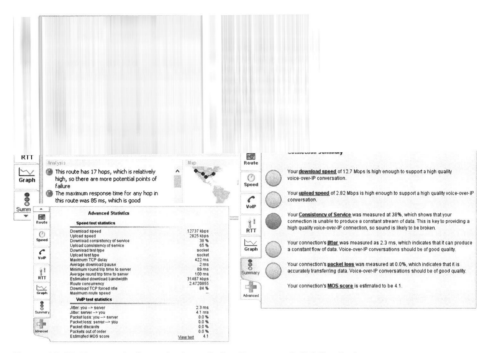

Figure 14-15 Test results from the Lync Online Transport Reliability Probe.

Determine ports and protocols

The first action that the Lync Online Transport Reliability Probe took was to test the firewall to make sure the required ports are open for the type of protocol needed by Lync Online. The information about ports and protocols is on the first tab. Figure 14-16 shows the ports and protocols tested.

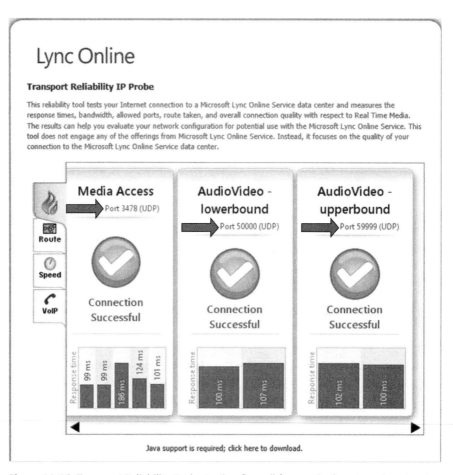

Figure 14-16 Transport Reliability Probe testing firewall for required ports and protocols.

Table 14-2 shows the ports that need to be open for the specified traffic type and the traffic direction for Lync Online.

TABLE 14-2 Ports and protocols needed by Lync Online

	Port	Protocol	Traffic direction
Audio, video, and application sharing	443	STUN/TCP	Outbound

<del>INSIDE OUT</del>   <del>Lync point-to-point communications are direct</del>

After Lync Online has established the point-to-point connection between two clients, the communication is then carried out directly between the endpoints, without having to go through the Lync servers in Office 365.

Allow outgoing connections

If you have a proxy server for your organization, ensure that you allow outgoing connections to the following destinations:

- *.lync.com

- *.outlook.com

- *.onmicrosoft.com

For performance, you might want to consider bypassing the proxy for these three destinations. These are trusted and secure locations, and a proxy will serve only as a bottleneck with minimal incremental security benefits.

Create DNS entries

The DNS settings for Lync Online can be found in the Office 365 admin center. To determine your DNS settings, follow the steps outlined in the Office 365 Lync Online 2010 or Office 365 Lync Online 2013 section, depending on which version of Office 365 your organization is currently using.

Chapter 14

INSIDE OUT Testing Lync Online without DNS Autodiscover

When you look at the DNS settings in the following section, you will notice that one of the DNS entries is an SRV record with a target of sipdir.online.lync.com. This SRV record enables Autodiscover, so you do not need to manually configure the Lync client. If you do not have access, are not ready to modify DNS, or want to test Lync Online, you can manually set the Lync client connection settings, as shown in Figure 14-17. This should be used for testing purposes only and is not ideal as a permanent, long-term configuration. Follow these steps that correspond to the steps labeled in Figure 14-17:

1. On the Lync client, click the gear icon.

2. Select Personal.

3. Click the Advanced button.

4. Select Manual configuration.

5. Enter sipdir.online.lync.com:443 for the internal and external server name.

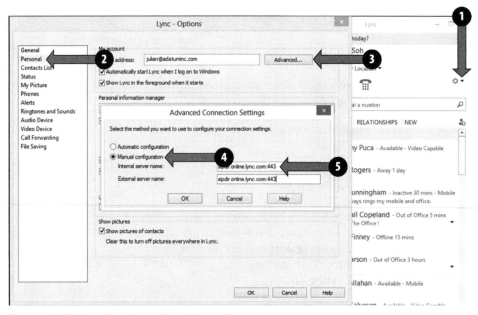

Figure 14-17 Manual configuration of Lync client connection settings.

DNS settings for Office 365 with Lync Online 2013

If your organization is using Office 365 with Lync Online 2013, follow these steps to determine the DNS settings required for Lync Online:

1. Log on to the Office 365 admin center at *https://portal.microsoftonline.com*.

2. Select domains from the left navigation pane, select the domain name that will be

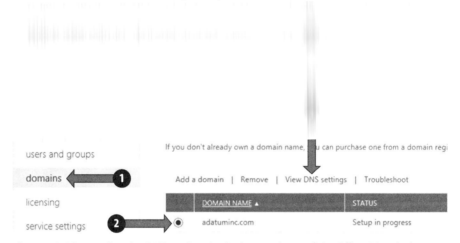

Figure 14-18 Locating the DNS settings in the latest release of the Office 365 admin center.

3. Expand View DNS settings by clicking the arrow and take note of the DNS records required for Lync Online, as shown in Figure 14-19.

Figure 14-19 Lync Online DNS settings.

4. Create the records in DNS.

DNS settings for Office 365 with Lync Online 2010

If your organization is using Office 365 with Lync Online 2010, follow these steps to determine the DNS settings required for Lync Online:

1. Log on to the Office 365 admin portal at *https://portal.microsoftonline.com*.

2. Select Domains from the left navigation pane, select the domain name that will be associated to Lync Online as the SIP URI, and click View DNS settings, as shown in Figure 14-20.

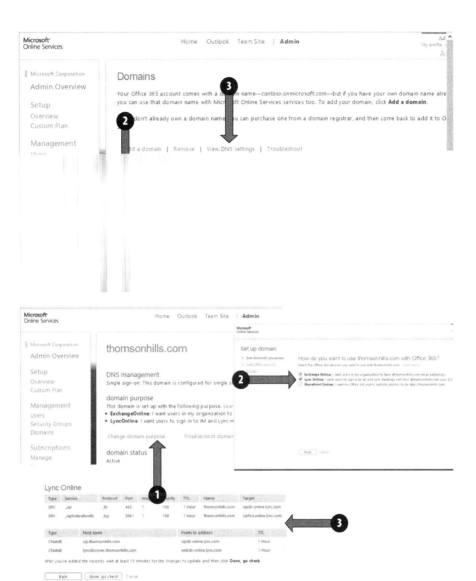

Figure 14-21 Locating the DNS settings for Lync Online 2010 in the admin portal.

4. Create the records in DNS.

Configuring and managing Lync Online

Lync Online is managed through the Office 365 admin center. Unlike the other services, there is currently no remote Windows PowerShell for Lync Online, although it is included in the Microsoft Office 365 roadmap to provide Windows PowerShell for Lync Online in the near future.

INSIDE OUT   Lync Online Windows PowerShell exception

There are a few scenarios that might require access to Lync Online remote Windows PowerShell. If you have a business need to access Lync Online Windows PowerShell, submit a support ticket with your request, and the request will be evaluated on a case-by-case basis. If what you need to do can indeed be carried out only through Windows PowerShell, the request might be granted on that basis. See *http://support.microsoft.com/kb/2824005/EN-US.*

Lync Online 2013

Follow these steps to explore the management capabilities of Lync Online 2013:

1. Log on to the Office 365 admin center at *https://portal.microsoftonline.com.*

2. Select service settings on the left navigation pane, and then click the Lync tab, as shown in Figure 14-22.

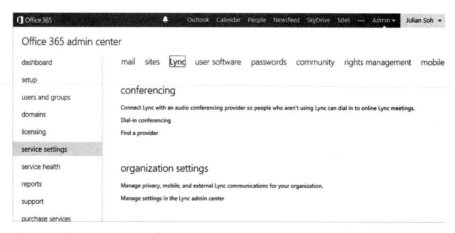

Figure 14-22 Service settings for Lync Online 2013.

3. Click Dial-in conferencing.

4. Assuming that you have not signed up for services with a conferencing provider, click export users wizard to export a list of users that you will provide to a conferencing provider. The conferencing provider will use the list to configure dial-in conferencing phone numbers and passcodes for the users.

5. Click Next.

1. getting started
2. select users
3. summary

Export all users
Export users with dial-in conferencing
Export users without dial-in conferencing
Export specific users

g, and then click Next.

Figure 14-23 Export options.

7. Save the .csv file, and then click Finish.

8. Click Find a provider and follow the instructions to acquire conferencing services. At some point, the provider will request a list of users, at which time you will provide the .csv file created in Step 7. Wait for the provider to return the file to you with the conferencing information and passcodes for the users, and then proceed to the next step.

9. Return to the dial-in conferencing set-up page as described in Step 3, and this time click import wizard.

10. Click Next.

11. Click the browse button, select the .csv file provided by the conferencing provider, and then click next.

12. The wizard will validate the file and show errors, if any. Otherwise, the information will be imported and all your users will now have conferencing dial-in phone numbers and passcodes. These will appear in the Lync meeting invitations they set up through Outlook or the Lync Web Scheduler. Click finish.

13. From the top menu, click Admin, and then select Lync to get to the Lync admin center, as shown in Figure 14-24.

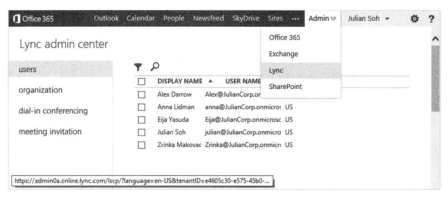

Figure 14-24 Lync Online admin center.

14. Select a user or users by selecting the boxes, and then click the pen icon to edit the users' Lync settings, as shown in Figure 14-25.

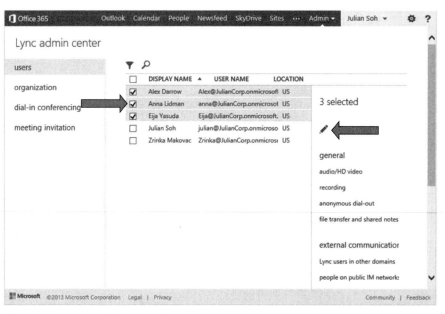

Figure 14-25 Lync Online user administration.

15. On the general page, as shown in Figure 14-26, set the following settings for the users:

   ❍   Ability to record conversations and meetings.

   ❍   Allow anonymous attendees to dial-out. When this option is selected, unau-thenticated meeting attendees can connect to the meeting's audio by having the conferencing service call them. If this option is not checked, anonymous

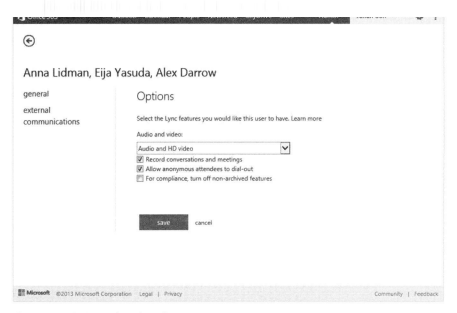

Figure 14-26 General settings for users.

16. Click save to save the users' settings.

17. As shown in Figure 14-27, click external communications, and then select the Lync users option if you want to allow the selected set of users to communicate with other organizations that are also on Lync Online, but in different tenants. Select the check box for People on public IM networks to allow the selected set of users to communicate with Skype and Live Messenger users. These are turned on by default for all users, but you can turn them off if desired.

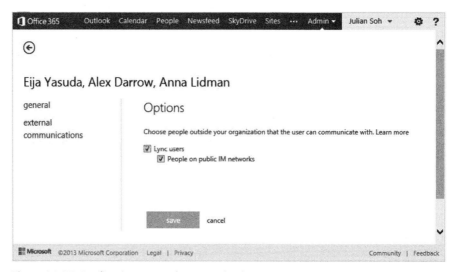

Figure 14-27 Configuring external communications.

18. Click the save button to save the settings for external communications.

19. Click organization from the left navigation pane in the Lync admin center. On the general page, determine the presence privacy mode for your organization and whether to push Lync alerts to mobile devices. The descriptions for these settings are clearly laid out on the page, as shown in Figure 14-28.

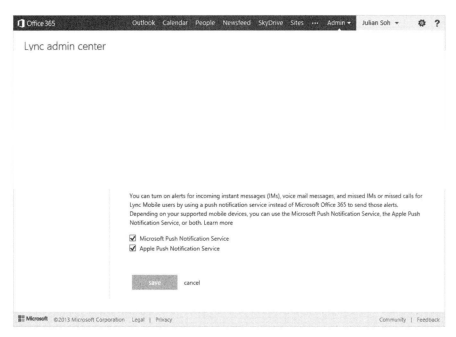

Figure 14-28 Presence privacy settings and mobile alerts.

20. If you made changes to the settings in Step 19, click save. Otherwise, click external communications at the top of the page.

21. Select whether to allow external access through federation, and then add the domains you want to federate with to federate Lync Online. Alternatively, you can choose to allow federation with all domains except the domains you list, as shown in Figure 14-29. The difference between the external settings here versus the one outlined in Step 17 is that the settings here are the default for the organization and include the detailed information of which domains to allow or block, while the one in Step 17 affects only the selected users. When enabled, it will use the domain information that is specified here.

Figure 14-29 Setting external communications (federation).

> **Note**
>
> It might take up to 48 hours for federation to take effect, so do not be surprised if presence information is not immediately blocked or made available to external users.

22. Click save if you made changes to the settings for external communications.

23. Select meeting invitation from the left navigation pane in the Lync admin center, and then enter the URLs to a logo file, Help page, legal page, and footer text, as shown in Figure 14-30. The information will be included in Lync meeting invitations, but it is optional and you do not have to set any of the fields if they do not apply.

Figure 14-30 Information to include in meeting invitations.

24. Click save if you modified the settings on the meeting invitation page.

This concludes all the configuration and management aspects for Lync Online 2013. As you can see, Lync Online is easy to implement and straightforward to configure and manage.

Lync Online 2010

Follow these steps to explore the management capabilities of Lync Online 2010:

1. Log on to the Office 365 admin portal at *https://portal.microsoftonline.com*.

2. Click Manage under the Lync section, as shown in Figure 14-31.

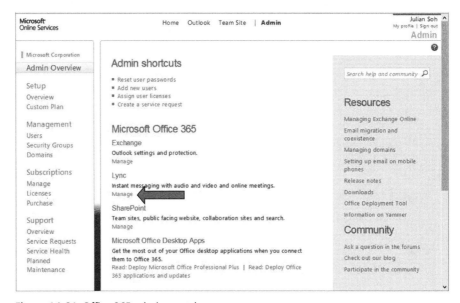

Figure 14-31 Office 365 admin portal.

3. On the Lync Online Control Panel, the Overview page provides a summary of your organization's current settings for Lync Online, as shown in Figure 14-32.

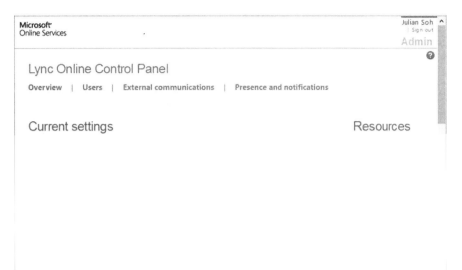

5. Click the down arrow next to Dial-in conferencing and select Export user list followed by Dial-in conferencing disabled, as shown in Figure 14-33. When prompted, click Save File to save the.xml file containing the user list, and then click OK.

Figure 14-33 Exporting a list of users with no dial-in conferencing information.

6. After the file has been saved, click Overview from the menu on the top of the page, and then select Find a dial-in conferencing provider under Resources on the right margin of the page.

7. Follow the instructions and pick a provider. At some point during the purchase of the service, you will be asked to provide a list of users to the provider. Provide the .xml file you created in Step 5. The dial-in conference provider will return the file to you with the dial-in numbers and passcodes for each user.

8. Repeat Steps 4 and 5, except this time select the down arrow next to Dial-in conferencing, and then select Import user configuration file.

9. Click the Browse button, and then navigate to and select the file provided by the dial-in conferencing provider. Click Next.

10. The wizard will report whether the file was uploaded successfully, as shown in Figure 14-34. Click Next to continue. The wizard will use the file to configure the users' dial-in conferencing settings. The results of the configuration will be displayed showing the number of users successfully provisioned as well as errors, if any. This is also shown in Figure 14-34. If there are errors, you have the option to click Download error file; otherwise, click Finish.

Figure 14-34 Uploading a configuration file for dial-in conferencing settings.

11. On the Lync Online Control Panel, select Users from the menu on the top of the page. Select one or more users by selecting the boxes next to the users, and then select the Edit user option on the top.

12. On the Edit user settings page, set the IM, Audio/Video, and Conferencing information, as shown in Figure 14-35.

Figure 14-35 Edit user settings for Lync Online.

13. In the External communications section, select the Lync users in other organizations check box if you want to turn on federation for the selected users, as shown in Figure 14-35. By checking this box, the organization-wide federation settings will be applied. You will set the organization-wide federation settings in Step 17. If you want to let the selected users communicate with users on Skype and Live Messenger, select the Users of public IM service providers check box.

14. You can also manually set the dial-in conferencing information for the selected users or use the import function described in Step 8.

15. Click Next, and then click Finish on the Summary page.

16. From the Lync Online Control Panel, select External communications from the menu on the top of the page, as shown in Figure 14-32.

17. As shown in Figure 14-33, federation is disabled by default. To turn it on, click the Edit button, and then select Turn off all external communications with all except allowed domains. Click OK. As shown in Figure 14-36, your other options are the following:

❍ Turn on external communications with all except blocked domains

❍ Turn off external communications with all except allowed domains

❍ Turn off all federation

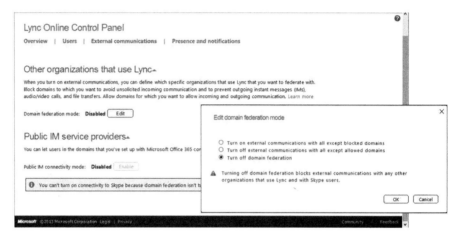

Figure 14-36 Modifying settings for Lync Federation (external communications).

18. After you have enabled federation, you will have the option to add domains, as shown in Figure 14-37. Click the add a domain link and enter a domain name to allow or block, depending on your selection in Step 17. For this exercise, because we selected Turn off external communication with all except allowed domains, the domains we add will be the ones allowed to federate with this Lync Online service.

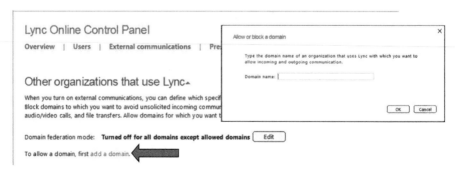

Figure 14-37 Adding domains to federate (or block).

19. Enter an SIP namespace, and then click OK.

> **Important**
>
> As with Lync Online 2013, it might take up to 48 hours for federation to take effect, even though some documentation says it might take up to 24 hours. Therefore, do not be surprised if presence information is not immediately blocked or made available to external users.

Other organizations that use Lync

When you turn on external communications, you can define which specific organizations that use Lync that you want to federate with. Block domains to which you want to avoid unsolicited incoming communication and to prevent outgoing instant messages (IMs), audio/video calls, and file transfers. Allow domains for which you want to allow incoming and outgoing communication. Learn more

Domain federation mode: **Turned off for all domains except allowed domains**   [Edit]

Add domain | Remove domain

☐	Domain name ▲	Status
☐	juliancorp.onmicrosoft.com	Allowed

Add domain | Remove domain

Figure 14-38 Adding and removing SIP domains to federate.

21. After you have enabled federation, you will have the option to also enable public IM connectivity with Skype and Live Messenger by clicking the Enable button located under Public IM service providers.

22. Click the Overview tab on the top of the page and verify that Domain federation and Public IM connectivity are enabled.

23. Click the Presence and notifications tab on the top of the page.

24. Configure the settings for Presence privacy mode and Mobile phone notifications.

This concludes all the configuration and management aspects for Lync Online 2010. As you can see, Lync Online is easy to implement and straightforward to configure and manage.

Lync IM conversation history and policy

The Lync client can be configured to archive IM conversations in Outlook. The IM conversations are stored in a folder titled Conversation History, as shown in Figure 14-39.

Figure 14-39 Conversation History folder in Outlook.

INSIDE OUT   Exchange eDiscovery and In-Place Hold

Contents in the Conversation History are treated like any other Exchange content. Therefore, your organization can include past IM conversations as part of eDiscovery and can also subject it to In-Place Holds.

Archiving of IM conversations is configured in the Lync client. Follow these steps to locate and configure the settings for IM conversation history:

1. From the Lync client, click the gear icon on the upper-right corner of the page.

2. Select Personal on the left navigation pane, and then select or clear the Save IM conversations in my email Conversation History folder check box, as shown in Figure 14-40.

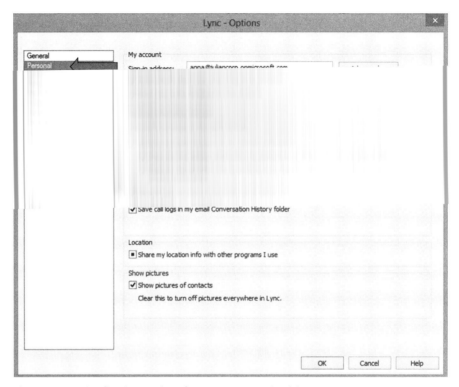

Figure 14-40 Configuring settings for Lync conversation history.

3. Click OK to save the settings.

In an enterprise environment where you might want to control and lock the settings for IM conversation history, you can use Group Policy Objects (GPOs) to create such a policy.

INSIDE OUT   Test before you leap

Incorrectly modifying GPOs and the registry can cause widespread system issues. Therefore, it is important to go through the following steps on a local machine's registry to test the impact of registry changes before making a system-wide change.

Before we configure the GPO, let us first understand how to control the conversation history settings for the Lync 2013 client by following these steps:

1. On a client machine, start the Registry Editor (Regedit).

2. Before proceeding, remember that these registry settings are for the Lync 2013 client. As shown in Figure 14-41, create the following registry key and value: [HKEY_LOCAL_MACHINE\SOFTWARE\Policies\Microsoft\Office\15.0\Lync] "IMAutoArchivingPolicy" REG_DWORD:00000000

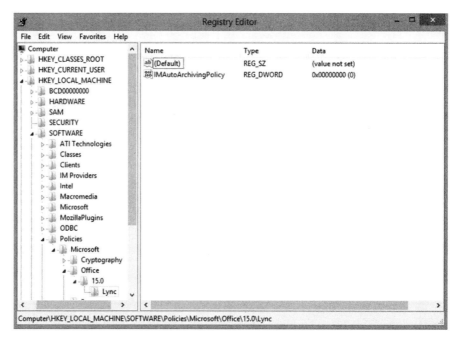

Figure 14-41 Using Regedit to create a key.

3. If the Lync client is running, exit the client and re-start it again.

4. Log on to Lync with the Lync client when it has re-started.

5. Click the gear icon and select Personal on the left navigation pane. You cannot make any changes to the Save IM conversations in my email Conversation History folder check box because it is unchecked and unavailable, as shown in Figure 14-42.

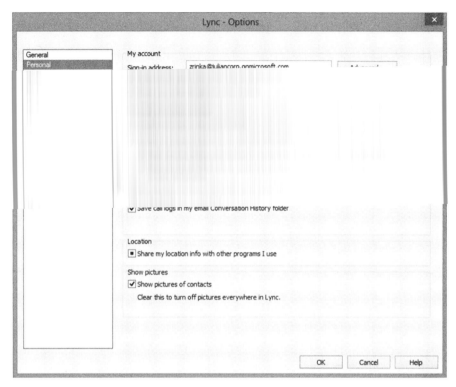

Figure 14-42 Save IM conversations in my email Conversation History folder check box is unchecked and unavailable.

6. Change the value of *IMAutoArchivingPolicy* from REG_DWORD:00000000 to REG_DWORD:00000001.

7. Exit the Lync client and re-start it again.

8. Log on and look at the setting for the Save IM conversations in my email Conversation History folder option. This time, it should be selected but still unavailable so you cannot deselect the box, as shown in Figure 14-43. Compare that to Figure 14-42.

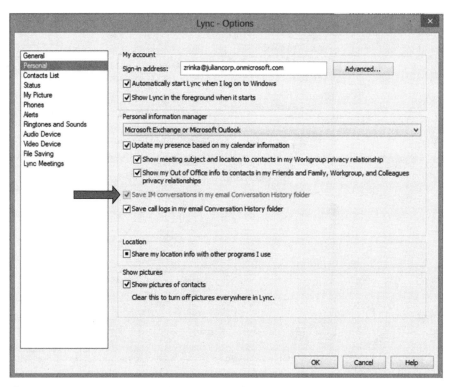

Figure 14-43 Save IM conversations in my email Conversation History folder check box is checked and unavailable.

Now that you have tested the registry keys to control the IM conversation history settings, you can deploy this policy to your organization through GPO by following these steps:

1. On a domain controller (DC), launch Group Policy Management.

2. Expand the Forest, Domain, and Group Policy Objects nodes. Right-click the applicable GPO object affecting the users you want to target, and then select Edit. For this example, we will use the default domain policy because we want to enforce this to all domain users, as shown in Figure 14-44. However, note the Inside Out comment about best practices when modifying GPOs.

Note

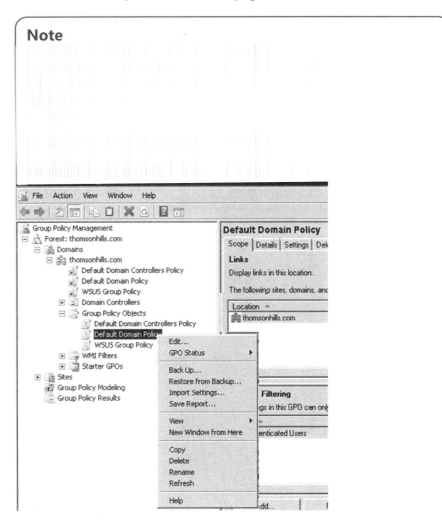

Figure 14-44 Editing a GPO.

3. In the Group Policy Management Editor, expand Preferences under User Configuration, and then expand Windows Settings. Right-click Registry, select New, and then select Registry Item, as shown in Figure 14-45. Refer again to the preceding Inside Out guidance on best practices for GPOs.

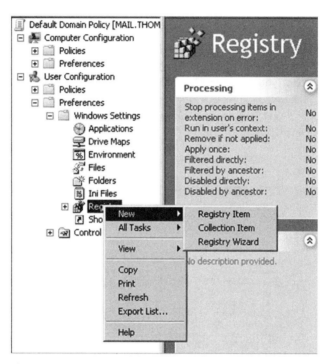

Figure 14-45 Create a new registry item.

4. As shown in Figure 14-46, in the New Registry Properties dialog box, select Replace for the Action and HKEY_LOCAL_MACHINE for the Hive. Type **SOFTWARE\Policies\ Microsoft\Office\15.0\Lync** in the Key Path box, type **IMAutoArchivingPolicy** in the Value name box, select REG_DWORD in the Value type drop-down box, and set the value data to 0 in the Value Data box. Click OK to save the new registry settings.

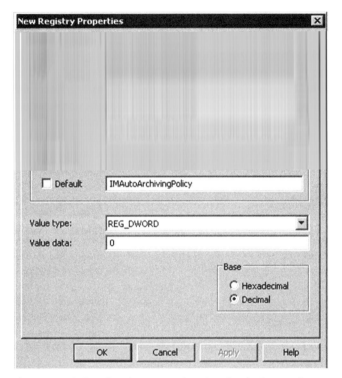

Figure 14-46 Creating the new registry key for the Lync policy.

At this point, you have used a GPO to affect user registry settings applied to domain users so that IMs will not be stored in the Conversation History folder in Outlook, nor will it allow users to enable the feature. If you changed the value of *IMAutoArchivingPolicy* in the GPO to 1, it will cause IMs to be stored in the Conversation History folder in Outlook, but users will still not be able to override that. This is the desired effect because we want to enforce this option.

As an alternative, you can also create an .adm or .admx file to deploy the Lync policy for archiving IMs in the Conversation History folder in Outlook. The .admx file is the new and preferred way; however, for this exercise we will walk you through creating a custom .adm file. Going into the details on the syntax and creation of custom .adm and .admx files is beyond the scope of this book, so we will simply present an .adm file you can reuse for the purposes of implementing this policy:

1. Copy and paste the following into a text file, and save it with an .adm extension. In this example, we will name the file CustomLync2013IMArchive.adm:

```
CLASS MACHINE
CATEGORY !!Lync2013_IMArchive_(CustomADM)
     POLICY !!PolicyConfigurationMode
     EXPLAIN !!ExplainText_ConfigurationMode
     KEYNAME "Software\Policies\Microsoft\Office\15.0\Lync"
       PART !!IMArchive_Configure DROPDOWNLIST REQUIRED
       VALUENAME "IMAutoArchivingPolicy"
       ITEMLIST
               NAME !!IMAutoArchivingOFF VALUE    NUMERIC 0 DEFAULT
               NAME !!IMAutoArchivingON VALUE     NUMERIC 1
       END ITEMLIST
       END PART
     END POLICY
  END CATEGORY

;;;;;;;;;;;;;;;;;;;;;;;;;;;;;;;;;;;;;;;;;;;;;;;;;;;;;;;;;;;;;;;;;;
[strings]
Lync2013_IMArchive_(CustomADM)="Microsoft Lync 2013 Custom Compliance Policy
Settings"

IMArchive_Configure="Configure IM Auto-Archiving"

CallLogArchivingPolicy="Configure Call Logging"

DisableSavingIMPolicy="Enable or Disable IM Saving"

PolicyConfigurationMode="Specify IM Logging in Outlook"

ExplainText_ConfigurationMode="Specifies and locks down the Personal Settings
for whether\nMicrosoft Lync archives IMs in the Conversation History folder in
Outlook."

 IMAutoArchivingOFF="Lock and turn off Auto Archiving for IMs"

 IMAutoArchivingON="Lock and turn on Auto Archiving for IMs"
```

In the following steps, note how the strings in the ADM script will correspond to the options and description when setting the policies in the Group Policy Management Editor. You can change the string values in the ADM if you prefer alternate text:

2. Start the Group Policy Management MMC and navigate to the applicable GPO. As in the preceding exercise, we will use the default domain policy for this as well; however, keep in mind what we mentioned earlier about how modifying the default domain policy is not a best practice and how you should create and link a new GPO. Right-

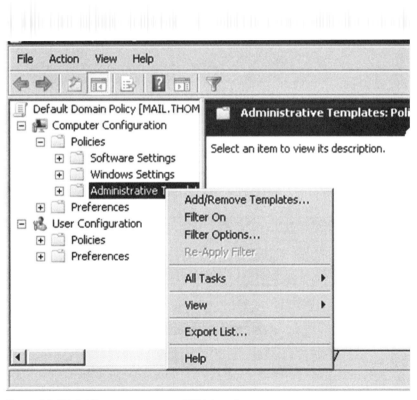

Figure 14-47 Adding a new custom ADM template.

4. Click Add and browse to the location where you saved the .adm file that you created in Step 1. Select the file, and then click Open.

5.   The file should now be listed as one of the current policy templates loaded, as shown in Figure 14-48.

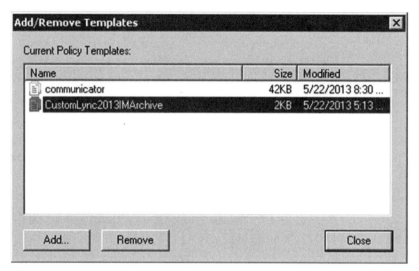

Figure 14-48 Loaded policy templates.

6.   Click Close.

7.   In the Group Policy Management Editor, expand Administrative Templates, and then expand Classic Administrative Templates (ADM). You should see the Microsoft Lync 2013 Custom Compliance Policy Settings folder, as shown in Figure 14-49.

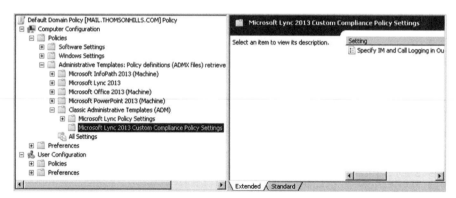

Figure 14-49 Setting the custom ADM.

8.   In the right pane, you should see the policy setting for IM Archiving. Double-click it.

9. In the Specify IM and Call Logging in Outlook dialog box, as shown in Figure 14-50, select Enabled, and then select Lock and turn off Auto Archiving for IMs in the drop-down box. Click OK.

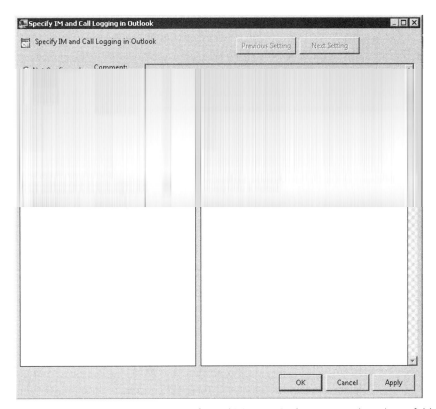

Figure 14-50 Setting the Lync policy for archiving IMs in the Conversation History folder.

10. Log out and log back on to a client machine to refresh the group policy for the user, or simply start a command prompt and enter the following command:

    ```
    gpupdate /force
    ```

11. Start the Lync client and verify that the Save IM conversations in my email Conversation History folder settings are set correctly.

INSIDE OUT   Other policy settings

There are a few more keys and values you can implement. These other registry settings will allow you to lock down the settings, disable the check box for the Save call logs in my email Conversation History folder option, and disable saving IMs:

```
[HKEY_LOCAL_MACHINE\SOFTWARE\Policies\Microsoft\Office\15.0\Lync]

Value Name: CallLogAutoArchivingPolicy
Value Data: REG_DWORD 00000000 or 00000001

Value Name: DisableSavingIM
Value Data: REG_DWORD 00000000 or 00000001
```

Configuring hybrid Lync

A true hybrid Lync implementation is a new feature in Lync 2013. To configure hybrid Lync, you must have met the following requirements:

- Have the latest Office 365 subscription, which comes with Lync Online 2013, and the appropriate Office 365 plan that supports directory synchronization and Active Directory Federation Services (AD FS)

- Implemented directory synchronization

- Implemented AD FS

We covered directory synchronization and AD FS in Chapters 2 and Chapter 3, "Active Directory Federation Services". You should also have on-premises Lync 2013. However, if your users are homed to a Lync 2010 on-premises server, you need to have a Lync 2013 edge server installed.

With these prerequisites met, you can follow these steps to start configuring hybrid Lync:

1. Log on to the Office 365 admin center at *https://portal.microsoftonline.com*, click the Admin menu, and select Lync.

2. Take note of the host name portion of the URL for your Lync admin center, as shown in Figure 14-51. This URL is also where the hosted migration services for Lync reside. You will need this information later, so write it down at this time. As you can see from Figure 14-51, the URL for our instance of the Lync Online admin center is *https:// admin0a.online.lync.com*.

Figure 14-51 URL of the Lync Online admin center.

3. Select organization on the left navigation pane, and then select external communications.

4. Turn on external communications by selecting On except for selected domains.

5. On your Lync 2013 edge server, run the following Windows PowerShell commands:

```
Set-CSAccessEdgeConfiguration -UseDNSSrvRouting -AllowOutsideUsers 1
-AllowFederatedUsers 1

New-CSHostingProvider -Identity LyncOnline -ProxyFqdn "sipfed.online.lync.com"
-Enabled $true -EnabledSharedAddressSpace $true -HostsOCSUsers $true
-VerificationLevel UseSourceVerification -IsLocal $false -AutodiscoverUrl
https://webdir.online.lync.com/Autodiscover/AutodiscoverService.svc/root
```

Notice the new *–EnabledSharedAddressSpace?* parameter. This parameter enables Lync to share a single SIP namespace.

6. You are now ready to move users to Lync Online. Start with a pilot group so you can verify communication across both Lync on-premises and Lync Online users. You can do so by entering the following commands from your Lync Server Management Shell:

```
$creds=Get-Credential
```

```
Move-CsUser -Identity <username@domain.com> -Target sipfed.online.lync.com
-Credentials $creds -HostedMigrationOverrideUrl
<URL>/HostedMigration/hostedmigrationService.svc
```

The *<URL>* for the *–HostedMigrationOverrideUrl* parameter is the URL of your Lync admin center. You took note of that in Step 2 and, in this case, it was *https://admin0a.online.lync.com*. Therefore, the command should look like this if the user you want to move is anna@adatum.com:

```
Move-CsUser -Identity anna@adatum.com -Target sipfed.online.lync.com
-Credentials $creds -HostedMigrationOverrideUrl
https://admin0a.online.lync.com/HostedMigration/hostedmigrationService.svc
```

7. Verify the successful move of the user by entering the following command. The output of the command should specify that the HostingProvider is sipfed.online.lync. com, as shown in Figure 14-52.

```
Get-CsUser -Identity <username@domain.com>
```

For example:

```
Get-CsUser -Identity anna@adatum.com
```

Figure 14-52 Output from *Get-CSUser*.

8. Test to make sure IM and presence are working between users homed to Lync on-premises and those homed to Lync Online.

In this hybrid Lync environment, you can move users from Lync Online back to Lync on-premises by entering the following command:

```
$cred=Get-Credentials
```

```
Move-CsUser -Identity username@domain.com -Target <On-premises Lync server URL>
-credentials $cred -HostedMicrationOverrideURL <URL>
```

For example:

```
Move-CsUser -Identity anna@adatum.com -Target lync.adatum.com -credentials
$cred -HostedMigrationOverrideURL
https://admin0a.online.lync.com/HostedMigration/hostedmigrationService.svc
```

Migration considerations

Traditionally, there is no data migration involved when going from Lync on-premises to Lync Online or from hosted services such as Live Meeting to Lync Online. Specifically, the type of data we are referring to are the users' contact lists and online meetings that have already been scheduled. Therefore, you need to take these into consideration during migration.

capabilities, and concepts. We demonstrated how to create policy files to be deployed through Microsoft Group Policy to enforce settings important for companies who have auditing requirements. Finally, we walked through the planning and deployment considerations necessary to successfully deploy Lync Online in both a dedicated and hybrid deployment.

Lync Online is one of the easiest workloads in Office 365 to deploy and, in many cases, significantly revolutionizes the way organizations communicate. The benefits of deploying Lync Online include tangible cost savings attributed to reduced carbon footprint and reduced printing cost with the use of electronic handouts. Intangible cost savings include increased employee productivity, improved morale, and better compliance through more effective training when using Lync Meeting as a training tool. Let us now proceed to the next chapter to cover the final service in Office 365, which is the Office Professional Plus subscription.

Office 365 Professional Plus

Introduction to the Microsoft Office editions 760   Patching Office 365 ProPlus 774

ProPlus, it contains new features aimed at addressing unique challenges brought on by the proliferation of non-PC, disconnected devices, such as tablets and smartphones. It also introduces a new way in which Office is delivered, activated, and patched through Office 365.

As a consumer, you can now acquire Office as a subscription. For the enterprise, the subscription edition is known as Office 365 ProPlus, which is what we will focus on. The latest version of Office 365 ProPlus is based on Microsoft Office 2013 technologies. In this chapter we will briefly cover the differences between Office 2013 editions, the licensing changes introduced with Office 365 ProPlus, the different deployment and management strategies, and how to customize your Office 365 ProPlus deployment.

The proliferation of tablets and smartphones over the last decade has led to an entire ecosystem of touch-enabled devices that present unique challenges with conventional applications. Office 2013 is designed to take touch computing into consideration. The challenge for Microsoft is to develop the new Office in a fashion that will allow it to be user friendly on touch devices, yet have the same look and feel on non-touch devices to make the cross-training or cross-use experience consistent. This change in Microsoft's direction of application development is most noticeable with the release of Windows 8, where the Start screen tiles are very easy to use on touch-enabled devices.

The trend of users having multiple devices also highlighted a new challenge for the traditional licensing model for Microsoft Office, which is per-device licensing. Microsoft needed a way to provide users the ability to run the Office applications they need, regardless of the device they are using them on. As such, with Office Subscription, Microsoft has shifted to a per-user licensing model, which we will take a closer look at later in the chapter.

Another challenge created by the proliferation of mobile platforms has been the processor architecture. The need for a version of Microsoft Office that can run on ARM-based processors was clear as it became the popular processor architecture for mobile devices due to form factor and low power consumption.

Finally, deployment of Microsoft Office has always been a daunting task for many organizations. Challenges associated with Microsoft Office upgrades include the following:

- Training users on the new Office graphical user interface (GUI)need any caps?

- Compatibility with third-party Office plug-ins or extensions

- Compatibility with the underlying operating system

- Managing deployments on growing number of devices because of the bring your own device (BYOD) trend

These are some of the primary industry trends and challenges that the new Microsoft Office seeks to address.

Introduction to the Microsoft Office editions

It is important to note that Microsoft Office 365 ProPlus, which is licensed and delivered through Office 365, is the fully functional, rich Office client application and should not be confused with Office Web Apps. Office 365 ProPlus is the Office 2013 software that actually gets installed on a computer. As such, all the hardware and operating system requirements for Office 2013 are needed.

Microsoft Office 2013 comes in twelve different editions, including three editions for retail outlets, two editions for volume licensing channels, and five subscription-based editions available through the Microsoft Office 365 program. Office Web Apps and Office RT are options for the Surface RT, tablets, and mobile devices.

There is a 32-bit and 64-bit version of Office 365 ProPlus. Traditional software deployment tools such as System Center Configuration manager can also be used to deploy Office 365 ProPlus. The primary differences between Office 365 ProPlus and volume licensing versions are the following:

- Microsoft Office 365 ProPlus is licensed per user, while the other versions are licensed per device.

- Activation of Office 365 ProPlus is handled by Office 365 using the user login credentials, while the other versions use a product key or a Key Management Server (KMS).

The following Microsoft Office 2013 editions cater to individuals, home users, or small business users:

- Office Home Premium

- Office Home & Student 2013

- Office Home & Business 2013

Office 365 ProPlus is designed for enterprises and can be purchased independently or through the A3, G3, or E3 Office 365 Suite. Office 365 ProPlus contains the following productivity tools:

- Microsoft Word 2013

- Microsoft PowerPoint 2013

- Microsoft Excel 2013

- Microsoft OneNote 2013

- Microsoft Outlook 2013

- Microsoft Access 2013

- Microsoft Publisher 2013

- Microsoft InfoPath Designer 2013

Some of the new features of Office 365 ProPlus are the following:

- Click-to-Run installation and software update management, which enables you to have Office up and running fast, often in less than two minutes.

- Coexistence with a previous version of Office.

- Updates delivered to users without interruption. Updates are cached in the background and applied the next time a user closes and re-starts Office.

Chapter 15

- The five instances of Office allowed per user are tracked by Office 365 through users' accounts, and therefore minimizes licensing issues and eliminates the risk of compromised software activation keys.

The improvements in Office 365 ProPlus based on Office 2013 technology should make it the easiest version of Office to deploy.

INSIDE OUT   Office for Mac

Microsoft recognizes that enterprise organizations might need Office for Mac computers. Therefore, Office 365 also provides access to Office for Mac 2011. See *http://community.office365.com/en-us/wikis/mac/default.aspx* **for more information about configuring Office 365 for the Mac.**

Office ProPlus Service Description

Like all the other services in Office 365, there is a Service Description for Office 365 ProPlus. See *http://technet.microsoft.com/en-us/library/jj819251.aspx* for more information on the Office 365 ProPlus Service Description.

Deploying Office 365 ProPlus

Office 365 ProPlus can be deployed in the following ways:

- Have users install Office 365 ProPlus Subscription from the Office 365 portal using the new Click-to-Run installation method. We will discuss Click-to-Run in detail in the "Office Click-to-Run and activations" section later in this chapter.

- Customize and deploy Click-to-Run through a file share.

The new Click-to-Run installation method for Office 365 ProPlus is different from deploying Office through a Microsoft Installer (MSI) package. Table 15-1 details the different deployment methods supported by the MSI deployment method versus the Click-to-Run method of deployment.

TABLE 15-1 Difference between MSI and Click-to-Run

Deployment method	Windows Installer (MSI)	Click-to-Run	More information
Local installation source	Yes	Yes	For Windows Installer-based versions of Office, Deploy Office 2013 from a local installation scripts: *http://technet.microsoft. com/en-us/library/ff602181.aspx.*
System Center 2012 Configuration Manager	Yes	Yes	*http://technet.microsoft.com/ library/gg682129.aspx*
Windows Intune	Yes	Yes	*http://go.microsoft.com/FWLink/ p/?LinkID=268147*
Remote Desktop Services	Yes	No	Remote Desktop Services in Windows Server 2008 R2: *http:// technet.microsoft.com/library/ dd647502(WS.10).aspx.* Remote Desktop Services in Windows Server 2012: *http://technet. microsoft.com/library/hh831447. aspx.*
Microsoft Application Virtualization (App-V) 5.0	No	Yes	Earlier versions of App-V are not supported to deploy Office 2013. Microsoft Office 2013 App-V packages: *http://www.microsoft. com/en-us/download/details. aspx?id=30423.*
Microsoft Deployment Toolkit (MDT) 2012	Yes	Yes	*http://technet.microsoft.com/ en-us/solutionaccelerators/ dd407791.aspx.*

Chapter 15

Office Click-to-Run and activations

The shift to a Microsoft Office per-user licensing model created a need to track and ensure that no more than five activations of Office are active at any point of time. A system of tracking this must not be burdensome to IT personnel, so the logical solution is to rely on each user's Office 365 account to track Office activations.

Office 365 ProPlus is activated at the time of execution and not during installation. This is done by prompting the user for their Office 365 logon credentials. If the user initiated the installation through the portal, that copy of the installation will be activated after installation is completed.

Office 365 ProPlus is streamed to the desktop in a persistent fashion through a process called Click-to-Run. Click-to-Run is based on Microsoft Application Virtualization (App-V) technology. The priority of Office features being streamed are based on usage analytics that Microsoft has gathered. That is why a user can start using Office within seconds instead of having to wait for many minutes for the entire installation to complete. The features are streamed in the background until the entire Office suite is streamed to the desktop. If a user selects a feature that has not been streamed yet, that feature will be re-prioritized and is immediately streamed. Figure 15-1 shows Office 365 ProPlus being streamed in the background through Click-to-Run. In the meantime, the user is able to start using Microsoft Word.

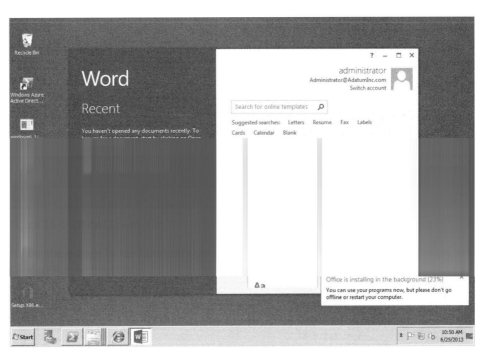

Figure 15-1 Office Click-to-Run.

Follow these steps to see how users can install Office 365 ProPlus from the portal using the Click-to-Run technology:

1. Log on to the Office 365 portal at *https://portal.microsoftonline.com*.

2. Click the gear at the upper-right corner and select Office 365 settings, as shown in Figure 15-2.

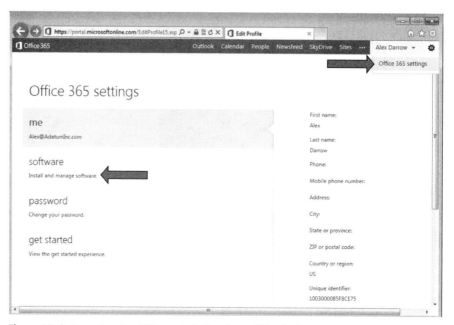

Figure 15-2 Accessing the Office installation from Office 365.

3. Select software from the Office 365 settings page.

4. Select Office, the language, and whether to install the 32-bit or 64-bit version. Then click install, as shown in Figure 15-3.

Figure 15-3 Office installation options.

After Office has been installed, the name of the computer that it was installed on is listed on the software page. The user can see all the computers that have Office 365 ProPlus installed and activated. There is also the option to deactivate a computer to release activation instances, as shown in Figure 15-4.

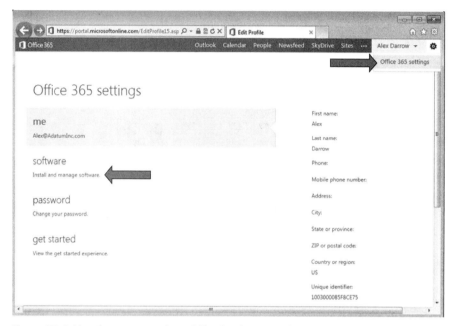

Figure 15-4 List of computers where Office has been activated.

INSIDE OUT Installation versus activation

As you can see, there is now a distinction between installation and activation of Office as a subscription. A mindset change is needed where you will no longer care about installations. After a computer is deactivated, it will not remove Office from the computer. It just releases one of the five licenses so that it can be activated on another computer. The deactivated computer will prompt for an Office 365 logon credential to reactivate the software. If no valid Office 365 credential is provided, a grace period of 30 days will be granted; after that, if Office is still not activated, it will revert to reduced functionality mode. Therefore, administrators and users no longer need to worry about uninstalling Office from computers to remain compliant with the number of purchased Office licenses.

Customizing Click-to-Run

Your organization's administrators can customize Click-to-Run by using the Office Deployment Tool. The Office Deployment Tool can be downloaded at the Microsoft Download Center at *http://www.microsoft.com/en-us/download/details.aspx?id=36778*.

With the Office Deployment Tool, administrators can perform the following tasks:

Modes

To use the Office Deployment Tool, your administrators will need to run it with one of the following command-line modes:

- */help*

- */download*

- */configure*

- */packager*

/help mode

The */help* mode provides detailed information about all the other modes. The following is the syntax for this command:

```
setup.exe /help
```

Setup.exe refers to the Office Deployment Tool executable.

/download mode

The */download* mode downloads Click-to-Run source files for Office 365 and is perhaps the most common mode that is used if there is a need to customize the behavior of Click-to-Run. The following is the syntax for this command:

```
setup.exe /download <path and name of configuration .xml file>
```

Chapter 15

The configuration .xml file is used to specify Click-to-Run update options, and the Office Deployment Tool package that you downloaded contains a sample Configuration.xml file that you can use as a template and modify to meet your organization's needs. The configuration .xml file allows you to specifically perform the following tasks:

- Add or remove products from the installation

- Add or remove languages from the installation

- Specify display options

- Set logging options

- Specify software updates behavior for Click-to-Run

A sample configuration .xml file is shown in Figure 15-5. This configuration file, when used with the */download* mode, will download Office 365 ProPlus Click-to-Run English source files to the *\\server\share* location.

```
<Configuration>
  <Add SourcePath="\\server\share" OfficeClientEdition="32">
    <Product ID="O365ProPlusRetail" >
      <Language ID="en-us" />
    </Product>
  </Add>
</Configuration>
```

Figure 15-5 Sample configuration .xml file for the Office Deployment Tool.

> **Note**
> A comprehensive Click-to-Run configuration .xml file reference is available at *http://technet.microsoft.com/en-us/library/jj219426.aspx*.

/configure mode

The */configure* mode installs or removes Click-to-Run Office 365 ProPlus products and languages and allows you to apply customized options. Like the */download* mode, the /

configure mode also relies on a configuration .xml file to specify the options. The following is the syntax for this command:

```
setup.exe /configure <path and name of configuration .xml file>
```

INSIDE OUT   **Using the same configuration .xml file**

The /packager mode creates App-V packages from Office 365 ProPlus Click-to-Run sources. This mode converts the Click-to-Run sources into an App-V package so that it can be used in an App-V environment. The following is the syntax for this command:

```
setup.exe /packager <path of Configuration.xml file> <output path>
```

The output path is the location to place the newly created App-V package.

> **Note**
>
> For a roadmap of Office 365 ProPlus deployment, see *http://technet.microsoft.com/en-us/library/jj839718.aspx*. The roadmap provides details and resources for the deployment of Office 365 ProPlus.

Difference between Click-to-Run and MSI

MSI deployment of Office is now applicable only for Office acquired through volume licensing. Office 365 ProPlus and retail versions of Office 2013 use the Click-to-Run deployment method. Because most readers are familiar with the MSI deployment, we have summarized the differences between Click-to-Run and MSI in Table 15-2.

Chapter 15

TABLE 15-2 Difference between MSI and Click-to-Run

Area of comparison	Windows Installer (MSI)	Click-to-Run
Applicable to which edition of Office?	Office acquired through volume licensing.	Subscription (for example, Office 365 ProPlus) and Retail (for example, Office Professional 2013).
Activation	Device-based.	User-based.
Installation time	You have to wait until the entire Office product is installed before you can open and start to use the product. If you also have to apply any updates or service packs, the required installation time increases.	You can start to use Office before the product is completely installed. Under normal conditions, you can have Office up and running in a few minutes.
Updates	Updates and service packs have to be downloaded and then applied. You can choose the updates and service packs that you want to apply to your Office installations. For example, you can decide that you want to apply all updates for Excel, but only apply critical updates for Word.	Click-to-Run products that you download and install from Microsoft are up-to-date from the start. You will not have to download and apply any updates or service packs immediately after you install the products. By default, Click-to-Run products are configured to be updated automatically over time. Users do not have to download or install updates. Updates are seamlessly applied in the background. You cannot specify which particular updates or service packs to apply to your Office installations. You cannot use standard update processes, such as Windows Update or Windows Server Update Services (WSUS), to apply updates.

Area of comparison	Windows Installer (MSI)	Click-to-Run
Customizations	Highly customizable. For example, you can specify which products and features to install or specify where product shortcuts are displayed. To customize installation settings,	Limited customization available. For example, you cannot specify the drive on which to install Office. You cannot specify which

fice-specific Adminis-
trative Template files
(ADMX/ADML)

Chapter 15

> **Note**
>
> "Who Moved My MSI" is a great video highlighting the differences between Click-to-Run and MSI. See *http://blogs.technet.com/b/office_resource_kit/archive/2013/03/05/ the-new-office-garage-series-who-moved-my-msi.aspx*.

Office on Demand

Office on Demand is a special instance of the Office 365 ProPlus being streamed to a computer without using one of the five licenses. Microsoft's strategy with Office and Office Web Apps is to ensure all mobile scenarios are addressed. This particular feature addresses the following scenario:

- The user has access to a computer that does not have Office installed but is connected to the Internet.

- The user needs *ad-hoc* use of an Office application.

If Office Web Apps is not sufficient in this situation, a user can access SkyDrive Pro and select the Use Office On Demand option, as shown in Figure 15-6. The user will then be provided with a page to select the Office application to stream.

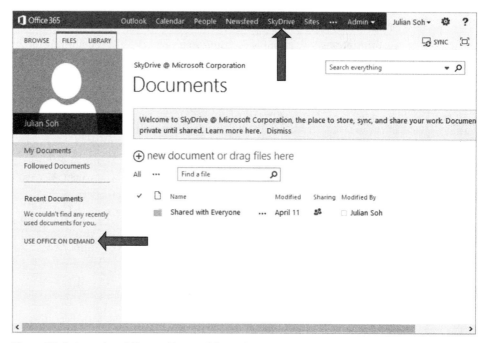

Figure 15-6 Accessing Office on Demand from SkyDrive Pro.

Office on Demand streams individual Office applications and is available only during the session. After the application is streamed, the user can use it offline and the application continues to be available until it is closed or the computer is shut down.

Patching Office 365 ProPlus

By default, Office 365 ProPlus is updated through Office 365 and features a new patching strategy:

- The Office rich client determines which updates are applicable from a single update package.

- The updates are applied in the background and become effective the next time Office is re-started, thereby minimizing interruption to the end user.

Instead of getting updates from Office 365, your administrators can use the Office Deployment Tool and the /configure command mode to specify the update path for Office 365 ProPlus. The configuration .xml file will need to contain the following setting:

```
<updates Enabled = "TRUE" UpdatePath="\\server01\updates">
```

Managing and deploying Office 365 ProPlus

There are additional options and requirements when planning to deploy the latest version of Office 365 ProPlus. This section details some universal considerations.

System requirements

Because the latest Office 365 ProPlus is based on Office 2013, the operating system require

doing complex tasks that might require using a lot of memory. There are some use cases where complex Excel files and Access applications will require the 64-bit version to perform adequately, in which case the 64-bit version should be deployed. The technical guideline is to deploy the 64-bit version if Office consumes more than 3 GB of memory when the user is using it. Careful evaluation of your environment's third-party software will identify if there will be potential application compatibility issues with the 64-bit version of Office 365 ProPlus.

Group Policy

You can use Office-specific Group Policy settings to create and enforce standard configurations of Office 365 ProPlus. These settings can be applied to users and computers that are in an Active Directory domain. These Group Policy settings apply whether Office 365 ProPlus is deployed from the Office 365 portal or from an on-premises location. The latest Office 2013 Group Policy Template files (ADMX) can be downloaded from the Microsoft Download Center at *http://www.microsoft.com/en-us/download/details.aspx?id=35554*. After installed, you can manage Office 365 ProPlus settings through Group Policy Objects (GPOs), as shown in Figure 15-7.

Chapter 15

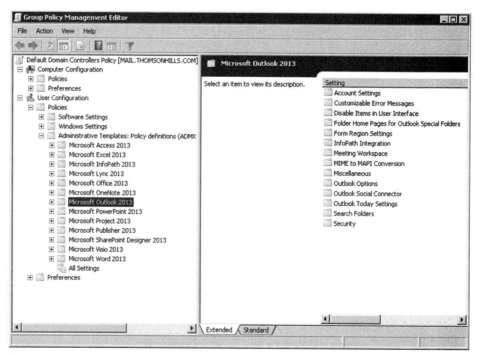

Figure 15-7 Office 2013 ADMX template.

Virtualization

You can deploy Office 365 ProPlus to a virtual desktop, but the virtual desktop must be assigned to a single user.

To use Remote Desktop Services, you must use a non-subscription version of Office Professional Plus 2013. The Office programs that are included with Office Professional Plus 2013 are the same programs that are included with Office 365 ProPlus.

The reason why a dedicated virtual desktop is required for Office 365 ProPlus is because of the requirement to associate an activated computer to an Office 365 user account. This is not possible if a virtual desktop is not persistently assigned to a user.

INSIDE OUT   Office subscription might not work for certain individuals

Sometimes, part of your organization might need to use Remote Desktop, or you might have employees who share computers. In such scenarios, Office 365 ProPlus installations might not work because of the per-user activation requirement. This does not necessarily mean that Office 365 is not the right program for you. Talk to your Microsoft representative because they might be able to help you justify exceptions for certain groups,

Visio, or SharePoint Designer because these are not part of Office 365 ProPlus.

Office 365 ProPlus common errors

There are some common errors a user might encounter with Office 365 ProPlus. The following sections describe the errors and recommend actions that might fix the problems.

Microsoft Office subscription error

When starting an Office application, the user encounters the Microsoft Office Subscription Error message. This error indicates there is a problem with the Office 365 ProPlus installation. Uninstalling and reinstalling Office 365 ProPlus should resolve this problem.

Office subscription removed

If a user sees the Office Subscription Removed error message, verify that the user's Office ProPlus licensing has not been removed. This error could also occur if the computer was de-provisioned by the user. Check these two conditions and uninstall and reinstall Office 365 ProPlus.

No subscription found

If a user sees the No Subscription Found error message, verify that the user has been provided with Office ProPlus licensing through Office 365. Then have the user click the retry button.

Activation error

If a user sees the Activation Error message, check the following:

- Verify that the computer has an Internet connection. This is needed only during activation. For other times, the computer can work offline with Office 365 ProPlus.

- Ensure that port 443 (HTTPS) of the Internet connection is not blocked.

- If your organization has a proxy server and the Automatically detect settings check box needs to be cleared for the local area network (LAN) settings in your browser, then run the following command:

```
bitsamin /util /setieproxy networkservice MANUAL_PROXY
<proxy_server_name>:<port>
```

> **Note**
>
> For more information about the BITSAdmin tool, see *http://msdn.microsoft.com/en-us/library/aa362813(VS.85).aspx*.

After checking all the preceding settings, if the user still sees the Activation Error message, then repair the Office 365 ProPlus installation.

Summary

In this chapter we introduced Click-to-Run, the new delivery method for Office 2013. We also highlighted the difference between Click-to-Run and the traditional MSI delivery method. We saw that Office 365 ProPlus can coexist with an older version of Office, thereby making transitions a lot smoother than before. We also introduced the concept of Office as a subscription and the shift from per-device licensing to per-user licensing. Finally, we introduced Office on Demand, an *ad-hoc* way to access Office applications. The key takeaway for Office 365 ProPlus is that it is designed for the modern mobile workforce and addresses the bring your own device (BYOD) phenomenon. Office 365 ProPlus is the simplest service to deploy because it is very similar to deploying another version of the Office rich client, only easier with Click-to-Run.

PART 5

Advanced topics: Incorporating Office 365 with

CHAPTER 16

Advanced concepts and scenarios for Office 365 . . . . **781**

Advanced concepts and scenarios for Office 365

Introduction to Forefront Identity Manager 783   Office 365 and FIM architecture to support multi-

vices. There are also new identity workloads, such as multi-factor authentication, that are being introduced in Office 365, so we will spend some time discussing these new services.

The following core technologies support these advanced Office 365 concepts and scenarios:

- Forefront Identity Manager (FIM)

- Windows Azure Infrastructure as a Service (IaaS)

- Windows Azure Multi-Factor Authentication (previously known as PhoneFactor)

Microsoft Windows Azure recently debuted its IaaS offering. Together with FIM, these technologies provide support for additional Office 365 adoption scenarios. Windows Azure IaaS should not be confused with Windows Azure Active Directory, nor should it be confused with Windows SQL Azure or other products that fall under the Windows Azure branding. In this chapter, when we refer to Windows Azure we are specifically referring to the Windows Azure IaaS offering.

> **Note**
> Going into the details of installing and configuring FIM or Windows Azure is beyond the scope of this book. In this chapter, we will introduce the concepts of how complex and more advanced scenarios are addressed in an Office 365 implementation. Implementing solutions for these advanced scenarios usually require specialized services such as Microsoft Cloud Vantage. For more information about Microsoft Cloud Vantage, see *http://www.microsoft.com/en-us/microsoftservices/cloud_vantage_services.aspx*.

Frequently, organizations undergo changes where mergers, acquisitions, growth, splits, collapses, and consolidations are part of their evolution. These changes in the organization's business usually require some level of restructuring. These changes impact the IT resources and users associated with them. Organizational changes have led to AD forests needing be merged, split, dissolved, and so on. As a result, there might be a need to temporarily or permanently support multiple AD forests, which in turn affects how Office 365 is being incorporated.

Users, groups, and computer objects, at a minimum, are stored in AD and need to be managed through any organizational changes. Each of these objects exists inside a Windows domain, which is a logical group of network objects (computers, users, and devices) that share the same AD database. Each person who uses computers within a domain receives his own unique account. This account can then be assigned access to resources within the domain and ultimately within Office 365.

Domain controllers (DCs) are responsible for managing all security-related aspects between a user and a domain, including authentication. Domain controllers replicate objects for redundancy and local service availability. AD is a hierarchical structure that consists of the forest at the topmost layer followed by trees and finally domains. A tree is a collection of one or more domains sharing the same namespace. A domain is defined as a logical group of objects such as computers and devices. In Office 365, there generally is a requirement for a 1:1 relationship between a forest and the Office 365 tenant. Multiple trees and domains within a single forest typically do not affect how Office 365 is incorporated. However, an organization with multiple AD forests will need to be handled differently. This is often referred to as a multi-forest Office 365 deployment. Figure 16-1 illustrates a forest with multiple trees and domains.

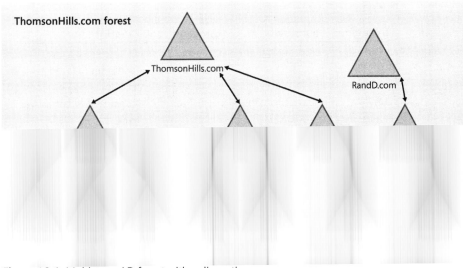

Figure 16-1 Multi-tree, AD forest with a discontinuous namespace.

Trusts

In multi-forest scenarios, trust is an important capability to understand when incorporating Office 365. Trusts are authentication pathways that must be present for users in one forest to access resources in another forest without additional authentication, much like single sign-on (SSO). When AD is initially set up, two transitive, two-way default trusts are established:

- **Parent and child**   Authentication requests made from subordinate domains flow upward through their parent to the trusting domain.

- **Tree-root**   Created when a new domain tree is created within the forest.

Frequently, when organizations go through changes such as acquisitions, they are left with multiple forests that need to trust one another to facilitate various business needs, such as seeing one another's calendar for free/busy times, granting access to SharePoint sites, and so on. To facilitate these requirements, additional trusts might need to be created. Four other types of trusts can be created using the New Trust Wizard or the Netdom command-line tool. Table 16-1 details the four trust types and their differences.

TABLE 16-1 Summary of trust types and options

Trust type	Transitivity	Direction	Description
External	Non-transitive	One-way or two-way	Use external trusts to provide access to resources located on a Windows domain or a domain located in a separate forest that is not joined by a forest trust.
Realm	Transitive or non-transitive	One-way or two-way	Use realm trusts to form a trust relationship between a non-Windows Kerberos realm and a Windows domain.
Forest	Transitive	One-way or two-way	Use forest trusts to share resources between forests. If a forest trust is a two-way trust, authentication requests made in either forest can reach the other forest.
Shortcut	Transitive	One-way or two-way	Use shortcut trusts to improve user logon times between two domains within a Windows forest. This is useful when two domains are separated by two domain trees.

When creating external, shortcut, realm, or forest trusts, you have the option to create each side of the trust separately or both sides of a trust simultaneously. If you choose to create each side of the trust separately, then you will need to run the New Trust Wizard twice, once for each domain. As a security best practice, all trust passwords should be strong passwords. You will need domain administrator credentials for each domain in which you are creating a trust.

INSIDE OUT   Trust setup tip

If you choose to create each side of the trust separately, you will need to use the same password for each side.

External and forest trusts will be the most common type of trust used with Office 365 due to the need to share one AD forest's security principals with another's. External trusts are individual trusts between a domain in one forest and a domain in another forest. This trust type is useful when you only want to share resources from a single domain in a forest with a single domain in another forest. If a forest has a single domain, it is in essence the same as a forest trust. Forest trusts are created at the root domain of a forest and connect to the root domain of the remote, or target, forest. As outlined in Table 16-1, forest trusts can be one-way or two-way.

One-way forest trusts

One-way forest trusts allow members of the "trusted" forest to access resources in the "trusting" forest. In a one-way trust, users in the trusted forest can access resources in the

For more information on AD trusts, see the following resources:

- General guidelines for trusts: *http://technet.microsoft.com/en-us/library/ cc786873(v=ws.10).aspx*

- When to create an external trust: *http://technet.microsoft.com/en-us/library/ cc755427(v=ws.10).aspx*

- When to create a forest trust: *http://technet.microsoft.com/en-us/library/ cc773010(v=ws.10).aspx*

- When to create a shortcut trust: *http://technet.microsoft.com/en-us/library/ cc737939(v=ws.10).aspx*

- When to create a realm trust: *http://technet.microsoft.com/en-us/library/ cc740052(v=ws.10).aspx*

- Trust transitivity: *http://technet.microsoft.com/en-us/library/cc739693(v=ws.10).aspx*

- Trust direction: *http://technet.microsoft.com/en-us/library/cc728024(v=ws.10).aspx*

Chapter 16

Introduction to Forefront Identity Manager

FIM 2010 R2 Service Pack 1 is an Identity Management (IDM) solution that provides users a common identity across heterogeneous systems. FIM provides a user management environment that can span systems, data centers, and companies' IDM repositories, enabling users to access what they need in a managed and auditable way. Although FIM is used only for Office 365 user provisioning in multi-forest scenarios, it can also be leveraged for other non-Office 365 capabilities, such as empowering users to be self-sufficient by allowing them to manage their own identities, group memberships, distribution list memberships, certificates, password recovery, and so on.

INSIDE OUT   FIM licensing

Like most Microsoft technologies, FIM has a server license component and a per user client access license (CAL) component. If you are using FIM for user provisioning in Office 365 without using any of the user self-service components, then only the server license is required. CALs are NOT required when using FIM for Office 365 directory synchronization in multi-forest scenarios, as long as the user portal and self-service capabilities of FIM are not being used.

FIM also includes the Microsoft BHOLD Suite, which adds Role Based Access Control (RBAC), as we discussed in Chapter 5, "Monitoring Office 365 with System Center", allowing admins the ability to audit access rights in the environment. FIM's key capabilities include the following:

- **Policy management**   SharePoint-based console for policy authoring, enforcement and auditing; extensible WS-* APIs; and Windows Workflow Foundation workflows and heterogeneous identity synchronization and consistency

- **Credential management**   Heterogeneous certificate management with third-party CA support, management of multiple credential types, self-service password reset integrated with Windows logon, as well as web-based tool and integrated provisioning of identities, credentials, and resources

- **User management**   Automated, codeless user provisioning and de-provisioning, and self-service user profile management

- **Group management**   Rich Office-based, self-service group management tools; offline approvals through Office; and group and distribution list management, which includes dynamic membership calculation in these groups and DLs based on a user's attributes

- **Access management**   Preventative role-based access control, rule enforcement through segregation of duties, and self-service access request and automated approval workflow

- **Compliance**   Rule-based analytics of access, access re-certification and attestation,

Figure 16-2 Forefront Identity Manager 2010 R2 web portal.

FIM uses Windows Workflow Foundation (WF), a Microsoft technology that provides an application program interface (API), an in-process workflow engine, and a designer to implement long-running processes such as workflows within .NET Framework applications. The use of WF allows FIM to run transactional workflows to manage and update changes to a user's identity.

FIM is a robust product, capable of consolidating IDs across cross-platform systems, centralizing smart card provisioning and management, centrally enforcing identity policy, and providing in-depth auditing and reporting using Microsoft SQL Server.

> **Note**
>
> For more information on Forefront Identity Manager 2012, see *http://technet.microsoft. com/en-us/library/ee621258(v=ws.10).aspx*.

Office 365 and FIM architecture to support multi-forest scenarios

The role of FIM with the Windows Azure Active Directory (AAD) connector in Office 365 is to specifically replace the free version of the Windows Azure Active Directory synchronization tool. FIM with AAD addresses scenarios that the latter cannot support. In such scenarios, FIM with AAD is responsible for synchronizing user accounts in AD and Office 365. Specifically, what FIM with AAD brings to the table that the Windows Azure Active Directory synchronization tool does not is the ability to handle complex, multiple AD forests or multiple, disparate identity management solutions. FIM also provides connectors, sometimes referred to as management agents, for various IDMs including SAP, Oracle, and PeopleSoft. The terms *connector* and *management agent* are used interchangeability and are synonymous, but to avoid confusion between the System Center Operations Manager (SCOM) management agent and the FIM management agent, we will try to refer to the latter as a connector. In fact, AAD is a type of FIM connector.

INSIDE OUT FIM management agents

Do not confuse FIM management agents with the System Center Operations Manager management agent for FIM. FIM management agents are the connectors to different IDMs. For a detailed list and discussion of FIM management agents, see *http://social. technet.microsoft.com/wiki/contents/articles/1589.fim-2010-management-agents-from-partners.aspx*. For more information about out-of-the-box FIM connectors, see *http:// technet.microsoft.com/en-us/library/jj863241(v=ws.10).aspx*.

Microsoft recommends using the Windows Azure Active Directory Sync tool whenever there are no technical requirements that can be addressed only by using FIM. The biggest issue with multiple IDMs in Office 365 is how a unique identifier can be established. On-premises IDM and Office 365 are bound by a unique identifier for user accounts. In a multi-forest environment, for example, there is a need to establish the unique identifier across all forests and then replicate it to Office 365.

Furthermore, replication is only part of the identity management process. There is still the authentication aspect and single sign on. If each forest remains responsible for authenticating users through SSO, then the users need to be identified with different namespaces. This is needed so Office 365 knows which Active Directory Federation Services (AD FS) service to use for authentication requests.

At the time of this writing, implementing FIM for multi-forest and multi-IDM Office 365 scenarios with multiple Exchange organizations is supported only with the engagement of Microsoft Cloud Vantage Services providing the implementation.

INSIDE OUT   **FIM version required for the AAD connector**

The FIM AAD connector will require FIM 2010 R2 with hotfix KB2849119 or later (*http://support.microsoft.com/kb/2849119*). This will be FIM version 4.1.3451. It must be this version or later to support the AAD connector. Contact your Microsoft representative if you are interested in evaluating the AAD connector prior to final release.

Let us look at a few scenarios in which FIM is deployed as the IDM management tool when incorporating Office 365.

Scenario 1: Direct synchronization

In this scenario, FIM is used to directly replicate identities from disparate IDMs into Office 365. Figure 16-3 depicts this scenario.

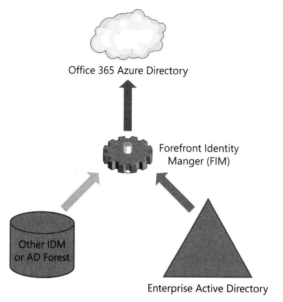

Office 365 Azure Directory

Forefront Identity Manger (FIM)

Other IDM or AD Forest

Enterprise Active Directory

Figure 16-3 FIM synchronizing a third-party IDM and AD identities into Office 365.

With FIM connectors specific to AD and the other IDM, FIM can connect to different identity solutions and then configure to replicate user identities through the AAD connector into Office 365. FIM uses a SQL database to track the state of synchronized objects, which is known as the FIM metaverse. Each time FIM runs, it will carry out only delta changes, thereby making the synchronization highly efficient. The metaverse is also where rules are created so that identity properties can be combined and transformed to create a well-formed, unique identifier.

The benefit of this approach is that it is straightforward, and the business requirement to keep the management of both directories separate is preserved.

Scenario 2: Indirect synchronization

This scenario uses FIM to first make a consolidated copy of all identities into an enterprise AD, and then replicate the identities into Office 365 through the AAD connector. Figure 16-4 depicts the workflow of this setup. Such scenarios are common when there is a concurrent AD consolidation project occurring as part of an Office 365 adoption.

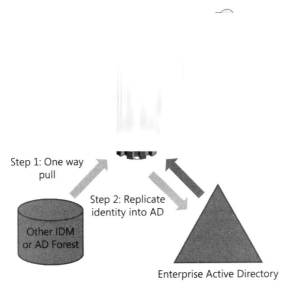

Figure 16-4 Creating copies of identities in AD before synchronization to Office 365.

With respect to Office 365, the end result with this scenario is the same as the one in the first scenario. Office 365 still gets a single view of the entire organization's identities, yet keeps the management of those identities separate in the respective IDMs. As mentioned earlier, because the accounts are synchronized into an AD, this model can also serve as a great approach for IDM consolidation initiatives.

Scenario 3: Account forest and resource forest scenario

Similar to scenario 1, an organization might have an AD forest that contains user accounts and a separate AD forest that is a resource forest that contains disabled accounts. A typical Exchange resource forest that is separate from an account forest is a common scenario. In this multi-forest scenario, FIM combines the AD properties from both forests to create a unique identifier for the user accounts with all the required properties, and then combines the information to provision the user in Office 365, as shown in Figure 16-5.

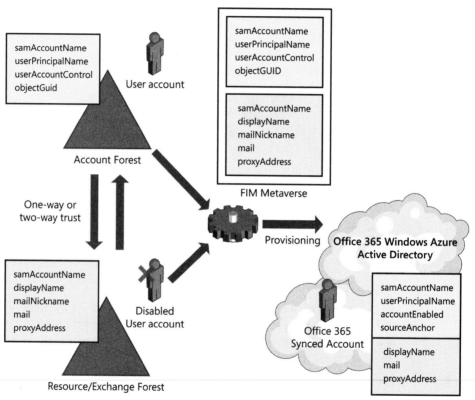

Figure 16-5 Provisioning users with FIM in an account-resource forest scenario.

FIM and the AAD are the primary user provisioning and de-provisioning tools for multi-forest and multi-IDM scenarios. FIM can also be used to transform identity properties prior to provisioning a user. For example, if you want to ensure that an office phone number has an area code included so everyone's contact information is consistent, you can achieve it with FIM. Finally, if you want to filter objects that should not be provisioned in Office 365, you can accomplish it by creating appropriate FIM filter rules.

Windows Azure

One of the challenges organizations face when adopting Office 365 is the conflict between service reliability versus convenient end-user experience. Specifically, organizations are very attracted to the level of scalability, reliability, and redundancy that Office 365 offers. These capabilities are usually at a level much higher than what an organization can independently achieve with on-premises infrastructure alone. However, there is also a desire to make

only domain controller (RODC) as well as AD FS within Windows Azure. Now, the AD FS service will be able to authenticate users for Office 365 even if the organization's on-premises infrastructure is down. This is also a great solution for organizations that want to minimize their on-premises infrastructure requirements.

Office 365 on-premises dependencies supported in Windows Azure

As we have seen throughout the book, there are several on-premises dependencies that Office 365 leverages. However, not all roles are supported in Windows Azure.

> **Note**
> KB 2721672 at *http://support.microsoft.com/kb/2721672* lists all the roles that are supported in Windows Azure. Any role that is not specifically mentioned should be considered as not supported in Windows Azure.

For Office 365, the following relevant roles are supported in Windows Azure:

- Windows Server
- Windows Server Active Directory Services (domain controllers)
- Windows Server AD FS

- Domain Name System (DNS) server

- FIM

The Exchange Server roles are not supported, so for hybrid Exchange scenarios you should not put the Exchange Central Authentication Service (CAS) server role in Windows Azure.

Identity and SSO for Office 365 in Windows Azure

As you can see from the preceding list, all identity roles can be deployed in Windows Azure. This provides two identity management scenarios in addition to one where everything is built on an on-premises infrastructure. Windows Azure enables the following two identity management scenarios:

- **Scenario 1**   All Office 365 identity management components deployed in Windows Azure. This is a complete cloud deployment of directory synchronization and AD FS in Windows Azure and eliminates the need for any on-premises servers.

- **Scenario 2**   Office 365 identity management components deployed in Windows Azure for disaster recovery and failover purposes. This is a hybrid cloud identity model with a duplication of identity components that are on-premises into Windows Azure, but used only for disaster recovery or failover purposes.

When deploying SSO in Windows Azure, it is highly recommended that both a DC and AD FS be deployed together. Although you can deploy just AD FS in Windows Azure and keep DCs on-premises, this may lead to authentication latency as AD FS communicates with on-premises DCs. Furthermore, if the connection between Windows Azure and the on-premises network is affected, then AD FS will not be able to communicate with the DCs and therefore will not be able to authenticate users. Thus, it does not meet heightened fault tolerance objectives that can be derived from cloud services if you just have AD FS without a corresponding DC replica in Windows Azure. Figure 16-6 shows this architecture. If the virtual private network (VPN) connection between on-premises and Windows Azure is severed, AD replication will be temporarily affected, but the continued availability of the DC replica in Windows Azure will ensure authentication services continue to be available to Office 365 federated users.

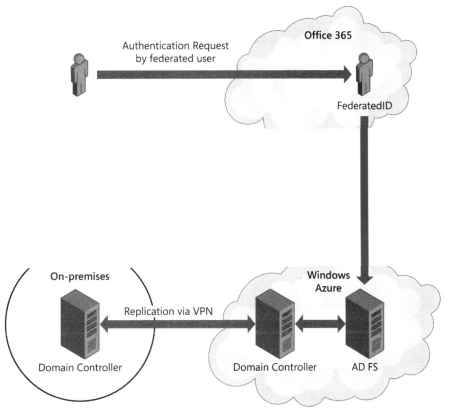

Figure 16-6 SSO authentication workflow with a DC and AD FS in Windows Azure.

INSIDE OUT   Guidelines for deploying AD roles in Windows Azure

Microsoft provides a guideline for deploying AD roles in Windows Azure that includes security best practices together with deployment scenarios. To view this guideline, see *http://msdn.microsoft.com/en-us/library/windowsazure/jj156090.aspx#BKMK_Scenarios*. In addition, if your forest has multiple domains, you will need to deploy at least one DC for each domain.

Scenario 1: All Office 365 identity management components deployed in Windows Azure

The architecture of Figure 16-6 can be expanded to include the directory synchronization workload so that all identity management components required for Office 365 provisioning and SSO can be fully accommodated in Windows Azure, as shown in Figure 16-7.

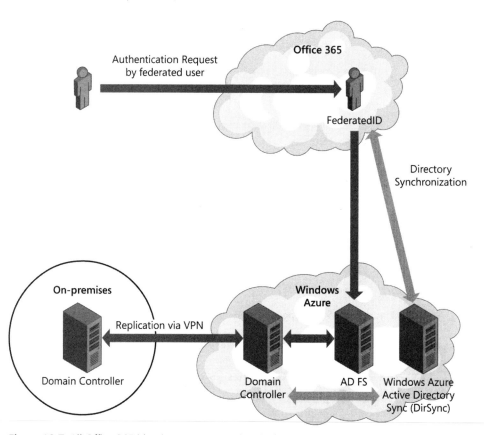

Figure 16-7 All Office 365 identity components in Windows Azure.

Scenario 2: Office 365 on-premises identity management components duplicated in Windows Azure for disaster recovery and failover

In this scenario, the on-premises identity components handle all provisioning and authentication requests. Therefore, Windows Azure Active Directory Sync, DC, and AD FS are all provided as on-premises services and serve as the primary identity infrastructure for Office

Azure can be operational, but not used for Office 365 provisioning and authentication until such time that a disaster recovery protocol would dictate their activation to serve as the primary activation workloads for Office 365.

Switching over from the on-premises identity infrastructure to the one hosted in Windows Azure is a manual process. This will also require DNS changes and DNS records to propagate so that the AD FS endpoint is resolved correctly in Windows Azure. In some cases, you might be able to tolerate not switching over the directory synchronization workload if you do not anticipate any significant provisioning changes during the outage period. The scenario also assumes that you have alternate Internet access to configure DNS and the components in Windows Azure. It is also important to note that an authoritative, Internet-facing DNS is available, so consideration should be made for a hosted DNS service or to also provision DNS within Windows Azure. Figure 16-8 depicts this scenario.

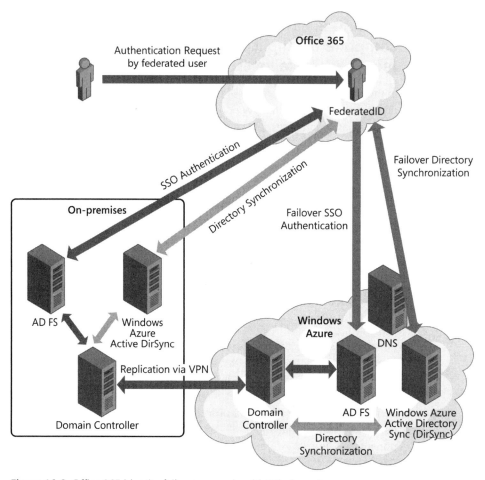

Figure 16-8 Office 365 identity failover scenario with Windows Azure.

Virtual machine sizing

Windows Azure classifies virtual machines (VMs) based on size. Because Windows Azure's cost structure is based in part on utilization, the size of the VM affects the cost. Therefore, it is important to correctly size your identity VMs in Windows Azure. Table 16-2 provides a guideline on the recommended VM size for the different Office 365 identity components based on organization size.

TABLE 16-2 Virtual machine sizing in Windows Azure

Server role	<5,000 users	5,001 – 15,000 users	15,001 – 50,000 users	>50,000 users
Domain controller	Small Plus 1 data disk	Medium Plus 1 data disk	Large Plus 1 data disk	Large Plus 1 data disk
AD FS server	Small	Small	Medium	Large
AD FS proxy	Small	Small	Medium	Medium

INSIDE OUT   Information on virtual machine sizing

For more information about the resources included in the small, medium, and large VM sizes, see *http://msdn.microsoft.com/en-us/library/windowsazure/jj156003.aspx*.

Implementing the identity components in Windows Azure is the same as building the same components on-premises; these tasks were covered in Chapter 2, "Planning and preparing to deploy Office 365", Chapter 3, "Active Directory Federation Services", and Chapter 4, "Directory synchronization". This chapter extends that knowledge to include options for building them in Windows Azure.

Multi-factor authentication

Multi-factor authentication is a heightened authentication method where a password is required in addition to the verification of physical possession of a token. A classic example of this is the use of a key fob, such as the one shown in Figure 16-9. The number currently shown on the key fob changes periodically and needs to be presented together with a password to facilitate a successful authentication attempt. Multi-factor authentication is available with Office 365 when AD FS is implemented.

Figure 16-9 Key fob.

On October 4, 2012, Microsoft acquired PhoneFactor. PhoneFactor provides phone-based authentication as a second-factor authentication method. Microsoft has started to integrate PhoneFactor into Windows Azure and Office 365 and plans to extend the service to other Microsoft software and services. In the summer of 2013, PhoneFactor began its transition to the Windows Azure brand and has been renamed Windows Azure Multi-Factor Authentication.

Windows Azure Multi-Factor Authentication provides a unique alternative to a key fob or smartcard. The concept is based on the assumption that many users are reachable by phone or a cellular device. Therefore, a phone number is used as the second-factor authentication that the service will use to contact the user. The user will answer the phone and press the pound (#) key to acknowledge the physical possession of a communication device associated with that number, thus achieving the multi-factor authentication requirement.

With the increase in cyber security threats, many organizations and regulatory authorities are starting to make multi-factor authentication a requirement.

Setting up Azure Multi-Factor Authentication

When an Office 365 tenant has been activated for Azure Multi-Factor Authentication, you will see the option when you visit the admin center.

> **Note**
>
> The steps and screen shots in this section are from the preview version of Azure Multi-Factor Authentication. In the release version, the steps and screen shots might differ from what is shown here.

To set up Azure Multi-Factor Authentication, follow these steps:

1. Select users and groups, and then click Set up for Set stronger verification requirements, as shown in Figure 16-10.

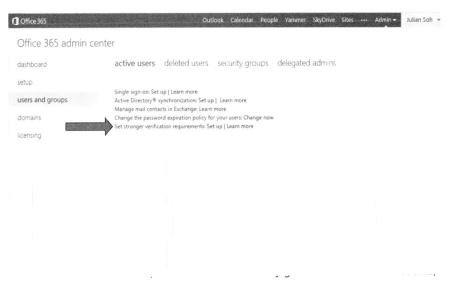

then we selected an account by selecting the check box next to the account.

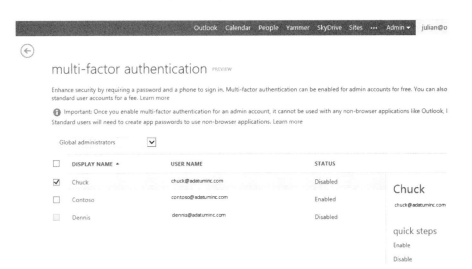

Figure 16-11 Check the box of the user you want to configure multi-factor authentication for.

3. When you select a user, the right pane shows the user's name and two items under quick steps. The action items are Enable and Disable. This is also shown in Figure 16-11. Click Enable.

4. On the Enable multi-factor authentication page, as shown in Figure 16-12, click yes.

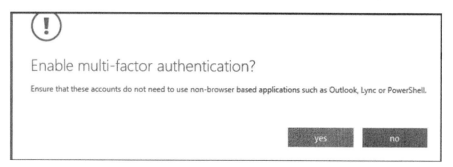

Figure 16-12 Enable multi-factor authentication prompt.

5. When the activation for the selected accounts is done, another dialog box will inform you that the updates are successful, as shown in Figure 16-13. Multi-factor authentication is now enabled for these accounts. Click close.

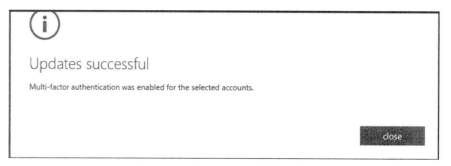

Figure 16-13 Dialog box stating that updates have been successful.

To disable multi-factor authentication, follow the same steps but select the Disable option in Step 2.

First time user experience

After a user has been enabled for multi-factor authentication, she will be guided to complete the configuration process. These steps outline the user's experience:

1. After the user has successful provided the correct password when logging on through the Office 365 portal page, she will be told she needs to set up additional security verification. She will need to click the Set it up now button, as shown in Figure 16-14.

Figure 16-14 User is prompted to set up additional security verification.

2. After the user has clicked Set it up now, she will be presented with the option to have the Azure Multi-Factor Authentication Service call a phone number or text a code to a mobile phone. The user also has the option to select the phone numbers that the service will use as the preferred method, as shown in Figure 16-15.

> **Note**
> Phone numbers are part of the users' settings in their accounts. Therefore, make sure the account already has phone numbers as part of the profile.

Figure 16-15 Configuring a security verification method.

3. Click save.

4. The user will be prompted to verify the settings, as shown in Figure 16-16.

Figure 16-16 Verification required dialog box.

5. The Azure Multi-Factor Authentication Service will call the phone number. While it is calling the number, the user will see the page shown in Figure 16-17. When the user receives the phone call and answers it, she will hear the following message: "Thank you for using the Microsoft verification system. Press the pound key to finish verifying your account." The user will press the pound (#) key on the phone. If for some reason the user is not able to do so, she will receive a verification failure dialog box, but will have the option to click a button labeled Retry.

the updates are successful, identical to what is shown in Figure 16-13. The user will then click close.

These steps detail the one-time process for the user that has just been enabled for Azure Multi-Factor Authentication. After this is done, users will not have to repeat this process. Their new Office 365 logon experience with Azure Multi-Factor Authentication is detailed in the next section.

Subsequent user experience

After the user has completed the initial verification process outlined in the previous section, her subsequent logon experience is as follows:

1. When the user has successfully provided the correct Office 365 logon password, she will see the Office 365 portal page informing her that she is being contacted, as shown in Figure 16-18. Notice that only the last two digits of the phone number are being displayed for security and privacy reasons. This page will remain active during the entire verification process.

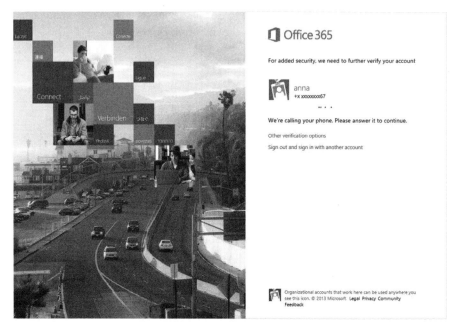

Figure 16-18 Office 365 portal page informing the user that the Azure Multi-Factor Authentication Service is calling the phone number.

2. When the user receives the call and answers it, she will hear the following greeting: "Thank you for using the Microsoft sign-in verification system. Press the pound key to finish signing in." The user will then click the # key on the phone.

3. The user will then hear the following message: "You have been signed in. Goodbye." At this point, the page that is shown in Figure 16-18 will change because the user will be redirected into Office 365 as a result of a successful dual-factor authentication.

4. If for some reason the user was not able to press the # key or did not receive the call, the authentication will fail and the user will see the page shown in Figure 16-19. Notice that the user has the option to select a different verification option.

Figure 16-19 Office 365 portal page when the attempted multi-factor authentication method failed.

5.   If the user clicks the Other verification option, she will see other options, as shown in Figure 16-20. She then will need to pick an alternate second-factor authentication method.

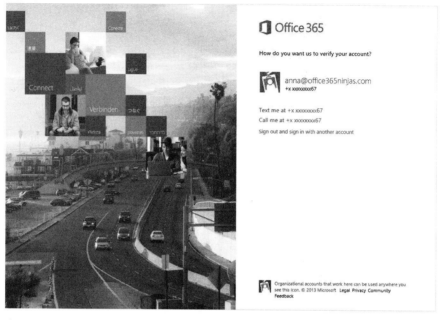

Figure 16-20 Office 365 portal page with other second-factor authentication options.

In summary, Azure Multi-Factor Authentication is simple to configure and consists of a two-step process:

●   A global administrator enables accounts for Azure Multi-Factor Authentication.

●   The users who are enabled for multi-factor authentication will go through a first time setup to configure the preferred phone number and verification method, which is either a phone call or a code sent through text messaging.

After the setup and configuration is done, the user experience is straightforward and easy to use.

> **Note**
> To learn more about Microsoft's acquisition of PhoneFactor and its integration into the Windows Azure brand, see *https://www.phonefactor.com/microsoft*. To learn more about using phone-based authentication as a multi-factor solution, request a whitepaper at *http://info.phonefactor.com/request-wp-auth-rev.html*.

Active Directory Sync roles.

Lastly, we introduced a new phone-based, multi-factor authentication method that Microsoft acquired. Previously known as PhoneFactor, Windows Azure Multi-Factor Authentication is being integrated with Office 365 and will provide an opportunity for organizations to do away with traditional physical security tokens.

These are all new and upcoming features of Office 365, many of which are either in the preview stage or already in the early deployment stage. If you have a business need to adopt these new services, contact your Microsoft representative or the Microsoft Cloud Vantage service.

Chapter 16

## PART 6

Appendix

Windows PowerShell scripts for Office 365

Introduction 813   Swapping licenses. 818

The way we approach presenting these Windows PowerShell scripts for Office 365 is through a build-up process. Each script will provide you with information you can use in subsequent scripts and tasks.

> ## INSIDE OUT   Creating .csv files
>
> The Flash Fill feature of Excel 2013 is a great tool to create .csv input files and combine values from several columns. This new feature allows you to easily create .csv files that can be used in conjunction with Windows PowerShell.

Determining the subscription name

It is important to learn the names of the subscriptions your organization owns because you will need that information when you use Windows PowerShell to add or remove licenses for your users.

The following script retrieves the value *AccountSkuID*, which takes the form *<AccountNam e>:<SubscriptionName>*. For example, our tenant name is AdatumInc, and we purchased the Office 365 E3 suite, which is known as the EnterprisePack SKU. Our *AccountSkuID* is *AdatumInc:EnterprisePack*. Your subscription name should be similar. Take note of it, as we will learn how it is used in other Windows PowerShell scripts:

```
Import-Module MSonline

$cred = Get-Credential
```

```
Connect-MsolService -Credential $cred

Get-MsolAccountSku
```

Creating cloud identities from a .csv file

If you are using cloud identities, which are Microsoft cloud services IDs, you can use Windows PowerShell to create accounts using a .csv file containing the account information. The first row of the .csv file comprises the column headers, which you will reference as $_.<HeaderName> in the script itself when creating the accounts.

The script at the end of this section does the following:

1. Imports a .csv file named user.csv located on the C drive

2. Creates each user by iterating through the rows in the file, using the values in $_.<Header> for the various user properties

3. Assigns the newly created user with a password that does not expire

4. Sets the user's location to the U.S.

5. Adds Office 365 licenses to the user

```
Import-Module MSonline

$cred = Get-Credential

Connect-MsolService -Credential $cred

Import-Csv 'C:user.csv' |

     ForEach {

                     New-MsolUser -UserPrincipalName $_.UPN -DisplayName
$_.UserName -FirstName $_.First -LastName $_.Last -Password "Change-Me" -Pass-
wordNeverExpires $true

                     Set-MsolUser -UserPrincipalName $_.UPN -UsageLocation us

                     Set-MsolUserLicense -UserPrincipalName $_.UPN -AddLi-
censes "ADATUMINC:ENTERPRISEPACK"

     }
```

Generating a user list

Generating a user list in .csv format with the corresponding user properties is important because the output can be imported into other Windows PowerShell scripts to carry out administrative tasks:

```
Import-Module MSonline
```

```
$FirstName = $User.FirstName

$LastName = $User.LastName

echo "$UPN,$FirstName,$LastName" | Out-File c:Users.csv -Append

}
```

Although this script is presented as a separate script, bear in mind that you can combine the output of a command and redirect it as an input for another command in a single sentence.

Generating a subscription assignment report

You might need to generate a report on which subscription a user is assigned to. The following script looks at each user in the tenant, determines the user's assigned *AccountSkuID*, and translates it into a descriptive name. The output of the report is in a .csv format:

```
#Script to see which users are assigned to which licenses

# Define Hashtables for lookup

$Sku = @{

    "DESKLESSPACK" = "Office 365 (Plan K1)"

    "DESKLESSWOFFPACK" = "Office 365 (Plan K2)"

    "LITEPACK" = "Office 365 (Plan P1)"

    "EXCHANGESTANDARD" = "Office 365 Exchange Online Only"

    "STANDARDPACK" = "Office 365 (Plan E1)"
```

```
      "STANDARDWOFFPACK" = "Office 365 (Plan E2)"

      "ENTERPRISEPACK" = "Office 365 (Plan E3)"

      "ENTERPRISEPACKLRG" = "Office 365 (Plan E3)"

      "ENTERPRISEWITHSCAL" = "Office 365 (Plan E4)"

      "STANDARDPACK_STUDENT" = "Office 365 (Plan A1) for Students"

      "STANDARDWOFFPACKPACK_STUDENT" = "Office 365 (Plan A2) for Students"

      "ENTERPRISEPACK_STUDENT" = "Office 365 (Plan A3) for Students"

      "ENTERPRISEWITHSCAL_STUDENT" = "Office 365 (Plan A4) for Students"

      "STANDARDPACK_FACULTY" = "Office 365 (Plan A1) for Faculty"

      "STANDARDWOFFPACKPACK_FACULTY" = "Office 365 (Plan A2) for Faculty"

      "ENTERPRISEPACK_FACULTY" = "Office 365 (Plan A3) for Faculty"

      "ENTERPRISEWITHSCAL_FACULTY" = "Office 365 (Plan A4) for Faculty"

      "ENTERPRISEPACK_B_PILOT" = "Office 365 (Enterprise Preview)"

      "STANDARD_B_PILOT" = "Office 365 (Small Business Preview)"

      }


# The output will be written to this file in the current working directory
$LogFile = "c:Office_365_Licenses.csv"


# Connect to Microsoft Online
Import-Module MSOnline
Connect-MsolService -Credential $Office365credentials


write-host "Connecting to Office 365..."
# Get a list of all licenses that exist within the tenant
$licensetype = Get-MsolAccountSku | Where {$_.ConsumedUnits -ge 1}


# Loop through all license types found in the tenant
foreach ($license in $licensetype)
```

```
{

    # Build and write the header for the .csv file

    $headerstring = "DisplayName,UserPrincipalName,AccountSku"


    foreach ($row in $($license.ServiceStatus))

    ʿ



            "MCO*" { $thisLicense = "Lync Online" }

            "LYN*" { $thisLicense = "Lync Online" }

            "OFF*" { $thisLicense = "Office Professional Plus" }

            "SHA*" { $thisLicense = "Sharepoint Online" }

            "*WAC*" { $thisLicense = "Office Web Apps" }

            "WAC*" { $thisLicense = "Office Web Apps" }

            default { $thisLicense = $row.ServicePlan.servicename }

        }



        $headerstring = ($headerstring + "," + $thisLicense)

    }



    Out-File -FilePath $LogFile -InputObject $headerstring -Encoding UTF8 -append

    write-host ("Gathering users with the following subscription: " + $license.
accountskuid)


    # Gather users for this particular AccountSku

    $users = Get-MsolUser -all | where {$_.isLicensed -eq "True" -and $_.licenses[0].
accountskuid.tostring() -eq $license.accountskuid}
```

```
# Loop through all users and write them to the .csv file

foreach ($user in $users) {


    write-host ("Processing " + $user.displayname)


        $datastring = ($user.displayname + "," + $user.userprincipalname + "," +
$Sku.Item($user.licenses[0].AccountSku.SkuPartNumber))


    foreach ($row in $($user.licenses[0].servicestatus)) {


        # Build the data string

        $datastring = ($datastring + "," + $($row.provisioningstatus))

        }


    Out-File -FilePath $LogFile -InputObject $datastring -Encoding UTF8 -append


    }

}



write-host ("Script Completed.  Results available in " + $LogFile)
```

Swapping licenses

You can have multiple subscription types in a single tenant. For example, you might have kiosk SKUs and E3 SKUs. In such a scenario, there might be a need for you to swap users' assigned licenses from one subscription type to another. The following script imports a list of users in a .csv file, sets their location, removes their existing license, and assigns a new license type:

```
Import-Module MSonline

Connect-MsolService

Import-Csv C:Users.csv |
```

```
    ForEach {

                    Set-MsolUser -UserPrincipalName $_.UPN -UsageLocation us

                    Set-MsolUserLicense -UserPrincipalName $_.UPN -RemoveLicenses
"ADATUMINC:STANDARDPACK"

                    Set-MsolUserLicense -UserPrincipalName $_.UPN -AddLicenses
"ADATUMINC:SHAREPOINTSTANDARD"
```

```
Import-Module MSonline

Connect-MsolService

#Get all the AccountSkuID and SkyPartNumber

Get-MsolAccountSku | Format-Table AccountSkuID, SkuPartNumber

$ServicePlans = Get-MsolAccountSku | Where {$_.SkuPartNumber -eq
"ENTERPRISEWITHSCAL"}

$ServicePlans.ServiceStatus

#Disable the services you do not want to assign by including it in the -DisabledPlans
parameter for the $myO365Sku variable

#RMS_S_Enterprise

#MCOVOICECONF

#OFFICESUBSCRIPTION

#MCOSTANDARD

#SHAREPOINTWAC

#SHAREPOINTENTERPRISE

#EXCHANGE_S_ENTERPRISE

#Assign Julian's account to E4 but turn off Lync, Exchange, and Voice

Set-MsolUser -UserPrincipalName julian@adatuminc.microsoftonline.com -UsageLocation
US
```

```
Set-MsolUserLicense -UserPrincipalName julian@adatuminc.microsoftonline.com -Remove-
Licenses ADATUMINC:SHAREPOINTSTANDARD

Set-MsolUserLicense -UserPrincipalName julian@adatuminc.microsoftonline.com -AddLi-
censes ADATUMINC:ENTERPRISEWITHSCAL

$myO365Sku = New-MsolLicenseOptions -AccountSkuId ADATUMINC:ENTERPRISEWITHSCAL -Dis-
abledPlans MCOVOICECONF, MCOSTANDARD, EXCHANGE_S_ENTERPRISE

Set-MsolUserLicense -UserPrincipalName julian @adatuminc.microsoftonline.com
-LicenseOptions $myO365Sku
```

Purging deleted users

When users are deleted, the accounts remain in the recycle bin for 30 days before being
purged, allowing an administrator to undelete a user. If you want to force purge by empty-
ing the recycle bin, you can accomplish it with the following Windows PowerShell script:

```
Import-Module MSonline

Connect-MsolService

$Users = Get-MsolUser -All -ReturnDeletedUsers|select userprincipalname,objectid

foreach ($User in $Users)

{

    Remove-MsolUser -ObjectId $user.objectid -RemoveFromRecycleBin -Force

    echo "Purged " $user.UserPrincipalName

    }

Echo "Done"
```

Sending bulk email to users

If you need to send a message such as a notification, you can use the following Windows
PowerShell script to accomplish a bulk send. This script uses a .csv file with two parameters:

- To column containing the email address of the recipients

- Message column containing the body of the email message

```
Import-Module MSonline

$cred = Get-Credential

$mailhost = "mail.messaging.microsoft.com"

$from = "julian@adatuminc.onmicrosoft.com"
```

```
$subj = "Notification regarding your email account"

#$service = new-object Microsoft.Exchange.WebServices.Data.ExchangeService

#$service.AutodiscoverUrl($user.Properties.mail)

Connect-MsolService -Credential $cred

$Session = New-PSSession -ConfigurationName Microsoft.Exchange-ConnectionUri https://
ps.outlook.com/powershell/ -Credential $cred -Authentication Basic -AllowRedirection
```

```
$mailmessage = New-Object net.mail.mailmessage

$mailmessage.from = ($from)

$mailmessage.To.add($to)

$mailmessage.Subject = $subj

$mailmessage.Body = $_.Message


$smtpclient.Send($mailmessage)

        }

Remove-PSSession $Session
```

Office 365 Windows PowerShell resources

Microsoft has provided sample Windows PowerShell scripts that can be downloaded and used. They are organized by function and can be found at *http://gallery.technet.microsoft. com/office365/*.

Index

Index

AAW (Application Approval Workflow), 222
Accepted Domain dialog box, 522
Access management, 787
account forest, 792
ACTIONS link, 658
activating services via script, 819–820
Activation Error message, 778
active-active synchronized configuration, 439
Active Alerts view, 289
Active Directory. *See* AD (Active Directory)
Active Directory Federation Services. *See* AD FS (Active
      Directory Federation Services)
Active Directory Integration Pack, 344
Active Directory User and Computer (ADUC) management
      console, 72, 89
ActiveSync, 36, 433, 512, 535
AD (Active Directory)
   Clean Up link, 24
   discovering information about, 23
   domain name, adding to Office 365
      DNS, configuring, 81–82
      domain purpose, setting, 81–82
      licenses, assigning, 80
      TXT records, entering, 77–79
      users, adding, 80
      verifying domain, 79–80
   module, 53
   schema, updating, 140–143
   and SSO, 71
   synchronizing account with Office 365 using
      PowerShell, 375
Adatum Inc., 678
Add a domain link, 75
Add Exchange Forest dialog box, 479

Add Features Wizard, 409

AD FS 2.0 Management snap-in, 106
AD FS (Active Directory Federation Services)
   architecture planning
      database, 101
      proxy, 100–101
      server farm, 100
   certificates
      creating requests, 93–97
      installing on Internet Information Server, 97–98
      protecting default website with, 98–99
      using enterprise certificate authority to issue, 97
   configuring, 106–112
   converting domain from standard authentication to identity
         federation
      server on remote Windows 7 workstation, 114–115
      server on Windows Server 2008 R2 or later, 113–114
      server on Windows Server 2008 SP2, 114–115
      verifying successful conversion, 115–117
   federation URL endpoint, updating, 117–121
   hybrid Lync environment, 754
   identity management in Windows Azure, 797
   installing, 101–106
   Internet Information Server role, installing, 92
   on-premises technologies, 207
   removing
      completely uninstalling, 125–135
      converting domain from identity federation to standard
            authentication, 123–124
   single sign on requirements, 84–86
   single sign on scenarios
      remote worker not logged on to corporate network, 84
      remote worker on virtual private network
            connection, 83–84

stand-alone AD FS server, 108
testing federation server, 112
user principal name suffix, remediating, 86–91
verifying successful domain conversion, 117–118
ADFSAppPool, 125
AdfsSetup.exe, 102
ADM (Classic Administrative Templates), 752
.adm file, 749
Admin Audit log, 421–422
admin center
    directory synchronization, activating through, 145–147
    directory synchronization, verifying through, 176–177
AdministrationConfig-en installation file, 57
Administration node, 256
admin resource center, 19
.admx file, 749
ADSIEdit.msc, 131
ADUC (Active Directory User and Computer) management
    console, 72, 89
ADVANCED option, 667
alert notifications (SCOM)
    creating alert recipients, 262–270
    creating subscription, 270–281
    customizing, 289–290
    resources for, 280–281
Alert Type window, 274
Alias attribute, 139
All Adatum Communications eDiscovery set, 687
Allow action, 446
All targeted objects setting, 298
anti-spam in Exchange Online, 443–445
App Catalog site, 634, 653
App Controller, System Center, 219–221
Apple iMessage, 433
Application Approval Workflow (AAW), 211
Application Pools node, 129
Application Virtualization (App-V) technology, 764
app licenses, managing, 657–659
App-V (Application Virtualization) technology, 764
architecture for SharePoint Online, 633
Archive Mailbox page, 546
ASP.NET 3.5, 225
Assign Licenses activity, 349
Assign Services to Certificate page, 502, 505
audio conferencing, dial-in, 717–718
Autodiscover service
    in Microsoft Remote Connectivity Analyzer Tool, 47
    resetting virtual directory, 539–542
    troubleshooting Exchange hybrid model
        deployment, 534–537
automated deletions in Exchange Online, 621
Availability Tracker, 310
Available classes box, 273
AVIcode, Inc., 213
Azure Active Directory (AAD) connector, 788

B

B2B (business-to-business) partners, 139
backup and recovery for Exchange Online, 439–441,
    449–450
bandwidth
    "burstable", 38
    and network latency, 26–27
    requirements for Lync Online, 45
    testing for Lync Online, 719–721
Basic authorization for WinRM listener, 402
BCS (Business Connectivity Services) Profile Pages
    feature, 634
BI (business intelligence), 632
Binary Tree, 601
BIS (Blackberry Internet Service), 436
bits per second (bps), 27
BitTitan, 601
Blackberry devices, 436
BlockedSendersHash attribute, 172
BPOS (Business Productivity Online Services), 147
bps (bits per second), 27
bring your own device (BYOD), 38, 438, 669, 760
British Telecom (BT), 717
Browse button, 569
Browse for Computer dialog box, 346
BT (British Telecom), 717
bulk emails
    sending responsibly, 439
    sending to users, 820–821
"burstable" bandwidth, 38
business case for Office 365
    core competency, 12
    economies of scale, 11
    redundancy, 11–12
    scalability, 11
    subscription model, 10–11
Business Connectivity Services (BCS) Profile Pages
    feature, 634
business intelligence (BI), 632
Business Productivity Online Services (BPOS), 147
Business Productivity Online Standard Suite, 49
business-to-business (B2B) partners, 139
BYOD (bring your own device), 38, 438, 669, 760

C

CA (certificate authority), 48, 93, 482
CAL (client access license), 11, 786
calendaring. *See also* Exchange Online
Can view option, 663
CAS (Client Access Server), 53, 207, 461, 591
Cemaphore, 601
centralized mail transport (hybrid Exchange)
    disabled, 558–559
    enabled, 560–562
    enabling/disabling, 562–564

CentralizedTransportEnabled, 564
certificate authority (CA), 48, 93, 482
Certificate Configuration page, 486, 493
certificates
    creating requests, 93–97
    Exchange hybrid model
        acquiring certificate, 495–497
        generating certificate request, 482–494
        importing purchased certificate, 498–506
        verifying certificates, 506–507

Complete Pending Request Wizard, 500
Completion page, Assign Services to Certificate Wizard, 506
Completion page, Manage Hybrid Configuration
        Wizard, 533
compliance
    automated deletions, 621
    enforced retention, 621
    holds
        creating, 625–627
        criteria-based hold, 624–625

Channel Type drop-down box, 267
Check Out Runbook option, 347
Chief Security Officer (CSO), 150
Citrix, 214
CJIS (Criminal Information Services) Security Addendum, 14
Classic Administrative Templates (ADM), 752
Clear Move Request action, 555
Click-to-Run installation method, 762
client access license (CAL), 11, 786
Client Access Server (CAS), 53, 207, 461, 591
Client Mix tab, 40, 43
client-side session, 403
Client tab, 47
cloud identities
    creating from csv file, 814
    defined, 72
Cloud Import List option, 599
cloud services, consumer vs. enterprise, 3–4
CMDB (Configuration Management Database), 217, 352, 366
cmd command, 397
cmdlets
    defined, 396
    general discussion, 53
    Office 365 commands listing, 424
CMS (content management system), 632
CN (common name), 139, 469
Collect Needed Information page, 466
Command Add-on library, 410, 411
Command Channel text box, 267
Command Pane in PowerShell ISE, 67, 410
Command Prompt program, 397
common name (CN), 139, 469
Community site, Office 365, 19
Complete-Migration cmdlet, 590

Configuration Management Database (CMDB), 217, 352, 366
Configuration Manager, System Center, 210–212
Configuration Results page, 110
Configuration.xml file, 770
Configure External Client Access Domain option, 508
Configure Prompts page, 389
ConfigWizard.exe file, 169
Confirm installation selections page, 234
Connection Configurations page, 552
Connect-MsolService cmdlet, 62, 113, 115, 121, 144
consumer vs. enterprise, 3–4
content management system (CMS), 632
conversation history for Lync Online, 742–754
converting users, 124
Convert-MSOLFederatedUser cmdlet, 123
copper cables, 27
CorpSQL, 159
Create a new Federation Service option, 107
Create a New Group option, Tasks pane, 284
Create App Catalog Site Collection page, 648
Create Certificate Request option, 94
Create Request Offering option, 387
Create Run As Account option, 293
Create Service Offering option, 390
Create User activity, 348
credentials
    in Manage Hybrid Configuration Wizard, 520
    management by FIM, 786
    storing in variable, 61
$cred variable, 60, 113, 144
Criminal Information Services (CJIS) Security Addendum, 14
criteria-based hold for Exchange Online data, 624–625
criteria for subscriptions, 271–272

Cryptographic Service Provider Properties page, 96
CSO (Chief Security Officer), 150
CSR (certificate signing request), 470, 482, 496, 507
CSV File Maker link, 25
.csv files
    creating cloud identities from, 814
    IMAP migration, 585
    staged migration, 574–575
Custom Compliance Policy Settings folder, 752
Customer Experience Improvement Program, 248
CustomLync2013IMArchive.adm file, 750
cutover migration
    with EAC, 570–573
    with ECP, 568–570
    overview, 566–567

D

dashboards (SCOM)
    creating, 312–317
    operator console dashboards, 311–312
    SLA dashboards, 317–323
databases, AD FS architecture planning, 101
Data Bus in Orchestrator, 370
data center locations, 28
Data Leakage Prevention (DLP), 422, 456, 460, 562, 617
Data Protection Manager, System Center. *See* DPM, System
    Center
Data Reader account, 249
Data Tables tab, 42
Data Warehouse Write account, 249
Data Writer account, 249
DC (domain controller), 84, 283, 746, 794
debugging
    in ISE, 406
    in PowerShell ISE, 66
decommissioning on-premises Exchange, 607
default website, protecting with certificates, 98–99
deleted users, purging, 820
Deliver with Bcc action, 446
Delta Confirming Import option, 190
Delta Import Delta Sync profile, 183, 186
Delta Import operation, 182
Delta Synchronization operation, 182
dependent servers, identifying, 283–286
Deploy IP to Runbook Server or Runbook Designer
    option, 345
deployment
    Deployment Guide, 18
    Deployment Readiness Toolkit, 18
    Exchange hybrid model
        capabilities, 460
        centralized mail transport disabled, 558–559
        centralized mail transport enabled, 560–562
        centralized mail transport, enabling/disabling, 562–564
        certificates, 482–507

changing MX record, 558
    configuring Exchange Web Services, 508–512
    configuring hybrid deployment, 517–534
    EMC configuration, 471–482
    establishing hybrid relationship, 514–516
    requirements, 460–462
    testing mailbox creation, 542–549
    testing mailbox move, 549–557
    troubleshooting, 534–542
    using Exchange Server Deployment Assistant, 462–471
Lync Online
    allowing outgoing connections, 723
    DNS entries, 723–727
    overview, 718
    policies, 742–754
    ports and protocols, 722–723
    testing network bandwidth and latency, 719–721
Microsoft Office 365 Deployment Readiness Toolkit, 21–26
Office 365 Deployment Guide, 20–21
Office 365 Professional Plus
    32-bit vs. 64-bit version, 775
    Group Policy, 775–776
    overview, 762–763
    system requirements, 775
    virtualization, 776–777
Office 365 Service Descriptions, 19–20
of OS, 211
tools for, 18–19
Depot PC scenario, 210
Details Information window, 348
Device Management node, 256
dial-in audio conferencing, 717–718
Differential configuration, 214
DigiCert, 495
directory-based blocking, 444
directory synchronization
    activating
        Active Directory schema, updating, 140–143
        through admin center, 145–147
        with Windows PowerShell, 144–145
    changing schedule, 195
    Directory Sync Setup Wizard, 164
    Directory Sync tool, 137
    forcing unscheduled
        run profiles and management agents, 182–183
        with Synchronization Service Manager, 183–192
        through Windows PowerShell, 191–195
    new feature, 138
    process of, 140–142
    troubleshooting common errors
        with MOSDAL toolkit, 199–204
        synchronization not running, 197–198
        unrecognized or invalid data in Active Directory, 198–199
    verifying
        through admin center, 176–177

Event Viewer, checking, 181–182
service status, 177
with Synchronization Service Manager, 178–181
Windows Azure Active Directory Sync
configuring, 170–176
installing with dedicated computer running SQL
Server, 151–163
installing with Windows Internal Database, 164–168
direct synchronization, 790
DirSync command, 327

DLs (distribution lists), 92, 198
DNS (Domain Name System)
configuring, 81–82
creating entries for Lync Online, 723–727
creating TXT record, 76
dependent technologies, 223
entering TXT records, 77–79
planning environment for Exchange Online, 461
domain controller (DC), 84, 283, 746, 794
domain names
adding to Office 365
DNS, configuring, 81–82
domain purpose, setting, 81–82
licenses, assigning, 80
TXT records, entering, 77–79
users, adding, 80
verifying domain, 79–80
associating multiple to tenant, 75
converting from identity federation to standard
authentication, 123–124
converting from standard authentication to identity
federation
AD FS server on remote Windows 7 workstation, 114–115
AD FS server on Windows Server 2008 R2 or
later, 113–114
AD FS server on Windows Server 2008 SP2, 114–115
verifying successful conversion, 115–117
Domain Name System. *See* **DNS**
Domain Proof of Ownership page, 524
Domain Scope page, 485
Domains page, Manage Hybrid Configuration Wizard, 521
downloading
Management Pack, 254
Microsoft Office 365 Deployment Readiness Toolkit, 22
Microsoft Online Service Module, 57

Microsoft Online Service Sign-in Assistant, 56
Microsoft Report Viewer Redistributable Package, 226
MOSDAL, 49
/download mode, 769
Download Report button, 691
Download Results button, 691
DPM (Data Protection Manager), System Center, 214–215
Dynamic Members page, 286

E

E-mail migration
IMAP migration with, 585–587
overview, 612–613
staged migration with, 575–579
Edge Transport server, 465
eDiscovery (electronic discovery)
Download Manager page, 692
multi-mailbox search in Exchange Online, 627–630
responsibility for, 612
Sets page, 687
in SharePoint Online, 674–693
Edit Bindings option, 98
Edit Federation Service Properties option, 118
Edit in Browser option, 670
editions of Microsoft Office, 760–762
Edit user settings page, Lync Online Control Panel, 738
Education suites, 6
EHE (Exchange Hosted Encryption), 438, 451–452
electronic discovery. *See* **eDiscovery (electronic discovery)**
email. *See also* **Exchange Online**
accounts
creating runbooks for, 346–349
mailbox access, granting, 417–418
time zones, changing, 418–419
campaigns, sending responsibly, 439
clients vs. server, 433
sending bulk email to users, 820–821
EmailAddress attribute, 574, 585
E-Mail Addresses tab, 556
E-Mail Migration page, 569, 576, 578
EMC (Exchange Management Console)
adding Exchange Online, 479–482
administration options, 53
installing, 469
migrating mailboxes, 603

overview, 468, 608–609
on server, 471
on workstation, 471–478
-EnabledSharedAddressSpace parameter, 755
Enable Exchange hybrid deployment check box, 173
Enable multi-factor authentication page, 802
Enable-OrganizationCustomization cmdlet, 423
Enable Password Sync check box, 174
Enable-PSRemoting cmdlet, 114
Enable User activity, 349
Enable wildcard certificate check box, 485
encryption for Exchange Online, 435
Endpoint Protection, System Center, 218–219
enterprise
    certificate authority, 97
    Enterprise suites, 6
    Enterprise Voice vs. peer-to-peer voice, 700
    vs. consumer, 3–4
environment, readiness, 21
EOA (Exchange Online Archiving)
    access, 450–451
    archive size, 448–449
    backup and recovery, 449–450
    compliance, 451
    hybrid archiving, 454
    overview, 434
    personal archives, 622
EOP (Exchange Online Protection)
    next release, 438
    overview, 620
Error Reporting page, 473
E suites, 7, 20
ESX, 214
Event Viewer, 181–182
EWS (Exchange Web Services)
    configuring for Exchange hybrid model, 508–512
    planning for deployment, 469
Exchange 2010 Pre-Deployment Analyzer (ExPDA), 462
Exchange Active Sync is enabled check box, 486
Exchange ActiveSync Services (EAS), 212, 435
Exchange admin center. See EAC
Exchange Client Network Bandwidth Calculator, 40
Exchange Control Panel. See ECP
ExchangeGUID property, 605, 607
Exchange Hosted Encryption (EHE), 438, 451–452
Exchange Hub Transport server, 561
Exchange hybrid model
    deploying
        capabilities, 460
        centralized mail transport disabled, 558–559
        centralized mail transport enabled, 560–562
        centralized mail transport, enabling/disabling, 562–564
        certificates, 482–508
        changing MX record, 558
        configuring Exchange Web Services, 508–512

configuring hybrid deployment, 517–534
EMC configuration, 471–482
establishing hybrid relationship, 514–516
requirements, 460–462
testing mailbox creation, 542–549
testing mailbox move, 549–557
troubleshooting, 534–542
using Exchange Server Deployment Assistant, 462–470
migrating mailboxes, 591
Exchange Management Console. See EMC
Exchange Management Shell window, 607
Exchange Online. See also Exchange hybrid model
    administration
        EAC, 617–619
        ECP, 612–613
        EMC, 608–609
        EOP, 620
        FOPE, 614–617
        remote Windows PowerShell, 611
    capabilities of
        backup and recovery, 439–441
        Data Leakage Prevention, 456–457
        messaging limits, 439
        Rights Management Service, 457–458
        service availability and redundancy, 441–442
    compliance
        automated deletions, 621
        enforced retention, 621
        holds, 623–627
        Messaging Records Management, 623
        multi-mailbox search (eDiscovery), 627–630
        personal archive, 622
        preserving content, 621
    core workloads and concepts
        archiving, 434
        communication between clients and Exchange
            Online, 435–436
        communication between Exchange Online and
            destination email servers, 436–437
        communication between Exchange Online
            customers, 437
        filtering, 438–439
        handling and transport, 435–437
        mailboxes and calendaring, 433–434
        security, 438
    Deployment Readiness tool, 24
    domain purpose, 81
    establishing Windows PowerShell session with, 414–416
    Exchange Hosted Encryption, 451–452
    Exchange Online Archiving
        access, 450–451
        archive size, 448–449
        backup and recovery, 449–450
        compliance, 451

Forefront Online Protection for Exchange
   anti-spam, 443–445
   layered protection, 443–444
   message handling, 446–447
   message quarantining, 445
   policies, 445–446
   reporting, 447–448
  hybrid environment, 20
  implementation options
   enabling hybrid deployment, 173

Exchange On-Premises node, 195
Exchange Server 2010 Setup Wizard, 473
Exchange Server Deployment Assistant, 462–470
Exchange Server Enterprise Edition, 431
Exchange Server Standard Edition, 431
Exchange Unified Communications Certificate, 484
Exchange Unified Messaging (UM), 173
Exchange Web Services. *See* EWS
Exchange Web Services is enabled check box, 487
Excluded Members page, 286
Exit And Show Files option, 200
ExPDA (Exchange 2010 Pre-Deployment Analyzer), 462
Export operation, 183
ExRCA (Microsoft Exchange Remote Connectivity
   Analyzer), 534
external collaboration with SkyDrive Pro, 660–664

F

Family Education Right and Privacy Act (FERPA), 14
Federal Information Security Management Act (FISMA), 13
Federal Trade Commission (FTC), 456
federated identities
  converting domain from standard authentication to
    AD FS server on Windows Server 2008 R2 or
    later, 113–114
    AD FS server on Windows Server 2008 SP2, 114–115
    verifying successful conversion, 115–117
  converting domain to standard authentication
    from, 123–124
  overview, 72–73
Federation server option, 104
federation URL endpoint, 117–121
FERPA (Family Education Right and Privacy Act), 14
fiber optic cable, 27
FILES tab, 668

file upload size for SharePoint Online, 637
FIM (Forefront Identity Manager)
  automating default UPN using, 90
  dependent technologies, 223
  directory synchronization, 138
  licensing, 786
  management agents, 788
  multi-forest scenarios
    account forest and resource forest scenario, 792
    direct synchronization, 790

anti-spam, 443–445
future releases, 438
layered protection, 443–444
message handling, 446–447
message quarantining, 445
overview, 614–616
policies, 445–446
prerequisite for EHE, 451
reporting, 447–448
vs. SCEP, 218
vs. Hub Transport, 445
ForceChangePassword attribute, 574
force TLS action, 446
Forefront Endpoint Protection 2010, 218
Forefront Identity Manager. *See* FIM (Forefront Identity
   Manager)
Forefront Online Protection for Exchange. *See* FOPE
Forefront Online Protection for Exchange Outbound
   Connector box, 530
Forefront Protection 2010 for Exchange Server (FPE), 438
forests, AD
  discovering information about, 23
  multi-forest scenarios
    account forest and resource forest scenario, 792
    direct synchronization, 790
    indirect synchronization, 791
    overview, 788–789
  one-way forest trusts, 785
  trusts, 785
  two-way forest trusts, 785
FPE (Forefront Protection 2010 for Exchange Server), 438
FQDN (fully qualified domain name), 74, 94, 96
FTC (Federal Trade Commission), 456
Full Backup configuration, 214

Full Import/Delta Synchronization operation, 183
Full Import/Full Synchronization operation, 183
Full Import operation, 182
Full Synchronization operation, 183
fully qualified domain name (FQDN), 74, 94, 96

G
GAL dialog box, 626
GAL (global address list), 92, 452, 460
gateways, 27
Gbps (gigabits per second), 27
GCC (Government Community Cloud), 8, 10
General page, Service Level Tracking Wizard, 318
General Properties page, Create Group Wizard, 285
General Properties page, Update Configuration Wizard, 315
geolocation, 29
geo-redundancy, 11, 442
Get-AutodiscoverVirtualDirectory cmdlet, 542
Get-Command cmdlet, 416
Get-Credentials cmdlet, 121, 403
Get-CSUser cmdlet, 756
Get-ExchangeCertificate cmdlet, 507
Get-ExecutionPolicy cmdlet, 64, 401
Get-FederationInformation cmdlet, 538, 539
Get-Group cmdlet, 419, 421
Get-HybridConfiguration cmdlet, 534
Get-HybridMailFlow cmdlet, 563, 564
Get-Mailbox cmdlet, 415
Get-MailboxPermission cmdlet, 418
GetMailboxRegionalConfiguration cmdlet, 418
Get-MsolDomainFederationSettings cmdlet, 116
Get-MsolSubscription cmdlet, 62
GetO365LicInfo.ps1 script, 63, 66
Get Object activity, 349
Get Relationship activity, 349
Get-RetentionPolicy cmdlet, 422
gigabits per second (Gbps), 27
GLBA (Gramm-Leach-Biley Act), 456
Global Address List dialog box, 626
global address list (GAL), 92, 452, 460
Global Administrator account, 150, 197
Go Daddy, 76
Government Community Cloud (GCC), 8, 10
Government suites, 6
GPOs (Group Policy Objects), 72, 743, 775
Gramm-Leach-Biley Act (GLBA), 456
Graphical User Interface (GUI), 52, 405
greater-than symbol (>), 422
Group management, 786
Group Membership tab, 201
Group Policy
    deploying Office 365 Professional Plus, 775–776
    Group Policy Management, 746
Group Policy Objects (GPOs), 72, 743, 775

groups
    creating distribution, 419–421
    viewing, 419
G-tenant, 10
GUI (Graphical User Interface), 52, 405

H
headquarters (HQ), 36
Health Insurance Portability and Accountability Act
    (HIPAA), 14, 438, 456
Heating Ventilation and Air Conditioning (HVAC)
    systems, 212
helper scripts, 68
Help files, updating, 416
/help mode, 769
HIPPA (Health Insurance Portability and Accountability
    Act), 14, 438, 456
holds (Exchange Online data)
    creating, 625–627
    criteria-based hold, 624–625
    overview, 623–624
    time-based hold, 624
hops, 27
-HostedMigrationOverrideUrl parameter, 756
HQ (headquarters), 36
HR (Human Resources) task, 325
HTTPS (Hypertext Transfer Protocol Sercure), 433, 435
Hub Transport
    email handling, 435
    Exchange hybrid deployment, 489, 530
    vs. FOPE, 445
Human Resources (HR) task, 325
HVAC (Heating Ventilation and Air Conditioning)
    systems, 212
Hybrid Configuration tab, 517
hybrid deployments
    defined, 9
    establishing hybrid relationship, 514–516
    Exchange Online
        configuring, 517–534
        general discussion, 20, 172
        hybrid archiving model, 454–455
        hybrid mailbox model, 452–453
        hybrid mail protection and routing model, 455
        planning for, 463
    Lync Online
        configuring, 754–756
        overview, 714–717
    SharePoint Online, 637
    SharePoint Online search
        one-way inbound topology, 697
        one-way outbound topology, 697
        two-way topology, 698
Hypertext Transfer Protocol Sercure (HTTPS), 433, 435

Hyper-V Dynamic Memory setting, 244
hypervisor, 215

I

IaaS (Infrastructure as a Service), 101, 209, 781
IBE (Identity-Based Encryption), 452
IDE (Integrated Development Environment), 410
Identity-Based Encryption (IBE), 452
Identity Management (IDM), 786
identity management in Windows Azure

requirement for Orchestrator, 351
restoring, 127–131
IMAP (Internet message access protocol)
   and EOA, 450
   Exhange Online protocol support, 433
   protocol, 585
IMAP migration
   creating .csv file, 585
   with EAC, 587–589
   with ECP, 585–587
IMAutoArchivingPolicy, 748
IM (Instant Message), 703
Import-ExchangeCertificate cmdlet, 501
importing
   Management Pack, 253–263
   purchased certificate, 498–506
Import-Module cmdlet, 414
Import-PSSession cmdlet, 405
Incremental Backup configuration, 214
indirect synchronization, 791
Infrastructure as a Service (IaaS), 101, 209, 781
Initialize Data activity, 348
In-Place Hold, 624, 626, 627, 684
Input tab, 42
Installation Type page, 474
installing
   Microsoft Exchange PST Capture, 593–600
   Microsoft Online Services Module, 54
   Microsoft Online Services Sign-in Assistant, 56
   selecting path Operations Manager installation, 240
Install-OnlineCoexistenceTool cmdlet, 160
Instant Message (IM), 703
Integrated Development Environment (IDE), 410
Integrated Scripting Environment. *See* PowerShell ISE
      (Integrated Scripting Environment)

Integration Packs (IPs)
   and Management Server, 325
   SCO, 216
   using with Office 365 automation, 344–346
IntelliSense, 66, 406, 408, 410
Intercall, 717
Internet backbone, 28
Internet Engineering Task Force (IETF), 700
Internet Information Server. *See* IIS
Internet message access protocol. *See* IMAP

ISE (Integrated Scripting Environment). *See* PowerShell ISE
      (Integrated Scripting Environment)
ISP (Internet Service Provider), 76
ITIL (IT Infrastructure Library), 217, 326, 352
ITPA (IT process automation), 325

J

Join Lync Meeting option, 705

K

KB (Knowledge Base), 112
Key Management Server (KMS), 760
key performance indicators (KPIs), 353, 632
Keyword Query Language (KQL), 625, 684
Kiosk plans, 6, 20
KMS (Key Management Server), 760
Knowledge Base (KB), 112
KPIs (key performance indicators), 353, 632
KQL (Keyword Query Language), 625, 684

L

LAN (Local Area Network), 36, 223
large VMs, 799
latency, network
   and bandwidth, 26–27
   testing for Lync Online, 719–721
Legal Hold, 624
LIBRARY tab, 668
Library workspace, 387
licenses
   accepting terms, 245
   assigning, 80
   script for swapping, 818–819
   stand-alone purchases, 5

suites, 6–8
limits, SharePoint Online
  file upload size, 637
  site collection limits, 636
  storage limits, 635–636
  users, 636–637
$LiveCred variable, 404
LOB (line-of-business), 632, 635
Local Area Network (LAN), 36, 223
Local System account, 249
Locations Mapper app, 651, 653, 657
locations of data centers, 28
Lock and turn off Auto Archiving for IMs option, 753
Log Location page, 541
Logon with default credential check box, 480
Long URL option, 487
Lotus Notes to Exchange Online, 20
Lync Federation, 713–714
Lync Online
  client, 702–704
  conversation history, 742–754
  deploying
    allowing outgoing connections, 723
    DNS entries, 723–727
    overview, 718
    policies, 742–754
    ports and protocols, 722–723
    testing network bandwidth and latency, 719–721
  dial-in audio conferencing, 717–718
  domain purpose, 81
  features, 713
  hybrid Lync Online
    configuring, 754–756
    overview, 714–717
  Lync Federation, 713–714
  Lync Web App, 708–712
  managing
    Lync Online 2010, 736–741
    Lync Online 2013, 728–735
  meetings, 704–707
  migration considerations, 757
  mobile, 707
  Outlook Web App and, 708–712
  and public-facing sites, 82
  terminology
    peer-to-peer voice vs. Enterprise Voice, 700
    SIP, 700
Lync Online Control Panel, 736
Lync Transport Reliability Probe, 19, 45, 719
Lync Voice Client Access Licenses, 699
Lync Web App, 708–712

M
mailboxes (Exchange Online)
  changing size of, 432

  cutover migration
    with EAC, 570–573
    with ECP, 568–570
    overview, 566–567
  decommissioning on-premises Exchange, 607
  Exchange hybrid model deployment
    creating, 542–549
    moving, 549–557
  IMAP migration
    creating .csv file, 585
    with EAC, 587–589
    with ECP, 585–587
  limits for Exchange Online plans, 431
  Microsoft Exchange PST Capture
    installing and using, 593–600
    overview, 592
  migration best practices
    performance, 601–602
    reducing TTL for MX records, 601
    service throttling, 602
    user throttling, 602
  migration overview, 565–566
  migration using remote Windows PowerShell, 590–591
  migration with Exchange hybrid environment, 591
  moving to on-premises Exchange
    originally created in Exchange Online, 605–607
    originally created on-premises, 603–605
  recovering deleted, 432
  staged migration
    creating .csv file, 574–575
    with EAC, 579–584
    with ECP, 575–579
  third-party migration tools, 601
Mailbox Replication Service (MRS), 591
mail-enabled user (MEU), 573
Mail Flow Security page, 531
Mail Flow Settings page, 530
malware, 218
Manage Hybrid Configuration Wizard, 517, 519
Manage License option, 659
management agents
  defined, 182–183
  FIM, 788
Management Agents tab, 184, 189
management groups, naming, 244
Management Packs (MPs). *See* MPs
Management Pack Templates node, 300
Management server action account, 249
Management Server component, 325
Manage My Organization option, 568
Manage Myself option, 568, 576, 586
Manage requests for apps task, 649
Manage Result Sources page, 679
MAN (Metropolitan Area Network), 36
manual activity, 386

Map Prompts page, 389, 390
Mbps (megabits per second), 27
medium VMs, 799
meetings, Lync Online, 704–707
megabits per second (Mbps), 27
Members attribute, 139
message quarantining, 445
Message Records Management (MRM), 422, 449
Metalogix, 601
Metropolitan Area Network (MAN), 36

installing and using, 593–600
overview, 592
Microsoft Exchange Remote Connectivity Analyzer
    (ExRCA), 534
Microsoft Federation Gateway, 516
Microsoft Hyper-V virtual machine, 214, 237
Microsoft Installer (MSI) package, 762
Microsoft Lync 2013 Custom Compliance Policy Settings
    folder, 752
Microsoft Management Console (MMC), 78, 405, 471
Microsoft .NET Framework 3.5.1, 55
Microsoft Office 365
    automation with Orchestrator
        applying runbook concept, 327–329
        creating runbooks for email accounts, 346–349
        installing, 330–346
        overiew of, 326–327
        using components of, 329–331
    automation with Service Manager
        components of, 352–353
        configuring, 369–394
        installing, 353–358
        Orchestrator connector, enabling, 367–369
        overview of, 351–352
        Self-Service Portal, installing, 358–365
        service catalog overview, 365–366
        service request automation, 366–367
    domain name, adding
        adding users and assigning licenses, 80
        DNS, configuring, 81–82
        licenses, assigning, 80
        setting domain purpose and configuring DNS, 81–82
        TXT records, entering, 77–79
        verifying domain, 79–80

user accounts
    cloud identities, 72
    federated identities, 72–73
Microsoft Office 365 Deployment Readiness Toolkit
    overview, 21–26
    troubleshooting data quality errors, 198
Microsoft Office Subscription Error message, 777
Microsoft.Online.DirSync.Scheduler.exe.Config file, 194
Microsoft Online Services Diagnostics and Logging
    Toolkit. *See* MOSDAL Toolkit

tool, 153, 165
Microsoft Software License Terms page, 473
Microsoft SQL Server
    directory synchronization, installing, 151–163
    installing, 334–335
Microsoft Updates, 218, 363
Microsoft Visual Studio, 410
Migrate to Exchange Online option, 571, 580
migrating mailboxes (Exchange Online)
    best practices
        performance, 601–602
        reducing TTL for MX records, 601
        user throttling, 602
    cutover migration
        with EAC, 570–573
        with ECP, 568–570
        overview, 566–567
    with Exchange hybrid environment, 591
    IMAP migration
        creating .csv file, 585
        with EAC, 587–589
        with ECP, 585–587
    Microsoft Exchange PST Capture
        installing and using, 593–600
        overview, 592
    moving to on-premises Exchange
        originally created in Exchange Online, 605–607
        originally created on-premises, 603–605
    overview, 565–566
    using remote Windows PowerShell, 590–591
    staged migration
        creating .csv file, 574–575
        with EAC, 579–584
        with ECP, 575–579

third-party migration tools, 601
using remote Windows PowerShell, 590–591
migration
Lync Online considerations, 757
options for Exchange Online, 566
MigrationErrors.csv, 567
MigrationStatistics.csv, 567
miisclient.exe graphical UI, 180
MMC (Microsoft Management Console), 78, 405, 471
mobile access to SkyDrive Pro, 669–670
mobile Lync Online, 707
MOF (Microsoft Operations Framework), 217, 326, 352
Monitor Folder activity, 327
Monitoring Overview pane, Operations Manager, 262
monitoring with System Center
alert notifications
creating alert recipients, 262–270
creating subscription, 270–281
resources for, 280–281
App Controller, 219–221
Configuration Manager, 210–212
Data Protection Manager, 214–215
Endpoint Protection, 218–219
importing Management Pack, 253–263
Operations Manager
downloading Service Pack 1 media, 236–237
installing, 225–235, 238–253
overview, 212–214
Orchestrator, 216
overview, 207–209
planning
administering monitoring solution, 224–225
evaluating what to monitor, 222–224
monitoring targets, 225
Service Manager, 217–218
Virtual Machine Manager, 214–215
MORE ACTIONS option, 659
More secure option, 295
MOSDALLog_Directory_Synchronization_Tool file, 200, 202
MOSDAL (Microsoft Online Services Diagnostics and Logging) Toolkit
overview, 48–52
troubleshooting data quality errors, 198
Windows PowerShell and, 52–54
Move configuration page, 588
Move Settings page, 553
MPs (Management Packs)
and monitoring, 222
catalog for, 253
configuring, 291–304
creating runbook automation activity, 380
defined, 253
importing, 253–263
and Operations Manager, 213
watcher nodes, 300–304

MRM (Messaging Records Management)
retention policies, 422, 623
retention tags, 623
time limits on, 449
MRS (Mailbox Replication Service), 591
MSDN (Microsoft Developer Network), 236
msExchArchiveStatus attribute, 172
msExchUCVoiceMailSettings attribute, 173
MSI (Microsoft Installer) package, 762
multi-factor authentication
Azure Multi-Factor Authentication, 800–802
initial verification process, 802–805
overview, 799–800
multi-forest scenarios
account forest and resource forest scenario, 792
direct synchronization, 790
indirect synchronization, 791
overview, 788–789
multi-mailbox search (eDiscovery), 627–630
MX records
Exchange hybrid model, 558
reducing TTL, 601
verifying DNS, 77

N

NAT (Network Address Translation), 536
NDR backscatter prevention, 444
NetBIOS method, 92
Netdom command-line tool, 783
network
latency, 26–27
performance statistics, 35
signal degradation, 27
testing speed, 29
Network Address Translation (NAT), 536
New Dashboard and Widget Wizard, 313, 321
New-DistributionGroup cmdlet, 419, 420
New Exchange Certificate Wizard, 483
New federation server farm option, 108
New Hybrid Configuration Wizard, 514, 515, 516
New Import List button, 599
New Lync Meeting option, 705
New Other Records option, 526
New PC scenario, 210
New PST Search Wizard, 596
New Registry Properties dialog box, 748
New Remote Mailbox Wizard, 542, 547
New Remote Move Request Wizard, 550, 604, 605
New-RetentionPolicyTag cmdlet, 423
New Site Collection dialog box, 644
New Trust Wizard, 783
non-ASCII characters, 575
No Subscription Found error message, 777
Notification node, Administration pane, 263

notifications
creating alert recipients, 262–270
creating subscription, 270–281
resources for, 280–281
Notification Subscriber Wizard, 264–271

O

O365 tab, 199
OAB (offline address book), 470, 512
Object Selection page, 286

stand-alone purchases, 5
suites, 6–8
overview, 4
portal page, 802
redundancy, 11–12
regulatory compliance, 14–15
scalability, 11
screen shots in book, 9
subscription model, 10–11
suite of tools in, 18
terminology
hybrid, 9
tenant, 8
tenant name, 8
vanity domain name, 9
waves, 9
Trust Center, 12–13
Office 365 Deployment Guide, 20–21
Office 365 Home Premium, 6
Office 365 Midsize Business, 6
Office 365 Professional Plus
Click-to-Run process
customizing, 769–771
modes for, 769–771
overview, 764–768
vs. MSI, 771–773
deploying
32-bit vs. 64-bit version, 775
Group Policy, 775–776
overview, 762–763
system requirements, 775
virtualization, 776–777
Microsoft Office editions, 760–762
Office on Demand, 773–774

patching, 774
Service Description, 762
troubleshooting
Activation Error, 778
Microsoft Office Subscription Error, 777
No Subscription Found, 777
Office Subscription Removed, 777
Office 365 Service Descriptions, 19–20
Office 365 Small Business Premium, 6
Office Customization Tool (OCT), 773

OperationsManagerDW, 305
**Operations tab, Synchronization Service Manager
window, 192**
operator console dashboards, 311–312
opportunistic TLS, 437
Orchestrator Exchange Admin Integration Pack, 344
Orchestrator, System Center
console port, 342
overview, 216
Product registration page, 336
runbook changes not updated, 379
Runbook Designer console, 347, 370
Setup window, 335
Organizational Unit (OU), 90
Organization and Location page, 492
OS (operating systems), 54, 210
Other New Records option, 78
Other verification option, 808
OU (Organizational Unit), 90
outgoing connections, 39
Outlook Anywhere is enabled check box, 487
outlook.com
geolocation information for, 31
pinging, 30
Outlook Web App (OWA)
and .pst files, 434
ECP, 612
Exchange Online plans, 431
hybrid Exchange environment, 460
Lync Online and, 708–712
traffic analysis, 36
Overview page, Lync Online Control Panel, 736

P

/packager mode, 771
packet loss, 46
PALs (Partner Access Licenses), 139, 636, 660
Password attribute, 574, 585
Password Synchronization screen, 174
Patriot Act, 456
PBX (Private Branch eXchange), 699
peer-to-peer voice vs. Enterprise Voice, 699, 700
performance, migrating mailboxes, 601–602
permissions
  changing using PowerShell, 417
  SharePoint Store, 655–657
PERMISSIONS tab, 668
personally identifiable information (PII), 456
Personal Storage Table (PST) files, 434, 622
PGi (Premiere Global), 717
PhoneFactor, 800
PII (personally identifiable information), 456
ping command, 30
pipe, defined, 422
PKI (private key infrastructure), 451
Plan 1/Plan 2, 20
planning for Office 365
  foundational planning and remediation tasks, 18
  Microsoft Office 365 Deployment Readiness Toolkit, 21–26
  Microsoft Online Services Diagnostics and Logging
    (MOSDAL) Support Toolkit, 48–52
  Microsoft Remote Connectivity Analyzer, 46–48
  Microsoft Windows PowerShell Integrated Scripting
    Environment (ISE) 3.0, 66–68
  network
    email traffic analysis, 39–43
    misconception about distance, 28
    quality vs. quantity, 27
    requirements for Lync Online, 44–46
    requirements for SharePoint Online, 43–44
    speed tests, 28–34
    traffic analysis, 35–39
  Office 365 Deployment Guide, 20–21
  Office 365 Service Descriptions, 19–20
  service-specific planning and remediation tasks, 18
  tools for, 18–19
  Windows PowerShell and
    Microsoft Online Services Module, 54–59
    overview, 52–53
    testing Microsoft Online Services Module, 60–66
POC (proof of concept), 330
Policies node, 751
Policy management, 786
POP (Post Office Protocol)
  and EOA, 450
  Exchange Online protocol support, 433
ports for Lync Online, 722–723
pound (#) key, 800

PowerShell
  closing sessions, 405
  cmdlets, 396
  customizing user interface, 403
  directory synchronization, activating with, 144–145
  directory synchronization, forcing unscheduled
    through, 191–195
  environment preparation
    configuring WinRM settings, 401–402
    connecting PowerShell to Office 365 service, 403–405
    pre-configured for workstation or server, 396–404
  examples and exercises
    Admin Audit log, using, 421–422
    Exchange Online, establishing session with, 414–416
    groups, creating distribution, 419–421
    groups, viewing, 419
    Help files, updating, 416
    mailbox access, granting, 417–418
    permissions, validating, 418
    retention policies, creating, 423–425
    retention policies, viewing, 422–423
    time zones, changing, 418–419
  as future interface, 405
  Integrated Scripting Environment
    navigating, 409–414
    starting from Windows 7, 407–408
    starting from Windows 8, 407
    starting from within Windows PowerShell, 407
  Microsoft Online Services Module
    overview, 54–59
    testing, 60–65
  Office 365 commands listing, 424
  online resources, 822
  overview, 52–53
  remoting, 53
  scripts
    activating services, 819–820
    creating cloud identities from csv file, 814
    determining subscription name, 813
    generating subscription assignment report, 815–818
    generating user list, 815
    purging deleted users, 820
    sending bulk email to users, 820–821
    swapping licenses, 818–819
  synchronizing AD account with Office 365, 375
  testing scripts on test tenant, 414
  underlying services, 395–396
  upgrading, 399
  verifying successful domain conversion, 115–116
PowerShell ISE (Integrated Scripting Environment)
  Command Pane, 410
  debugging in, 406
  executing scripts in, 91
  Module view in, 424
  navigating, 409–414

overview, 66–68
required tools, 53
starting from Windows 7, 407–408
starting from Windows 8, 407
starting from within Windows PowerShell, 407
upgrading, 409
using as Administrator, 399
Preboot Execution Environment (PXE), 210
Preferred Server drop-down box, 32
Premiere Global (PGi), 717

proxy role, 100–101
PSTN (public switched telephone network), 700
PST (Personal Storage Table) files, 434, 622
public-facing website, 82
public switched telephone network (PSTN), 700
purging deleted users, 820
PXE (Preboot Execution Environment), 210

Q

QoS (Quality of Service), 35
Quarantine action, 446
Quest Software, 601
Quick Links, 24

R

RAM (random-access memory), 244
RBAC (Role Based Access Control), 224, 612, 786
Readiness Checks page, 476
read-only domain controller (RODC), 793
Recipient Configuration node, 543, 550, 604
recipients, limits on, 439
Recoverable Items folder, 440
recovering deleted items, 440
Recover License option, 659
Recovery Point Objective (RPO), 442
Recovery Time Objective (RTO), 442
Redirect action, 446
redundancy
    business case for cloud, 11–12
    data center locations and, 28
Refresh PC scenario, 210
Registry Editor (Regedit), 744
regulatory compliance, 14–15
Reject action, 446
released to manufacturing (RTM), 429

Relying Party Trust option, 117
remediation tasks
    defined, 18
    foundational planning and, 18
    service-specific planning and, 18
Remote-AutodiscoverVirtualDirectory cmdlet, 542
Remote Procedure Call (RPC), 48, 435
Remote Target Database box, 604
remote workers, single sign on scenarios
    not logged on to corporate network, 84

request offering
    creating, 387–390
    in Self-Service Portal, 392–394
Request timed out error message, 30
Require sign-in check box, 664
re-routing of connections, 28
Research In Motion (RIM), 436
Resolution State window, 275
resource forest, 792
Resource Record Type dialog box, 78
resources, SCOM notifications, 281
Restart Manager, 408
retention of data
    enforced, 621
    policies
        creating, 423–425
        defined, 623
        viewing, 422–423
    tags, 623
Return on Investment (ROI), 4, 222, 325
Return to site link, 651
Rights Management Service (RMS), 457–458
RIM (Research In Motion), 436
RODC (read-only domain controller), 793
ROI (Return on Investment), 4, 222, 325
Role Based Access Control (RBAC), 224, 612, 786
Roles & Auditing page, 613
Roles Summary pane, 92
RootCAType, 507
routers, 27
RPC (Remote Procedure Call), 48, 435
RPO (Recovery Point Objective), 442
RTM (released to manufacturing), 429
RTO (Recovery Time Objective), 442

Run As Account Creation Progress page, 296
Run As Account Credentials page, 294
Run As Account Distribution Security page, 295
Run as Administrator icon, 398
Run As Configuration node, 293
runbook automation
   creating activity template, 379–383
   flow of, 367
   Orchestrator Runbook Designer console, 370
   process overview, 369
Runbook Control Integration Pack folder, 348
Runbook Designer, 216, 325, 329, 341
runbooks
   applying concept to office 365, 327–329
   creating for Office 365 email accounts, 346–349
   defined, 216
   finalizing, 371–379
   modifying for testing, 379
   naming, 372
   not updating in Orchestrator database, 379
Run Management Agent dialog box, 190
run profiles, 182–183
Run the query every option, 302

S

SaaS (Software as a Service), 720
SafeRecipientHash attribute, 172
SafeSendersHash attribute, 172
samAccountName attribute, 139
SAML (Security Assertion Markup Language) toke, 119
SANs (subject alternative names), 496, 537
Save Policy Rule on the Actions pane, 616
scalability
   business case for cloud, 11
   economy of, 11
SCO. See Orchestrator, System Center
SCOM (System Center 2012 Operations Manager)
   alert views, 289–290
   dashboards
      creating, 312–317
      operator console dashboards, 311–312
      SLA dashboards, 317–323
   downloading Service Pack 1 media, 236–237
   identifying dependent servers, 283–286
   installing, 225–235, 238–253
   management pack
      configuring, 291–304
      watcher nodes, 300–304
   overview, 212–214
   reports, 305–310
   state views, 287–288
SCOM Web Application Monitoring Wizard, 291
screen shots in book, 9
scripts
   authoring pane in PowerShell ISE, 67

executing, 64
helper scripts, 68
in Operations Manager, 213
PowerShell
   activating services, 819–820
   creating cloud identities from csv file, 814
   determining subscription name, 813
   generating subscription assignment report, 815–818
   generating user list, 815
   purging deleted users, 820
   sending bulk email to users, 820–821
   swapping licenses, 818–819
   saving, 68
SDK (Software Development Kit), 328
Search-AdminAuditLog cmdlet, 421, 422
Search All Now button, 598
searching
   EOA mailboxes, 451
   multi-mailbox in Exchange Online, 627–630
   primary mailbox, 433
   SharePoint Online hybrid environment
      one-way inbound topology, 697
      one-way outbound topology, 697
      two-way topology, 698
secondary federation servers, 101
Secure Sockets Layer (SSL), 27, 700
Security Assertion Markup Language (SAML) toke, 119
Select a Target Class page, 319
Select a well known Naming Context option, 133
Select Client Access Server dialog box, 529
Select features page, 231
Select Management Packs page, 256
Select Services page, 504
Select Stand-Alone or Farm Deployment page, 108
self-repairing connections, 28
Self-Service Portal
   installing, 358–365
   request offering in, 392–394
   service offering in, 392–394
   Silverlight required, 365
Self Signed column, 498
Send Instant Message icon, 710
Send Mail activity, 327
Server Certificates option, 93
Server Configuration node, 483, 498, 508, 540, 608
server farm, 100
Server Role selection page, 475
server-side session, 403
Service Descriptions
   downloading, 430
   for Exchange Online, 430
   for Office 365 Professional Plus, 762
   for SharePoint Online, 633–635
Service Level Agreement. See SLA
Service Level Objectives page, 320

Service Manager Integration Pack, 344
Service Manager, System Center, 217–218
service offering
    creating and publishing, 390–392
    in Self-Service Portal, 392
service request template, 383–387
Service Request Template form, 384
services, activating via script, 819–820
service (SRV) records, 461
service throttling, 602

Set up and manage Active Directory synchronization
        page, 145
Set up link for Active Directory synchronization, 149
SharePoint 2010, 359
SharePoint Foundation 2010, 359
SharePoint Foundation 2013 Server, 359
SharePoint Online
    architecture, 633
    compliance with eDiscovery, 674–693
    domain purpose, 81
    hybrid model, 637
    limits
        file upload size, 637
        site collection limits, 636
        storage limits, 635–636
        users, 636–637
    managing
        SharePoint Online 2010, 642–645
        SharePoint Online 2013, 638–641
    Office Web Apps, 670–674
    overview, 631–632
    and public-facing sites, 82
    search in hybrid environment
        one-way inbound topology, 697
        one-way outbound topology, 697
        two-way topology, 698
    Service Description, 633–635
    SharePoint Online Management Shell, 694–696
    SharePoint Store
        adding apps to sites, 655–657
        managing app licenses, 657–659
        overview, 646–654
        permissions, 655–657
    SkyDrive Pro
        external collaboration capabilities, 660–664

    managing external sharing, 664–669
    mobility, 669–670
    overview, 659–660
    storage, 660
SharePoint Online Management Shell, 694–696
SharePoint Store
    adding apps to sites, 655–657
    managing app licenses, 657–659
    overview, 646–654
    permissions, 655–657

    remote worker not logged on to corporate network, 84
    remote worker on virtual private network
            connection, 83–84
    SLA and, 224
    when to implement, 73
    in Windows Azure, 794–795
SIP (Session Initiation Protocol)
    overview, 699–700
    URIs, 700
site collections, limits on, 636
sites, SharePoint Online, 655–657
-SkipUserConversion parameter, 123, 124
SkyDrive Pro
    external collaboration capabilities, 660–664
    managing external sharing, 664–669
    mobility, 669–670
    overview, 659–660
SLA (Service Level Agreement)
    and Service Descriptions, 19
    dashboards displaying, 317–323
    financial obligations, 441
    for EOA, 449
    leveraging with Windows Azure, 101
    monitoring, 224, 293
small VMs, 799
SMS (Systems Management Server) 1.0, 210
SMTP (Simple Mail Transfer Protocol), 48, 278, 436
SNMP (Simple Network Management Protocol), 212
Software as a Service (SaaS), 720
Software Development Kit (SDK), 328
SourceAD Delta Import Delta Sync operation, 193
SourceAD Export Sync operation, 193
SourceAD Management Agent, 187
SourceAD update, 185

spam
  blacklists, 444
  FOPE protection, 218, 438, 443
Specify a Service Account page, 109
Specify IM and Call Logging in Outlook dialog box, 753
speedtest.net, 31
SPN (service principal name), 111
SQL Reporting Services report, 309
SQL Server
  Installation Center, 334
  installing, 354
  Management Studio console, 379
  Native Client, 156
SQL Server Reporting Service (SSRS). *See* SSRS
SRV (service) records, 461
SSL (Secure Sockets Layer), 27, 361, 700
SSO (single sign on). *See* single sign on (SSO)
  hybrid Exchange environment, 465
SSRS (SQL Server Reporting Service)
  Configuration Manager reporting, 212
  Operations Manager reporting, 250
staged migration
  creating .csv file, 574–575
  with EAC, 579–584
  with ECP, 575–579
stand-alone AD FS server, 108
stand-alone purchases, 5
Start Configuration Wizard now option, 156, 168
Start-OnlineCoexistenceSync cmdlet, 192, 607
star topology, 27
Start-Process cmdlet, 407
Start Test button, 719
StateAlertPerformance dashboard, 304
state views (SCOM), 287–288
storage
  SharePoint Online limits, 635–636
  SkyDrive Pro, 660
Stored Conversations folder, 433
Subgroups page, 286
subject alternative names (SANs), 496, 537
Subscriber Addresses page, 269
Subscriber Name text box, Notification Subscriber
     Wizard, 264
subscription assignment report, 815–818
subscription model, 10–11
subscription name, determining, 813
subscriptions, creating, 270–281
Suffixes tab, UPN, 88
suites, 6–8
Summary Dashboard option, 313
Summary page, 280
-SupportMultipleDomain parameter, 114, 115
swapping licenses, 818–819
Synchronization Service Manager
  directory synchronization, forcing unscheduled
     with, 183–192

directory synchronization, verifying with, 178–181
Synchronization Statistics pane, 188
SyncTimeInterval key value, 195
System Center
  alert notifications
    creating alert recipients, 262–270
    creating subscription, 270–281
    resources for, 280–281
  App Controller, 219–221
  Configuration Manager, 210–212
  Data Protection Manager, 214–215
  Endpoint Protection, 218–219
  importing Management Pack, 253–263
  Operations Manager
    downloading Service Pack 1 media, 236–237
    installing, 225–235, 238–253
    overview, 212–214
  Orchestrator, 216
  overview, 207–209
  planning for monitoring
    administering monitoring solution, 224–225
    evaluating what to monitor, 222–224
    monitoring targets, 225
  Service Manager, 217–218
  Virtual Machine Manager, 214–215
System Center 2012 Orchestrator
  Data Bus in, 370
  installing
    completing installation, 335–344
    installing Microsoft SQL Server, 334–335
    Integration Packs, 344–346
    prerequisites for, 331–333
  overiew of, 326–327
  runbooks
    applying concept, 327–329
    automation, 367
    creating for email accounts, 346–349
  System Center connector, completing integration, 370–373
  System Center connector, enabling, 367–369
  using components of, 329–331
System Center 2012 Service Manager
  and SharePoint Foundation 2013 Server, 359
  architecture of, 352
  components of, 352–353
  configuring automation
    completing Orchestrator integration, 370–371
    request offering, creating, 387–390
    request offering, in Self-Service Portal, 392–394
    runbook automation activity template, creating, 379–383
    runbooks, finalizing, 371–379
    service offering, creating and publishing, 390–392
    service offering, in Self-Service Portal, 392–394
    service request template, creating, 383–387
  hardware requirements, 353
  installing, 353–358

Orchestrator connector, enabling, 367–369
overview of, 351–352
runbook automation, 367
Self-Service Portal, installing, 358–365
service catalog overview, 365–366
service request automation, 366–367
software requirements, 353
System Center connector, completing integration, 370–371
Systems Management Server (SMS) 1.0, 210

technical contact, 196
tenant, 8
tenant name, 8
tenants
for testing, 414
terminology
hybrid, 9
Lync Online
peer-to-peer voice vs. Enterprise Voice, 700
SIP, 700
tenant, 8
tenant name, 8
vanity domain name, 9
waves, 9
testing, 60–65
test tenant, 414
TFS (Team Foundation Services) Online, 4
ThirdParty certificate type, 507
throttling limits, 19
ticketing systems, 214
Tier 1 networks, 28
time-based hold, 624
Time To Live (TTL), 601
time zones, changing, 418–419
TLDs (top-level domains), 114, 115
TLS (Transport Layer Security), 27, 437, 700
top-level domains (TLDs), 114, 115
tracing email messages, 448
Transport Layer Security (TLS), 27, 437, 700
troubleshooting
Exchange hybrid model
Autodiscover service, 534–537
resetting Autodiscover virtual directory, 539–542
virtual directory security settings, 537–539

Office 365 Professional Plus
Activation Error, 778
Microsoft Office Subscription Error, 777
No Subscription Found, 777
Office Subscription Removed, 777
tools for, 18–19
Trust Center, 12–13
Trust Relationships node, 117
trusts
one-way forest trusts, 785

UM (Unified Messaging), 431
Unified Communications certificate, 494, 495, 537
Unified Messaging (UM), 431
Uninterruptable Power Supplies (UPS), 213
unlimited storage, 449
Update Activity activity, 349
Update-Help cmdlet, 416
Update-HybridConfiguration cmdlet, 539
Update-SCSMConnector cmdlet, 369
Update Sequence Number (USN), 183
UPN Suffixes tab, 88
UPN (User Principal Name)
common problems, 86
format, 137, 171
remediating suffix, 86–91
UPS (Uninterruptable Power Supplies), 213
uptime
for EOA, 449
guaranteed by FOPE, 442
Use AutoDiscover check box, 680
Use Microsoft Update option, 363
Use mutual TLS to help secure Internet mail check box, 489
Use Office On Demand option, 773
User Account Control (UAC), 397
user accounts
adding users and assigning licenses, 80
cloud identities, 72
federated identities, 72–73
User Administration portal page, 549
user list, generating via script, 815
User management, 786
UserName attribute, 585
User Principal Name (UPN). *See* UPN
User Prompts page, 388

users
purging deleted, 820
sending bulk email to, 820–821
throttling, 602
Users & Groups page, 569, 576
USN (Update Sequence Number), 183

V

vanity domain name, 9
verbose console pane, 67
Verification required dialog box, 804
Verify Prerequisites Again option, 242
View Installed Updates link, 127
virtual directory security settings
troubleshooting Exchange hybrid model
deployment, 537–539
virtualization
deploying Office 365 Professional Plus, 776–777
VM sizing in Windows Azure, 798–799
Virtual Machine Manager, System Center. *See* VMM, System
Center
virtual private network (VPN), 83
Virtual Server hosts, 328
virus protection, 218, 442
VMM (Virtual Machine Manager), System Center, 214–215
VMs (virtual machines), 244
VMware, 214
voice quality, Lync Online, 46
VoIP (Voice over IP), 700
Voltage Security, 438
Volume Shadow Service (VSS) API, 214
VPN (virtual private network), 83
VSS (Volume Shadow Service) API, 214

W

watcher nodes, 300–304
waves, 9
Web Application Editor, 301
Web App Transaction Monitoring pane, 300, 301
Web Management Tools node, 472
Web Server Role page, 232
Web Service port, 342
Welcome page, Configuration Wizard, 170
Welcome page, Directory Sync Setup Wizard, 152, 164
-whatif parameter, 91
WID (Windows Internal Database). *See* Windows Internal
Database
Wildcard certificate, 485
wildcard certificates, 95
Windows 7
PowerShell ISE in, 407–408
remote workstations, 114–115
WinRM versions, 397
Windows 8
PowerShell ISE in, 407, 409
WinRM versions, 397

Windows Authentication, 231
Windows Azure
App Controller and, 219, 220
identity and SSO for Office 365, 794–795
identity management components all deployed in, 796
identity management components duplicated in, 797–798
on-premises dependencies supported in, 793–794
VM sizing, 798–799
**Windows Azure Active Directory Module for Windows
PowerShell**
converting domain from identity federation to, 123–124
downloading, 113
installing, 401
Windows Azure Active Directory Sync
configuring, 170–176
installing with dedicated computer running SQL
Server, 151–163
installing with Windows Internal Database, 164–168
service for, 177
Windows Computer state view, 288
Windows Internal Database (WID)
directory synchronization, installing, 164–168
planning architecture, 99
system requirements, 148
Windows InTune, 212
Windows PowerShell. *See* PowerShell
**Windows PowerShell Integrated Scripting Environment
(ISE) 3.0.** *See* PowerShell ISE (Integrated Scripting
Environment)
Windows Presentation Foundation (WPF), 408
Windows Remote Management. *See* WinRM
Windows Server 2008 R2
converting domain from standard authentication to identity
federation, 113–114
PowerShell ISE in, 409
WinRM versions, 397
Windows Server 2008 SP2, 114–115
Windows Server 2012, 397
Windows Server Update Services (WSUS),, 772
Windows WF (Workflow Foundation), 787
WinRM (Windows Remote Management)
Basic authorization, 402
configuring settings, 401–402
determining version, 397–399
listener service, 114
upgrading, 399
verifying running status, 399–401
versions, 397
WPF (Windows Presentation Foundation), 408
Write Web Page activity, 327
WSUS (Windows Server Update Services), 772

X

XenServer, 215

About the authors

Julian Soh, MCITP, is currently the Microsoft Office 365 Architect for the Microsoft Western U.S. Account Teams. In this capacity, Julian works with Microsoft's largest and most prominent public sector customers to address challenging business, security, and technical requirements for adopting Office 365 as part of their IT portfolio. Julian has been involved with Office 365 since its introduction as the Business Productivity Online Services (BPOS)

ate of Washington State University and currently resides with his family in the Puget Sound area of the State of Washington.

Anthony Puca is a Microsoft data center specialist. Anthony currently spends his days consulting for U.S. state and local government accounts on Microsoft Windows Server, System Center, and private, public, and hybrid cloud technologies. Anthony's IT career started 24 years ago as a Mainframe Librarian for American Express. Anthony has spent the last 17 years in IT, primarily as a consultant for Perot Systems, Avanade, and EMC Corporation fulfilling duties including enterprise architecture, system engineering, network engineering, and database administration. Anthony's last project at EMC in 2010 was consulting VMware about how to efficiently monitor and deploy operating systems in a virtual infrastructure. In the last eight years, Anthony has presented at Microsoft's TechReady, Microsoft's TechEd, Microsoft's Management Summit, Microsoft's Security Summit, VMworld, and various CIO summits across the U.S. Anthony co-wrote three MOF white papers about change, configuration, and release management and the SAMS/Pearson book *Microsoft System Center Configuration Manager 2007 R2 Unleashed*, focusing on inventory management, software distribution, and operating system deployments. Anthony was recognized and awarded with Microsoft's Most Valuable Professional (MVP) award from 2004-2010. These MVP awards were for data center monitoring with Microsoft System Center Operations Manager and Windows Management Instrumentation. Anthony's other certifications include MCSE, MCP+I, and numerous MCTS certifications. Anthony's customer demographics over the last decade include vehicle rental, retail, financial services, food processing, manufacturing, mining, health care, government, and energy. Anthony spends his free time flying general aviation and radio-controlled aircraft and enjoying the Rocky Mountains.

Marshall Copeland, MCT, MCSA (Windows Server 2012), MCSE (Private Cloud) is currently a Microsoft data center and Azure specialist focusing on management of business services and applications. Marshall currently provides technical conversations with Microsoft Western U.S. State and Local Government customers for cloud security, Azure, and data center application health monitoring. He has been working with Microsoft core infrastructure technologies including Windows Server, Hyper-V, System Center, Azure, Office 365, and other Microsoft technologies for more than 15 years. Marshall has presented at the Microsoft SharePoint conference and Microsoft Management Summit and has been a trainer at the Management Summit. He has contributed to Windows IT Pro Magazine and creates technology videos for customer industry events. Marshall is advancing security and identity conversations with customers supporting computer forensics while pursuing a master's degree in Information Assurance at Dakota State University. Marshall graduated from Southern MS and resides with his family in Denver, Colorado.

How to download

To download your eBook, go to http://aka.ms/PressEbook
and follow the instructions.

Please note: You will be asked to create a free online account and enter the access code below.

ACCESS CODE:

XJPJPNM

Microsoft Office 365 Administration Inside Out

Your PDF eBook allows you to:

- search the full text
- print
- copy and paste

Best yet, you will be notified about free updates to your eBook.

If you ever lose your eBook file, you can download it again just by logging in to your account.

Need help? Please contact:
msinput@microsoft.com